90° to Zamboanga

*Memoirs of a 20-year
Marijuana Smuggling Adventure*

by

Rick Bibbero

Disclaimer

In this memoir I have tried to recreate events, locales and conversations from my memories of them. In order to maintain their anonymity in some instances I have changed the names of individuals and places. I also changed some identifying characteristics and details such as, but not limited to, physical properties, occupations and places of residence. Because of the nature of this story, such changes were created to protect the identity and privacy of the people involved.

My goal here is to tell my story as it relates to me and to societal attitudes regarding marijuana at the time and in the places during which this adventure takes place and is intended solely to give the reader a vivid sense of what was going on at the time. This story has been recreated from my memories and the memories of others whom I interviewed of events that took place between thirty and fifty years ago and thus may or may not be entirely accurate as to all recreated conversations and vignettes as they appear throughout this book.

The reader should not presume that any person described herein is a real person, living or dead, other than those who can positively be identified by the exact name given as it appears in the book.

Credits:
Original logo design concept, Melissa Vaio
Book Cover and logo designs, Lauren Taylor / LTDesignco.com

90degreestozamboanga.com

LUCKY SHIRT PRESS

Dedication

This book is dedicated to the memory of Father John Sorce whose guidance, spirituality, friendship and counsel helped me enjoy what could have otherwise been a rough time in my life.

Father had many sayings he used to bestow on me. Some were inspirational, some spiritual, some were funny and some were simply appropriate at the time. My favorite was:

> "Listen and learn from the wisdom of the other guy… you don't have to go to the electric chair to know that's a place where you don't want to go!"

Fr. John J. Sorce
1924–2011

Contents

Introduction

When historians of the future look back and study social issues of today and of the past 50 years, certainly analyzing and examining the War on Drugs will be one of the main subjects of their interest. Future scholars on the subject of marijuana will have as much to say about it and its history as current intellectuals and historians do regarding any of America's past social conflicts and wars.

What they will find is that today's attitudes with respect to marijuana and its legalization did not just happen in a vacuum or simply fall out of the sky. This current awareness is the result of nearly half a century of the risks a few adventure-seeking pioneers and daredevils took and the consequences they faced and experienced at a time when there was absolutely no tolerance for illegal drugs, especially marijuana. *90° to Zamboanga* portrays an integral part of marijuana's history. It chronicles the 20-year saga of a pioneering marijuana trafficking operation as seen through the eyes of one of its principals.

90° to Zamboanga is a fast-paced, sometimes comedic, and often deadly serious story about the adventures and misadventures of a group of free-thinking entrepreneurial college students who built a contraband empire. It is not only a tale laced with action and suspense, but also the story of relationships with family, friends, business partners who wanted it all, parents who didn't understand and the women who gravitated to the 'bad boys'. Greed, power, ruthlessness and deceit all come into play.

Written in the first person, and seen through my eyes, I have tried to tell this story in an easy to read and engaging manner. I detail my 20-year experience as smuggler, marijuana entrepreneur, and ultimately, a convicted felon. It is the tale of my life and times; the fun and excitement, the insanity, the relationships, the consequences and the aftermath stemming from the rise and fall of a criminal international marijuana enterprise.

90° to Zamboanga is a saga from another era, akin to historians studying and authors writing about the adventures of the swashbucklers and pirates dating back to the 16th century. It is an adventure story and history lesson of what it really took to make it all happen and what led to bringing the discussion of marijuana use to the forefront of subjects of today's conversations and media coverage, and is of major significance today for a society just beginning to finally legitimize the use of marijuana.

I hope the reader of these memoirs will enjoy it as much as I have both telling and re-living it.

Rick Bibbero

Section 1

Border Brown
(1969–1970)

First Crossing

Mid-Summer 1969

"One small step for (a) man, one giant leap for mankind!" Those immortal words from Neil Armstrong as he stepped onto the surface of the moon on July 20, 1969, crackled on our TV set in the hot summer afternoon in Stockton, California. I watched the event in my apartment having just returned from a morning of water skiing on the San Joaquin Delta with my roommate Del Carlucci and several other buddies attending summer school at the University of the Pacific (UOP). We were sitting in the living room on giant multi-colored paisley pillows enjoying multiple joints of marijuana. Through a smoke-filled haze we stared in amazement and in a trance, watching the moon landing events unfold before our unbelieving eyes.

Right then our stupor was broken by the sound of the phone ringing. I answered it. It was my old childhood friend Willie Sherman calling me from Tempe, Arizona.

Willie and I had grown up together in the chic San Francisco neighborhood of Sea Cliff where we were neighbors. He was several years younger than me and the youngest of five children, another Jew from the neighborhood whose grandparents emigrated from Prussia. Willie was the epitome of tall, dark and handsome and much the ladies man. Six feet tall, thin as a rail with curly dark shoulder length hair and a wild spirit, Willie was the most gifted natural athlete I ever knew. The son of orthodox Jews, William was given his nickname by the baseball great Willie Mays, a friend of his family from when the Giants first came to San Francisco in 1959. The nickname stuck and he was forever Willie, spelled with an 'ie' and not a 'y'. Golf, tennis, football, baseball, or basketball. Willie had a future in any of those sports. He was a natural.

In looks and physical appearance Willie kind of reminded me of a taller, thinner version of myself. Both of us with dark curly hair, dark complected and typical Mediterranean Jewish features, although his heritage was Ashkenazi from Central and Eastern Europe and mine Sephardic from the Iberian Peninsula. I too was an athlete, being on the high school swimming team and good skier, although not nearly as accomplished in team sports as Willie.

In the spring of 1969 both Willie and I were stuck by similar tragedies. In separate but eerily coincidental incidents our longtime girlfriends both passed away. Willie lost Judy Kinnealey to cancer and I lost my first love and childhood sweetheart Sally Brown, who died in a car accident. Neither had reached the age of 22.

I suppose we were both adrift in a sea of subliminal depression which drew us together and possibly led us on a different, adventurous and rebellious path.

"Rick, you've got to come down here right away. A couple of friends of mine are making some serious money running dope across the Mexican border. They score a few kilos from a Mexican contact and walk it back across the border. It's easy, fun and a real adventure. Get down here, now!"

In Stockton, I was smoking dope regularly with my friends and selling a few 'lids' (one ounce bags) so I could smoke for free. This could be my opportunity to have some really good weed and provide my friends with it as well.

For me, the seed was planted and Willie's opportunity was a way to get better weed and lots of it. It was also a way to gain independence and hopefully move on from my depression surrounding the death of Sally.

I asked Del if he would be interested in going down to Arizona to see what it was all about. Intrigued by the prospect of an adventure and curious about the possibility of making some serious money, Del agreed to accompany me on the trip down to the hot desert of Arizona. As intrigued and curious as he seemed with the romantic idea of clandestinely smuggling pot across the U.S./Mexican border, I would soon discover that when push came to shove, the reality of actually doing it would prove, for Del, to be much more than he could mentally or psychologically handle.

Del, whose ancestry was a mixture of Scottish and Italian, was a student from Southern California studying at UOP. Tall, curly blonde hair, a thin athlete's body and John Lennon wire-rimmed granny style glasses resting on the bridge of his aquiline nose, Del was the life of the party. Del was an all-star baseball player in high school and a natural athlete. He was enrolled in UOP's Pharmacy School; however, he wasn't a natural student and had to study very hard to get through his difficult pharmacy curriculum. Most pharmacy students had access to a virtual smorgasbord of pharmaceutical drugs, mostly uppers and downers, which helped Del and most of his friends study and cram late into the night, then crash afterwards. Anyway, three days later we departed Stockton bound for Tempe, Arizona, in my blue Fiat 128.

Willie had a very persuasive nature about him, one you couldn't resist. His enthusiasm was infectious. Although he was quite conceited, he also had the ability to laugh at himself and had a great sense of humor. Del and I met Willie a couple of days later at Willie's apartment on the outskirts of Tempe. There we all hooked up with Willie and a couple of his Arizona State University (ASU) classmates, JP and Bill, two students/pot smugglers from back East. While Bill stayed behind in Tempe, JP accompanied the three of us as we traveled 150 or so miles south down to Nogales, Arizona, to scope out the smuggling plan. JP took us up to an observation point atop a large hill in Western Nogales by a water tank where we could see Nogales, Arizona, to the east and west and Nogales, Mexico, to the south. He pointed out some large white buildings in the distance to the west and told us it was the Holy Cross Hospital located just a couple of miles west of the main highway at the U.S./Mexican border crossing. He said, what he had done was to park his car in the hospital parking lot and simply walk down the ravine and into Mexico. It was an easy stroll, as he put it, across the desert for just about a mile or so where he could meet his contact, a Mexican cab driver named Jesse, pick up a few kilos and simply walk back the same route in reverse to the parking lot with a load of good Mexican pot. That's all there was to it. It sure sounded simple enough.

It was at dusk when I snapped a picture of Willie, Del and JP at the water tank, ready to embark on an adventure which would change our lives forever.

Nogales is a large border town bisected by the U.S./Mexican border. The similarity of the two sides of Nogales stops in name only. Nogales, Arizona, is a relatively clean, sleepy place with clean fast food restaurants, hotels and motels, paved streets, clean hospitals and generally all of the amenities of any other small sized American southwestern town. Nogales, Mexico, located at the northern edge of the Mexican state of Sonora, is a much larger city than its American namesake. Its population is sprawled out across the hilly, dry, dusty, hot Sonoran Desert. Honky-tonk bars, taco vendors, cheap hustlers, pimps, hookers, child beggars offering packets of Chiclets gum for a few cents and macho looking Mexican 'cholos' (Hispanic looking, heavily tattooed males in sleeveless wife beater tee shirts) riding in lowered, beat-up cars with no mufflers are the town's signature. Noise is everywhere and the pervading foul sewer stench permeates the air and immediately makes one aware you have just entered the Third World.

In Willie's 1967 Plymouth Barracuda, with himself at the wheel, the four of us drove the main highway to the Mexican border and after a perfunctory check at Mexican customs we crossed into Nogales, Mexico. I immediately noticed, despite the one hundred degree heat, the streets were teeming with people and humanity wheeling and dealing, begging and hawking. Loud music and some kind of political mishmash was blaring from the roofs of garishly painted, unmuffled taxis, emanating from large attached speakers. Blinking neon signs advertised Mexican beer at the entrances of countless bars which lined both sides of the street. Scantily dressed women were standing around the bar entrances enticing customers to come in and enjoy whatever piqued their fancy. But, the overall smell was revolting; a combination of heat, beer, urine, sweat and sewer effluent permeated the air. It was one which stuck to the follicles inside of your nose and would last for days before dissipating.

"I've never seen anything like this and that smell... Jesus, what is it?" I said.

"This, amigo, is Mexico," replied JP, arms gesturing wildly in every direction. "Land of tequila, fast money, women and some mighty good weed. Everybody hustles. Everybody is corrupt, even the cops can be bought. Here they call it 'la mordita'... the bite. Everyone gets their share, but you don't want to piss off the Federales (the uniformed federal police). From what I hear the jails are rotten, rat-infested hell holes and if you get caught and thrown in there you'll be eating half cooked frijoles until hell freezes over... which, in this heat, ain't never gonna happen!"

Willie and I were fascinated and amazed by what was going on around us; all the commotion and activity, Del however was freaking out. Perspiration dripped from his face, his glasses were fogging up, the ever present happy-go-lucky attitude was gone, replaced by fear, apprehension and nervousness. He began with a series of rapid-fire questions and statements: "Do we know what we're doing? How many times have you done this before? How well do you know the contact? Do you know anyone who has been busted trying this? I don't want to get arrested! We gotta be super careful, don't we? What about the food? I don't want to get dysentery. Didn't the customs agent at the border look at us like we're up to something? I don't like it!"

This in turn got JP nervous about us and Del specifically. "Willie, how well do you know these guys? I'm not sure I want to continue if this guy's going to freak out on us."

"Calm down JP," said Willie. "I've known them forever, Del is just a bit nervous. We'll get him a couple of cervezas and that should cool him off!"

JP ran into the supermercado and came out with two frosty six packs of Carta Blanca. We then drove up a dusty dirt road to the top of a barren desert hill. It was high enough to have a panoramic view of Nogales, the border and the overall landscape as viewed from the Mexican side. It was dusk and JP pulled out a pair of binoculars and handed them to Willie. As he panned the horizon, JP pointed out the border station below and to the north, shanty towns spreading like a spider web to the northwest and northeast, and Nogales, Arizona, to the north. A few miles northwest across the wind-swept barren hills and shanty towns across a dry river bed and empty desert, Willie saw some small white buildings shimmering in the hot desert setting sunlight. "That's the hospital in the distance you're looking at," said JP. "You park your car in the parking lot right behind those buildings and walk down the dry river bed and out through the shanty town to a low-life bar right there called the Tropicana. You can't see it from here but we will go there now and meet our contact, Jesse, who I'll introduce you to and he'll score the weed for us. Jesse will then drive you back to the edge of the shanty town and you'll walk out the way you came and back to your car. We've never had any trouble and neither will you."

"How many kilos do you carry across the border? How much does it cost? Are there any snakes in the dry river bed? How do you know the border patrol won't be back in the parking lot to greet us? Who's going to bail us out if we get caught?" Again Del with his nervous, staccato, rapid-fire questions and wiping his granny glasses with a handkerchief.

"What is this, the fucking Inquisition?" asked JP, who for the second time in a matter of minutes became wary of his new potential smuggling buddies. Willie was again able to calm JP down and we drove down to the Tropicana.

The Tropicana was a typical Mexican bar, flashing neon sign with a blinking arrow pointing towards a set of double-swinging western style doors. It was located on a dirt road at the edge of the shanty town we had just driven through. It was complete with a mean looking Mexican bouncer in a dirty Corona tee shirt with the sleeves rolled up and a pack of Marlboros sticking out of his torn shirt pocket. He was straddling the doorway. He knew JP and smiled revealing a grill of gold teeth and waved us in as if we were old friends and regulars.

At the bar sat a fat Mexican man in a cowboy hat and plaid cowboy shirt missing two buttons revealing a huge beer belly jiggling as he laughed and greeted us.

"Hola. Buenos noches señor JP. These are your Amigos who you tell me about?"

"Si, si Jesse. Hola y como estas? This is Guillermo (Willie), Ricardo (Rick) and Del, my amigos from the Universidad in California. They are here for some of your good 'mota'. Can you score some kilos for them when they come back tomorrow night?"

"Si, si. No problema. Que hora (what time) mañana?"

"They will meet you here at 11:00 tomorrow night," said JP.

"Nice to meet you Jesse," said Willie. "Do you have a sample of what we will be getting tomorrow?"

"Si, si señor. I have some here." He reached into a paper bag and brought out a large rolled joint which he lit and passed to Willie who took a long pull and passed it to me, then to JP and then to Del. In the bag he had a package wrapped in brown wrapping paper. It appeared to be about a foot long by eight inches wide and two or three inches thick. He carefully opened it to reveal a pressed brick of marijuana flower tops, dry and tightly packed together, light brown in color exuding a rich fresh pungent smell.

"This is some pretty good shit!" I said. "How much will it cost?"

"Feefty dolores por kilo."

"I think the three of us can handle 50 kilos." I said. "If we get 50 can we get them for $10 apiece?"

"No señors, forty dolores," countered Jesse.

"That's way too much, Jesse! We're just college kids working our way through school."

"I have to feed my señora and ocho (eight) ninos too. I cannot go any lower. Everybody has to eat, including me," laughed Jesse grabbing his big belly protruding from his shirt and shaking it. "Thirty five and no less!"

"Come on Willie, Del. Let's go," I said. "It's useless. The price is too high and he won't come down. We're outta here. Come on JP, maybe we can find someone else who's more reasonable."

"Uno momento, amigos," cried Jesse taking a piece of paper and pencil from the bar and scribbling some figures. "We can make a deal. Especiale price just for you because you are JP's amigos. Thirty dolares."

"Twenty five is the most I can pay."

"No problemas, amigos," the fat man chuckled. "But give me four dolores a kilo more for my driver, Juanito. He has a new baby who is very hungry."

"No, only three dollars more, Jesse!" I said emphatically. "It's that or we walk."

"Si, si señor Ricardo," the taxi driver conceded. Jesse threw up his hands as if to say 'you win'. "You guys are the toughest I've played this game with. Viente ocho (twenty eight) a kilo it is. Mucho bueno!"

We settled for twenty-eight dollars a kilo. But, more importantly, we gained Jesse's respect. We agreed to rendezvous back with Jesse the following evening between 11 and midnight at the Tropicana. We then all piled into the Barracuda and headed back across the border and back to Tempe. After dropping JP off the three of us went to

Willie's apartment to reconnoiter and plan the following evening's adventure. A fly in the ointment quickly developed as Del didn't want to go back. He claimed he couldn't risk jeopardizing his pharmacy career and would simply wait back at Willie's place until we returned. We agreed, however, that his share would be reduced from the previously agreed 33% to 20% since he wouldn't be involved in the actual smuggling of the pot. JP was to receive 10% for the introduction to Jesse and for showing us the route and how to do the smuggle. This would later become known as 'OTO' (original turn-on), which would prove to become a bone of contention in later dealings in the marijuana business. It was agreed JP would receive his OTO as a one-time payment unless he actually participated in the future.

Del's absence in the forthcoming evening's adventure presented another problem for us. We had agreed with Jesse to buy 50 kilos of pot (110 pounds). This meant Willie and I would now be stuck carrying fifty five pounds apiece rather than thirty six, if the load were to have been divided up three ways. There was also no way to alert Jesse in advance of the news there would only be two of us carrying all the weight, so we just went with it. 'C'est la vie!'

At around 10:30 the following evening we pulled into the Holy Cross Hospital parking lot and parked the Barracuda in a far corner of the lot away from the other few cars which were already there. Our parking spot was right at the edge of an embankment leading down to an arroyo (dry river bed) taking us to our destination, the Mexican shanty town roughly two miles in the distance.

The arroyo seemed to amplify the strange unfamiliar night sounds. A thin crescent moon hung in the sky like a silver scimitar. A coyote howled somewhere in the distance and the otherwise quiet of the night reverberated like a silent screaming banshee in our ears as we walked through the night.

"Maybe we should have had JP go with us," I said.

"Maybe Del was right being concerned about snakes. Wonder if they come out at night. What about tarantulas, scorpions and gila monsters? If one of those things bites you or me, we're fucked. No medical kit or anything," said Willie.

"I didn't think about water. We don't even have a canteen," I said licking my parched lips. "I was a Boy Scout and so were you. Guess we just re-interpreted the motto to Be Unprepared!" I joked.

"Not funny. This is serious. Plus how are we going to carry all of that weight between just the two of us?"

"I guess we'll manage somehow! Maybe next time we should consider sled dogs!" I joshed.

"Idiot," Willie responded. "More people and equipment would be better." Willie always had a way of putting me down, but I got used to it, to a point, before I would come unglued. It was our way of banter between us. It carried through for all of our time together… which would come to be over 50 years.

Before attending UOP, I had spent almost a year on active duty as part of my training in the California Army National Guard. I joined The Guard in 1966 to avoid being drafted and almost certainly being sent to Viet Nam. As a private first class, I trained with the Regular Army in boot camp and in advanced training where I became a combat medic then a surgical technician. However, I mustered out in early 1968 after having had surgery on my shoulder due to an old skiing accident. I served only two years and was subsequently reclassified 4-F, medically unfit for military service... now and forever.

At this point in the journey across the desert in the arroyo, I was beginning to have deja vu visions of my time in Army basic training at Fort Polk, Louisiana, back in 1967. A few of us Army buddies had been smoking pot and had gotten severely stoned out on bivouac in the Louisiana bayou country. Ultimately we had gotten hopelessly lost on the edge of a swamp whose inhabitants included alligators, snakes and mosquitos. Mosquitos everywhere! We had also been warned to be on the lookout for quicksand. There was no telling which direction was which and there was no point of reference to get your bearings. I was having those same feelings now as Willie and I trundled in the desert. The high dune walls in the arroyo prevented us from seeing our destination and except for the sliver of moon it was pretty much pitch black. We were becoming disoriented when the unmistakable smell of the Mexican shantytown began to permeate the air. We knew we were close!

As we climbed out of the dry river bed the smell of excrement, rotted vegetables and wood smoke soon assailed our parched nostrils. Raw sewage was backed up in fetid pools, spilling a rancid sludge-like ooze down the embankment and into the arroyo which suddenly had become a slick and slippery slope.

"Jesus, watch your step. Fall into that shit and I'm leaving you here," said Willie. "I guarantee you'll never set foot in my car again!" Thankfully, I didn't; assuring myself of a ride back home... if we made it back!

Kerosene lamps glowed faintly through thin cardboard, plywood and corrugated tin walls of the shacks lining the dirt roadway where we now found ourselves. The sounds of silence we had just come through in the arroyo were now broken by babies crying, dogs barking and a television broadcasting a soccer game in Spanish. Shadows seemed to move somewhere in the gloom as we became suddenly aware we weren't alone. Maybe it was our hypersensitivity or maybe just paranoia, we didn't know, but the fact was, we were two long-haired college students wandering alone in a Mexican shantytown late at night carrying a couple of thousand dollars in one hundred dollar bills. Certainly easy targets if someone had bad intentions toward us.

We skirted around a rusted pipe, then down a narrow dingy alley, past a bloated, ripe-smelling dog's carcass just lying on the side of the filthy dirt road. A sullen old man in a mule-drawn cart passed us going the opposite way. He was sipping from a bottle and muttering to himself in Spanish. I don't think he even noticed us.

Willie said, "Hell, I wouldn't feel safe here even if I was carrying a gun. Thank God we aren't stoned. And we're carrying an awful lot of money, to boot. What if someone tries to rip us off?"

"Man, don't even start to think that way," I replied. "Just keep walking. Look straight ahead. Just think good thoughts and we'll be fine." This would become my mantra in the years ahead: 'Just think good thoughts...'

The street dead-ended and we turned a corner and there before us, a half a block away, were the bright glitzy lights of La Tropicana. We had arrived. It was almost midnight. We had come out of the shantytown and into what seemed like a hub of activity and noise. Loud, off-key Mariachi music blared out into the streets. A sign which I hadn't noticed the previous night, maybe because it hadn't been turned on until the witching hour of midnight, sat next to the arrow pointing to the Tropicana's entrance. It was a marquis showing neon palm trees with topless hula dancers with red lights blinking on their breasts. The same bouncer stood at the doorway. He obviously recognized us from last night and motioned us to enter.

"Buenos noches señors. Nice to see you again. Por favor, come inside and see the pretty ladies. For you especial por este noche."

"Muchas gracias, but we're here to see Jesse," I said trying to conceal my nervousness.

"He's in back. Have a couple of cervezas at the bar. I will get him for you."

We walked into the low-lit room and moved to the bar. A mangy quartet wearing sombreros and red sequin and satin suits which had seen better days were playing Mariachi sounding music wheezed as if it came out of a squeeze box. A group of exotic looking Latin women with brightly painted fingernails and lips, wearing black flowing Mexican dresses and stiletto high heels, sat in a corner at a dimly lit table.

"God damn! That shantytown gave me the creeps. Any moment I thought we would get our throats slit, robbed and left in some gutter to rot like that dog back there we almost stumbled over. I need a drink, right now!" cried Willie as he motioned to the bartender. "I'm parched."

"Me too."

Willie ordered an anejo tequilla shooter with two Cerveza Pacifico backs and I had a Modelo Especial.

"Slow down, you jerk," I said pointing to Willie's second tequila shooter. "We've got business and have to keep our wits about us. I don't want to have to drag you back across the desert."

Just then Willie turned to find one of the fine ladies had taken a seat next to him at the bar and began to suggestively rub his leg aiming for his crotch. Up close I noticed she wasn't nearly as nice looking as from a distance. She was heavily made up concealing a beauty which had long ago left her. She looked like miles and miles of bad road. But Willie was immediately turned on and reached for her heavily endowed breast.

"Hey, pretty boy. I make you feel good. Come upstairs with me."

Before he could even answer, I said, "Whoa amigo! We don't have time for any of that nonsense. Tell her you'll be back tomorrow or something."

"Aw, come on. Don't be a party pooper."

I looked the other direction and saw Jesse appear from some back recess in the bar. 'Saved by the bell,' I thought. Jesse's belly jiggled over his belt as he threw his head back and laughed loudly at something the bartender said. The fat cab driver then sidled up to a bar stool to join us for a beer.

"We are going to go back to my cousin's casita. I have everything ready for you. You can count the kilos and give me the 'dinero' (money). I have boxes for you to put the mota in to carry back home. Then I take you to the arroyo. No problema! No policia!" Jesse relayed.

Jesse drove us in his battered taxi back to a house in the middle of the shantytown where we entered a large dimly lit room. On the floor were the fifty kilos wrapped with a red cellophane outer layer, under brown wrapping paper which appeared to be the same as the one we had sampled the previous evening.

"Jesus, fucking Christ!" I exclaimed, staring wild-eyed at the huge pile of packages stacked on the floor. "How the hell are we supposed to carry all that dope back to the car? I didn't realize there would be so much and now there are only two of us! What the fuck are we going to do? Maybe we should only take half."

"Nah, I think we can handle it. Look at you. You're buffed from all of the water skiing you've been doing. This will be your chance to prove how strong you are. I've been lifting some weights too, so I think we'll be OK. Let's go for it!" Willie replied.

"Si señors. Like I said, No problema."

Jesse put twelve kilos each in four cardboard egg boxes and put the two additional kilos on top of one box. I pulled a wad of hundred dollar bills out of my pants pocket and counted out 14 which I gave to Jesse.

"Por favor, señor Ricardo. One more for Juanito. He work very hard to get you this stuff, and his family is very poor," Jesse begged.

"OK, OK." I said handing him one more Franklin. "Tell him muchas gracias, too."

"Muchas gracias y vaya con dios (thank you and go with God)," said Jesse.

Back outside we put the boxes in the trunk and piled into Jesse's cab. He then drove us back to the edge of the embankment leading to the dry arroyo below.

"Well, this is it," I said. "Muchas gracias."

"Adios muchachos. Hasta luego (see you later)!" The fat cabbie extracted himself from the driver's seat and smartly saluted.

We hoisted the boxes on our shoulders and descended the bank, half stumbling, half sliding trying to avoid the raw sewage which cascaded down beside us until we reached the arroyo at the bottom. It was nearly an ink black night, but the stars glowed brightly, the moon a narrow waxing crescent low in the west giving very little ambient light. We stumbled only a few paces down the gully when I promptly ran into a cactus and my boxes went flying.

"Fuck!" broke the silence and echoed across the desert. "Hey Will, give me a hand. I think one of my boxes might have come apart. Mother Fucker!"

Willie set his boxes down and helped me recover the spilled packages. One of my egg cartons indeed had a tear in one of the corners where it hit the ground. We were able to get all of the packages back into the box. We continued.

"Try not to be so clumsy. If your boxes break any further you'll really be up shit creek."

Trudging across the desert, carrying the two egg cartons at about 25 pounds apiece, we had to stop frequently to shift our loads, and catch our breath. It felt like I was juggling bowling balls while walking across a tightrope, blindfolded. One step in front of the other. Try not to trip or fall.

"If my old man could see me now," I said. "He'd have a fucking heart attack."

"Yeah, but he'd like the money we're going to make," answered Willie.

"That's true. It's all he thinks about. But don't count your chickens. We have a long way to go. One step in front of the other and don't think about the money. Contrary to what my father thinks, there's got to be more to life than just the fucking money."

"You got it, man. Except in my world; it's fucking and money. Christ, if you'd have given me fifteen minutes back at the bar I could have put another notch in my belt."

"What was that?" I nervously asked and cocked my head to one side, listening intently. A distant howl broke the night's stillness. Maybe it was a coyote, maybe not… I never knew.

One step in front of the other… keep walking.

We lapsed into silence. The night was still, so quiet we could almost hear the mad whoosh of adrenaline pumping through our veins as our hearts pounded like red-lined locomotive pistons.

'When have I hung it out this far?' I thought. 'There's just too much on the line, but this is really a gas! This is more than just a high school prank. Very heavy dues to pay if we picked the wrong card. We could go to jail or get robbed and killed out here and nobody'd ever know. Willie just thinks this is some kind of fun kid's game. No consequences in his mind at all. All he thinks about getting laid. Another notch on his bedpost.'

At 3:30 in the morning, tired and sweaty but pumped with energy, we cautiously climbed up the embankment, shifting the two cumbersome boxes which now felt like 50 pounds each, and saw the silhouette of the hospital. We quietly slunk to the car, opened the trunk and deposited the boxes. Willie took a second to grab a six pack of Coors out of the ice chest in the trunk. He opened one and guzzled. So did I. We were the only car in the parking lot.

"This is really stupid. We look like a couple of idiots or maybe we look like exactly what we are, a couple of smugglers," I said. "If we ever do this again, we have to park over there by the emergency room where the night staff parks, so we won't be the only car left in the parking lot standing out like a sore thumb." … if we ever do this again?

Willie started his Barracuda. The customized glass packed muffler system broke the night's silence and solitude, sounding similar to the Indianapolis Motor Speedway at the start of the 500. Varoom, varoom!

"Do you have to rev this piece of shit up? Can't you just go quietly?" I said as the car crept out of the parking lot. Willie was looking in his rear and side view mirrors almost simultaneously, while my head spun wildly on its axis, probably resembling an out of control gun turret.

"Be cool. Don't look around as if there are cops hiding behind every cactus. JP said it's cool… it's cool," Willie cautioned. "Relax you jerk! Pop a couple of beers and let's fire up a joint."

Driving the three miles east away from the hospital, we then turned north onto the main highway and slowly drove the one hundred and fifty miles back toward Tempe.

"Can you believe it, Rick? Can you believe what we just did?" asked Willie, taking another hit from the joint while holding his second beer between his legs as the smoke drifted upwards and we began to finally relax a bit. "I'm going to get a motorcycle and maybe a boat too. Then I'm going to rent a really nice ranch out in the desert where I can get loaded, turn the stereo up full blast and run around naked with my lady friends and not get hassled. This is going to be a blast. Welcome to our new world, Ricky my boy!"

"Again, better not count your chickens, you fool. We haven't made it back yet and still have a ways to go before we see any money."

"You always worry too much, Rick. Just cool it. Have another hit. We'll be OK." Willie said as he turned up his custom installed stereo to the Rolling Stones.

'Jumpin' Jack Flash, it's a gas, gas, gas…' [1]

---

1 Referenced Songs & Music, Item 1, Page 530.

Chapter 2

Sticky Clumps

Meanwhile, back at the ranch… in Willie's apartment Del was waiting anxiously for our return. He paced the living room of the tiny apartment around and around until the carpet looked like it had doubled as a thoroughbred race track. At every bit of noise made by neighboring tenants of the apartment building, Del nearly jumped out of his skin anticipating the cops had busted his friends and would burst into the room to capture him as well. 'My pharmacy career, which I haven't even started yet, is over,' he thought. 'I'm doomed to a job as a grocery clerk, if I can even get that!'

Just as he began to mumble his onsetting panic out loud, Willie and I stumbled through the door, dead tired but high on the residual energy from the evening's adventure.

"It went great," I told Del, "but, we have to get some sleep. We're exhausted. We had to carry your share of the load… since you weren't there… thanks! I'm beat! We'll tell you all about it later. I've got to get a few hours of sleep."

"I am going over to Julie's apartment a few doors down and burn off some of my nervous energy," Willie said. "I'll be back in a few hours."

"Wait, wait, you guys. I want to hear all about it. I've been a nervous wreck waiting here," cried Del.

"Later," I said. "There's plenty of time for storytelling. Like I said, I'm getting some sleep right now!"

Del just stood there slack jawed and stupefied as both of us newly christened smugglers left the room.

After I'd slept for a few hours, Willie returned looking pretty much relaxed and rejuvenated. The three of us then went down the back stairs to the garage. Luckily Willie had a separate garage space which he had pulled into the night before. We opened the garage door and I backed my Fiat up to the back of his Barracuda so we could transfer the load between vehicles' trunks. Immediately it became obvious, all of the packages wouldn't fit into the small trunk of my Fiat. Another miscalculation! So we piled the remaining six or so packages into a duffel bag with some dirty clothes thrown in on top as camouflage and threw it in the back seat.

"Oh, my God!" exclaimed a distraught Del. "We aren't going to drive all the way back to Stockton with that shit just in the back seat. What if we get pulled over and searched? What if they want to check us thoroughly at the California Agricultural Station? I'm fucked!"

"Just relax. Maybe take a downer, you pharmacy guys always have some," I said. "If we don't do anything stupid on the way home, no one is going to stop us for anything. And by the way, I have a secret way to avoid the Inspection Station in Truckee anyway. So don't sweat it. Just think good thoughts!"

"OK, OK. I will try and relax. You drive. Maybe I can settle down and take over after a few hours." Del pulled a red capsule from his shave kit and popped it. It was a Seconal and it was the last I heard from him for the next seven hours.

We crossed from Arizona into Utah then into northern Nevada without incident, taking a circuitous route which led us to Lake Tahoe's eastern shore, then around the lake's northern shore to Highway 89 past the entrance to Squaw Valley, site of the 1960 Winter Olympics.

I had spent many years skiing at all of the resorts around Lake Tahoe. In the mid-1960s when my skiing buddies and I started smoking pot while taking to the slopes around the lake, and specifically at Squaw Valley, we became increasingly paranoid about the drive back to the Bay Area so stoned after smoking pot all day. Squaw Valley is located just off of Highway 89 midway between the North Shore of Lake Tahoe and Interstate 80, the main east-west freeway which connects Northern California to the west with the rest of the United States to the east. When traveling back to California from Squaw Valley via this route, located just west of the cloverleaf connecting the two highways is the California Agricultural Inspection Station. All traffic on the interstate is funneled into two lanes which must pass through a building with kiosks adjacent to each lane. All traffic is required to stop at the kiosks whereupon a uniformed officer comes out and asks where you are coming from and if you have any plants or fruit in the vehicle. If you have out-of-state plates, if they are suspicious of anything, if they suspect you are hiding something or for any other unspecified reason seemingly at a whim, they will ask you to pull into a specially designated parking area and will search your vehicle. However, if you knew the way around the Inspection Station, it could be avoided by taking a back route through the railroad town of Truckee which bypasses the Inspection Station.

One of my skiing buddies who I had regularly skied with and who I also had smoked weed with while skiing had shown it to me last winter when we were returning home from skiing at Squaw Valley. Even though he usually wasn't carrying anything more than a personal stash with him, unlike Del and me, he too felt paranoid about having to go through the station and possibly being searched. Some of his friends had shown him the 'secret' bypass route and he in turn showed me. It led around the north side of Truckee through a residential neighborhood and to a freeway onramp which was located just west of the station at the east end of Donner Lake. From there it was over Donner Pass, the route through the Sierra Nevada mountain range named for the fateful Donner Party, a group of westward bound covered wagon pioneers who in the winter of 1846 became snowbound and ultimately resorted to cannibalism, eating their dead, to stay alive. The road today, however, was clear and we passed over it without having to resort to eating each other.

It was hot as we came down the western side of the Sierra and entered the Central Valley bound for Stockton. "It seemed so easy, Del. The only hassle was in my mind. I tell you, I was scared shitless walking through the shanty town, not knowing who was lurking behind any corner ready to jump and rob us. I felt like a lamb walking to a slaughter. And in the arroyo, carrying all that shit in the middle of the night; it was pretty scary, but I liked the way it made me feel… really in tune and totally alive. Kind of like we were invincible, Willie and I. But we sure would have liked to have had you there at least to carry your share of the load, like we agreed to before we started this craziness."

"I know. I was just too scared to even go and realized it the night before at that seedy bar. My whole life flashed before my eyes. I was ready to shit in my pants. All I could think about was my pharmacy career going down the toilet. All those years of study. My parents footing the bill and everything. I just chickened out. Sorry," said Del.

I could hear his voice becoming choked up as he explained it. He continued, "But there should be some pretty good bucks from this, don't you think?"

"I do. If we can get rid of this stuff easily," I answered. "I wonder if we should try it again?"

"Don't know about you, but I'm not running the border, ever! No way! I'll just package it and sell it back in Stockton. Tell you what. Let's just finish this and get it sold."

"I'd say, it's worth another shot, just to prove we can do it again," I said. "Maybe we can bring more back next time. Willie and I would have to figure out a better way of hauling the stuff across the desert. Fumbling around with those awkward egg cartons just doesn't cut it. Maybe some sort of specially designed backpacks or duffel bags. Hey, check this out! How about sled dogs dragging a sled with wheels?"

"How about a rocket sled? No need for dogs!"

"Just pass the joint, shut up and let's try to make it home without getting in a wreck while you're daydreaming about going Walter Mitty!" I said, referring to the fictionalized character depicted as an ordinary, hapless man and ineffectual dreamer having fantastic dreams of personal triumphs.

After a couple of hours of silent contemplation fantasizing about what a future in marijuana smuggling might hold for us we finally arrived back in Stockton exhausted but pumped with excitement and anticipation. Parking in the carport below our apartment, Del and I unloaded the boxes from the trunk and carried them along with the duffel bag from the back seat upstairs and into the living room and dumped the load onto the floor. Del then carefully opened one of the red cellophane packages from the pile and for a minute we just stared dumbfounded at its contents. The brick was loaded with seeds, sticks and stems and had a sticky Coca Cola-like substance adhering to it.

"What the fuck? I can't believe it," cried Del. "This stuff is shit! We've been fucked!

That motherfucker Jesse double crossed us and pulled the old switcheroo on us. How the hell are we ever gonna get rid of this crap?"

I was speechless as we tore into package after package with all of them appearing to contain pretty much the same garbage.

"I can't believe it either," I finally gasped. "But I think, if we sort it and clean it we can maybe salvage at least enough to make something for all of our effort. Look, there are some buds here, but this is going to be a mess going through all of this. And here we thought we had just done the hard part. I know, I know; before you say it Del, we should have checked everything on the spot. It's my fault!"

"Lighten up Rick and don't be so hard on yourself," Del said. "You aren't responsible. You said it was dark and you two had to get back across the border. Remember, it did get us stoned when we tried it the night before. And even as bad as it looks, it's better than most of the other shit that's around here. Some of it has been harvested in the mid-west and only gives you a headache. At least this gets you high."

"It looks sort of like the same stuff we tried, but this must have been the bottom of the barrel," I said. "Let's get started, we've got work to do. This shit isn't going to clean itself."

We then proceeded to break apart each kilo in the bathtub so we could contain the mess. We carefully separated the stems and overly sticky clumps and were able to salvage a little over half of the load or about 60 pounds.

Our first intention was to sell it by the kilo, but we scrapped the idea in favor of going back to our old method of selling it by the ounce to try and minimize our losses. It would take more time but it was what we had to do, especially if we wanted to do it again and have enough capital to improve our trip for next time.

Each ounce was weighed on an Ohaus Triple Beam scale Del had borrowed from the pharmacy lab. The 'triple beam', a delicate and precision instrument of weights and measures primarily used in the preparation of legitimate chemical and pharmaceutical compounds, now had become an integral component in the illicit marijuana trade. We weighed the ounces, known as 'lids', and then packed them in plastic sandwich bags. Each ounce or multiple ounces were then advanced or 'fronted' to friends, all students at UOP and surrounding schools, who in turn sold them and paid us in the following days or weeks. We were beginning to build a distribution network and, as the story of our adventure spread, we were also becoming legendary within our circle of friends.

Selling the weed in ounces was a much slower process than we had originally imagined, as we had hoped to unload it by the kilo. However, within two months all the weed was gone, except for a modest personal stash, and everything we'd fronted out was paid for by our friends, their friends, and friends of friends in various college campuses around the San Francisco Bay area. We sold each lid for $10 apiece. Out of the approximate 1000 ounces sold, we grossed nearly $10,000. After deducting expenses and paying JP for the OTO, Willie and I were able to net about $3,000 apiece and Del about $2,000. Not what we had expected but not bad either, considering.

My father had many sayings he bestowed on me through the years, one of which was "Good judgement is based on experience and experience is based on bad judgement." We had learned a valuable lesson in this first smuggling adventure based on our inexperience and which would carry on for me for more than the next decade. What I learned is a cardinal rule of marijuana smuggling. It is impossible to score weed out of season. The Mexican marijuana growing season is in the fall and winter and harvest is in the spring. All of the good stuff is then sold. In the summer it is nearly impossible to score anything decent. Everything left over by summer is garbage and we were lucky to even be able to salvage anything from this first adventure.

Chapter 3

Dodging Bullets

"Hello, this is the operator. I have a collect call to Alvin Lee from Ted Schwartz in Tempe, Arizona. Will you accept the call?"

"No. Mr. Lee is not home. Can he call back later?"

I put down the phone and walked three blocks down Pacific Avenue to a phone booth at a gas station to return Willie's call. He and I had worked out a system of telephone communication which was private and free. He would call me person to person/collect using the Alvin Lee to Ted Schwartz code names; I being Alvin Lee and he being Ted Schwartz. I'm not sure where we came up with 'Ted Schwartz', but Alvin Lee was the lead guitarist for the rock group Ten Years After. Anyway, I would refuse the call then walk to a nearby phone booth and return Willie's call where he would be waiting at a pre-arranged phone booth in Arizona. Since I already knew the number, I would call him back using a fake telephone credit card number. Then talking phone booth to phone booth we could freely discuss our newly formed marijuana business without being overheard and without paying for the call.

"Jesse fucked us," I said. "That shit was crap! From now on I'm only going to buy quality; and I mean the good stuff. The weed we bought was poor because it was left over from the previous winter's harvest. This stuff is a seasonal crop and can only be bought at harvest time. No more garbage. JP should have known that as well and told us. We should have cut his percentage to five percent. For christ sakes, we lost half of the load. For all of that risk, we need to maximize our profits. I can't believe we were so naive and trusting!"

"I know what you mean. I'll bet it was hard to sell," replied Willie.

"Yeah, we got rid of it all in about two months instead of two weeks and had to sell it by the lid instead of by the kilo. We lost almost half of the load because of sticks and stems. They must have poured whatever the sticky shit was, over what remained of the actual weed to hold it together. What a fucking mess. The good news is, it did get us stoned, but a lot of people complained. I never want to have to go through that again," I said.

"We have a good thing going and there's a future in it. The way we bring it in is easy and, so far, there are no hassles. We will have to let Jesse know when we're coming and how much we need beforehand, so we don't get stuck again with that dog shit border brown," replied Willie.

"Since you're already down there, maybe you can take responsibility for going down and giving Jesse advance notice of when we will be there and how much to have ready for us. On second thought, maybe we should both go talk to him about the quality so he knows exactly what we want. I think we should work out something with him which makes him responsible as well, if we don't get the quality we want," I said.

"OK, OK. Get your ass back down here as soon as you can and we'll go talk to him and get this all worked out. Plus, I don't like discussing all of this on the phone," said Willie. "This conversation is over!" and he hung up.

And so it was. Willie and I drifted from nickel and dime campus drug dealing into the high-risk world of marijuana smuggling. 'As long as it stays fun and we're making money, I'm gonna keep doing it,' I rationalized to myself.

Between November of 1969 and March of 1970, Willie and I made five more runs across the border, each a little bolder than the last. We established new ways of hauling up to 70 kilos at a time between us, using customized backpacks and duffel bags, so we could hike the dry river bed and rocky terrain more swiftly and with greater ease. We had steel-toed hiking boots so if we ran into a cactus in the night it wouldn't puncture and cut our feet, like the first time when we were only wearing tennis shoes. We also carried army canteens filled with water and had military style flashlights with red lenses to help us see the arroyo better in the dark.

Following the long drive back to California after the first and second smuggling episodes, Willie and I streamlined the transportation back to the West Coast by deciding to fly the loads as checked baggage on commercial airlines.

"Don't you think this is a pretty risky idea?" I asked Willie.

"JP and Bill do it all the time to New York. They said it's a piece of cake, and saves plenty of time and a lot of exposure on the road."

"I don't know. I like the road," I said. "I don't like putting the trip into someone else's hands. At the airport you lose control and, to me, I think it's very risky. Fifty-fifty at best and I don't like those odds."

"We should at least try it and see how it goes. Like I said, those guys do it and haven't had any problems. If we don't feel good about it, we can go back to driving; but if it works just think how much time we will save," suggested Willie.

"Yeah, but on the other hand, if we get busted, just think of how much time we'll lose!"

"Jesus Christ, Rick! Will you stop worrying? Like you always say: 'Just think good thoughts'."

"Oh fuck you! You know I worry because I don't like taking any more unnecessary risks than we are already taking, for christ sakes!" I said. "But, you win, let's try it at least once and go from there."

We purchased two large footlockers at an army surplus store in Phoenix. In Willie's garage in Tempe we packed both olive drab footlockers with the freshly smuggled kilo packages of pungent marijuana which Jesse was now procuring for us following the dressing down he'd been given following the first load. In order to mask the smell, we sprinkled Johnson's Baby Powder over the wrapped kilos.

"What happens if this shit leaks into the weed? You ever tried to smoke baby powdered weed?" I asked.

"JP said that this is what they do so the footlockers don't smell like one giant kilo at the airport or on the plane. Anyway, will you stop worrying, God dammit Rick, you're driving me nuts!"

"I think you're already there," I countered.

At the Phoenix Airport curbside baggage stand, we checked the footlockers with an overly friendly skycap and I gave him a twenty dollar tip. Each footlocker weighed nearly 85 pounds. While I called Del back in Stockton to tell him we had checked the weed and were ready to board, Willie stood at the concourse bar and hastily downed two double Tanquerays on the rocks. We then boarded the San Francisco bound plane. In the cargo hold of the PSA 727, the airline which featured a smiling face painted on the aircraft's nose section, was 170 pounds of top-grade Mexican marijuana.

The plane was smiling for a good reason!

At cruising altitude and approximately three seconds after the 'No Smoking' and 'Fasten Seatbelt' signs were extinguished Willie and I bolted out of our seats and headed for the two restrooms located in the tail section of the plane. In the adjoining bathrooms we each pulled out 'bomber' joints from our shirt pockets and lit up. After taking huge hits off the joints we would depress the sink drain plunger and exhale into the washbasin drain so the pungent marijuana smoke was vacuumed into space. Willie then released the plunger and squirted a quick blast of Ozium room freshener from his pocket sized aerosol canister into the airplane's small bathroom. He then exited the washroom and before returning to his seat, he rapped twice on the door to my bathroom. I opened it slightly and he passed me the Ozium container. I did likewise and a few seconds later returned to my seat.

"Another double Tanqueray please and a Coke for my friend," a bleary-eyed Willie slurred to the blonde stewardess.

"The Dead are going to be playing at Winterland this weekend," I said. "I'll get the acid, you get the tickets."

We spent the remainder of the flight with Willie drinking doubles as we listened to music blasting over the complimentary inflight headsets provided by PSA. Both of us were tuned to channel 6, rock music, our volumes adjusted to the maximum setting, 10.

As the stewardess bent to serve Willie a last drink before the descent into SFO, his face suddenly went pale, chalky white and ashen. His lips began to quiver as he reached frantically for an airsick bag in the seat pocket in front of him. Fumbling around in the seat pocket, instead of an airsick bag he pulled out an inflight magazine, managed to open it just as a dry metallic bile taste began to fill his mouth and uncontrollably, a fountain of vomit erupted like a volcano from his gullet, showering the serving tray, the magazine which he miraculously positioned to partially deflect most of the mess, but not all of it. The remainder, which I estimated to be about a pint, splattered all over the front of the young woman's uniform.

"Aarrggh! Holy shit!" I gagged as the aromatic colorful chunks cascaded into Willie's lap.

"Must be the sudden turbulence," said Willie, reaching for his handkerchief and his composure. "They ought to re-name this flight the 'Vomit Comet'."

"Right. The only turbulence is in your hand because you've got the shakes so bad, you screwball. I have to say, you've got some style! Now who's the idiot? That's a real classy move. Do you impress all the women like this?"

"Asshole!"

"Let me get you a wet cloth, sir," the flight attendant said. As she turned and fled down the aisle, under her breath I heard her say, "What a loser."

"Please fasten your seat belts, extinguish all cigarettes and prepare for arrival in San Francisco," came the voice over the loudspeaker.

Another stewardess proffered Willie a wet towel.

"We're beginning our approach into San Francisco. Please try and clean yourself off as best you can," the woman said to Willie, handing him the scented damp cloth.

"Huh?" mumbled Willie as his rheumy eyes gazed into hers. "What are you doing tonight, sweetheart?"

"I'm married, thank you," answered the flight attendant, showing Willie the gold band on her left hand. "Please fasten your seatbelt, close your tray table and bring your seat-back to the upright and locked position. We're almost on the ground."

"Too bad. We could have had some fun," said Willie as he fumbled to snap his seat-belt over his damp reeking trousers.

He still smelled like puke as I helped him stumble off of the plane onto the jetway and through the crowded mass of deplaning passengers who parted a passageway for us like Moses parting the Red Sea. We headed down the escalator to the baggage claim area to retrieve the checked footlockers. Arriving at SFO's baggage claim area, the two footlockers came up the conveyer belt following one another amid the mass of other suitcases, duffel bags and other checked baggage. The two 85 pound cases dropped one after the other onto the revolving stainless steel carousel then smashed into the protective rubber bumper at the bottom of the carousel chute with two loud thuds squirting powder from both footlockers' every seam.

We both managed to corral the footlockers and hoist them off the carousel to the baggage area floor. We then managed to awkwardly manhandle the first footlocker half-carrying, half-dragging it outside the terminal to the curb, leaving a Hansel and Gretel-like trail of baby powder in its wake. We then went back inside and repeated the same fiasco a minute later with the second footlocker.

"Look at us," I exclaimed. "We look like the dumb brothers covered in powder. At least it covers the barf all over your slacks."

"This is all your fault, you idiot. I told you not to use so much. Look what you've done! If a cop cruises by and sees this, were finished," scolded Willie in his usual fashion of not taking any responsibility and always trying to blame me for his own ineptness.

"Fuck you. Don't forget, this was your idea in the first place. But let's not worry about it right now. Just try and at least attempt to look somewhat together in case a cop does cruise by. Hopefully he'll just think you wet your pants and are waiting for a ride. Try to be cool while I go and rent us a car."

I said a quick silent prayer to myself and left him standing at the curb with the lockers. Drenched with sweat and dusted with a fine white powdery layer I brushed myself off as best I could as I approached the Hertz counter. To my dismay, the only car available was a red Toyota Corolla, 2-door coupe. I had no other choice, so I took it.

Loading the car was another Keystone Cop-like comedy. The Toyota Corolla was one of the first sub-compact cars featuring a streamlined body style, great gas mileage but a very small trunk and cramped back seat. We put the first footlocker in the trunk but it was too big so the trunk lid wouldn't close all the way. Rather than leaving the trunk lid open, we managed to keep it at least partially shut using Willie's barf smelling, wet belt. The second locker we managed to squeeze through the passenger door and into the small cramped back seat area. In order to do this, the passenger seat, which Willie currently occupied, had to be pushed forward all the way so his long spindly legs were almost bent double, forcing his knees to his chin.

"Nice car. You've done it again. Don't you think you could have gotten something smaller?" Willie said sarcastically as his knee banged against his chin causing him to bite his tongue. "Ouch!" he cried as we went over a speed bump while driving away from the airport. For the icing on the cake, he then proceeded to hock a loogie composed of alcohol, dried vomit laced saliva and blood out of the window in disgust.

"Jesus! Do I have to think for both of us all the time?" Willie said as he lit a joint and tried to relax. "At least you could have reserved a station wagon!"

"Fuck you! We're fortunate to even get this piece of shit. It was the last car they had. So don't try to heap all of this shit on me. Again, remember this was all your cocka-mamie idea, in the first place. You could have at least thought it through, you jackass," I retorted.

Shipping the kilos by the footlocker/checked baggage method was refined so as not to have a repeat of powder spewing out of the footlockers in a Three Stooges-like smuggling scenario. For subsequent shipments we devised a method of sealing the footlocker's seams with silicone sealant and enclosing the entire contents inside the containers with plastic bags taped shut with gray duct tape. We also made sure the receiving vehicle at SFO airport was reserved and large enough; avoiding the rather insane way we had driven the dope from the airport back up to Stockton the first time.

We also made several other changes to improve our burgeoning smuggling business. After a couple of deals, a degree of trust with Jesse was established. Willie would drive to Nogales, Mexico, and tell Jesse how much weed we wanted and when we would cross the border to pick it up. Willie always relished the prospect of going to Nogales as he could always mix business with pleasure. This always involved meeting with Jesse to provide him with the details of our requests, throwing down a few shots of tequila and enjoying the pleasures of the local bar fly/hookers who seemed to make La Tropicana their home. The ladies now treated Willie as a preferred regular customer as he was always a generous tipper as well as one who was fun to be with. Jesse now knew we would only buy the best quality. No more border brown. Jesse said he could get much better 'mota' down in Culiacan, about 500 miles south of the border, if Willie could give him one week's advance notice. We were also able to charge a higher price for the better quality pot. If sold by the lid, it could bring up to $20 per ounce for singles. If sold by the pound, it would fetch around $200 to as much as $350 per kilo.

Meanwhile, Del, true to his word, never came back to Arizona but stayed in Stockton and handled distribution. Breaking down the loads out of the footlockers, he occasionally sold by the ounce, but more often by the kilo or in multi-kilo lots. By the Spring of 1970 we were starting to make some real money, at least for a couple of college students with no other visible means of support. Willie now had rented the ranch property he had spoken of, way out in the country in the rural area north of Scottsdale between Carefree and Cave Creek, Arizona. This would be a much better place from which to stage our operation rather than the crowded apartment complex where Willie had lived previously.

Up until this point everything for us was going smoothly, no hiccups or bumps in the road. The trip was becoming more and more refined with each successful venture.

However, we were soon in for a rude awakening.

On our next run, I decided it would be a better plan for me to drive down to Arizona so we wouldn't be using Willie's Barracuda each time. My parents were vacationing in Europe, so I decided to 'borrow' my father's new Ford Thunderbird to make the trip. It was a gunmetal gray, new four door Landau model with a black vinyl roof. It had less than 5,000 miles on it and still had the new car smell. It was without so much as a dent or scratch anywhere on it. In perfect condition. I had figured since I would only be gone a few days there was no way it would be missed. They wouldn't be back for a couple of weeks. I drove it down to Willie's Cave Creek ranch and from there we proceeded to do our run the following evening. It was a great trip across the scorching desert. The air conditioning was blasting cool air on us as we approached the border crossing station in Nogales. It was just as we passed through the custom's kiosk when I noticed the customs officer jot down our license plate number as we crossed the border into Mexico.

"That's weird. It looked like the guy wrote our license plate number down. It's never happened before," I said. "I wonder if it's because we have California plates, or what?"

"I didn't really notice anything unusual," answered Willie. "But, there you go again, worrying about everything. What else is new?"

Regardless of what Willie was saying, alarm bells started ringing in my head. It was like the yellow light of an overhead traffic light, between the red and green had come on: 'Caution, caution'!

We met Jesse, as usual, at La Tropicana to arrange the pick-up time for later that night. Jesse was his normal jovial self. We made all of the arrangements as planned and I put the incident at the border out of my mind, at least momentarily, that is, until later when we re-crossed the border back into the U.S. where we were summarily stopped at customs.

A black customs officer holding a clipboard in his left hand approached the car.

"Please drive forward and park over there by the yellow line and get out of the car," he requested in a noticeably southern accent. Drive sounded like 'draav' and yellow line sounded like 'yella li-ine'.

"Let's see some I-dentifaa-kay-shun, li-icense and vee-heckle registration, pel-heeze," he continued.

The previous caution warning light in my head was now on bright red.

I maneuvered the Thunderbird into the designated space and both of us got out of the car, licenses in hand.

"Where have y'all been and what were y'all doin' down in Mexico?" he drawled.

"We just came down from school to have a little fun in Nogales, sir," I answered.

"Did you bring anything back? Do you have anything to declare?"

"I hope not," joked Willie.

"Now what the hell zat s'pose ta mean, smart ass?"

Before the conversation could turn into a tit-for-tat, I interjected: "Excuse me sir. I'm sorry. He was just trying to be funny. We just had a few beers and saw a couple of nice Mexican ladies at the bar. He didn't mean anything and was just trying to be funny. That'll never happen again, sorry."

However while this exchange was happening, I glanced at the officer's clipboard which now was facing me in his relaxed giant hand and recognized the California license plate number of my dad's car followed by the words 'gray 1969 Thunderbird four door' which had been highlighted by a fluorescent yellow highlighter marker. It stood out on the otherwise white print-out sheet like a yellow dandelion sticking out in a field of freshly fallen snow. My internal alarm bells were now shrieking and screaming at me in bright red… 'Stop'.

"OK, y'all can go now. Ha-ave a nii-ce evenin'," said the officer as he walked back to the customs booth. As we pulled away, I noticed him back in the kiosk talking on his walkie-talkie.

"You got a little too funny with the cop, you idiot. That wasn't too smart, even though it was probably the multiple beers talking," I said.

"Probably just a routine stop. It was bound to happen sooner or later. I'm not really concerned. He was nice enough anyway and just let us go. Don't sweat it," said Willie.

"Yeah, maybe," I said. "But when I looked at his clipboard while you were making that stupid joke you moron, I saw he had a printout sheet attached to it with our car's license plate number and a description of this car on it highlighted in bright neon yellow. What do you think of that, Mr. Smartass?"

As we drove out to the hospital, both of us felt uneasy about what had happened at the border and at U.S. Customs. Maybe it was intuition, maybe not, but we decided to call off this night's deal and just do a dry-run. Parking our car in the night staff's small lot by the emergency room, we left our backpacks and several duffel bags one stuffed inside another and those two inside of the third in the trunk along with the ice chest full of ice containing two cold sixes of Buds. We also searched the car thoroughly, in the trunk, under the seats, in the ashtrays or anywhere to make sure there were absolutely no traces of any marijuana absently left behind in the car. Satisfied, we exited the parking lot, descended down the embankment and into the dark arroyo. We snuck across the border, stealthily traversing the dry river bed, up the fetid embankment and out through the wretched shantytown we walked. We were thinking and discussing how we would break the news to Jesse, that the run had to be cancelled.

Arriving a few minutes later at La Tropicana, we found Jesse on his usual barstool a bottle of Corona in his hand. Jesse went crazy when we gave him the news.

"You amigos have to take the stuff… tonight! It has all been arranged," yelled Jesse, slamming his beer bottle down on the bar.

"Relax, Jesse, just calm down," I said. "We don't want to get into trouble and something's not right. We think we've been followed today. We got pulled over at customs after we left you earlier and they had our license plate number written down. They let us go, but it doesn't feel right for tonight. We don't want to get caught. If we do, we're finished and they'll be no more dinero for any of us, including you. If everything's alright we'll be back tomorrow night or the next at the latest and we'll pick up the load then. OK? Comprende amigo?"

"Si, si. No problema amigos. Tomorrow or the next night is OK for me, but you will have to pay my cousin another $3 per kilo for storage. It will make him happy," replied Jesse as the familiar gold plated smile returned to his pudgy reddened face. He then drove us to the edge of the shantytown, dropping us off near the dry river bed.

"Vaya con dios," he yelled as we again descended the embankment.

We hiked back down the river bed and everything seemed normal and quiet as usual.

"Maybe we're just being overly paranoid," said Willie.

"It sure seemed like the cops and customs were on to us," I answered.

'Something's just not right,' I just kept thinking, 'and Willie doesn't seem to be picking up on it.' It was if my early warning system was articulating a vague indefinable message I just couldn't put a name to. It was as if some spirit was calling to me from just beyond my reality alerting me to some unforeseen impending doom.

When we finally arrived back at the hospital parking lot and exited as usual, turning right (east) and heading towards the main highway, we noticed a pair of headlights in the rear view mirror. It appeared as if some car was following us. This had never happened before as we had always been alone on this road this late at night. Never any other vehicles in either direction. Then a second set of headlights appeared, and a third set. About a mile down the road, suddenly, four more cars, tires screeching, came tearing out of two dirt roads which intersected the road we were on and blocked our exit onto the main highway leading back to Tucson and Phoenix. Red and blue lights were now flashing from the roof bars atop the police cars which surrounded us. Angry looking men in military camo outfits and police tactical gear jumped out of the cars and approached us with handguns drawn. There were snickering sounds coming from some of the other military clad soldiers in the attack group, as slides racked shells into shotguns. Bright lights were trained on us, directly pointing into our eyes, blinding us from seeing exactly what was going on.

From beyond the lights in the darkness boomed an authoritarian voice: "Get out of the car now! Put your hands on the top of the car where I can see them and freeze, motherfuckers!"

My heart thumped like a pneumatic ram trying to pound its way out of my chest: ka'bam, ka'bam, ka'bam. 'I knew it, I knew it,' I thought.

"What seems to be the problem here officer?" lamely answered Willie, trying hard to stop the uncontrollable shaking in his legs. He knew there was not a thing the cops could do. He and I were clean; squeaky clean.

The camo clad man grabbed Willie's outstretched arm and spun him around so they faced each other. "Let's see some I.D. boys and the vehicle's registration. Like, now!"

"What the fuck are you two yo-yo's doing out here in the middle of the night?" barked a crew-cut military looking man suddenly appearing out of the darkness wearing a blue jacket with a U.S. Customs insignia emblazoned on the back.

"We were down in Nogales visiting with some ladies and having a few beers. We had car trouble and then we got lost, and now this. What's going on?" snapped Willie dizzily off the top of his head.

"What's going on here anyway?" I repeated. "Have we done anything wrong?"

"You just shut up, boy," drawled the angry looking agent. "I'll ask the questions around here."

Customs agents, local police officers and what appeared to be some federal agents clad in camo outfits appearing as if they had just emerged from the jungles of Viet Nam swarmed around us and the car like a cloud of angry bees. They searched the car thoroughly, opening the hood, checking the engine, looking under the seats, in the trunk and all over the vehicle. All they could find were the empty backpacks, the three empty duffel bags one stuffed inside of the other inside of the other, and an ice chest filled with ice and the two six packs of Budweisers.

Another agent overturned the ice chest, spilling ice all over the trunk. The man pulled two cans of beer free from the six pack held together with a plastic yoke which held each can in the six pack configuration and shook them, to see if they were actually beer and not some ingenious concealed stash. He then popped the tabs like hand grenade pins and the beer squirted and foamed out in a spray showering the agent and Willie standing next to him. "What the fuck?" the agent screamed as he threw the half empty cans at my feet. He was soaked with beer dripping from his face and onto his camo shirt.

"What the hell are these?" the now exasperated and angry customs man asked, holding up the backpacks and empty duffel bags in the glare of the headlights.

"Just our camping gear," Willie answered wiping his face with the front of his dirty tee shirt which he pulled up exposing his rail thin stomach. "We went camping a few days ago and left our stuff in the trunk. Anything wrong with that, officer?"

"Just get the fuck outta here!" the officer yelled, throwing the packs and bags into the ice strewn trunk with disgust. He returned our driver's licenses and car registration after writing down the information. It was the only thing he could do.

Twenty miles down the road, and just off of the main highway, Willie appeared to be shaking uncontrollably. I stopped the car, he got out unsteadily, took a piss on the side of the road and proceeded to retrieve the remaining six pack of Budweiser from the trunk. As I began to drive, he slammed down three beers, one after another, throwing the empty cans out the open window onto the empty highway. I nursed one. My heart was still pounding. My mind racing. Everything seemed crystal clear, as if my head was full of bennies (pharmaceutical speed).

"We dodged a bullet this time!" I said, now a master of the obvious. I was in a trance and those were the only words spoken until we arrived back in the Phoenix area some two hours later as dawn was breaking. It was a beautiful morning in the desert southwest as the sun rays shone over the Superstition Mountains lying to the east of Phoenix. Indeed it had been a close call, but by some miracle we had escaped certain capture and the situation needed some serious reflection.

Before attending UOP, I had spent two years at the University of Colorado after graduating high school in 1964. In my second year at CU back in 1965, I had come close to a serious if not fatal skiing accident. I was a good skier and a natural athlete and had always skied the expert slopes. Never one for too much caution, I had been skiing the deep powder in a back bowl at Vail which had only recently been opened following an avalanche. Dangerous parts of the bowl were still closed. I completely missed the 'Run Closed Due to Avalanche' sign which had previously been knocked down by wind and buried.

Coming out of the powder, I shot down the closed cat-walk at dusk, close to forty miles an hour and finally, at the last possible second, saw the slope straight ahead of me was completely gone: only twilight space and evergreen trees two hundred feet below was all that remained between me and certain annihilation. There was barely enough time to dig in my edges and come to a frantic stop, or I would, without question, have hurtled into the void. For the next twenty minutes I shook and shivered, but it was not from the cold. It was from what could have been. When I returned to the ski lodge, I felt disembodied, floating, as if I were walking in zero gravity. My head felt like a balloon filled with laughing gas; things seemed rarefied, transparent, but there was no laughter, only a silent awareness. I had tap danced 'on the edge.'

Sitting in the car headed for Tempe and Cave Creek beyond, I shivered as I realized again I was on the same razor sharp edge. 'Is this fun?' I silently wondered. Yet as the adrenaline had worn off, I suddenly became very tired and pulled over to take a leak and let Willie drive. I lay back exhausted, feeling a warm syrupy glow flood my body as I drifted into unconsciousness. I awoke as we pulled into Willie's ranch. It all seemed like a dream… but it was real.

The next night, Willie and I got together with JP at Willie's ranch in Cave Creek. We told him about the previous night's fiasco and that Jesse still had a load waiting for us. Since JP knew Jesse, he seemed the obvious choice to ask for assistance in helping us out of the jam we knew we were in.

"Can you help us out JP?" asked Willie. "Jesse is impatient and wants to get rid of the load as soon as possible. Can you do us a favor and pick it up for us?"

"We can't use our cars, since they have taken down all of the info on our I.D.'s and we can't go near the hospital," I added. "There's just too much heat on us right now."

"I can't help you. I've got something going on for the next few days, but Bill, my partner who you met before, can set you up with a buddy of ours, George, who runs his stuff over the dry river bed route. We don't know him too well, but we've done business with him before so I don't think there will be any problems."

"I don't know. It sounds a little flaky to me," I said. "You really don't know him very well, but what choice do we have? If we screw Jesse over, he won't trust us and do any more business with us. We're kind of over a barrel, at this point."

"There's a 'Y' in the dry river bed. One fork to the east comes out at the hospital and the other to the west comes out by an old abandoned quarry on the U.S. side. Maybe this guy George could drop us off at La Tropicana and then meet us at about 3 in the morning off the dirt road at the quarry," replied Willie.

"Sounds like it might work," said JP. I'll have Bill get in touch with George and set something up for tonight or tomorrow night."

George, a tall, acne-scarred, Ichabod Crane-looking man who appeared to be about 25 years old, was an out of work electrician. He was dressed in faded and torn at the knee blue jeans and a Harley-Davidson sleeveless white stained tee shirt. He wore work boots and had a polyester windbreaker slung over his shoulder. His Adam's apple bobbed up and down like a ratchet when he spoke. His dark hair was cut short, rather military style and his fingernails were chewed to the quick. Needless to say, he was a rather rough and seedy looking character, but having been given the OK by JP and Bill, we thought we could trust him.

Boy, were we in for a surprise.

George picked us up at JP's Tempe duplex in his battered white GMC van early the next evening before sunset. The van looked like it had been used in a demolition derby with dents everywhere, the front bumper missing and the rear doors bent inwards which were tied together with what appeared to be an old frayed water ski pull rope to hold them closed. We piled into the back seat of the van, as the front passenger seat had been removed and replaced with a bag of George's tools. Near the border, we drove down the dirt road passing adjacent to the hospital to the road's terminus at the abandoned quarry. Willie scanned the abandoned quarry with his binoculars. There were no other cars in sight. The only things moving were a few vultures, circling, riding the hot desert evening updrafts.

"Did you guys bring a heater?" George asked after we left the quarry, still on the dirt road which paralleled the main road where the hospital was.

"Why would we want to bring a heater? It's probably still over a hundred degrees outside and it's only a quarter to eight," I said confused and glancing at my watch.

"No, no. Not that kind of heater. A 'heater' is a gun. What are you guys, a couple of amateurs?"

"No, we didn't bring a gun," Willie said. I started to get an anxious queasy feeling in my stomach.

As we continued down the lonely bumpy dirt road, the same road the cops used as they descended, literally out of nowhere, upon us a couple of nights before, George swerved the van into a clump of bushes lying on the side of the road. Dust was flying as the van came to a sudden stop at the edge of the road. George set the parking brake.

"What the fuck?" I exclaimed.

"Dammit! The engine's overheating! Say, will one of you guys hand me the water bag in the back?" George asked.

Willie passed him the burlap water bag. George put on his windbreaker which was thrown over his tool bag and got out, walked around the front of the van and pulled up the hood. The desert was still and quiet. The only sound was George rattling around under the hood. He set the water bag down and withdrew a snub-nose .38 caliber revolver he wore in a holster tucked into the small of his back which was hidden by the windbreaker. Keeping the pistol at his side, George walked around the van, and opened the sliding door with his free hand, and in one quick motion swung the pistol up, stopping three inches from Willie's astonished face. Willie's mouth moved open and shut like a fish out of water struggling to breathe. I was speechless.

"Now, this is a heater," said George with a tone of finality, gesturing with the revolver. "Let's have the money, guys."

I pulled up my shirt and unfastened a money belt I wore around my waist. I unzipped the canvas belt and with shaking hands gave George three banded wads of one-hundred dollar bills which was our 'buy' money. All I could see was the revolver's small dark hole and George's silhouette. Willie's mouth still was open and closing, his lips making little silent O's.

"Let me give you fools some advice, since you just paid for it," George continued as he stuffed the bills into the jacket's inside pocket. "You both are a couple of stupid, real lame dicks. I don't know how you ever got this far without getting busted or shot dead. In this business, never trust anybody, not a fucking soul. Now get out of the van and start walking."

We grabbed our back packs and exited the van as George, still pointing his revolver in our direction, got back in the driver's seat and took off in a cloud of dust leaving us dumbfounded on the side of the dirt road. We then walked three miles into Nogales, Arizona. Since George had not asked for our wallets, fortunately we had enough money to catch a bus back to Phoenix. We sat in the back of the darkened coach, passing a bottle of Tequila back and forth, quiet for a long time, each of us lost in his own thoughts. There were no recriminations, no shouting, no friendly banter. The game had suddenly turned deadly serious, and this was beginning to sink in.

'Only the gods love gamblers, those guys who push it to the razor's edge, but nobody loves a couple of fools. We were damn lucky,' I thought, tipping the bottle to my parched lips.

"That asshole was right, man. Never trust anybody. We could have gotten killed! Shot dead in some slum. This is serious shit!" said Willie.

"Yeah, don't forget what happened the other night at the hospital. If we'd have been carrying, we'd be in the slammer right now. They were waiting for us. Maybe we'd better cool it for awhile."

"Perhaps. What I'd like to do is find George and get our money back."

"Forget it man! It's gone, lost. What are you gonna do, Willie? Get a gun, find him and stick the barrel in his face? Let's just drop it right here and say we learned a very expensive lesson," I said. "We were very lucky."

Later we questioned JP and Bill, but they never heard from George again. He simply vanished into thin air like some ghostly vapor trail.

Completely dejected and empty, without the load I had anticipated bringing back, I drove the Thunderbird back to the Bay Area. On the return trip, I got a flat tire out in the Arizona desert. I changed it and threw the flat into the trunk. For some absent-minded reason, even to this day I can't remember 'why' I forgot it there, and returned the car to the garage of my parents' home after washing it at a drive-thru car wash. Two weeks later upon my parents return, my father discovered the flat tire in the trunk and, of course, questioned me about it on the phone. I had to confess, or rather lie to him. I told him I had 'borrowed' his new car and had gotten a flat while driving it back from Stockton.

"Sorry, Dad," I told him. "No big deal. I'll pay for a new one."

"You could have at least asked me if you could borrow it," he said.

"How could I? You were gone and my car was in the shop," I lied.

"Right! And I suppose a round trip to Stockton and back is 2,000 miles!" he said sarcastically and slammed down the phone in my ear.

I had always felt like a square peg being forced into a round hole by my overbearing father. He was a self-made man who'd earned his chops by hard work and dedication and rose to the top in his field of business. He was eventually appointed by a governor and two U.S. presidents to serve on their advisory counsels. Since I was the first born and only son of Jewish parents it was indeed a hard, if not impossible, act to follow.

Sarcastic remarks from my father were nothing new to me. I grew up listening to them and was almost constantly the target of such comments. I called it 'sarcasm with a bite.'

One such comment has forever stuck in my mind.

One day when I was still in high school, I rather optimistically suggested to my father the possibility of following in his footsteps by applying to Stanford University, which he had graduated from in 1937. It was a long shot at best considering my less than stellar academic grades. His response was typical of what I'd grown up with and had to endure on a regular basis.

"Son, the only way you'll get into Stanford is in their museum with your head in a pickle jar labeled: 'The Man With No Brain.'"

So much for my self esteem.

Chapter 4

Ditch Weed

February 1970
Stockton, California

Among the frequent friends and customers who visited our apartment was another UOP student named Phil Erikson. Phil had a full head of perfectly combed brownish colored hair and was a light complected clean cut business student. He and I had become the best of friends and had bought a water ski boat together and enjoyed water skiing with Del and other students in the San Joaquin River delta on the hot days of the preceding summer when we both attended summer school. Phil was a handsome young man who had grown up in a small San Joaquin Valley farming town where his well-to-do family grew seasonal fruit on their farm of nearly 100 acres. Phil was the second of two children and was his parents' favorite child, the 'good son.'

Phil was polite, easy going and very popular among his high school friends. He was a better than average tennis player and a good skier. He played wide receiver on his high school's varsity football team and was voted 'Most Likely to Succeed' and 'Best Dressed Senior' of his graduating class in 1966. The lanky, six foot tall young man then went off to college at the University of the Pacific in Stockton. Phil was very conservative. He dressed in slacks, button down shirts and always sported two tone saddle shoes. Phil was also a prankster, a practical joker and needled his friends whenever he could with a certain quirky sense of humor, making him a very popular man about campus. A real ladies' man, Phil was always surrounded by some of the best looking women on campus… cheerleaders and sorority beauties were commonplace on his arm. As one would suspect, he bedded many of them and had quite a reputation as a real 'Don Juan'.

Del, Phil and I had skied together many times up at Lake Tahoe for the past couple of ski seasons. On one of our ski trips to Squaw Valley, Phil ran into one of his oldest friends who he had grown up with named Ciro Mancuso. Phil introduced us to Ciro who was living in Tahoe and attending Tahoe Paradise College, a small private school located in Meyers, South Lake Tahoe, where most of the other students were skiers as well, a few of whom were accomplished enough to be on a path to ski in the Winter Olympics.

Twice the previous summer, at the same time Willie and I were first humping kilos across the Mexican border, Ciro, Phil and two of Ciro's college buddies from Tahoe had driven their pickup trucks to Kansas where they had heard stories of marijuana growing wild along backroads and river beds.[1] They harvested a little over 100 pounds of the wild marijuana on each trip, cutting down the ten-foot-tall plants with machetes and carefully putting the plants in the back of two pickups whose beds were covered with camper shells to conceal the load. On the return trips they stopped and spent a couple of days camping off of isolated roads in the hot, dry desert of Northern Nevada. There they spread out huge sheets of plastic on the ground and dried the marijuana for two scorching days in the hot Nevada sun. They manicured the plants once they dried, cutting away the huge stems leaving the very green leafy-looking flower tops which they carefully bagged in large Ziplock bags each weighing about one pound. They repacked the trucks and drove back to Lake Tahoe and sold the load to their friends for about $75 per pound. Phil had fronted Del a few pounds of the Kansas weed to sell. I tried it as Del had it around the apartment. The bright green pot looked good, was very fresh and smelled nice with a faintly pungent characteristic weed smell. However, when I smoked it, it only gave me a sore throat and a dull headache. Even though Phil tried to convince us it was good, those of us who smoked the Kansas so-called pot generally only did it once and often made comments such as: "instead of getting high, we only got sore throats and headaches." It also made us very cranky and irritated to boot!

I often wondered why Ciro's Kansas 'bunk' weed looked so nice but didn't have the same effect as what Willie and I were bringing up from Mexico. Most likely, unknown to the inexperienced Lake Tahoe skiers and would be smugglers, was the scientific fact that there are many strains of cannabis all related to each other. Just like the fact that all canines, no matter how similar or different from each other they appear, are genetically related; i.e., Great Danes are related to Chihuahuas and both are related to wolves.

As far back as the Revolutionary and Civil Wars, hemp was grown commercially throughout the United States. Its production was significantly curtailed and nearly eliminated in 1937 with the passage of the Marihuana Tax Act. During World War II, production was renewed primarily in the mid-western U.S. in states like Nebraska, Indiana and Kansas to fuel the war effort as it was mainly used in the production of rope. This strain of Cannabis, known as 'Ditch Weed', is hemp growing in the wild, usually in close proximity to where it was once cultivated commercially. The difference between the two strains is in the THC content, the chemical element which gets you stoned. Marijuana's THC content is anywhere from 3 percent to 22 percent, while 'Ditch Weed' or hemp has a very low THC level, less than one percent. Most certainly this was what Ciro and his friends were harvesting and selling as marijuana. No wonder all you got was a headache, sore throat and increased irritability! It was indeed 'bunk' and no amount of verbal convincing from Phil, Ciro or anyone else trying to market it as marijuana could change that reality.

Ciro Mancuso was the son of an Italian immigrant, Ciro Sr., who had emigrated to the United States in the 1930s. The family roots were Sicilian and, it was rumored, Ciro

1 Referenced Books, Item 1, Page 532.

Sr. had connections to the Italian Mafia and was probably into some nefarious activities before coming to the U.S. The family settled in California's fertile central valley where Ciro Sr. became a successful cherry farmer and raised his family, a wife and two children: Ciro Jr. and his younger sister.

Ciro Jr. was dark eyed and of medium height and build and played football with Phil in high school. He was the starting varsity halfback. He also proved to be a brilliant student, excelling in history and foreign languages. Since his parents' native tongue was Italian, which was spoken at home, Ciro gravitated to both Italian and its close relative Spanish, and he became fluent in both. Extremely competitive by nature, Ciro was hard driven to succeed at whatever he pursued regardless of the consequences. He was not a person to lose graciously. His competitiveness would sometimes turn ugly and like his father, a menacing ruthlessness would come into play based upon Ciro's manipulation of other people. Ciro had an eye for quality and he was obsessed on acquiring the best of everything whether it was cars, sports gear, houses or whatever and he never missed the opportunity to boast about it. Friends from childhood, Ciro and Phil were as close as two peas in a pod.

Because of his excellent academic achievement in high school, Ciro was positioned to receive academic scholarships to numerous major universities, but he chose Tahoe Paradise College because of his love for the Sierra Nevada Mountains and skiing in particular. There in the winter he was able to ski nearly every day at the nearby ski resort of Heavenly Valley located on Lake Tahoe's south shore. One of his friends, Walter Brugger, also a student at Tahoe Paradise, was a member of the U.S. National Junior Ski Team. Even though he was outmatched as a skier, Ciro nonetheless continually tried in vain to compete against Walter. It was a hopeless effort, but off the slopes the two classmates began a partnership to smuggle marijuana and, for nearly two decades hence, would become a legendary smuggling operation, certainly the biggest in Lake Tahoe and one of the largest in the entire United States. It was the mutual passion for skiing which brought me together with Ciro and Walter through our mutual friend Phil Erikson.

Ciro and Walter were envisioning a potential 'Fortune 500' career in the fledgling smuggling business. At Lake Tahoe, they built detachable 'stash boxes' hidden underneath two automobiles with false bottoms built into the trunks. During the harvest season, they ran dope across the Mexican border, carrying between 25 and 50 kilos a run per vehicle. Enough money was gained from this venture and from several Kansas harvests to enable Ciro, being fluent in Spanish, to purchase a small avocado rancho outside of Tlaquepaque, not far from the city of Guadalajara in central Mexico.

After several successful trips their ventures escalated and in a rented warehouse with the help of a foreign exchange student from Thailand named Phassakorn 'Pat' Suraghoomkol, an excellent woodworker and craftsman, they now took small recreational trailers, and into each built hidden 'stash' compartments. A converted trailer could safely accommodate around 200 kilos of marijuana.

Walter, for his part, would scour the raunchiest of Nevada casinos located around the South Shore of Lake Tahoe to find elderly derelicts and winos, usually unkempt compulsive gamblers hopelessly feeding one-armed bandits. These consisted of both elderly, disheveled men and overweight, haggard-looking women, down and out on their luck, hoping beyond hope to hit a jackpot. He'd study them for hours and would make small conversation to assure himself they were hopeless enough to be right for the job. He'd then entice and recruit them to take a camping vacation to Mexico, all expenses paid. Intrigued by such an offer, they'd usually accept on-the-spot.

First, he'd get them all spiffed up; sending the men for haircuts and shaves to barber shops and the women coiffed and prettied at beauty shops in the South Tahoe area. Then, to complete the ensemble and transform them to respectability, he would send them to Parker's Western Store in Reno, outfitting these folks in fashionable western attire, making them appear as upstanding retired couples, cruising America and Mexico in their pickup truck towing their trailer and enjoying the rest of their waning years. In a matter of a couple of weeks, Walter had counseled and transformed these down-and-outers into respectable looking 'mules' to smuggle loads of marijuana across the border. Compared to their present mostly broke and otherwise hopeless situations, it was a hard offer to turn down. Each member of each team of couples would be paid $1,500 plus expenses per trip.

Once the trailer 'remodel' was completed, Pat would fly down to Guadalajara and stay at Ciro's rancho. The 'respectable' retired couple would drive the trailer down to Mexico, vacation for a few days at a nearby resort while Pat dismantled the trailer, loaded it with marijuana and put it back together. The 'couple' would then drive the trailer back, crossing the border usually at Tijuana or Nogales along with thousands of other tourists and people commuting to and from Mexico completely unnoticed and usually waved through without even a cursory check at customs. They would then proceed to a designated spot near the rented warehouse. Walter would meet them and drive the load to its warehouse destination where Pat, having flown back to the Bay Area, would unload it, then re-assemble it for the next round trip, which would usually commence immediately.

Two such trailers with two sets of respectable looking drivers and passengers were in constant motion back and forth, to and from the Bay Area to Guadalajara. Ciro and Walter were starting to make serious money. Walter brokered most of the loads, which were now up to between 250 to 500 pounds per week. It was beginning to almost resemble a production line at an automobile assembly plant. Pat was also in constant motion; assembling, disassembling and re-assembling the trailers and flying back and forth to and from Mexico. Both Ciro and Walter bought extravagant houses around Lake Tahoe with spectacular views and moved out of the dormitory, a converted motel, where they had previously been living. Ciro got his pilot's license and purchased a small airplane. He would sometimes make weekend trips to the rancho from Lake Tahoe to inspect his operation while still a senior in college.

Following the near bust and the money rip-off in Nogales, I was thinking about a new route, using more people, so Willie and I wouldn't have to make so many trips to accommodate our rapidly growing market. Phil seemed to fit perfectly, I thought, and he was willing to run the border wearing a weed-filled backpack.

Chapter 5

Boraxo

In March of 1970, I flew back down to Phoenix and was met by Willie at Phoenix Sky Harbor Airport. He picked me up on his new Triumph 650 c.c. Bonneville motorcycle. It had a bright red painted gas tank with accompanying red front and rear fenders. With its polished chrome spokes, it was definitely a 'mean machine'. Juggling my small carry on suitcase, I climbed on the back, put the suitcase between us, and held on tight as we headed back to Willie's Cave Creek ranch. We weren't wearing helmets and I was very nervous as Willie weaved in and out of traffic. I was relieved when we arrived. The ranch was located in a very isolated area north of Scottsdale and offered complete privacy. It was surrounded by bone white desert and cactus.

We were greeted at the entrance by a beautiful Golden Retriever, who barked as we pulled up. This was Willie's new dog, Sunshine. She was named after a particularly potent variety of LSD called 'Orange Sunshine.'

The reason for my visit was to scout out a new smuggling route. We both felt the old dry river bed and Holy Cross Hospital parking lot or even the abandoned quarry where we had gotten ripped off were known by too many people and were proving to be too much risk. Even the cops seemed to know about it, so our goal was to find a new way to get from Nogales, Mexico, back to Nogales, Arizona. We envisioned bringing more people as well, so we wanted a much less-known and less-traveled route.

The following day, Willie with me on the back of the Triumph sped south towards Nogales. Even in March, temperatures in the desert southwest could reach 90 degrees at mid-day. And it was hot as we cruised at speeds up to 110 miles per hour. I was petrified.

"Just because this thing is a Bonneville, are we trying to break the land speed record?" I asked, yelling into his ear from behind and referring to the Bonneville Salt Flats in western Utah, site of where the world's land speed records were broken. "If you hit a rock or anything and lay this down, we're fucked. No, I take it back… 'fucked' would be a good place. We'll be hamburger!"

"Relax, we'll be fine," Willie said, ignoring me. "At this speed we'll be down there in half an hour and out of this heat. I can't wait for a beer when we get to 'Nogo'."

"Just slow down, will you please? I'd like to get there and back in one piece, if you don't mind."

I've never really liked motorcycles and have always liked four wheels beneath me rather than two, but Willie on the other hand seemed completely fearless on his bike. It scared the hell out of me.

We arrived in Nogales and proceeded to the water tank, where we had made the original reconnaissance before our first run. As we scanned the terrain with binoculars, I came to rest on some buildings in the distance to the east. All alone in the hilly desert scrub lay a new housing subdivision under construction. Houses were in various stages of being built. Some were only poured concrete foundations, some were framed with two by fours with no walls, and others were simply vacant lots. None of the buildings were completed and no one appeared to be working. It seemed as if the project was abandoned. This looked good, at least from the standpoint of being a spot to arrive to when we finished our run. However, the hills to the south of the subdivision appeared steep and somewhat rocky and a long distance from anything appearing on the Mexican side, from what we could see.

We came off the hill for a closer look. We drove through the subdivision and it seemed perfect. Then we drove a few miles east, dismounted the bike and climbed the steep jumbled hills lying to the south of the subdivision, scanning the area with binoculars as we hiked. It was all up and down, none of it level; barrancas, dry arroyos, cactus and miles of bleached, broken rock. The distance from the partially constructed subdivision across the border into Mexico to another disconsolate cardboard and tin-roofed shanty town appeared to be about 4 miles, almost twice as long as the original run and appearing more than twice as difficult a trek.

"If say, ten guys or so, each carrying 25 kilos or so were to cross down there, we would have quite a score," I said swinging the binoculars in a slow arc.

"Yeah, we could cut down on the number of runs we make. Of course then I wouldn't get to go to Mexico as often… the ladies, you know," replied Willie, taking a long pull from the water-filled canteen he'd removed from the military utility belt he was wearing.

"Try to focus. All you have is a one track mind. See if you can, for the moment, attempt to think with the big head, rather than the little one in your pants," I said. "It looks a hell of a lot harder than the dry river bed run. We need to make sure nobody, not JP, not Jesse, I mean nobody knows about this new route. It stays completely secret. We almost got popped last time. Who could have tipped them off?"

"It doesn't matter how the cops knew. The old route is blown," answered Willie flatly.

However, we had to reconnoiter on the Mexican side to get a perspective of where we would be starting from. We then crossed the border to check it out. On Willie's motorcycle we were simply waved through with customs not even giving us a second glance. We then meandered through the shanty town which lay on the eastern side of

Nogales to a spot we had sighted from the other side of the border. It was a deserted rocky outcropping appearing as the knob we had originally seen from the north. It looked like just the right spot from where to start our trek.

"Let's stop for a couple of cervezas," Willie said. "We need to clear the air with Jesse from last time when George really fucked us. No 'buy' money, no run. Jesse was probably really pissed."

"We need to actually do a run by ourselves and check out this route before bringing anyone else down here," I said. "We have to bring our own driver so Jesse won't know our new route."

"I've got just the guy," Willie said. "He knows about our trip and really wants to get involved and make some extra money. I know we can trust him; not like George. I've known him for a long time, he's a classmate of mine and I know he won't fuck us over."

We then dropped in at La Tropicana. Jesse's battered cab was parked out front and as we entered we saw him sitting, as usual, on the bar stool which he seemed to own. He was amiable, happy and jovial as ever as we sheepishly explained to him what had happened.

"Pobrocito amigos" (poor friends), Jesse said. "No problema. Business is good and I had no problem unloading the 'mota'." We put together a 50 kilo deal for a few nights later. He said this would give him enough time to go down to Culiacan to get us the quality he knew we wanted.

Later in the week, we drove down to Nogales with a college friend of Willie's, nick-named Nape. He was blonde, short, about 5'5" tall and with the physique of a wrestler, very stocky, built like a fireplug. He wore jeans and a tank top revealing his bulging biceps and athletic torso. He was quiet, but very friendly and eager to do as we asked. Willie told me he was nicknamed 'Nape' because of his huge neck size which made it seem as if his face was connected directly to his upper body. His job was to drive his car, a blue Chevy Malibu, into Mexico to La Tropicana, then to Jesse's cousin's house to pick up the load and finally to our drop-off spot where we would begin our trek. He would then re-cross the border and meet us in about three hours at the subdivision and drive us back to Willie's ranch. He said it sounded simple enough and he was ready and excited to get involved.

After dropping us off at the knob east of the shanty town, Nape went back to the subdivision to wait the anticipated three hours for us to arrive.

Crossing the border was a nightmare. Almost from the start, things went wrong. Willie and I immediately got lost. The hills seemed much steeper at night than had appeared during the daytime reconnaissance, and now both of us were carrying 25 kilo backpacks. Also, we had not considered the fact there was no moon, and there were no lights from the new unfinished subdivision for us to pinpoint and use as a landmark.

For four or five hours, Willie and I wandered the lonely and forbidding hills, each of us blaming the other for getting lost. As the sky lightened in the east, we finally saw the subdivision's ghostlike framing silhouetted in the violet dawn. Nape was nervous, and on the verge of leaving his post at the entrance to the subdivision, when we finally showed up. We were both totally exhausted, cut and bruised from stumbling into sagebrush and cactus and falling on the dry shale rock. Several times each of us fell and nearly tumbled into oblivion down the steep, rocky pitched slopes. But somehow we managed and arrived back battered and bruised, but happy, confident and secure in the knowledge we were the only ones who knew of this new route. The trek had been much more difficult than either of us had anticipated. We guzzled water and beer as Nape drove the Malibu back to Cave Creek on the bright spring morning.

To prevent getting lost again, we subsequently plotted the route with topographical maps I had picked up from the U.S. Geological Survey Office and laid out a compass course to follow at night. We made another run two weeks later. With the aid of a partial moon and armed with a map, compass, good hiking boots, and a rudimentary awareness of celestial navigation I had learned years earlier as an Explorer after the Boy Scouts, the trek went off without a hitch. We rendezvoused with Nape at the subdivision in just over two and a half hours. Nape then drove us back to Cave Creek where we packed the load into odor proof footlockers. This time I alone accompanied the footlockers back to California aboard a 'happy face' PSA jet. Del met me at SFO driving the family station wagon he had borrowed from his parents with the excuse that he needed to move a bunch of books and lab equipment from school to our apartment. Together we drove back to Stockton. The entire 50 kilo load was sold in three days and we were ready to go again.

Over the next two months the same uneventful scenario was repeated four more times. We clocked our border crossing each trip. Our best time for the tough four mile nighttime trek over the parched jumbled hills, each carrying 25 kilos in our specially designed backpacks, was one hour and fifty-nine minutes from the time Nape dropped us off on the Mexican side until he met us at the subdivision. The whole operation was running like a finely tuned Swiss watch and we were starting to rake in considerable money. The going wholesale price for this high grade marijuana was $150 per pound and each of these runs on the new route was grossing about $16,000 per load. By May of 1970, the three of us, Willie, Del and I, now in our senior year of college, had together made nearly $100,000.

Willie and I spent the better part of May organizing all of the various facets required to pull off what we came to call 'the Boraxo scam', evoking memories of the twenty mule team Boraxo commercials featured on the TV show Death Valley Days. The logistics for this venture began to look like a paramilitary unit preparing for a night mission in some lost Ethiopian desert valley.

"Something positive came from George robbing us," I said, writing another item on the list I was compiling during a late night planning session. That incident's impact was never far from my mind.

"Hmm? George was a motherfucker and nothing else. What are we running, a charity here? In my book he gets no credit. If I ever see him again…" Willie left the thought hanging and continued, "What, are you going all philosopher on me, Rick?" angrily crushing the joint he'd been rolling in his hand.

"No." I replied disregarding his temper tantrum. "First, we learned never trust anybody in this business. Second, I figure you can't plan for every conceivable contingency;

unexpected stuff always happens. The best you can do is to try and have as many bases covered as possible."

"Kind of like the Scout motto, 'Be Prepared'?" Willie said, rolling another joint.

"Exactly. In the Army they told us 'prior planning prevents poor performance'," I said making another notation in the list I was preparing.

Another saying my father always used and constantly reminded me of was: 'Plan your work and work your plan.' He also used to tell me to always have alternate plans: 'If Plan A fails, have Plan B and if Plan B fails, have Plan C which now will become Plan B'… it went something like that, anyway.

The list of required items included multiple vans and drivers, compasses, maps, walkie-talkies, sophisticated custom-made backpacks, web belts with knives, canteens and military flashlights with red filters attached, and cases of beer and soft drinks in ice chests in the back of each van.

As I was compiling the list, which also included the clothes I would be wearing, I came to realize that inadvertently during each of the previous smuggling trips I had done, I had worn the same dark blue T-shirt each time. I suppose the first few times I wore it was because of its homogeneous dark color with no other markings or writings anywhere on it and because of its breathable light-weight material. This was not the ordinary cotton T-shirt we all wore, but was rather a very light polyester knit golf-type shirt without a collar. The brand was Munsingware and it had a small white insignia embroidered on the breast. As I reflected on this coincidence I had an epiphany, whether real or imagined I was never sure. The common denominator for each of our successes could at least be partially attributed to my wearing this shirt, now named my 'Lucky Shirt'. Upon coming to this realization, now and in the future, the 'Lucky Shirt' would be an integral component of every successive smuggling venture I was to ever participate in.

The moment for the Boraxo score was ripe. Willie and I knew this would be the last trip of the year as the supply of fresh weed from this season's harvest was at an end. The profits from this one trip would equal all the profits from all the trips to date combined.

The 'mule team' was recruited from both Willie's and my college campuses. It seemed like everyone we knew who had the slightest bit of daring in them wanted to be involved. It consisted of both Willie and me, Phil and three of Del's pharmacy classmates and four of Willie's classmates from ASU. The two drivers were Nape and one of Willie's friends named Scooter. Jesse's part of the operation also became much more complicated and required more people on his end to accommodate the 250 kilo load.

The trek was set for a night early in the month of June, 1970. The vehicles and people were assembled at Willie's desert house at Cave Creek. The 'mule crew' from Stockton had flown down to Phoenix the previous day, with the exception of Phil and I who had driven down in one of Phil's father's ranch pickups. Willie had gone to Nogales the previous evening and had inspected the load. He met with Jesse and arranged for the pickup and the packing of each man's duffel bag-style backpack with 25 kilos of marijuana. The ten backpacks were left with Jesse to be filled and packed, as Willie had instructed, and were to be ready for the pickup the following night.

Everybody was primed; the energy level was high. The two vans, loaded with the team of twelve student smugglers, left the Cave Creek house in the late afternoon and headed South for the border. Willie and I met with Jesse at the fat Mexican's cousin's place at about 10 PM to complete the money transaction. We had negotiated this load for $25 per kilo. The entire cost was $6,250 for the load plus another $750 for Jesse to have his compadre, Juanito, bring the load up in a truck from Culiacan. Juanito made all of 500 Pesos (the equivalent of $25 U.S.) for his work. The backpacks were then loaded into a van at Jesse's cousin's while the other vehicle was at the edge of the eastern shanty town with the squad. The 250 kilos arrived at the jumping off point near the Mexican end of the border and each of the ten of us slipped on our 25 kilo packs and started off.

It was close to midnight when Willie looked at the luminous dial on his compass, then at his wrist watch, and crawled under the barbed-wire border fence located in a suspiciously hollowed-out arroyo, probably man-made and previously used by illegal aliens sneaking into the U.S. There was barely enough room to maneuver as the top of Willie's dope-filled pack scraped the wire.

"OK," he whispered to the next man in line. "Take your pack off, scoot it under the fence, stay low and keep it quiet."

It was no more than five minutes before all ten men had crawled beneath the barbed wire fence and were slowly climbing up the first ridge line.

Back in Stockton and at ASU in Tempe, the students' talk and bravado had been cheap while they sat around their frat houses smoking dope and drinking beer. Now the reality of the situation began to rest heavily upon their out of shape arms and shoulders as their uncomfortable packs, which they continually struggled to adjust, shifted with each unsteady step in the cool, dark desert night. A couple of pharmacy students had popped Bennies (Benzedrine tablets), yet their bodies still flagged, and the only thing racing was adrenaline in their fearful minds. Each pound represented another year added on to their potential prison sentences if they got caught at this moment. The aroma of paranoia was as pungent as the stink from their sweat covered bodies. It was a piece of cake for Willie and me, as we were already in top shape from our previous runs.

An hour into the trek, the line of struggling smugglers stretched for what seemed like half a mile, with some having to stop and rest, waiting for the slower guys, while those toward the rear occasionally had to be assisted by me. I was walking 'tail-end Charlie', taking up the rear of the procession. Willie kept in contact with me by walkie-talkie.

"How's it going back there?" Willie said into the hand-held radio.

There was the crackle of static, then my reply: "The column is bunched up. Climbing the second ridge by the big boulder, some of the guys are straggling. Too bad I don't have an electric cattle prod to move this along. You just keep going and we'll be along shortly."

"If we do this again, maybe we should have these guys train for a few weeks in advance with packs filled with 50 pounds of gravel," came Willie's voice out of my walkie-talkie.

"Enough chatter. Stop talking and keep walking!" I replied.

Those in the column's middle and toward the end kept in sight of the others and in single file by following the red filtered flashlight signals of the man immediately ahead. The broken column seemed to inch itself forward like some handicapped centipede over the desolate barrancas.

Willie, Phil and one of Willie's classmates were the first to arrive at the subdivision on the U.S. side of the border. It was 2:45 in the morning. The rest of us arrived about half an hour later led by me with the others following behind; dog tired. No one had gotten lost in the desert that night, but the trip had taken its toll. All but Willie and I were exhausted, beat-up and emotionally and physically drained. A pharmacy student named Jake limped to the van pulling off a tennis shoe and bloody sock. "Jesus Christ," he screamed, "That fuckin' hurts!"

"Shut up!" I whispered, extracting a one inch cactus thorn from Jake's throbbing toe. "Or you'll wake the dead and bring a raft of heat on us." Jake bit his lip as I grabbed the first aid kit I'd tossed into the back of the van earlier and dabbed on an antibiotic ointment and bandaged the puncture.

All of us piled the loaded backpacks into the van driven by Scooter with Willie riding shotgun and the rest of us climbed into Nape's van for the trip back to Cave Creek. We arrived back at Willie's ranch house just as the sun peaked over the Superstition Mountains and the distant desert buttes. Sunshine, Willie's faithful golden retriever, was there as usual to greet us, her tail wagging excitedly back and forth.

Later, Phil and I packed the load neatly into the bed of Phil's 'borrowed' Ford pick-up truck. The truck had a camper shell on it, and the load fit entirely into the truck's bed beneath the rim where the bottom of the shell was attached to the truck bed. The camper shell had windows in each side and a glass window/door hinged at the top that swung upwards to open. Anyone passing us could see inside through the windows. However, on top of the load we put three plywood sheets down, cut to fit precisely over the truck bed which concealed the load of marijuana bricks below. Phil had also brought some farm equipment with him which he'd tossed into the back of the pick-up on the trip down from the valley. These implements—a couple of shovels, picks, wooden fence posts, coils of barbed wire, some various fencing tools, a ladder and a couple of old tires—were then placed on top of the plywood sheets and were clearly visible through the windows of the camper shell. Phil and I wore cowboy hats and headed back to Stockton, looking just like a couple of inconspicuous ranch hands hauling farm equipment. Just like the first trip with Del, Phil and I skirted the eastern shore of Lake Tahoe and surreptitiously entered California on the 'secret' back road through Truckee, avoiding the California-Nevada border Agriculture Inspection Station.

Eighteen hours after dragging ourselves across the high, dry desert, Phil and I safely pulled the truck into a barn at Phil's parent's ranch. His parents wouldn't be home from Europe for another three weeks, so the load would be safe and undisturbed until it could be sold; most likely within the next week to ten days. The rest of the crew flew home on the big 'smiling' jet plane. They, too, all sported smiles; except Jake whose toe had become infected. After a few drinks in flight, their voices became loud and they had to constantly remind each other to "Keep it down" and not talk about the previous night's coup.

Del, Phil and I sold the entire load within ten days. Part of it went to my cousin Marty who lived in San Francisco and who had brokered some of the weed I had previously brought across the border. Everyone kept one kilo for their own personal stash which, hopefully, would last through the dry summer months ahead, until hopefully we all could get back down for the next late fall or early winter marijuana harvest. The net profits from the 'Boraxo' venture amounted to approximately $75,000. Willie, Del and I each pocketed about $20,000 and Phil, who had been let into the group as a minor investor, made about $10,000. Each of the others on the team was paid $1,500 plus expenses plus the kilo personal stash. Some of the crew also sold some of the load to their friends and contacts and were able to make additional profits from the trip as well.

I washed then carefully folded and placed the now revered Lucky Shirt in a special place at the bottom of my nightstand next to my bed to await the next smuggling escapade.

Chapter 6

First Heat

The Summer of 1970 was one of those rare, slow, carefree times that would forever stand out in our minds. Del, Phil and I all stayed in Stockton and attended summer school as we all needed to make up some college credits for an anticipated December graduation. We rented an old Victorian house in a fashionable area in North Stockton which had a beautiful veranda surrounding it. It was the site of many afternoon and evening gatherings where alcohol and drugs flowed freely. Our routine was to attend classes in the morning when it was rather cool, then as the day heated up, usually to over 100 degrees, we'd take our ski boat over to Ladd's Marina, the local boat launching ramp located on the north side of the channel across from the Port of Stockton and launch it into Stockton's deep water channel and head directly to the sloughs where the water skiing was perfect.

On any Sunday afternoon, it was always a three-ringed circus and we enjoyed sitting on the grassy knoll overlooking the Ladd's Marina boat ramp where drunken boaters who had spent the day fishing or water skiing in the scorching sun would be pulling their boats out of the water. The chaotic scene always resembled a cross between divorce court and a bases-emptying brawl after a pitcher had intentionally hit a batter at a San Francisco Giants' baseball game. The screaming was intense and invariably a scene devolved into a fist fight as the current in the channel combined with the prevailing westerly afternoon winds blowing in from the Bay to make launching or pulling a boat out of the water a challenge even for the most experienced boater, not to mention those who were so drunk they could hardly stand or focus on the situation ahead.

One of many such Laurel and Hardy-style launching incidents we watched unfold before our eyes one Sunday afternoon was highlighted by two falling-down drunken, would-be skiers who arrived at the ramp at 4 PM. One of them was in the truck which was backed down the ramp and the other was in the boat resting on the trailer behind the truck. As the boat floated off the trailer it quickly began to sink as they had, in their stupor, obviously forgotten to put in the boat's drain plug, located at the rear of the ski craft. Before either of them knew what was happening, the boat disappeared beneath the surface and came to rest in six feet of water at the base of the loading ramp. At the same time the thoroughly inebriated driver of the truck panicked. Forgetting to put the vehicle's shift lever back into the 'drive' position from 'reverse', he gunned the truck's accelerator, backing it into the water with a burst of speed and before he knew what was happening the submerged trailer rammed into the sunken boat, holing its bow and pushing it into deeper water just as a flood of water cascaded into the truck's bed and into the cab through the open rear window. By the time the driver remotely came to his senses, the truck's engine became waterlogged and died and now the truck had rolled backwards most of the way into the water. It was only by some miracle neither man was injured.

Ten minutes later the Coast Guard arrived followed by a crane-bearing tug. After nearly three quarters of an hour, the wreckage was removed. However, at least 50 other mostly drunken boaters, in boats, were waiting to pull their boats out and were stacked up in the channel, fighting the winds and current and angry as hornets whose nest had been poked with a stick. The Coast Guard then had to direct traffic to the ramp and attempt to calm the angry boaters into an orderly procession. On any Sunday afternoon, chaotic scenes like this were commonplace at Ladd's and quite a crowd always showed up to watch the weekly summer follies devolve into chaos.

The San Joaquin and Sacramento river delta is composed of over one thousand miles of brackish inland waterways. Ocean-going ships are able to enter the delta waterways from the San Francisco Bay and transit from all parts of the world to the deep water Ports of Stockton and Sacramento to load and unload cargo. The delta also consists of numerous islands which are surrounded by sloughs, many of which have ten to fifteen-foot grasses, trees and crops growing on their banks. This area usually is windy in the afternoons; however this tall vegetation at the slough's banks keeps the water in the sloughs smooth as glass. Because of all of the agriculture on the delta islands and all of the other floating debris in the river, the water is anything but clean. You can't even see your hand even one foot beneath the surface. It's that dirty! However, the water is warm and smooth and despite its murkiness it is nevertheless one of the most fantastic places to waterski in the world. Thousands of skiers gravitate to the delta to ski, but because it is so large it is easy to find isolated sloughs where anything goes! During the hot summer months drugs, sex and loud rock and roll music blaring were commonplace among skiers in the delta sloughs. And as we later learned, it was also a great place to grow pot, unload boats carrying pot and other drugs, as well as other illicit cargo, human cargo included, from places all over the world.

But while it was party time for us in Stockton, there was trouble brewing down in the Arizona desert. Willie's buddies JP and Bill and one of their drivers named Benji had been busted in a house they were renting in the rural outskirts of Scottsdale. There had been over a ton of Mexican weed stored in the garage which was being readied for shipment back to New York when the local police, men from the Bureau of Narcotics and Dangerous Drugs (the BNDD, soon to become known as the DEA), Border Patrol and U.S. Customs agents conducted a pre-dawn raid on the high-rent Scottsdale property. All three were immediately jailed, held without bail and interrogated for fifteen solid hours, before Benji finally broke. He told the police of JP and Bill's entire smuggling operation including all of the known border crossing routes in the Nogales area. When asked what he knew of other people in the marijuana business, he told the BNDD agents, who were furiously grilling him, about a friend of JP's named Willie Sherman who lived in a ranch house in the Cave Creek area.

Willie was attending Arizona State summer school when, at 6 AM on the morning of July 10, 1970, ten agents and sheriff's deputies with guns drawn raided his rented ranch home. Fortunately, for Willie his Golden Retriever, Sunshine, began barking when she heard cars coming up the long dirt driveway leading up to the isolated ranch home.

"This is the Scottsdale Sheriff's Department. Open the door immediately! We have a search warrant!" shouted a loud voice from the other side of the large double wooden front doors decoratively adorning the ranch's entrance.

Willie had woken up to the barking and the incessant banging on the door. He was badly hung over and just barely had enough time to hide his personal three-pound marijuana stash, some LSD tablets and peyote buttons, and the nearly $25,000 in cash, he had haphazardly thrown into his top dresser drawer, into a specially constructed hidden floor compartment located beneath his bedroom closet.

He came to the door wearing nothing but a pair of psychedelic tie-dyed boxer shorts. When Willie opened the door a BNDD agent thrust the search warrant into his hand, spun him around and roughly pinned him, spread eagled, to the wall.

"What's the meaning of this?" a stunned Willie exclaimed.

"Are they here to get rid of the giant bat and the odd colored pterodactyls?" said Chloe, his blonde girlfriend for this week, still hallucinating from the extremely powerful hit of acid she had taken the night before. "Fumigate the kitchen first. The pterodactyls are guarding the rutabagas, and I need to get past them to make some jasmine tea. Willie, I'm still really dizzy."

The agent was momentarily disconcerted as his intense gaze fell upon the spaced-out blonde clad only in a pair of pink panties and matching bra.

"Are you William Sherman?" he said, returning his attention to Willie.

"Yes?"

"We have a warrant to search this place. We're looking for the drugs you are hiding."

"You obviously have the wrong address. There's nothing here and I don't peddle dope."

The agent quickly handcuffed Willie's arms behind his back and took him into the bedroom where he was interrogated. A young puffy faced sheriff's deputy gently took Chloe's arm and led her into the kitchen.

"Let's go and see what we can do about that giant bat, honey," he said, still fixated on the scantily clad young woman. "Maybe you can make me a cup of tea, while you're at it."

Luckily for Willie, Chloe knew nothing. She barely knew her own name. Although the cops combed the residence for nearly two hours, while Sunshine was locked in the bathroom wildly barking, they found nothing. The agents debated whether to call the paramedics for Chloe. Willie vehemently denied the accusations. Once again, he escaped disaster by the skin of his teeth.

From then on, the 'heat' was closing in. Willie was followed constantly by the police. Two days later, he finally eluded his 'tail' long enough to place the 'Alvin Lee to Ted Schwartz' coded telephone call to me and apprised me of the situation. He told me of JP and Bill's bust and he suspected their driver, Benji, might have confessed to the police. He later learned both JP and Bill had 'held their mud' and kept quiet about everything and had not cooperated with the police whatsoever. Both of them pled guilty and were sentenced to a year in state prison with five years' probation. Benji was released and became a campus informant at ASU and later in the summer 'ratted' on several student smuggling groups.

I later told Willie I had hoped George had been arrested in the dragnet too. He wasn't.

I knew right then we would have to re-think the whole desert smuggling operation and possibly find a new way to get weed smuggled across the border, if we were going to continue safely in the future.

Chapter 7

Graduation

December 1970
Stockton, California

It had been a mild winter in California's Central Valley. Graduation was held outdoors in front of the University library. It was a beautiful crisp winter afternoon. The
last semester at UOP had been filled with term papers, final examinations and, for Del,
pharmacy board examinations. He passed, and the three of us proudly accepted our
diplomas from the University president on a temporary stage which had been erected
in front of the stately building. The campus of UOP looked like an Ivy League college
set amid evergreen trees with meandering walkways and students dressed in black caps
and gowns.

The day following graduation, Del, Phil and I planned to move to Aspen, Colorado
to ski, rock and roll and consider our futures. Willie still had another year to go to complete his business degree at Arizona State.

Our three families gathered separately to bask in the glow of this proud occasion. If
one could view the snapshots taken of this moment, a subtle insight about individual
family dynamics could be seen. While the Erikson and Carlucci clans hugged, kissed
and were close physically and emotionally, my family was all too cerebral. They stood
there emotionally distant and physically connecting only with a handshake or peck on
the cheek. Where George Erikson wanted the very best for his son, Phil, my father
Richard Sr. (Dick) expected the best from me.

"Good job Rick," said Dick, giving me a firm handshake. "Now, what's your plan,
son? Have you given a thought to when you will take the pre-med exam? You know, I
have it all set for you to attend U.C. Irvine Medical School. The Commanding Officer
of your former National Guard unit is now the dean of admissions at Irvine and has
given you the green light. You're as good as in. How's that sound?"

"Huh?" I mumbled, not really paying attention to his usual diatribe. This was typical
of the 'receding finish line' my sisters and I had grown up with. We were never allowed

a moment's rest before the next challenge was foisted upon us by our father in his overbearing way.

"I have a place for you in my business where you can start right away since you've finally finished all of this," said my father, as he gestured at the campus and graduation stage behind me. "It'll be a great place for you to finally do something productive in your life, while getting ready for med school in the fall."

This happy scene depicting my father and me was taken on the UOP campus grounds following my graduation. It was shot moments before I informed him that I would be leaving for Aspen the following morning. Had the picture been taken five minutes later one could probably see the steam coming out of his ears and no doubt he certainly wouldn't have been able to even muster a smile.

"Dad, this may come as a shock to you. I'm moving to Aspen tomorrow. I'm going to live there and at least ski through the winter. I'll figure it all out, maybe in the spring."

"What? Do you mean you are going to throw your education away?" said Dick, his voice now starting to rise and his face starting to flush crimson with anger. "We've sent you through college. Dammit! We pulled you together after you almost skied your way out of the University of Colorado. We financed you through school. Your mother and I spent a fucking fortune…"

"Look Dad, you've never heard me," I interrupted. "You never asked me what I wanted to do. You just assumed I would be the dutiful son and trudge off to medical school straight away. I just need some time. I want to find out what I want to do. I'm out the door first thing tomorrow morning. I've made up my own mind for once, and I'm going to ski for awhile. That's it!"

"Skiing!" he nearly yelled at me. "I worked my ass off at your age and was nearly

50 before I ever took so much time off. When I visited you mid-way through your freshman year at Colorado five years ago, all you were doing was skiing. Your books hadn't even been cracked opened yet. The glue was still on the bindings, for God's sakes. I pulled some strings and got your sorry ass into the National Guard or you'd have flunked out and would have gone straight to Viet Nam. Then, again I went to bat for you and got you in here because of your shitty previous grade point average. You'd have been lucky to even have gotten into the school of hard knocks, if it weren't for me. Is this the thanks I get for all I've done for you? For Christ sakes! How much skiing do you need? Rick, nothing about you has changed except the amount of new ski equipment you have! I suppose that's where all the money that I've given you went. Your mother will be very disappointed, to say the least!"

"Dad, my mind is made up."

"Fine, go to Aspen or wherever. Do whatever you're going to do, but don't look to me for any financial support!" Dick said, his voice filled with venom and disgust. "Just don't write or call me asking for money."

"I don't need your money, Dad."

"That's a first! And by the way, don't ever use my car again. You not only didn't pay me back for the tire you ruined, but I had to get a new set of brakes on a brand new car! What the hell did you do?"

"Rick, Dick!" My mother, Helen broke in half weeping. "Can't we enjoy the moment, and be a family just for this once?"

* * *

I had traded in my Fiat for a Volkswagen Station Wagon as I had figured it would be a better vehicle for travel and for use in the snow and mountains of Colorado. The following day, Phil and I loaded all of our belongings into the VW and with the skis on the roof rack we set out for Aspen. We drove for twenty-four hours straight, arriving in Aspen the following day. Del had already secured a spot for us to live in and he had flown out to complete the final arrangements earlier in the day.

Arriving in Aspen, the house Del had arranged for was an old Victorian miner's cabin located at the top of Mill Street, six blocks up from the famous Jerome Hotel. The cabin was built in the late 1800s and was located up on Aspen's Ajax Mountain, above the #1 Chairlift. The only heat was from a wood burning stove in the living room. My living quarters consisted of a bed in the living room with virtually no privacy. It was surrounded only by a paisley colored piece of material attached to a ceiling rod, like a shower curtain. I had a window right next to my bed and during some nights it was so cold, icicles formed on the inside of the window above my head. I was always warm though and slept with two down quilts and sometimes in my down Everest mummy sleeping bag on really cold nights.

We had three other roommates, one of whom was a longtime Aspen local who was able to secure jobs for us cleaning up the kitchen at the best restaurant in Aspen, The Copper Kettle. Phil, Del and I would work in alternating shifts from eight in the evening until midnight. We ate like kings, eating the gourmet food pre-cooked but unordered still in the kitchen or left on guest's plates uneaten. Because we were now employed, we were given free ski lift passes to ski daily on Aspen Mountain. The pay was negligible, but it was a skier's dream. One of our roommates was employed as a member of Aspen Mountain's Trail Crew and most every morning I'd get an opportunity to join them on the mountain at 7:30 to help open the trails before the mountain opened at 9:00. Armed with a pocket-full of pre-rolled joints which I shared with the Trail Crew, this gave me the opportunity to ski miles of untracked powder with only the crew before the mountain even opened. I would then ski the entire day, always sharing joints on the chairlift with friends and strangers alike.

Our house was located right on the slopes of Ajax Mountain, where in the morning I could put on my skis in our back yard and ski down to the chairlift. At the end of the day I could ski right up to our back door, take my skis off and set them inside our back porch. It was an unbelievable time and the perfect place for what was to come next.

This was the old Victorian miner's cabin where we lived in Aspen in the early 1970s. At the time we could have bought it for around a couple of hundred thousand. It has since been demolished and replaced by an upscale condominium and is now worth upwards of ten million dollars. Ouch!

Section 2

Mexican Waters
(1970–1973)

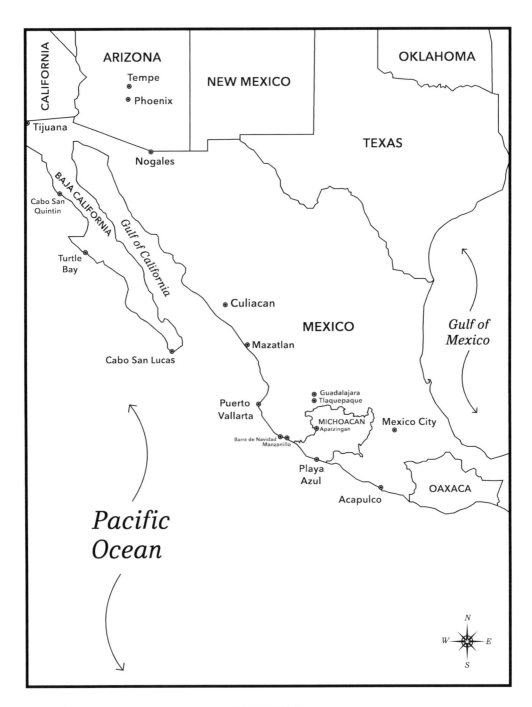

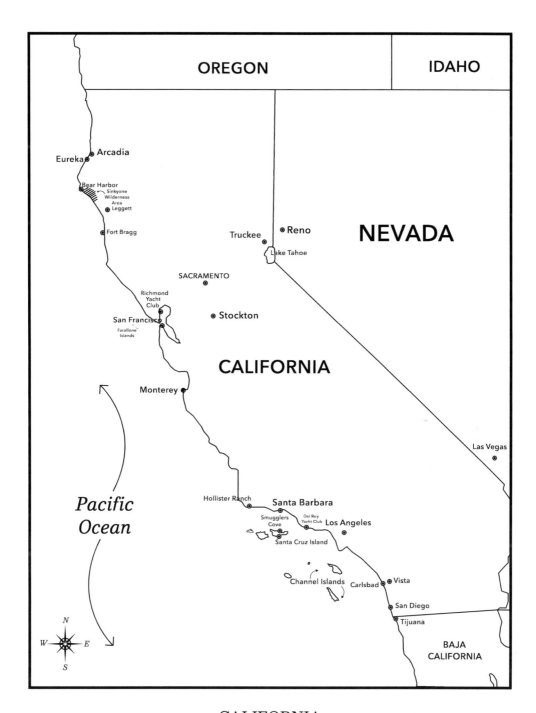

CALIFORNIA

Chapter 8

Any Port In The Storm

January 1971
Aspen, Colorado

Mark Wozenberg and I had grown up together. He lived in San Francisco's exclusive St. Francis Woods. Yet another Jew from The City treading into the world of marijuana smuggling. Mark, like Willie, was a third generation San Franciscan, whose grandfathers, like mine, had emigrated to the United States from Europe just before the turn of the 20th century.

Both of our fathers also served in World War II and were military officers. Mine had a stateside desk job in the Army. Mark's dad was a Navy fighter pilot who flew missions in both the European and Pacific theaters. Mark Wozenberg Sr. continued his love of flying after the service and flew regularly as a private pilot during the remainder of his life. They were also members of The Jewish Community Center in The City where I first met Mark Jr. and where we both learned to swim and to participate in team sports as boys. As a youngster, I would also accompany the Wozenberg family on many of their ski vacations in Northern California where both Woz and I learned to ski.

We went to different high schools in The City, but remained friends and saw each other frequently as our rival schools met often in athletic competition. I was on the swimming team in the lightweight division and Woz, being much bigger physically than me, played football and rugby. We were both successful athletes in high school, however he always used to 'rub-it-in' and never let me forget that he played on the varsity teams while I was only, in his view, just a puny 'lightweight'. We both graduated from high school in 1964 where Woz matriculated to a university on Florida's east coast where he learned how to sail, continued his athletics in the sport of lacrosse and majored in philosophy. Philosophy seemed to be the perfect major for Woz as his head was usually in the clouds. He loved to prattle on endlessly discussing his philosophical living experiences to whom ever would listen. My mother, who knew him well as a young man, used to say he marched to a different drummer and he must love the sound of his own voice, because he was always talking to hear himself talk.

Following his college graduation, Woz returned to the West Coast and crewed on a few sailboats racing in ocean regattas to both Hawaii and Mexico. He had twice raced to Hawaii from San Francisco in the annual Transpac Sailboat Race and had also crewed in races from Southern California to the Mexican ports of Mazatlan, Cabo San Lucas, Puerto Vallarta and Acapulco. He was building a reputation on the West Coast as an able-bodied crew member and at the same time learning the finer points of the art of sailing. His dream was to someday be a crew member on an America's Cup yacht. It might have happened if he hadn't taken a different path…

Being fully aware of my recent smuggling activities, Woz came to Aspen in the Winter of 1970/71 to seek me out and present me, his old lifelong friend, with new possibilities.

* * *

Our chairlift rolled through a drifting whiteout that clung to the ski slopes of Aspen's Ajax Mountain, making it appear as if we were suspended in time and space; no up or down just stationary in a seemingly endless white nothing. We had been skiing the very steep expert run appropriately called Elevator Shaft on this particular morning when the fog rolled in from nowhere, leaving us to decide which run to ski next where the visibility might be better. It looked like it would be the face of Bell Mountain which appeared to at least have enough 'vis' to be able to see the Volkswagen-sized moguls in front of you. We were both up to the challenge as we loosely played the competitive ego ski game of 'who's the best?' Having not skied together for the past few years, it was a good question. As we were riding up the chair together sharing the usual things that friends who have not seen each other in a while discuss—girlfriends, who's in better physical condition, who was going to win the Superbowl and such—Mark made his proposal.

"I have a friend who is delivering a yacht back from the Los Angeles to Mazatlan sailboat race in a couple of months. I've talked to him about bringing a load of weed back on the boat," Mark said. "Would you like to come along?"

"I've never sailed before," I replied.

"That's not a problem. My friend has taught sailing for years and I'm getting pretty good at it myself. We'll teach you."

"Is this guy reliable?" I asked.

"Well, he's a little bit strange, but he's a really good skipper and one of the best sailors around. I really think we can do it, Rick."

"What exactly do you mean by 'strange'?" I asked. "I need trustworthy people, not rip-off artists or flakes. I got fucked over once and got ripped off. I'm not going to let it happen again, if I can help it."

"No, no. He's reliable and a real stand-up guy and, as I said, a great sailor. What I meant by 'strange' is he's a switch hitter. He bats from both sides of the plate, if you get my drift. He's bi-sexual."

"Jesus Christ, Mark! What are you getting me into? I don't know about this," I said.

The chairlift deposited us at the top of Bell Mountain where we both wiped off our fogged up goggles and took off for 'the face' where the huge moguls awaited us. We then both began 'dancing' down the mogul field, kind of showing off to each other, when I missed a turn, caught an edge and went flying down the next set of bumps on my face, coming to rest on a relatively flat spot. I gathered myself and looked up to see Mark standing beside me ready to help.

"You OK?" he said.

"I'm fine. So this guy's queer?" I asked, changing the subject.

"Well, I guess you could say that, but he likes women too. He's bi. You know, 'any port in a storm'."

I winced. "I think this boat thing has potential. The old border route I've been using is finished. It's a bust. If we can depend on this guy, Captain Bi, I don't care if he's bisexual or whatever, as long as he can do the job and he doesn't try any 'funny business' with me. I'm really not in to that sort of stuff. Get it? What's his name anyway?"

"David B. Killian," Mark said laughing. He pulled a joint out of his parka, lit it, took a long hit off of it and passed it to me, still sitting on the ground and finally getting up to take a hit too. Mark gazed down the slope through the high thin air and suddenly broke the stillness with a loud long-drawn-out yodel, sounding more like the 'caw, caw, caw' of a psychotic raven's squawk. He then planted his poles firmly in the snow and with a tremendous lunge, took off full speed downhill.

Late January 1971
San Francisco, California

The white hulled sailboat *Sirius II*, its name emblazoned on the stern in raised gold letters, bobbed and tugged at her mooring lines at her berth in the exclusive San Francisco Yacht Club located on the San Francisco Bay in Belvedere, California. She moved like an impatient thoroughbred getting ready to run in the Kentucky Derby. *Sirius II* was a Cal 40 sloop by its original design; however, she had been radically altered by her owner and came to be known as the fastest ocean racer in her class. She had previously won Transpac and finished in the top three in two Mexican races. The modification of this Cal 40 included increasing the size of the mast to afford her more sail area plus shortening the stern three feet and reversing the transom making her appear sleek, riding low in the water, and much faster. This radical and very expensive alteration gave *Sirius II* a definite advantage over other Cal 40s and boats of similar design in her class. Her owner, Dr. Wellman Fortay IV, was a cardiac surgeon at Stanford who had pioneered aortic valve replacement and was wealthy beyond belief. The only time he was aboard the boat was during a race. He left the day-to-day running of the vessel, the maintenance and all of the return deliveries back home to the sailing master, Dave Killian.

Dave Killian was a hulking bear of a man standing at 6'4" and weighing in at over 240 pounds. He was 32 years old with thinning blonde wavy hair bleached to a reddened hue by the sun. Killian sported a perpetual tan on his massive frame and his nose was in a constant state of peeling, highlighted by red and sometimes pus-like bleeding scabs, which he always picked. Most of the time he covered it with a piece of specially fashioned metal, padded with foam on the inside, which attached to the bridge of his sunglasses making him look like the reincarnation of Tycho Brahe, the 16th century wealthy Danish astronomer who was best known for the copper prosthetic nose he wore after losing his real one in a sword fight. Killian was known throughout the local sailing world as one who guzzled beer and gin in epic proportions, but somehow always remained functional when sailing, even when he was falling-down dead drunk. His blue eyes had a piercing laser quality, unless he was deep into the booze. Then they appeared pink, unfocused and rheumy like a bunny rabbit's eyes. His handshake was like a vice which could crush your fingers when his massive meaty paw closed around yours.

I flew out from Aspen to meet Killian, check out the boat, and to contact a former classmate of mine from Stockton to arrange for procuring the load in Mexico, while Woz looked for the last crew member, as a crew of four was required for a safe return trip.

It was one of those rare winter days in the San Francisco Bay Area, brisk, perfectly clear with a light, prevailing northerly wind blowing, as Killian took me through *Sirius II* for my first inspection of any sailboat. As in all racing sailboats, I would soon learn, space was at a premium and cramped quarters were the norm.

Dave was expecting me and invited me aboard. He nearly crushed my hand as he enthusiastically shook it as I stepped over the rail and onto the teak deck.

"You must be Rick, I'm Dave, skipper and sailing master of this yacht. Mark has told me all about you. You've never sailed before?"

"I am and no I haven't," I said. "But I'm really eager to learn and am a quick learner."

"Great. I've taught sailing to greenhorns for years and the first thing you need to know is, when you're out at sea the lives of all of us onboard depend on each other not to fuck up. But, don't worry. You'll learn the ropes quick enough," he said with a hearty belly laugh.

"Woz told me all about it and I'm up for the challenge," I replied. As nervous as I was at the prospect of trying something completely new to me, I felt relaxed as Dave exuded a quiet and strong confidence about him which was very different from what I had expected, as well as also being different from Woz, who could be unpredictable and volatile at any moment.

Dave followed me through the opened hatchway and down the steep set of beautifully finished wooden stairs into the main salon.

As we stood at the bottom of the companionway, Dave reached out and grabbed something off of a table to my right, the chart table.

"You need to learn the language of sailing," Dave said. "Here. I've bought you a book," he said, handing me a paperback with a green cover and the drawing of a sailboat on it. "It's Royce's Sailing Illustrated [1], the sailor's bible as far as I'm concerned. Read it, study it and learn it as quickly as you can. When we get to sea you'll be tested, and knowing all the sailing terms and jargon is half the battle. Things happen fast out

1 Referenced Books, Item 6, Page 532.

there and I don't want to be explaining to you what's what when I need you to do something quickly. Everything onboard has a name. It's not just 'a thing on a thing'."

"Thanks. I'll start studying it tonight."

"Another thing is, although it's sometimes very peaceful and quiet out at sea, it can be very noisy as well. If I sound like I'm yelling at you, I'm not. So don't get offended. I just need to be heard and understood at all times and I tend to raise my voice. So don't worry about that either."

"OK."

"To your right, looking forward, is called 'starboard' and to your left is called 'port'," Dave said. "The front is 'forward' towards the bow and the rear is 'aft' towards the stern. Don't say left and right or front and back. It can be confusing depending on which way you're standing. So, it's port or starboard, forward or aft, bow or stern. Got it?"

"I'll try to remember."

The boat was much smaller than any apartment I'd ever been in. Thirty-seven feet, front to back—oops, I meant 'bow to stern'—is a very small space to be confined in for a month with four guys, it seemed. But I knew I'd have to get used to it as it was shortly going to be my world.

Forward from where I stood was the navigation table or 'nav station' on the starboard side which had a stool beneath it, charts in wooden tubes next to it and a radio with a microphone attached suspended above it. Next to the radio was a gray two foot square box called a LORAN, which is used for navigation. Also there was a black faced compass on a gyro attached to the table surface. Forward were two pilot berths, stacked similar to staggered narrow bunk beds, each having a small cotton net or hammock for personal belongings stretched and suspended above. As I turned to port, I saw a small galley opposite the nav station with a stainless steel propane stove which seemed to move from side to side, keeping pots and pans from spilling when the boat tipped or heeled, as it's called, to either port or starboard when in motion.

Dave answered the question before I had a chance to ask it. "I know what you're thinking. The stove is gimbaled so when we heel over, shit doesn't fly off it."

Forward of the stove was a small refrigerator, more like an ice chest with a lacquered wooden lid which had a stainless finger pull on it.

"On racing boats like this, the refrigeration unit usually has been removed for weight. We just put block ice in there to keep the beer cold and the vegetables fresh for a few days anyway. After that, it's warm beer and hard tack. You'll love it!" Dave chuckled.

Ahead on the port side was a small mahogany table surrounded by a booth. The table had a gimbaled box attached to it to keep drinks from spilling. The booth had cushions where another crew member could sleep. Next to the table by the bulkhead I saw the base of the aluminum mast which came through the deck above and extended through the teak floor below. On the wall or bulkhead forward of the table were two round brass nautical instruments; one a barometer and the other a clock. They were polished to a sparkling luster and both had brass spokes radiating outwards imitating two mini-versions of an old sailing schooner's steering wheel.

We then moved forward to a smaller compartment on the other side of the bulkhead. On the port side was a very small bathroom, called 'the head.' In it was an extremely small pumped toilet and next to it was a pumped wash basin. On the floor were various valves and knobs which I'd later learn were through-hull fitting valves attached to pumps so they could be opened to flush the toilet or empty the sink. It would be a quick learning curve to always be sure I remembered to close those valves so as not to let water in and potentially sink the ship! There was a small hanging locker opposite 'the head' adorned with louvered mahogany doors so clothes could hang with ventilation.

In the most forward part of the boat, known as the forepeak, there was another double berth with cushions on top of it. There were at least 10 sails in sail bags to be used for different amounts of wind and when sailing in various directions relative to the wind. I noticed there was no extra room for anyone to sleep in there. And, as Dave pointed out, below it was the anchor and chain attached to it.

I took all of it in and tried to remember as best I could what was what.

There was a pilot berth aft of the nav station and next to it, under the stairs, was the engine, an Atomic 4. This was a lightweight and very unreliable gasoline power plant most racing sailboats used. It was mostly used for charging the batteries, which had to be done on a daily basis and could never be relied on for motoring of any distance. Another problem with the Atomic 4 is that it runs on gasoline, which is a highly flammable substance and very dangerous to keep aboard in any large quantities.

Back up on deck and in the cockpit under the seating cushions were two large sail stowage lockers on either side of the tiller, a polished wooden handle used to steer the boat. And mounted on both sides of the companionway in the cockpit's forward bulkhead were gimbaled compasses with red lights inside to protect the helmsman's night vision.

"We can safely stow a ton of weed on *Sirius*," Dave said as we sat in the cockpit having a beer. "The trip home will be headed into the wind for the most part. It's called 'beating to weather' and the boat will be heeled over to the side. Not a very comfortable point of sail."

"A ton?" I said surprised. Privately, I had thought it would not be more than a third of that, about 300 kilos.

"Yeah, I figure about 2,000 pounds. It comes in bricks, right? We just pack it in sail bags and stash them everywhere. You might not see it right off, but this boat has lots of space and lockers of all size. The stuff's got to be packed securely so it won't fly around in rough weather, which we always seem to have going back 'uphill'. A beat is a tough point of sail; tough on the boat and tough on the crew because you're always pounding and seemingly 'on your ear', getting your fillings rattled with each wave," Killian said lighting a Winston with his Zippo in a theatrical gesture.

"Want one?" he asked offering me a smoke.

"Nope. The only thing I smoke is weed. Those cancer sticks will kill ya."

"Well, we all gotta die sometime," Dave replied.

"You sure you can do this?" I asked.

"Hey, no problem. It's just cargo to me," Dave said. "You're handling the load, right?"

"Right. I've got a man on it," I replied. "Dave, this is kind of embarrassing, but I gotta ask you, since we'll be sailing together."

"What? Go ahead and ask."

"Umm, Woz kind of told me about your, um proclivities. I have to lay it on the table 'cause I don't want any misunderstandings later on. He told me," I stammered trying to find the right words; "that you, um, had certain peculiarities sexually. I'm straight and am not into any 'funny business'. Please, let's just keep it that way. OK?"

"Oh, no problem. Everything will be on the up-and-up. What you do ashore is your business and what I do is mine. No worries, man!"

"OK, that's behind us," I said, relieved.

"Tell you what, you get your man down to Mazatlan to score the load. Then, when the race is finished and all the hoopla's over, and the owner and the rest of the race crew have flown home, I'll have Mark phone you. Fly down there. We'll load the boat and take off," Killian concluded.

In Stockton, one of the guys I had sold to and bought weed from was a classmate of mine named Rob Farnsworth. Rob and I had spent time together driving back across country when both of us attended summer school last August, after Willie and I had made our first run across the border. That summer I spent a couple of weeks taking a class at Dartmouth while Rob attended another Ivy League school over on the East Coast. We had met the previous year as Rob was involved in a large smuggling operation bringing hashish in from Afghanistan. I had dealt several pounds of it to friends of mine, and just as I was starting to gear up to move more, he ran out. We stayed in close contact and later discovered we were both going to attend summer school in the east and agreed to meet there. We ended up driving back to Stockton together where the main topic of discussion was smuggling as I told him of my adventure in Mexico. He was a much more experienced smuggler than me as he had already done several loads of hashish from Morocco and now Afghanistan. He also had told me he had contacts in Mexico, so after meeting with Killian, I went to Stockton where I broached the idea to him about getting involved in our upcoming boat trip. Rob said he was interested, his contact in Mexico could score the load for us and he had the capital to finance it as well. He and I agreed to split the load evenly; so I was covered for my part.

For his part, Woz had very little trouble lining up the third crew member. Steve Morrison was a local San Franciscan who both Mark and I knew casually from childhood. Steve had grown up in the affluent area of Telegraph Hill, most notably known for Coit Tower, one of the famous San Francisco landmarks. Sporting a shock of surfer blonde hair and a stocky build, Steve, at 5'8" tall, was a young man who had dropped out of high school in his senior year and joined the U.S. Coast Guard. This proved to be an extremely smart move as it kept him from being drafted and certainly going to Viet Nam as his lottery number came to be in the first 25. Steve spent the first half of his four year stint serving on small Coast Guard water craft cruising in the San Francisco Bay doing random boat safety checks and studying the currents and tides in the Bay. One of his duties also was to fish out the bodies of Golden Gate Bridge 'jumpers', those who had taken the final suicide plunge off of the famous span joining San Francisco with Marin County to the north. He also cut his chops by regularly servicing and sometimes manning the old Mile Rock Lighthouse, located in the ocean a mile off San Francisco's Land's End. This assignment gave him the lighthouse tending experience which the last eighteen months of his enlistment would entail. Steve became the U.S. Coast Guard's solitary keeper of a lighthouse station located on an uninhabited island in the Alaskan inland waterways. It was there he had developed a certifiable mania for kayaking, scuba diving for abalone and smoking copious amounts of pot to alleviate the boredom. He had brought three kilos of Mexican's finest to get him through his eighteen months on the island.

When his enlistment was up, Steve successfully completed his high school GED (graduate education diploma) and thought he would attend college to further his education. After auditing a couple of classes at Colorado State University in Fort Collins where he also did his share of skiing and chasing coeds, he realized he just wasn't cut out for any more formal education. So he departed Colorado and went directly to Mexico where he was able to use one of his Coast Guard skills, scuba diving, to conduct diving tours in the Mazatlan area. Woz and Steve had several close friends in common and one of them told Woz of Steve's history and thought he would be perfect for the sailing adventure. Woz liked the fact that Steve was adventurous, smoked pot, had nautical experience and had connections in Mexico.

Steve jumped at the opportunity.

Late February 1971
Mazatlan, Mexico

Sirius II lay anchored at the north end of Mazatlan harbor. The afternoon was hot and sultry. A few little light puffs of wind on the water called cat's paws scurried over the otherwise listless Mazatlan Bay. For the captain, 'Happy Hour' had gotten an unusually early start that day. At about 10:30 in the morning, Killian began a liquid 'breakfast' with several slugs of Bloody Marys, which dissolved into gin and lime on the rocks at about noon followed by just the gin on the rocks at 2. It was now half past four and the quart of Oso Negro, cheap Mexican gin featuring as its signature a small black plastic bull on a chain around the bottleneck, was empty and tossed haphazardly on the cockpit's floor. Killian lay sprawled half in and half out of the cockpit. The lower half of his body rested on the cockpit cushion and then bent back at an awkward angle so the top half lay draped on the deck next to the main sheet winch. His golden brown huge stomach rose and fell with his labored breathing as he peacefully rested in that position like a half baked soused beached whale. He was wearing nothing but a fire engine red French G-string bikini, a floppy Greek sailor captain's hat garnished with scrambled egg gold braid and his black rimmed Buddy Holly-style sunglasses with the ever-present attached metal nose covering.

Three hours earlier Rob Farnsworth had arrived from California and had come aboard *Sirius II* hoping to find me, but the only one onboard was Killian already half snockered. Rob, now thoroughly drunk, had been for the past hour forced to keep constantly on the move over the unfamiliar deck to avoid Killian's not-so-subtle advances. Rob had arrived at the Mazatlan airport, took a cab to the dock and hired a water taxi to ferry him to *Sirius II* lying at anchor in the bay. He came with bad news to tell me: his connection had some serious heat on him and couldn't score the load as promised. However, all he found aboard the boat was a lecherous drunken bisexual sea captain.

Woz had rowed ashore in the rented dinghy, had done some shopping then had taken a taxi to the airport to meet Steve Morrison and me. We were arriving on the afternoon direct Mexicana Airlines flight from San Francisco. Woz had a taxi waiting for us and we returned to the dock, picked up the dinghy and were rowing out to the boat sitting serenely by itself in the bay. All I can say is, thank God there were no other boats in the near vicinity of *Sirius II*, because as we approached, a blood curdling yell erupted from the yacht. If any others had witnessed the goings on, the Mexican police would have surely been on scene to investigate.

"I told you to stay away from me, you faggot!" screamed Rob. Then he lunged at Killian who stumbled backwards and plunged overboard, landing in the water flat on his back followed by a whoosh sound as the air in his lungs rushed out of his mouth. He sank immediately then re-surfaced looking completely dazed and confused.

"What's going on here?" I yelled from the dinghy.

"That fruit was all over me! The bastard actually asked if he could give me a blow job!" screamed Rob, his face red with anger.

"Jesus Christ! I'm not even in Mexico twenty minutes and look what's happening. I wouldn't be surprised if the harbor master can probably hear or see all this commotion." I yelled. "I thought we were going to try and keep a low profile and not draw any unnecessary attention to us."

"Killian! What the fuck is going on here?"

Dave, looking sheepish, grabbed the boarding ladder and sputtered, "Hey, I didn't mean any harm. I was just trying to be hospitable."

"If he comes near me again, I swear I'll kill him."

"If this grab-ass continues we will get tossed out of here, for sure." I said. "Dave, I thought we already had this discussion, remember… if you can. You obviously forgot what you said. Let me refresh your memory. 'Everything will be on the up-and-up and what happens on shore is nobody's business.' You said it and last time I looked this is not 'on shore'. Unless this is over and done with right now, you're done."

"This is great! Is this what I have to look forward to on the trip home?" chimed Steve, his eyes as big as saucers. "I'm not sure if I want to go through with this."

Dave mumbled something unintelligible and disappeared below deck, presumably to sleep it off.

"Row me back to shore, Rick," said Rob. "I've got to go to my hotel room, sober up and get the essence of that queer off me. Let's meet in a couple of hours for dinner, but please, leave the weirdo back on the boat."

"He's harmless. I've sailed with him before. He's just testing the water," said Woz laughing.

Steve, Woz and I sat in the cockpit drinking the few remaining Carta Blancas and watching the sunset while down below the reverberation of Killian's snoring could almost be felt by the three of us sitting up on deck.

"I thought this guy, Rob, had his shit together?" said Woz. "You told me he was some big time smuggler."

"I know," I said. "I don't know exactly what happened. He said his connection got busted and his people have too much heat on them and are lying low. We'll find out more tonight. In the meantime, we're going to have to scramble around and see what we can put together."

"I have a Mexican diving buddy who lives down here in Mazatlan. He can probably get us anything we want," said Steve. "Why don't I go ashore and give him a call? I'll meet you for dinner."

Later at La Posada, a waterfront hotel and restaurant, the four of us sat eating fresh shrimp and drinking beer. Rob drank strong black coffee.

"We're in luck. Mario said he can get us a load. He said, 'No problema'. He can deliver us a ton in a week. He wants $10,000 up front and $10,000 on delivery. He said it's high quality and he can get us a sample tomorrow," Steve said. "I told him I was having dinner tonight and I'd let him know tomorrow."

"I'm still willing to be the money man for this," said Rob. "I feel bad my end fell through. How do I know we can trust this guy, if I front him ten grand?"

"I saved his life diving last year. I know him and his whole family. They are well-to-do, educated and well established here in Mazatlan. They treat me like a son. Mario is not going anywhere, and he's as honest as they come. The price does seem a bit on the high side, but let's see what he's got, then decide," Steve replied.

Mario and his brother Luis owned a scuba diving shop on the main tourist beach. We met him at eleven the next morning. Mario was about 25 years old, dark complected with longish black hair. He was 5'7" tall, had a deep brown suntan and a very muscular physique. He wore a pair of red and blue surfer-style trunks, had on a white tank top advertising Sol Beer on the front and wore leather huarache sandals with old tire soles stitched on the bottom. His left forearm sported a faded tattoo of an anchor and his right hand was deformed, probably at birth. It looked like a dolphin flipper with no fingers and hung limply from his wrist.

After the introductions, Mario led the four of us into a back room in the dive shop, behind a wall of compressors, weight belts and diving regulators. He retrieved a box from the corner and produced five kilo packages of marijuana each wrapped in red and green cellophane paper. He carefully opened each package and at one glance I could tell this was very high-grade weed. The individual flower tops were pungent, resinous and green-brown in color and were laid together and packed loosely into nice uniform bricks.

"Now, this is more like it. Way better than anything I got at the border or even from Culiacan," I said.

"But twenty grand is way too steep at a wholesale ton-price," added Rob.

"You guys come to me at the last minute, because your guys fucked up and couldn't score. You beg me to put something together of only the finest quality, which I do,"

Mario said pointing to the bricks spread on the floor. "Now you tell me it's too expensive. Maybe you guys should just go fuck yourselves and try to get something going on the streets of Mazatlan, where the Federales will certainly bust you rookies, right now!"

"Come on old friend. This is just the beginning. Can't you give us a little better deal? For old time's sake?" said Steve.

"All right, all right. Just because you saved my life. I kind of owe you one. I'll knock off a couple of grand and do the whole ton for eighteen G's. No less," replied Mario.

"OK," said Rob. "Eight now and ten on delivery."

"No. I don't think so. I need ten now to get things working and then eight on delivery one week from tonight at the small fishing dock at the north end of town."

"OK. It's a deal," said Rob. He offered his hand and Mario shook it with his deformed hand. Rob then handed him a neatly bound stack of one hundred $100 bills.

As we left the dive shop, Steve turned and said, "Rob, you kind of act as if you think he's a liability with that flipper hand of his. Let me tell ya, he's a better swimmer and dive master than you'll ever be."

Six days later, Mario met Steve at a thatched-hut beach bar known as a 'palapa', located behind La Playa Hotel.

"There's a slight problema. The load's ready to go, but it's been raining in the mountains and the road is too muddy to bring the truck out. We are going to have to wait. I think, in three or four days it should be OK."

"So, we wait. No problem," answered Steve.

Finally, at sunset on the third evening, Mario came out to the boat and said, "We're ready to go now. We'll meet you at the pier in two hours."

We were ready. Decked in a pair of cutoff jeans, flip-flop sandals and, of course, my Lucky Shirt, I went ashore and contacted Rob at his hotel who said he would be at the pier with the final payment. Everything was set, except there was only one small hang-up. Dave Killian was three sheets to the wind and twenty minutes into his late afternoon nap sprawled unconscious in his pilot berth. Woz shook him awake and gave him a cup of black mud-like coffee laced with two Dexadrine tablets which he gulped down like water.

"My god! Look at this guy. He's a mess. He's totally fucked up, Rick." Woz ordered, "get over here and see to this dickhead. Steve, you go topsides and get the lines ready. I'll get the engine going and take us to the dock."

"The hell you will!" Killian roared, now totally alert and in obvious control. "Wozenberg! Get me a gin on the rocks, get the engine started and stand by the anchor, in that order! Let's get this straight, right now! Only one man gives the orders on this boat, and that's me! Got it, Dickhead?"

There are those rare individuals who, when the chips are down and everything's on the line, have the capacity to rise up from a complete drunken stupor and deliver. Dave Killian was such a person.

A full goblet sized plastic glass of gin and cigarette in one hand, the other on the tiller, Killian precisely steered the boat a mile up the bay to the old fishing dock. There was a moderate cross wind and a strong ebb tide. A lesser sailor might not have made the docking appear as easy as Killian did. In near-total darkness, he maneuvered *Sirius II* effortlessly to the end of the pier on the first attempt. With Steve on the bow and Woz on the stern, they just had to step off the boat, as if getting off of a city bus, and cleat the lines. Killian didn't miss a beat.

Rob was standing there waiting for us.

Ten minutes later, headlights appeared at the street end of the pier. The ten-wheeler turned around. Mario jumped out of the truck and waved his deformed arm, guiding the vehicle to the dock's seaward end where the yacht was tied. About ten Mexicans jumped out of the covered military style truck and began heaving down heavy gunnysacks to us on the boat. Within five minutes all forty-four, fifty pound burlap sacks were deposited onboard, heaped on deck, with the Mexicans back in the truck. Rob shook hands with Mario, giving him the eight grand they had agreed upon. As the truck rolled away, Rob started walking back toward his rental car parked at the end of the pier. After a few paces he stopped and slowly turned around to see the silhouette of a huge blimp-shaped mound laboriously ease away from the pier with Killian fully in command at the helm.

Chapter 9

Becalmed

After departing Mazatlan the first night had been a mad scramble until dawn to stow the ton of marijuana. Working in shorts and tank tops Steve, Woz and I, in my Lucky Shirt had unloaded the fifty pound gunnysacks, throwing the empty burlap bags overboard, then stacking the individual kilo packages in every locker and available space aboard the boat.

When the lockers were filled, each of us was drenched with sweat and covered by a fine green resinous layer of marijuana dust. Next, we put the remaining bricks into empty sail bags, twenty-five kilo packages per bag, and stashed them securely in the forepeak, the hanging locker, the cockpit sail lockers located under the cockpit cushions and in the lazarette (the stern-most compartment aft of the cockpit). Still more packages remained to be stowed. We then packed Killian's quarter berth tunnel with a few sail bags. He would have to sleep in what room remained in the fetal position as the aft area of his bunk was crammed with weed. We even packed two sail bags into the small head, so anyone wanting to use the toilet had to squeeze into the minuscule area. Use of the washbasin was impossible. Every surface we sat or lay upon had kilos of weed beneath it.

When Killian was satisfied everything was securely stowed, he set the watch shifts. "All right, we are going to use what's known as the Swedish watch system. That'll give each person two-on-six-off," he said referring to the number of hours a crew member stood watch then the number of hours he had in-between. "Since we have a couple of sailing novices, we'll pair up for the first few days. Rick, you and I will stand watch together until you get the hang of it and can stand watch alone. Woz, you and Steve pair up as well for your watch. We'll rotate watch mates in a few days. Make sure each of you have hot coffee ready for your replacements late at night. I'm sure after a few days even you, Rick, will be able to stand watch by yourself. Any questions?"

"Dave, remember I've never sailed before," I said. "I really don't know my ass from a hole in the wall. I did read the book you gave me and I think I am pretty aware of some of the sailing language, though."

"Don't worry. Just do what you're told and ask questions later. If you know the sailing terms, like I said, that's half the battle," Killian replied.

Daybreak, some eight hours after departing Mazatlan, the predictable Atomic 4 engine, known for its unreliability, coughed up a smoky belch, seized up and simply quit. We were headed in a northwesterly direction crossing the Sea of Cortez, aiming for a point roughly fifty miles offshore to round the tip of the Baja Peninsula. The wind was blowing from the north-northwest at about fifteen knots off the starboard bow and the seas were choppy with small whitecaps. With the engine now suddenly silent, I found the lack of the engine's drone a very welcome change. Dave, who had been off watch plotting our dawn position, did a cursory check of the engine and couldn't find the problem. He consulted with Steve, the only one of us with any real, albeit rudimentary, engine mechanic knowledge and they still couldn't figure it out.

"Might be the carburetor, which could mean a fuel flow issue," Woz suggested looking over Steve's shoulder gazing at the Atomic 4. "Mind if I take a look?"

Steve simply shrugged his shoulders and moved aside.

Woz crept forward in the tight engine compartment, rubbing his hands together gleefully like some mad Frankenstein-like scientist preparing for an experiment on a dead corpse. He theorized the fuel pump might also be affected. Within ten minutes he had removed and disassembled both the carburetor and fuel pump but still was perplexed and couldn't find the baffling problem.

"I don't know, might be a bearing or valve problem. I might have to get deeper into this," Woz said.

"How do you know where all those parts go, since now you've got it all torn apart?" Steve questioned.

"What, do you think I'm stupid? I know where they all go." Woz arrogantly snapped.

"Whatever. We'll see," Steve replied.

Steve was right. After putting the carburetor back together and re-assembling the engine components, Woz, the would-be philosopher and aspiring yachtsman now turned pseudo engine mechanic, found he still had a spring, two very small machine screws and a small ball bearing left over, resting in his greasy hand. There was also a torn gasket he had accidentally snapped in two while taking apart the carburetor. Steve recognized it as an integral seal. We had no spare and thus even if the carb was re-installed properly it could never seat without leaking.

"Well, nobody else could fix it either!" Woz said seeing the silent laughter in Steve's eyes. "Hey, I gave it my best shot," he continued wiping the engine oil off his hands.

"I'd say, it's toast. Great job, Woz. Remind me to never let you work on my Volvo," Steve snickered to the bumbling mechanic.

The mainsail and jib were immediately raised and set. *Sirius II* took the bit in her teeth, heeled over and galloped forward northwesterly, close hauled, thirty degrees west of the wind blowing from due north.

"Holy shit, we're going to tip over," I exclaimed and was spooked as the boat started heeling. "What's that noise? Sounds like we're starting to crack too." I said as the rig made creaking and little popping sounds as the stress was taken up on the sails. I just watched, staying out of the way as the sails were raised.

"Relax Rick. It's OK," said Woz on the tiller. "It's impossible to tip over. The keel acts as a counterbalance. You'll get used to the feeling in a couple of days. This point of sail is called beating to weather and the boat is heeled over, which is normal. But it's probably going to get worse as I saw an LA newspaper back in Mazatlan. Said to expect unusually strong gusting winds."

"What? How strong?" interrupted Killian. "Thanks for letting me know."

"Well, you were as usual stewed to the gills. I couldn't tell you anything. The paper said to expect gusts up to fifty knots."

"Fifty! Holy shit! Thanks for the prompt weather update, asshole. Did you even try to tell me?" questioned Killian.

"Well, I thought I tried. Anyway, I thought we'd just monitor the situation on WWV on our way north," Woz answered referring to the call sign of the National Bureau of Standards weather station and time signal radio broadcast out of Fort Collins, Colorado, and Hawaii.

"That would be great," replied Killian. "But since you really fixed the engine, which now we can't even start, we can't charge the batteries so you won't be using the radio to monitor anything, Mr. Know-It-All. Please, don't even try to think. That's what the owner pays me for, besides we have to save any juice we have left for the running lights or we'll be pulled over for sure at night by the Coast Guard once we hit the U.S."

"Dave!" I yelled breaking into the conversation. "I can see a sailboat. It's off the port bow at ten o'clock." I was really beginning to learn the sailing terms now as Dave gazed into the distance where I told him in nautical terms. He grabbed the binoculars from the cockpit utility locker pushing aside several kilos.

"Whoa. I recognize her," Killian exclaimed looking through the powerful binoculars. "That's *Sleeping Beauty* out of the San Diego Yacht Club. She looks really fucked-up. She's a one-design race boat and was in the Mazatlan race with us and I saw her leave yesterday. Looks like she's headed back to Mazatlan. Check this out. Her mast is broken and lying on deck. She must have hit those winds you forgot to tell me about," Killian said, looking straight at Mark.

"OK," Killian continued. "We'd better prepare for this. Looks like we're in for it too. I can see it coming this way. Look at the wind on the water… they're whitecaps and building. Woz, you and Steve get the 150 (the light wind headsail) down and put up the storm jib. I'll put a single reef in the main too, just to be safe," Killian said, referring to shortening the mainsail so as not to overpower the rig. "Rick, you are going to get your first actual sailing lesson right now. Take the tiller and when I say 'head up,' swing the boat directly into the wind and hold her there until Woz and Steve get one sail down and run the other up and I'll get the main reefed." "Head-up, now!"

Sirius II was into her third day at sea and was hard on the wind making eight knots on a northwest beat still under the storm jib and a reefed mainsail. Now on a night watch under a corrugated cloud layer covering the moon, the wind had risen to twenty-five knots with gusts to thirty. It seemed every third wave broke over the bow throwing phosphorescent colored spray aft toward the cockpit. If it weren't for the canvas dodger covering the cockpit and deflecting the ocean spray we would have been soaked standing watch.

I was wearing a safety harness over my foul-weather gear as I sat in the cockpit under the shelter of the dodger. The large plastic windows on the forward side of the dodger allowed us to see the foredeck and, at this moment, the large waves crashing on it. Dave was at the helm, as usual holding the tiller with one hand and a drink and cigarette in the other. He had the boat trimmed, so in spite of the heel angle and the wind force, the steering was comfortable and could be done with one finger; there was no wrestling with the helm.

"You know, Rick, I think I got a bad rap back there in Mazatlan," Dave said.

"Whaddya mean?" I questioned.

"Well, let me ask you first, how well do you know Rob?"

"I knew him from UOP, we were classmates and sold and bought weed from each other. I drove cross country with him when we both took summer school classes on the East Coast. I've been to his house in Stockton and had dinner with him and his wife. Where's this going anyway?" I asked.

"Rick, he's gay." Dave said flatly.

"What? Are you kidding me? He's married to a beautiful lady. I don't believe it."

"Let me tell you. The incident in Mazatlan. It was all bullshit. He put on a show for you guys returning in the dinghy. What really happened was he came on the boat in the early afternoon. I was pretty well lit. Been drinking since the morning, but I was OK. Anyway, I welcomed him aboard and told you guys would be back later and offered him a drink, which he accepted. Have you ever heard of the term 'Gaydar'?"

"Nope. What is it?"

"Well, it's not too common and it sounds stupid, but it's real, believe me. It's like a sixth sense gay people have, like radar, where they can spot another gay person instantly. Certain mannerisms, speech, movements, or whatever. I have it and am not ashamed to admit it. Look, I know where you stand on the subject and don't worry about me. OK?"

"Yeah, this is kind of an uncomfortable subject for me, but go on."

"Anyway, I hand him a drink and notice immediately my Gaydar is 'off the charts'. Something about him. Well, we start talking and he moves closer to me here in the cockpit and the next thing, he has his hand on my leg. Well, I get the message and respond kind of affectionately towards him by putting my arm around him. He then asks me if I want to give him a blow job. He asks me! I say, 'sure' just as you guys come rowing up. Then he freaks out, we both stand up and he pushes me overboard and starts yelling I'm a faggot and such. You saw it. So did Woz and Steve. It was all a show, man, for your benefit. I think he was embarrassed and didn't want to be 'outted'. I fell into the water and I admit, I was pretty well looped by then, but totally aware of what was going on. I surfaced and just figured I'd act totally out of it and not bust him because I knew he was footing the bill for this project and if I exposed him he might walk."

"I'm totally blown away," I said. "He never came onto me in any way and he's married, for Christ's sake."

"Well, he wouldn't because he knows you and you'd freak out if he did. It's a gay thing. And the fact he's married is probably just a cover. I know several of my 'buddies' who are gay and married. I know it's weird but, 'it is what it is'. I'm just telling you so you'll be aware. That's it."

"Wow! Guess if I ever travel with him again, I'd better not drop the soap in the shower," I laughed, although in reality, I didn't think it was really very funny.

We continued the watch in silence. I was just contemplating this revelation in stunned disbelief. Remember this was the early 1970s and the gay thing was still pretty much in the closet and had just started to crack open. My naiveté on the subject had just gotten a rude awakening.

Sirius II continued her beat up the Baja Coast for the next couple of days. The wind had dropped to a steady twelve to eighteen knots. Under Killian's tutelage, I had become adept at handling sheets and halyards during sail changes. I could work the foredeck alone, bending on a new jib by myself. I learned the rudiments of piloting, using dividers and parallel rulers to plot the boat's position. With Killian's twenty-five years of sailing experience, he proved to be an excellent teacher and I a fast learner, if I could catch him early enough in the day, before 'Happy Hour.'

We switched watch mates and I was now on watch with my old friend, Woz. It was interesting, educational, and somewhat unusual, to say the least. Sometimes he would be completely lucid and our conversation would be rational and cogent, such as our first evening on watch together when we had a discussion revolving around the money we'd hope to make from this trip.

"Our share is probably close to one-hundred fifty thousand," Woz said.

"My old man would take notice of that kind of money. In his mind, money equals success. He's spent his whole life making money and he's done pretty well. But it's all he seems to have done. It does seem like fun to him. You ask me, there's more to life; like this," I said gesturing to the boat and the surrounding nothingness but ocean.

"Money means everything to my dad, but at least he knows how to have fun doing other things as well. He loves to fly and play golf and he's crazy about fishing."

"Dad always wanted me to succeed. By his standards, I'm successful, but I can't tell him. What we're doing now would blow his mind," I said.

"Me being a success," I said as I took another toke off of the giant six paper marijuana cigar, "was like always being in a footrace where I could never reach the finish line, because it always kept moving further and further away from me, no matter how fast I ran. The receding finish line! Nothing I did was ever good enough for the old bastard, yet I tried so hard. There was always something wrong. Never any praise from him, only criticism. All I wanted was his love and respect and nothing more. As a Boy Scout when I achieved the rank of Life Scout I was so proud of myself, for one second. But Dad ruined the moment for me when he said, 'if you had only worked a little harder and gotten more merit badges you'd be an Eagle Scout. I would have been so proud of you Rick'."

Nothing I did was ever good enough for him. This time it would be different!

Everyone aboard smoked dope from one of the kilos we had broken into for the trip home. Steve and I had a joint rolling contest; from pencil-lead thin 'pinners' to huge submarine shaped behemoth 'bombers' made from as many as ten ZigZag wheat straw cigarette rolling papers. Killian had stashed a case of them aboard *Sirius II* before the race, which I had given him, so we wouldn't run out on the voyage home. The mood was as mellow as a Mexican sunset, with the ebb and flow of our daily lives revolving around the two-on-six-off watch changes.

Then on the other hand it inevitably came to pass, usually after smoking bombers or zeppelin-sized joints, Woz would don his pseudo-philosopher hat and theorize in the ridiculous abstract, making no sense to anyone whatsoever. I often wondered if any of his verbal gibberish and nonsense even made sense to him.

"If Timothy Leary had only read Bowditch's chapter entitled, 'Introduction to the History of Navigation', he could have been able to plot a cerebral chart using relevant psychedelic data gleaned through mind altering drug experiments related to polar opposites of the human condition; man's desire to do good juxtaposed with his propensity to do evil. Take for example quotes from the 'Tibetan book of the Dead' and from Paramahansa Yogananda's book 'Autobiography of a Yogi' when coupled together..."

"Whoa! Time out, Coolbreeze! What the fuck are you babbling about?" Steve asked.

I added: "Get a grip on yourself, Woz. You're really over the edge this time."

Killian took another slug straight from the Oso Negro bottle as he rummaged through the first pages of Nathaniel Bowditch's famous book, *American Practical Navigator*.[1] "Here it is, I think I've found it."

Woz's face had a dazed and vacant expression on it as he took another large hit. "You guys just don't get it. I tell you, Leary was onto something. If he could plot the pre-death experience followed by the post-death state on a polyconic projection...."

"Lemme see that book, Dave," I interrupted and grabbed the volume from Killian's lap. "Here it is in Chapter 3. Just take this polyconic projection of the earth and roll it into a cone pointed at the top and open wide on the bottom; it looks exactly like what Woz should be wearing. A dunce cap!"

What Woz's incoherent rambling had to do with piloting a vessel across the sea from point A to point B on planet Earth nobody knew. It was nowhere to be found on any page in the large green volume that was simply known as Bowditch. Woz, now in the realm of intergalactic theoretician, hastily leaped out of the cockpit and scurried forward onto the foredeck vainly searching for something to fix which wasn't broken, but in reality trying to escape the jeers, cat-calls and rude laughter coming from us sitting there awestruck at such nonsensical blather.

After six days at sea, Killian decided we would pull in at Bahia de Tortuga (Turtle Bay) for supplies. By supplies he meant he was low on gin and cigarettes. We had run out of ice on the third day, which didn't seem to matter to Killian. Warm gin did the trick as well as on the rocks.

It didn't take long for me to realize Killian was a lush. A real alcoholic in every sense of the word. I asked him if he ever drank water instead of gin. He replied, "Never, it rusts the pipes!" I rest my case, which became more apparent the longer I knew him and the more time we spent sailing together.

---

1 Referenced Books, Item 7, Page 532.

"Making this stop is unnecessary and too risky," I protested. "We can't stand the chance of being boarded. After all we're nothing but a floating ton of unconcealed weed, sort of like the van that was actually made of marijuana in the Cheech and Chong movie *'Up In Smoke'*.[2] It would be a disaster if the authorities came aboard."

"Turtle Bay is safe. Don't worry about it. We stop here on the way back from every Mexican race. Matter of fact it would be weird if we didn't stop," Killian replied. "Some other race boat might start to worry and put out a call to come looking for us."

Killian was right. Bahia de Tortuga was a sleepy little Mexican fishing village located about halfway up the Baja peninsula. It was famous among yachtsman for cheap and plentiful lobster and abalone. There were no customs officials, Federales or local police apparent. There were a few other yachts anchored in the sheltered bay. *Sirius II* dropped the hook an inconspicuous distance from the other returning race boats. Killian hailed a dinghy from shore and a young Mexican boy rowed out to the boat. He took Dave and Steve ashore. They returned a couple of hours later with kerosene for the lamps and the emergency running lights since we had no engine to charge the batteries and run the electric running lights, plus some fruit, vegetables, blocks of ice, cases of beer, cartons of cigarettes and several gallons of gin. Unknown to Steve and the rest of the crew, Killian had also brought back a capsule of organic mescaline he had picked up from a friend off of another boat whom he had met while shopping.

That evening while *Sirius II* was sitting peacefully in the bay, Killian went berserk. Complaining of a bad back and tension, he got into the ship's well stocked first aid kit and took several methaqualone tablets, better known as Quaaludes or simply Ludes, that the owner, Dr. Fortay, must have absentmindedly forgotten to remove after the race. Whether it was the gin, the weed, the Ludes, the head full of mescaline or the unholy combination of all the substances in totality was a moot point. What cannot be discounted was the adrenaline-producing response I experienced when Killian, totally out of control and mumbling incoherently, loaded the Very pistol and started shooting emergency distress parachute flares into the moonless night sky.

"Phummp!" broke the silence as the flare shot out from the pistol sounding like mortar fire and leaving a bright red trail behind as it arced over the water. Then suddenly at its apogee it exploded into a brilliant Fourth-of-July-fireworks-like star cluster, with each smaller burst illuminating the harbor and falling back harmlessly into the inky black water.

I was below playing backgammon with Steve. Woz was taking a snooze in the forepeak wedged in-between several sail bags loaded with kilos. At first I was stunned and didn't quite know what was going on, but then an instant later a second flare erupted from on deck. As the second star cluster exploded above, I vaulted up the ladder and burst into the cockpit. There I saw Killian on his knees on the floor of the cockpit, flare pistol in his hand with the emergency flare kit open beside him. He was reaching for a third flare as I kicked the flare kit to the side and out of his reach.

"Just what the fuck do you think you're doing, Dave?" I yelled. "Are you out of your fucking mind? Are you trying to get us busted, or what? If the Mexican Navy sees

2 Referenced Television & Movies, Item 4, Page 533.

this bullshit, we're fucked." I was beside myself and wanted to kill the stupid asshole. "Gimme that fucking flare pistol, right now. I might not know much about sailing, but what I do know is that this isn't cool," I said taking the gun as he handed it to me. "Regardless of what we're doing, I can't imagine the good doctor who owns this yacht would condone such reckless behavior.

"Nah, Nah!" Killian blubbered. "We always do this stuff at Turtle. It's no problem."

"Well, it is for me. We're trying to keep a low profile and you're doing your best to screw up everything," I said glaring at Killian. "I've got better things to do than spend the next twenty years in some Mexican hellhole prison, which is exactly what's going to happen if you ever again get so stoned or drunk that your behavior puts the load and everyone aboard in jeopardy."

All hands were now on deck.

"What the fuck," both Steve and Woz both said almost simultaneously.

"This drunken asshole is firing the flare pistol, as if you didn't notice!"

Right then, there was a muzzle flash in the distance as another flare gun's popping sound rolled across the anchorage emanating from a race boat nearly one-hundred yards away. "Give 'em hell. Take no prisoners. Yeehaw!" a drunken chorus shouted as an answering parachute flare burst high above, red sparkles drifting down. A green star cluster followed. More loud voices in the distance, and ooh's and ah's from the obviously trashed crew on the other boat. Then a splash, as presumably someone went overboard.

"Looks like the crew aboard *Maybelle* are in about the same shape as Killian. Let's hope the Mexicans don't take any of this shit seriously," Steve said.

"They don't. It's business as usual when we come to town. Don't worry about it!" Killian popped in as if his condition suddenly had reversed itself, and he seemed like his old normal self again.

"They're used to this kind of craziness from the race boat crews," Woz added. "Be a different story if the flare had gone up while we were sailing. Still, it's really stupid drawing attention to ourselves with all this dope aboard."

"Ya think so, Sherlock?" I sarcastically replied.

We departed Turtle Bay the following morning without further incident and continued north. Approaching Cabo San Quintin still about 200 miles south of the U.S./Mexican border, the wind slackened, then abruptly died. Woz had fixed our position, using his chronometer to ascertain the accurate time and his sextant to shoot evening star sights. Using those instruments coupled with his mathematical calculations, Woz placed *Sirius II* fifty miles off the Baja coast with plenty of sea room to spare. Although he might have considered himself the combination of the second comings of both Copernicus, the 16th century Polish astronomer and mathematician, and Magellan, the famous Portuguese navigator who first circumnavigated the earth in the early 1500s, Woz's astronomical observations, mathematical calculations and navigational skills seemingly proved dangerously inaccurate and incorrect as we were soon to find out.

The entire day was spent on a flat sullen sea with no wind. The only sound was from the slack sails slatting back and forth and the water's low lap against the hull. With no engine, the only hope of forward motion was from the wind, of which there was none.

There was, however, a current which could not be felt aboard the boat, but was evident on the sailing charts, if one noticed, which apparently Woz didn't. As evening fell, the usually spectacular Mexican sunset was obliterated by a cloud cover on the western horizon which soon covered the entire sky. Still no wind. As the clouds moved off to the east, the early morning sky started to lighten and the foggy, smoke-colored dawn slowly became visible. Faintly, ever so faintly, a rumbling sound could be heard somewhere in the indeterminate distance.

I was on watch with Steve, as we had switched watch mates the previous day. Steve was the first to hear the distant sound.

"Rick! Wake up!" Steve said rousing me from a cat-nap.

"Huh? What is it?"

"Listen!" Steve exclaimed.

"I don't hear anything."

"Shut up, Rick! Listen."

"Dave! Dave! Get up here!" I yelled. The unmistakable booming sound was now clear and coming directly due east of our position.

Killian was on deck almost instantly, nude and looking haggard. He had taken a moment to look at *Sirius II*'s position on the chart below before scrambling up on deck. Killian surveyed the scene in a glance, his every sense reading the situation instinctively: no wind, the sound of waves crashing somewhere in the distance, the becalmed boat drifting toward an unsuspected lee shore caught in a swift three and a half knot current. It was among the worst possible situations for a captain and his vessel to encounter.

"Wozenberg!" he yelled. "You plotted our position less than six hours ago at 0100 hours as fifty miles off Cabo San Quintin. Do you hear the shore break?"

"Well, my star sights were accurate!" Mark Wozenberg said defensively.

"Accurate, my ass! Waves crashing against a lee shore can only be heard from less than ten miles. You either fouled up shooting the sight or making the calculations. Something was fucked up. You should have gotten a three star fix."

"My calculations were correct!" insisted Woz.

"Horse shit! Where was your common sense? Did you even bother to read the Sailing Directions for this part of Baja? It says clearly and specifically there is a three and a half knot current off Cabo San Quintin. Even without a fix you should have placed our position using dead reckoning from when we left Turtle Bay much more accurately, and you should have taken into account this current. That's what piloting is all about. I don't have time to argue with you. As of now, you are no longer navigating this boat," Killian said.

"I can see waves breaking against cliffs to starboard!" Steve cried, passing the binoculars to Killian.

"Settle down. There's plenty of time for panic. Looks like we're about three miles off the cliffs. The breakers are about twelve feet and coming in about every thirty seconds or so. We've got perhaps an hour or so to find some wind or the boat ends up on the rocks," Killian said matter-of-factly scanning the shore through the intermittent drifting fog.

"What are we going to do?" I questioned, trying to force from my mind the image of *Sirius II*, broken hull, a thousand kilos washing up on some desolate beach and us standing there dumbfounded looking like four Robinson Crusoes marooned and wondering what to do next.

"Steve, you and Woz get the lightest drifter set this instant. We might get some sort of off-shore wind or even blow-back from the wave action. Rick, you get the bow anchor ready, but keep it secure on deck. We may have to try and anchor outside the breakers as a last chance. Also loosen the hold-downs on the life raft, just in case. I'll take the helm," Killian commanded, now fully in charge. "Hey, Rick. Grab my smokes and lighter off the chart table, too. Will ya?"

For the next hour, we sat on pins and needles silently hoping for some sort of miracle, while Killian nervously chain smoked. Still becalmed and caught in the fast moving current, *Sirius II* drifted to within one hundred and fifty yards of the breaking surf. By now the early morning fog had lifted and to our horror we clearly saw fifteen foot steep glassy waves exploding against a vertical wall of two hundred foot white cliffs. There was no beach whatsoever; just the waves breaking directly onto a solid massive rock face. I could read Killian's mind. He was contemplating his next move. Drop the hook and hope the bottom was good enough to hold the boat outside of the breakers. If not, cut the life raft loose from the deck chalks and pile into it. And pray...

There was nothing I could do but watch the drama unfold. Killian, so intense as to seem one with nature, sensed the faintest breeze tickle the follicles of his nose hairs. He looked directly northwest and into the wind and felt the ever-so-slight breeze blowing evenly over both ears.

"Sheet out two inches on the drifter! Don't let her luff!" Killian shouted to Steve who sat tending the jib sheet. The huge light sail popped full and ever so slowly *Sirius II* started to inch seaward away from the thrashing surf line. The light air miraculously held and with Killian on the tiller and Steve continuously trimming the jib sheet, within thirty minutes *Sirius II* was heeled over making seven and a half knots, beating her way north and out to sea.

Hard on the northwest wind, *Sirius II* continued to beat northward as she plowed through moderate size seas. She would hit a wave and shudder, slowing fractionally as she dropped off the crest and plunged into the trough. As a twelve-foot wall of water sloughed aft it would break over the dodger, cascade into the cockpit then back out via the cockpit's self bailing system and deck scuppers. Killian ordered us to shorten sail, because of the stress on the hull.

"Hoist the lapper and put a reef in the main," Killian boomed. Instantly, both Woz and Steve jumped into action following his commands. The task was completed within two minutes.

"Dave, why can't we leave the main unreefed and keep the genoa up?" I asked.

"You should have picked up on that part of sailing theory in Royce's. Anyway, since you might have missed it, I'll enlighten you. By flying the jenny now, we're carrying too much sail for this amount of wind and this point of sail and we don't want to overpower her. There's another issue here, a point surely not included in Royce's. We are carrying an extra ton of weed. Carrying so much sail combined with the force of these seas and the extra weight puts too much stress on the hull. I'm not sacrificing safety for speed. Other's aboard might not agree, but since I'm running this show, what I say goes!"

Indeed, Killian was right. 'What else is new?' I thought realizing the obvious. Shortening the sails made the boat ride more comfortably with less pounding to weather. Our speed slowed about one knot to five and a half, but we were still making good time with the U.S. border less than a day's sail away.

Killian suggested all of us should abandon any sort of long hair hippy-look, as well as shave clean and look like normal yachtsmen. I was the only one with rather long shoulder length curly hair and a handlebar mustache. Steve and Woz both had maintained short hair and were clean shaven as was Killian, whose hair was thinning anyway. I first shaved clean then, stupidly, let Woz proceed to cut my hair with the deft precision of a drunken tonsorial apprentice. He cut first the left side short then the right side shorter trying to match the left. He failed miserably, cutting the right even shorter. Additionally he left spots where you could see right through to my scalp. He then cut the back unevenly. When finished I looked like a radiation survivor from Hiroshima. God, I was pissed and of course, he just laughed as he always did when making fun of someone else. However, he could dish it out, but couldn't take it when the tables were turned and the joke was on him. Then he could, and most likely would morph into defensive, irrational, unpredictable and often violent behavior in the blink of an eye.

The day passed to evening, then to night smoothly without further incident. Next morning Steve spotted a Mexican Navy patrol boat two to three miles west of *Sirius II*. The World War II surplus American PT boat, made famous in the 1963 movie *'PT 109'* [3] about John F. Kennedy as a U.S. Navy officer who captains a PT boat in the Pacific in WWII, appeared to be on a southerly course and when she came abeam of our position she suddenly veered due east and headed directly toward us. We all saw the trail in the water as she arced eastward and couldn't help but observe the increase in the size of her bow wake as she accelerated, now coming straight at us at something near twenty-five knots. She would be on us in a matter of five minutes. As the Mexican vessel drew nearer our anxiety level rose to a near panic state, yet there was nothing anybody could do. If for some reason, any reason, they wanted to board us there was no denying the ton of virtually unconcealed weed packed below deck.

"Just wait 'em out," I said as calmly as I could. "See what they want." Then my old desert mantra came back and I continued: "Just think good thoughts. We may just be able to 'vibe' them away. Don't even think that they may come aboard."

"Smile and wave," said Killian. We all waved and saluted with raised coffee mugs.

The Mexicans waved back and one-hundred yards from *Sirius II*, the coxswain spun the wheel and the patrol boat turned sharply to starboard, resuming its original course. *Sirius II* gently rocked side-to-side over the patrol boat's wake and collectively we breathed a sigh of relief. Whew!

The northwesterly winds became light, five to seven knots, as we crossed into U.S. waters a few hours later. With the San Diego skyline in the distance to the east, we

---

3 Referenced Television & Movies, Item 2, Page 533.

entered the outbound shipping lane and were passed to port by a huge aircraft carrier loaded with planes probably headed to its station off North Viet Nam's coast. With lit joints cupped behind our backs we waved to the small uniformed figures gathered on the carrier's flight deck.

Our plan was to make a night approach into Santa Monica Bay, west of Los Angeles, then head up into Marina Del Rey estuary which terminated at Del Rey Yacht Club.

Killian, having sailed and raced in Southern California and Mexican races for years, was well known and had guest privileges at the exclusive gated Del Rey Yacht Club. If ever in the area he could always tie up at the transient berth and stay for a few days. We would dock, tie up, then call Rob Farnsworth from the pay phone there, who was waiting in the LA area, by a phone number he had given me. He would then meet us with a camper shell covered pickup truck to receive the load.

It was two in the morning. Southern California is known for light sailing breezes and as we approached the breakwater outside the estuary, the wind dropped to almost nothing, greatly complicating matters. We dropped and hastily furled the mainsail atop the boom. Sailing under the lightest headsail alone, the drifter, with the ever-so-slight breeze blowing right down the channel in our face, without an engine, and lit only by the kerosene bow running lights, green on the starboard side and red to port, we began what seemed like an endless series of precision short tacks up Marina Del Rey's main channel. It seemed like as soon as the starboard tack was set we would immediately be coming about to set the port tack. Back and forth, back and forth. The channel was lined on both sides with countless docked sail and power boats, both large and small resting peacefully in the glassy water. The Del Rey Yacht Club lay at the end of the long channel, perhaps a mile and a half to two miles up the waterway. It was surrounded by a fence with an electric gate for which Rob had been given Killian's laminated plastic guest card, affording him entry by inserting the card into the slot at the call box.

Furiously short tacking the long channel as the sail fluttered and the winches clattered and whirred, *Sirius II* had negotiated half the distance to the yacht club. Steve, working the port jib sheet, happened to glance back and, to his astonishment, saw we were being followed by a harbor police boat, twenty-five yards dead astern. "Fuck!" was whispered by Steve. Except Killian, the rest of us aboard *Sirius II* felt flashing hot paranoid jolts and a sinking feeling of imminent doom. The police boat inched to within twenty yards of us when Killian, on the helm turned around and casually waved. His gin fueled smile, like the Great Pumpkin's, lit the afterdeck now bathed in the beam of the police boat's searchlight.

"Returning from the Mazatlan yacht race with no engine. Everything's under control here. Heading for the Del Rey Yacht Club. Thanks for your concern." Killian's voice thundered across the silent harbor.

"Very well, sir. Have a good night," the tinny voice responded over a loudspeaker megaphone.

"Boy, you are some cool dude," I said in admiration.

"Done it a million times. Nothin' to it. As you said, 'think good thoughts'." Killian replied.

At exactly the right moment, Killian ordered the jib dropped as he glided *Sirius II* into the yacht club's guest dock slowing perfectly at the dockside, allowing Woz and me to step off and cleat her without any effort, stopping her forward movement completely.

There was no time for a collective sigh of relief. I hurried off to call Rob, while Woz and Steve went below and began unloading the kilo packed lockers, forepeak and head, piling the packages on the floor of the main salon. Killian, fresh gin in hand, stood by the helm smoking another cigarette.

Rob came through the club's security gate at about 3:30 in the morning driving a one ton, long bed pickup truck. He parked in the parking lot as close as he could to the ramp leading from the guest dock, a distance of about one hundred feet, first on a floating wooden slatted dock and then up a sloped ramp to the parking lot. Fortunately for us, at that hour the yacht club and parking lot were deserted.

The three of us were all 'assholes and elbows' stuffing kilos into white heavy sailcloth sail bags, each containing about 40 to 50 kilos. I then left the boat and went to the truck and climbed into the back inside the camper shell. Steve and Woz then brought two loaded sail bags up on deck put them into the yacht club's small two-wheel wooden cart used to load and unload supplies from boats docked at the club. Steve then wheeled the hand cart off the dock, up the ramp to the rear of the truck and hoisted them to me in the camper shell. I quickly unloaded the sail bags and stacked the packages neatly in the truck bed and returned the bags to Steve, who with Woz's help repeated the process again and again with Killian standing guard in the cockpit and on watch like the Sphinx guarding the Egyptian pyramids.

By sunrise, Woz and Steve had made about twenty to twenty-five trips up the dock with the cart. Approximately 2,200 pounds of high-grade Mexican marijuana had been transferred from the boat to the truck, where I had packed them securely with no room to spare. Rob shook hands with all of us and drove back through the gate to begin the drive back to the San Francisco Bay area where the load would be split.

The last item on the agenda, before the mandatory check-in call to U.S. Customs, was to sanitize the boat from bow to stern, making sure there were absolutely no traces of any weed, seeds, rolling papers or joints left aboard.

At 7:30 AM Killian called the harbor master and Customs office to report in. We all had our personal belongings lined up on the deck ready for customs inspection and waiting for the custom inspector's arrival. The officer showed up fifteen minutes later at dockside right next to *Sirius II*.

"Do you have anything to declare?" the tired-looking officer asked Killian.

"No, we're just returning from the Mazatlan race," replied Killian.

"No fruit or vegetables?"

"Nope. All that stuff was finished or thrown overboard before we entered U.S. waters," Killian answered.

"OK. Have a nice day."

The customs officer left, never having boarded the boat nor having checked our personal belongings.

Chapter 10

Think Of All The Money

Following our clearance by U.S. Customs, the three of us, Steve, Woz and I, called a taxi to take us to LAX for our flight back to San Francisco. We left Killian to find another crew to finish the delivery of *Sirius II* back to her home berth in Belvedere, since it was necessary for us to meet Rob and discuss the splitting of the load and receiving of our share.

Rob had arranged for the load to be brought to a friend's house in the Berkeley Hills where it would supposedly be safe to stash and work out of for selling and getting rid of the load. This would be ideal for Woz and me since we didn't have a stash house of our own.

Rob arrived at the East Bay hills stash house, unloaded the pickup and divided the load evenly into two 1,100 pound piles on the garage floor. Each pile contained 500 kilo packages which he then stacked neatly against the garage wall into his share and our share. Each stack consisted of rows of packaged bricks, ten high by ten wide by five deep. This volume amounted to two and a half feet high by ten feet wide by three and a half feet deep or about 90 cubic feet, about the size of, as we were to soon find out, what would fit into the bed of a full sized pickup truck.

"I just got a call from the guy who owns this house. He told me to get this shit out of here as soon as possible, tonight. It's not safe here." Rob said on the phone to me. "He told me there was some heat on him from an Afghan trip he had just done. It would be best if you guys took your share right now as I don't want to be responsible if it goes down. I'll pick you guys up in The City and you can use my truck to move it wherever you want. It's all counted and divided up. I'll pick you up in an hour in front of the Ferry Building on Embarcadero. Be there and don't be late!" His parting words to me: "I hope I'm not followed!"

"Holy shit, Woz. We're not set up for this and we've got to get our share outta there. Rob's going to let us use his truck, but we've got to move it somewhere. You got any ideas?" I asked.

"Yeah, I do. My folks just left on an a deep sea fishing trip to Hawaii and won't be back for a week. No one else will be there so we can put the load at their place, in their garage, until then. It gives us a week to figure out what to do next," Woz replied.

"OK. We have to meet him in front of the Ferry Building in forty-five minutes. Let's go!" I sensed another fiasco, but we had little choice of what to do so we just went with it. We had just shared a huge zeppelin-sized joint and were pretty well stoned. 'Just think good thoughts.'

March 1971
Berkeley, California

It was a dark drizzly night as we arrived at Rob's stash house. We counted and quickly loaded the packages in Rob's truck and left immediately, fearing the worst. We might have been followed or who knows what. We were stoned and paranoid, to say the least.

The streets were curvy and slick descending from the Berkeley hills in Rob Farnsworth's Ford pickup. We didn't have time to stack everything neatly in the back of the truck as Rob wanted us out of there as quickly as possible, so Woz got in back to re-arrange everything and I drove. We screeched around a corner and onto Berkeley's Telegraph Avenue as I had taken the turn way too wide and Woz in the truck bed was flung to the opposite side, pasted against the camper shell wall. Immediately, there was banging on the rear wall of the cab.

"Slow down, you idiot! Slow down!" Woz's muffled yells came through the cab's closed sliding rear window. Then more pounding as Woz banged his hand more violently against the cab's rear wall.

Distracted, stoned and hopelessly lost, I was trying to find a through street leading to the on-ramp onto the Bay Bridge. Another corner, another wild turn too fast, this time narrowly avoiding a parked police car waiting in the dark. This time, my eyes and mouth wide open with mostly the whites showing, like some 'Little Orphan Annie' character, I could almost read the angry officer's lips "Slow down!" through the rain soaked windshield. In the back, more kilos flew through the air hitting Woz who could not believe what he had just witnessed looking out the camper shell's side window.

More pounding on the cab wall. With one hand on the wheel, I reached around and slid the rear window open behind me.

"Nice turn, numb nuts! You always this careful driving in the rain with half a ton of dope in the back and the cops watching?" an irritated and red-faced Woz asked.

"How do I get to the bridge?" I asked, ignoring the sarcasm.

Woz finally gave up on the futile effort of trying to re-organize the load with me at the wheel, stuck his head and shoulders through the window separating the cab from the truck bed and started slithering his six foot frame into the front like a Komodo dragon.

"Make a right, then after the next block, turn left onto University. Go all the way down to the freeway, but shit, Rick, slow the fuck down!" Woz said, his chin now sliding down the seat to the truck's floor, while his feet scraped upside down and backwards through the window into the cab. He pivoted his head upon the floor, while rotating his body, scrunching and sitting up together, finally facing forward in his seat looking comfortable.

"Maybe you should apply at the circus as a contortionist. Want to try it again?" I asked. "I'll pull over and let you in the back again, if you want."

"Ha ha. Very funny, you moron! Just try and not get us into a wreck, like you almost did back there. OK?"

Arriving at Woz's parents house, the one where he'd grown up, in San Francisco's fashionable St. Francis Woods neighborhood, I pulled the truck into the alley behind the house to access the garage. It was a basement drive-in garage located under the two story house with two parking spaces, one in front of the other. Adjacent to the garage were two small rooms: one for storage and the other a laundry room. On the southern side of the laundry room above a block retaining wall and behind some unfinished wooden beams was a small raised area, shrouded with cobwebs, directly above the house's dirt foundation. It was an area nobody was likely to enter.

I backed down the narrow driveway into the basement garage and we unloaded the truck. We then neatly stacked the 500 kilos, ninety cubic feet of weed, in the thirty foot deep dirt space and sealed it off from the laundry room with a large piece of black plastic visqueen sheeting, which we tacked to the wood beams. It seemed like we were safe at least for the moment and hopefully for the foreseeable future. Even if Woz's mother came into the laundry room when they returned, as the lighting was only marginal, she would never notice anything amiss in the darkened, unlit foundation area where we had created a new false black plastic wall about fifteen feet back from the retaining wall. The carefully concealed weed occupied the deeper fifteen feet.

We'd agreed to give Steve one hundred pounds as his payment for crewing on the boat. So, our first order of business was delivering it to him in Santa Cruz and getting him paid off. Secondly, we fronted fifty pounds to my cousin Marty.

Cousin Marty Bibbero pictured here in about 1971. The clean cut San Francisco banker and pot distributor before getting involved in the cocaine business.

At twenty-six years old, my balding, chubby, bank teller cousin had become one of my most reliable dealers brokering some of the 'Border Brown' Willie and I had smuggled from Nogales the previous year. Now, part of the San Francisco hippie scene, with an odd assortment of 'friends' hanging out at his Noe Valley flat, Marty had become increasingly dependent upon cocaine. He had transitioned from a recreational to habitual user in less than six months. His efficiency as a dealer decreased proportionally to his increase in cocaine use. Since Marty had not been making the quick turnaround from pot to money like he used to, I began to search for a new sales outlet to handle our increased thousand pound volume.

Woz's younger brother Jacob, Jake, introduced us to a friend of his, William Greenberg, who lived in San Francisco's Mission district. Billy had grown up in New York, moved to San Francisco in the mid-1960s and in the span of two short years had become one of San Francisco's large-volume marijuana dealers. Many of his clients and customers had also migrated from New York during the San Francisco Summer of Love and were following the local music scene. A few of his customers had friends and customers of theirs who were among the most famous local rock and roll musicians of the time, such as Grace Slick, Paul Kantner and Marty Balin of the Jefferson Airplane, Jerry Garcia and Bob Weir of the Grateful Dead and Janis Joplin of Big Brother and the Holding Company, to name only a few. Talking with a distinctive New York accent, the 5 foot 8 inch, rather heavy set, bearded young man was a virtual bundle of energy. With short curly hair, tortoise shell dark glasses and a bald spot always covered by a French Fedora-style hat, 'Yorktown' Billy resembled a Hassidic Rabbi, in Levi's, brown penny loafers, and a black turtleneck over which he wore a corduroy sports coat.

Jake introduced Woz and me to Billy at an espresso bar in San Francisco's North Beach, a few doors down from the Condor Club, made famous by the busty, topless and later bottomless stripper Carol Doda in the mid-1960s. After the introductions were made, Jake departed for a Country Joe and the Fish concert at the Fillmore Auditorium. We sat in a small booth by the window, sipping espressos and watching the nighttime hustle and bustle up and down Columbus Avenue. 'Yorktown' Billy and I took an immediate liking to one another; however, an air of friction between Billy and Woz seemed to develop almost right off the bat.

"I gather you really don't have any business experience," Billy said to Woz.

"My major in college was philosophy, and I think business is only a reflection of a specific philosophical outlook," a red-eyed and stoned Woz replied. "Take for example the philosopher Nietzsche… ."

I rolled my eyes and glanced at Billy, but said nothing.

"Spare me the lecture, Socrates," Billy broke in. "Dude, my business philosophy is 'money talks and bullshit walks.' I buy weed cheap and sell high volume, simple as that. I don't give a damn about whoever the fuck you're talking about… Nietzsche, Schmietzsche! If you guys want to do business, let's do it. If you want to philosophize then I can turn you on to the guy on the soap box standing in front of City Lights Book Store, right over there," he said pointing across the street at Lawrence Ferlinghetti's legendary bookstore made famous and notorious by the poet Alan Ginsberg's poem *Howl*, which embroiled the bookstore in an obscenity trial in the late 1950s.

"Can you handle half a ton of good quality Michoacan?" I asked. "I have a couple of bricks here in my flight bag as samples of our load."

"I can handle whatever you've got as long as the price is right so I can move it fast.

That's my speciality. Pricing is everything and you have to be competitive because you're not the only game in town. Half a ton will take no longer than a week," Billy said. "Let's go out to my van and have a look."

The 1965 brown VW bus was parked around the corner in an alley off Broadway Street. Inside, with psychedelic curtains drawn, I unzipped my blue PanAm flight bag and put two red cellophane wrapped kilos on the small table.

'Yorktown' Billy carefully undid the cellophane and smelled one of the bricks. He pulled off a flower top and rubbed it between his fingers, feeling the sticky resin.

"Nice bud!" the hefty dealer said approvingly. "A little leafy, but definitely salable. Are all the bricks consistent?"

"I'm not sure, but it looks so," I replied. "We've opened around ten of them and they all look the same to me. If maybe some aren't, we'd certainly make some sort of adjustment for those in the price."

Billy pulled out a pack of orange Zig-Zag rolling papers and expertly rolled a joint. He lit up, taking a long hit, holding the pungent smoke deep in his lungs. He slowly exhaled.

"Good flavor," Billy said, smoke still trailing from his mouth. "And, what's the cost per pound?"

"Billy, it's really worth a lot, man. We sailed a ton of the stuff all the way up from Mazatlan. We almost lost the boat on the rocks," Woz said. "It's expensive stuff. It had to be packed out of the hills by burros. We went through all kinds of hassles getting here. The boat captain is a drunken fag and…"

"Whoa, pal!" Billy cut in. "Now I see for myself, you have zero business experience. Do you think any of that shit matters? I just asked for the price, not your story. My customers don't care if you brought it here by camel from the moon."

"OK, OK, I get it. I think it should be at least a couple of hundred a pound," Woz responded.

"You're way off the mark, Woz, or whatever they call you. At that rate, you'll die of old age and you'll be buried in the ninety five percent of it you'll still have. I can show you right now a similar load I'm selling for one-fifty and I'm only putting a dime on it. If you want to do business with me, it's one and a quarter, and no more. That's why I can move the stuff so quickly. Here, let me show you something." Billy reached into a drawer and pulled out a small brown paper bag containing five ounces of the most beautiful, pungent flower tops of 'Panama Red' I'd ever seen.

"Billy, sell it to me right now. That's what I want to be smoking," I said with a connoisseur's eye.

"Fifty an ounce."

I handed Billy two hundreds and a fifty dollar bill as quickly as I could get them out of my wallet. It was an unheard of price and I couldn't pay for them fast enough. I put all five ounces of the 'Panama Red' into the now empty flight bag.

"How about one-forty, and you can still sell it for one-fifty?" I said.

"No. I still think it should be more for all the trouble we went through," Woz interjected.

"Don't you listen?" Billy said. "None of that matters and, if that's what you want, then we can't do business."

"Look, Woz," I said, "this is our chance to move it quickly and in volume. I want to get back to Aspen and be done with this, first of all, to minimize our risk and exposure. Haven't we been through enough already? And secondly, I'd like to do some more skiing before they close the mountain at the end of the season. Come to your senses, man. This is a fair wholesale price. Don't get greedy."

It reminded me of another of my father's old sayings: 'Sometimes the bulls win and sometimes the bears win; but the pigs are always slaughtered and never win.'

"OK." Woz conceded with a rather dejected look on his face.

"One-forty is stretching it, but I'll go for it," Billy said. "Let's start with one hundred pounds and see how it goes. Cash and carry."

"Done. Can we meet you tomorrow at 10 in the morning at the parking lot next to Fleishacker Pool by the San Francisco Zoo? You know where it is, don't you? Go west on Sloat Boulevard which dead ends at the Great Highway. Turn left and park right there by the pool entrance. We'll take your van, fill it and be back in about a half hour."

"I'll find it. See you at 10. Now get outta here!" Billy said in his New York accent.

Our first deal came off without a hitch.

Two days later, I was at Marty's Noe Valley flat on 22nd Street. It was late in the afternoon, around 5:30 PM, and I was just starting to get the characteristic metallic taste in my mouth and beginning to feel the first effects from the initial rush from the Orange Sunshine LSD I had popped half an hour earlier. I was sequestered in Marty's back bedroom with a beautiful raven haired girl whose name I can't quite remember. It might have been Star. We were sitting on the edge of his waterbed sharing a joint, trying to mellow into the onslaught of the acid we had both taken. On the record player I had just started to play in the bedroom was one of my favorite songs: Jefferson Airplane's *White Rabbit*[1] with Grace Slick's wonderful melodic voice singing…

> 'One pill makes you larger, and one pill makes you small.
> And the one that mother gives you, don't do anything at all…'

In the softly lit room, I could actually see each golden colored note rise like a bubbling musical score from Star's open mouth. Just as I put my arm around her, there was a loud banging on the bedroom door. It sounded like the staccato beat of a jackhammer. "Rick!" Marty yelled. "Open up. It's Woz on the phone."

"Not now. Tell him to call back later."

"Get the fuck out here, right now. He says it's a matter of life and death."

"Rick, you'd better get over here right away. My parents came home early. The wind blew out their fishing trip. We're in big trouble! They found the load!"

Sylvia and Mark Wozenberg Sr. had arrived home three hours earlier, having had their Hawaiian fishing trip cut short because of bad weather and choppy seas. Tired from the long flight, they had stopped at the veterinary hospital on the way home from the airport to pick up Precious, their miniature poodle, who had been kenneled there

---

1 Referenced Songs & Music, Item 2, Page 530.

while they were on vacation. Sylvia had just put a last load of wet clothes into the dryer and was heading out of the laundry room to go back upstairs and find something to cook for dinner.

"Yip, yip, yip," barked Precious.

"You miss me? My cute little baby. Mommy missed you too." Sylvia cooed.

"Yip, yip, yip," the barking continued.

"Come on Precious, let's go upstairs and find you some dinner," Sylvia said as she turned around to leave and turn off the light.

"Yip, yip, yip," Precious barked as she now was standing with her front legs up on the retaining wall at the far end of the laundry room.

"What is it girl? What's back there? Let me get a flashlight off of Daddy's workbench and see." Sylvia returned a few seconds later with a flashlight and put Precious on top of the retaining wall. Immediately the little dog started pawing at the black plastic sheet, tearing a hole in it as she spun around in a circle wildly barking. Then she disappeared through the hole. Shining the beam at the plastic, Sylvia frowned. She then retrieved a small stepladder she kept in the adjacent garage, climbed over the small retaining wall, pulled down one corner of the tacked plastic sheet and ducked under the rough wooden beams following the little dog.

Sylvia emerged from the small enclosed space brushing cobwebs out of her hair with one hand and holding a red wrapped cellophane package in the other. Her brown eyes were filled with rage as she ran up the backstairs as if chased by demons from Hell.

"Mark! Maarrkk!" Sylvia shrieked at the top of her high pitched voice to her sleeping husband, who had settled in for a nap to recover from jet-lag. Since his service in the war and probably from being a pilot himself, he always had trouble sleeping on planes. Now only an hour into his nap, he was jolted awake by the wailing of his wife as she trundled upstairs with 'the goods'.

Driving my VW wagon from Marty's flat in Noe Valley to the Wozenbergs' home in St. Francis Woods, a distance of some five miles from one side of San Francisco to the other, and now completely in the throes of the LSD, everything appeared to me as if I was in a psychedelic circus. Automobile headlights and taillights looked like unbroken ribbons of light, appearing exactly like out-of-focus time lapsed photography seen as if looking through reverse binoculars. I kept saying to myself, 'Keep it together… just keep it the fuck together.' Rolling the window down helped as I gulped for some fresh night air. Somehow I managed to negotiate the way across town as if being drawn there by some unseen magnet pulling me uncontrollably to what I envisioned as 'the house of doom'.

Parking the car in front of the Wozenberg home required a supreme effort and felt like I was docking the Queen Mary at a dock the size of a kitchen sponge, cranking the steering wheel one way then the other and trying not to jump the curb nor hit the street lamp. I hadn't noticed when I first docked my VW, but as I looked around I saw that the only other vehicle on the street was of the same make and model as the one which belonged to my parents. 'Uh oh. Not a good sign,' I said to myself somehow managing a cogent thought given my condition. The thick fog now swirling through the area, coupled with the distant foghorn bellowing, made for an even more surrealistic scene, as I stepped out of the car and onto the street in front of their home. It was like a foreboding scene out of a Dracula movie. The ground seemed to be moving in waves and I sensed I was no longer walking, but floating and being pulled toward the vampire's castle. Right then, I knew the full force of the acid had hit me and I was peaking.

My father answered the door. In my acid-warped reality, I saw the top of his toupee-covered head was completely gone, absolutely flattened. In its place there appeared to be a boiling cauldron of bubbling red hot lava from which thick black smoke and fiery red and yellow sparks spewed into the hallway behind where he was standing. He was trying to say something, but the erupting-like sound created from the volcanic activity emanating from his head drowned out the words. He turned on his heel, in a military-like, about-face maneuver and marched theatrically into the adjacent living room as if still in the Army. I followed.

As I then stood at the entrance to the living room I saw what was a completely chaotic and totally demented scene, something appearing to be straight out of *Dante's Inferno*. Everyone seated in the room, Sylvia and both Mark Wozenbergs, Junior and Senior, and my mother now joined by my father, seemed to be shouting at each other simultaneously. I was stunned. 'Is this real', I thought. All of their faces were melting like wax, dripping down the front of their clothes. Nobody's face had any features; just streams of molten flesh in different stages of disintegration. "Wow," I thought I heard myself saying out loud. My own voice sounded alien, hollow, tinny and distant as if coming from a ventriloquist in another room.

"Get in here and sit down, son. The two of you are in deep shit," Dick said pointing at both Woz and me with both hands gyrating and shaking as if trying to maintain his balance so as not to fall onto the carpet which seemed like a bubbling pool of yellow shag liquid.

"Huh? What?" I said, completely shaken.

There on the coffee table lay three red wrapped kilos, two untouched and one ripped open revealing the marijuana neatly packed inside. Next to it was my blue unzipped PanAm flight bag with the four gorgeous ounces of 'Panama Red' setting beside it. They were lying side-by-side each in clear plastic one quart Ziplock bags.

"What have you two done?" said my mother, Helen. Her face appeared like a large rodent's head with an elongated quivering snout from which protruded silver whiskers. She gulped vodka from a tumbler. "We raised you to be good boys. We sent you to college. Gave you everything and now look at you, common criminals! Dope peddlers!"

"I guess that's what your sailboat trip from Mexico was all about," said an unusually calm Mark Sr.

"What's all this stuff worth, anyway?" asked Dick.

"A lot. Over six figures," I said, barely aware I'd even spoken.

The black smoke and ash emanating from his head had now turned green as dollar signs now replaced the red bubbling molten lava. I could hear my mother's mind making sharp clicking and clacking sounds like abacus beads changing into dollars.

"Well you two are going to be sadly disappointed, because we're getting rid of all of it, right now," said Helen. "It's the only decent thing to do." Her nostrils flared and the silver whiskers trembled.

"And just how do you propose to do that?" Woz inquired with a quizzical smirk.

"This isn't funny," Mark Sr. now glaring looking directly at his son. "We're going to load up our station wagon and drive out to Land's End and dump it over the cliff into the ocean. I'm going downstairs and start loading, right now."

I immediately erupted into almost uncontrollable laughter. Between gasps I was able to say: "Do you see how much marijuana is there and how many trips back and forth to the cliff you're going to have to make? Do you even realize or can you even imagine what it's going to look like if somebody sees you in a Chinese fire drill bucket brigade lobbing all of those packages off the edge in the middle of the night in this fog?" I was helplessly laughing.

"There's close to a thousand pounds!" Woz chimed in with emphasis. "Probably take four maybe five trips. Any less and the station wagon will sag like if you are hauling an elephant in the back!"

Now with tears in my eyes, I still couldn't stop the uncontrollable laughing.

Mark Sr. turned and headed for the backstairs leading down to the basement garage. Sylvia heavily rose from the couch, uttering short gasping sobs and blindly following her husband. Parts of her body ballooned and contracted randomly, like the female version of the Michelin Man, seemingly unaffected by the madness transpiring around her.

Trying to somewhat control my laughter I said, "Dad, can we take a walk? I need some fresh air." We stepped out into the evening fog and started walking a short distance up the street.

"Dad, this is a great business opportunity. Mark and I stand to make close to one-hundred fifty thousand on this one transaction alone. Everybody's smoking," I said, reaching into my shirt pocket and pulling out a joint of 'Panama Red' and sticking it in my mouth.

"Put that away!" Dick ordered. "Don't you know all of this is totally illegal? You and Mark can go to prison for this, lose everything and bring nothing but shame on both of our families."

"This is the wave of the future. Millions can be made, Dad. Think of it! We can go into business together and make a fortune, like the Kennedys did during Prohibition. It's the opportunity of a lifetime, plus it's going to be legal soon and we'll be on the leading edge of it. We'll be rich beyond belief." In my acid-soaked mind, the father-son business scheme seemed totally right for the moment. Nothing seemed too grandiose. Hitler had probably felt this way on the eve of his catastrophic Russian invasion. Nothing could possibly go wrong.

"Have you totally lost your mind? I don't want to have anything to do with this. Everything I do is legitimate, above board. I pay my taxes. I don't break the law. If this is the direction you're heading, son, then I don't want to have anything to do with you!"

I felt deflated as we both returned to the house. Upon entering we could hear voices coming from the basement. Everyone had gone downstairs. Mark Sr. was attempting to load the station wagon, but with close to five hundred kilos piled on the basement floor but only a few in the back of the car, he slowly realized the futility of his plan. In his mind's eye he began to envision the potential fiasco on the cliffs which I had probably gotten him to think about earlier.

"You know, Dad," Woz addressed his father, "this stuff really isn't ours to get rid of. It belongs to the guy who actually bought it; a very heavy underworld figure. Probably Mafia. When he finds out it's gone, Rick and I are as good as dead."

Seeing Woz's rare burst of genius I followed his lead. "This guy is Mr. Big. Our lives are on the line here. You want to be responsible for our deaths?"

"I'm calling Jeffrey Cohen this minute to get his legal advice," Mark Sr. said, referring to Sylvia's brother who was one of San Francisco's high-powered corporate attorneys. "Jesus Christ! Your stupidity has really jeopardized both of our families here!"

As we marched single file back up the narrow staircase, Helen turned and sarcastically said to me following right behind her: "Think of all the money, think of all the money." Even after we were back in the living room I could hear these words reverberating in my ears, sounding like a row of shuffling Tibetan monks, slowly and together, droning a monotone Tibetan chant: "Think-of-all-the-mon-ey, think-of-all-the-money, think-of-all-the-mon-ey."

Mark was in the den talking on the phone to Jeffrey Cohen, discussing the situation and assessing the various options. Cohen advised that giving the marijuana back to us would probably be the safest choice, and logistically, trying to get rid of it by throwing it over the cliff just didn't make any sense and was, at best, a very risky scheme. Cohen then told Mark Sr. he wanted to speak personally to both Mark Jr. and me.

First Woz took the phone from his father's hand and was severely reprimanded by the attorney.

"Yes sir. Yes sir. Yes sir. I understand sir. It won't happen again. I give you my word, Uncle Jeff. I promise." Standing next to him, I could only hear Woz's side of the conversation. He then handed the phone to me saying: "He wants to speak with you."

With the LSD molecules still shaking every cell of my cerebral cortex and warping my cognitive thought, I took the phone and said: "Mr. Cohen, is it possible for Mark Jr. and me to retain your services for future endeavors in this business?"

Jeffrey Cohen hit the roof, demanding to speak to Mark Sr. "These boys are incorrigible. They are going to get themselves in serious trouble and wind up in prison. I want nothing to do with them and if you were smart, Mark, neither would you!" He slammed down the receiver.

I returned to the living room just as my mother and Sylvia emerged together from the adjacent powder room.

"At least we got rid of something," Sylvia said to Helen, sniffling as she wrung out her soaked handkerchief.

"What's going on?" I asked guardedly.

My mother turned to me and said smugly, "We flushed those four small bags of marijuana down the toilet."

My jaw dropped as I realized my precious Panama Red was gone. Nearly bursting into tears, I cried: "How could you? That was the best grass in the world, and I can't get any more! How am I ever going to mellow out? I can't believe what you did!"

"One more word out of you and I'm going to personally call the cops and you'll learn a lesson you'll never forget," Dick snarled. "Now shut up and get the rest of that dope out of the house by tomorrow, before I simply kick the shit out of you!"

Later, I called Rob Farnsworth who said he'd be over as soon as he could get there. At 7 the following morning Rob arrived from the East Bay in his covered pickup that we had used to unload *Sirius II*. Rob stashed the load at his friend's garage where it would be safe for a week.

During the next five days, I ferried about one hundred kilos a day to 'Yorktown' Billy. On one of those days, he invited me to accompany him and meet one of his customers who lived over in Marin County.

We crossed the Golden Gate Bridge and went up to the town of Fairfax, where we met a real hippie looking character who Billy introduced as Woodacre Bob, nicknamed for the tiny Marin village of Woodacre, located west of Fairfax. I immediately liked his carefree attitude and just called him Woody Bob. Bob was about six feet tall, with a full head of blondish-brown curly hair which flowed in tight ringlets down the middle of his back, had leather sandals, white pajama bottom pants with a drawstring holding them up and wore a tie-dyed purple, green, red and blue tank top which looked like he'd just thrown up down the front of it. We followed him in Billy's brown VW bus. Woody Bob also drove a VW bus, but his was painted from bumper-to-bumper with bright psychedelic swirls causing any passerby to nearly suffer a broken neck from gawking at him as he passed.

We headed west into the Marin countryside then turned off the main road. We went about a quarter of a mile on a dirt road and through a locked wooden ranch-type gate, then climbed up the Marin hills for several miles to a barren mountaintop surrounded by nothing but blue sky, tall brown grass and clean fresh air. We all got out of our vans and Bob proceeded to remove all of his clothes. Now he was totally nude and we proceeded with the transaction, like it was nothing out of the ordinary. Coincidentally, this was not the last time Woody Bob and my paths would cross. Many years later we would meet again in rather unusual but predictable circumstances.

"What the fuck?" I asked Billy.

"Oh, don't mind him. This is what he always does. He's just getting in touch with nature. I just had to let you see this. He is one of the biggest dealers in Marin and one of my best customers. We transferred the load to his 'hippie van' and he gave Billy a paper bag full of cash. "We don't need to count it here. I guarantee it's all in there. I've never lost a penny with any of my customers. Now you can see how it's done. And, please don't ever bring your fool of a partner around me. I really can't stand him, his holier-than-thou attitude or his philosophizing nonsense."

"You got it!"

On the fifth day I got a call from Billy. "I've got something for you over at my place. Why don't you come by and pick it up?"

"OK. Is now convenient?"

"Yeah, 'Bro'. Come on over."

I drove to Billy's Mission District home. Inside Billy handed me a brown paper bag on which was printed with the slogan, 'Safeway – Nobody Does It Better'. Inside the bag was $135,000 in cash. The bills were mostly $20s and $100s. Some neat clean and new and some crumpled, faintly smelling of mildew.

I counted the money as we passed a joint back and forth. Each thousand dollar stack was banded with a rubber band and five of those stacks were banded together with paper bank bands imprinted with $5,000 on each. There were twenty seven of them in the bag and the counting took an hour.

"By the way, Billy, is there any more 'Panama Red'?"

"Sorry man, it's all gone. It was some of the best ever."

"Bummer!"

Chapter 11

Sinsemilla

April 1971

Woz and I flew out to Aspen to catch the last few days of spring skiing before the mountain closed for the season. Those last few days of the season were some of the most beautiful spring skiing days imaginable with crispy corn snow, crystal blue skies and shirt sleeve temperatures reaching almost seventy degrees. Before leaving for Aspen we both met with Killian to pay him off, plus he was given a sizable bonus over and above the agreed upon contract fee.

Following our return to the Bay Area, Woz and I rented a two story houseboat in Sausalito. It was located near the end of the dock and had an unobstructed view of Richardson Bay Bridge and the seaplane port. At the suggestion of Woz's father, Mark Sr., an advocate of having numerous salable skills, we both enrolled in flight school at Oakland Airport and two months later received our single engine pilot's licenses. Since the seaplane port was practically in our back yard, I took enough instruction there to get checked out and certified in a seaplane as well. I was also spending time water skiing on the San Joaquin Delta with my old college friend and Aspen roommate Phil Erikson, who'd run in the 'Boraxo' scam with Willie and me the previous year.

Currently, Phil was working with his old childhood friend, Ciro Mancuso. Ciro and his partner, Walter Brugger, had set up a business to import handmade furniture from Mexico. Each piece was stamped with the words 'Hecho en Mexico' and was crafted by inmates inside the federal prison at Guadalajara. Ciro had procured the furniture contract from the prison authorities and arranged for shipment into the United States. Phil had rented a warehouse near SFO airport and received the shipments, handled all of the customs paperwork and importation procedures and stored the goods for U.S. wholesale distribution. The operation was designed as a legitimate 'front' business for Ciro so he could continue to make frequent trips to and from Mexico having a bonafide reason for his travel. Our houseboat, Phil's house and Walter's stash houses were all fashionably appointed with the handmade couches, chairs, chests of drawers, dressers, bed frames and nightstands manufactured in the prison. The nightstands were specially constructed with hinged fake side panels to conceal a secret handgun or weed stash cubbyhole accessed from bedside.

Early in the summer of 1971, while on the ski boat Phil and I had purchased while still in college, Phil told me about Ciro's operation.

"Ciro and his partner Walter bring in weekly shipments of weed from Mexico. Ciro has the connections for the really good stuff," said Phil. "I just happen to have some with me here. It's called Sinsemilla. It's a special seedless strain of Mexican weed grown in the state of Oaxaca and is very strong. I got some from their last trip. Here, I'll roll a joint and you tell me."

Phil produced a one gallon Ziplock baggie containing only one Sinsemilla marijuana bud. It was a huge, very pungent flower top which looked like a miniature Christmas tree. By far the most beautiful weed I'd ever seen. It alone measured nine inches long and took up the bottom one-third of the bag. It had not been compressed at all, as most weed was when it was put into brick form. The sparkling resin on the bud glistened in the afternoon sunlight like tiny mirrors.

"Boy, I'd sure like to get some," I said taking a long toke off the joint, holding it deep in my lungs and exhaling slowly. "I have a great connection set up. He can sell all you can get me. His name is 'Yorktown' Billy and he's one of the biggest dealers in San Francisco and has connections all over the U.S."

"Ciro's got about five hundred pounds of this from Oaxaca and they brought it up last week. I'm sure I can get you some. Walt is selling it for $250 a pound," Phil said. "But I can get it for $200 and I'm sure we can sell it for $275 to $300."

"We'll have to cut Wozenberg in on it," I said. "Since we met Billy through Woz's brother it probably wouldn't be right to exclude him and might really upset the apple cart for future boat trips. The price seems kind of high, but for this quality we can move it without a doubt. The good news is, even with Woz cut in for a share, we can still each make $25 per pound which is not bad for being a middleman. Ya think we can get a couple of hundred pounds?"

"Shouldn't be a problem. When we get back to the dock, I'll give Walt a call and arrange it. Hey, save me some of that joint!"

"Oops, sorry. I didn't mean to 'bogart' all of it. Here you go," I said as I had almost forgotten I still had the joint in my hand since I was now thoroughly stoned and staring blankly at the water gently lapping against the side of the ski boat's hull.

It was nearly 90° as we sat in the sun on Fourteen Mile Slough. Phil continued: "I just got back from 'Guad' and you should see Ciro's setup down there. He has a ten acre avocado ranch and hacienda outside of a little town named Tlaquepaque, near Guadalajara. Kind of reminds me of a postcard picture of old Mexico. Lush, beautiful bougainvillea growing everywhere around his two story stone and wooden hacienda. There is a central courtyard and fountain and he has a maid and servants at the beckon of his every command. He lives like a king. He's installing an intercom and video surveillance camera for security. You should see the place. It's really something," rambled Phil as he tossed the roach into the water and began rolling another joint.

"Sounds great, I'd like to see it someday."

"You probably will," replied Phil. "His ranch is the perfect place to do their thing. I don't think we'll ever have a 'summer drought' of weed in Northern California again, because Ciro can store tons of pot at his place year round. In fact, summer's even better than during the growing season for doing the actual smuggle. For one, there's generally no other weed around then, so we can get the best price. And two, even more importantly, there are so many more people out traveling and crossing the border, customs just can't check everybody as closely."

"I'm sure you remember the shit we got during the summer when Willie and I first ran the border," I said. "Sounds like we won't have to go through that cluster-fuck again, thank God."

"Ditto. And that crap from Kansas. That's history too. It's sure nothing like this," Phil said passing me the joint which was now almost burning my fingers.

"Let me tell you," Phil went on. "Their operation is so slick. They have this guy from Thailand, Pat, who works for them. He's an an excellent craftsman who builds stashes for them in their trailers so perfectly it's impossible to tell. Ciro and Walter rented a warehouse in an industrial area in Redwood City where Pat does all of his trailer 'remodeling' work. Nobody's the wiser as the area is filled with auto repair shops, welding shops and the like. Repairing trailers fits right in. Anyway, they bring a trailer to the warehouse where Pat completely dismantles it and removes the inside of it leaving nothing but a bare shell. Then he remakes all of the removed parts only a few inches smaller than they had originally been but perfectly proportional to each other and puts it all back together leaving a space of about 8 inches between the exterior wall and the newly fashioned interior. The walls of the stash are coated and sealed so no smell can penetrate through them. The furniture and all of the interior is then screwed and bolted back together so it has the illusion of being a normal trailer with nothing out of place. It looks the same as any trailer and fools even the most scrupulous customs officer. They can put at least 300 pounds of weed in the stash. It's really amazing. Pat's their guy. They fly him back and forth, to and from Mexico for each loading and unloading. I saw the whole thing when I was at the ranch last week."

"Personally, I like our idea of sailing the loads," I responded. "Even though we really don't conceal the weed, I think it's much safer. It's an awfully big ocean and we're just a tiny speck out there and there's virtually no customs at all to go through. Hell, when we came back last time, we called customs and they sent a guy down to the boat who said 'hi, goodbye' and never even came aboard. Never inspected a thing. Just made a note on his clipboard and left. But, I guess, whatever works and Ciro's rigs haven't been busted. I just hope we can get some of the Sinsemilla before it's all gone."

"Don't sweat it. Let's go in and I'll call Walter," said Phil, pulling two ice cold Heinekens out of a cooler. "I'm sure we can have some by tomorrow morning."

I started the engine and we roared out of the sloughs and into the Delta's main channel. The sun was beginning to set and the water was smooth as glass. It was 6:30 in the evening and the temperature was still well above 90°.

"You should see some of these rummies Walter digs up to drive their trailers across the border. He calls them his 'tarnished casino nuggets.' Mostly they're down-and-outers from the casinos. Sometimes he finds couples, ya know, Ma and Pa Kettle types," Phil continued. "I met this one dude, named Jimmy Phelps. Now this guy is a real piece of work! Walt must have found him in a garbage can, behind the casino. On his good days or when he's driving a load he looks great, a real 'dapper Dan'; but on his bad days, 'Katie bar the door'. He's a real skid row bum, all smelly and strung out on coke or smack. Walt's had to bail him out of jail more than once. Still, Jimmy's a good guy, but he and Pat sure don't get along. Pat can be temperamental and Jimmy always seems to rub him the wrong way. I saw Pat kick the shit out of poor Jimmy a few weeks ago in a hotel elevator in Guadalajara. Jimmy said something which really pissed Pat off and Pat did a couple of Thai kick boxing moves and flattened ole Jimmy. It was ugly."

We arrived back at the ramp at Ladd's Marina a few minutes later and pulled the boat out of the water and headed back to Phil's house. On the way we stopped at a pay phone where Phil called Walter and arranged to pick up 200 pounds of Sinsemilla the following day at Walter's new stash house in the swank Los Altos Hills on the Peninsula, thirty miles south of San Francisco.

The next morning at Walter's house, Phil and I were greeted at the front door by Walt's number one gofer, Mike Duncan, a young ski racer from Lake Tahoe and one of Walter's skiing proteges. Mike was 5'10" tall, slim with what appeared to be zero body fat, but muscular with short sandy hair and a thin mustache. He was barefoot and wore cut-off jeans and a tank top and had a cast on his left leg which he had broken in a hang gliding accident two weeks previously.

"Hey, Mike. How's the leg?" Phil asked.

"Better. But sure can't wait to get this fucking block off my leg. Slows me down. Come on in," Mike said inviting us into the kitchen.

"This is Rick," Phil said as we went through the modern living room and into the kitchen.

Mike introduced me to Pat who was busy making coffee. Pat was about my height, maybe an inch taller at 5'6". He had dark longish black hair which fell loosely over the collar of his white Lacoste polo shirt. He wore faded blue jeans and white Adidas running shoes with three green stripes on the side. I noticed a large brown mole on the right side of his upper lip and his markedly Asian features were highlighted by a broad, warm friendly smile. Pat and I shook hands, sized each other up and immediately took a liking to one another.

"Have seat. How you like coffee?" asked Pat in heavily accented pidgin English.

"Black," I said.

"Phil?"

"Black for me too, Pat."

"Where's Walt?" Phil asked.

"Taking shower. He be down in minute," answered Pat. "Mike, put those four duffel bags in Phil's trunk. Phil, you have keys to car?"

Phil handed Mike the keys to his Chevelle parked in the driveway next to the garage. Mike hobbled out of the room and I saw him through the kitchen window putting four large red Rossignol ski equipment bags into Phil's trunk. Mike returned a minute or two later and handed Phil back his keys just as Walter came downstairs and entered the kitchen. He was drying his blond hair with a towel.

Walter was about 5'9" tall and appeared to be in good physical condition, but not nearly as athletic looking or muscular as Mike. He had on tan Dockers, a blue polo shirt and wore a pair of Nike running shoes with no socks. His open collar revealed a gold chain and he wore a stainless steel Rolex Submariner watch. Walter had an angular shaped face with a rather large nose that extended outwards then bent sharply down in the middle. He had blue rather shifty eyes and seemed to take in everything at once, probably characteristic of the world class ski racer looking downhill for the next slalom gate.

"So this is Rick, eh?" said Walter extending his hand to greet me. "You tried any of this Sinsemilla yet? It's dynamite, don't you think?"

"Looks like Christmas in June." I said picking up one of the miniature Christmas tree-like Sinsemilla flower tops lying on a rectangular silver serving platter which doubled as a joint rolling tray. "All that's missing are the ornaments. I've never seen such perfect buds."

"Mike put about 200 pounds in your trunk, Phil. There's an accounting in one of the bags. Don't worry, it's all there. Each package is marked and inventoried on the list," said Walter.

Phil reached into his pocket and pulled out a wad of one-hundred dollar bills and handed them to Walter. "Here's ten grand. Looks like we owe you about another thirty or so. We'll do the exact accounting when we get back to Sausalito and will have the balance for you in a week, give or take."

"No problem, Phil," Walt said. "Get back to me when you can. Hey, it's after 10, I've got to run and Mike has to hobble to keep up."

"Hobble, my ass. We'll see who is hobbling on the slopes this winter when you're eating my exhaust, old man," Mike replied laughing.

"We sure will. You might want to put your money where your mouth is, big shot. Now, cut the crap, and let's boogie. You put the other hundred pounds in my trunk, didn't you? Pat, we'll be back in a couple of hours. Get the rig ready to go south. It has to leave by tomorrow."

"Yes, sahib," Pat said sarcastically with a smile on his face and a crisp salute, clicking his heels together. I could tell in that instant Pat did not like being ordered around.

Phil and I left Walter's house, drove down his long winding driveway and through the electric gate. In under two minutes we were on Interstate 280 heading north.

Back at the houseboat in Sausalito, Woz was anxiously waiting for us. In anticipation of our return, he had opened up the houseboat's pontoons and was waiting to fill them with the weed. The pontoons, upon which the houseboat floated, had access doors located underneath the carpets of the two first floor closets located on either side of the living room. Arriving back at the dock, Phil and I each carried one ski bag while Woz carried the other two from the car through the gated entrance, down the sloping wooden ramp, along the floating dock and up into the houseboat.

It was a beautiful, cloudless sunny morning as we entered the houseboat. The morning sunlight streaming into the living room was filtered through the glass French doors on the south side which opened to a sitting deck right on the water. We eagerly opened the bags and checked the list against the packages neatly stacked inside. Everything was in order as promised by Walter. In the sunlight, the weed was the most beautiful any of us had ever seen. Each 'cola', the Mexican word for flower top, was bright green, perfectly manicured and glistened with sparkling resin. Each package contained several 'colas' packed very loosely together so as not to damage the gorgeous buds. The packages were each wrapped first in white tissue paper then with an outer layer of green cellophane paper and carefully taped shut with a piece of off white masking tape with the weight marked on it in grams. The average weight of the packages was about 750 grams, a little over a pound and a half, and there were about 30 in each of the four ski bags now sitting on the living room floor.

Woz's eyes seemed as large as silver dollars as he gazed at the packages. He picked up one and opening it very carefully, put it up to his nose and inhaled deeply. "Holy, mother of God!" he exclaimed. "This is outrageous! I'll bet we can get $500 a pound for this. Just look at these tops!"

"Now, let's be realistic Woz," I said. "If we sell them to Billy for $275 we each make $25 a pound and he can sell them for $300, they'll probably be gone in a couple of days. We would each make five grand. Not bad for two days' work."

"I think we should try and make as much as we possibly can and maximize our investment," Woz replied. "Isn't that what business is all about?"

"What are you talking about?" Phil said, rather irritated. "Most of this was 'fronted' to us. Our investment was minimal. I'm with you, Rick. What this business is about, Mark, is the sooner we get it all sold, the less risk we are taking plus I want to pay Walter back as soon as possible, so we look good and establish ourselves. What this business is not all about is trying to make it all for ourselves on one shipment. I would've thought you'd have figured that out by now. These guys have loads coming in every week and this could start looking pretty nice for us… if we get off on the right foot and not try and get greedy."

I was again thinking about my father's words regarding 'the bulls, the bears and the pigs' and feeling Woz's answer would be putting us in the role of 'pigs'. Not a good place to be!

Phil continued: "I don't think there will be any more Sinsemilla till next year, but they have plenty of good weed stashed at Ciro's ranch and there should be more in a couple of weeks. So, I think the vote is two to one here and the price is $275. Right? Agreed." We all nodded, albeit Woz reluctantly. "So let's get to work."

'Yorktown' Billy couldn't get enough and almost couldn't get rid of it fast enough. It was gone nearly overnight and four days later Phil paid Walter the balance owed and we were ready for the next load. It seemed as if in virtually no time at all we were one of Walter's best customers. Phil, Woz and I formed a loose partnership to broker the weekly loads Phil got from Ciro via Walter.

Soon, the loaded trailers rolled from the avocado ranch at Tlaquepaque into the

Bay Area weekly. After a shipment arrived at a pre-arranged spot, usually a large shopping center like Hillsdale or Tanforan on the Peninsula, Walter sent Mike Duncan to retrieve the load and drive the vehicle to the Redwood City warehouse for unloading and processing. There Pat disassembled the trailer, then he, Mike and Walter removed the load, weighed the weed, labeled and inventoried it for distribution. Walter then divided it among four or five key distributors, of which we were one, in 50 to 100 kilo lots. Meanwhile, Pat reassembled the trailer, fixed and touched up any dings and sent it back to Mexico to reload. The 'Ma & Pa Kettle' drivers were alternated so as not to arouse suspicion by making too many back and forth trips.

The whole operation was growing rapidly. New trailers were purchased and converted by Pat Suraghoomkol. New drivers were being recruited. Money was constantly ferried back and forth between Walter's stash pad and Ciro's ranch in Mexico. Walter opened a trendy furniture store in downtown Palo Alto which Phil stocked from the SFO warehouse with Mexican furniture. 'Sombrero Imports' furniture store was now Ciro and Walter's legitimate 'front' business for their growing marijuana smuggling operation.

Phil, in addition to clearing and receiving the furniture, was also busy helping to convey money down to Ciro in Mexico. He and an assistant driver would make 36-hour non-stop runs from the Bay Area to Mexico with cash concealed in a hidden compartment Pat had made in a Chrysler station wagon known as 'the Goon' which Phil used specifically for that purpose. On one such return trip after delivering the money to Ciro, Phil, with his out-of-place rather longish hair, mustache and European good looks, was stopped by Federales at a checkpoint and detained for three days in a local jail in the Mexican town of Ciudad Obregon, on Mexico's west coast highway. He was starved with only small daily portions of burnt frijoles, rice and sour smelling water and threatened with a prison sentence and only released after finally being allowed to make a phone call to Ciro whose Mexican connection obtained his freedom in exchange for a $5,000 ransom paid to his Mexican jailer. It was another example of 'la mordida', the bite, and the Mexican way.

Following Phil's return after narrowly escaping what could have been a much worse situation, it was decided to retire the old reliable 'Goon' from any more trips to Mexico. It wasn't worth the risk, since possibly now its make, model and license number might be on some border crossing watch list and vulnerable to further scrutiny. Phil and I decided we'd just use 'the Goon' for making weed deliveries for our part of the business.

Although now running like a finely tuned Swiss watch, Ciro's operation nearly suffered what could have been a fatal blow later in the summer.

Weekly shipments were arriving on schedule throughout the months of May, June and July, coming off without a hitch. However, the first shipment in August somehow got heat on it following the border crossing in Nogales. The seasoned 'Ma & Pa Kettle' drivers with several successful trips under their belt saw nothing unusual following the cursory customs examination and clearance into Arizona on a bright, hot August morning. What they didn't know was, most likely because this was their fifth border crossing in five months, they had attracted the attention of U.S. Customs. And what they obviously didn't see was that they had been followed by several unmarked cars all the way back from Nogales to their rendezvous drop-off point at Tanforan Shopping Center in Burlingame, California.

'Ma Kettle' casually got out and went into the shopping center to a pay phone and called Walt with a coded message indicating they had safely arrived. She was on the phone no more than ten seconds. She then went next door into Macy's department store and bought a change of clothes for her and 'Pa Kettle', then returned to the rig to wait. It was only by sheer luck that none of the officers who had tailed them up from Arizona had time to follow her into the shopping center without being noticed. 'Ma' returned to the truck pulling the trailer carrying a red Macy's bag of clothes, got inside where she and 'Pa' smoked cigarettes and waited.

About an hour later, Jimmy Phelps, Walter's most trusted 'tarnished casino nugget', arrived at Tanforan Shopping Center as planned, followed at a safe distance behind by Mike Duncan as an observer. Jimmy, in a rented car, was to pick up the trailer and give his vehicle to the drivers who were to return it to the rental car agency at SFO, check into a nearby motel where they would be paid and given plane tickets for a month's vacation before their next planned smuggling trip. Jimmy pulled into the parking lot and parked next to the rig while Mike parked outside the lot on an adjacent street located on a hill above the shopping center parking lot where he could observe the transfer at a safe distance through binoculars. No one noticed the now five unmarked sedans parked nearby in the crowded parking lot. Smoking a cigarette as well, Jimmy nonchalantly got out of his car and went to the driver's side of the truck and opened the door. Almost as if out of nowhere, lights and sirens came blazing up and surrounded the vehicles. Ten agents from the U.S. Customs, FBI, BNDD (Bureau of Narcotics and Dangerous Drugs) and local sheriff's department jumped out with guns drawn, yanked Jimmy away from the truck and ordered 'Ma & Pa Kettle' out of the truck. All were placed face down on the pavement and handcuffed with guns pointed at their heads and agents yelling in their faces: "You're under arrest! Where are the drugs?"

Jimmy and the drivers responded with complete surprise and ignorance of any drugs. All produced driver's licenses and stuck to their story of innocent travel to Mexico and meeting Jimmy, a friend, just to say 'hello' and welcome them home. No one noticed as Mike casually drove away from his lookout spot to report back to Walter what had just happened.

The three were summarily taken to San Mateo County jail and held in separate cells. The trailer, truck and rented vehicle were then taken to an impound lot at the San Mateo County Sheriffs Department. All of the vehicles were thoroughly searched during the following two days. In the trailer, all of the interior space: the cabinets, the closets, the compartments below the living area, and every conceivable nook and cranny was thoroughly searched and inspected by agents who were literally crawling all over the rig. A drug sniffing dog was brought in to aid in the search.

At the same time that all of this was going on, Walter, Pat and Mike went into a state of panic followed quickly by Walter regaining his cool-headed composure and giving the orders to go into emergency action mode. They scrambled and cleared out everything from all locations which could possibly lead the cops back to Walter. All of the equipment and tools were removed from the Redwood City warehouse and Walter's stash house was emptied of any evidence of the clandestine operation; scales, bags, lists, rolling trays, cigarette rolling papers, and any marijuana was hastily put into Walter's pickup and driven to the safety of the SFO airport warehouse used for furniture storage. Walter was confident the drivers knew virtually nothing of the workings of the operation. The only possible 'loose cannon' was Jimmy, but Walter had conditioned and counseled him over and over during the previous year to keep his mouth shut and wait out any trouble which might come. He was assured he would be taken care of if he just 'held his mud.'

Miraculously, after two or three days, nothing was found in any of the seized vehicles. Not a seed, nor any trace of any drugs could be found or detected. Pat's genius at total concealment of the load had worked and even fooled the drug-sniffing dog. All three stuck to their story and were subsequently released on Day 3 following their arrest for lack of evidence. No charges were brought, although all names, addresses, and VIN numbers were duly noted. Walter and Company were sweating bullets for the next two weeks while the truck and trailer remained in the Sheriff's impound lot. Finally, on Day 14, Walter had Jimmy summon up all of his courage and go the sheriff's department to retrieve the truck and trailer. With Mike again following at a safe distance, Jimmy picked up the trailer, drove around the Bay Area with Mike tailing and observing and finally to another 'safe house' in the East Bay Hills where the trailer was safely parked and unloaded a few days later. It was during the unloading process where Pat discovered several half inch holes that the agents had apparently randomly drilled into the interior walls of the trailer. It was only by some miracle, that the drill bit had missed the concealed pot hidden in Pat's secret stash area between the trailer's interior and exterior walls. It had missed by mere millimeters. Pat then restored the trailer to its original condition and it was taken to a used car lot and sold.

After a few days, Jimmy delivered our share of the load to me. I was waiting for him behind some dilapidated buildings at an old abandoned quarry near Larkspur in Marin County. We transferred our share into 'the Goon' and I returned to the houseboat to stash and later delivered the weed to our primary customer, 'Yorktown' Billy, plus a small amount to my cousin Marty and a larger amount to a new customer to our business, an old friend and college classmate, John Quinn, who went by the initials JQ. Jimmy would from now on always be the one to deliver Walter's loads to me and he would be the one to whom I would give money for him to give to Walter.

I didn't know it at the time, as you never do when it's happening, but my getting to know Jimmy Phelps as I did would, in the future, prove to be one of my most valuable introductions and a blessing in disguise.

Mid-summer, after brokering several loads, Phil and I were simultaneously beginning to feel Woz was getting in the way of a smooth operation. We both felt our partnership with Woz just wasn't working. His lack of business acumen, his constant quibbling about trying to squeeze more money out of each pound, coupled with our main customer's reluctance to even see him, forced us to re-evaluate the situation. Woz

really wasn't doing anything to further the operation. He was busy building up his
flying hours and occasionally sitting on the load in the houseboat, but not making any
pickups or deliveries and whenever he'd accompany me to 'Yorktown' Billy's, he would
always make some 'off-the-wall' comment, driving Billy nuts.

"I'm afraid he could jeopardize the relationship with Billy," I said one evening as
Phil and I were driving back to the Sausalito houseboat with another 200 pounds of
primo weed we'd just picked up from Walter's stash house. "He's got to go. This three-
way partnership is just not working."

"This probably won't end well," Phil said. "He's your partner and one of your oldest
friends."

"I know, I know," I replied. "But in this part of the operation, he's as useless as
'tits on a boar'. Look, Phil, we both have college degrees in business and understand
the basics of such business concepts as 'supply and demand' and marketing, but our
partner, Mr. Philosopher, just doesn't get it. He's always got his head in the clouds and
is always making some cockamamie non-sequitur statement. My Dad was famous for
his sayings, you know, and he always use to say: 'Better to keep your mouth shut and be
thought an idiot, rather than open it and remove all doubt.' And, I'll tell you, there's no
doubt in Billy's mind when it comes to Woz. He goes around to Billy saying he wants
to set the market price, since he brought the weed into the States and went through
whatever troubles he did to do it. That's total bullshit! Billy knows it and both you
and I know it. The price is set by what the market will bear, plain and simple. And,
yes, we might get a little more by jacking up the price, but at what cost? We turn the
loads in mere days and are making great money. He'd have us nickel and dime-ing and
selling piecemeal and risking everything. It ain't working! I don't need the aggravation
of smoothing Billy's feathers each time he talks with Woz."

"Isn't it a little ruthless, dumping an old friend?" asked Phil.

"For Christ sakes, Phil, I'm not dumping an old friend, I'm suggesting we re-organize here. My thought is, we ease Woz out of the distribution part of this operation and
just let him handle the boat transportation from Ciro's people in Mexico up to us. He
handles the transportation, we handle the distribution. We all make great money doing
what we do best. It's about specialization. It's true in any business and it applies here as
well. You wouldn't want a podiatrist doing brain surgery on you. Would you?"

"Yeah, I see your point. OK. I'll back you, but you're the one who has to tell Woz."

"All right. I think I can reason with him and hopefully get him to understand. I'll
do my best to try and keep him from coming unhinged. It's risky, but what can we do?
We have to make this run smoothly. Look, Ciro handles his end and Walt handles his
end of their trip. Shouldn't we do likewise? Hey, it's not my intention to hurt the guy. I
want what's best for all of us. We all want to make more money and not have one guy
who's out of his element gum up the works for the rest of us, don't we?"

Woz's interference was made even more apparent by 'Yorktown' Billy's specific
request to do business exclusively with me, and only me. "Please do me a favor," pleaded
Billy. "Keep the philosopher away from me. I just can't handle his spacey gibberish anymore, and he totally lacks any business sense whatsoever. He's really in the way."

Two days later I tactfully approached Woz. "I think it would be best for us to reorganize. You just handle the sailing and organizing the boat trips and I'll deal with brokering the loads and distribution. It would be in everybody's best interest if we specialize and things will run more smoothly."

"Well," said Woz, "if that's the way you want it, OK. Fine by me! I'll just do the smuggling and you don't need to have any part of it! You do your thing and I'll do mine! As a matter of fact, you don't need to have anything to do with me. Anyway, I'll deal directly with Ciro! I don't need you, or Phil, for that matter!" Woz abruptly turned on his heels and stormed out of the houseboat, down the dock toward the parking lot.

'Uh,oh', I said to myself. 'I think I blew it.' I could feel Woz's bitterness and resentment, but it was too late to turn back now. The die was cast. 'Maybe when he cools down, I can reason with him and get him to see the wisdom of what I was suggesting', I optimistically thought. At any rate, the only appropriate thing for me to do now would be to move out of the houseboat and set up on my own.

I found an art-deco style house for rent which was advertised in the San Francisco Chronicle newspaper. It was located in San Francisco's Twin Peaks area on scenic Grandview Street. Our new one story house was set into the hillside with an attached two car garage below, accessed from the street by an electric garage door. The home itself was characterized with a flat roof and a spectacular east facing view of downtown San Francisco, the Bay Bridge and beyond to the East Bay hills in the distance. Looking up the hill to the southwest was the giant radio antenna tower atop Twin Peaks. This house would be much more suited to efficiently store Walter's weekly loads. Besides, I was becoming increasingly paranoid at having to trundle loaded bags from my car down the dock to the houseboat and back out again in plain view of anybody who happened to be watching.

At this time, I had been dealing exclusively with 'Yorktown' Billy and my cousin Marty. I now had a new customer who I knew from college and who'd been away for some time, but had been a former customer during the time of Willie and my Nogales runs.

JQ, John Quinn, was a former college football player at UOP. He had played both on the defensive line and at tight-end. He had just returned from a year spent motorcycling across Europe and the United States. A year earlier, he had graduated and left for his motorcycle adventures at an imposing 6'5" tall and weighing 235 pounds. He had short crew cut blondish hair, a pencil thin 'Boston Blackie' mustache and was in top physical condition. However, now following his return to the United States, JQ was a gaunt shadow of his former self. He weighed about 175 pounds and though still an impressive figure, he now sported shoulder length red hair with a huge handlebar mustache. He wore faded jeans, a leather motorcycle jacket and black motorcycle boots. It looked like he might have cultivated a methamphetamine or cocaine habit during his travels, he was so thin and pale white complected. He was eager to rekindle his friendship with both Phil and me and looked forward to doing business with us again.

JQ had extensive connections in Colorado, Texas and the Bay Area. He was a local competitor of 'Yorktown' Billy and in addition, they shared common clients. JQ could get the same weed as Billy but was now one step closer to me. Hopefully, it wouldn't create a conflict.

As it was, everybody's 'marijuana trip' was getting bigger, snowballing through the 'old boy' school network, with connections that intertwined and crisscrossed. The volume of weed and cash flow rose dramatically. Rob Farnsworth, the financier behind our first Mexican boat trip, was now smuggling hashish from Nepal in handmade woven carpets which I sold to 'Yorktown' Billy, JQ, Walter and my cousin Marty. 'Yorktown' Billy had South American connections and sold marijuana from Panama and Columbia to me, which in turn I sold to JQ, Walter and Marty. Cousin Marty had connections who were smuggling hashish in from Afghanistan which he sold to me, and in turn I sold it to Billy and Walter. I also expanded my distribution network to include an old Army buddy from Boston and a college friend from my days at Colorado who had a commercial pilot's license and would fly kilos back East in a private twin engine Cessna.

Since both JQ and cousin Marty both lived in The City, I introduced them to each other and JQ became a frequent visitor at Marty's Noe Valley flat on 22nd Street. Both of them also had friends who were smuggling cocaine from Peru and Columbia and they both tried to get me interested. However, I wanted nothing to do with the 'dumb dust' business, as I called it. I felt that dealing coke was bad karma, involved an entirely different mind-set, a much 'heavier' group of people, and was just bad news. It was the type of venture which was likely to get someone killed in the process and I wanted nothing to do with it.

"It's so much easier to smuggle. It's smaller and worth much more than weed," said JQ, placing a rolled up hundred dollar bill to his nose and snorting a line of pure Peruvian flake one afternoon at Marty's flat. "It's the wave of the future." It seemed like I had used the same logic to try and entice my father to get involved in the marijuana business. Now it was coming full circle back to me.

"I have a friend who has a very reliable connection in Peru and we could load a boat for you," said Marty. "It would only take you a couple of weeks longer sail than from Mexico and just think of the unloading. A couple of duffel bags. Nothing to it!" Marty bent his balding head to the mirror, vacuuming two huge lines up his congested nose, which made a gurgling sound like water rushing from a toilet being flushed.

"You guys are nuts!" I exclaimed pausing to take the rolled up bill and snort a couple of lines. "I want nothing to do with smuggling this shit. I just like doing what I do. From what I know, smuggling coke isn't mellow, like the weed trip. First of all, you can't tell what you have by just looking at it. You have to test it chemically. It could be cut with cyanide or you could be buying five pounds of salt, for all I know. Secondly, I've heard the people down there in South America would just as soon kill you as look at you and they sell you the stuff, then turn you in for the reward. It's a very ruthless business. Count me out!"

"Oh sure! Don't stand on ceremony and say you want nothing to do with it, Rick," replied Marty. "You buy it. I've sold you an ounce or two. You know it's not that bad. You sound like such a hypocrite, using it and at the same time saying you don't want to get involved. What gives?"

"Sure, I like it occasionally. Makes for some good times and I kind of like the effect, but I'm not into smuggling it or being in that business, period. You guys can do what you want," I said, "but without me."

"I've brought in a couple of kilos of coco myself from Columbia," JQ said. "It was no sweat. Ricky, my boy, you'd be a natural for it, with your sailing experience and all, it would be easy as pie. Why don't you give it some thought?"

"Coco my ass! Look, JQ, you and I have known each other for a long time and don't give me that 'Ricky, my boy' shit to try and butter me up. I said NO and I meant it. And, please don't insult my intelligence by sugar coating this proposition and trying to make it sound like all I have to do is bring in a load of chocolate. So, I don't have to give it more thought. I said NO and I meant it and nothing you can say or do will change my mind. Again, absolutely NO! Get it?"

"Come on Rick! There's lots of money to be made," wheedled Marty.

"Are you that stupid or just deaf? What part of NO don't you understand?"

I just couldn't take the haranguing anymore and left the flat shaking my head. 'What a loser!' I thought as I got into my car and was driving away. 'He can't leave that powder alone even for a day. It's changing his personality. Marty's headed for big trouble and I don't want to be anywhere near him when it all comes down. Dealing coke's just too heavy; there are too many gun carrying crazies, coked-up to the gills in that business. Everything about weed is much more laid back: the high, the business and the people. Marty just doesn't see it. Well, better him than me!'

Marty was becoming wilder, much looser with his parties, snorting copious amounts of the crystalline white powder and not being very selective about new relationships or the people coming to and from his flat. There were always coke whores or musicians flitting about the Noe Valley flat and his 'parties' were becoming a well known function throughout The City and into Marin County as well. I was becoming very worried about my cousin and what was becoming of him. And, more importantly for my sake, I was becoming extremely paranoid about being seen anywhere near Marty's flat especially doing what I was doing. There were just too many strangers. So, I began distancing myself from Marty, his flat, his business and his so-called friends. As far as I was concerned he could cultivate his coke business, but I was cutting him loose from any of my dealings as of this instant.

In the early fall of 1971, Woz and I had pretty much made amends and it seemed like he'd come to his senses through a good deal of persuasion on my part and, for once, listening to reason on his part. It appeared Woz had accepted the concept of specialization and his role of being in charge of transportation. With it settled, at least in my mind, we decided to get a place in Aspen for the upcoming winter. Since we now both had our pilot's licenses and a hundred or so hours under our belts, we felt confident enough with our flying experience to charter an airplane and fly ourselves back to Colorado.

We chose a Piper Arrow, a Piper Cherokee with retractable gear, for the trip. The first day we flew to the Grand Canyon and landed at the South Rim airport. We stayed the night camped in our sleeping bags under the wing of the airplane tied down in guest parking on the edge of the runway. The airport is located to the south of the canyon itself and at dawn we arose and took off heading northeast and flew out over the canyon. It totally blew our minds when one minute we were a couple of hundred feet over the scrub desert and the next moment we were thousands of feet over the Colorado River located at the bottom of the Grand Canyon. We continued on and later in the day we arrived at Aspen. There we rented a studio condominium on the north side of town which had a spectacular view of Aspen Mountain from our living room window. It was a giant step up from my primitive accommodations from the previous winter where I had lived in the small Victorian house built in the 1800s at the top of Mill Street actually on Ajax Mountain.

"I'm really looking forward to at least having some modern conveniences, like heat, this winter," I said as we departed Aspen on our return trip to San Francisco.

"Yeah. Should be good skiing, when I get back from Mexico. Too bad you won't be sailing this year," chided Woz. "We could have read Mixter and Bowditch together and I could have taught you celestial navigation and how to use the sextant."

"I'm not sure I want to learn from you. Remember, you almost navigated *Sirius II* onto the rocks at Cabo San Quintin," I quipped. "Anyway, I'm busy enough and really don't have time to go sailing this year."

"My sights were perfect," Woz responded.

"That may be so," I said. "But one thing's for sure; you didn't account for the current and… Hey, I don't even want to go there. We both know we dodged a bullet. It's water under the bridge and hopefully you learned from it. My dad used to say: 'Good judgment is based on experience and experience is based on bad judgment.' So, hopefully you won't make the same mistake again since transportation is now solely your responsibility."

In the pilot's seat, I put the Piper into a steep left bank and set a heading for San Francisco while Woz plotted our course on the air navigation chart spread out in his lap.

In 1971, from May through November Phil and I brokered Ciro's trailer loads and we were also middle-manning other people's loads as well. We could make between $25 and $30 on each pound we sold. From the rented house on Grandview, we had stashed and sold about two tons of Ciro and Walter's Mexican weed; about half a ton of black Nepalese Temple Balls and finger-shaped hash from Rob Farnsworth; about 500 pounds of dark golden brown Afghani 'Primo' hash known as 'surfboards' from cousin Marty; and a ton of Colombian 'Santa Marta' gold marijuana from 'Yorktown' Billy. In those six months I had turned a hefty seven figures worth of marijuana and hashish and had pocketed a nice six figure income which Phil and I split. If I put the deal together with my connections, Marty, Billy or Rob I would get the lion's share of the split and if it was through Phil's connection with Ciro, he would get the larger percentage. It was a great arrangement for both of us and much simpler without including Woz, as we had done previously. There were no arguments as we both knew what to do and how to do it.

Phil and I rented several safe deposit boxes in various San Francisco Bay Area banks to store the cash, but we became increasingly nervous about it. First of all we were concerned about being seen making too many trips in and out of a bank and secondly if we were being followed, someone might know where we were hiding the money. So we decided to find another place to store cash.

Phil had recently bought a small house in a residential neighborhood in one of California's rural central valley towns. The house, located on a typical quiet street, was made of adobe slump stone and was of Southwest or Mexican design which we nicknamed 'Adobe House'. The interior was adorned completely with the Mexican furniture Phil had imported from Ciro's prison furniture factory. Ciro had also counseled Phil regarding the safe storing of money since there was such a continual and growing flow of it. It was now an ongoing problem for all of us. "Stay away from banks in this country," Ciro had told Phil. He said in foreign countries cash was a way of life, but here it draws too much attention. Even safe deposit boxes are not really safe. Just bury it or build a secret stash was his solution. Phil said Ciro had done it in all of his houses both here and in Mexico. Phil's new Adobe House would be perfect.

Underneath the house was a concrete perimeter foundation which surrounded a compacted dirt floor. The floor joists were supported by concrete piers with two foot tall 4" x 4" posts spread throughout. This left roughly two feet of crawl space underneath the entire house which would be an ideal place to bury the money. We went to an Army surplus store and bought several watertight ammunition boxes. We then rigged up several portable construction lights to fully illuminate the crawl space area and taped black plastic sheets over the foundation vents so when we had to go in there at night, no light would be seen through the vents which might arouse suspicion to a passerby on the street. With folding military entrenchment shovels in hand, dressed in coverall 'monkey suits' normally used by mechanics working on cars, bandannas wrapped around our heads and wearing respirator masks and work gloves, we both squeezed through a small wood covered access hatchway located under the carpet in the master bedroom closet. Working on our knees and on our stomachs we dug several 3' x 3' x 3' holes in the hard and compacted dirt.

"Shit, Phil, this is a lot of work! You think it's worth it?" I said, taking off my bandanna and wiping my sweaty dirt caked forehead.

"I think it's definitely worth it. Ciro told me it's much safer than any bank. Running into the bank with satchels of money every day is asking for trouble. Also, doing this, there are no bank records or suspicious eyes who might notice us. It's all low profile."

After filling each ammo box with banded bundles of cash and closing and securing the watertight lid we then put each box into several garbage bags, sealing each with grey duct tape to keep them as clean as possible. Then we put them into the holes, re-filled the holes with dirt and smoothed the area so it appeared totally undisturbed. We then drew two 'treasure maps' to indicate the precise location of each of the money boxes and inconspicuously numbered each joist and support post for reference. Emerging from under the house we looked like a couple of raccoon eyed coal miners.

During the late summer, Woz started making preparations for the upcoming Los Angeles to Puerto Vallarta sailboat race scheduled for early November. Dave Killian was to be sailing master on a red colored, Ericson 37 racing sailboat, appropriately named *Frankly Scarlett,* out of Newport Beach. He was to deliver the boat back to SoCal following the race. Woz had also arranged through Phil to meet and deal directly with Ciro to discuss the plan with him since he would be supplying the load. His intention was to completely shut me out of the sailboat venture as payback for him being cut out of the brokering and distribution aspect of our partnership, earlier in the summer. Unbeknownst to Woz, Phil had already met and clued Ciro in on his intentions so Ciro wouldn't get caught blindsided by Woz's attempt to cut us out of the venture.

Woz met Ciro in a bar outside of Tahoe City. It was agreed Ciro would supply and load *Scarlett* in Mexico with 3000 pounds of high-quality Mexican pot only under certain specified conditions; his conditions, take it or leave it.

"The load will be divided into thirds; 1000 pounds to you for your part in transporting the load by boat, 1000 pounds for me and Walter, and 1000 pounds for Phil and Rick who will work with Walter on the unloading and who will be investing for their share. Additionally, I am going to have two of my guys sail with you as crew members aboard *Scarlett.*"

"What?" responded Woz. "This is my trip and I just want to do a 50-50 split between you and me. You guys supply the load and handle distribution and I will be responsible for sailing and unloading. Fifty-fifty, OK?"

"No. It's not OK. I said, take it or leave it. It's not up for negotiation. I heard that last time your contact in Mexico proved unreliable and you know already I'm solid, so if you want me to supply your boat those are my conditions. Period."

"Well, it wasn't my contact who fucked up, it was Rick's, and Steve Morrison, the guy I chose for crew, bailed it. I'd like to use him again and I have another guy in mind for crew who I've sailed with before, who I'd also like to use," said Woz. "Don't you trust me? I know how to pick a good crew who can all work together and already know each other. And, I can handle the offloading, like last time. That part of it came off without a hitch."

"Hey, it's not a matter of trust. This is strictly business. If I didn't trust you, I'd get rid of you," said Ciro matter-of-factly. He continued: "Let me educate you. There are two kinds of mistakes. The first is not so bad if you don't repeat it. The second is unforgivable and generally results in violence or death. I want to spare you from any more mistakes. Understand?"

"What do you mean?" asked Woz, not immediately grasping Ciro's veiled meaning.

Then the light went on and he suddenly remembered Phil had told him that Ciro's family was originally from Sicily and said to have Mafia connections.

"Um…" Woz tried to reconnoiter, but Ciro continued, cutting him off mid-thought. "Look, Woz, you're a solid guy and I consider you a friend, but the word is out, you always seem to be stepping in your own shit, if you know what I mean. You're stepping on lots of toes making stupid mistakes, blundering about with good intentions, and creating unnecessary hassles. I can't afford any screw-ups. Your one-third share is for transportation and that's it. I will take care of the rest including offloading. And two of my people will be sailing with you. Both are trusted, very good guys and well-seasoned, excellent sailors. Don't worry about that. So, if you agree, let's get it on, if not, we're done!"

"OK," said a rather deflated but resigned Woz, now knowing his original intention had been undermined, probably by Phil. On the other hand he was now confident he would be able to get a good load without having to scramble as before.

Phil and I were to work with Walter to arrange for *Scarlett's* offloading. It was decided the best area to offload would be in the Channel Islands, an archipelago of islands located west of Santa Barbara where the winds were generally predictable, usually light and variable, and the currents negligible. The topography consists of a rugged coastline, steep cliffs, hidden coves and sandy beaches.

Historically, the Channel Islands were a known location for bootleggers and smugglers, offering a spot close to the mainland yet isolated and remote with protected coves, hideaways, beaches and safe anchorages where smuggled goods could be unloaded and stored then ferried to the coast along with and in numerous fishing vessels undetected and in relative safety. Specifically, Santa Cruz Island, the largest in the chain, would offer the best location and ironically Smuggler's Cove would be the spot for the clandestine offloading.

Our plan called for a trailerable 30-foot fishing boat to be launched from a ramp north of Santa Barbara. The fishing boat would rendezvous with the anchored yacht, *Frankly Scarlett*, at Smuggler's Cove where the load would be transferred. The fishing boat would then return to the ramp, be pulled out of the water, covered with a full boat cover and trailered back to Walter's warehouse in Redwood City.

November 1971
Puerto Vallarta

The race ended in mid-November as scheduled in Puerto Vallarta. Woz flew down from San Francisco and met Killian at the Vallarta Yacht Club located on beautiful Banderas Bay on Mexico's west coast, where the race ending parties were in full swing. *Scarlett* finished second in her class by a mere two minutes and twelve seconds behind the leader, who caught a puff of fresh wind at the finish line to edge out *Scarlett*.

Woz told Killian about his troubles with me and that I would not be making the return trip. "I would have preferred Steve Morrison and another guy of my choosing for crew but Ciro vetoed it, since he is providing us with the load, and instead requested two of his men accompany us. He assured me they're both well accomplished sailors... we'll see."

That night, Killian, up to his usual tricks, got stumbling drunk, and returned to the boat at daybreak. He appeared disheveled with a large bruise on the side of his face. His hands were cut and scraped. Killian lurched aboard *Scarlett* as Woz was having his morning coffee.

"My God, Killian! What happened? Looks like you got into a fight and came up on the short end."

"Not exactly sure. I don't remember much, but somebody said I was hanging onto one of the halyards used for raising the flag at the yacht club when I apparently lost my grip and fell onto the concrete dock. Guess I must have slept it off right there," Killian said, pouring a cup of hot coffee then doctoring it with a healthy slug of Bushmills Irish Whiskey and lighting a cigarette from a crushed pack he pulled from the pocket of his blood and dirt stained white pants.

"Great! That's all you need. More booze! Why not make it a double? Hey, do you have to smoke cigarettes down here?" Woz said, theatrically fanning the air with his hand. "Can't you at least smoke up on deck, for Christ sakes?"

"Give me a fucking break, Wozenberg!" Killian said slamming his coffee mug down on the mahogany chart table. "Who the hell do you think you are, anyway, Admiral fucking Nimitz? You may have put this load together, but aboard this vessel I'm the only one giving orders. If I say 'jump', the only thing I want to hear from you is 'how high?' But, please, let's not get off on the wrong foot again. OK?"

Woz turned and ascended up the companionway stairs alighting on deck mildly fuming and without responding.

A couple of days later the two other crew members Ciro had chosen arrived in Puerto Vallarta.

Mike Stallings and Jeremy Fromriko, who everyone called 'Rico from Rico', came aboard *Scarlett* after arriving on the afternoon flight from SFO. The two experienced sailors were very big men, ex-collegiate football players and both well over 6'3" tall. Mike was blonde, lean, agile and athletic looking and had played at wide receiver while Rico, also tall, was rather heavyset, had dark curly hair, a lumbering appearance, weighing in at about 265 pounds and played at offensive tackle. Both had been sailors since childhood and were friendly and enthusiastic about the upcoming voyage. At first blush, it seemed like everyone would get along.

Two days later Mike contacted Ciro at his ranch, who told him everything was ready and to depart the following day. On the afternoon of the third day, *Scarlett* departed Puerto Vallarta under full sail striking a northerly course as she sailed out of Banderas Bay. She rounded the northern end of Banderas Bay at Punta Mita at sunset, and turned westerly for three hours until night fell and they were well out of the sight of land. In the dark, Scarlett made a 180° turn and proceeded due south heading for the pre-arranged rendezvous spot, 100 miles south to a well protected bay north of Manzanillo, off the Mexican coast between the quiet towns of Tenacatita and Barra de Navidad. The bay was highlighted by quiet beaches and offshore by large rocks sticking out of the water like huge prehistoric dinosaurs, which afforded a loading site whose view was obstructed from shore.

Ciro's two main gofers, a 6'2" lanky West Texas cowboy type named Brad and a tall, thin, long haired blonde California surfer, Jeff, were in charge of the loading operation. Accompanying them was a crew of Mexicans who loaded 65 pound gunnysacks of weed into two inflatable Zodiac boats, capable of holding eight sacks apiece. They had driven down from Guadalajara the night before in two large ten-wheeled trucks, unloaded the boats and weed and camped on an isolated beach to await the morning rendezvous.

The inflatable boats were powered by 25 hp Mercury outboards. Each Zodiac tore across the flat turquoise water that morning to meet up with *Scarlett* which lay at anchor west of the large rocks. With Brad and Jeff each driving a Zodiac, they pulled along-side the yacht and transferred the gunnysacks to Mike, Rico and Woz awaiting on deck. After three round trips each, three thousand pounds of weed were successfully transferred out to the waiting sailboat.

At around noon, on a hot and cloudless day, *Frankly Scarlett*, now lying low in the water just at the black waterline mark, weighed anchor, raised her sails and headed north on a compass course set to round the tip of the Baja Peninsula. Killian was at the helm in the familiar pose of cigarette and gin-filled tumbler in one hand and the other on the steering wheel. The crew was working busily below deck stowing the dope as the gentle northwesterly warm Mexican breeze filled the sails while the tropical seawater gently lapped against the red hulled yacht slowly beating northward.

Chapter 12

Poleaxed

Frankly Scarlett beat her way northward carrying a cargo of dollars and dreams, a ton and a half of high-grade marijuana stashed in every nook and cranny. The winds were light, fairly typical mid-November weather in Mexican waters.

It had been decided beforehand that the trip would be non-stop to avoid any possible high risk behavior in port like the Killian/Turtle Bay fiasco of the last boat trip. Killian had several cases of liter-sized bottles of Oso Negro gin, a dozen cartons of Winstons to last the entire trip and a ton and a half of weed to smoke. Hopefully he wouldn't go through all of the pot, as well. Mike Stallings had thoughtfully brought an ounce of cocaine along to keep the crew alert and 'on its toes' as he put it.

Halfway up the Baja coast, Mike developed throbbing chest pains. As a certified equine farrier and erstwhile horseman, Woz was familiar with animal anatomy and physiology as well as with equine veterinarian techniques and practices. With such purported knowledge in his quiver, he felt human medical techniques were probably not much different. Woz had the ship's medical kit open and strewn about the settee while he attended to Mike Stallings. He was prepping to begin administering Mike with an I.V. solution of saline combined with ground up nitroglycerine tablets.

"What is going on?" Killian demanded, descending the ladder from the cockpit.

"From his symptoms, it's obvious Mike's had a massive heart attack. I'm going to start an I.V. right now," said Woz.

"Fuck the I.V.!" Killian grabbed a morphine syrette from the open medical kit, pulled off the safety cap, and plunged the needle into the stricken man's arm. "Just keep him calm and don't let him do any more coke," he continued. "We're half a day out of Turtle Bay. I'm heading in. Then we'll get him to a hospital. Get back on deck, and let the poor guy rest, Wozenberg. If you don't mellow out and stop being a panic merchant, I'm going to sedate you too!" Killian turned and climbed the ladder back into the cockpit.

Mike Stallings was put ashore at Turtle Bay. The closest hospital was on Cedros Island, thirty miles offshore. The following day he was medevac'd to the island for medical treatment, released and flew home two days later. The doctors had diagnosed the chest pains as an anxiety attack.

Now, only three crew members remained aboard *Scarlett* for the duration. For the rest of the voyage Mark Wozenberg and Dave Killian were constantly at each other's throats. Woz felt he was in overall command of the operation, having merely chosen Killian as the man to bring the load back, thus was in a superior position in terms of chain-of-command. Killian conversely dictated, as skipper, anything that went on aboard *Scarlett* was at his discretion, and solely in his domain regardless of whatever command theory Woz fantasized about.

With the fourth crew member now gone, each man had an extra hour tacked onto his watch, making three hour watch periods instead of two. One morning when Killian came on deck to relieve Woz at the 6 AM shift change, he found Woz at the helm in front of the binnacle compass pedestal, facing backwards, toward the stern.

"What the hell are you doing? Why are you facing aft while steering the boat? Have you gone crazy?" yelled an exasperated Killian.

"I was getting in touch with the wind and the waves, so I am trying something different. Our course is 346°. I figure, if I steer 166°, the reciprocal compass direction, we will be dead on course and I can effectively steer facing the opposite direction."

"You idiot! You almost beached us last trip on *Sirius II* with your obtuse piloting antics. How about just trying to steer in the direction you're going? Keep it simple. I think that's all you can handle," said Killian sarcastically.

"Don't call me an idiot, Killian! I know what I'm doing. I'm just trying to keep from getting bored."

"Hey, just do what I say and don't give me any lip! When you're ashore, you can drive your car backwards or sideways, for all I care. Out here it's by the book," Killian said. "Now, get off the wheel. You're relieved!"

Rico was also tired of Woz's constant barrage of criticism and haranguing, so one night while Woz slept, he and Killian came up with a contingent remedy to alleviate the situation once and for all.

"I tell you, Dave, that asshole is always on my case. In his eyes, I can't do anything right. I've been sailing, racing and crewing on sailboats since I was sixteen, three times as long as that jerk, yet he's always ragging on me about something. My lines aren't coiled properly. I don't fold the sails right. I can't even steer the boat right."

"I know what you mean, Rico. Hey, I'm only the skipper here and that dickhead thinks he's the grand fucking admiral of the deep. And who's he talking about steering properly? I caught Mr. Bass Ackwards steering the boat and facing the wrong way, backwards at the helm, to keep from getting bored!"

"Tell you what, Dave. Why don't we spike his tea with about 20 valiums and when he falls asleep, we just dump him over the side?"

"It's a thought," mused Killian smiling.

Early December, 1971
Smuggler's Cove, Santa Cruz Island

Two weeks later, after a strained passage, *Scarlett* arrived at Santa Cruz Island. As Killian steered the boat into the cove, Woz dropped the anchor and secured it, after he made sure the Danforth plow anchor had firmly taken hold on the sand bottom.

Killian had placed a ship-to-shore call to me the day before to give me an expected time of arrival. He used the pre-arranged telephone code system I had worked out with Willie two years earlier.

"This is the marine operator. I have a collect call for Mr. John Bonham from the yacht *Frankly Scarlett*."

"Mr. Bonham is not at home," I said. I then walked to a phone booth at a small 'mom and pop' grocery store down the hill from my Grandview home, on Twin Peaks. Ten minutes later Killian called the phone booth.

"This is Ralph Beefeater," Killian said, ironically. Beefeater's was a brand of gin he loved when he was home and wasn't having to settle for 'rotgut' Oso Negro in Mexico.

"Hey Ralph," I replied. "Catch any fish?"

"Yup, we caught our limit of albacore," Killian replied. The code name 'albacore' meant *Scarlett* would arrive by dusk the following day. If Killian used the phrase 'striped bass', that would mean they would arrive by dusk in two days. If he had said, 'we got skunked' it would mean there was a problem and he would call back later to explain and figure out what to do next.

Following the coded call, I set the wheels in motion for the rendezvous and the pick up. That evening two separate teams headed south for Santa Barbara to meet *Frankly Scarlett*.

That night, wave action caused *Scarlett* to drag anchor. Apparently the sand bottom wouldn't hold *Scarlett* fast against an inflowing wave set fueled by a strong onshore breeze. Killian had let Woz talk him into setting just a single anchor rather than setting both bow and stern anchors. At about three thirty in the morning, Rico from Rico fortunately had awakened to the sound of crashing waves. He hurried on deck in time to see the boat drifting toward a rocky promontory.

"Killian, Woz! We're dragging anchor!" shouted Rico. Wearing only a T-shirt and jockey shorts he scrambled onto the foredeck and tried to reset the hook.

"Wozenberg!" Killian yelled, more to himself than to anyone else. "Why did I let you talk me into setting only a single anchor? Fuck! This is all my fault!"

Woz, in the darkened cabin, attempted unsuccessfully to put on his sea boots, each on the wrong foot. Frustrated he hurled the boots, one by one, through the companionway hatch and into the water. He appeared at the head of the ladder barefoot where he spied Killian, calm as ever, starting the engine. As Rico tended the anchor, Killian slowly moved the boat safely away from the shore. Woz hopped frantically about looking like a unicyclist jester-like clown trying unsuccessfully to maintain his balance in a three ring circus.

Next day, the unloading team of Mike Duncan and Pat Suraghoomkol launched the 30-foot fishing boat from a ramp north of Santa Barbara and sped across the Santa Barbara Channel to Santa Cruz Island at twenty five knots. Phil stayed at the launch ramp and waited for the fishing boat's return.

I chartered a Cessna 182 at the Santa Barbara Airport and with Walter in the right co-pilot's seat we headed off to fly surveillance over the unloading operation.

It was early afternoon when the plan came together. Pat and Mike rafted the fishing boat to *Scarlett* and tied the two craft together fast against *Scarlett's* bumpers so as to avoid any damage to either boat as they rocked in unison in the now gentle wave action in Smuggler's Cove. Both crews worked tirelessly for the next half hour unloading the three thousand pounds of weed from the sailboat to the fishing boat. At the controls of the Cessna, I circled the vessels at one-thousand feet above the water while Walter, the spotter, talked on his walkie-talkie to Pat.

"All is George," Walter said into the radio. The code word 'George' meant everything was OK. Had he used the word 'Sam', then there was trouble.

"George here," responded Pat on the fishing boat.

"Get us down to two hundred feet, will you Rick?" asked Walter.

Having only received my pilot's license the past summer, I felt comfortable piloting the aircraft at a height of one-thousand feet. As I descended to two-hundred feet and flying at one-hundred-twenty miles per hour, I was terrified.

"Can you take us a little lower, so I can get a better view?"

"No way! Any lower and we'll need a snorkel and periscope," I answered.

"OK. All is George. We're wrapping it up and heading for home," Walter squawked to Pat as he gazed at the water below just as the fishing boat was seen to have clear sailing back to the launch ramp. I took the plane up to one-thousand feet, banked steeply to the left and fixed my heading back to the Santa Barbara Airport.

Back at the launch ramp, the fishing boat was pulled out of the water, hosed off, and immediately covered with a full length boat cover which was tightly secured to prevent any billowing on the trip back to the Bay Area. The load was caravanned back to the Bay Area with Phil leading the procession in his pickup truck, Pat and Mike in the middle pulling the trailered fishing boat, and Walter and I bringing up the rear. Again, Walter and Pat communicated by walkie-talkie. The return trip was 'George' except for a stop to repair a broken taillight on the boat trailer which Walter spotted and reported to Pat. It was fixed at a truck stop just off the highway and the trip proceeded without further incident.

At the Redwood City warehouse, the load was removed from the fishing boat and split three ways. Phil and I took two thousand pounds, half of which belonged to Woz and half was ours, and went back to the Grandview stash house. The other thousand pounds was weighed, labeled, inventoried and fronted out to Walter's other connections.

Woz arrived back in San Francisco the following day. He demanded he be allowed to sell his thousand pounds to 'Yorktown' Billy first since, he argued, Billy was his original contact. Reluctantly, Phil and I agreed.

Woz met 'Yorktown' Billy at his Mission District Victorian. Woz had brought a sample kilo with him in a brown leather briefcase.

"Smells great," Billy said holding the kilo still wrapped in red butcher paper up to his nose. "How much have you got, Mark?" he continued.

"I've got a thousand pounds," Woz said. He somehow conveniently failed to mention the fact that Phil and I also had a thousand pounds of our own.

"OK. How much per pound?" Billy cautiously asked, unwrapping the red paper, and gently pulling apart a resinous bud. Billy was wary of Woz, and his New York street sense silently screamed that the sailor-philosopher was a loose cannon with a propensity for sudden violence.

"One-eighty a pound seems reasonable."

"Reasonable? You're outta your fucking mind, sport," the short heavy-set man exclaimed, throwing caution to the wind. "That's thirty dollars more than I've been paying for the exact same stuff. The last couple of months I've been buying similar weed from your partner, Rick," Billy said gesturing at the kilo, "and I've been paying him one-fifty a pound."

Woz frowned. His quick-kill fantasy, a fast turn-around from dope into money at a high price, disappeared quicker than snake shit.

"I don't know where you come up with your figures, man. You're way off the mark here," Billy said.

"Hey, I plug other factors into the equation like how tough it was getting it into the country and I'm working with some real evil dudes who…"

"Whoa, pardner. No fucking way! This doesn't work," Billy stopped fondling the bud and hastily began re-wrapping the brick. "We've had this discussion before. Why can't you get it through your foggy head, you're not the only game in town. You can't dictate the price when there's plenty of weed on the market. I've had two other calls just this week for similar stuff. You ever read about supply and demand in college? Tell you what: I'll give you what I give Rick, one-fifty a pound. Take it or leave it."

"I'll leave it," Woz replied angrily. He put the brick back into his briefcase and slammed the lid down, snapping the latches shut. Bursting onto the street, he neglected to see there was a strip of red butcher paper sticking out of the side of the briefcase, caught between the top lid and the bottom body of the briefcase.

While Woz had been meeting with Billy, Phil and I doled out a small quantity of our share, mainly in twenty-five kilo lots, to JQ and a few packages to Marty just to keep him in the loop and not upset him by thinking he'd been cut out completely. Just then, Woz roared into the Twin Peaks pad like a mad bull in a rodeo.

"That filthy thief won't pay me one-eighty a pound," raged Woz, his face red with fury.

"Don't take it personal, Woz. Nobody's gonna get one-eighty a pound wholesale. You're not somebody special and it's not about you. It's the market. This is a business just like any other. Just chill out," said Phil, who was trying his best to remain calm in the face of the lull before the storm.

"Why don't you just leave the dope with Phil and me and go back to Aspen and relax. You've just had a long trip, now it's time to go skiing. You've successfully done your part, why don't you let us do what we do. We'll sell your share and you won't have to worry about it. We'll only put a dime on it and you'll get one-forty a pound which is a very fair wholesale price. Go skiing and enjoy. You deserve it," I said.

"What? Are you trying to rip me off too? Billy said he'd pay one-fifty! Are you trying to fuck with me, Rick?" Woz yelled.

Phil and I exchanged bewildered glances at each other. Without a spoken word between us, we could clearly see Woz was losing it.

"Look Woz," I said in a soft voice, as if trying to explain a complicated theoretical idea to a three-year-old child who barely understood English. "The going rate is one-fifty wholesale. What wholesaler, in their right mind, is going to pay one-eighty for a commodity, any commodity including weed, when they can get the same product for one-fifty? And, on top of that, you're not a wholesaler, you're a smuggler. I thought we already had this discussion about specialization. Let me deal with Billy. Hey, I will make you even a better deal and I'll only make seven dollars a pound out of this, which by the way, is unheard of moving this kind of weight. It's normally ten or more. You'll be spared all the hassle and will be able to go and relax with no worries. Look at you! The veins are sticking out of your neck. You're all pumped up, a twenty-five year old heart attack candidate. Just walk away from this right now and calm down. I'll take care of it and you won't have to worry."

"No!"

Now resigned to the fact I wasn't getting anywhere, I sighed and continued: "OK then, if that's your decision, I think it would be better if you take all of your share out of my garage. Since you'll probably be piecemealing your share at your price, I don't want that kind of frequent activity going on here. It's not safe and won't be a quick turnover; besides, it will be easier for you when you finally find a buyer. Then you can deal with it at your own pace."

"I know you guys are fucking with me!" screamed Woz.

Now totally exasperated, Phil exploded. "Mark, you're totally paranoid and are becoming a fucking menace. If you don't get your share out of the garage right now, I am going to do what your parents wanted to do. I'm going to personally dump both you and your load over the cliff at Land's End."

Five days later, 'Yorktown' Billy had sold our remaining kilos and we collected the rest of the money from Marty and JQ. So before heading back to Aspen, Phil and I made a stop in the valley and safely buried our combined profits beneath three feet of Adobe House's foundation dirt.

Woz remained in San Francisco, where he contacted Rob Farnsworth, my old class-mate and our financier from the *Sirius II* load. Rob was fronted two hundred fifty kilos from Woz's share, which was later ripped off by some of Rob's contacts. One month later, Woz showed up in Aspen with two-thirds of his thousand pound share still unsold. It would be another five months before the balance was sold. He sold a little at a time and at a price substantially lower than either Billy or I had originally offered, so only small amounts of cash trickled in.

January 1972
Aspen, Colorado

Maria Farnsworth, barely a novice having skied only once previously, snow-plowed down the bunny slope hopelessly out of control. Suddenly she veered from the groomed trail and plunged headfirst into a snowbank. Trying not to burst out laughing, I chuckled as I skied toward her. Maria was covered in snow from head to waist, and looked like 'Frosty the Snowman' as she tried to extricate herself.

Maria was Rob Farnsworth's wife. Much neglected and bored, the attractive Cher look-alike had accepted Woz's invitation to accompany him to Aspen where he promised to teach her how to ski.

Upon their arrival in Aspen, Woz completely ignored the raven-haired beauty and seemed to forget his promise to her. In his mind, he was just babysitting the woman, doing Rob a favor, getting the man's wife out of his hair and hopefully, in doing so, facilitating a quicker movement of his share of the load. Rob was indeed trying to unload Woz's weed at an exorbitant price; however it was only a sidelight for him as he was otherwise busy organizing his main business venture, smuggling tons of hashish in from Nepal. Rather selfishly, I thought, as Woz was leaving the condo at 7:30 the morning after arriving, to head off to god knows where at that hour, he seemed to all of a sudden remember he had company and had made her a promise.

"Hey, Rick, I have to do a couple of things since I just got back. Why don't you teach Maria to ski and I'll catch up with you later?"

"Um… I was planning on meeting up with a group of guys today at Aspen Highlands for some great out-of-bounds powder, but, what the hell. Sure," I said not wanting to leave her alone and trying to go out of my way to be nice. She was, after all, a friend of mine as well. I had had dinner at their house and had casually known her during my days in Stockton, though I was surprised when she showed up with Woz and not accompanied by Rob.

I skied to a stop right beside her lying helplessly in the snowbank. "Look at you. Let's get you back on your feet and try again. You almost did a stem christie, but caught an edge. It happens. Don't get discouraged. You're doing great," I said in my best ski instructor mode. Reaching down to help her up, I grabbed her hand and pulled her to her feet whereupon she immediately crossed her skis and lost her balance again, pitching to the side and pulling both of us back into the soft snowbank. Hopelessly entangled we both lay there for a second or two.

"Oops," I said trying not to lose my cool at the compromising situation.

"What do you mean, oops? This is rather nice," Maria responded looking at me coquettishly. We were both silent. For an instant, there was unspoken communication as we looked into each other's eyes; nothing promised, spoken or expected, but completely open to the moment. Right then, I realized, the look lasted a little longer than it should have. 'Uh oh', I thought.

"I think we'd better get back to the lesson," I heard myself say in a rather husky voice.

"Spoilsport!"

The small studio condo Woz and I had leased looked like a high rent crash pad. It featured a kitchenette the size of a shoebox, a bathroom and the remainder an over-sized living room with a fantastic view of the town of Aspen and the ski area and surrounding mountains dwarfing it above. There were sleeping bags unrolled upon three bare mattresses which lay in opposite corners of the living room. I had placed a large folding four-panel Japanese dressing screen with translucent rice paper inserts at the foot of my mattress which afforded a modicum of privacy.

Woz, Maria and I dined that night at the Hotel Jerome. Since Woz had arrived the day before, I had taken every available opportunity to needle and chide him regarding his foolishness in not letting me sell his share.

"You'd be spending your money and enjoying yourself, if only you'd have come to your senses," I quipped. "The only way you are going to come close to getting your price is if you sell it by the ounce. You might even get a bit more if you sell it by the joint. Is that what you plan on doing, Woz?"

Woz ignored the jest, twirling his wine glass by the stem as he appraised the vintage. He took a sip as if he were a fine wine connoisseur. "I've decided to employ a waiting strategy. I'm fronting out just a small portion of my share, waiting for the glut on the market to thin out. Then, when the supply's down, I'll control the market and will get my price or even more," he said lecturing us like he was some Wall Street wiz kid and financial guru.

"Sounds like you've really thought this strategy through, Einstein," I teased. "It's a great idea of yours. I only hope you've stashed your share in a hermetically sealed time capsule so it doesn't rot or mildew. It'll have to keep for about oh, say twenty years, because, if you're lucky, then maybe you'll finally get your price, just before the government legalizes it and weed will be as cheap as cigarettes."

"Oh, hush you two! Can't we just enjoy this dinner?" admonished Maria between bites of her rack of lamb. Under the table she started stroking my leg with her ankle.

Following dinner we all smoked a couple of joints, before Woz for the second time in 24 hours abandoned Maria and left to see The New Riders of the Purple Sage who were appearing live at Little Nells, the locals' bar and nightclub located at the base of Ajax Mountain. Maria and I returned to the condo. She went into the bathroom and took a bath. Exhausted, I collapsed in a heap on my mattress and was immediately asleep.

I had been asleep for what seemed like an hour, but was probably only a few minutes when I awakened to a ruffling sound as the top of my sleeping bag was pulled back and a warm body smelling of bubble bath snuggled in next to me.

"Maria! What the…"

"Ssssh…"

Maria stayed in Aspen for a week. During the day, I helped her progress on the bunny slopes from novice to beginner while at night, she became the instructor and, in my naiveté, I became the pupil. It was snowing hard the day Maria left. She managed to catch the last plane out of Aspen before the airport was shut down. The Arctic storm, one of the most severe in years, charged through the Rockies with a vengeance.

Forty to fifty-mile-an-hour gusts ripped down the empty streets, blowing the snow horizontally past our living room picture window. Around one in the morning, the doorbell began ringing incessantly. In only my long underwear bottoms, I awoke and stumbled out of bed to the door. When I opened it, the wind, a billow of snow and Willie Sherman blew into the small studio.

"Hey, Rick! We just drove up from Arizona. It was eighty when we left. This is colder than hell," he said taking off a Russian Cossack-style fur hat and running his hand through his curly hair.

Willie's golden retriever Sunshine burst into the room followed by a gaggle of ten small puppies. The animals shook themselves off, wet snow flying, then jumped upon the mattresses and a sleeping Woz.

"Willie!" I exclaimed. "What are you doing here?"

"I just graduated from ASU and wanted to party and ski a bit before I start law school. This is my friend Julie," said Willie, introducing me to his latest girlfriend, a lithesome brunette. It was then I noticed another couple standing behind Willie and Julie. They stood there and the guy was holding an Irish setter next to him on a leash. "Oh, and these are friends of mine from ASU who wanted to join the party. Al and Sara, this is Rick. This is their dog Lucky. We couldn't just leave him behind. Boy, this is going to be cozy."

Al was short, about my height, thin, dark complected and, I could tell at once, very Italian. Sara was a beautiful petite blonde and Lucky appeared very obedient, unlike Sunshine.

I pointed to the other side of the room. "That lump on the floor in the sleeping bag is Mark Wozenberg. Everybody calls him 'Woz.'"

"Hey, sport, what's up? Long time no see, Woz. Looks like old home week," said Willie as he stomped clumps of snow from his boots onto our carpet.

"Hi, Woz!" said Julie flashing an ear-to-ear grin.

Woz mumbled "hello" as he curled up in his sleeping bag, putting a pillow over his head. Three or four puppies frolicked over him, simultaneously biting at the pillow and the zippered edge of the sleeping bag covering him.

One little golden ball of fur grabbed the cuff of my long underwear bottom and began tugging at it in reverse. I picked the puppy up and the animal immediately started licking my face. I held the little dog under my arm and stroked its furry head. "What a cutie. Is this one mine?"

"Rick, you've got to try some special stuff I brought. Julie, where's my Destructo Kit?" asked Willie.

Julie reached into her large woven Navajo shoulder bag, pulling out a small black leather dob kit. Willie took the kit from her, unzipped it and laid out its contents on the kitchen counter. In it were an assortment of pill filled bottles, vials of powder and what looked like a marijuana-filled baggie.

"Just the thing for the well traveled stoner," Willie said pointing to the bag with his outstretched finger. "And in this corner wearing the red trunks, we've got…" intoning the words spoken by the ring announcer at the start of a boxing match "... bennies from Mexico, some pharmaceutical coke, valium, reds, Quacks (quaaludes) and some opium balls. And in this corner, wearing the blue trunks, we've got Windowpane acid, and this little baggie of special goodies. Julie, take out the mirror and carve us a few lines of this coke to wake up these sleepyheads while I prepare the pipe. Hey Rick, how about some sounds?"

"It's two in the morning so I can't play it very loud or we'll get booted out of here," I said. "But, OK." I put on the Moody Blues' song *Ride My See-Saw*[1] from the album entitled *In Search of the Lost Chord*.

> 'Riiide, ride my see-saw,
> Take this place on this trip just for me...'

"Woz, you want some of this nose candy?" Julie asked.

"I just want to get some sleep," growled a sleepy Woz as he attempted to shoo away the puppies tormenting his futile slumber. It was a losing battle.

Willie undid his belt buckle from his black leather stitched cowboy belt. Now for the first time, I noticed the dull gold colored belt buckle that apparently doubled as a brass pipe which appeared to have a well-used blackened bowl with a small fine mesh screen wedged down inside. Julie withdrew the mirror and tapped a small mountain shaped pile of glistening white powder out of a vial. She chopped the flake with a razor blade she had proffered from a side-zippered compartment in the Destructo kit and produced ten, four-inch-long evenly spaced lines of coke.

Except for Woz, we all snorted a couple of long lines. The cocaine instantly brushed the sleepiness from my head.

"Nice pipe, Willie," I said, picking up the little brass pipe and turning it over in my hand. Julie shook some more coke out of the vial onto the mirror.

"Here, gimme that." Willie took the mini pipe and filled it with what appeared to be bright green leafy parsley flakes from the baggie.

"What's that?" I asked.

"Shut up and take a hit," Willie replied.

I put the pipe to my mouth and as Willie held up a Bic lighter to the bowl I took a long hit. The next thing I knew, I was flat on my back looking up as if underwater peering to the surface. The same little golden puppy was licking my face. I have no idea how much time had passed, but in my head thick with fuzziness I could hear the reverberating sound of the Moody Blues' song *Legend of a Mind* [2]:

> 'Timothy Leary's dead
> No... , no no no he's outside looking in...'

Through the haze, I saw Willie, Julie, Al, Sara and now Woz standing above me looking down, their mouths were moving but I couldn't hear what they were saying. The fog slowly lifted out of my head as if an eastern wind were blowing it out of the

---

1 Referenced Songs & Music, Item 3, Page 530.
2 Referenced Songs & Music, Item 4, Page 530.

Golden Gate and I finally heard Woz's words strike the tympanic membrane of my inner ear: "My God, Willie! What happened?"

"Aww, he's OK," Julie replied giggling.

"What is that stuff?" I somehow managed to ask.

Laughing almost uncontrollably, Willie said, "That's Angel's Dust! You've been dusted!"

The storm's center passed by early the next morning. As light snow fell in the storm's aftermath we all skied Ajax Mountain in knee deep powder that afternoon. Realizing the cramped quarters in our condo, Al, Sara and Lucky left us after skiing and found a hotel room for the rest of their stay in Aspen. I didn't see them again, but this would not be the last time I saw Al.

As evening came the four of us all dined at Galena Street restaurant. Before leaving the condo, Willie put all ten puppies into the closet and I dismantled the top stereo shelf. Then using the empty shelf and two cinder blocks I created a 'puppy-proof' barricade in front of the open closet doorway. While we were gone, Sunshine easily leapt over the barricade, went into the kitchen, jumped up on the kitchen counter and ate an entire box of twenty-four Gainsburgers, packaged dog food. In our haste to get to dinner we had forgotten to remove the full box of dog food which had been left unopened on the counter.

Sunshine, the sly devil, had an evening feast and devoured all the dog food.

During the early morning hours Woz awakened to the smell of fresh dog shit. Rolling over, he opened his eyes to the sight of an enormous pile of steaming dog excrement less than one foot from his face.

"Aggh!" gagged Woz. "What the… Rick! Rick!" he shrieked.

I was jolted awake by Woz's loud voice. "What's going on? What happened?"

"Get over here and clean up this mess your friend's dog made!" Woz barked, ordering me as if I were a private in his own personal army.

"Huh? What are you talking about?"

"That fucking dog almost dumped in my face! Clean it up now!" Woz loomed over my prone figure as I was trying to gather my thoughts coming out of a deep sleep. His fists were clenching and unclenching and a wild look filled his eyes.

I slowly slid out of my sleeping bag and got to my feet. "I don't take orders. You're a big boy, Woz. Clean it up yourself. The maid has the morning off."

"Clean it up before I use your face to wipe this shit up!" Woz screamed pointing at the pile, his hand shaking with rage.

"No!"

Woz's fist clenched and his right arm shot out like a piston, catching me squarely in the forehead. Poleaxed, I dropped on my sleeping bag as if my knees had turned to Jello.

Woz stood over me, every muscle in his body vibrating as if he were holding a pneumatic jackhammer. "Clean it up right now, fuckhead!"

I saw stars. My head throbbed and my vision was blurred. I was seeing double. Wobbly, I slowly stood up attempting to regroup and gather myself. "Go fuck yourself and then you can kiss my ass."

The commotion had awakened Willie. He jumped behind Woz and grabbed both arms, pinning them to his side, before he could fire off another punch.

Unsteadily, I slowly spun behind the kitchen counter and grabbed a large carving knife from the kitchen drawer. I whirled again and stood knife extended facing Woz who was still in Willie's grasp.

"Touch me again and I'll kill you. I swear it," I said softly.

"Whoa guys! Cool it, before somebody really gets hurt," Willie said.

"I hope you make a fortune on your share of the load, because you'll never work again in this business with anyone I know. That's a promise." I said in a menacing voice.

Woz turned, hurriedly dressed, and left the condominium. His hand throbbed and the knuckle on his right hand was red, distended and oddly misshapen. It was obviously broken. "Have that shit cleaned up before I get back."

"Fuck you!"

In less than two hours, I had gathered all of my belongings, moved out of the studio and back into the Old Victorian at the top of Mill Street where I'd lived the year before. In my wake, I left Woz, our twenty-year friendship and our Aspen condo complete with the untouched pile of dog shit on the living room floor. After that I really had no desire to see him again and haven't since.

Upon reflection, it truly saddened me to see a twenty-year friendship come to an end just like that. And what made this situation even more of a bummer was the fact that it was Woz's OTO that first introduced me to Killian and 'Yorktown' Billy both of whom were critical to my current and future success in the marijuana smuggling business. However, given Woz's unstable nature, it seemed inevitable and the culmination of the series of the previous year's conflicts between us that resulted in his predictably unpredictable violent reactions. The bottom line, I felt, was that friends don't beat up friends no matter what and that his behavior was inexcusable given at minimum our size differences. Right then it became unmistakably clear to me that as a result of such violence I could no longer trust Woz ever again under any circumstances, period. Since this was the only time in my life that I had been struck in the head with such force, I often hypothesized that the blow had resulted in a concussion and was the source of subsequent frequent headaches I was now experiencing. Now back at the old Victorian miner's cabin and gazing at the lump on my swollen forehead and the black eye now forming in my right eye, Phil remarked, "I saw this coming from a hundred miles out. I always knew that it was just a matter of time before this psycho would finally lose it, and this was the straw that broke the camel's back. Consider yourself lucky… it could have been much worse."

* * *

At the 19th-century miner's cabin, my former quarters were now rented to an old friend of Phil's, Joe Schroder. Joe had just graduated from Chico State College and had come to Aspen to ski. His father, Joseph Schroder Sr., was a full bird colonel and commanding officer of an Air Force Reserve unit at Mather Air Force Base in Sacramento. Both Joe and Phil were in the unit and held the rank of Airman 1st Class. Joe was a good skier and athlete who had played linebacker on his high school football team in the central California valley town of Turlock, but was considered too small to play in college. At 5'10" with shoulder-length dark brown hair, a stocky fire-plug-like build, a full drooping Yosemite Sam mustache and an outrageous sense of humor, the muscled-up prankster fit the mold perfectly as a future player in our growing smuggling venture. He was enthusiastic, had a willingness to do whatever was required of him and would make a valuable asset in both Phil's and my eyes—one of which was now blackened just below a huge red knot on my forehead.

So now with my moving back to the old miner's cabin it created an even more cramped living space for the three of us, plus two other skiers who were on the Aspen Mountain trail crew, but as enthusiastic skiers we all enjoyed every moment of it. We all still had part-time work at the Copper Kettle Restaurant, skied everyday with reckless abandon and partied at night when not working. Sometimes we'd stop at the Hotel Jerome for evening drinks and later go to Little Nells to continue drinking and to watch live music. It wasn't an uncommon event for us to return home pretty looped on those cold winter nights and it turned out Phil could be a pretty mean drunk on occasion.

On one raucous freezing evening Phil came home completely inebriated and stumbling down drunk. He was particularly annoying to both Joe and me and while attempting to climb up the ladder to the loft, lost his balance and fell off, just missing by inches the corner of the thick cedar planked living room coffee table with his head, landing hard on the wooden floor. He continued his slurred blather at both of us until we threatened to tie him up outside in the sub-freezing cold to the large spruce tree in our front yard. After, he calmed down and slunk away and passed out in his room. The following morning, he remembered nothing of the previous night.

It was later in the year when Willie again showed up in Aspen during his first and what would prove to be his last and only spring break from law school. He gladly accepted our hospitality and slept on the floor in his down sleeping bag. At the time Phil was dating a pretty blonde who was also living in Aspen for the winter. Her name was Rene Polard and she was from Florida, enjoying a winter of skiing after graduating from college. Somehow, but not surprisingly, Willie ended up with Rene after an evening of partying at Little Nells, while Phil and I were busy cleaning up the kitchen at the Copper Kettle. Phil came back to the cabin only to find Willie and Rene in his room and in his bed. Apparently it was during that time of the month and Rene had bled profusely during the evening's frolicking with Willie. Phil slept on the floor that night in Willie's sleeping bag and in the morning went into his room, now vacated and exclaimed, "God, it looks like someone slaughtered a pig in there!" Willie seemed to always end up with someone else's lady. This was his forte and would continue for years to come. I guess for Willie, like the horndog he was, food always tasted better out of someone else's bowl.

Such were the good times in Aspen, except for me getting my ass kicked by Woz, but we all survived and lived to see another day.

Chapter 13

Bad Moon Rising

February 1972
Tlaquepaque, Mexico

It was a crisp winter sunrise. Roosters crowed as the darkness became a thin yellow band rising over the rolling hills of central Mexico. Behind the twelve foot walls of Ciro's avocado ranch, campasinos were lighting their cooking fires. Sleepy servants gathered in the hacienda's kitchen for morning coffee before attending to their routine daily chores. Ciro, the ranch's patron, owner and master, was awake but still lying in bed in the hacienda's lavish master suite. It was just after the dawn, but before the sun had cleared the hills to the east, when a squad of uniformed soldiers, using ladders, climbed over the wall and opened the locked gate. The twenty-five Mexican Federales had been in position, sequestered in surrounding bushes and in unmarked cars parked on nearby streets, since before dawn. The rancho's intercom and surveillance video cameras had not yet been installed. Ciro's gofers, Brad and Jeff, were away in the mountains conferring with Ciro's main marijuana procurer and negotiator, a well connected Mexican aristocrat named Heriberto Torres, who directed and organized the local pot growers. They were preparing to score another ton of marijuana for the upcoming weekly trailer trips. The raid came as a complete surprise.

One squad ransacked the main house as two other squads fanned out searching the outbuildings. There they discovered approximately one ton of marijuana hidden in a basement storeroom. What they failed to find was another two tons of weed which had been cleverly hidden behind a false wall Pat had constructed at the far end of the storeroom. Pat's magic worked again and the only reason any marijuana was found at all was because it had been removed from the hidden secret stash and was being readied for the three shipments scheduled to occur in the upcoming weeks. Luckily, the trailer, which was en route on its return trip from the States, had not yet arrived back at the rancho. The servants were lined up and perfunctorily questioned. They were terrified and sobbingly confessed they knew nothing and were only local employees who were working hand-to-mouth to support their families.

Ciro was dragged from his bedroom shirtless and wearing only a pair of drawstring white peasant-style pajama bottoms. He was summarily beaten by two soldiers while being transported downstairs and into the hacienda's ornately decorated dining room. Nervously, he sat in one of the brightly cushioned handmade dining room chairs he had just acquired from the Guadalajara prison furniture factory. His arms were hand-cuffed behind his back, his left eye was red and beginning to swell and a trickle of blood dripped from the side of his mouth.

"My men have found what appears to be about 1,150 kilos of marijuana," the Federale Police Colonel said glaring and stern faced as he stood facing Ciro. The two soldiers who had brought Ciro downstairs stood behind him, unsmiling and in a parade rest position. Their rifles with bayonets affixed were leaning up against the dining room wall underneath a hand-painted mural depicting a sleepy Mexican village at sunset. The officer continued: "Where did you get these illegal drugs?"

Ciro slumped, head hung low, but said nothing.

"By the way, we opened a safe located behind the bar and found $35,000 in U.S. dollars. I have confiscated the money and will personally see to its safekeeping." A thin smile formed at the corner of the officer's mouth. "Again, where did you get the marijuana?"

Ciro remained silent staring blankly at the floor and his bruised bare feet.

The colonel sighed, nodded to the sergeant standing to the left behind Ciro who came to attention, saluted, then marched out of the room. The other soldier picked up his rifle and with his bayonet cut the drawstring on Ciro's pajamas, roughly yanked them off of his legs and then tied each ankle to a chair leg with strips of gray duct tape.

"So, it looks like we do it the hard way, but I promise you Señor Mancuso, you will tell me where you got the drugs. Of this you can be certain." The colonel lit a thin brown cigarillo.

The sergeant returned carrying an old army field telephone which had a black crank handle under the receiver and two coiled electrical wires terminated with alligator clips attached to the side. He set the phone box on the ornate handmade dining room table, uncoiled the wires and attached one electrode to one of Ciro's nipples and the other to his scrotum, snapping the loose skin tight between the alligator clips' jagged rusted metal teeth. The colonel nodded again. The sergeant cranked the handle for a long moment and Ciro screamed.

"Please, please keep the money. Just get these wires off," howled Ciro, tears running down his cheeks.

"I have no intention of returning the money Señor Mancuso. You see, a colonel's pay is not so good, and I have expensive tastes. Now then, where did you get the marijuana?"

Ciro screamed again as another long electric jolt hit his body. He lost control of both his bowels and bladder. The colonel wrinkled his nose in disgust.

"Oh, please, PLEASE! I'll tell you everything, just stop! The weed's not mine," lied Ciro, somehow managing to keep his wits about him. "It belongs to a couple of guys from California. I'm just keeping it for them."

"You know, things will go easier for you if you just tell me to whom the marijuana belongs."

"I don't know. I swear it! Please tell your men to take these wires off."

The colonel reluctantly accepted Ciro's story, but privately felt he was lying. 'Not bad for an early morning's work', the colonel thought, 'a quick $35,000. Let somebody else have a bite of this rich gringo's ass.'

Ciro was hauled into court and pled guilty to simple possession. Through his family's well connected government contacts, Heriberto was able to secure the right attorney to handle Ciro's case. A thick dollar-filled envelope was quietly passed to a friendly judge who expedited his case and gave him the minimum sentence allowable, which was only one year in the Guadalajara Federal Prison. Ciro would later remark that in Mexico, the color of justice was green.

News of Ciro's bust filtered up to Walter from Brad and Jeff who had learned about it from Heriberto. Fortunately, with advance notice, they learned of the bust before returning to the ranch as scheduled, thus avoiding walking into the middle of it. Walter disseminated the information to Phil, me and his other contacts and friends and to Ciro's family in Central California. The story with multiple photographs of Ciro in custody, the avocado ranch and hacienda, and the load of stacked kilos of marijuana surrounded by Mexican Federales appeared in a Mexican tabloid called Alarma. I was able to purchase a copy of this issue from a Mexican grocery store in San Francisco's Mission District.

With Ciro busted, all aspects of his marijuana business came to an abrupt halt. Everybody laid low. There was just too much 'heat'. I made plans to rent a 50 foot sailboat and spend two weeks cruising the Virgin Islands with several friends on a bareboat charter. I was also looking forward to attending the 1972 Summer Olympics in Munich with Willie, who claimed a cousin of his was competing on the United States' Swim Team and could get us front row seats to all events. Willie had a tendency to exaggerate, but I believed him and in any event, whether we got great seats or not, it would be a great experience to finally get to attend an Olympic Games. Previously, in 1960, I had missed attending the Squaw Valley Olympics. My parents nixed it because my grades did not meet their standards, so I was really excited to finally get the chance to go.

All of Ciro's ventures, including his legitimate Sombrero Imports, were now put on hold while everyone adopted a wait-and-see attitude. Phil, who'd been in charge of the SFO warehouse and customs clearance, was out of a job and now devoted his time to working in his family's fruit orchards. He too was looking forward to going to the Summer Olympics, but would keep a very low profile and hope none of Ciro's Mexican 'heat' would somehow come to the U.S. and drift in his direction. It was certainly a time of 'pins-and-needles' for all of us.

Inside Guadalajara Federal Prison, Ciro was treated like royalty. A large double cell, leased at considerable cost from the warden, provided a luxurious setup for Ciro in which to do his jail time. His prison accommodations measured 10-feet wide by 20-feet deep and featured a high 16-foot ceiling. Ciro had a specially constructed loft installed in the rear half of the cell, accessed by a handmade wooden ladder. The loft served as a private bedroom which was made even more private by a large colorful Mexican blanket hung as a curtain from a brass ceiling rod, attached by hand-fashioned wooden rings. The 'upstairs' was adorned with a television sitting atop a wooden handmade dresser, a telephone, king sized mattress and box spring nestled in an ornate handmade wooden bed frame with a matching nightstand, all under a lighted ceiling fan hanging from above, suspended by a brass chain. The 'downstairs' main floor contained a small kitchen with a counter and two leather covered bar stools and a corner private bathroom containing a sink, shower, toilet and mirrored wooden medicine cabinet. In the living room was a handmade wooden couch and matching chair and ottoman with colorful cushions made from Mexican blankets, a desk and executive leather chair and wooden file cabinet which served as a quasi-office where he could oversee his prison furniture business. There was also a 'downstairs' television and telephone. The cell door was covered with an ornately hand carved wooden panel made of mahogany. The only items reminding you it was a prison cell were the bars installed on the kitchen window and on the entry door. He also had a maid and servant who could come and go as they pleased and brought him food from outside street vendors as well as special platters of meat, vegetables and seafood from high-end Guadalajara restaurants. He was allowed visitors at any hour, and special arrangements were made so prostitutes could visit him day or night.

After a few months, Heriberto felt the 'heat' had cooled. So, cautiously at first, trailers were again set in motion and loads began rolling to start moving the other tons which had escaped capture during the bust. Brad and Jeff, acting under Ciro's orders, ran the Tlaquepaque ranch headquartered smuggling operation and continued loading trailers with Pat as before, and commenced returning to the Michoacan mountains to score more loads. The operation was back up-and-running almost as if nothing had changed.

April 1972
San Francisco

Cousin Marty just couldn't say 'no'. The tall, thin to the point of almost skeletal, balding bank teller and small-time dealer had become fixated on running his own smuggling venture. Over the past year, Marty had seen me consistently making a considerable amount of money smuggling marijuana and brokering other peoples loads: sixty thousand here, forty thousand there and so on. Marty, on the other hand, spent his days in a teller cage handling other people's money. Financial security was his ultimate goal. Marty had become very jealous of me and also had become enthralled with the smuggler's lifestyle and mystique: fast cars, faster women, briefcases stuffed with bundles of hundred dollar bills, luxurious houses, European vacations, and always overflowing piles of coke to snort and kilos of weed to smoke. Smuggling a few kilos of Peruvian cocaine seemed Marty's obvious solution.

Marty knew I wanted no part of the cocaine business. In his warped, drug induced mind, he felt my refusal to participate was short sighted, so, feeling a new sense, invincibility, he became convinced he could pull off what he considered to be a bold, foolproof scheme to smuggle cocaine into the United States.

Of the many visitors and gatherings which had taken place in Marty's flat over the past year, one visitor whom he had gotten particularly close to was a sleazy, dropout, druggie named Peter Pipe. Pipe was a fallen-from-grace, Marin County attorney whose claim to fame had been established at an appearance before a judge in court in the Marin County Civic Center where he had been charged with contempt of court for refusing to comply with the judge's court order. The event had been reported in the *Marin Independent Journal,* the local newspaper, complete with his picture. He instantly became sort of a local hero in Marin's counterculture for his defiance of 'the man' in such a public setting. Marty too, was seduced and infatuated at having such a quasi-famous character as a regular face at his flat. Peter would bring both girls and drugs to Marty's get-togethers and soon became the primary source for Marty's growing drug habit.

If one's mental image could conjure up a picture of a sleazy lawyer and reprobate it was personified by Peter Pipe, Esq., as he liked to be called. In 1967 at 35 years old, the 5'9", scrawny 140-pound man with short dark curly hair migrated to the San Francisco Bay Area from Seattle and was admitted to the California State Bar Association. Having formerly practiced law in the State of Washington, he saw an opportunity to come to San Francisco during the Summer of Love in hopes of gaining new clientele who might need his services in the drug infested growing hippie counterculture. The upstart, straight looking young attorney set up a practice and small office in the Marin County town of Fairfax and quickly got a reputation in the Marin drug scene as a lawyer who would help locals in trouble with the law for minor drug offenses. His notoriety elevated him to cult hero status; however, soon his law practice began to spin out of control as his proclivities devolved into a serious cocaine 'jones' and his once respectable appearance transitioned into a disheveled mess. His business-like crew cut grew into an unkempt scraggly set of black curly strands running down the middle of his back. His teeth yellowed from his chain smoking habit. It seemed as if he never bathed as he always reeked of stagnant body odor. He became increasingly paranoid and his shifty eyes seemed to be looking everywhere at once. He turned in his three-piece Brooks Brothers suits for a ragged pair of cut-off jeans, flip-flops and tie-dyed t-shirts. He spoke with a high pitched monotone voice at such a rapid pace that it was hard to understand him or, if you did, it was difficult to comprehend what he was saying. And when he spoke, which was all the time, white foamy spittle would appear at both sides of his mouth. The only semblance of respectability was that he still drove a rather new BMW 2002 acquired earlier during the time of his successful law practice. How Marty ever trusted this degenerate or let him into his life was always a mystery to me, yet he was a frequent visitor and almost a permanent fixture at the Noe Valley flat. If he was there, which he usually was, I couldn't wait to get out of there. His presence really made me nervous.

What Marty apparently didn't know was that Peter, himself, had been busted in

Marin for possession of cocaine and heroin. He was taken to the San Rafael police station and interrogated by a drug enforcement detective who knew of him because of his reputation. During the questioning, Peter folded like a cheap suit and confessed to his use and dealing of drugs and to the fact that he knew of a major smuggling operation now in the works. Under the threat of the loss of his law license, his career ruined, and with the prospect of a jail sentence, Peter agreed to become the detective's personal snitch. The case was quietly shuffled under the rug with the understanding that if Peter didn't deliver the proposed smuggling operation's details, he would have the book thrown at him and his reputation crushed. A secret deal was struck and he was never charged for the incident.

Marty's smuggling plan called for him and Peter to travel down to Peru and, using Peter's contacts, they would score ten kilos of cocaine. Marty would then conceal the drugs in a specially constructed false-bottom valise and fly to Mexico by commercial airline via Colombia. Once in Mexico, where airport customs were virtually nonexistent, he would then rendezvous with Peter's driver who would drive the load through Mexico in a specially concealed compartment hidden in the trunk of a Volkswagen Karmann-Ghia, crossing the border at Tijuana and then back to San Francisco. Marty had hoped to net a quick couple of hundred grand by pulling off this scam. Before putting the plan into motion he decided to run it by his cousin, me.

I hadn't seen Marty for quite some time and the first sight of him visibly shook me to the core. Marty, normally the clean shaven, professional looking, rather paunchy bank teller, now appeared bone thin and sporting a beard. He looked like a radical college professor in his tattered Levi's, t-shirt and Birkenstock sandals.

Cousin Marty supposedly looking like a 'professor' before he was busted in Mexico. Looking like this, it's no wonder he didn't arouse suspicion on his hippie-like looks alone.

At his Noe Valley flat, Marty related to me the plans for his proposed scam. I listened silently until he had finished, then I commented: "I can't believe you'd try something like this, Marty. Look at you! You're a walking bust. With that ridiculous-looking beard, you look like a communist. The Peruvians, Colombians, and even Mexicans aren't exactly enamored with radical left-wingers."

"Hey Rick, don't you see it? I look like a professor. Latinos respect academics," replied Marty, chopping some mother of pearl flake cocaine on a mirror with a razor blade and carving a thick long line. He snorted the white sparkling powder through his clogged nose. Unfolding a small paper bindle, Marty then laid out a tiny mound of tan-looking powder on the now clean mirror.

"You're going to blow it, man, and wind up in deep shit. One of my first rules is never to use public transportation for the actual smuggle. The trip never wants to be out of your hands. If it is, it's 50/50, and those are not good odds in this business. Commercial airlines are also a bad choice. At least you could charter a private plane and increase your odds. Plus, bottom line, I never liked your friend Peter Pipe, Esq. He's a sleazeball and has the smell of a rat. If there's trouble, he'd sell you down the river in a heartbeat."

Then, as if some strange malevolent premonition, a bizarre precursor of inevitable doom, KSAN, the hip San Francisco FM radio station which had been playing on the radio in the background, came on with an old Creedence Clearwater Revival song:[1]

'I see a bad moon rising. I see trouble on the way…
Don't go around tonight, it's bound to take your life, there's a bad moon on the rise…'

It stopped both of us dead in our tracks as we ceased talking and listened. It was a split second when we both stared deep into each other's eyes, wondering and questioning the significance of such a song coming on at this particular moment. The trance was broken as Marty dismissed the eerie feeling and drew a small line of the tan powder on the mirror. A shiver ran through my whole body and the hair on the back of my neck pricked up. There were goosebumps on both of my arms.

"Aww… that's bullshit! Just cool it, Rick! We'll be fine. Peter has done this once before and I'm sure it'll work again. I need to build up some quick capital anyway." Marty bent his head to the mirror and like a Hoover, vacuumed up the tan powder through a silver straw.

"Wait a minute!" I responded. "If you're getting into this smuggling business just for the money, then you're in it for all the wrong reasons. The money will be there if you have a sound plan, good trusting people around you and you execute the plan well. In my opinion, you don't have any of those components. It's a hare-brained scheme. There's bound to be some kind of trouble. There always is. It never goes as smoothly as you think, sitting here stoned in your San Francisco apartment. Just let Peter do the trip and you can stay here and sell it and not have all the risk. There's plenty of money if you do it that way. Come on, Marty, be sensible," I pleaded. "Hey, what's that tan stuff, anyway?"

---

1 Referenced Songs & Music, Item 5, Page 530.

"Oh, that. It's Persian heroin. Peter is into it and got it for me just to take the edge off. Don't worry, I've got it under control. I only do it occasionally, now and then."

"Knowing you Marty, it's probably more 'now' and less 'then'. And if Peter is into it as well, why are you two smackheads even considering concocting a suicide mission like this? I told you, I don't trust him, and this just reinforces it. You're outta your fucking mind!"

Marty wouldn't listen and four days later he was off on his South American cocaine smuggling escapade. Three weeks later I got word, Marty had been busted coming through customs into Mexico City on a flight from Bogota, Colombia, with five kilos of cocaine hidden in a false-bottomed suitcase.

Apparently what had happened was that Marty had also related his proposed plan to John Quinn, JQ, my old college classmate who had previously done a cocaine run and was looking to do one again. JQ had met Peter at one of Marty's parties but never liked nor trusted the 'sleazy opportunist' as he called him, and when Marty proposed that he join the venture, he declined. However, after scoring the ten kilos in Peru, Marty realized a ten kilo load couldn't nearly fit concealed into his false bottom suitcase. So, after he and Peter had split up, Marty had contacted JQ and offered to sell him half the load. JQ was in search of a load himself and contemplating another run, and since he would only be meeting Marty, not Peter, accepted and flew to Peru, where they met in Marty's hotel and he took the five kilos.

When JQ returned, having successfully brought back his five kilos, he relayed the story to me. Gone were JQ's shoulder length red hair and handlebar mustache. His hair was still short, having grown out only a month beyond the crew cut stage. JQ had entered South America looking like a Catholic priest doing missionary work. He carried a Bible and missionary pamphlets in the unconcealed top part of his false-bottom suitcase. He told me that wearing thick non-prescription Buddy Holly style glasses, black priest-looking clothes, and sporting a detachable priest's clerical collar, he had traveled overland, never using airports, through Central America and Mexico and back to the U.S., taking taxis, trains and buses. Dressed in his priest costume he was waved through customs in all countries without a second glance. He said he even crossed himself saying "Bless you my son" to the obviously Catholic Central American and Mexican border customs officers at each border crossing station, and even at U.S. customs in Tijuana. Explicitly, he never consumed alcohol or drugs and never partied before or during a smuggle. He totally fit into character and played his role to a T, unlike Marty, who did exactly the opposite.

"Marty blew it, Rick. He wasn't cool. From the start he just wouldn't listen, even though I begged him to shave off that stupid beard. He insisted on looking like an intellectual rather than a religious person, like I suggested. From what I heard, he just went wild and got way too loose. He got into the coke he had scored, drank heavily and was snorting the smack he brought down with him. I could see bad craziness coming down, so I told him I didn't want any part of what he was doing, especially with Peter. When he called and told me he had five keys and said I could come and get it from him, I went with the understanding I would only meet him and no one else would know. That happened. The story I got was, someone Marty knew or who he'd partied with turned out to be an informant. I always suspected it was Peter, the opportunist, who'd set up Marty in the first place for a ten kilo reward. I'd even heard through the grapevine, Peter was secretly working for the man. Couldn't prove it, but knowing him, I wouldn't doubt it. Two days later Marty was busted at the Mexico City airport. They knew he was coming and they were waiting for him, Ricky."

"How come you didn't get popped?" I asked suspiciously.

"Hey Rick, I know what you're thinking, but you're wrong. I never even saw him after I met him at the hotel in Lima. Later, I heard he was getting drunk and loaded down there like there was no tomorrow and partying to beat the band. I set my role up and was visiting churches, attending mass and playing the role. I even made calls to the Peruvian Ministry of the Interior inquiring about doing missionary work in remote Peruvian villages. If Marty was going to be a professor or academic he should have been visiting universities and libraries and not mingling and partying. And where was Peter when all of this was going on? Now in retrospect, I think he was making a deal to 'rat' Marty out and set him up for the reward money. For Christ sakes, Rick, they were both junkies and junkies will do anything for money to support their habit. Marty was just too stupid or naive to see it."

"OK, JQ. I had to know. And I did know about the heroin. He said he had it under control. Obviously he didn't. Also, JQ, I always wondered, where was Peter when all this was going down and what was his role? I thought the Peruvian contact was his man. You know I never liked or trusted that asshole. I think you're right and he could have set it up for the money and to save his ass. I never thought Marty could have come up with this on his own. He was conned."

"It's weird, Rick. I made it and he didn't. You know, there's a moment of truth when you're at the customs window and 'the man' in the booth is holding your passport in his hand and he starts asking you questions looking directly into your eyes: 'What is the purpose of your visit? Do you have anything to declare? Are you traveling alone? Etc. He might glance at a computer screen, but generally he stares right at you. He's measuring you. Seeing how you answer his questions. Your body language. Your nervousness. Now, in my role as a priest, I was totally into the mind-set and playing the role. I was living it and had the backup paperwork in my bag to prove it. I actually looked like a man of the cloth and mentally I believed it with every fiber of my body. It was the vibe I was giving off. I'm sure of it. I think you understand that. I tell you, when you walk through customs, the rush is incredible. Maybe a part of him was scared because Marty just couldn't see getting completely into character, doing it all the way. From what I heard, for some stupid reason he wanted to get into the Peruvian party scene and now that dumb bastard is in one of the worst possible places in the whole world, Lecumberri Prison in Mexico City. It's a true hell on earth. Forget him Rick, he's as good as dead. He looking at thirty years. He's gone forever."

"I know what you mean JQ, the rush is better than any drug I've ever done. Sometimes I think it's the only reason why I'm in the game. The money is the bonus. It's there if you keep your eye on the ball and don't screw up. But, Marty, I can't forget him. He's my first cousin. This is going to hit my folks, his grandparents and his family real hard, like a ton of bricks. I can tell you, as sure as I'm sitting here, 'dollars to donuts', they'll hold me responsible for his stupidity. I'm sure they'll think I was behind all of this. I warned him against doing this trip more than once. I even pleaded and begged him not to do it. He just wouldn't listen. He knew it all and I think he was jealous of me and what I was doing and was out to try and prove himself. But I'll tell you this: Marty was not cut out for smuggling and I don't think he can survive a Mexican prison." I pondered this for a second. "Hell JQ, I don't think I could either."

May 1972
Acapulco, Mexico

Helen and Dick, my parents, checked into the Acapulco Hilton having arrived on the afternoon Mexicana Airlines flight from San Francisco. It was a hot, balmy day with white tropical afternoon cumulus clouds building, signaling typical squally thundershowers weren't far off. It usually happened every afternoon in the coastal Mexican resort, then it would clear and the evenings were a pleasant relief after the cool rain.

At the concierge desk, a spit-polished uniformed official greeted them.

"Buenos tardes, Señor and Señora Bibbero. Welcome to the Acapulco Hilton and Happy Anniversary." It was their 28th wedding anniversary and they had planned the trip for months. "I hope you will enjoy your stay with us. We have prepared a lovely suite for you with a magnificent view of the harbor. By the way, there is a message for you at the front desk."

Dick strode to the front desk and retrieved an official looking envelope with a return name and address embossed in raised letters on the outside: Juan Xavier Batista, Abogado, Mexico D.F.

"What is 'Abogado'?" Dick asked the concierge. Helen, now at Dick's side frowned as the impeccably dressed concierge responded.

"This letter appears to be from a lawyer from Mexico City. The word 'abogado' means attorney in Spanish." The smartly dressed man then snapped his fingers and a bellboy appeared instantly. The concierge handed the bellboy the key to the suite. "Please escort Señor and Señora Bibbero to their suite, Miguel."

"Hmmm, this doesn't look good. Who even knows we're here?" Dick wondered aloud as he and Helen were escorted to their 5th floor corner suite with a phenomenal western-facing ocean view.

"What's going on dear?" asked Helen. The frown on her face had now transformed to a look of nervous anticipation.

"Just give me a moment, sweetheart." Dick answered impatiently.

They entered the beautiful suite with a panoramic view, but Dick scarcely noticed as he was preoccupied with the mysterious letter he now opened and read:

> *Señor Bibbero,*
> *Please contact me at once.*

It is extremely urgent.
Sincerely, Juan Xavier Batista

There was a Mexico City address and telephone number printed across the bottom of the letter. Dick picked up the telephone and a minute later the English speaking hotel operator had reached the offices of Juan Xavier Batista

"Mr. Batista, this is Richard Bibbero. I am here in Acapulco and am in receipt of a rather cryptic letter you sent me. Who are you and what is this about?"

"Thank you for calling. I am an attorney here in Mexico City. This concerns your son, Martin Herbert Bibbero."

"What? Marty is not my son. He is my brother Donald's son, my nephew. What has happened to Marty? Is he OK?"

"No, Señor Bibbero," Batista replied. "I'm afraid Martin Herbert is not OK. He was arrested last week at Mexico City International Airport on a flight arriving from Bogata, Colombia. He was carrying a large quantity of illegal narcotics concealed in a false bottom suitcase. The official arrest papers state he was carrying five kilograms of cocaine. In Mexico, this is an extremely serious matter. Martin Herbert is now in Lecumberri Prison here in Mexico City and is facing at least thirty years in prison."

"Oh, my God!" anguished Dick. Stunned, he slumped, nearly falling into a leather covered desk chair.

"Apparently some person informed on him in Peru, because the authorities were waiting for him here in Mexico City. I have been asked to represent him at his trial and I think I can get him out, but it will be very expensive. I know the presiding judge. He will want $20,000 in U.S. dollars. It shouldn't be a problem if we act quickly. If you can please get me the money this week, we'll have Martin Herbert out in a few days," said Batista.

"I will see what I can do," answered Dick. "I'll get back to you within a couple of days. By the way, Mr. Batista, my wife and I are here celebrating our wedding anniversary. How did you know I was here in Acapulco?"

"I asked Martin Herbert if there was anyone in his family who could possibly help him, and he told me, perhaps his Grandfather might be of assistance. I contacted his Grandfather, Señor Herbert Salinger, at his office in San Francisco. He informed me that both you and Señora Bibbero were on your way to Acapulco and he said you'd be staying at the Hilton."

"Mr. Batista, one more question please. How is Marty doing in there?"

"I'm afraid Martin Herbert is not doing very well at all. You see Lecumberri is not a very nice place. It is in fact the worst of all Mexican prisons. At present, Martin Herbert has no money, and his living conditions are, well, you might say, less than sub-standard. Make no mistake, Señor, in prison here in Mexico, money is a necessity. He needs help desperately."

"Thank you, Mr. Batista. I'll be in touch with you." Dick hung up the phone visibly shaken, now exhibiting ashen pallor. He turned to his wife and told her of Marty's predicament.

"I wonder if Rick is somehow involved in all this?" questioned Helen.

"Wouldn't surprise me a bit," snapped Dick. "It's a marvelous way to start our vacation. Guess we'll have to go to Mexico City and pay Marty a visit. We'd better call Mother and Herb. No doubt they're beside themselves. You know, Marty is their favorite grandchild."

Helen and Dick spent the next couple of days trying to enjoy Acapulco while inwardly preparing to steel themselves for what lay ahead. On the third day, Helen suggested they stop the charade of pretending to enjoy themselves, cut their vacation short and go to Mexico City to see what could be done for Marty.

The Bibberos, accompanied by Juan Xavier Batista, stood bewildered at the prison's entrance. Palacio de Lecumberri, also known as The Black Palace of Lecumberri, was adorned with foreboding walls which loomed above them like the Wicked Witch of the West's castle as graphically depicted in L. Frank Baum's famous novel, *The Wizard of Oz*. In its ninety year history only two inmates were said to have escaped, one being the notorious Pancho Villa. They shuffled up to the guard station, almost appearing as if in a zombie-like trance, and approached a sinister looking fat Mexican guard sporting a holstered .45 caliber automatic pistol on his Sam Brown belt complete with a shiny gold buckle.

"Ah, Señor Batista, I see you have guests today. How can I be of service to you?" queried the guard.

"Sergeant Garcia, nice to see you again," Batista said graciously, shaking the guard's hand. "I have brought Señor and Señora Bibbero to visit the son of Señor Bibbero's brother, Martin Herbert Bibbero. I hope Señora Garcia is feeling better. Please give her my best wishes." Señor Batista slipped him a 500 Peso note and the three were expeditiously escorted around fifty people lined up at a barricade waiting to visit prisoners. The trio entered a fenced sally port topped with jagged concertina wire, passed through a Judas door in the high wooden gate and went into the prison.

Helen's insides were quaking as they entered the stone castle. Dick could only relate in terms of words he had read in a literature class at Stanford University years ago, appearing in Dante's *Divine Comedy* as he entered the gates of hell: 'Abandon all hope, ye who enter here.' There was a large central courtyard where prisoners were receiving visitors. It was there they found Marty. The once well-dressed, pudgy bank teller and small-time drug dealer now appeared a disheveled, broken-spirited, gaunt figure reminiscent of a Nazi concentration camp victim. Marty's front tooth was missing and his eyes were glassy as they shifted around nervously. He walked with a slight limp and had noticeable purplish colored bruises on his face and arms. His right eye was red and swollen and he had a large goose-egg, third eye, cyclops-looking knot bulging in the center of his forehead.

Helen was horrified at the sight of Marty and uttered a small guttural cry. Embracing her nephew, Helen burst into tears. Dick shook Marty's hand.

"This must be terrible for you, Marty. Is there anything we can do to help?" asked Helen. She took a handkerchief out of her purse and blew her nose.

Marty's fear-glazed eyes darted around the courtyard scanning the other prisoners as trying to seek out potential threats. Then they seemed to focus on Helen. "Please get me out of here! My life is in danger. I can't survive this brutality much longer. I am threatened and beaten every day, both by prisoners and guards. A murderer hit me in the mouth last week and knocked out my tooth. I think my jaw is broken. Rape is common and I'm sure it will happen to me sooner or later. Oh, please Aunt Helen, please save me!" Marty blurted out.

"How did you get into this mess? And is Rick involved?" asked Dick.

"No, he wasn't involved. I was set up and I got in with the wrong people. I made a big mistake and I'm very sorry about it all. But that's not important now. Just get me out of here. Mr. Batista says if I can come up with $20,000 for the judge I will be released. Can you or Grandpa help me before it's too late and I get sentenced to thirty years in here?" pleaded Marty.

Batista interrupted, "Yesterday, I spoke to the judge who will be presiding over Martin Herbert's case. He is a personal friend of mine and told me, very confidentially mind you, our trial will be held next week, and if we can get him $20,000 before the trial, the case will, most assuredly, be conveniently dropped. But we cannot waste any time. If we go to trial, there is almost no chance for leniency, and from that point on it will be virtually out of our 'friendly' judge's hands. The Mexican government is treating American narcotrafficanos very seriously and, let me be very clear, five kilos of cocaine is a very serious crime here in Mexico."

"Your Grandmother will be devastated, but I think I can convince Grandpa to put up the money," said Dick. "I will call him as soon as we get back to Mr. Batista's office."

"Oh, thank you, thank you, Aunt Helen and Uncle Richard! I know I made a terrible mistake and I'll never do anything wrong again. I promise. Just please get me out of here!" The words rushed out of Marty's gap-toothed mouth like a water faucet that couldn't be turned off. His wild eyes spied a group of rough looking, completely tattooed Mexican prisoners all with shaved heads standing in a circle nearby. They were spasmodically miming his waving arm gestures and laughing loudly.

"When de familia goes, we gonna give you what you want!" teased one of the tough looking Cholos as he grabbed another of the group from behind and began rhythmically dry humping him as he laughed hysterically.

"Oh! Oh! Oh!," mimicked another in a high pitched falsetto voice as he too laughed evilly, when he saw he had Marty's undivided attention.

"Please, get me outta here!" wailed Marty desperately.

An hour later, back at Batista's office, Dick phoned his stepfather, Herbert Salinger, and arranged for $20,000 to be transferred to the bank account of Juan Xavier Batista at Banco Nacional de Mexico in Mexico City.

Two days later, Juan Xavier Batista, having just purchased two round-trip first-class tickets, boarded an Iberia Airlines 747 bound for Spain. He was accompanied arm-in-arm by a raven haired, stunningly beautiful, high-class Latino call girl for a three-day fling at one of Costa del Sol's finest luxury hotels, Hotel Globales Reina Cristina. Upon returning, Batista gave the presiding judge $10,000, all the money he had left over from his 'fun-in-the-sun' trip to Spain. Angered at not having received the requested

$20,000, the judge now upped the ante to $50,000. This time a fuming 'Uncle Richard' refused to pay the extortion. So, the following Monday morning a shackled Martin Herbert Bibbero was taken before the presiding Mexican federal judge and summarily sentenced to thirty years in prison.

As happened, the Bibbero family had been swindled out of $20,000 by individuals of the Mexican judicial system. Roughly two hundred and fifty Americans held in Mexican prisons, arrested on drug trafficking charges, were similarly blackmailed. Nearly all paid bribes to Mexican lawyers and officials and almost none of the imprisoned Americans were released.

Other than the legendary Pancho Villa in 1912, the only other person to have ever escaped from Lecumberri Prison was an American cocaine smuggler by the name of Dwight Worker. Worker ironically was incarcerated at Lecumberri in a situation very similar to Marty's during the same time period and surely knew Marty as one of the other Americans imprisoned there. Worker escaped by casually walking out of the prison in 1975 disguised as a woman. His story was captured in a book[2] and made-for-TV movie entitled *Escape*[3] and was later re-told in a 2012 TV episode of National Geographic's *Locked Up Abroad*.[4]

July 1972
Chicago, Illinois

Willie Sherman, through his San Francisco sports connections, procured five sets of tickets and press passes to all of the main events at the 1972 Summer Olympic Games to be held in Munich, West Germany. He invited me, Phil Erikson, Del Carlucci and Jordan 'Jordy' Hoffman, the son of a wealthy San Francisco banker, to accompany him to the games. Following the games, the five of us then planned to travel through Europe for a month. Jordy and I decided to leave a few days before the rest so we could pick up a car in Munich. We planned to meet the others prior to the opening ceremonies.

We boarded a TWA flight at San Francisco International Airport bound for Chicago. Our tickets routed us through Chicago with a change of planes and onward, non-stop to Munich.

As soon as we were settled into our first-class seats and airborne, the stewardess came by to serve drinks. I ordered a gin and tonic while Jordy chose a Cutty Sark on the rocks. I reached into my carry-on bag and retrieved a small bottle containing four Quaaludes, two of which I swallowed, chasing them with my gin and tonic. I gave the other two to Jordy, who did likewise.

Twenty minutes later I nodded out. I was completely unaware of the time and before I knew it, we were landing at Chicago's O'Hare Field. We both wobbly emerged from the plane and headed down the concourse to catch the connecting flight bound for Europe.

---

2 Referenced Books, Item 9, Page 532.
3 Referenced Television & Movies, Item 6, Page 533.
4 Referenced Television & Movies, Item 10, Page 533.

As I passed through the metal detector at the security station, a loud buzzer sounded and the uniformed security officer manning the detector ordered me to stop.

"Empty your pockets into the tray and go back through the metal detector," barked the guard.

Still loaded from the Quaaludes, I unthinkingly emptied all of the contents from my trouser pockets into the tray and as I turned to go back through the metal detector the guard said, "Stop right there! What's this?"

The officer was holding up a small vial of white powder I had taken from my pocket and placed into the tray along with my keys and change. I blinked twice and paled, suddenly realizing I had inadvertently put my cocaine vial into the inspection tray.

"Huh," I stammered. "Oh, that's, ah, ah, just some baking soda for my upset stomach. It helps keep my ulcer in check."

"Yeah, right. Just wait over there," the guard said motioning me to a side bench adjacent to the inspection station. He pulled his two way radio from his belt, placed it to his mouth and depressed the talk button, "Security, we have a code five at gate 19B."

Within seconds, three uniformed Chicago policemen appeared and surrounded me. Before I knew what was happening, my hands were cuffed behind my back and I was led away through a side door, downstairs and into a small smoky interrogation room on the ground level at O'Hare. One cop went through my pockets, placing the articles on a table, then seated me roughly in a chair. The door slammed again as in came another plainclothes policeman.

Showing me his badge and credentials, he said, "I'm Detective Chuck McDermott from the Chicago Narcotics Bureau and I'd say, offhand, you're in big trouble, son." He went through the items on the table, examining the contents of my wallet, my alligator leather passport case and airplane ticket with keen interest. He then paused and lit a cigarette.

Blowing the smoke in my face he said, "The way I see it, you're a drug dealer. Twenty-five hundred in cash, a fancy leather passport case, a ticket to Germany which shows you paid for it in cash, a passport and a vial of what appears to be cocaine in your pocket." The hefty, pudgy faced, crew cut detective theatrically paused and exhaled a cloud of cigarette smoke. "Son, you ain't going nowhere except downtown to jail. Where did you get all this cash? Where did you get the drugs? Who is traveling with you? Why were you headed to Europe with all this money? Come clean right now!"

"Hold on a second, detective," I answered. "Some hippie-looking fellow just gave me the vial at the San Francisco Airport. I'm not sure what's in it. I was just going to the Olympics in Munich and the cash is to buy a car in Europe to travel around in. I'm not a drug dealer."

"Thought you told the security guard that it was baking soda for your stomach. Now you tell me, you got it from some character at San Francisco Airport and you don't know what it is. Tell you what I think, son. You're lying to me. You're a goddamn drug dealer and you're going down. I don't know what you think you can get away with in San Francisco, but we don't put up with that shit here in Chicago. You're under arrest for possession of narcotics. You have the right to remain silent. Anything you say can be held against you in a court of law." He then turned to the uniformed cop standing by the door and said, "Book this douche bag into Cook County Jail." Returning his attention to me, "We'll continue this discussion later after you've had a chance to think about it for awhile, where your surroundings won't be so pleasant."

I felt as if I was in a movie scene looking at myself from a distance as I was put into the back seat of a caged squad car with my hands handcuffed behind my back. I was taken to Cook County Jail in downtown Chicago where I was booked, fingerprinted and put into a holding cell. Finally coming back to reality and off the effects of the Quaaludes, I began to recognize the gravity of my situation as I sat alone in the holding cell. A few minutes later a guard came by and gave me a soggy cookie and a cup of coffee, which somehow I promptly spilled down the front of the white sweater I was wearing. It was about two hours later that the guard returned to tell me I had a visitor. I was taken to a small cubicle where I saw Jordan Hoffman sitting on the other side of the two inch thick piece of glass separating us. We both picked up the wall-hung phones at the same time.

"Good to see you Jordy. Guess I really fucked up," I said trying not to sound too despondent. "Sorry you had to re-schedule your travel itinerary to come here and see me."

"Don't worry about it. This could have happened to anybody. I think your silver and turquoise belt buckle set off the metal detector and you were still pretty wasted. I was standing right behind you and you looked a little spaced out and just didn't think and emptied everything out of your pockets, including the vial," replied Jordan. "You know we were both 'holding' and I'd probably have done the same thing, if you hadn't been in front of me."

"I think you'd better make a call and get me a lawyer. If my folks find out about this, I'm up shit creek without a paddle."

"Do you know a lawyer?" asked Jordy.

"Del Carlucci used a lawyer from L.A. named Michael Lumanski. He helped Del beat the draft and he's a criminal lawyer. I think he's listed in the L.A. phone book. Maybe you can give him a call and hopefully he can come out here and get me out. Looks like the Olympics are out for me. They took my passport and all my cash."

"The good news is, they have the Olympic Games every four years. You can always go to the 1976 games in Montreal. Anyway, try not to worry about things for now and don't be so hard on yourself. I'll get hold of the lawyer and see you in the morning. OK?"

"Yeah. I'll be OK."

An hour later a uniformed officer came to my cell and led me down a long pale green hallway and into a small interrogation room. Seated at the interrogation table waiting for me was Detective Chuck McDermott. I could see he'd been there for awhile because there was already a crushed cigarette in the ashtray and he was smoking another. He pulled a pack of Camels out of his shirt pocket, shook one up and offered it to me.

"No thanks. I don't smoke."

In early 1972 this photo was taken in Colorado just after I had purchased the silver and turquoise belt buckle that I am wearing. It was this belt buckle that set off the alarm as I passed through the metal detector security station at Chicago's O'Hare Airport that led to my arrest for possession of cocaine.

McDermott shrugged his shoulders. "Suit yourself. So, now do you want to tell me where you got the drugs and who you're involved with. We analyzed the powder and it's cocaine, just as I thought. You're in a heap of trouble unless you talk right now."

"I'm waiting for my lawyer to come from L.A. Until I consult with him, I have nothing to say. I'm sorry, I won't say anything to anyone without my lawyer present."

"OK wise guy, have it your way." McDermott's face reddened and he raised his voice. "We're going to throw the book at your dope peddling ass. Go ahead and bring fifty lawyers from L.A.! It ain't gonna do you a bit of good. Hope you like it here, 'cause you're in for a long stay."

I wanted to say: 'We'll see about that,' but held my tongue, figuring I'd just inflame the asshole, so instead just shrugged as if to say, 'whatever.'

I was returned to the holding cell where I spent a long sleepless night on a metal bench without so much as a blanket or pillow. This was the first time I'd ever been arrested and to say I was a bit fearful about what lay ahead was an understatement. I began to think of Marty in kind of a different light and contemplated what it might be like if I were forced to survive behind bars for an indeterminate period of time. I guess at least it's probably better than in Mexico, I thought: 'What a fucking stupid jerk I was. I let my guard down for a second and now look at me. I guess this is no longer just a game,' or if it was, the stakes had suddenly been dramatically raised. My experience of being on the 'edge', as I had previously pondered, had just decidedly taken a down-ward twist.

Around 10 the next morning a guard again came and this time escorted me to the jail's visiting room. I took a seat at a table and sat across from a long haired man with

John Lennon-style glasses and dressed in perfectly pressed Levi jeans, a blue Brooks Brothers button down shirt, a tweed sport coat and paisley tie.

"I'm Michael Lumanski. I got the call yesterday from your friend Jordan Hoffman and came as soon as I could catch a flight from L.A. I caught the red-eye, but don't mind me if I seem a little bushed. I'm your lawyer."

"Well, I'm pleased to meet you. You helped get a friend of mine beat the draft and I hope you can help to get me out of this mess."

"Here's the situation. I met with the prosecutor before I came here. They're charging you with possession of cocaine. It would be nothing if this was San Francisco or Los Angeles, probably just probation. It's a different story here in Chicago. They're recommending three years in jail."

"I can't believe they'd be so bummed out about less than one gram of coke."

"Drugs are drugs here and they just want to slam you," replied Lumanski. "You are scheduled for arraignment at three this afternoon. I can get you out on bail, which will probably be ten grand and will cost a grand, ten percent. My fee is twenty-five grand. Twenty-five hundred up front and the rest later when we figure out the best defense. At the arraignment, just stand up and plead 'not guilty'. That's all you have to do. I'll handle the rest and you'll be out today, just relax and don't worry about anything else."

At the arraignment, things went as Lumanski predicted and I was released on bail. I flew back to San Francisco and Jordy went on to Europe.

I went to my parents' Sea Cliff house the following evening for dinner. It was cocktail hour and my father and I were in the library which doubled as a TV room and bar. As he poured himself a tumbler of single malt scotch I told him about what had happened in Chicago.

"Why didn't you come to us first?" asked Dick, taking a long sip of the whiskey. "We can help you. You've gotten yourself mixed up with a shyster lawyer. All this guy wants is money and you are going to end up spending time in a Chicago jail. You'll have a criminal conviction on your record, no doubt a felony, and you'll be screwed for life. I knew something like this was bound to happen to you sooner or later. The sands of time have run out on your fooling around and your frittering away all of the opportunities you've been given. You fucked around and fucked around and finally got caught. I ought to let you go down. It would be a good lesson for you. First your cousin Marty, now you."

"Hold on a second, Dad. Let's clear something up right now," I said angrily. "I had absolutely nothing to do with Marty's cocaine smuggling. In fact, when Marty came to me and told me about it, I pleaded with him not to go through with it. I want you, Mom, Grandma and Grandpa to understand that. I feel like everybody has pointed the finger at me for Marty's stupid decision. I will not be blamed for what he freely did."

Dick's eyes narrowed and focused on me like gunsight lasers. "Look at you! Your life is ruined. If you want my help, Son, we are going to have an understanding between us. If not, you can rot in jail for all I care."

"Dad, I don't want to go to jail. You know I need your help. What do you have in mind?"

"One of your mother's relatives, Walter Tipman, is a top lawyer in Chicago. Chicago is where, if you know the right people, you can get things done. I'll call Walter and see what he can do."

"That's great, Dad! I'd really appreciate it if you would help me out."

"I know you would, but like I said before, you and I are going to have an understanding. No, better than that, a contract. I am going to draft an agreement, stating in black and white, you are immediately coming to work for me. I will train you in our business first, then you will move to Cleveland and set up offices there. It will be a great opportunity for you, if you don't fuck it up."

"Sounds interesting," I replied. Having been a San Francisco 49er football fan for all of my life, I added: "I guess I'll now have to become a Cleveland Browns fan. Wonderful!"

"There's more," he said. "You will not associate with any of your so-called friends again. Do I make myself clear?"

"Yes, sir."

"And you'll agree to that in writing?"

"Yes, sir."

Dick shifted his corpulent frame in the brown leather-covered easy chair. He leaned forward. His glare had softened a bit. "OK. I'll have my secretary draw up the agreement in the morning. You sign it and then let's give Walter a ring and see if he can get you out of this mess you've gotten yourself into. I hope you won't have to end up like your cousin Marty."

Walter Tipman got the cocaine possession case against me moved to San Francisco where the charges were summarily dropped with no more than a stern lecture from a local probation officer and the entire incident was, for all intents and purposes, swept under the rug. I paid Michael Lumanski $4,500 for his services. Walter Tipman charged nothing.

I went to work for my father in his San Francisco office, but was stalling for time. Although I was learning the rudimentary aspects of his consulting business to doctors, I was reluctant to give up my unique lifestyle. As a show of good faith, I did, however, study and pass the exams to become both a real estate and insurance broker. But I was really in a quandary.

'It's dullsville if I go to work for him,' I thought. 'In fucking Cleveland of all places. I'll be trapped behind a desk living a hollow programmed life: Yes, sir. No, sir. I'll find out, sir. No more fun. No more skiing. No more traveling. The old bastard will be monitoring my every move. Definitely, no more trips to Mexico and no more sailing. I don't think I can go through with it. That'd be a fucked life. Fuck it,' I concluded. 'Just fuck it!' I wasn't particularly proud of the decision and the prospect of going back on my promise to my father, but, on the other hand, I knew I was also just on the verge of making it big and striking it rich in the marijuana business. In my mind, I knew the adventure was just too great to pass up.

I told my father, I needed a little more time to put my affairs in order. I just needed to buy time. When Phil came back from the Olympics, we leased a home together on the San Francisco Peninsula in the upscale neighborhood of Belmont Hills. Willie was selling Sunshine's litter and he gave me the puppy I'd taken a fancy to in Aspen. Willie had named him Ace, but after he escaped from our yard twice, I changed his name to Papillon after reading the book by the same name.[5] It is the true autobiography of Henri Charriere, known as Papillon, written about his escape from the notorious Devil's Island prison in French Guiana in the early 1930s. The name Papillon or 'Papi' for short seemed fitting.

In early November 1972, with my legal troubles behind me, I double-crossed my father, breaking both the agreement and his trust. I left for Mexico to help put together the next boat trip. My sudden departure occurred when my father had anticipated my eminent relocation to Cleveland and starting to work in earnest as the contract stipulated.

At my parents' home, Dick turned to Helen at the dinner table and angrily said, "That little son of a bitch went back on his word and broke our agreement. He lied to my face. I'm through with him! He's out! I'm having our attorneys cut him out of the will and removed from all family business interests!" Dick slammed his fist down on the dining room table knocking over a wine glass. "He's disowned. As of this moment, I have no son."

Helen began sobbing uncontrollably.

---

5 Referenced Books, Item 12, Page 532.

Chapter 14

Green Tea In The Cockpit

Late October 1972
Belmont, California

Having made the conscious decision to break the written contract I had made with my father, when Phil and I rented the Belmont Hills house, I had not anticipated my father's venomous response. Clearly, I had not thought it through, but in retrospect; given who he was and how he had reacted previously, really, what else could I expect? Even so, in my junkie-like thought process I rationalized 'there is just no way I can stop doing this, short of a medical or legal catastrophe.' I viewed what had happened in Chicago as a mere 'speed bump' and again my father's words, 'good judgment is based on experience and experience is based on bad judgment,' reverberated clearly in my mind. If I couldn't live and learn from such an experience, I was doomed. Thirty-plus hours in Cook County Jail had given me just enough experience to fully understand the consequences of my actions, but it was not enough to dissuade me from continuing. In the future I would just have to be more careful and extremely mindful of what I was doing. Certainly, marijuana smuggling's monetary rewards were enticing, but more so, it was the adventure and danger I was hooked on, as gradually and surely as if I'd been sticking needles into my arm. Before I left for Mexico, Phil and I made preliminary plans and coordinated the logistics for another sailboat smuggling trip.

Dave Killian had called me at the Belmont house and said he would be sailing master on *Sequoia*, a Cal 40 racing sloop, sailing the mid-November Los Angeles to Acapulco Race, and there appeared to be a window of opportunity for smuggling another load.

"Sounds good Dave! Just what we all need right now, but there have been a few changes to the program," I said.

Killian was ecstatic to hear of my break with Mark Wozenberg, although I did not go into the actual details of the split.

"I tell you, the trip will be a hell of a lot easier without Wozenberg," Killian said over the phone from his small East Bay apartment. "Every moment won't be a potential mutiny or a disaster in the making."

"Say Dave, I've got a couple of guys who would work out real well for crew. They are enthusiastic, hard workers, and do what they're told. Only problem is, they don't know how to sail," I said, referring to Willie Sherman and Joe Schroder.

"You know that's not a problem. Don't sweat it. Remember you didn't know your ass from a hole in the wall about sailing before the trip aboard *Sirius II*. Have these guys fly down to Acapulco and meet the boat after the race. I've also got a man, Pete Newman, a quiet reserved guy from Point Richmond who will be racing down with race crew on *Sequoia*. He's very cool and can navigate. He'll make a good navigator for the return trip. I've sailed with him in the San Francisco Bay Big Boat Series and he's an extremely competent sailor plus I trust him with my life."

Willie Sherman just couldn't pass up another opportunity to make big money and have some fun to boot. The handsome, lanky, lady's man had tried law school in Southern California but just couldn't concentrate because of his usual distractions: women, drugs and more recently, the maddening thought of how successful I'd become in the marijuana business he and I started together. The thought that I was making lots and lots of money really got to him. He'd missed out on the past two years and this was his chance to get back in the game and play catch-up. Willie was currently staying at his parents' Sea Cliff home in San Francisco.

Both Phil and I had thought Joe Schroder was a natural for the business. The first time I had met Joe was on the beach in Mazatlan during a Spring Break while I was at UOP. Phil and I had traveled together to Mexico in the spring of 1970 and had run into Joe, who Phil knew from childhood and in the Air Force Reserves. We met again in Aspen and skied together, then following the 'Woz incident' had lived together. Phil and I had both commented on Joe's enthusiasm and loyalty. However, the stocky, brown-haired joker with the drooping walrus mustache had a couple of liabilities. Joe was more than an occasional cocaine user. He was rarely without at least a couple of grams, but more likely an ounce or so. These he scooped into his nose with the Swiss Army knife screw driver blade much like a Chinese with chopsticks shoveling rice from a bowl. Joe, constantly sniffling from a runny nose, sounded as though he had a perpetual cold. His vehicle, pockets and general surrounding areas were always littered with crumpled, wadded and booger incrusted Kleenex tissues, some rolled into a point to be used to twirl, swab and ream out his nose. More often than not, these tissues were striped with blood. Upon seeing this he would always laugh and exclaim: "Yikes, stripes!" Joe rarely smoked marijuana. He was one of those individuals who, when he smoked weed, became extremely stupid. Joe knew his limitations and, for the most part, accepted them.

Phil was dispatched to find a location where *Sequoia* could be safely loaded. He reported that he had found the ideal place, an isolated beach one day's sail north of Acapulco. Phil said the loading zone was an uninhabited beach located at the bottom of a cliff, accessible only by a narrow mule trail. He said the water was 'smooth as glass', as he put it, and loading off the beach and ferrying the load in Zodiacs to the yacht anchored offshore should be a piece of cake. There were no villages, houses or people nearby and none were likely to be there due to the inaccessibility of the location. The nearest village, Playa Azul, was about five miles north.

Even though Ciro was still incarcerated, the trailer smuggling operation was back in full swing as before, with Jeff and Brad running the show at the ranch with the help of Heriberto scoring the loads in the mountains. For the *Sequoia* load, I was to coordinate with Phil at Ciro's Tlaquepaque ranch. I would then travel to Acapulco to meet Willie and Joe, introduce them to Dave and sail with the crew north to the loading site and assist in getting the ton and a half on board. Leaving the boat to sail north, I would then return to Guadalajara with the loading crew. The site chosen to unload the boat was the Long Beach Yacht Club, where Killian was well known and had guest privileges. We did not want to risk using Del Rey Yacht Club twice. Long Beach was another ideal yacht club unloading spot with a gated entry and private guest dock. When *Sequoia* was due in, I would be waiting at a nearby hotel with Killian's laminated gate card. We would unload and I would drive the truck north to the Belmont Hills stash house, followed by Phil in his truck. We would use walkie-talkies to communicate with each other, if we needed to.

Late November 1972
Acapulco, Mexico

The crew arrived in Acapulco ready to go. I was down from Tlaquepaque, where three thousand pounds had been put into gunny sacks and were set to load on a ten-wheeled truck. The following day was spent stocking the boat with provisions for the trip home. Pete Newman had taken a few moments to show Joe and Willie a few basic nautical knots: the square knot, a clove hitch, the sheepshank and the bowline.

"Looks easy enough," replied Willie.

"It's just a question of knowing where to use a particular knot," said Pete. "The bowline is your best knot."

Before lunch, everybody, including Joe smoked a hefty six-paper joint rolled from some weed I had brought down from the hills. Lunch consisted of numerous Carta Blanca beers, ham and cheese sandwiches, potato salad, fresh pineapple and more hits off the joint for dessert.

"This is the stuff we will be carrying," I said, taking the giant reefer from Willie. "Three thousand pounds. Try to, at least, have some of it left to sell back home."

"Boy, that's mighty good weed!" replied Willie, exhaling the pungent smoke. "Much better than anything Jesse ever got us from Culiacan."

"Yeah, this stuff comes from around the town of Apanzingan, in the mountains of Michoacan between Guadalajara and the coast," I said as I passed the multi-paper joint to Joe. "Jesse, Culiacan and Nogales seem like another lifetime."

'What the hell, why not? What can happen to me while we're still in port?' Joe thought, as he took the joint and inhaled deeply, scrunching the smoke down deep to the lowest lobes in his lungs, holding it there as his face reddened, then exhaling slowly in two puffs, like an Indian sending smoke signals into the air. He then passed the reefer to Dave. Its diameter was the size of a Greyhound bus's wheel lug nut.

Half an hour later Joe rowed ashore in the dinghy to pick up more ice. Killian was almost as phobic about running out of ice as he was about running out of gin or cigarettes. It took Joe almost the whole hundred yards from the boat to the beach to coordinate both oars into a single fluid stroke. After procuring the ice, Joe again strangely rowed back across the harbor to the *Sequoia*, came aboard and went down below for a siesta.

Thirty minutes later there was a yell across the water from someone aboard *Howdy Doody*, another yacht which had also finished the race and was lying at anchor fifty yards away.

"Hey *Sequoia*! Your dinghy's drifting away! If you don't get her soon, she'll get caught in the outgoing tide and you'll lose her!" the voice from the other boat shouted.

Killian came on deck, He had been overseeing the stowing of supplies, personally handling his cases of Oso Negro gin and cartons of Winstons. He yelled across to *Howdy Doody*, "Could you go fetch it for me. We don't have time to inflate our Zodiac, before it'll be gone."

"Hey, no problem," came the reply.

'Hummm, I wonder how it got loose,' I mused, glancing down through the open main hatch at the napping Joe, open mouthed, flat on his back in the salon's pilot berth and snoring loudly.

When the dinghy was returned, the mystery was solved. After Joe had rowed back to *Sequoia*, he had tied the perfect bowline in the dinghy's bow line, showing a rapid mastery of the knot. The only problem was, he had overlooked tying the bowline's loop around the stanchion, leaving the perfectly tied knot secured to nothing but thin air. Everybody, including Joe, had a good belly laugh and that small bit of weed engendered lunacy became known amongst us as 'the dinghy to air bowline incident.' More seriously though, it also served as a constant reminder to Joe, by any and all of us who witnessed the incident, to be mindful of his limitations.

Sequoia, stocked with provisions, crew aboard, and me in my lucky shirt, left Acapulco at daybreak the following morning. The winds were light and steady, as the boat settled onto a comfortable beam reach. I had the same queasy feeling in the pit of my stomach about Phil's 'ideal' loading spot that I had had back at Tlaquepaque when Phil first showed me the location. There I had spread out a nautical chart on Ciro's dining room table and questioned Phil about the spot.

"Is the loading spot on open coastline or in a protective cove?" I had asked Phil.

Phil had pointed to a crescent-shaped stretch of beach with his forefinger. "Open coastline, Rick, but not to worry because the water there is 'smooth as glass', like in the sloughs on the Delta."

"I've seen places like that. One day it looks like a millpond and the next day it's like Hawaii's North Shore. Wave faces over ten feet," I said.

"Trust me," Phil replied. "It'll be dead calm."

A shot of me taken on an isolated beach north of Acapulco in 1972. I am wearing my Lucky Shirt which I wore on every smuggling venture I participated in.

Willie in 1972 on the Acapulco trip. It seems obvious from this picture why Willie always ended up with the women. With his natural good looks combined with his magnetic personality, women loved him, and he reciprocated smoothly and with irresistible maximum charm.

"It would have been better if you'd picked a spot where it had natural protection, like the lee of a point, here," I said pointing to a spot to the north. "Something sheltered."

"I looked at that spot, but we'd have to drive through Playa Azul to get there. This spot is much better, as you can see the road from the mountains leads right to it. You always worry too much. We'll be fine," said Phil.

Now arriving near the loading beach, the sails were dropped and furled, and the engine engaged. Killian eased the boat to a point just outside the surf line and my worst fears were confirmed. Big waves were breaking in sets of five. The waves' backsides were between four and seven feet in height, which meant that the wave faces were eight to fourteen feet behemoths.

"There's no fucking way they're gonna ride the Zodiac out through that surf, especially loaded with gunny sacks," Killian yelled. "Willie, bring me that chart and let me see if there's a better looking spot somewhere nearby."

Standing on deck looking through binoculars, I could see the loading crew on the beach pondering their quandary. Killian examined the chart.

"Just north of here, maybe ten miles, is an inlet and protected cove. It looks perfectly protected from this south swell by that cape," Killian said pointing to a spot on the chart with his cigarette.

"How are we going to tell the loading crew about the change?" questioned Willie.

"There are some swim fins on board. I can swim in with the chart and show them where to go and then we can meet you there," I said.

"Are you nuts?" asked Killian. He shook his head, "Never mind, don't answer that. We all know you are! And since we're short on carrier pigeons go ahead, but get ashore as quickly as possible and be careful of a current or rip-tide."

As I put on my swimsuit, Pete wrapped the chart in Saran Wrap and put it into a plastic bag he sealed with gray duct tape. I stuck the chart in the swimsuit's elastic waistband, put on my blue and yellow Churchill fins and dove overboard. As I swam the hundred yards to just outside the impact zone, I could hear a rumbling explosive sound like the battery of 105 Howitzers firing at enemy targets as I remembered from every World War II movie I'd grown up with. Treading water, I let a complete set of five waves pass, observing each individually to see if they were breaking to the right, or the left, or just 'closing out'.

On the boat, the crew was growing impatient. Both Willie and Pete thought I'd lost my nerve, while the men on the shore probably assumed I was just crazy.

The waves appeared to be breaking to the right. Swimming to the peak, I let three steep waves break, pulling back at the last second. Each wave I let pass was 'closing out', breaking all at once, and if I had taken one of them, I would have risked free falling twelve feet where I would then have been pummeled severely by perhaps two tons of water which might have driven me into the sloping ocean floor like a tent stake.

The fourth wave looked good. I took off kicking hard with my fins, going over the crest at a sharp forty-five degree angle perpendicular to the beach. With my chest thrust out and right arm extended, I shot down the wave's face, speeding just a few feet ahead of the curling white frothy lip which almost tubed me.

I emerged from the water, heart pounding, adrenaline supercharging my cardiovascular system and breathing hard like a racehorse at Churchill Downs. With my fins in my left hand and the plastic wrapped chart in my right, I walked toward the huge pile of marijuana filled gunnysacks lying at the cliff's base. Jeff, Brad and ten Mexicans, some wearing large sombreros, were cheering loudly, clapping and grinning like pirates who had just discovered a treasure chest filled with gold doubloons.

"There's been a change of plans," I said as I opened the baggie and began taking off the plastic and tape surrounding the chart. "We're going to move the loading up to this little inlet and cove right here," I continued, pointing to the spot on the chart.

"Hell, we'll have to pack this ton and a half back up the cliff and reload the truck. It could take maybe two hours. No, let's try it here. I think we can make it between sets, if we time it just right," Jeff said pointing his well worn cowboy hat at the waves. His shoulder length blond hair blew in the wind. "What do you think, Brad?"

The laconic cowboy spat a brown jet of tobacco juice onto the sand. "Don't wanna haul all tha shit up the cliff, along wi tha Zodiac and engine. Les giv 'er a try, Rick," he said in a Texas drawl.

"Not a chance! We'll never make it. Those waves are too big and coming too fast. We'll get crunched." I responded.

"I want to give 'er a try," insisted Jeff.

"OK, ok," I said. "But our timing has to be perfect to get past the impact zone."

The Mexicans loaded eight fifty pound gunny sacks into the Zodiac, four on each side to balance the weight. Everybody on the beach helped slide the loaded craft across the wet sand into the foamy water. Jeff, in the stern on the starboard side, got the Mercury 25 outboard running while I sat in the bow. Several Mexicans gave the small inflatable a shove and we were off into the shore break with just enough depth to submerge the prop in the water. Jeff gunned the engine and it roared to life, but the small boat barely moved out into the surf. The prop couldn't bite into the foam-filled water and just spun wildly, producing a high pitched whine, but the Zodiac only inched forward towards the oncoming breakers.

I looked up horrified, to see the feathering crest of a steep ten foot wave approaching us head-on. From my position in the bow of the inflatable rubber boat, the monstrous wave rose like a moving version of the Eiger's North Face sweeping down on us and I realized, we had absolutely no chance. Jeff saw it too, and his blue eyes widened three times their normal size. His mouth opened into a silent scream as the wave broke, impacting on the bow of the Zodiac and tossing the five hundred pound, weed-laden vessel into the sky as if it was light as a piece driftwood or flotsam. Jeff flew off the stern, high into the air, his cowboy hat in hand like he was riding a bronco. Still clinging to the bow line with one hand and trying to hold on to the two gunnies at my feet with the other, my body was suddenly hurled over the tumbling gunnysacks and as the boat hit the water upside down, somehow I managed to hold onto the line. Six waterlogged gunnysacks rolled around in the surf. Two sacks had already been washed ashore. The upside-down boat and the remaining gunnysacks crashed ashore, with the next exploding wave.

Pounded to the sandy bottom by the second eight foot breaker, I felt neck vertebrae and my shoulder joint pop. 'This is it. I'm finished, paralyzed,' I thought, as I was tossed about like a dry twig, eyes closed tight, lungs burning for oxygen. More than amazed, I broke the water's surface and gulped air. 'Fucking Phil and his ideal spot,' I thought, as I worked the kinks out of my neck and shoulder.

It took about an hour and a half to haul all the dope, the Zodiac and engine up the cliffside mule trail to a green rusted 1948 Chevy flatbed ten-wheel truck parked by the side of the dirt road. The long bed truck which had six-foot wooden stake sides attached to the bed was guarded by a fierce looking, bandito-like Mexican strongman. At 6'4" and appearing to be about 270 pounds adorned with a colorful sombrero on his head, the man looked like a huge version of Pancho Villa with a holstered .45 revolver on his hip, and two sets of crisscrossing leather pouched bandoliers slung loosely across his shoulders which held bullets for the well cared-for bolt action Mauser rifle he carried comfortably in his left hand.

The Mexicans piled all the weed haphazardly onto the truck, including the eight soggy bales. The load stuck out above the truck's wooden stake sides, leaning precariously to the driver's side. All ten Mexican loaders plus the 'Pancho Villa' strongman got on top of the load to hold it down and keep the sacks from falling off. Jeff, Brad and I squeezed into the cab beside the Mexican driver, and with gears grinding, the old ten wheeler headed north in a red dusty cloud toward the quaint coastal village of Playa Azul.

The only road through Playa Azul was a paved section which was currently blocked by local youths using the blacktopped surface as a basketball court. The truck slowed to a halt, gunnysacks swaying dangerously. 'Pancho Villa' jumped down off the truck and began waving the Mauser rifle wildly and yelling: "Vamanos chingaderos (get outta here, fuckers)! Andele, andele, ahora mismo, pronto!" The youths scattered like a rack of pool balls struck by the cue ball. The truck started forward and passed slowly through the village, stopping two miles north on a grassy bluff overlooking a protected little cove and beach.

Brad took out his binoculars and scanned the cove. A trail disappeared into a grove of trees, finally emerging down on the white sandy beach. The water looked like a mirror. He could see *Sequoia's* gleaming white hull at anchor, with Killian relaxing, drinking gin in his black French G-string bikini and his garish looking floppy captain's hat.

"What the…?" Brad suddenly exclaimed. He focused the binoculars on a beach encampment of eight to ten nude hippie-looking gringo men and women. They were resting on folding beach chairs and lying upon brightly colored beach towels spread out by an open beach fire. They appeared to be cooking lunch and passing around joints. Brad passed me the binoculars.

"We gotta get them hippies outta here right pronto," Brad said. "This could be a bust if they see us loading the boat 'n go fer the Federales."

"Let me just keel them," 'Pancho Villa' said as he worked the Mauser's bolt, jacking a round into the chamber. "I can have it done in no more than dos minutos," the huge Mexican continued, popping up the rifle's rear sight.

"Nah, not this time, amigo," replied Brad. "Gimme yer rifle, yer sombrero and one o' them bandoliers."

'Pancho' handed him the sombrero, and a leather belt of bullets, but the huge Mexican would not part with his rifle. Instead he offered Brad his .45 revolver. The Texan donned the huge sombrero, slung the bandolier across his shoulder, stuck the pistol into his belt, and walked toward the trailhead. Now, looking like a bad-ass Mexican, a tall lean version of the real Pancho Villa, Brad disappeared into the trees below.

He emerged from the trees and onto the beach running toward the stunned group waving the .45, and yelling like some crazed madman: "Git off th beach! Thiz beach is closed!" Brad punctuated his wild approach by firing two shots into the air. The hippies fled to the far end of the beach, hastily gathered their gear, and within five minutes they had piled into their VW bus and were gone.

The equipment and ton and a half of weed was then packed down the trail to the beach, and loaded into the Zodiac, eight bags at a time. On the first run out to the Cal 40, Jeff and I took the wet gunnysacks. We heaved them aboard to Willie and Joe. Killian, standing by the port rail bellowed, "There's green tea in the cockpit," as the wet sacks slid to the bottom of the cockpit, dripping a dark green viscous liquid into the scuppers.

"Get that wet stuff out of the way for the next batch. Keep it separate," I told Willie. "We'll find a way to dry it later." As the Zodiac sped back to the beach, I was making a mental note, we needed a waterproof way of packaging the kilos in the future.

Within an hour, the three thousand pounds of marijuana were aboard *Sequoia*. Fifteen minutes later they hauled anchor and set sail. In his usual pose and now changed into more modest sailing attire, beer in one hand, Killian spun the wheel to port, and motored the yacht out to sea on a northwesterly course.

Killian at the wheel.

Chapter 15

When All The Laughter Turns To Tears

Late November 1972
Guadalajara, Mexico

Guadalajara Federal Prison was built like a fortress with its concertina razor wire strung atop high brick walls and guard tower castle-like turrets at each corner. Although a foreboding structure in appearance it had little of the oppressive, castle-like, nightmarish feeling Lecumberri Prison possessed. Nonetheless, like its Mexico City counterpart, it was almost impossible for an American to survive, let alone get released from inside the stone walls.

The morning following *Sequoia's* loading, Jeff escorted me to visit the imprisoned Ciro Mancuso. We passed through the main guard post, through the gates and into the prison yard. Most prisoners congregated in wolf packs, while some sat on rough wooden benches talking. A few younger men were kicking a soccer ball. I sensed an atmosphere of fear and hopelessness, as thick as the hot, humid morning.

"There's a couple of dormitories over there to the left," Jeff said pointing to a building as we walked across the yard. "Ciro has a special deal with the warden. He rents a luxury cell, and dig this Rick, the whole setup costs him around twenty grand a month. That's a quarter of a million for one year! For him it's a small price to pay so, at least he doesn't have to mingle with these gangsters and lowlifes. Believe me, he's got it really good in here. You'll see."

Entering the cellblock, we walked down the long, dark dungeon corridor. Many cells were empty with most of the prisoners out in the yard. At the corridor's end was the luxury cell. Jeff nodded to Ciro's bodyguard seated on a chair outside a large wooden door smoking American Marlboro cigarettes and looking at a copy of *Hustler* magazine.

"I've got some errands to run for Ciro. I'll be back to pick you up around two o'clock," said Jeff.

The guard opened the door and I entered a parallel universe from where I had just been. Ciro was getting a shave. He sat with his back to his desk in a swivel leather covered chair, a towel tucked around the collar of his white Lacoste polo shirt. A small white haired man wearing a faded bleached out prison uniform made the finishing touches to Ciro's dark sideburns with a cutthroat straight razor.

Ciro saw me approaching. "Leave us, please" he said in Spanish to the barber. Ciro stood, took the towel from his collar and wiped the remaining lather from his face.

"Rick! Good to see you!" said Ciro graciously, peeling off a couple of notes from a big wad of Pesos he took from his Levi jeans pocket. He handed the bills to the barber with the towel. The well groomed curly haired marijuana entrepreneur came forward with a smile on his freshly shaved face and embraced me.

"Ciro, you're looking good. Looks like you've been working out," I said, taking note of his now well defined physique. This was a significant change I observed at first glance, remembering his rather scrawny stature the last time I'd seen him. He also seemed kind of cocky, which I guess he had to be, given his situation.

Ciro motioned me to a chair. Phil had previously told me Ciro lived like a king in prison, but as I sat there and took in the surroundings I was truly flabbergasted. The remodeled double cell featured a living room complete with carpets and custom made furniture, cushions and pillows. A color television and stereo system were stacked in a wooden entertainment cabinet with Grateful Dead music playing quietly in the background, blotting out any other ambient prison noise. The kitchen had a modern stove and refrigerator and counter with an overhang under which sat four leather covered barstools. Above the kitchen sink was a three foot square double hung window overlooking the prison yard. Through the window a blooming jacaranda tree was visible. The sweet scent of the purple blossoms permeated the room. To the left was a Talavera tiled bathroom with a toilet, sink, shower and door for privacy. The otherwise concrete floor in the cell was covered in rust colored Saltillo tile squares. A ladder led up to a bedroom loft with a king size bed, dresser and nightstand. Original watercolor paintings, mostly of quaint Mexican village scenes, covered nearly every inch of the otherwise drab concrete encasing Ciro's lavish quarters. The only evidence which reminded me I was in a prison and not in some luxury condominium was, there were bars covering the window; however, the window was high enough so as not to be able to see other prisoners in the courtyard below.

"Yeah, the weight pile's in the yard. Still, I've got too much time on my hands, even though I'm running my furniture factory. That's the big lesson in the joint. You've got to know how to do your time or else you go crazy. But I read a lot," he said directing my attention to his well stocked library over his desk. "Like the drunks in AA say, 'it's one day at a time'," Ciro laughed, looking at his expensive black faced military style dive watch on his wrist.

"Doesn't look like you're doing too badly in here, considering the circumstances," I said.

"I had to do an extensive remodeling job. Didn't used to be this way when I first got here. It was pretty much an empty shell. Hey, I even have my favorite Dr. Bronner's Castile Soap in the bathroom. Recognize the furniture?"

I nodded my head. "Yeah, we have some of it at home. This is the furniture from your prison factory, Phil has been sending up to Walter. Looks like you really can have hands-on operation now," I said with a chuckle.

"Mario," Ciro said to his bodyguard. "My amigo will be staying for lunch. Seafood from Carlos at Casa Bonita. Por favor."

"Si, padron," Mario responded instantly.

The beefy Mexican put down the girlie magazine and walked down the long corridor.

"Beer, Rick?"

"Thanks."

"So, did the load get aboard the boat OK?" Ciro asked as he walked to the refrigerator and got two cold Coronas.

I related the details of the Playa Azul loading. Ciro started laughing when I came to the part about when the Zodiac was overturned by the wave.

"It's not really that funny, Ciro. And it sure wasn't when it was happening. Jeff and I could have been killed. I'm still a little bit sore from the beach fiasco, but we're both OK, thank God. Right now we've got about four hundred pounds of waterlogged weed which is about as smokeable as a wet teabag," I said. "I don't know if the stuff can be dried out or not or if it's even salable, for that matter. The point is, we can't afford to let this happen again. We need a waterproof, airtight way to transport the stuff by boat. It's way different than overland in a trailer. Triple bag and seal each kilo with gray duct tape, so each package is completely waterproof."

The conversation turned to Ciro's bust. I had only heard third hand information from Phil and Walter.

"A Mexican guy who works for me driving loads ratted to the Federales. The cocksucker sold me down the river for money. Rick, you know I take care of my people, pay 'em really good, and look after their families, especially if the kids are sick or something. They've never had it so good. But this rat got greedy. I'm going to make an example out of the little spic motherfucker. You wait and see. It will send a message that nobody will ever fuck with me again!" Ciro snarled. His dark hooded eyes looked like burning coal.

My eyebrows arched. "What are you going to do?"

"Look, I'm not going to get into the details. That's all you need to know. Just know this, Rick. The guy is a rat. Hell, I was tortured with electrodes clipped to my nuts and I kept my mouth shut! They don't know anything unless you tell them. The fucker sold me to the Federales like Judas for thirty fucking pieces of silver. If I ever ratted on a friend, I couldn't live with myself. My integrity would be gone. I'd be paranoid for the rest of my life, looking over my shoulder waiting for somebody to turn up and even the score."

Ciro turned and got a bag of fresh tortilla chips from a cabinet and a small ceramic jar of fresh Pico de Gallo salsa from the refrigerator.

"That's all pretty heavy stuff, Ciro," I said.

"Rick, what am I going to do with you?" Ciro chuckled good-naturedly. "You are too nice a guy! You are a good organizer with great business sense and a real adventurer, but a little naive about dealing with the people in our business. If you want to stay free and alive, you've got to be as ruthless as the people with whom you are dealing… or even more so, to discourage any hint of disloyalty."

We chatted and drank beer until Mario returned followed by a thin man carrying a large tray.

"Ah, Carlos! What have you brought today?" Ciro said conversationally. "Carlos runs a great seafood restaurant on the outside," Ciro said for my benefit.

We lunched on avocados stuffed with tiny shrimp with an oil and vinegar dressing at the kitchen counter. For the main course, we ate large succulent lobsters with drawn butter and french fries. Carlos served us fresh papayas for dessert. To me Ciro's prison arrangement seemed exactly like a Mafia don probably might live under these circumstances.

Following lunch, we smoked a joint and snorted some cocaine. When Jeff returned to the cellblock, Ciro stood up and warmly embraced me.

"Jeff and Brad can only do so much for me while I'm in the joint. You, Phil and Walt will have to see the whole operation runs smoothly up there."

"Don't worry, Ciro. We'll handle things." I hated to see my business associate and friend behind bars. Tears welled up in my eyes as I turned to leave.

"And Rick. To be very good in this business, you sometimes have to be very bad. Remember what I said today."

Two days later I flew from Guadalajara to Mexico City to visit Marty in Lecumberri Prison. I had received two letters from Marty begging for help. I had written back, saying I would visit the next time I was in Mexico.

Marty's longtime girlfriend, Carol Goldstein, had moved to Mexico City to be near her boyfriend. It was difficult for Carol, who was suffering from the first stages of multiple sclerosis, to give Marty the emotional support he needed. I had telephoned Carol from Tlaquepaque to say I was coming to Mexico City.

"Marty's in bad shape, Rick," Carol had said on the phone. "He's lost over fifty pounds and sick from dysentery and scabies. Other prisoners beat him up. What little money I can afford to give him he spends on heroin, not on food like I tell him. For God's sake Rick, do not repeat what I am going to tell you. Promise?"

"OK."

"Marty was gang raped by three Mexicans. He is withdrawn and I think he is losing the will to live. He probably will die or go insane. I don't think I can take much more of this," Carol said, suddenly bursting into tears.

"Take it easy, Carol. I'll be down day after tomorrow and I'll bring some things for him."

Carol continued crying. "Be sure to give the guard at the gate some money. They'll let you bring stuff into the prison. Food and clothes."

"OK. Keep your chin up, which I know is easy for me to say. But, try to be strong."

I checked into the Mexico City Sheraton Hotel. On the way to the prison, I had the cab driver stop at a department store where I purchased a sweatshirt, some Levi's and underwear and a pair of tennis shoes. Carol had given me Marty's clothes and shoe size. At a pharmacia, I brought several bottles of vitamins, some antibiotic capsules, a razor and shaving soap.

When the cab driver let me off at the prison, I looked up at the castle's high walls and guard towers. 'Looks like the movie set of Dracula's castle,' I thought. 'All we need is a full moon and bats circling the tower.' I shuddered. This was going to be much different than my visit with Ciro.

I had to bribe the guard twice the normal amount of five hundred Pesos to allow me to bring the vitamins, and antibiotics into the prison.

Marty sat in the dirt, his back against the prison wall, staring vacantly. Looking tattered and dejected, like a concentration camp inmate, Marty absently brushed away flies from buzzing around his face. Scabs and open sores festooned his scalp and there was a large knot in the middle of his forehead. He smelled like an unswept stable mixed with the pungent aroma of dried urine.

"Hello, Marty," I said softly. I was shocked at his appearance.

"Rick! Rick! My God, what are you doing here? Did you get busted?" Marty said, his glazed eyes focusing upon me.

"No, I came to visit you. Get up. Let's go to the table over there. I've got some things for you."

Marty's head swiveled around nervously scanning the prison yard for predators.

"It's OK, Marty," I said reaching down with my right arm and helping him to his feet. Marty shuffled across the yard, appearing to barely be able to pick up his feet more than an inch or two off the ground.

I laid the large shopping bag on the wood table. Marty looked blankly at the bag.

"If I had only listened to you, Rick."

"I know. Let's not even go there. It's water under the bridge. Are you willing to listen to me now?"

"What do you mean, Rick?"

"Marty, if you don't get your shit together, you are going to die in here. That much is certain. Look at you! You've got to eat as best as you can and get some exercise. Try and keep yourself clean. I brought you vitamins. Take care of your body and it will take care of you. I know I sound like some guru, but it's true. I am going to see Carol has at least enough money so she can shop for you, buy you food and clothes and toiletries and whatnot. But the money is not for smack or toot or any other drugs. Do you understand?"

Suddenly, Marty's thin frame seemed to draw in upon itself and he broke down sobbing.

"They raped me, Rick. Two guys held me down, while a third… ."

"Listen," I interrupted. "I get the picture. I really don't need the graphic details. I'm really sorry."

"Then they switched places and each one took his turn. There was nothing I could do. Oh, God! Oh, God!"

I put my arm around my cousin. I felt Marty's body shaking and convulsing with each soul wracking sob.

"I wrote my dad for help, and do you know what he did?" Marty sniffled, wiping the tears and snot away with his shirt-sleeve. Then he started laughing, a bitter, black sardonic laugh. "Dad sent a priest! He sent a fucking priest to see me! Can you imagine?"

I also began laughing. We both laughed at this bit of insanity. Both Marty's parents, had fifteen years earlier rejected Judaism and had become Catholics. They attended church mass and tried to even re-write the roots of his Jewish heritage, by telling their children, my first cousins, they were ancestrally Christians from Genoa, Italy, instead of Jews from Spain and Prussia. And through his father, Donald's, constant brainwashing, they actually believed it; which was probably the underlying reason behind sending the priest in the first place.

"The main thing, Marty, is not to lose hope. Carol is constantly nagging the U.S. Consulate and writing letters to senators and congressmen."

A shrill alarm horn sounded, which meant the visiting session had ended. Guards started clearing the yard, separating prisoners and their guests.

"I guess I've got to leave," I said standing.

Marty stood up. When I offered my hand for a handshake, Marty embraced me. Hugging was not a Bibbero family characteristic. As I returned Marty's embrace, I choked up, on the verge of tears. Crying had also been discouraged in my childhood and adolescence. I had been taught the less emotion shown, the better.

As I departed, I said to Marty, "Remember what I said, Marty. Be strong. Take care of yourself and this will be over soon. Don't give up hope."

I walked out through the prison gates thoroughly depressed. No matter how a guy rolled the dice, I now realized jail was a real possibility if I stayed in the drug smuggling business. I had now visited two men in Mexican prisons, plus I had my own very brief experience behind bars in Chicago's Cook County Jail. It seemed to me while Ciro could afford to do his time in a plush, gilded cage without any real discomfort, very hard time was doing Marty, and most likely doing him in. It now seemed crystal clear to me the obvious dichotomy of both situations. Ciro would emerge from the experience a stronger and much more ruthless, cagy character while Marty, on the other hand, would be lucky to survive at all, and if he did, would most likely return from his 'hell on earth' a hopeless neurotic mess. I knew he was never cut out for the drug smuggling business and he should have stayed home like I had pleaded with him to do. Again, I felt like a master of the obvious with 20/20 hindsight. For a fleeting moment, I wondered where I would end up if it all came down and how I would deal with it.

Chapter 16

Don't Keep All The Eggs In One Basket

The third boat trip north was uneventful. I met *Sequoia* in the early hours of a Tuesday morning at The Long Beach Yacht Club. Three thousand pounds were unloaded, which Joe drove up to the San Francisco Bay Area in my new pickup. His experience as a truck driver, where he had once been employed hauling 18-wheelers loaded with tomatoes and pickup trucks loaded with heavy farm equipment, was proving to be an essential component to our operation. I followed behind in Phil's pickup.

At the Belmont Hills stash house, the weed was unloaded and the eight wet gunnysacks were opened and spread out on the garage floor. All the cracks in the garage door opening and all of the vents under the adjacent house foundation were sealed with sheets of black plastic so no light could be seen outside at night. Joe, Phil and I rigged up six 300-watt heat lamps to dry the four hundred pounds of wet dope. The process took a week, with the marijuana turned hourly and constantly separated to dry. The trick was to avoid over-drying, which would leave the weed brittle and powdery.

"I told Ciro we need to have each kilo triple bagged and individually sealed with gray duct tape. The people down at the ranch will have to do it before putting the weed into gunnysacks for the next boat trip," I said.

"Yeah, we'll need about a million rolls of the stuff. Why don't we buy stock in the company?" Joe joked.

The bulk of the load was split with Walter taking one third and Phil and I taking two thirds. Phil, Walter and I all agreed we would dry the wet kilos and split it according to the formula later, after we'd dried it. During the week in which the four hundred pounds were drying, 'Yorktown' Billy brokered all seventeen hundred pounds. He later sold the dried formerly wet weed as well for a discounted half price to one of his old customers who couldn't afford the one-fifty per pound going rate. All told Phil and I each pocketed in the low six figures, after expenses. Killian was given $25,000 while Joe and Willie each received $20,000. Pete Newman, being the rookie, made $7,500.

In February of 1973, immediately following Ciro's release from prison, Dave Killian again skippered *Sequoia* with Joe, Willie and Pete Newman as crew. This time they sailed from Puerto Vallarta back to Marina del Rey. The boat had loaded just north of the small fishing village of Zihuataneo on a beautifully calm day. Twenty-two days later, a ton and a half of potent Sinsemilla was brought ashore at the Del Rey Yacht Club and then transported back to Belmont.

With Ciro again back firmly at the helm of his enterprise, this load was the best quality Phil and I would ever smuggle into the U.S. from Mexico. Under Ciro's supervision, each kilo had been meticulously wrapped according to my triple bag/gray tape specifications. This time each pound sold wholesale for a phenomenal and previously unheard of price of $225 per pound. Phil and I each netted a hefty six figure profit and, because of the increased value of the load, we were able to double the crew's salary from what they had made on the last run.

On an unusually warm winter day in the low 70s in California's Central Valley, Phil and I each buried our share of the returns safely and securely under two feet of dirt, carefully marking the joists and columns for transcribing the info to our sacred 'treasure maps'.

Until now my standard of living had been rather modest. With my buried share now having grown exponentially, it was time to think about spending some money and moving a portion of it to a new location. Phil was thinking about something Walter Brugger had recently suggested to us, while the three of us were dining at the world famous Julius' Castle Restaurant perched on the side of Telegraph Hill in San Francisco. Of all the five-star Bay Area restaurants we frequented, Julius' Castle was by far my favorite.

It was after an exquisitely prepared abalone dinner. The three of us sat there relaxing and drinking Napoleon brandy with coffee, gazing at the lights of both the Golden Gate and Bay Bridges from our table surrounded by 270° of windows that sat secluded and private in one of the castle's turrets and away from the other patrons. At the time I was just recovering from a nasty cold. Walt had a rather quirky sense of humor and said, as he surreptitiously removed a vial of cocaine from his pants pocket, took a healthy sniff on the blade of his pocket Swiss Army knife, then handed me the small bottle, "Here Rick, just burn the cold out with coke. It works every time."

"That's a novel and, I'm sure, a scientific approach for the cure of the common cold. Maybe you should be nominated for the Nobel prize," I quipped, as I took a sniff, hoping maybe he was onto something.

Walt continued without missing a beat, "I have a safe deposit box in a Swiss bank. I fly to Europe with cash stuffed in my cowboy boots and convert the dollars into gold and European currency."

"Why do that?" Phil had asked.

"You know the cliche about 'keeping all your eggs in one basket'?" Walter had said.

"So what?" I questioned, taking a sip from my brandy snifter and simultaneously wiping my nose.

"Well, Mr. Naive, let me explain it to you. I like to take some of my money to Switzerland and put it in different currencies including gold, to cover the dollar's fluctuating rate on the international money market. It's also a great place to have fun. I can really lead the high life: fly first class, stay in all the best hotels and bank my assets without arousing suspicion. In Europe, spending cash, and lots of it, is a normal way of life. Here in the States, a hundred dollar bill raises eyebrows. But over there, nobody bats an eye."

"Whaddya think? We need a vacation anyway and Joe can handle things with Billy while we are gone," Phil said.

"I've heard there is great spring skiing. Let's go!"

Late April 1973
Geneva, Switzerland

Swiss Air Flight 111 touched down at The Geneva International Airport on schedule at 8:52 AM. Phil and I had flown to New York on United, then changed planes at Kennedy Airport. We then went first class non-stop on the trans-Atlantic 747. This time, I took no drugs whatsoever and passed through the metal detector without any of the problems I'd experienced in Chicago.

Having nothing to declare at Swiss customs, we were waved right through. Both of us agreed, one hundred and fifty thousand dollars would be a comfortable amount to carry. A Mercedes Benz taxicab took us to the posh Richmond Hotel, the finest in the city. Our reserved accommodations were a two bedroom suite connected by a central living room overlooking Lake Geneva. The rooms were adorned with the finest quality Louis XIV antique European furniture.

My feet ached. I pulled off my black custom-made Tony Lama ostrich skin cowboy boots. In each boot was $75,000, banded in five stacks of hundred dollar bills, fifteen thousand per bundle. I put the money into my brown leather attache case and left the hotel. Phil and I decided we'd use different banks.

At precisely ten o'clock in the morning, the huge gold doors of the bank's main branch were opened and I was escorted inside. I was shown to the far side of the bank to the exchange teller's cage. I set my attache case on the counter.

"I have U.S. dollars and I'd like to purchase one hundred thousand dollars worth of South African Krugerrands and fifty thousand in Swiss Francs, please," I said trying to appear as relaxed and nonchalant as I possibly could, while actually quaking in my boots. 'Just think good thoughts' my subconscious was screaming at me.

"Certainly, monsieur."

I fought an attack of nervous jitters as I withdrew the banded stacks of one hundred dollar bills from my briefcase and placed the money neatly upon the counter. The teller took the Franklins and placed them in an automatic money counting machine. The machine whirred and within one minute the notes were counted and the digital readout on the machine's face confirmed it had just correctly counted all of the one hundred dollar notes.

The teller then efficiently banded the stacked notes and placed them in a drawer beneath the counter. He then did a quick calculation on his desktop calculator and looked up at me. "One moment please, monsieur," the man said, locking the drawer with a key. He turned and left for the vault.

Returning a couple of minutes later, he carried a polished Mahogany wooden tray containing numerous rolls of shiny newly minted 1973 gold Krugerrand coins and several bundles of Swiss Francs. The Krugerrand's were about the size of a U.S. half dollar and came in rolls of ten coins per roll, each roll sheathed in a plastic casing. Each gold coin was valued at a slight premium over spot gold bullion price. The man counted out the rolls on the tray, and passed them to me through a slot beneath the one-inch-thick bulletproof glass.

"Thank you and have a nice day," I said, breathing an inward sigh of relief.

"Oui, monsieur," he smartly replied.

I filled the briefcase with the gold coins and banknotes and was ushered over to the ornate, old-fashioned gilded elevator cage by a stodgy looking official wearing a black three piece pin-striped suit. He served as both an usher and elevator operator.

The elevator descended one floor into what seemed like the bowels of the bank, beneath the street's surface, where I was directed across the foyer to a woman seated behind a desk. I gently set the now nearly twenty-five pound gold-filled briefcase down on the marble floor trying to make it appear light as a feather, as if I had nothing but paperwork in it. I'm sure that fooled her, like this was her first day on the job… right! Actually she looked like she had worked there forever and had seen everything.

"I'd like to rent a safe deposit box, please," I said.

The woman, dressed in a gray pants suit with a white shirt and black tie and whose silver/gray hair was tied in a bun, asked to see my passport, then showed me three sizes of boxes.

"Ve rent ze boxes by ze year, sir. Ve alzo have valk-in lockers," she said in a thick German accent.

"I'll take this size please," I said pointing to the mid-size box. I'll pay for two years."

I paid cash for the box, was given a key, and then was shown through a two-foot-thick vault door with a gigantic locking wheel into the main vault. The vault was the size of a small auditorium with rows upon rows of varying-sized safety deposit boxes and huge walk-in safety deposit vaults. We walked down several rows of polished stainless steel boxes exuding Swiss business-like perfection.

The woman stopped and put her key into one of two key slots on the door to the box number she had assigned me. She then instructed me to put my key into the other key slot and she turned both keys simultaneously. Opening the door she withdrew the metal box and handed it to me. She led me to a small adjacent room and closed the door, giving me complete privacy within the vault auditorium. I transferred the contents of the briefcase into the metal box and she accompanied me back to the secure slot where I replaced the box. Again, as I carried the box back to its home, I tried to act as if it contained nothing but paperwork and was virtually light as a feather.

Locking the box, we returned through the vault door to the woman's desk, where I handed her my key. Unlike American banks, Swiss banks kept their depositor's safety deposit key. She placed my key into a small manila envelope which had a white string and two grommets. Licking the envelope's flap, she sealed it and drew the string around both grommets in a figure 8, securely closing it. Next she placed the envelope underneath a machine, which at the touch of a lever attached to the side released a red-colored glob of hot sealing wax over the sealed flap and string-secured grommets. She then took a metal cylinder with a flat head and stamped it upon the hot wax, smearing it completely across the envelope's sealed flap and attached string. Drying the glob with a small dryer which looked like a miniature hair dryer, she instructed me to write my signature across the red waxed envelope flap. The whole process insured only the properly designated customer would have access to the key.

Phil and I spent three days in Geneva sightseeing, shopping and dining in some of the best restaurants. We each purchased Rolex watches and several cashmere sweaters. We rented a new Mercedes Benz 450 sedan and drove to two of Europe's most celebrated ski areas: Chamonix and Verbier. We stayed in only the most exclusive hotels while enjoying a week of absolutely perfect late spring skiing.

The trip's only unpleasantness occurred at Kennedy International Airport in New York, when, after getting off the returning Swiss Air 747 flight and claiming my suitcase, I was briefly detained at the U.S. Customs and Immigration kiosk. Phil passed through without incident, but when I presented my passport, a Customs officer checked my name and passport number against those on the computer's 'stop list'.

The officer saw my passport number had been red flagged. He pressed a red button alerting two other Customs officers in the duty office who arrived immediately and confiscated my passport and escorted me to a holding room.

"Please, open your suitcase," said a bald-headed Custom's officer.

"Get undressed," said the second uniformed officer.

While I complied, the officer began a through search of the suitcase, looking not only at each item of clothing, but checking the seams of the bag and cuffs of the trousers and shirts in it, going through my toilet kit and attaché case. The officer ran the ski boots, a pair of brown penny loafers, the cowboy boots I was wearing and the attaché case through a fluoroscope.

"What's going on?" I again asked, taking off my trousers.

"Just a routine check, sir," the man said in a monotone as he began to examine the trousers.

"What was the purpose of your trip to Europe?" asked the bullet headed officer scanning the images appearing on the fluoroscope screen.

"A skiing vacation," I replied.

"Did you take any U.S. currency out of the country?"

"No."

Finishing their search, the officers, finding nothing during their examination, released me back into the terminal. In the years to come, every time I re-entered the United States, my name was flagged by the computers as a result of 'the Chicago incident.' I was routinely subjected to a strip search and asked a barrage of questions regarding my travels. Over time I was able to adopt a confident and very indignant attitude about it which would usually put the officers on the defensive and they would summarily release me from their custody.

April 1973
Tlaquepaque, Mexico

Ciro was released from prison in January 1973. He desperately wanted to make up for lost time and the quarter of a million dollars he had spent paying off the warden in prison.

He again began to acquire and store large quantities of high-grade marijuana at the avocado ranch through his main contact and confidant Heriberto Torres. Heriberto had faithfully supported him and had helped the operation run as smoothly as possible while Ciro was incarcerated. Ciro began a rapid production line-like operation shipping marijuana north weekly in one of four trailers Pat Suraghoomkol had modified. Between April and June of 1973, one trailer per week rolled from the rancho into the U.S. Pat was commuting between the rancho and Walter Brugger's Los Altos Hills stash house, sealing and unsealing the loads into the trailers before and after each smuggle.

It was rumored throughout our small group that Ciro had somehow 'taken care of' the individual who had informed on him. It was never discussed openly, but whispers continued to float amongst us, the rat was given his just deserts. Those who routinely came and went from the ranch never saw him again.

June 1973
Homewood, California, on Lake Tahoe's west shore

Blue jays were squawking, raucously calling to each other. A woodpecker's staccato tapping could be heard in the distance. There was the scent of pine in the light breeze. Ciro walked through the open French doors of his wood paneled living room onto the porch carrying a pitcher of ice tea. Walter Brugger and Pat Suraghoomkol sat comfortably in deck chairs taking in the early afternoon sun.

"The way I see it, we need to make a real big push and try to get two trailers a week running from the ranch up to the Bay Area. I've got a big supply stored at the ranch. Walt, check into getting a second stash house, OK?" Ciro said, setting the pitcher on a table. "Pat, you will have to see about buying and outfitting three or four new trailers."

"I'll look into it. Do you think you could get another load of Sinsemilla like the one we had back in February? It really knocked everyone's socks off. Rick and Phil unloaded their share in a week," Walter replied.

"I'll look into it," Ciro said. "You have to order it in advance and it's probably too late for this season. Next growing season it shouldn't be a problem though. I've got the best contacts in Mexico for it now."

"Ciro, this is not good time for me. I burn out real bad. I work very hard for last two months, maybe eighteen hour a day. You owe me lotsa moneys since February, sixty-fi thousand dollas. I want to go Hawaii, just two weeks for mellowing. Can you please pay the sixty-fi thou you owe me?" asked Pat.

"Not now, Pat. This isn't the time," Walter said in a low voice.

"Hang tough, Pat. Another real big effort for a couple of months and then we can all coast for a while," Ciro said, disregarding the Thai's request.

"No. I am very exhausted. Need to go away now. Just two weeks. Visit friends on Maui. Want to get shit together. Need to do something for myself. Mabbe buy house over there. Please pay me the sixty-fi you owe me, now," Pat insisted.

Ciro saw this was going to be a losing battle. He sighed, turned and walked into the house and went to his study where he opened a safe hidden beneath the closet floor. Ciro removed fifteen thousand dollars in hundred dollar bills from several stacks of money and put the money into a manila envelope. He made a notation in a ledger and closed the safe.

"OK Pat," Ciro said returning to the porch. He dropped the manila envelope onto the table in front of Pat. "There's fifteen thousand. I'll pay you the other fifty I owe you in a couple of months. Little problem with cash flow right now. Gotta make up for all the money I spent in prison. There's also the expenses for the new trailers. Things are pretty tight."

"No good. In past three months we make twelve loads. It's plenty money for all workers. I want all my money now. Can't buy nothing with only fifteen," Pat said his voice rising.

"Come on Pat, cool your jets! Everybody's biting the bullet right now. Take the fifteen G's and go to Hawaii for a week or two. Don't worry. We'll pay you everything you're owed. Be reasonable," Walter said.

"No! I not work until all money is paid to me. I quit! You guys get another coolie to build your trailers!" Pat was visibly excited. He stood up, and put the envelope into his windbreaker pocket.

Ciro took off his Vuarnet sunglasses, tossed them onto the table and got to his feet. "Listen zipperhead, you don't fucking threaten me! That greasy Mexican motherfucker who ratted me out… well let's just say he won't do that again. Don't even think about messing with me!"

"Jet ma mung!" Pat swore in Thai, meaning 'Fuck your mother.'

Walter stood up and got between him and Ciro. Abruptly, Pat spat onto the wood deck, turned on his heels and strode down the steps to his black Karmann-Ghia. With a loud whine, the car sped down the dirt driveway, with gravel and clouds of dust flying. 'If I can ever fuck those guys over, I will,' Pat thought in Thai. 'And I will get every dollar they owe me, no matter how long it takes!'

Arriving back in the Bay Area, Pat immediately packed his bags and moved out of Walter's Los Altos Hills house. He telephoned me and asked if he could stay with me in Belmont for a couple of days while he sorted things out.

"No problem," was my reply.

Pat and I had known each other for the past two years. Though not close friends, we liked each other and found our dispositions were complementary, lighthearted and breezy. We joked with each other and I always found time to patiently help Pat with his English while Pat, a fanatic about cars, would give me tips about the best car wax or spark plugs. I loved Thai food and Pat knew the best Thai restaurants serving authentic

Thai food which hadn't been Americanized. These restaurants were not high class but places where local Thais ate and the food was fantastic. He taught me the Thai words so I could order the delicious food myself.

One night at dinner at a San Francisco Thai restaurant Pat related his blowup with Ciro and Walter. I offered to loan Pat some money.

"How about me lending you the fifty? This way you will have something to get started with when you return to Thailand. You can pay me back whenever," I offered.

"Thank you my friend. Ciro and Walt take advantage of me. I get even with them someday. They treat me very poorly. I work harder than Mike, yet he get more money," Pat said referring to Mike Duncan, Walter's number one gofer. He helped me to another serving of Tom Yum Goong, shrimp and lemongrass soup.

"Maybe it will turn out for the best. Hey, this is great soup and the squid salad is outrageous."

"If you think this good, you not believe the food in Thailand. Fruit is unbelievable. I promise you never had anything like it. I'm going back home in two days. Mabbe sometime you come visit me?"

"Really?"

"Sure, why not?" Pat laughed. "We 'bi-tio' (the Thai phrase for 'go on vacation'). I take you all over. We go India, Nepal, Singapore, Malaysia. Have great time," Pat said with a huge smile on his face. This was probably the first time he'd relaxed and felt at ease in weeks.

"The guy who financed my first boat trip brings in hash from Nepal once in a while," I said.

"I went to boarding school in Northern India, near Nepal, in town called Darjeeling. I know lots of people up there."

"Hmmm. The guy who sells my loads got a little weed from an Air Force friend of his stationed at an Air Force Base over there called Ootapoo-poo or something like that. The guy shipped it home in stereo speakers. Billy said it was the absolute best weed in the world."

Pat laughed and said: "It's Utapao Air Force Base. It's located near Chanthaburi in Southern Thailand. My family have big ranch there. One-hundred acres. He right. Thai weed best ever. Number one in all the world!"

"Maybe I will come visit. I could leave here at the end of this month. We could travel and check things out. Perhaps you and I could put some sort of scam together. Who knows?" I said smiling.

Three weeks later, I bought a first class ticket and boarded Pan Am's 747 flight #1 bound for Hong Kong. On June 30, 1973, I got off a Thai International Airlines flight at Bangkok's Don Muang Airport. It felt like I had just landed on the moon or another planet. It was the start of an adventure which would change my life, and the large, high-quality marijuana smuggling business was about to 'take a giant leap for mankind.'

Section 3

Across the Pacific
(1973–1976)

Chapter 17

Nepal or Thailand?

Bangkok, Thailand
July 1973

S outheast Asia was a violent assault upon my senses. As the airplane hatch opened, I felt like I had been thrust into a blast furnace. My 'lucky' shirt was soaked and stuck to my back even before I had left my seat. The temperature was 98 degrees and the relative humidity was at 92 percent. Going the short distance from the air conditioned interior of the airplane's cabin to the mobile air stair platform and down to the bus waiting to transport passengers to the terminal building, the oppressive heat and humidity hit me like a ton of bricks. It was then I became aware of the smell which instantly reached up and corroded my sinuses. It was the most unusual smell I had ever encountered and was exacerbated by the oppressive heat and humidity. The stench-like aroma filling the air was a mixture of rotting garbage, wood smoke, jet fuel, automobile exhaust fumes and the excrement of Bangkok's four million souls.

I cleared customs and took a thirty-minute cab ride from the airport to Bangkok's Siam Intercontinental Hotel. The automobiles were righthand drive and drove on the opposite side of the road from what I had been used to. The road was a modern four lane highway with all different types of vehicles headed for the city: luxury Mercedes Benz and BMWs, Japanese pickup trucks, three-wheeled open-air jitneys called 'tuck-tucks', motorcycles zooming in and out of traffic at suicide speeds, and brightly colored ten-wheel trucks with pictures of Clint Eastwood or Charles Bronson emblazoned on their mud flaps. The roads were actually built atop levies which had been constructed above and bordered by canals called 'klongs'. The water in the klongs was the color of sewer water, yellowish brown, and I could see young boys wading chest deep in the mire, scooping the greenish scum floating on the surface with what appeared to be giant butterfly nets. The landscape was flat and in the distance as far as the eye could see lay endless bright green rice fields.

'This is way different than anything I've ever seen. It might as well be a city on the

Moon', I thought, noticing the large advertising billboards with hieroglyphic looking script. Strange music characterized by odd sounding sing-song-like voices blared from the cab's radio.

"You wan girls? Fuckie, Fuckie," the cabbie asked with a smile revealing a grill of gold teeth. "You wan white powder? Ganja? You wan, I get for you. Numbah one!"

"No thanks," I said blandly. "Just get me to the Intercontinental. I need a hot shower and cold beer."

"Aaaah!" the man intoned as if suddenly comprehending an elusive cosmic riddle.

After checking into the hotel, I phoned Pat who was living with an uncle and aunt along with their grade-school daughter in a middle-class house, out on Sukhumvit Road. Pat was overjoyed to hear from me and proposed we get together the following day.

First thing next morning, we went to a local bank where we rented a safe deposit box in both of our names and were each issued a key. I had brought $50,000 in hundred dollar bills, stuffed in my boots and in a money belt around my waist, so Pat and I could travel in comfort, stay in good hotels, fly anywhere and have whatever cash we might need readily available.

Pat gave me the grand tour. I noticed Bangkok's automobile traffic moved at two speeds. Either not at all, with vehicles stopped and intersections terminally gridlocked as each driver leaned upon his horn, producing a blaring cacophony of different tones; or they madly raced their cars and rice-rocket-style motorcycles like contestants in a Grand Prix for the insane, with extra points scored for narrowly missing pedestrians.

Having lived in the United States for the past fifteen years, Pat was still not entirely comfortable with Thai traffic rules. In right-hand drive countries like England, Australia and Thailand traffic travels on the opposite or left side of the road. This is exactly backwards from what we are used to in the United States. Later in the day and now on foot in downtown Bangkok, we were crossing a major street and Pat stepped off the curb. Instead of looking to his right for oncoming traffic, he looked left, the wrong way, and was nearly run over by a bus. I saw it coming and reached out and grabbed him by the shirt collar, jerking him back onto the curb as the bus passed with no more than six inches to spare.

The incident left Pat pale and completely shaken, suddenly realizing I had just saved his life.

We visited the Royal Palace and saw the Temple of the Emerald Buddha, then Wat Arun, the Temple of The Dawn on the banks of the coffee colored Chao Phraya River, bisecting the city of Bangkok, locally known as 'Krung Thep'. We took a ride on the river in a long, narrow, shallow draft wooden speedboat with a huge engine and long pole-like drive shaft extending aft from the stern about six feet in length where the prop was attached. The brightly colored boats roared up and down the Chao Phraya at speeds of 25 to 30 knots, sometimes narrowly avoiding head-on collisions by mere feet. We veered off the main river and sped down the klongs, now dwindling in number. Bangkok had once been known as 'Venice of the Orient' and these canals which had once been the city's major highways were now in the process of being drained and paved over. We went to the Snake Farm on the other side of the river and I had a photograph taken with a twelve-foot boa constrictor draped around my neck and over each shoulder with its head in one of my hands and tail in the other. We ate lunch at a sidewalk stall and when I asked what the deliciously marinated barbecued meat was, Pat smiled and said, "Ling," the Thai word for monkey.

At sunset, we sat drinking ice cold Singha Beer in the colonial atmosphere on the verandah of the exotic Oriental Hotel, located on the Chao Phraya's banks.

"I'm fried Pat. Bangkok is like a crazy madhouse. Just twenty-four hours in this city and I'm ready to get out of town. I'd like to get to the beach and relax," I said.

"Tomorrow we go to Pattaya," Pat responded. "I've rented a bungalow right on the beach. You'll love it there. Much more relaxed."

The resort town of Pattaya is located about two hours' driving time southeast of Bangkok on the Gulf of Siam. It is a favorite tourist resort, especially with Europeans, featuring first class hotels and gleaming white sand beaches. It is also a frequent R and R spot for sailors off 6th Fleet warships and airmen up from the big United States Air Force Base at Utapao. There is a promenade running parallel to the beach lined with curio shops selling every type of tourist trinket, and there are countless bars and massage parlors servicing the visiting tourist's and military men's every carnal whim.

Pat drove his Toyota Corolla and on the drive to the coast, we talked about putting together our own smuggling venture. Both of us were certain we did not want to work with Ciro anymore.

"I hate the man. He used me like third rate coolie. After all I did for his trip, he became very greedy man and screwed me out of fifty thousand. I think prison changed him, because he act like big shot after he get out. He not like the same mellow person I used to know. Now, he order everyone around like an arrogant prick. Walt, he OK, but Ciro is clearly running things and Walt just go along with it. I think he afraid to say anything against him," Pat said.

"I know what you mean. He's really full of himself. His ego is totally out of control. I think he's power tripping, trying to make everybody afraid of him. When I visited him in prison, he said he was going to make an example of the guy who ratted him out," I said.

"The asshole threatened me too! I overheard Walt saying to his man Mike, Ciro actually did make an example of him and he said, the guy probably would never do it again. I can only imagine what it really meant. And I don't want to know. All I know is, somehow, someday, I get the money back he not pay me."

"What we need to do, Pat, is check things out. See what kind of options there are. Maybe we can put something together ourselves. We sure don't need those guys. We probably should go to Nepal and check out hash trips. What do you think?"

"Yeah, Rick. I agree. I think we see my old schoolmate from when I went to high school at St. Patrick's School in Darjeeling, India. He lives in Nepal and his name is Bhanubhakta Phanindra. His father is in the Nepalese government and he lives in Kathmandu."

The beach bungalow was flanked with frangipani trees with their pink and white blossoms offering complete privacy. Pat had scored some Thai stick marijuana, ganja as it was called, and it was indeed the best I'd ever smoked. Pat and I were both the unusual type of people who could function normally while stoned. Everyday we'd roll a few joints for the road and take them with us as we took trips around the countryside. We'd usually eat at roadside stands on the way. The food was fabulous. In the evenings we'd drive south from Pattaya to the fishing village of Sattahip to eat at a small local fish restaurant or where we'd get a late night dessert called roti. It was a crepe made on a roadside grill, laced with coconut milk and sometimes papaya. It was delicious. Sattahip was directly adjacent to the big Utapao air base which was a scene of constant military activity. In 1973, the 'secret' bombing of Cambodia was in full swing and the B-52s flying on their nightly missions were based at Utapao.

There were thousands of U.S. military and government personnel in Thailand and the economy was geared to provide them with everything they wanted including women, ganja, tailor-made clothes, opium and heroin down from the golden Triangle, sapphires and jade from Burma, and rubies from the southeastern part of the country. Everybody was after the U.S. dollar. It was a virtual free-for-all. For the Thais it was a great opportunity to fleece as many servicemen as possible. The Viet Nam War and the war in Cambodia were winding down all too soon.

This is the runway at Utapao Air Force Base located in Sattahip, right across from the small fish restaurant where Pat and I frequently dined while enjoying the sights and sounds of B-52s taking off and readying for takeoff to make their bombing runs over Cambodia.

The entire country was on a war footing. It was a staging area for much of the land-based air war over North Viet Nam and the 'secret war' conducted by the CIA and their airline, Air America, in neighboring Cambodia and Laos across the banks of the thousand mile long Mekong River. The outlawed Communist Party of Thailand had active guerrilla units who would periodically blow up rural police stations or power plants. On every major road and highway there were military checkpoints with sandbagged machine gun emplacements and barricades of barbed wire guarded by units of the Royal Thai Army, all armed with M-16 automatic rifles slung over their shoulders and Colt model 1911 .45s holstered on their web belts. Pat and I routinely had no trouble passing through the checkpoints on our various trips around the countryside.

Eating dinner in Sattahip at the small outdoor fish restaurant, we would enjoy mouth-watering lobster and fresh fish while listening to the rumble of B-52 bombers taking off for their nightly sorties over neighboring Cambodia. They would leave at a rate of about one per minute, bank over us and head south. The main road south led right past the airfield and during the day, as we drove past the airbase, we'd see some-where between fifty and a hundred B-52s lined up with just their tail section visible over the jungle foliage bordering the road. They looked like rows and rows of menacing black shark fins waiting to feast on their upcoming evening's prey, less than one hun-dred air miles to the south in Cambodia.

Pat's grandfather owned a one-hundred-acre farm southeast of Pattaya, a few miles north of Chanthaburi, site of Thailand's famous ruby mines. We drove there one day to inspect it and spent a couple of days camping out in one of the dilapidated buildings.

The farm once had been a prospering agricultural entity growing coconuts and rambutan, a delicious spiny tropical fruit. Now, however, it had fallen into a state of dis-repair and was abandoned. It was mostly overgrown jungle with a few buildings located on a hill in the center of the property. In nearby Chanthaburi, we bought two 125cc Suzuki dirt bikes and took them back to the farm, where we explored hidden jungle trails, streams and waterfalls. Some of the overgrown paths had to be cleared, which we did with machetes we carried with us in scabbards attached to the bikes.

"This would be a great place from which to base a smuggling trip. It would provide perfect cover and it's so remote we could come and go as we please, without anyone being any the wiser," I said, peeling a tasty rambutan, 'ngaw' as it was called in Thai, and popped it into my mouth.

We sat at the base of a waterfall on a rock jutting out into a stream. Our feet soaked in the cool water while the afternoon heat and humidity beat down on us, in spite of the thick jungle canopy overhead. It seemed to me to be a thousand shades of green, with tropical sounds of birds cawing and monkeys chattering somewhere hidden above in the jungle. Pat was rolling a joint of the powerful resinous Thai weed.

"Mabbe so. It not difficult to get farm working again. Very little upkeep. Just fix leaky roofs and hire people to cut back jungle. I think now we go up north, up to Chieng Mai in the Golden Triangle. Opium poppies grow in Burma and transported to Chieng Mai. Heroin come from there," Pat said taking a toke off the freshly rolled reefer and passing it to me.

"I don't want to mess with that shit, Pat. Heroin is very bad karma. I know, it would bring a phenomenal amount of money, better than any other drug scam, but it's not mellow. The people you deal with are heavy, most of them Mafia or psychotic killers. Same with cocaine. I've had plenty of opportunities to do coke trips and turned them down. It's not just the money, Pat. I only want to be involved in something I'm person-ally into and is mellow. My cousin, Marty, tried to get me involved in a coke smuggling trip. I wanted no part of it. Someone set him up and ratted him out and now he's doing thirty years, rotting in a Mexican prison."

"I not want to do heroin smuggle either. Big time heroin smugglers who get caught here are shot by firing squad. Doesn't matter if you're Thai or 'farang' (the Thai word for foreigner). You get shot, just the same. That's Thai law. We go to Chieng Mai, anyway. Prettiest girls in Thailand are from there. Hill country people very poor. If you like, you can buy them from their parents for only a few thousand 'baht' (the name for Thai currency)," Pat said smiling.

"Can't wait to see it," I said. "Let's go!"

We left early the next morning and drove nine hours from Bangkok up north to Chieng Mai. The weather was slightly cooler in the northern hill country. We went to the famous Buddhist temple, Wat Doi Sutip, situated on a mountain and visited a school training elephants to haul mahogany and teak logs through the tall rain forests. On the second day, we took a trip into the hills past Mae Tang to see one of the Meo hill tribes who grew opium.

Returning to Bangkok, we booked a flight to India. That evening, Pat took me to a first class massage parlor off Phaya Thai Road. We 'bought' four of the attractive women out of the massage parlor for twenty four hours, spending less than one hundred U.S. dollars. It was a night I would never forget. The next day Pat and I played golf at the local country club with the mini-skirted women acting as our caddies, retrieving golf balls and serving us cold Singha beer.

* * *

We flew first to Calcutta, where we stayed at the beautiful Grand Oberoi Hotel, the city's finest luxury hotel amid one of the filthiest overcrowd places on earth. The streets were teeming with beggars, outcasts and low caste 'untouchables.' Outside the hotel, I tried to give a small child a few rupees and I was immediately mobbed by a ragged horde of youngsters grabbing and pawing at me whereupon I had to forcibly push my way back into the hotel's sanctuary.

The flight the following day brought us to the city of Patna in the northern part of India. Patna was unbearably hot. Drifting clouds of boiling red dust irritated our eyes and got into our mouths and nostrils. A six hour taxi ride over a winding two lane road in a taxi with nonexistent suspension took us into the mountains. Vehicular traffic thinned the higher we climbed on the steep sometimes cliffside road, constantly dodging oxen drawn carts hogging the middle of the road. The vehicle in which we were riding bounced and bobbed up and down like a destroyer in heavy seas. Thick, gray summer monsoon clouds cloaked the Himalayas and as we came into Darjeeling, clouds hung over the mountains almost totally obscuring the view of the majestic twenty-five thousand foot Mt. Kangchenjunga, which rose spectacularly to the west of Darjeeling. It was disappointing we never had a clear view of the mountain during the five days we stayed there. I later learned that the best time to travel in the Himalayas is late fall or early spring when the weather is usually clear... not in the summer when the monsoons set in.

There are many Tibetan refugees in the northern part of India and Nepal who had fled their native homeland on foot in 1960, when the Chinese invaded their country. Walking south, they climbed wind-whipped mountain passes, over miles of frozen rock, across flimsy braided-rope footbridges spanning deep gorges with jade colored, glacially fed rivers tumbling below. With what they could carry on their backs, the refugees survived as best they could. At the Tibetan Self Help Centre in Darjeeling, I asked a young man if there were any old Tibetan carpets for sale. The youth, named Tenzin, said there were none at the Centre, but his family had an old rug at home, his grandfather might be willing to sell. His family had brought it from Tibet. We agreed to meet the next day at the Centre and Tenzin would escort us to his home.

Tenzin's Tibetan family lived outside Darjeeling up the road in a small village named Ghoom not far from Tiger Tops, a popular Himalayan viewing spot.

"This is my home," Tenzin proudly said pointing to a muddy cave. It's entrance was carved into the side of a mountain. Grass was growing upon the slopes and the cave's entrance was covered with a crudely made wooden door.

Pat and I followed Tenzin into the cave. The passageway led into a series of sculpted catacomb chambers. Kerosene lamps and candles illuminated these larger rooms, some separated from each other by beaded curtains, the same style many of San Francisco's Haight-Ashbury residences also had. It was probably where hippies in the Bay Area got the idea in the first place. There were at least fifteen family members living in the cave. A small cooking fire heightened the foul smell of kerosene, burning animal fat and unwashed bodies. The people were very friendly and made Pat and me feel comfortable and 'at home'. A very old man with long gray hairs growing out of a wart on his chin sat in the chamber's far corner.

"This is my grandfather," Tenzin said to me.

The old man motioned me to sit. A woman dressed in native Tibetan garb poured Pat and me cups of tea. The hot liquid was covered with a layer of thick yak butter. I tasted the greasy brew and nodded my approval. It had a wretched taste and I nearly gagged at the fetid liquid. I was offered a refill, but politely declined. The old man smiled and began talking with his grandson, who translated for me.

"My grandfather say carpet in our family for many generations, over one hundred years," Tenzin said pointing to the rug lying at the old man's feet. It was filthy, covered with dirt and dried mud and looked like a raggedy old piece of worn burlap. "My grandfather say he not want to sell carpet, but family is very poor. He sell to you for one hundred U.S. dollars."

"Please tell your grandfather, I understand," I said. "I agree to the price." I thought, even if the carpet was just an old rag scrap, it would be worth it. The old man's bearing and sense of pride had deeply touched me. I would have bargained for such a commodity as I normally would have done like in Mexico, bargaining for blankets on the beach, but in this situation I just couldn't do it and was only happy to be able to help these destitute people.

On the return trip back to our hotel in Darjeeling, Pat started laughing. "What a sucker! Looks like you really got rooked. It's nothing but a filthy old piece of burlap,

Rick. You were an easy mark and got totally scammed."

"Maybe so, but I feel good about giving them the money. These people are like the Native American Indians. Very dignified and proud people. Both the Indians and the Tibetans have been kicked out of their homelands and have been viciously exploited. I can't imagine living in a cave like that. Can you? Even the poorest people in America have no idea how good their lifestyle is compared to how these people live. No, Pat, I really feel good about it."

Back at the hotel, we took the carpet outdoors and hung it from a clothesline and began beating it with a couple of brooms. Dirt billowed from the rug in clouds of dust which nearly choked us. Half an hour later it was relatively clean. The rug was navy blue with several lighter shades of blue yarn woven into a characteristic Tibetan coin design. I later found out, the carpet was truly a treasure, well over a hundred years old and valued at more than $5,000 dollars. Upon my return back home, the carpet became my dog Papi's favorite thing. He would crumple it up, circle around it, and paw it into just the right pile. Then he would just flop down and lie on top of it and, with his nose, burrow into its blue woolen depths, seemingly 'grooving' in the essence and scent of generations of Tibetan feet.

Traveling back down the mountains to Patna, we caught an Indian Airline flight to New Delhi where we intended to visit Agra and the Taj Mahal. When the plane reached its cruising altitude, I went forward to the Boeing 727's cockpit to visit with the pilots. They welcomed me and when I told them I was a fellow pilot, albeit of a small Cessna, they laughed and let me sit in the co-pilot's seat. We chatted amiably for twenty minutes talking about flying and air navigation. The landscape below was burnt brown but we could see little of it, as it was mostly obscured by blowing dust.

"Excuse me just a second, sir," the pilot said in a clipped English accent, typical of the sing-song Indian lilt. His attention was drawn to his gauges. He put on his headset and radioed New Delhi tower. He frowned when he realized he had flown past the New Delhi airport and he wasn't exactly sure where we were.

"Please strap yourself in, nice and tight my friend," the pilot said to me. After he flipped on the 'Fasten Seatbelt' switch, he executed a radical 'bat turn' and the plane plunged into a steep dive to get low enough for the pilot to visually inspect the terrain, to determine our position. We went from 37,000 feet to 12,000 feet within one minute. My stomach felt like it was at the back of my throat.

"Ah, got it now. Not to worry," the pilot said when he recognized some familiar landmarks, hauling back on the control yoke and leveling the aircraft out. I thanked him and nervously returned to my seat, where Pat, along with most of the other passengers, had gone ghostly white, feeling we were about to crash.

After sightseeing at the Taj Majal and the nearby Red Fort, we boarded a plane for Kathmandu, Nepal, where one of Pat's classmates with whom he'd attended St. Patrick's School in Darjeeling was living. Bhanubhakta Phanindra's father was the former Nepalese minister of trade and part of Nepal's official delegation to the United Nations. His name was a mouthful, but Pat said everyone called him Bakta for short.

Bakta gave us a guided tour of the city with its temples, bells and shrines. The summer monsoon had set into the Himalayas and had veiled some of the world's tallest mountains from view. Bakta took Pat and me to the famous hashish houses of Kathmandu where it was legal to buy the drug from vendors who advertised their wares on signs posted outside of their shops. All grades of Nepalese hash were offered for sale. In the Eden Hashish Center located on one of Kathmandu's main streets, I sampled and then purchased a couple of the finest and most potent of the Nepalese Temple Ball hash for our personal use. Each black sphere was about the size of a golf ball.

"I think we need to consider the pros and cons of a hash smuggling trip out of Nepal versus a Thai weed trip," I said. The three of us sat outside the Oberoi Hotel at an open air teahouse enjoying Kathmandu's afternoon sunshine.

"Do you think you could come up with two tons of the finest grade hashish?" I asked Bakta.

"For the right price it could be arranged," the short wiry Nepalese replied.

"There would have to be two different smuggles. Since Nepal is landlocked, one smuggle would be from Nepal down to the Indian coast, and the other would be from India by boat back to the United States," Pat said.

This is one of several hashish bazaars located throughout Kathmandu where it is a legal commodity. One can procure all grades of Nepalese hashish sold by an ancient Indian unit of measure called a tola which equals 11.6 grams or 4/10ths of an ounce.

"We've a lot to think about, Bakta. If we decide to put together a hash smuggling venture we would want you to be the man who scores the load. If we go ahead, we will let you know," I concluded.

We left Nepal and returned to Thailand and the beach bungalow at Pattaya. We discussed and evaluated each individual point thoroughly, writing everything down. We had topographical maps of Nepal, India, Thailand and South-East Asia. Plus I had brought along sailing charts of the world so we could actually plot out what a potential voyage would look like.

One significant advantage of a Nepalese smuggle I mentioned was that hashish, by nature, is a much denser and durable product and probably would survive a long sea voyage better than the more fragile Thai stick marijuana.

Pat pointed out that we could package the load, whatever it was, Nepalese hash or Thai stick marijuana, in a manner so the risk of water damage and mildew would be greatly reduced.

I thought back to the 'green tea in the cockpit episode' at Playa Azul when four hundred pounds of marijuana got wet. This was not like a Mexican smuggle, where the product was in the hands of the consumer one month after being harvested. A sea voyage from Asia would take two to three months of prolonged exposure to the elements, so the time from harvesting to smoking would be a minimum of three to four months.

There was another unavoidable factor when considering a smuggling scam in this part of the world: pirates. The voyages from Mexico had been a series of long tacks; beating up the Mexican coastline, the Baja Peninsula and coast of California. This however would be a long journey across thousands of miles of open ocean, part of which would pass through South-East Asia and extremely hazardous waters. There were hundreds of small islands scattered through the Sulu Sea off the southern Philippines and northeastern Malaysia, and many islands along the coasts of Viet Nam, Cambodia and in the Gulf of Siam. They all posed a vast danger zone plagued not only by shallow dangerous ground and shoals, but by pirates as well. I had heard stories of sailboats in these waters being hijacked. The yachtsmen had been brutally killed by pirates using fast boats and automatic weapons.

"If we're to stand a chance against such scoundrels in these waters, we've got to have at least as much firepower as they do," I said.

"No problem. I know a few officers in the Thai Army. Not difficult to get M-16s or M-72 grenade launchers. Mabbe even light anti-tank guns or shoulder fired rocket launchers. Over here cash speaks and cuts through red tape," Pat responded.

We also took into account that the war was still going on all around us, in Viet Nam, less than fifty miles to the east, in Cambodia to the east, south and southeast as well as in Laos to the north. I observed the strange paradox, where our proposed base of operations for a Thai weed scam, Pat's grandfather's farm near Chanthaburi, was no more than twenty-five miles from the Thai-Cambodian border. And the source where the weed is predominantly grown is in the northeast part of Thailand, only a few kilometers from the Thai/Laotian border. In fact some of the best weed is actually grown in Laos.

Here in the quiet restful setting on the deck of Pat's beach house in Pattaya with the sun setting into the calm Gulf of Siam, Singha beers on the table and a joint in the ashtray, Pat and I peacefully discussed an exciting new business venture while at the same time, paradoxically, in every compass direction and in relative close proximity, we were surrounded by chaos, war and hostile waters.

"Maybe the war might work to our advantage. Perhaps in all the chaos and confusion, the authorities will be too tangled up to even worry about drug smugglers and our boat might just slip through the cracks, so to speak," I said.

A yacht sailing in the Gulf of Siam or crossing the South China Sea might stick out like a sore thumb, if it was ever observed, or it might not be seen at all. When smuggling loads up from Mexico, we had legitimate reasons for each voyage and the vessel's presence was inconspicuous. It was always being delivered back to the U.S. from a particular sailboat race. There were no sanctioned yacht races from India or Thailand back to the United States. The closest yacht races were from Hong Kong to Manila and the Southern Ocean Racing Series in Australia.

After lengthy evaluation, it was decided that a smuggling venture from Thailand would be the best of the two alternatives. Everything considered, we figured, the scam would take perhaps one year or a year and a half to put together and pull off and would cost between three hundred and fifty thousand and half a million dollars to finance.

I had seen Thai weed before from one of 'Yorktown' Billy's people and knew it sold for a fantastic $1,500 per pound or more, but it had never been available in the quantities Pat and I were contemplating. The estimated gross proceeds from such a venture would amount to over three million dollars per ton, if the scam could be pulled off without us: getting caught by a patrol boat from one of the nearby countries we were at war with, held as prisoners of war or simply executed as spies, or being caught in waters of a country whose penalty for any kind of drug offense was death either by firing squad or hanging. We could be overtaken by pirates and summarily executed. We might be simply lost at sea and never be heard from again. We also faced the possibility of finally getting home after spending all the time, money and effort required to actually complete the ocean voyage, only to find out the weed had gone stale from the amount of time elapsed between harvest and consumer. Or it might be ruined due to over-exposure, mildew, infusion with saltwater or simply waterlogged, thus rendering the entire venture worthless.

Other than those 'minor' obstacles, we both felt that the monetary rewards, the adventure, the freedom from Ciro Mancuso and his people presented a worthwhile risk. Phil and I had enough combined resources to purchase and outfit a boat and finance the scoring of the load.

I made arrangements to return to the United States, where I planned to locate and buy a used sailboat and do one final Mexican load with the new vessel as a shakedown cruise. It would also build up some needed capital which would surely be required to pull off a smuggle from Thailand, so we wouldn't get in a financial pinch due to the unexpected, which always seemed to happen in this business. Pat agreed to start getting things organized on the Thai end. The growing season was determined to be August through March, with the prime harvesting months November through February. It was now late August 1973 and a smuggle for this current year was out of the question. So we figured we would shoot for the following year, which would give us plenty of time to put every aspect of the plan into operation.

After coming up with a workable plan, we both flew to Hong Kong and got a two room suite at the world famous Peninsula Hotel overlooking the harbor. From our balcony we could see the Star Ferry coming and going to Hong Kong and Kowloon almost every ten minutes. Planes just outside of our window were on final approach to Kai Tak Airport bringing tourists and business people from all parts of the world. The harbor was a beehive of activity both from commerce and ferrying gamblers to nearby Macao. We got a safe deposit box at the offices of one of the world's biggest international banking institutions which we would use as a storage facility for ferrying money over. We also went on a buying binge in the world's premier shopping capital. We had suits tailor-made so that we would look like international businessmen. We bought leather briefcases, binoculars, radios and cameras for use in the planned adventure. More importantly we had spent the past two months traveling and forming a strong bond of friendship and trust, made plans for a globe trotting adventure and started a wild business venture which was to consume the next decade of our lives.

Chapter 18

The Cook's Trophy

I returned home via Pan American flight #2 direct from Hong Kong non-stop to San Francisco, a grueling thirteen-hour flight. Upon arrival at SFO, I collected my military-style B-4 flight bag which was laden with collectibles I accumulated from Nepal, India and Thailand: carpets, thangkas and other Nepalese and Tibetan artwork. The bag weighed almost eighty pounds and was bulging at the seams. I knew I was in for trouble.

I presented my passport to a friendly looking female customs agent standing behind the counter who punched my passport number into a computer. All of a sudden all the friendliness vanished, as she stared at the computer screen. With her left hand, she reached next to the computer and pressed an ominous red button, which I noticed illuminated a red lightbulb over the line in which I was standing. She frowned as she looked up at me and then down at my passport and customs declaration forms in her hand.

"One minute, please, sir," she said as three other uniformed customs officers appeared at the counter. The woman handed my passport and declarations form to a stern looking officer who said: "Bring your bags and come with us, Mr. Bibbero."

The three officers escorted me to a small holding room.

"Where have you been?" demanded an agent with a crew cut. He had the disposition of a pit bull.

"I see you've had some trouble in the past. Any drugs here?" asked a Hispanic officer pointing to my bag.

"I've been traveling in the Orient, and no, I don't have any drugs," I answered.

"Right. Now, open your bag and let's have a look. Sit down and remove your shoes," the crew cut agent growled.

"Look pal," I said, "you don't have any right..."

"Yes, I do have a right," snapped the agent. The mottled red splotches on his face deepened in color.

"No, you don't have a right to be rude. I'll do as you request. I've declared everything

I purchased abroad. It's all here on the declaration form. There's nothing else. I'll subject myself to your search. As far as I'm concerned you can turn me inside-out, if you like, but you won't find anything that's not listed on the form. The past is the past and I made a mistake, but that's no reason for your rudeness. I don't need to listen to your veiled accusations. Just get on with your business," I said, thoroughly annoyed.

The agents backed off at my assertiveness and then quietly proceeded to search my B-4 bag. They examined my Tibetan carpet and the Tibetan scrolls known as thangkas, and all of the trinkets I'd purchased. They cross-checked everything with my customs declaration form and then inspected my shoes. They found nothing.

"I'm sorry for the inconvenience, Mr. Bibbero," the Hispanic officer said.

"That's OK," I said. "I know you are only doing your job. Have a nice day." I repacked my bag and left the room.

Later in the day, I got together with Phil at our Belmont house and told him of my travels with Pat and of our prospective plans.

"This seems like the perfect opportunity to do something on a scale that's never been done before: bring a ton of the highest quality Thai weed into the States. I've seen it before, but never in quantities like this. It would be a first. We'd be putting this trip together from scratch, just the three of us and we'd handle the entire operation ourselves. Just our small little group and no one else. We'd handle the scoring, loading, transportation, unloading and sales ourselves. It'll probably take over a year to put it all together. The financial rewards alone would justify it. The money we'd make from this venture alone would equal what we'd make from five Mexican trips and we wouldn't have to split it with anyone else. Pat's farm in southern Thailand is a natural place where the load can safely be received from the growers in the north, then packaged and stored right there. We found the perfect isolated spot to load. Phil, I know we can do this"

"So this would leave us totally independent from Ciro and his outfit," Phil said. "We would have our own thing, just the three of us, you, Pat and me."

"That's right. Look Phil, I know, you and Ciro have been friends forever, but this scam is just us, not him. Pat hates him and won't have anything to do with him. Ciro fucked him over and ripped him off for peanuts of what he was worth to them. If we can keep this operation small and just between the three of us, we can have a gold mine for a long time to come. You have to promise not to say anything to him, or Pat's out."

"OK, I promise."

"Good, I think, between the two of us, we might have the money to buy a boat and have enough funds to give Pat to score the load, as well."

"OK," Phil said. "But I don't think the boat should be in either of our names. If Killian wants in, we set him up with a 'front' company and put the boat's name into the dummy business. That way we keep everybody separate. Looks like the first order of business is to find a boat."

Killian agreed to the plan, and he and I began looking for a suitable boat. We scoured the Bay Area marinas and most of the yacht brokerages, but came up empty. A few possibilities but for one reason or another, nothing seemed to be exactly what we were looking for. Most were either too expensive or needed too much work. So, after a couple of weeks of searching in vain we flew down to Los Angeles where the southern California sailboat market was much larger. Killian knew several yacht brokers there and had a long time association with a number of people in the SoCal racing circuit.

One of these yacht brokers came up with an ideal boat suited to our purposes. The vessel was a forty-one foot, one design yacht, which had previously been raced, but now was outclassed by the faster, lighter displacement boats. The boat named *Nepenthe* was designed by the noted naval architect and yacht designer Paul Kettenburg and had been built in 1967 by Kettenburg Marine in San Diego. *Nepenthe* had a fiberglass hull with a classic keel. The cabin top and sides were made of beautifully varnished mahogany. She had been campaigned in several Mexican races as well as the Transpac Race to Hawaii. Killian thought that *Nepenthe* was a very appropriate name.

"This is a good omen, Rick," Killian said. "Our voyages on this yacht will always be happy. I went to the library last night and did some research on the meaning of the name *Nepenthe* and I can't believe the coincidence. According to the legend in the *Iliad* and the *Odyssey* written by the Greek poet Homer in about 850 BC, the drug *Nepenthe* was used by Helen of Troy as a potion to eliminate sorrow by inducing forgetfulness, similar to marijuana. It actually could have been marijuana. Can you believe that? This is definitely our boat," Killian beamed.

The asking price was $32,500. Killian and I had the boat surveyed and she was found to be sound and in good condition, although as with any boat, minor repairs were needed. After some negotiations, the broker agreed upon a cash selling price of $28,500. Cash transactions under $10,000 at banks went unreported, with no paper-work or identification required. So I went into three different banks in the Marina Del Rey area and got three cashier's checks each in the amount of $9,500 and later in the afternoon Killian and I took possession of *Nepenthe*, using Killian's new company, 'Round The World Yacht Delivery Service,' as title holder.

The boat was temporarily berthed at the Del Rey Yacht Club's guest dock where Killian figured we could stay and get her ready for the upcoming Los Angeles to La Paz race scheduled for November. *Nepenthe* was a racing sloop, but she had not been campaigned in several years and had been mainly used for cruising the light airs of Southern California waters. She was sorely in need of a new set of sails, as well as deck repair.

"Owning a boat is like pouring one hundred dollar bills into a hole in the ocean," Killian remarked as we brought *Nepenthe* into the yacht club's guest dock.

I soon learned that if the word 'marine' prefixed any piece of gear, it was triple the price of the exact same item found at a regular hardware store. Killian told me that all hardware must be stainless steel, and not just any stainless steel but American or German stainless steel, because Japanese or Chinese stainless steel rusts.

We stayed aboard *Nepenthe* and got her ready for the La Paz race. The refitting cost another $15,000. We changed the rigging, leading all the sheets and halyards aft to the cockpit for safety and ease of handling. We had the mast anodized. New more efficient self-tailing Barient winches replaced the rusted old ones. A local loft cut new sails, including two multi-colored spinnakers. Killian and I would frequently sail *Nepenthe* out of Del Rey into the SoCal waters. I began to quickly assimilate more sailing knowledge and my instinctual responses were constantly being refined. By now I had almost completely memorized *Royce's Sailing Illustrated*, the book Killian had given me at our first meeting a couple of years ago. Most all of the sailing lingo and jargon was now as common to me as the English language.

It was during this time that Killian and I got to know each other a little better. I had to occasionally warn him to keep his distance. Killian was very considerate of the homosexual aspect of his bisexuality and would not force his opinions on me; however, he liked to walk around below deck in the raw. One morning as I had just awakened, the first sight filling my eyes was Killian making a breakfast omelet in the galley with his drooping genital package swinging back and forth below his blubbery belly like some kind of obscene metronome.

"Hey, Dave, would you please put on some shorts and not run around naked when we're aboard this boat?" I asked. "It's really kind of bumming me out and the sight of you making breakfast with your 'junk' so close to my food is making me lose my appetite."

"Oh, sorry. I didn't know it bothered you," Killian said laughing, with a rather lecherous grin on his face.

"Hey, it's not that funny to me. Get your schlong away from the omelet and put some clothes on. Right now!" I commanded.

Killian acquiesced, donning his French G-string bikini. His gut hung over the scanty black bathing suit, jiggling whenever he moved. I also prevailed upon him to only smoke cigarettes up on deck and not down below. With those two issues out of the way, we got along great. He was the sailing master and I was the attentive pupil. I soaked it up like a sponge.

Killian was in his element aboard the sloop, completely at home, moving nimbly on deck with the grace of a fleet-footed two hundred forty pound ballerina, but once on land he was hopelessly out of control. He would drink incessantly during the day and by Happy Hour he was almost always three sheets to the wind. On one occasion, Killian, cut and bruised, staggered back aboard *Nepenthe* a day and a half after leaving the boat at sunset. He had been beaten up and robbed on the Long Beach docks outside a topless bar known as the VIP Lounge, with little recollection of the previous night's events. I quickly came to the conclusion that the only way to ensure Killian's safety and the safety of our future venture was to keep him aboard the boat at all times. After that episode and forever in the future, 'Never get off the boat' was the strict rule I insisted on for Killian, especially in foreign ports. He was OK with it, so long as I kept him well stocked with gin, ice and cigarettes.

Phil made frequent trips to Los Angeles to bring money and assist me in combing the local ship chandleries for needed parts. In a month and a half *Nepenthe* was ready for the race. I decided not to accompany them as there was other work to be done. Killian was to skipper with Pete Newman navigating and four other veteran racers crewing. Willie and Joe planned to fly to La Paz, meet the boat after the race and accompany Killian and Pete on the smuggle home. Phil had secured three thousand five hundred pounds of top quality Michoacan and Oaxacan marijuana from Ciro at the usual split, one third to Ciro and two thirds to Phil and me.

Ciro's main lieutenant, Jeff, had found a suitable loading spot on the Mexican coast just north of Manzanillo, at a protected bay called Bahia de Tenacatita near Barra de Navidad, close to where they had loaded us once before. This time, as per my instructions, each kilo was to be triple-bagged and sealed with gray duct tape to ensure nothing got wet.

Meanwhile, Joe and Phil had rented a new house in Belmont Hills where we would stash the forthcoming load. Joe and his new girlfriend Jenny Stiles moved in, blending comfortably into the middle-class neighborhood. Jenny, a tall buxom brunette, was the sister of John 'JQ' Quinn's wife Michelle. Along with 'Yorktown' Billy, JQ had become one of my best customers, brokering loads for me as well as doing cocaine loads for himself. Between the two of them they had distribution networks spread across the entire country.

The new Belmont stash house was a three bedroom, two bath home with an attached garage. Inside, adjacent to the garage, was an unfinished room approximately fifteen feet long by ten feet wide with an eight foot ceiling. The room had been plumbed for a laundry room. I took one look at it and right away realized, with a little work, I could turn it into the perfect secret stash room. Using the ingenuity of concealment I had learned from Pat, I built an eighteen inch deep, five shelved, painted linen closet into a wooden frame the size of the doorway and mounted it on a sliding track. With folded towels and sheets neatly placed on the shelves, the whole affair looked just like a bathroom linen closet when you opened the door, but when two screws were removed the whole cabinet slid to one side revealing a 960 cubic foot hidden room. It would easily accommodate and totally conceal two tons of marijuana and unless someone had architectural plans of the house, chances were slim to none that anyone would find it.

Everything was all set and on the tenth of November, the race started with about seventy five boats participating. It was anticipated that the race would take five days, due to the light winds. Killian felt *Nepenthe* could be competitive, provided they got a few breaks and if the wind picked up and held for the race's duration.

On the day of the race I emphasized to Killian: winning was not important.

"Dave, please don't put any unnecessary pressure on the rig or do anything which might damage the boat. Hell, it doesn't matter if you finish last, just as long as you finish," I pleaded.

"Don't worry, Rick," Killian responded, double gin on the rocks in hand. "They even give an award for last place. It's called the Cook's Trophy. I've never won one, but there's always a first time."

"Just keep it mellow, Dave," I cautioned. "We've got a bigger prize waiting for us across the Pacific than just a damn trophy. We'll be the ones who'll be the big winners. Just keep that in mind."

"OK, OK. You just take care of your end and I'll take care of mine. Have I ever let you down?"

"No you haven't. Please keep it that way. Good luck and I'll see you in La Paz."

Killian took his time getting to La Paz and *Nepenthe* arrived nearly thirty-six hours behind the rest of the fleet. Some of the other skippers were beginning to worry, but on the morning of the seventh day, *Nepenthe* pulled into La Paz harbor.

I was there to greet Killian and the boat.

"I said take your time, but this is embarrassing."

"Just following your orders, Rick. The trip was very mellow. We went outside the others trying to find the wind, but it died and we just stayed there and enjoyed it," Killian said.

Nepenthe was awarded the Cook's Trophy at the awards banquet, memorializing her last place finish. The following day Joe and Willie arrived in La Paz and two days later *Nepenthe* departed south for Bahia de Tenacatita with me aboard to oversee the loading. As with every smuggle since 1969, I was wearing my special talisman, the 'lucky' blue shirt.

The loading operation came off without a hitch, with Jeff coordinating from the shore. *Nepenthe* was waiting about a half mile offshore as two Zodiacs, each ferrying ten gunnysacks at a time, sped across the smooth, glassy waters under a blazing sun and clear blue sky. There was not a breath of wind. Within an hour *Nepenthe* was loaded with thirty five hundred pounds of marijuana and powering her way offshore.

The trip up the coast took eleven days and the usual late-night unloading procedure was repeated at the Del Rey Yacht Club. Joe drove the load north with me following. The load was stashed in the converted laundry room of the new Belmont house. Within ten days, 'Yorktown' Billy had sold about seventy percent and JQ had sold the other thirty percent of our share. This time we made nearly 400 grand which would be plenty to finance our new venture.

Killian took the boat down to San Diego to Kettenburg Marine. It had been decided to convert *Nepenthe* from a single mast sloop rig into a two masted yawl in preparation for the long trans-Pacific voyage that lay ahead. Killian had advised that it would be safer if *Nepenthe* was a yawl, because of easier handling under storm conditions. We could drop the mainsail and still maintain headway with a storm jib and mizzen sail raised and not put too much pressure on the boat laden with heavy cargo. *Nepenthe* also needed a new engine. The old gasoline-fueled Atomic 4 was replaced by a new more fuel-efficient Perkins diesel. Also diesel was not as flammable as gasoline and would be much safer to store in barrels on deck during the long voyage.

During this time period skiing had taken a back seat to smuggling and I missed it terribly. So, while *Nepenthe* was being refitted in San Diego I took the opportunity to take a couple of weeks and go skiing in Aspen. I took Joe and Papi with me as the dog seemed to enjoy the snow as much as we did. He was now a fully grown, beautiful perfectly trained, nearly 100-pound Golden Retriever. We all were able to stay in the old Victorian miner's cabin up on Mill Street. We had a great time with weather and snow conditions perfect, but sadly it ended all too soon as we had to get back to San Diego, if nothing else to keep an eye on Killian and keep him out of trouble.

Papi and me in Aspen in early 1974, while *Nepenthe* was being refitted in San Diego.

The conversion took two months,, after which Killian and I along with Joe, Willie and Phil, on his first ocean sailing experience, took the boat on a shakedown cruise north, up the California Coast to the Bay Area. *Nepenthe* handled perfectly, rounding Point Conception, a particularly nasty spot located north of Santa Barbara, in forty knots of wind. She did not heel nearly as much as when she was sloop rigged and passed the test with flying colors. Phil, however, did not. His only color was green. He was seasick, puking over the side every few minutes and groaning miserably from the short choppy seas, the pounding of the waves and the heeling of the boat as she beat northward. Killian finally relented and we pulled into Morro Bay and let the poor guy off. He rented a car and drove the rest of the way home.

Nepenthe arrived at Richmond Yacht Club, Killian's home club located in Point Richmond. We stayed at the guest dock while arrangements were made for other modifications required to transform *Nepenthe* into an ocean cruiser. At nearby Richmond Boat Works, an Avon life raft canister was mounted to the deck, aft of the mainmast. The large viewing windows in the main salon were refitted on the outside with Lexan storm windows to protect the glass windows if a wave hit them. All the halyards were replaced and new lines and sheets were strung with Samson braided rope, the strongest available. A new dodger was fabricated, resembling a Porsche Speedster convertible top with a Lexan window in front and supported by strong 3/4-inch stainless tubing.

The boat was then hauled out and the bottom sanded and repainted with a coat of copper-based anti-fouling paint to slow down the growth of barnacles which were more prevalent in the warm tropical waters where we were headed. In addition, we raised the water line, painting the blue striped boot top six inches higher, so that when the boat was fully loaded it would not appear to be sitting low in the water.

A rather comical incident, from my perspective, happened in Richmond one day as I was driving Dave from his house to the boat. Killian was virtually a chain smoker and had to be constantly reminded, by me, not to smoke down below on the boat, or indoors, or in the car or upwind of where I was sitting, ever! I had just picked him up in my Mercedes and he immediately put a cigarette in his mouth and started to light it.

"Not in my car, you're not doing that." I commanded. "Don't you dare light up in here!"

"I'll just hang it out the window. You'll never know it's there," Killian responded.

"Ain't gonna happen. No way!" I answered. With that, as I rolled to a stop at a red light on Richmond's Cutting Boulevard, in a very undesirable section of town, Killian bolted out of the car, lit his cigarette and started walking. I simply left him and drove off. He arrived at the boat half an hour later, madder than a wet hen. I simply shrugged it off, saying, "I meant what I said about smoking in my car." He never did it again!

The boat was then moved to a small private boat harbor located on Richmond's Cutting Boulevard, a short distance from Point Richmond where 'unique' and 'special' work could be preformed on *Nepenthe* in a mellow and private setting. Pat Suraghoomkol had come over from Thailand to work his ingenious magic of modifying existing spaces in the boat so the load could be completely hidden in case we had to stop or were boarded on the long voyage home. Pat, with my assistance, made the sail lockers smaller, using the spaces underneath for stashes. We redid the forepeak and chain locker in a similar manner. New cushions and covers were cut by a sail maker to make the new smaller spaces look normal in size. It was a masterpiece of illusion. The port quarter-berth was virtually eliminated and converted into a sitting area hiding a particularly large stash space capable of concealing at least a couple of hundred pounds or more.

The idea was, after the weed had been loaded into the specially constructed stashes, I would then seal these spaces with pre-cut, pre-fitted, painted pieces of wood. Screws, silicone sealant and a fresh coat of paint would then completely fasten, seal off and camouflage the stashes. We calculated a thousand kilos, also known as a long ton (twenty-two hundred pounds) of potent Thai stick could be loaded and completely hidden from sight. At a wholesale price of $1,650 per pound, the value of the load would amount to over three and a half million dollars.

Slowly and with great patience, Pat and I fashioned the hidden compartments. It proved to be much more tedious and difficult than his previous work on trailers, as the hull of the boat contained many double-curved sides and irregular spaces. By the end of June 1974, we were for all intents and purposes ready to set sail and anxious to leave in order to get across the Pacific in time for a late fall loading in Thailand. The final touches could be made in Hawaii, and the run to the Islands would be a good test for *Nepenthe* and her crew.

Chapter 19

Relieved From Watch

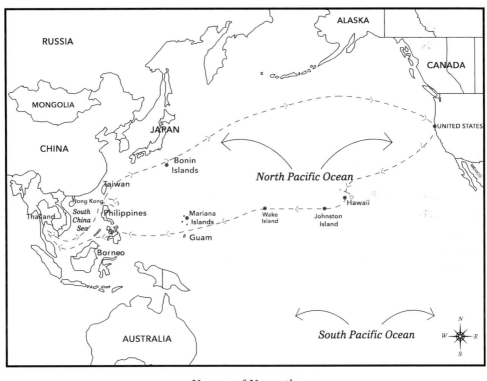

—————— Voyage of Nepenthe ——————

July 1974 - March 1975

July 1974

Pat and Phil left for Thailand each carrying one hundred and fifty thousand dollars in their cowboy boots and tucked in between pages of business magazines in their briefcases. Copies of *Forbes*, *The Economist*, and *Business Weekly* and various corporate prospectus brochures were stacked neatly with only the binding visible in the inner folds and pockets of their high-end leather-covered briefcases. In every couple of pages one hundred dollar bills, Franklins, were laid side-to-side, four to a page. In all the magazines and brochures, they were able to comfortably conceal at least $80,000 amid miscellaneous paperwork, business folders and magazines in each of their brief cases alone. The rest of the money was stuffed into cowboy boots and worn in money belts around their waists. They looked like a couple of Pacific Rim businessmen who frequently traveled to and from the Orient. Businessmen aroused no suspicion at Customs and Immigration either in San Francisco, Hong Kong or when they finally deplaned the next afternoon in Bangkok. The money they had brought would be enough to score the twenty-two hundred pound load of prime Thai stick marijuana and transport it from one end of Thailand to the other, hire a local crew to repair the farm buildings, then package, safely store the weed and finally load the boat. The money would also be used to acquire any equipment, tools, or vehicles and for construction and general repairs to the Chanthaburi property, or whatever else was needed to facilitate the overall operation.

My father used to tell me, 'you always need extra money in business for G-O-K, God Only Knows'. Again he was right. Funny how it is; some of his profound sayings took a long time to 'get through my thick skull', as he use to call it, but it all made sense to me now.

They also needed to lease a beachfront 'safe house' in Pattaya where the load could be held and stored for a day or two prior to *Nepenthe*'s expected arrival and loading. It could then be carried from the house across about ten or fifteen yards of the beach to a waiting fishing boat. Since the beach sloped to water's edge, then dropped off quickly at the shoreline, fishing boats normally could be seen 'beached' with their bows in the sand and the stern floating. When departing, they would simply put it into reverse and back off the beach. Once aboard the fishing boat with the load, the weed would be delivered to *Nepenthe* anchored in a protected cove on the Island of Ko Lan about five miles west in the Gulf of Siam.

After initiating everything in Thailand, Pat and Phil would then fly back to Honolulu and meet *Nepenthe*. If more money was needed, Phil could fly back to California and retrieve whatever was needed from the funds buried beneath Adobe House. Pat was to be on hand to put the finishing touches on the stash compartments. There was plenty of time to get everything organized on the Thai end because the load could not be procured until the end of October or the beginning of November when the first cutting would be ready for harvest. All time parameters were structured so there would be a minimum of pressure on the Thai crew and enough leeway so, depending on the winds and the weather, *Nepenthe* could make it to the Far East with a month or two to spare.

Nepenthe's four crew members, Killian, myself, Willie and Joe had readied ourselves, both mentally and physically, for the prospective four to six months at sea as best we could. The boat was ready to go. All the supplies had been bought and stowed below. Willie's current girlfriend, Melinda Southwick, had agreed to look after Sunshine and Papi, both of our golden retrievers, mother and son. I made a special point to pack my lucky blue shirt into my duffel.

A large supply of cassette tapes were prepared and recorded. The dubbing took nearly two months with Phil, Joe and me making tapes in every spare moment from my extensive record collection. Dubbing sessions would invariably go late into the night, in a cloud of marijuana smoke, trying to get the right music to everyone's taste and to be able to set the mood for any eventuality which might occur at sea. Everything from Bach and Beethoven to the Rolling Stones, Led Zeppelin, the Who, the Beatles and the Grateful Dead, along with country songs from Willie Nelson, Hank Williams and Tanya Tucker were taped, catalogued and boxed in plastic waterproof containers. Over two hundred tapes were available.

Since both Willie and I were licorice fanatics, we contacted The American Licorice Company in the East Bay to see if they would be interested in sponsoring us or at least supplying the boat with an endless supply. They declined sponsorship, but we at least stocked up directly from the factory.

Pat and I had installed an elaborate stereo sound system with miniature Bose speakers both in and outside of the main cabin with external jacks for removable speakers in the cockpit. Much to Killian's consternation, we also installed a special headphone jack on deck so the helmsman could have his music on during night watch without disturbing any of the other crewmen, who were most likely asleep. Killian particularly frowned on this because he felt the helmsman should be alert, with all his senses attuned in case anything went wrong. He didn't relish the thought of the helmsman at two o'clock in the morning, stoned to the gills, listening to Led Zeppelin on the headphones with the spinnaker flying under hazardous squall conditions. His objection centered around a vision he told me he had one night, one of the few he actually remembered.

"I just can't get the mental image out of my mind of Willie, alone at the helm late at night on a downwind run with the sails wing-and-wing, stoned out of his mind with yet another doobie in his hand, the headphones on and him singing aloud and way out of tune to the Led Zepplin classic, *Stairway to Heaven*:[1]

> 'There's a lady who's sure all that glitters is gold
> And she's buying a stairway to heaven...'

"All of a sudden the wind shifts from dead aft to ninety degrees off the port beam and Willie's too stoned to notice or prepare. The wind gets behind the main and we do a flying jibe, breaking the mast. Then a rogue wave hits dead astern and we pitch pole, ass over teakettle and sink. All is lost. And that's why I'm paranoid about putting the headphone jack in the cockpit. You guys need to pay attention all the time when you're on watch." This philosophy was also, by the way, the reason Killian wouldn't allow me to install an autopilot or self-steering device on *Nepenthe*. He said: "One hundred percent attention, one hundred percent of the time."

I replied: "Sorry, we'll just have to be careful, but I'm not going to be up there at night and not have at least background music. It doesn't have to play full blast. We're all college graduates and I think, or at least hope, we can be taught something." Although Willie seemed to know everything; in fact, I'd always say, jokingly, but with some truth

---

1 Referenced Songs & Music, Item 6, Page 530.

to it: "He knows so much about so little, he knows everything about nothing!"

"We'll try to educate everyone on the safe use of the headphones. You can be the teacher on that one as well as everything else! Don't worry," I said. "It was only a dream."

All good-byes were said and on July 7, 1974, *Nepenthe* departed Richmond, sailing beneath the Golden Gate Bridge on an afternoon ebb tide. We cleared the Farallon Islands with me at the tiller and Killian at the chart table plotting our course.

"Bring her to 225 degrees when you pass the southern tip of the Farallones. We'll stay on that course until we hit the Northeast trades. It should be no more than four or five days," Killian boomed.

"Jesus Christ, Dave, I know you're excited to finally get this show on the road, but I'm right here, only five feet away," I responded. "You don't have to yell!"

"Sorry, Rick. You ought to know me well enough by now to know I unconsciously raise my voice when I'm at sea to make sure I'm heard. I'll try and tone it down."

The first days at sea were overcast, cold, dreary and rough, with all of us either down below or huddled beneath the canvas dodger wearing foul gear and ducking spray. Things down below in the main cabin were wet and damp and drips of water from ceiling condensation or leaks were constantly a problem. Killian said: "The ocean's job is trying to get in the boat, and your job is trying to keep the ocean out. But the ocean always wins!"

Killian was always very polite with his demands, that is, when not giving a direct order. He always said please and thank you. His usual demand, repeated almost constantly, was for paper towels to stop the ceiling drips. "Paper towel, please. Thank you." Five minutes later, "Paper towel, please. Thank you." And on and on and on, until I could hear it subconsciously, even when I was sleeping.

The atmosphere was relaxed with everybody in high spirits, grooving to music as *Nepenthe* hauled offshore at seven to eight knots. We had brought plenty of pot to smoke and Joe had a few ounces of cocaine sealed airtight in plastic bags to protect it from the dampness. Unfortunately Willie was seasick from the moment *Nepenthe* rolled over the southernmost end of the Potato Patch shoals, a one-mile-square rough section of water, located just west of the Golden Gate Bridge and Marin Headlands. He had been throwing up and turning every imaginable shade of green. At first he threw up solids, until finally there was only gut wrenching dry heaves. Marijuana seemed to calm his nausea.

Miraculously on the fifth day Willie's seasickness disappeared, and as Killian predicted we hit the Northeast trades. The short, steep coastal waves were replaced by long rolling ocean swells as *Nepenthe* charged beyond the continental shelf. The sheets were eased out and *Nepenthe* cracked off from a close reach to a broad reach with the wind swinging aft from the bow to the starboard beam at a steady fifteen to eighteen knots. The course was adjusted to 240 degrees. The sun came out and the foul weather gear was stowed and replaced by shorts and T-shirts.

After a week or so at sea, I began to understand the enormity of our undertaking. This was not the same as the previous Mexican trips, where land was just over the horizon. We were now in open ocean and its vastness was overwhelming. If anything happened out here, we were on our own. Help, if we ever needed it, could be days away or never.

My mindset was now geared to self-sufficiency. If something broke at sea we had to fix it ourselves. Killian had sailed the Transpac several times and had counseled and helped me provision the boat. We had no shortage of food and other supplies, especially numerous rolls of gray tape. Dave said: "the world is held together with gray tape." It looked like we'd never run out.

I had accumulated an adequate spare parts kit including numerous stainless steel nuts and bolts of various sizes, spare fittings and shackles, as well as hoses, gaskets, belts, clamps and other spare engine parts which I stored in watertight plastic containers. I also had a complete mechanics engine manual, so as not to repeat the same fiasco as happened on *Sirius II*. Additionally, I procured an emergency medical kit containing everything from Army field surgery supplies to bandages and various prescription drugs including morphine syrettes, which hopefully would only be used in case of emergency.

We were indeed stepping off the edge into the unknown. All of us, except Killian, were novices at blue water sailing and had some of the same feelings of apprehension and trepidation as most likely were experienced by astronauts being shot into space for the first time.

At five o'clock every afternoon, Killian announced 'Happy Hour' and poured himself a large water goblet of gin over ice. The rest of us drank Corona beer and smoked joints.

On the twelfth day, Killian was perched atop a stool at the chart table poring over a nautical chart of the Pacific Ocean with dividers and parallel rulers spread out in front of him on the chart. He scratched his head, staring intently as he puzzled as to *Nepenthe*'s exact position.

"You mean to tell me, you don't know where we are?" I asked, stunned.

"I said, I have an idea, but I don't know exactly. Remember most of my experience has been coastal piloting. On Transpac we had a professional navigator. Plus I'm not up on all that electronic gear," Killian said gesturing toward the LORAN; a radio navigation system receiver developed by the Navy in WWII. The LORAN would receive signals sent from land or sea based numerically indicated beacons, whose beacon numbers were drawn on a special LORAN nautical chart. If one could receive signals from three different stations, triangulation could be drawn on the chart and at the intersecting point would be your location.

"Are you kidding me?" I snapped. "Well, an idea of where we are just won't cut it, Killian. I figure roughly, we should be in Hawaii about now. Where the hell are we? You say you're not sure, well… Guess what? You're no longer navigator."

"Who's gonna navigate then?" asked Joe, in the process of sticking his nose deep into a pint-sized Ziplock bag of cocaine.

"I will," I said nonchalantly.

"Oh great!" chortled Willie sarcastically from his position on the tiller. "The blind leading the blind!"

I got out the radio directional finder, the RDF, a radio with a directional antenna mounted atop it which could be rotated in a 360° circle and had an arrow which could be pointed to the broadcast source of an AM, FM or short wave radio station it was receiving. A meter on the front showed exactly where the signal was strongest. I was then able to triangulate our exact position from radio station broadcasts I was able to pick up coming from AM stations: one from Honolulu, one from Hilo on the Island of Hawaii and one from Lihue on the Island of Kauai. I then plotted our position and confirmed it on the LORAN. We had actually passed Honolulu, which I determined to be some two hundred miles to the southeast and we were on a course which would have missed the Islands completely. Next stop China!

This was not just some piloting error, but a gross navigational miscalculation on Killian's part. I was determined to not let something like this happen again, if I could help it. An error like this could have drastic consequences, especially if we were close to land. Luckily this time we were in open ocean.

For days we had been sailing a course of 240°, west southwest on a beam reach in the northeast trade winds, blowing a steady 10 to 15 knots. From our current position the Hawaiian Islands were two hundred miles in an east southeast direction and almost dead downwind.

Willie was driving the boat. "Hang a hard left immediately. Bring her to 160 degrees, Professor," I ordered from my seat at the chart table.

"Jawohl, Herr Navigator," Willie replied. This mockingly pseudo-intellectual moniker stuck and from that moment on Willie was known as 'The Professor'.

"Hold on, Professor!" Killian barked. "Let's get the chute up. This is the perfect time for you guys to learn how to sail downwind with a spinnaker."

Nepenthe pictured here running with the wind, is proudly flying her massive blue and white spinnaker with a full racing crew on a cloudless SoCal day. Photo, taken sometime after we'd sold her in 1977, was the only picture I could find of her under sail.

Killian and Joe scurried up on the foredeck, dropped the jib and set the spinnaker. The mainsail was sheeted out all the way over the port rail. As the chute filled, I looked up from the chart table to see a huge grin appear on Willie's face, which was immediately replaced by intensity, as he began to chew on his tongue, realizing his total concentration was required at that moment. He tossed the joint he'd been smoking over the side as he became transfixed on the sail's newly set configuration in front of him. It was the first time we'd used it and the sail was brand new. It was pure white with a giant blue star stitched in the center and it billowed out in front of us.

"At this point of sail, Professor, you can't fuck up," Killian instructed. "You only have about ten degrees on either side of the wind to play with. Anything more than that and the chute will start to collapse. And, whatever you do, don't let the wind get behind the mainsail or you'll do a flying jibe and break the mast. Keep the spinnaker full at all times and pay close attention to where the wind is. And watch the water, for wind shifts. That's an order."

Like a racehorse taking a bit in its teeth, *Nepenthe*'s spinnaker filled with a large 'pop', capturing the 15 knot tailwind as if she was instantly accelerating from a canter into a full blown gallop as she literally flew headlong downwind. The sea was calm but characterized by long gentle six-foot-high ocean swells, giving us an opportunity to actually surf *Nepenthe* for the first time. We were hauling-ass on what was like a mini-roller coaster ride in slow motion. The exhilaration was breathtaking as the knot meter dial moved past the ten knot mark. We were literally dancing up and down the ocean rollers. We all took turns at the helm, each totally exhausted following our intense two hour watches.

Twenty four hours later, on a beautiful cloudless morning, *Nepenthe*, with the chute up and the steady tropical breeze at her back, flew through the 26 mile wide Molokai Channel that separated the island of Molokai from the island of Oahu. She then screamed past Diamond Head peak, the beachfront hotels of Waikiki and the high-rise buildings of downtown Honolulu. We were now on an inbound run headed directly for the breakwater and channel markers leading to the Ala Wai Harbor and our destination at the Ala Wai Yacht Club.

"All right, ladies," Killian roared in a particularly good mood. "Let's drop the chute, and slow this baby down before we ram the dock." Turning to me he said: "By the way, you did a fine job getting us here. I guess you will be the navigator from now on."

"I already told you that yesterday. Where the hell have you been?" I said lightheartedly. My tanned face was beaming.

"Thanks for the vote of confidence anyway, Dave," I said slapping the big man on the back.

Killian had the Ala Wai Yacht Club wired from previous Transpac races and in spite of his dubious reputation as a notorious drunk, *Nepenthe* was given a berth at the guest dock.

Phil and Pat flew into Honolulu from Bangkok the next day. Pat had already set the Thai part of the operation rolling. He'd made contact with a local marijuana dealer in Pattaya named Suay, who would be able to score the load. On Pat's grandfather's farm a crew was already at work cutting back the jungle from the buildings and rehabbing them, clearing the overgrown entrance road, and upgrading the electrical service. It was there the load would be received, packaged, securely stored and ready to go. They had also rented a private beach house near Pattaya, where they could hang out and relax and from where the loading operation would be staged.

It didn't take long for both Willie and Dave to live up to their reputations once we settled in at the dock. Willie found a new girlfriend and Killian found a long lost bar-stool at the outdoor bar at the Ala Wai Yacht Club. In the three weeks or so that we were in Honolulu, we rarely saw Willie, who'd checked into a nearby hotel where he proceeded to make up for lost time with his new lady friend.

I couldn't let Killian roam around unchaperoned, therefore he became a perma-nent fixture at the outdoor tropical bar overlooking the guest dock. I had to re-think my 'Killian never gets off the boat' policy and suggested he go to the bar at the yacht club, always in plain sight, so as I explained to him, "we could keep an eye on each other." He could be found almost all the time planted on his barstool perch like King Tut overlooking his domain, *Nepenthe*, while Pat and I, his minions, were working on board putting the finishing touches on the stashes. In case we had to rescue him if a situation surrounding him devolved into chaos, at least I was right there to drag him back to the boat if necessary, rather than the usual scenario of finding him slumped on some unknown dock having gotten the shit kicked out of him again. Joe and Phil ran around gathering parts.

Phil had arranged to have some additional required items shipped to him in Hawaii from the Bay Area. He delivered to the boat a 12-gauge pump-action police 'riot-style' shotgun, an M-2 military-sniper style carbine and a 'Dirty Harry'-like .44-caliber revolver, with plenty of ammunition for each weapon. These items were already broken down, cleaned, greased thoroughly and stowed in airtight plastic bags which Pat took aboard and fashioned an 'invisible-but-in-plain-sight' stash below the dinette.

Everything was ready and new stores had been purchased including fresh vegeta-bles, tropical fruit, more beer, more ice—Killian already had plenty of gin so we didn't need any more… yet—beef jerky, and a case of Zig-Zag Wheat Straw rolling papers with the age old iconic image of the French Zouave soldier emblazoned on the orange packets. Pat cleaned up the final loose ends and finished his work and on August 15, we said our good-byes, raised the mainsail and departed on the morning tide. We motored out of the Ala Wai over a mirror flat sea, southwest on a compass course of 240°. The prevailing northeast trades were unusually light, forcing us to power rather than be stuck for who knows how long in these doldrum-like conditions.

During the day, we trailed a fishing line astern. Willie of course, Mr. Fisherman (what else is new?), prepared the line with a bright colored 'hoochie' and 'flasher' lure and threw it overboard, tying it off to a piece of shock cord with a little bell attached to it, which was attached to a stanchion near where the helmsman sat. When the fish hit the line the shock cord would stretch out, the little bell would ring like 'Jingle Bells' and we'd pull in bonito or dorado, called mahimahi in Hawaii. After our first successful catch, attempting to get Willie to admit that this fishing procedure was not his original idea was like trying to pull teeth out of a chicken.

"Told you we'd catch 'em, Rick. You just have to think like a fish. I knew you'd like my idea," Willie bragged to me while at the helm and me pulling in the fish.

"Right Professor! And you invented this based on all your years of experience deep sea fishing off sailboats," I sarcastically responded.

Killian had an unusual method of filleting fish for sashimi, sushi, or broiled fish dinners. The fish would be hauled up on deck and Killian would take a large razor-sharp fish knife and surgically remove one large filet from either side of the fish's backbone while it was still alive, then would casually toss the fish overboard. The entire process took less than a minute and the fish would actually swim away appearing to be unaware that the main part of its body was gone.

Sailing south of Hawaii, we seemed to be entering an area of very little wind known as The Doldrums. The weather was hot, the ocean was flat, the skies were cloudless and blue and the scorching sun baked our bodies to a golden tan. On deck we were sweating like pigs when I came up with the bright idea to go for a swim. I tied about a thirty-foot length of rope to the stern and threw it over the side so that it trailed behind the boat. We then slowed down to about three or four knots and I walked up to the bow pulpit and dove overboard. Just as the boat passed me amidships, I glanced up at Joe who was standing up on deck, with a big grin on his face and yelling something to me, which at first I couldn't understand. I lifted my head up to hear him yelling, "Boom, boom! Boom, boom! Boom, boom!" He was laughing and mimicking the foreboding music from the movie *Jaws*.[2]

At that point, I just couldn't get out of the water fast enough. All that flashed through my mind was the image portrayed in an article I had recently read about of the sinking of the U.S.S. *Indianapolis* in the Pacific in World War II and her 900 surviving crew members in the water who were attacked by sharks. She was sunk in 1945 by a Japanese submarine and was the greatest single loss of life in U.S. Naval history. I literally ran through the water to get to the stern rope and hauled myself back aboard in what seemed like merely an instant.

Standing on *Nepenthe*'s stern, dripping wet, I turned to Joe. "Very funny, Asshole. You scared the shit outta me," I cried.

"That'll teach you not to enter the food chain, you idiot," Joe replied, laughing in near hysterics.

The water looked so inviting on such a hot and sultry day, however, it was the first and last time I ever pulled a move like that. Upon reflection, Joe was right. It was amazing how small, stupid and insignificant I felt in that vast ocean, exposed to whatever might have been lurking just below the surface. I could have been devoured in the blink of an eye!

Joe was truly the joker among us and many times he would come up with insightful but hilarious anecdotes to explain the obvious. We called it 'the world according to Joe'. For example in explaining where experience was necessary to do something technical, Joe would say, "You have to learn to crawl before you can fly a Lear jet." When

---

2 Referenced Television & Movies, Item 3, Page 533.

pontificating about his cocaine habit and the reason that his baggie of coke was always empty, he would say, "Take-a-___, sniff-a-___. You fill in the blanks and they're both the same."

One time I was driving my two-wheel-drive truck into soft, wet grass in my front yard when I sank up to the frame and my wheels were spinning hopelessly in the wet slush and muck. I asked Joe if I might be able to rock it back-and-forth by alternately shifting from reverse into drive. Joe replied, "it's stuck." I continued to pursue my theory upon which Joe said, "Rick, you moron, I don't think you get it. Do you really understand the meaning of the word 'stuck'?" Joe was one of those people who always had to keep moving. He could never sit still and when I questioned him about it, his reply was "I'll sleep when I'm dead." This was 'the world according to Joe' and he could always be counted on for such minor bits of insanity-laced truths.

A typical shot of Joe at the helm of *Nepenthe* in 1974 during our ocean crossing.

Three days under power made refueling the diesel tank a priority. Burning nearly a gallon per hour put a pretty big dent in our total fuel supply of a 65-gallon fuel tank, plus the two blue plastic 55-gallon drums lashed on deck at the stern above the lazarette. I consulted the chart as to where we might stop and pick up more fuel. Johnston Island, seven hundred miles southwest of Honolulu, was only a couple of days' sail from our present position.

Two days later a tiny speck of land appeared on the western horizon. The morning was crystal clear, the temperature in the high 80s to low 90s, the ocean swells a rich deep blue color and the wind virtually nonexistent. As *Nepenthe* closed in on the small atoll with Dave asleep coming off the graveyard shift and Joe on the helm, me at the chart table, Willie surveyed the shore with my powerful 10 x 70 Nikon binoculars.

"Look at all those barrels stacked up on the beach," he said handing the binoculars to Joe.

"Those are fifty-five gallon drums. There are thousands of 'em stacked three high.

Damn! Here, Dave get up here and take a look," Joe exclaimed.

Killian appeared and stuck his tan balding head up at the top of the companionway. "This island is a U.S. military installation. There's a truck which appears to be following us along the beach. There are people in the back of the truck who seem to be checking us out through binoculars. I wouldn't be surprised if those barrels weren't filled with some kind of poisonous gas or napalm or something. When I was in the Coast Guard and stationed on Kwajalein Atoll in the Marshall Islands out in the western Pacific, we used to store nerve gas just like that. It was all very hush-hush. Now there are two more trucks following the lead one," Killian observed.

Nepenthe rounded the tip of the island and came into the harbor. Fifteen Marines were standing on the dock, each with an M-16 automatic rifle slung over his shoulder. A captain with twin silver bars on the epaulettes of his white shirt and stitched on his baseball cap stood in front of his men as *Nepenthe* slowly approached the dock.

"This is a United States Government installation and you are trespassing. State your business," the captain shouted as *Nepenthe* was twenty yards from the dock.

"We are a U.S. documented yacht, the *Nepenthe* out of San Francisco," Killian boomed across the ten feet of water now separating the boat from the dock. Killian had changed from being bare foot, bare chested and wrapped in a blue Hawaiian lava lava with a little white palm tree pattern to a white short sleeve dress shirt with *Nepenthe* printed in blue lettering over the breast pocket, white duck trousers and off-white Sperry Top-sider lace up deck shoes. The silly looking white yachting hat with scrambled eggs on the black brim covered his thinning blonde hair. His dark glasses with the attached metal nose piece hung from a string around his neck and lay dangling on his chest. He had a cigarette in hand. "We left Honolulu five days ago and the winds were so light, if we could find any, so we had to use our engine to get anywhere. We're low on diesel fuel. Any chance of buying 75 gallons?"

"This installation is off limits to civilians, gentlemen, but I think we can accommodate you this time," the officer said. "Tie your vessel up here."

He said something to two Marines who proceeded to tie off the dock lines which Joe and Willie, standing on the bow and stern, had thrown over.

"Welcome aboard, Captain. I'm Dave Killian, skipper of this vessel, and this is my crew. We're on our way to Australia to campaign my boat in the Southern Ocean Racing Series."

"I'm Captain Ben Peterson, United States Marine Corps," the officer said extending his hand to Killian, as he stepped onto the deck. "I'll see to it you get your fuel. You and your crew will not venture any farther on this base than this guest dock. Understand?"

"Aye, aye, sir. I understand," Killian said, snapping a smart military salute. Killian ducked below and came back up with two bottles of wine in his hand. "Here Captain, I'd like you to accept these bottles of California Cabernet for your hospitality.

The mood lightened considerably as the officer took the wine.

"This is against regulations, but I appreciate it. We'll fill you up and you can be on your way," the Marine officer said. "Hey, Smith," the captain yelled. "Bring the fuel hose over here, on the double!"

"Much obliged," Killian replied.

"What are all those barrels stacked up on the beach, Captain?" I asked.

"That's classified. But…" he let the word hang for a moment, "let's just say, there's some nasty shit in 'em used in warfare and, believe me, you don't even want to know."

"Wow," I said. "Mind if we come ashore and stretch our legs?"

"Go ahead. Just stay right here by the dock."

Willie grabbed the football from the forward hanging locker and the two of us tossed it back and forth next to the dock.

"Go long," Willie said arcing a thirty yard spiral in the air to me running after it.

"Hey you two. I said, no further than the end of the dock," the captain warned.

"Oops. OK. Sorry, that one got away," Willie apologized.

Joe undid the fuel cap and was handed the fuel nozzle from the Marine on the dock. He proceeded to fill both blue deck tanks.

"How much do we owe you?" Killian asked when the fueling was complete.

"Aw, forget it. It's on the house. Compliments of the United States Government. Hey, I appreciate the wine. Now you boys best be on your way. Have a nice trip." The captain and his squad remained on the dock until *Nepenthe* had departed and had motored out beyond the harbor.

The trade winds finally came alive and blew from astern at twelve knots. Killian ordered the spinnaker raised and at my direction, the course was set to 280° toward Wake Island, the next landfall some eight hundred miles distant.

It seemed like my knowledge of sailing and my sailing ability grew with each day spent at sea. I studied Dave and watched him like a hawk, not only to keep him in check and on the straight and narrow, but to try and soak up all the subtleties and nuances of sailing he'd accumulated over the past 30 years.

I picked up on the finer points of yachting such as being able to determine the precise direction from which the wind is blowing. Killian said, "without the aid of any instruments, if you look directly into the wind and can feel it blowing evenly over both ears, that's where the wind is coming from."

It sounds so simple and logical, but it is probably one of the most important basic concepts of sailing. A miscalculation of wind speed or direction can have disastrous consequences at sea.

"Don't rely on your instruments alone," Killian lectured. "Use all your senses as well. Watch the water and you'll see wind shifts coming before they actually hit you. It'll give you a chance to adjust or change sail before you get blindsided by an unexpected wind shift or approaching squall."

Of course all of this was great advice in the daytime when you could see what was going on. At night it was another story.

It was common in tropical waters to see squalls in the distance. They appeared as isolated tall cumulus thunderheads towering on the horizon on an otherwise cloudless, hot sunny day. It always seemed, no matter where a squall appeared, it would always be on top of you within a half hour or so… and you'd better be ready for it. Again, not a problem in daylight. If something weird was going to happen, it almost always happened at night. A dramatic wind shift or squall would be on top of you with little or no advance warning because it was dark and you couldn't see it coming. One minute you'd be sailing along comfortably and the next minute all hell would break loose. It would be pouring rain and wind gusting to 30 knots or more, mid-squall. Then, just as fast, it'd be all calm again.

Out there, the weather was predictably unpredictable. Killian was right about always paying attention 100% of the time, but I still needed my music when on watch, at least in the background regardless of his admonition and his foreboding dream.

One of Killian's favorite hobbies was cooking. He fancied himself a gourmet cook, claiming he'd cooked 'all over the world'; in reality it was only during his stint in the Coast Guard on Kwajalein Atoll, the remote Pacific Island chain inhabited only by other sailors and natives, and on sailboat races cooking for hungry yachtsmen, who really didn't care what they ate. Anyway, while there were still fresh eggs, he whipped up omelets for breakfast and on one occasion a spectacular nautical rendition of Eggs Benedict. He stood before the hot gimbaled stove dressed in his other red Tahitian lava-lava with drops of sweat rolling down his gorilla-like fat hairy belly. Droplets from his forehead splashed into the skillet, as he fastidiously poached or boiled fish and con-cocted his special sauces. Gourmet cook... rather questionable.

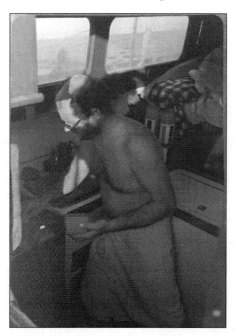

Dave Killian cooking aboard *Nepenthe* during our ocean crossing in 1973.

The rest of us never let on how much we enjoyed his cooking; instead we had a particular way of getting the 'culinary master's' goat. Poor Dave. We just tortured him.

"Say Dave, would you please pass the Tabasco sauce?" Willie said with a straight face. "This broiled mahimahi seems a little flat."

Joe was shaking what seemed like half a tin of pepper over his portion and I madly rummaged through the condiment shelf looking for the salsa.

Killian exploded. "Goddammit!" I spent a good hour preparing that fish and teriyaki sauce and you fucking peasants are ruining it! You might as well spread shit on the fish!"

"Well, if I used enough Tabasco, I could even eat that!" Willie said, taking another mouthful of fish then shaking out more drops of the spicy hot sauce.

* * *

For six days the wind held, and *Nepenthe* made good time running steadily downhill with the Northeast trades and her multi-colored spinnaker full. Killian took the opportunity to teach us the finer points of downwind yacht racing.

One morning Joe was knocked down to his knees on the foredeck, and sustained a nasty bump on his forehead and a bloody nose when he failed to pay close attention to the spinnaker pole during the critical moments of a spinnaker jibe. It was like his head was the baseball and the spinnaker pole was Hank Aaron's bat hitting a home run. Joe was lucky he didn't get knocked overboard or wasn't more seriously hurt. Things happen fast and as Killian reiterated over and over, "You have to pay attention one hundred percent of the time." No shit! All in the world according to Joe.

We stopped at Wake Island to top off *Nepenthe*'s water tank and to replenish our stock of beer, ice, fuel and gin. The military attitude was more relaxed than at Johnston Island and we were allowed to shop at the base PX, where Willie immediately started hustling one of the commissary employees. She was a rather mousy looking bespectacled brunette dressed in a camo outfit who seemed genuinely interested in the tall, smooth-talking yachtsman with the deep brown tan, blue eyes, dark brown shoulder length curls dressed casually in a yellow tank top, red swimming shorts and wearing a pair of well-worn tan leather Sperry Top-sider moccasins.

"Give it a rest, Willie! Ten more minutes of this and I'll have to turn a garden hose on you like a dog humping a bitch in heat," I said dragging him from the air-conditioned PX. "Why don't you consider this voyage as a sort of floating monastic retreat?"

"Oh, just leave me alone!" Willie said moodily. "I know I could have gotten into her pants by evening. If I don't get my rocks off soon, even Killian will probably start looking good to me!"

Nepenthe left Wake Island and continued running with the spinnaker flying both night and day. It was one of those miraculous times a sailor dreams of, running with the wind, chute up day and night and virtually flying through the warm tropical waters. For the man at the helm, though, the two-hour shift was physically and mentally exhausting. With a spinnaker flying and the wind blowing from astern, the helmsman has only about ten degrees of fluctuation on a course relative to the wind direction. Anything more in either direction and the chute will start to collapse or jibe. The tremendous pressure exerted from accidentally letting the wind get on the wrong side of the spinnaker is called an accidental or flying jibe and could break the mast.

On the seventh night out of Wake Island, following Killian's most prized culinary masterpiece, Beef Stroganoff with wine sauce, he basked in the glow of its exquisite presentation and rewarded himself by gulping continuous rounds of an after dinner

aperitif consisting of five parts rum to one part Rose's Lime Juice. We watched a spectacular sunset which crescendoed in an amazing pop of the green flash as the upper
limb of the sun sank into the ocean, amid a perfect crystal clear haze-free horizon.
Killian continued to pound down his 'aperitifs' as darkness fell.

At around midnight while Killian was on watch, Joe was awakened by the continuous deep popping sound of the spinnaker collapsing and filling. Boom! The mast and
spinnaker pole shook with every canvas explosion. Joe sleepily rose from his berth and
climbed topside for a look, where he found Killian slumped over the tiller, passed out.
Somehow, perhaps by instinct, Killian was apparently able to keep the boat from doing
a flying jibe, by unconsciously heading up into the wind and then falling back off just
before disaster struck, over and over again.

Boom! The spinnaker popped again and the rigging rattled as Joe stood in the companionway dumbfounded, taking in the potential catastrophic situation before him.

"What the fuck is going on here? Are you OK?" cried Joe trying to rouse Killian.

"Yesh, I'm jez fine, shank you. Now g'wan back to bed. Everyshing's jez fine up
here," slurred Killian.

"Like hell it is!" Joe said thoroughly steamed. "You're drunk as a skunk! You're putting all of our lives at risk. Get the fuck down below. I'm taking over. You are relieved
of watch!" Joe was so mad he was shaking.

Killian stumbled down the hatch and slumped behind the chart table and began
to log in at 12:17 AM. In barely legible handwriting he scrawled in the ship's log book,
'Relieved from watch. I'm sorry'. There were none of the other required notations in the
log book such as course, speed, wind direction or sea conditions. Killian then plunged
into his shortened bunk in the port quarter berth and passed out in the fetal position.

Twelve hours later, I called a crew meeting. While Killian slept in the hours preceding the meeting, the rest of us discussed what to do about his drinking. By noon,
Killian had sufficiently recovered by drinking two pots of strong black coffee with a
handful of aspirin washed down by a quart of canned pineapple juice. He had shaved
and taken a bucket bath on deck. Everybody was gathered in the cockpit. The atmosphere was charged with tension.

"I've reached a decision as owner of this boat," I began. "Dave, your drinking has
gone far enough. Last night you put this trip in jeopardy, not to mention our lives with
your out of control behavior. We've spent nearly half a million dollars so far on this
venture and I'm not willing to risk the boat, our lives or this opportunity due to your
drunkenness." I took a breath and continued, "I'm giving you a choice, Killian, right
here, five hundred miles from our nearest landfall, which is Guam. Either all the booze
goes over the side or you go over the side. There are no other choices. You have exactly
one minute to make a decision."

Joe, looking very intense, stood blocking the companionway hatch, the cords in
his neck tight and the muscles in his upper arms taut, ready for anything, including
throwing Killian overboard.

Killian let out a deep sigh. He slumped wearily, and rubbed his aching head with
both hands. "That's not much of a choice, Rick. I admit, it's not like me to be in the

condition I was in last night. I normally don't do that at sea. How about if I agree to only have one drink at 'Happy Hour'? I'll sign an agreement to that effect; in blood if that's what you want."

"The only alcohol you'll be consuming at 'Happy Hour' will be what you can take with you during your swim from here to Guam. Unfortunately that's not one of your options. I've collected all the alcohol in a box and, if you choose to stay here with us, you can do the honors. The beer is not included here and, again if you choose to stay, you will be entitled to one beer per day, because the beer belongs to the crew and I am not going to deprive everybody of beer because of your irresponsibility," I said.

Joe turned and stepped down the companionway ladder. Within seconds, he reappeared with a cardboard box containing a half dozen 1.5-liter bottles of Beefeater London Dry Gin and five 750-ml. bottles of Captain Morgan Deluxe Dark Rum.

"Let's have it Killian. No more wriggling around like a rat in a trap. What'll it be before the three of us make the decision for you?" I demanded with a hard-edged voice.

There was only the hiss of the boat gliding through the water, the clattering of the halyards against the mast and a creaking noise as fittings continued to chafe somewhere in the distance.

Killian reached down, picked up the cardboard box and heaved it over the stern railing. It landed right side up as the glass bottles clanked together. The box drifted away in the frothy wake, the glass sparkling in the afternoon sunlight. Without saying a word, he turned and went below and lay upon his bunk, thoroughly dejected. He buried his face in the pillow and softly began to cry.

We made a quick stop in Agana, Guam, for fresh fruit and vegetables, departing a few hours later for the Philippine Islands. Thirty years after a vicious World War II battle on Guam, its main harbor Agana was still littered with the rusted, half-sunken hulls of many ships which had fought there.

Both Willie and I were avid sports fans and we took great pleasure listening to football and baseball games which were broadcast over the Armed Forces Radio Network. We were able to pick it up on our world band shortwave radio, another item I had picked up on my Hong Kong shopping spree. We both eagerly awaited the upcoming Mohammed Ali–George Foreman Heavyweight Boxing Match from Kinshasa, Zaire—'The Rumble in the Jungle'. It would be broadcast in our time zone at two in the morning on the shortwave. Listening to a shortwave at sea can be a challenge as the frequencies fade in and out seemingly with each movement of the boat. For the fight broadcast we were able to pick up a station broadcast from Subic Bay in the Philippines.

We sat in the cockpit in the middle of the night intently listening to the fight— Willie driving and me holding the large bulky radio trying to keep it perfectly level so as not to lose the signal as the boat moved up and down the long sea swells. The fight, said to be 'the greatest boxing match ever' went on and on for well over an hour as Willie and I sat next to each other virtually in total darkness. With the radio antenna fully extended combined with the gentle rocking motion of the boat, it was a challenge to maintain a clear broadcast signal, keep the radio level and not poke Willie in the eye with the wildly swinging antenna. Ali won at the end of the eighth round.

The following night was Halloween. *Nepenthe* was pushing westward on an inbound course toward the Surigao Straits, the eastern passageway into the southern Philippines. The water was smooth as glass and mirror-like as we stealthily knifed through the phosphorescent Western Pacific in light air blowing eight to ten knots under a full moon. The huge brilliant orange-white moon rose over our stern as I calculated our exact position to be directly over the dark waters of the Philippine Trench. At nearly 35,000 feet below sea level, it is one of the deepest spots in the world. Out in the ocean, all water is not the same and here you could feel the vast depth as we sailed over what seemed like a bottomless black pit. Just black deep nothingness. It was something strange and different from any waters we had previously been in and we all noticed it.

Willie had decided this would be the perfect setting to 'kill two birds with one stone', as he put it; simultaneously celebrating his dog Sunshine's birthday and Halloween. The celebration would be in commemoration of his fifth annual 'Peaking Pumpkin Party', a yearly quasi-Halloween affair on the full moon which he had started while he was an undergraduate at Arizona State. The general theme of the party was to take LSD and celebrate while peaking under the full moon on the powerful hallucinogen. He had brought along a few hits of the famous 'orange sunshine' acid.

We both took the acid about eight o'clock in the evening, and by quarter to nine, the familiar bitter copper taste was in our mouths as the drug started taking effect. To me, it was as if every neural cell suddenly expanded, all synapses firing impulses two times faster than the speed of light. Joe and Killian appeared flat, two-dimensional clownish figures while Willie's body seemed to be glowing, discharging yellow sparks and purple lightening flashes like St. Elmo's fire. The sky above was a vast serene blackness filled with an infinite number of pulsating white hot diamonds.

Gravity seemed to be playing a strange trick on me. My body felt ridiculously heavy, as if it was ten thousand pounds. Unable to stand, I slowly sank to my hands and knees and began crawling forward toward the bow. The moon climbed higher in the black sky. The ghostly white orb was now the color of bleached bones.

With my arms and legs locked around the bowsprit, I looked down into the curling bow wave. Glowing green phosphorescent shapes darted past the boat leaving a vanishing day-glow trail in their wake as they disappeared into the inky deep. 'This can't be real,' I thought. 'It has to be the acid playing tricks with me.' I wondered what psychedelic unreal vision would be next, but the same image kept repeating itself before my unbelieving eyes. It was then I heard through the sound of the bow sloshing through the water what seemed like a million chirps coming to life beneath me. Dozens of porpoises were playing in the bow wave, their black shiny bodies arching out of the water in incandescent flashes. I leaned down as far as I could without falling in, put my mouth close to the rushing water and began to whistle as if I were whistling for my dog Papi. The chirping noise I was hearing was their squeaking replies to my presence. I looked down, less than one foot beneath me and gazed deep into one of the eyes of a porpoise who had rolled on his side and was looking directly at me. I reached down and stroked its shiny black skin. It just stayed right there as I gently stroked it and continued softly whistling to it. It was squeaking back to me. The edges of its mouth were turned up at the corners and it was smiling up at me and taking in the entire scene.

Willie had been sitting in the cockpit descending into a maelstrom of fear. Where I had been awe filled, connecting with the natural forces surrounding me, Willie had allowed his terror-struck mind to whirl him downward toward the darker primal reaches of his imagination. He was obsessing on what might lie far beneath the jet black waters of the Philippine Trench nearly seven miles below. An unspeakable slimy thing might come swimming up from the lightless depths and devour the boat and all the crew.

He didn't seem to notice Joe sitting next to him wearing headphones and steering the boat. It was only ten o'clock. Suddenly Willie noticed I was missing. He tried to stand, but became aware of a bone crushing weight forcing him to his knees. He, too, crawled forward on his hands and knees to where he saw me lying prone out on the bowsprit, one arm wrapped around the teak extrusion which the upper part of my body was lying on and the other arm extended down in the water. My hand was gone!

"Ahhh! God! No!" Willie shrieked. In his drug-ravaged mind the porpoise I was reaching out to and stroking was not a porpoise at all, but a Loch Ness sea monster who seemed to be on the verge of eating his best friend and had already taken off my hand.

"Rick! Rick! Get back or you'll be eaten by Ness!" Willie wailed. The porpoises had put him tottering on the edge of the abyss.

I turned, a quizzical look on my face. I sensed Willie was having a bad trip. From far away I could hear myself shouting to my friend, "Willie, they're porpoises, not sea monsters! They're our friends!"

Right then, the jib directly above us filled with a loud pop. Both Willie and I looked up to see the moon explode, crumbling into pieces of sparkling white bone which tumbled into the sea.

Now, with all luminescence gone, Willie's mind panicked. His senses went wild as he tipped over the edge. A rotten putrefying smell of decay at the back of his throat seemed to come from over the weather rail. Beyond all reason, with the drug flooding every cell, he looked up to see a giant scaly repulsive looking thing, three times the size of the fifty foot mast having the body of Godzilla and the laughing head of a jack-o-lantern lurching toward the boat.

"Oh, no! That's it. We're finished! Abandon ship!" Willie screamed.

"What's going on? What happened?" Killian shouted from the companionway hatch. He had been awakened by Willie's blood curdling cry.

"Willie's having a bum trip. Go on back to bed, Dave," I yelled from the bowsprit. I was starting to come down.

I inched backward from the bowsprit speaking reassuringly as we both slowly crawled aft toward the cockpit. Willie continued to rave as I tried my best to calm him down.

Only after opening up the medical kit and forcing twenty milligrams of Valium and a Seconal capsule down Willie's throat did the 'Peaking Pumpkin Party' begin to wane forty-five minutes later.

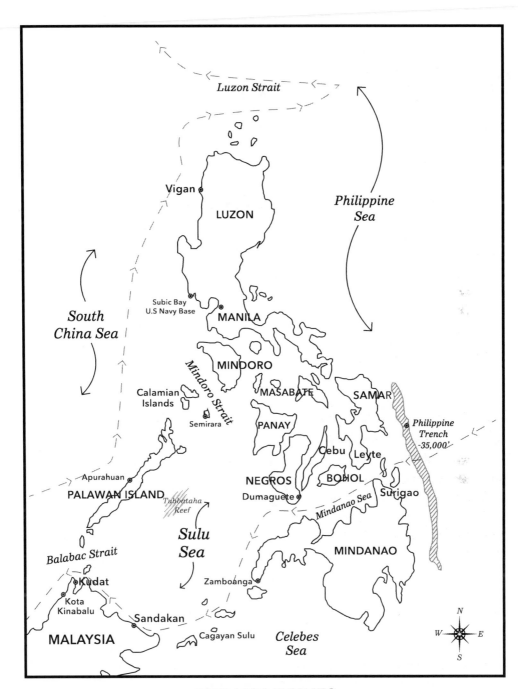

THE PHILIPPINES

Nepenthe's Track: November 1974

Chapter 20

90° To Zamboanga

Nepenthe passed through the Surigao Straits and into the Mindanao Sea. To the north lay the islands of Leyte, Bohol, Cebu, Sequijor and Negros. To the south was the largest of the southern Philippine Islands, Mindanao, known for its frequent political unrest, communist insurgency and pirates. Using the LORAN navigation system, I plotted our course and predicted every landfall with pinpoint accuracy. As a backup to the electronic navigation system, I had been teaching myself how to use the sextant and became adept at taking noon latitude sun sights. I found shooting three star fixes was extremely challenging. The mental concentration of sighting and shooting a minutely small celestial body required much more balance and physical coordination. I was, however, very determined and promised myself I would master it during the trip.

We stopped at Dumaguete, the southernmost town on the island of Negros, for fresh fruit and vegetables. Joe, Willie and I went ashore leaving Killian on the boat. I knew from experience, if Killian went ashore, anything was possible and would most likely happen. Killian was more than happy to remain aboard alone, getting some much needed peace and quiet from the rest of the crew. Although Dave tried to be one of the guys, he was definitely an outsider as Willie, Joe and I had much more in common. But Dave was OK with it and accepted his role as Captain and sailing master, even though he had been deprived of one of his lifelong major staples, alcohol.

The Filipino people were helpful and generous, some of the nicest we would ever meet. At a local grocery store, in addition to buying a box of the most unusual tropical fruit I had ever seen, jackfruit, red bananas, mangosteen and star fruit, I picked up two crucial pieces of information. First, the Sulu Sea, which *Nepenthe* was about to enter, was notorious for pirates, and secondly, the weather in this area was subject to very rapid change. It was not uncommon for a typhoon to blow through the southern islands this time of year. These storms usually originated in the Caroline Islands to the southeast, then followed a northwesterly track up through the Philippines where they generally dissipated across the South China Sea. The larger and fiercer typhoons sometimes reached as far as mainland China and Hong Kong.

As it happened, the grocer told me, there was indeed a tropical depression being tracked in the Molucca Sea. The storm system appeared to be gaining strength as it approached the Celebese Sea, six hundred miles to the south. It should not be a problem if *Nepenthe* was able to make a fast passage across the Sulu Sea.

The water and fuel tanks were topped off and we departed at noon. The plan was to make a beeline across the Sulu in two days and out through the Balabac Straits into the South China Sea. *Nepenthe* quickly rounded the tip of Negros and plowed into the Sulu Sea. There was a steady fifteen knot wind and a violet sunset. Around midnight, the wind started picking up and by morning was a thirty-four knot gale. The smooth blue water of the previous days had now become a sinister-looking slate colored chop.

"The storm appears to have gained speed and it looks like it's overtaking us," Killian said as I relieved him at the tiller. I showed him the copy of a weather fax I had just received and printed from our onboard radio-facsimile machine. I held the curly fax paper for Dave to see and it showed a cyclonic storm system of tight concentric barometric pressure lines now centered over the southern Philippines with the outer edges in the Sulu, over our exact position. There was an edgy, unsettled tone to his voice as all four of us shared an unspoken feeling of dread.

Killian then decided to double reef the mainsail and put up the storm jib. "Be sure you are wearing your safety harnesses. I don't want anybody on deck without one," Killian ordered. Joe and Willie bent to the task while I steered. When it was rough, like now, we wore bright orange float coats which we all had specially made at the sailmakers loft. Each custom-made coat had an exterior layer of rip-stop nylon which incased a form fitting piece of Thinsulate floatation material stitched inside. It also had two 'D' rings double-stitched on either side of the zipper and attached to two inch webbing also double-stitched around the coat's middle. The 'D' rings were then attached to a ten foot rope lifeline with snap shackles braided into each end, which each of us all carried in our float coat pocket. One end of the lifeline attached to the railing stanchion and the other to the 'D' rings in the float coat in case you went over the side. In this fashion we could work anywhere, upon deck, at the bow during a headsail change or in the cockpit while on watch, and at the same time remain safely secured to the boat. Each of us also carried a red and white emergency beacon light in one of the zippered pockets. Just in case.

One hour into my watch, Killian made another decision. "There's too much sail up. Take everything down. We'll try and run with the typhoon. Make sure every hatch and dorade vent is secured tight," Killian shouted to Joe and Willie. The dorades are plastic cowlings attached to brass deck fittings which funnel fresh air below, allowing for ventilation to circulate in the cabin, great in light weather, but in heavy seas they are a primary source of water getting into the boat. They were now sealed with tight fitting brass deck plates.

The howling wind now shrieked and groaned like a tortured beast.

The gale had dramatically risen to typhoon strength, a steady sixty to sixty-five knots with gusts approaching eighty or more. There were no distinct wave patterns, the sea was in a state of wild confusion with dark towering mountains of water, some almost as high as the fifty foot mast, appearing out of nowhere. Rain and spray were blowing horizontally, making it very difficult to see anything through the dodger window. For the helmsman, he was alone in the cockpit with the lee boards and companionway hatch securely shut. He was in his own world, huddled against the bulkhead and virtually hanging on, trying to keep the boat on course and hopefully not hit anything in front of us, which you couldn't see anyway. Even though the wind was blowing at typhoon strength, the air temperature was still in the balmy mid-seventy degree range. With all of the fresh ventilation ports closed, down below the ship's cabin was beginning to reek like a high-school gymnasium locker room permeated with the stagnant aroma of sweat and fear.

For two days *Nepenthe* ran under bare poles, and the knot meter always showed a speed of between five and seven knots per hour. Sailing under 'bare poles', with no sails up, was amazing and at the same time frightening to realize, we were moving at 5 to 6 knots simply by the force of the wind pushing only against *Nepenthe*'s hull. The noise was deafening and scary to say the least. It even gave Killian cause for alarm.

All of us tried to steer 260°, the course I had plotted to the Balabac Straits, but it was impossible. We were constantly blown off course and headed by the winds which had taken on a palpable personality, evil and malevolent. We were all fearful, yet there was no time for fear. Sleep was virtually impossible, with the boat's insane pitching and rolling and the horrible alien noise of the wind and crashing seas. Off watch, each of us tried to dry off as best we could and would climb into our bunks exhausted, fastening the rolling canvas leeboards which prevented us from being thrown onto the cabin floor. I was short enough so I was able to sleep athwart ships, perpendicular to the fore and aft direction of my upper bunk with my feet propped against the hull and head resting inboard on the rolling canvas. There were no hot meals, only cold soggy corned beef sandwiches, canned pudding and lukewarm coffee.

On the fourth day of the storm, during the late afternoon watch change, the boat unexpectedly pitched to starboard at the same time as a wave broke over the port beam. A wall of water cascaded through the partially opened companionway hatch, drenching the chart table, rendering the stereo and, more importantly, the LORAN inoperable.

"We are truly fucked," I said to Killian, after we had wiped up the seawater and sponged the navigation station dry. "With the LORAN out, we can't get our position. There's no way to get a sight with the sextant. In the day there's no sun and at night the sky's as black as a well digger's ass. Even if the cloud cover broke, it would be impossible to hold the sextant steady enough to shoot an accurate fix."

"Our only option then is dead reckoning," Killian replied. "Go from our last known position and pay very close attention to our course and speed. Thank God our electrical system wasn't affected, so the knot meter still works. Also check the charts carefully and read the sailing directions to see if there are any currents in these waters which may have pushed us off course. Remember, the storm came from the south and blew to the north, so if anything, we have been shoved northward."

"What really worries me," I said, sitting behind the chart table, "to the north there are all sorts of shallow coral reefs," pointing to an area on the chart known as Tubbataha

Reefs. "To the south there are a group of islands called Cayguyan Sulu. These are some of the most well known pirate-infested waters on earth. We're somewhere in the middle, but I don't know exactly where," I said tapping my finger on the chart. "We're lost in the Sulu Sea. The worst part of all this is, there could be a reef or an island directly in our path and with this visibility near zero, we might not know about it until we hit it."

"So what you're saying is, without any warning we might go 'boink' then directly to Davy Jones' locker!" Joe said from the helm trying to make light of our dire circumstances with another comment from 'the world according to Joe'.

"Not a good situation, Rick," said Willie.

"Since when did you become a master of the obvious, Professor?" I quipped.

Right then, 'Boing'. It was a loud bang-like sound we all heard coming from somewhere above us. It was like a pistol shot, followed by a harsh metallic rapping on the mast. Joe, on the tiller, yelled, "I think something broke at the top of the mast and whatever it is, it's banging against the masthead antenna."

Willie, Killian and I exchanged glances as if to ask, 'Well, what else can go wrong?'

"Somebody has to go aloft and fix it before it tears up the antenna and anemometer," said Killian, referring to the mast-top wind direction and speed measuring instrument.

"Rick, you're the shortest and lightest," Willie quickly reasoned.

We rigged up a bosun's chair, where I was to sit while being hauled aloft. Joe and Killian, being the strongest, began to winch me up the mast with the chair attached to the main halyard, while Willie steered the boat. Although the storm had weakened somewhat, it was by no means over. With each pull of the line, as I ascended, I felt an increased violent rocking motion until, three quarters up the mast, I was holding on for dear life. *Nepenthe* pitched and yawed like a cork in boiling water. At the top, I clung to the mast, my legs wrapped tightly around the cold wet aluminum spar. I took a spare piece of line from my float coat pocket and lashed the chair to the mast.

Inspecting the damage, I found, the spinnaker halyard turnbuckle had come loose at the mast top and smashed into the radio antenna which was almost broken off, so I removed it and tied it to the chair. The motion at the top of the mast was wilder than any amusement park ride I had ever been on. The mast swung fifteen feet to each side with a whipping motion that threatened to catapult me out into the black raging sea like a rock slung from David's slingshot.

Finally with the turnbuckle firmly pinned and secured, I yelled for Joe and Killian to lower me down. They let the line out a little at a time and slowly I descended, holding on with both my arms and legs, virtually shinnying down the mast. By the time I reached the deck, the insides of my legs were rubbed raw and by my next watch my entire upper torso and legs down to my ankles were black and blue with yellowish-purple splotches around the bruises.

The following morning, the storm broke and the wind slackened. It was only by sheer luck we hadn't hit anything in the night. With the sky still overcast, I set out to find our position by the only real means available, the radio directional finder. I took the RDF up on deck and started turning the dial trying to find a station from which I could identify its broadcast location. The only station I could pick up came from 90 degrees or due east relative to our present position. Wherever that was! The station was being broadcast in a language I couldn't understand. The only word which sounded remotely familiar was 'Zamboanga'. I heard it repeated through the static several times during the next few minutes.

"Blah, blah, blah, Zamboanga. Blah, blah, blah, Zamboanga" was what I could understand as the voice over the radio spoke. From it, I surmised the broadcast originated from a place called Zamboanga. I went below and consulted my navigational charts.

"All I can determine is, from our current position, it's ninety degrees to Zamboanga," I said to Killian. "Zamboanga is in southern Mindanao, and I figure we were blown about two hundred miles to the south during the storm. I'm still not sure where we are. But, so much for your theory of the storm pushing us northward. The only way Zamboanga is ninety degrees from us is if we are smack dab in the middle of Cagayan Sulu and likely to be attacked at any minute. Man the deck artillery!"

"Well, at least we have one relative bearing. If the cloud cover breaks, you can try and get a shot with the sextant," Killian responded.

The light faded and the sky turned orange and then gold, finally paling to blackness behind the high overcast. In the distant west, Willie thought he could make out land on the horizon, but he wasn't sure if it was land or just more clouds.

Unsure of our position, and possibly heading toward a lee shore and a midnight 'boink', Killian decided to stand off in the relative safety of deep water. We spent the night tacking back and forth, sailing a reciprocal course to just maintain our position until well after dawn, when we were finally able to see that it was indeed land... but what land?

As *Nepenthe* drew closer to land, the waters became populated with native fishing boats. Willie looked through the binoculars at the stern of two of these boats, and saw the inscription 'S-d-n, B-r-n'. It meant nothing to me as I continued poring over the charts, still without a clue.

The closer we got to land, the more fishing boats we saw working the shallow coastal waters. Finally, in mid-afternoon, with lush green jungle covering the hills above us, *Nepenthe* rounded a steep promontory, and to our complete surprise, we found ourselves in a large city's harbor. I still didn't know where we were, but Killian spotted the name 'Sandakan' printed on the side of a large water storage tank looming above the city. Again I looked at the chart and this time I found the city of Sandakan on the northeast coast of the island of Borneo.

"Borneo!" I exclaimed, as I burst out laughing. I had never contemplated being in Borneo and had not noticed it being the land to the south of the Balabac Straits. As a child, I had been enchanted by the exotic sounding name, a strange mysterious island inhabited by wild men... 'The Wild Man of Borneo'! Now, here my crewmates and I were: blown off course by a typhoon, lost in the Sulu Sea for five days, our navigational equipment down, with our only point of reference being a radio station broadcasting from Zamboanga, ninety degrees relative to our unknown position. There had been a risk of running aground on an unsuspected coral reef or onto some island pirate's nest and yet we had rounded an unknown jungle headland to find ourselves in a major city on the coast of Borneo. I continued laughing at the folly and absurdity of it all.

To digress for a moment, *90° to Zamboanga,* the title of this story, became a metaphor for the entire voyage and for the story as a whole. Here we were at the mercy of mother nature's wild fury. We had been caught in a typhoon and lost in the Sulu Sea for what seemed at the time, like days on end. It is one of the most dangerous and far off corners of the world. Our instruments were broken and we had been blown about two hundred miles off course. Using the only navigational tool left, we discovered ourselves to be squarely in the middle of the most notorious pirate-infested area in the entire region, not to mention an area surrounded by reefs, islands and dangerous shoal grounds. It was only by some miracle that we averted disaster. We survived it and unexpectedly found ourselves in the wilds of Borneo, another surprise. This characterized and highlighted the unpredictability of the entire voyage and served as a message of just how lucky we had been.

Later research indicated that 1974 was a particularly active typhoon season in the Western Pacific. Although there were no super Category 5 typhoons of winds greater than 156 miles per hour, there were sixteen storms that reached typhoon intensity with winds greater than 74 mph.

We entered the Sulu Sea on about November 5th, the same time that Typhoon Gloria, a Category-4 with winds up to 140 mph, struck the Northern Philippines. It appears that we had only been hit by the outer edges of the storm, as its primary track and eye passed well to our north. However with the counter-clockwise cyclonic movement of such a storm combined with the 75-mile-per-hour winds we experienced coming from mainly the northeast, it is no wonder we were blown off course and pushed to the southwest, which is indeed where we found ourselves.

Nepenthe pulled into port and tied up at the shipping docks. Killian and I made our way to the harbormaster's tower above the waterfront to check in. We found out that Singapore was the closest place to have the LORAN, stereo and antenna repaired. The nearest airport from Sandakan was a day's drive around the northeast tip of Borneo to a place called Kota Kinabalu where there were daily flights to Singapore.

The harbormaster told me he had a friend who was going to Kota Kinabalu later that day by helicopter and there was room for another passenger. I went back to *Nepenthe,* gathering up the antenna and its mounting bracket. I also removed both the LORAN and stereo from their brackets and unplugged all their electrical leads and packed everything securely in a box. I also packed a duffel bag with some clothes and by late afternoon had made my way to a grassy field where the helicopter stood waiting to transport a ship's captain and myself to Kota Kinabalu.

The helicopter lifted off and flew over the dense jungle, heading west toward a tall snow capped mountain.

"That's Mt. Kinabalu," the pilot told me. "It's the highest mountain in this part of the world. Kota is at the foot of the mountain."

"Is there any skiing there? That looks like a perfect bowl of untracked powder off there to the right," I said.

"No mate," the Australian pilot answered. "The mountain is not developed for that sport. It's pretty rugged, over 13,000 feet, but it's a favorite for mountain climbers."

The helicopter landed at the airport. The plane for Singapore had already departed, so I got a hotel room and spent the night. I ate dinner at a local Indonesian restaurant, which was a welcome change from the sailboat cuisine I had been eating for the past couple of months. The following day I flew to Singapore, bought a new stereo to replace the damaged one and took the LORAN and broken antenna to an electronics shop to be repaired. The service technician said he had a new antenna in stock, but it would take a week to fix the LORAN, so I decided to fly up to Thailand and check on the status of the load with Pat and Phil.

Checking into the Raffles Hotel, the grand dowager of all South-East Asia hotels, I telephoned back to Sandakan and through the harbormaster's office talked to Killian.

"I want you to sail the boat over to Kota Kinabalu," I said. "Get any local charts you need from the harbormaster."

"OK, Rick. We can leave tomorrow. We'll pass through the Balabac Straits, round the tip of Borneo and be in Kota Kinabalu in a couple of days. It's just a coastal piloting job. Piece of cake."

"I want you to stay on board Dave. Let Joe and Willie handle any provisioning," I said diplomatically. "The LORAN will take a week to fix, so I may go visit Pat and Phil. Just have things ready to go when I return."

"No problem, Rick."

'I hope not,' I thought as I rang off.

Next, I called Pat's aunt in Bangkok and told her I would be flying into Don Muang Airport the following day. I gave her my flight number and estimated time of arrival and asked that Pat meet me at the airport. It had previously been arranged for Pat to check with his aunt daily for telephone messages, as there were no phones down at the farm.

The main ranch building on Pat's grandfather's ranch located just outside of the Southern Thai city of Chanthaburi, famous throughout the world for its sapphire and ruby mines.

Pat met me at the airport and together we made the four hour drive down to the farm outside Chanthaburi. The final thousand pounds had just arrived the day before from the Northeastern part of Thailand where it had been grown. The marijuana had been brought down by a ten-wheeler and was being re-packaged and readied for shipment by Pat, Phil and several Thais.

I inspected the load and rolled up some weed from an opened package to sample an average joint. It was the most potent weed I had ever seen or smoked. It had a beautiful sparkling green-gold color. Its characteristic pungent odor filled the jungle warehouse.

The individual buds of marijuana, all flower tops, had been neatly wrapped around a thin bamboo stick and were held together by a fine thread of hemp twine. Twenty of these sticks were in one bundle, ten to a layer, and two of these layers were packed together into a package weighing about one kilo apiece. Phil and Pat had devised a method of vacuum-sealing each package by using a vacuum cleaner to suck all of the air out of each plastic bag, and then a hot iron was used to seal the plastic bag closed.

Every package was then double-bagged and wrapped with gray tape in case the vacuum seal did not hold. Thirty packages were put into a gunnysack which was sewn closed and piled in another room. Each gunnysack was filled with about fifty-five pounds of weed. The real weight of each sack, including the weight of the plastic bags and the weight of the burlap, came to between sixty and seventy pounds. I saw the final sack of the forty gunnysack load sewn closed, weighed, labeled and stacked in the adjacent room with the others ready for transport to the beach house. Everything was running according to schedule.

Pat decided to move the load to the beach house at Pattaya about a week prior to *Nepenthe*'s arrival. The load was to be kept small and inconspicuously transported to the beach house in two trips because of the Thai Army checkpoints on the road from Chanthaburi to Pattaya and especially around the U.S. Air Force Base at Utapao. One of Suay's friends had a ten-wheeler with high stake sides and a canvas cover to contain the cargo. Like most of the trucks in Thailand, it was gaudily painted. On each mud flap behind the rear tires were pictures of Clint Eastwood from his role in the spaghetti westerns. The flint and steel in his slightly narrowed eyes, a cigarillo stuck in his mouth and a hard expression on his bearded face, showed he was ready for anything.

Twenty-five gunnysacks of weed were placed on the truck bed's center and then covered with large plastic sheets. Then, the truck's cargo area was completely filled with loose stinking cow manure burying the precious marijuana beneath. The manure's presence and smell usually allowed free passage through the checkpoints without unloading the cargo. A few baht given to the inspecting officer helped speed the process.

With the load secured, Phil joined me and a week later we returned to Singapore, and subsequently flew on to Kota Kinabalu with the repaired LORAN and new stereo. In Kota, Phil came across an old 1930's vintage Bentley racing car in perfect condition for sale, but we were too busy readying the boat for him to do anything about it. To this day, he regrets not buying it on the spot. The asking price was $35,000 and today it would be worth well over a million dollars. The following day Phil left to return to Thailand for the upcoming loading.

The load was then moved to the beach house in two trips without incident. It was figured that it would take about two weeks from when I left until I returned to Thailand aboard *Nepenthe*. We then sailed *Nepenthe* from the island of Borneo into the South China Sea. The winds were light, the sky was cloudless and the sea a sparkling bluish green.

It was obviously something I ate during my time away from the boat because I'd been sick to my stomach with the runs since arriving back aboard *Nepenthe*. While sitting at the chart table plotting our course across the South China Sea, I suddenly was overcome by severe stomach cramps and had to rush to the head… again. The South China Sea is treacherous and dotted with numerous shoals and seamounts, requiring careful plotting and concentration. In my haste to get to the head, I failed to see that I had plotted our course directly over some very tiny 'x's that appeared on the chart, fifty miles west of Kota Kinabalu. Ten hours later, in the clear late afternoon on a flat and glassy sea, *Nepenthe*, on a southwest course heading directly into the sun with engine purring and sails up doing a comfortable six knots, ran aground.

"What the… ," Joe said, as the tiller became sluggish and the boat made an ungodly lurch. The boat leapt forward and, startled, I jumped up from my seat in the cockpit, dropping my chart and pencil, and promptly fell back to the seat as the boat almost came to a dead stop. I plunged back on the cushion and landed on the freshly sharpened point of the pencil. The pencil point went into my thigh and the tip broke off in my leg.

"We're on the bottom!" Joe yelled as he quickly turned off the engine.

Killian rushed up from preparing a fish dinner, saw immediately what was happening and virtually pirouetted around the cockpit, danced up on deck and dropped the main sail. "Turn in to the wind and release the jib," he yelled dropping both sails on deck. *Nepenthe* came to a stop and it appeared as if we were back on the San Joaquin Delta resting peacefully on a glassy slough in the hot afternoon valley sun.

"Now look what you've done!" Willie said to me. "Who's the Professor now, Professor? You just ran us aground. You fucking idiot!"

Fortunately we had run into a sandy bottom and no damage was done. Had it been a coral reef, *Nepenthe* might have been holed or at the very least suffered severe damage to her propeller or rudder, a spade rudder which hung by itself aft of the keel.

As he was prone to do, Willie chided and berated me for my error in navigation, just as he had done in the old days on our treks across the Mexican border.

"What's the matter with you? Is that Paregoric you've been swilling for the squirts making you dizzy, Herr Navigator?" Willie chided, holding up the bottle of the pink narcotic liquid I'd been chugging for my diarrhea, for all to see. "I guess those little 'x's' on the chart were just Christmas decorations, you could just 'twinkle' over… and take the rest of us with you. Moron," Willie continued, with an unusually derisive tone to his voice. Perhaps we had been at sea too long.

"Look, Willie, I'm sorry. I was wrong. No excuses. I fucked up. Next time I'll pay more attention… if there is a next time," I added.

A few minutes later Killian was able to back *Nepenthe* off the sandy bottom by putting the engine in reverse and giving it full throttle. Willie was on a roll.

"Remember a few years ago when we were scouting that new route across the border from Nogales and you got us lost? This is almost an instant replay. I wouldn't be too surprised if tomorrow night we sailed past the Statue of Liberty and underneath the Brooklyn Bridge. Wouldn't surprise me a bit! Perhaps we should put Killian back as navigator."

"OK, OK, all right. Now stop beating a dead horse. I learned a lesson. The South China Sea is a treacherous place and I'll pay more attention to those little 'x's' on the chart. And, no, Killian will not be the navigator. I'm still the navigator," I replied. "I won't fuck up again. That's it! Can't you just leave it alone and not rub it into the ground. I get it, Dickhead!"

Basically, I was an apprentice navigator, learning as I went and by the seat of my pants. However, running aground in the South China Sea, a million miles from nowhere, gave me a new respect for the position I had chosen to assume. Right then, I clearly realized, everyone's life was in my hands and one mistake like this could have been my last.

For me, this was another deja vu moment, just like what had happened two years previous at Chicago's O'Hare Airport. I could never let my guard down, even for one moment, without possible disastrous consequences.

Nepenthe passed across the South China Sea without further incident and made for a point called Mui Bai Bung on the southern tip of Viet Nam. We wanted to stay at least one hundred miles offshore to avoid any possibility of running into patrol boats. The winds were light, so Killian elected to motor, which expedited our time in crossing but burned most of our fuel. With the winds as light as they were, almost nonexistent, it soon became apparent we would have to stop and take on more diesel before reaching Pattaya. I checked the chart and consulted the local sailing directions and it appeared that a small coastal town in Cambodia might be our only opportunity to pull into a dock and fuel up. We headed into the protected harbor in Kampong Som Bay.

The sun dipped below the jungle hills as *Nepenthe* motored into the bay. The twilight was hot and sultry. There was not a breath of wind. We saw black oily smoke rising from a burning hillside village. On the bay's other side we could see Sihanoukville and the opulent summer palace of Cambodia's deposed leader, Prince Norodom Sihanouk. From somewhere inland, there was the dull flat sound of outgoing artillery fire followed by a distant rumbling and a concussion-like boom.

"Hey, there's a war going on here. Do you think it's wise to pull in here? Señor Professor," Willie said sarcastically, half joking, half not.

"We don't have much of an option. There's no wind, and I figure we have less than ten gallons of fuel left. We've got another day powering ahead of us and burning at a rate of a gallon or so an hour, we'll run out before we get to Thailand. It could take us days with no wind or fuel. We might make it if we slow down to one or two knots, but I don't like going so slow in these waters. Might look like we're in trouble and could draw attention to us. Attract the wrong people, if you know what I mean. There's really no other safe choice," Killian replied from his position at the helm.

"I agree with Dave. We get in, find some fuel and get out as fast as we can. I'm going down below to make sure all the boat's documentation papers are in order. From what I read in the papers in Singapore and Thailand, it's a virtual free-for-all in here. God only knows who's in charge of this asylum," I said. "Say Joe, make sure our gun stash is well secured and didn't come loose in the typhoon."

A rag-tag bunch of Cambodian soldiers, their weapons ill cared for and slung loosely over their shoulders, and a couple of army officers stood on the quay as *Nepenthe* tied up. A stern looking colonel had followed our progress into the bay with binoculars, which were passed back-and-forth with the other mean and serious looking officers of junior rank. It was fortunate that Willie spoke a little French to communicate our peaceful intentions. The Cambodians had a history of xenophobia and were very suspicious of all visitors. Currently, the Khmer Rouge were conducting a guerrilla war, much like the Viet Cong, and terrorizing the population, while the United States B-52's bombed the countryside.

Now was where Willie really proved his mettle. During the previous eight to ten years of both high school and college, Willie, when required, had taken French and somehow through all the years and drugs had managed to retain at least enough to have a rudimentary conversation with the officers standing at the dock while we tied up. They only spoke French and Cambodian.

"Bonsoir, monsieur," Willie said. "Avez-vous, petrol? Diesel?" he asked now running short of the rest of his French vocabulary. He lapsed into a combination of broken French and broken English accentuated by wild gesturing and pointing.

The colonel who greeted the boat softened after he was invited aboard and offered a glass of wine. Willie made it clear, our only purpose was to refuel and be on our way.

The officer wearing military fatigues reminded me of 'Odd Job' without the top hat, from the James Bond movie *Goldfinger*, a stocky fireplug of a man with a flattened boxer's nose. He accommodated us by requisitioning a three-wheeled jitney with a rusted fifty-five gallon drum lashed to the back. While Willie and Dave stayed on the boat, Joe and I accompanied the colonel and an M-16 toting soldier on a fifteen minute ride to a nearby jungle village where we procured diesel by siphoning it from a tank located behind an abandoned village store. The only lights showing in the otherwise black night were from a string of 25-watt light bulbs strung along the dirt road from an overhead wire. It seemed like only one out of every ten bulbs was lit. The village appeared to be deserted. The night was dark and humid.

At first we thought it was lightning illuminating the sky in the distance followed by rumbling thunder, then we came to realize what we were seeing and hearing were explosions from B-52's carpet bombing the countryside, followed by the bark of heavy machine guns and the throaty cough of mortar fire. Dropping their bombs from high altitude you couldn't even see the planes overhead. You could only hear as the bombs struck with thundering reverberation. The return fire was practically for show only, as the targets were at such an altitude there was no chance of hitting them. The whole scene was surreal and seemed as if we were viewing it on a Hollywood stage lot, but this was war and we were in the middle of it, out in the jungle in the middle of the night accompanied by fierce looking Cambodian soldiers on a three wheeled jitney, not knowing who might attack us from the dense jungle overgrowth.

"I'd be a lot more comfortable if we were ten miles offshore right now," Joe said shakily, loosely screwing the cap back on the fifty-five gallon drum.

"For once I'd have to agree with you," I replied.

As I reflect on this Cambodian wartime scene it was eerily reminiscent of many of the chaotic Southeast Asian jungle scenes depicted in the 1979 Viet Nam War classic film *Apocalypse Now*.[1]

Upon our return to the dock, Willie asked the colonel what the charge was for the fuel. The colonel gave a Gallic shrug. Before he could calculate a price, I proffered a crisp one hundred dollar bill toward the officer and a bottle of California Cabernet.

In the distance we could hear the thud of exploding rocket propelled grenades, distant automatic gunfire and the continued earthshaking rumbling from the bombing above. On the dock, there was an atmosphere of urgency.

By this time, Killian had connected a hand pump and hose to the diesel drum and had run it across to Joe who had already unscrewed both of *Nepenthe*'s gas caps. As soon as Joe had the fuel nozzle inserted, Killian began feverishly cranking the pump handle. The gas was filtered into a funnel covered with a section of cheesecloth, because Asian fuel is notorious for impurities and water contamination.

"Merci beaucoup," Willie said to the officer. Then turning to me, muttered under his breath, "Let's get this show on the road, right now. Before it's too late and we either get hit by one of those bombs or these 'wonderful' people decide to change their mind and hold us hostage."

It was close to midnight when *Nepenthe* motored out of Kampong Som harbor. A few fires illuminated the blacked out port city and more explosions could be heard in the distance. Killian pushed the throttle forward as far as it would go.

It was only later we learned that Kampong Som was the site of two incidents which happened within a year of our visit. It was the site of the famous 1975 *Mayaguez* Incident where U.S. Marines rescued the crew of a merchant marine ship, the *Mayaguez*, after it was captured in those waters by the Khmer Rouge. Later it became known where, right in this area, two American sailors on a sailboat en-route to score a load of Thai weed were captured in international waters west of this town. They were tortured, imprisoned, ultimately executed and the bodies were burned beyond recognition by soldiers of the Khmer Rouge.[2] We were indeed very lucky, and someone must have been looking over us, to get out of there unscathed.

The following evening *Nepenthe* arrived off Pattaya Beach. We anchored just beyond the small surf line on a flat listless sea. When both the bow and stern anchors were set, Willie, Joe and I rowed ashore in the inflatable, leaving Killian to look after the boat.

We decided to spend two days at anchor, not to arouse any undue suspicion by a rapid arrival and departure. I flagged down a samlor, a three-wheeled pedicab, and set off for the beach house. Joe and Willie immediately headed for the massage parlor. An hour later the two crewmen were relaxing in the soothing waters of a Japanese style hot

---

1 Referenced Television & Movies, Item 20, Page 533.

2 Referenced Books, Item 4, Page 532.

tub. Two beautiful Thai women sat alongside them in the hot water washing their salt encrusted bodies, kneading their developed muscles and tanned frames.

"God, this is absolute paradise!" Joe exclaimed. He reached over and picked up his Singha beer and took a long swallow.

"Ahh!" was all Willie could say. His female companion's hand was moving beneath the water.

"And to think, yesterday we were in a war zone with bombs, artillery, mortars and RPG's going off." Joe continued. "And now look at us!"

Ko Lan Island, Thailand
Mid-November 1974

Nepenthe departed Pattaya after three days at anchor and headed five miles or so offshore to the island of Ko Lan. Pat and Phil had previously reconnoitered the island and had selected a small cove for the loading operation. At ten o'clock a fishing boat drew alongside *Nepenthe*. I could clearly hear Pat's voice shouting commands in Thai, as oil-streaked cork and braided Manila hemp bumpers were put over the side. Lines fore and aft were thrown across to *Nepenthe*. When the two boats were securely rafted together, Pat came aboard the sailboat.

The Thai crew began heaving gunnysacks aboard *Nepenthe* and within twenty minutes one ton of weed had been transferred. Pat yelled back to the fishing boat and a Thai handed him two duffel bags.

"I bring you something special. Something to keep you safe," Pat said as he unzipped the larger bag. He withdrew an M-16 automatic rifle. There was a second M-16 in the bag. Both were in excellent condition, covered with an almost invisible layer of sweet smelling gun oil. There were a number of loaded thirty round magazines in the bag. The magazines had been taped end to end for rapid reloading. Pat unzipped the smaller bag. Joe stepped forward, put his hand into the satchel and pulled out an M-79 grenade launcher. It too was in mint condition. There was a smaller canvas bag filled with swollen looking 40 millimeter rounds.

"Fucking A! A 'bloop' gun!" Joe exclaimed. He broke open the breech and examined the weapon. "We got to fire these during Advanced Infantry Training. This will definitely discourage anybody who has naughty motives," Joe said as he lovingly creased the wooden stock.

"OK," I said. "Stow those things below and let's get to work filling the stash compartments."

As dawn broke, each package of marijuana had been neatly placed into the numerous stash compartments and sealed. Pat had fit the pre-cut pieces of wood to each individual compartment, sealed it with silicone sealant and seated each piece with stainless steel screws. I followed him, painting each area with a coat of white paint. Our calculations had been perfect and the whole load was completely concealed except for a couple of pounds we kept out to smoke on the return voyage home.

By nine in the morning, the fishing boat had also resupplied *Nepenthe* with canned food, water, fresh fruit and vegetables, Singha beer and more diesel fuel. We all said goodbyes as *Nepenthe* weighed anchor and motored out into the Gulf of Siam in light winds under a deep blue cloudless sky. We anticipated the return trip would take about two months.

We motored south in the typical light winds of the Gulf of Siam. Nothing out of the ordinary. On the second day we spotted a fishing boat which was obviously in distress and listing badly to port. The crew was waving at us.

"Hey Dave," exclaimed Willie at the helm. "Look at that scow off the starboard bow at 2 o'clock. Looks like they're in trouble."

The three of us scrambled up on deck to have a look.

"I think we should give assistance," replied Dave. "It's the law of the sea."

"What the fuck are you talking about?" I answered. "It could be a trap. You see that skiff on the other side of the fishing boat, kind of hiding in its lee. There's no way in the world we're stopping. I don't give a damn what their problems are."

"If we were in that situation, we'd sure like help," said Dave. "I still think we should check it out."

"In this instance, I really don't care what you think," I said. "We ain't stopping. No way. We just loaded and we aren't going to risk it. And, this is not a democracy. If it were, you were just outvoted, three to one. So forget it."

We all watched, passing the binoculars back and forth as we continued south. I kind of felt bad, but with the skiff they could save themselves anyway. I wasn't about to risk our trip or fall for a possible ruse, if that's what was going on.

I was very careful plotting our course back across the South China Sea. The winds were light, so we were again forced to rely on what Killian called 'the iron jib', the engine. It took us one week from the time we left Ko Lan to when we pulled into the small village of Apurahuan on the southern Philippine island of Palawan to refuel.

It was a quick in and out stop. While Joe and Killian oversaw the transfer of diesel fuel from the dock to *Nepenthe*, Willie and I went to the local market and purchased more soft drinks, beer, fresh fruit and vegetables.

"I got a funny feeling from that place. The people in the market seemed very uptight and not friendly at all, like the people in Dumaguete," I said as we powered out of Apurahuan a little after noon.

"Yeah. The fishermen at the dock were very nosey. They asked questions about what electronic gear we had on board, and they kept asking me how much stuff cost," Killian added. "One guy wanted to go aboard to look around and he kept pressing me until I physically pushed him back and said, 'No way Jose'."

"Another guy asked me if we had any guns. I said we had an old bolt action hunting rifle for sharks," Joe said.

"I think it would be a good idea to get the weapons out of their stashes. You never know. Keep them hidden from sight, but readily available. Since you've fired a grenade launcher before, Joe, she's your baby. Rick, you're probably familiar with the M-16 from Basic Training. Why don't you get reacquainted? Willie, I want you to really keep a good watch, OK? You're our eyes," Killian said.

The Palawan Passage is a stretch of coastal waters west of the island of Palawan. Three hours after leaving Apurahuan, Willie, sitting on the cabin top, spotted two native 'bancas'. The long narrow outrigger boats powered by fast outboard engines were overtaking *Nepenthe*, whose cruising speed under power was at best six or seven knots.

"Uh, oh, we've got company," Willie said. "Two native boats moving up astern real fast. I'd say they are doing at least twelve to fifteen knots."

Killian came up on deck from down below where he had been making sandwiches. Willie handed him the binoculars.

"Humm, these guys are closing quickly," Killian said. He made a snap decision. "Joe, Rick. Get the weapons up here right now but keep them out of sight. Make sure you have enough ammunition. If these guys get closer than three hundred yards I am going to start maneuvering to see what they do. Willie keep alert and see if you spot any weapons."

I had been steering the boat, but, following Killian's orders, I turned the helm over to him and along with Joe went below and readied our weapons. Joe took the M-79 grenade launcher and the canvas bag with the 40-millimeter rounds and placed them on the deck aft of Killian. I inserted a full thirty-round magazine into one of the M-16 rifles and laid it on the cockpit cushion. Joe passed me another two magazines which had been taped end to end.

The bancas were rapidly drawing closer. Through the binoculars, Willie now could make out individual figures.

"There's four mofo's in one boat and five in the other. I see a guy in one of the boats fiddling around with something. It looks like a rifle. Another guy is definitely wearing a set of crossed bandoliers," said Willie.

"Rick, if you have to shoot, lie prone on the cushion facing the stern and rest the gun barrel against the cockpit combing, to compensate for the boat's movement. Be sure to aim low enough. I don't want anybody shooting unless I say so. Joe, I want you to fire first, but wait until I give you the word. I am going to let them come no closer than a hundred and fifty yards," said Killian, who had pushed the throttle forward and was now turning the boat fifty degrees to port toward the deeper water of the South China Sea.

The bancas also swung to port. They appeared to have closed to less than five hundred yards.

"I see guns," said Willie. His voice had gone up an octave. "Men in both boats have rifles!"

"OK, Professor. Get down off the cabin top so you won't be a target. Stand in the companionway. Joe and Rick stand by. Load the grenade launcher and get set," said Killian glancing astern.

Joe got behind Killian and sat facing forward, so the M-79 was concealed. He broke open the breech and inserted one of the oversize bullets. Snapping the weapon shut, he pulled up the adjustable rear sight. I pulled the bolt back on the M-16, jacking a round into the chamber. I put the safety on and set the rifle across my lap.

"Ready, Joe! You can fire!" shouted Killian when the bancas were about two hundred yards astern.

"Right!" Joe stood up and turned around. He raised the M-79 to his right shoulder, the stock barely touching his cheek, adjusted the rear sight and squeezed the trigger.

There was a loud crump-like sound, and an exploding ten-foot geyser maybe fifty feet to the right of the outside banca.

"Again!" yelled Killian. "Rick, you fire after Joe's second shot."

Joe quickly reloaded, raised the weapon, and fired again. This time the exploding round burst within twenty feet of the boat and there was another geyser-like fountain of water. Both bancas were now veering to starboard, trying desperately to get out of range.

Lying in the prone position on the cockpit cushion, I thumbed the safety off, switched the fire selector to full automatic and started firing short bursts. The noise was deafening.

"Shit!" cried Killian, as a hot shell casing from the rifle's ejection port struck his bare back.

Several of the men in both bancas raised their weapons and fired erratically in *Nepenthe*'s general direction. Small pops could be seen in the water some 50 feet away. Not even close!

"If this is the best they can do, they should be in a different line of work," said Willie in a loud voice, monitoring the action through binoculars from his station in the companionway.

I fired another long burst which emptied the magazine. The water around both bancas looked like a hail storm. Willie noticed one man who was standing up shooting at us, fall overboard, as the banca on the right abruptly swerved to port.

"You missed, Rick! You're not as good a shot as you thought, 'cause I see the man overboard swimming back to the boat," Willie exclaimed, looking closely at the scene through the high powered binoculars. "Looks like he just lost his balance. Must have dropped his rifle. I don't see it anymore. At least you didn't kill anybody. That's all we need. It'd be the icing on the cake and you'd have really fucked us!"

"There you go again," I replied. "Always blaming others. Maybe you could have scared them away by just throwing the binoculars at 'em. I'm sure that would have worked. Believe me, I wasn't aiming to hit them. Just trying to scare them away. Look Screwball, if I really wanted to hit 'em, the only direction they'd all be going is down!"

One longboat stopped to retrieve the pirate from the water, who hastily scrambled back aboard, while the other vessel cranked on the speed, beating a swift retreat.

Joe fired a third grenade which landed between both boats.

"OK, guys. That's enough. Looks like they got the point. Save your ammo. We might not have seen the last of these fuckers," said Killian.

I withdrew the empty magazine from the M-16 and took the weapon down below. Willie maintained a vigilant watch until the pirates had disappeared from view.

With grins and high fives all around, each of us breathed a sigh of relief, silently hoping we'd seen the last of them but vowing to remain alert and on guard, especially in these waters.

"I've been saving this for a special occasion," I said, climbing back up the companionway ladder with a bottle of Myers Rum in my right hand.

"God bless you, Rick! I really need this," Killian exclaimed, totally astounded.

"Don't get any ideas, Dave. Everybody gets just one glass," I replied.

I had four coffee mugs in my left hand.

"Wrong!" Killian said, as he grabbed one of the mugs. He ducked down below and quickly reappeared, a huge grin on his face. In his outstretched hand he held his special large 20-ounce plastic drinking glass with smiling dolphins jumping through hoops depicted on the cup's side. Both the cup and Killian had been dry for the past two months.

I relented and filled his goblet, then tossed the empty rum bottle over the side. He deserved a break. We all did, as we 'clinked' in celebration.

Chapter 21

Mt. Everest of Water

The distant noise was a sound like pebbles rolling down a long metal pipe. I was on watch and very stoned in the middle of smoking a joint of Thai weed while steering the boat and listening to a Grateful Dead tape.

It was eight thirty on a beautiful morning. The wind was fresh at eighteen knots, the sea a deep royal blue color. Flying fish scudded across the bow. *Nepenthe* was thirty miles off the Bataan Peninsula, northwest of Manila and south of the U.S. Naval Base at Subic Bay located on the main Philippine island of Luzon.

The Dead song playing on the cockpit speakers was *Unbroken Chain*[1] written and sung by the group's bass player Phil Lesh.

> 'Blue light rain, whoa, unbroken chain
> Looking for familiar faces in an empty window pane
> Listening for the secret, searching for the sound...'

At that point in the song, the sound of chains can be heard. I listened for the next line in the song:

> '... But I could only hear the preacher and the baying of his hounds.'

And the 'chain' sound, which should have melded into the other music was still there, only getting louder. I thought it was part of the song which somehow I'd missed in the umpteen times I'd heard it before, but as the noise amplified, I turned and looked toward the stern and squinted into the horizon. At first I saw nothing, but then I saw two silver specks very close to the water approaching us at tremendous speed.

When the two U.S. Navy F-14 Tomcats, no more than fifty feet above the sea, were parallel with *Nepenthe*, one on either side of the boat, each pilot pulled his stick back and in unison hit the afterburners and rocketed skyward. Flames shot out of the tail pipes of each plane with a deafening roar, like a prehistoric dragon with a bad case of gas as the jets shot straight up. I could feel the heat blast wash over me and could smell

---

1 Referenced Songs & Music, Item 7, Page 530.

the fumes as I saw the orange exhaust flames trail behind the speeding bullets. Both Joe and Willie were now on deck and Willie with his camera, wildly snapping away trying to get photos of the twin tailed Navy jets. Joe quickly got our American flag and put it in the stern mounted flag holder. The pilots executed a series of barrel-roll maneuvers for us, the three stunned observers. As a closing act to the brief private two and a half minute air show, the two F-14 jet fighters again passed over us, rocking their wings side-to-side then disappearing at four hundred and fifty knots toward the northeast and the Naval Air Station at Subic Bay.

The air show was over, but *Unbroken Chain* was still playing in the cockpit speakers with a rather prophetic message:

> 'Out on the mountain it'll drive you insane
> Listening to the winds howl'

Followed by the familiar sound of chains, sounding like F-14 Tomcats, indelibly etched into the recesses of my brain.

Two days later, we made our last stop at the northern Luzon town of Vigan where we took on water, diesel and supplies in preparation for the long non-stop sail across the North Pacific. Again the three of us went ashore while Killian remained on board. He requested ten cartons of cigarettes to be added to our shopping list.

"Let's just get him only one carton," Willie said as we entered the grocery store. "Even though he only smokes up on deck, the air down below reeks of stale cigarettes."

"I don't know, Willie. First the booze and now the cigarettes. We really don't have the right… ," Joe replied.

"Fuck the right, as far as he's concerned this is a dictatorship," I said laughing.

"When Killian's not smoking, which only happens when he's asleep, he still smells like a wet ashtray," Willie said.

At the counter, coincidentally, there was only one carton of Winstons, the brand Killian favored. There were assorted brands of Philippine cigarettes. We bought the sole carton of Winstons and about ten packets of long thin brown cigarillos.

"Well, at least we won't be lying to him," I rationalized as we unloaded the cases of supplies from the taxicab, back at the dock.

Aboard *Nepenthe*, I put the carton of Winstons and the packets of cigarillos down on the chart table.

"They only had one carton of Winstons, Dave, and we bought it specially for you. Got you a few packs of these brown things," I told a very disappointed Killian.

Killian looked broken hearted. "You guys have taken away all of my pleasures, first drinking and now smoking. I guess the good news is, I might even get healthy after all is said and done."

"I doubt it, Dave. I really doubt it. You're too far gone, unless you sign up for a liver transplant the moment we reach San Francisco," Willie replied. In retrospect and years later I would come to recall this conversation between Willie and Dave and reflect that it was 'like the pot calling the kettle black!'

Departing Vigan, we headed north for the Luzon Strait. We rounded the tip of

Luzon and started heading east back across the Pacific at 20° north latitude bound for San Francisco. For four days, *Nepenthe* was hit by thirty to thirty-five knot headwinds.

It was depressing now as I had thought that we'd finally made it back to open ocean and were headed home. But we weren't getting anywhere in the direction we wanted to go. The seas were choppy and we were beating to weather, heeled over basically on our collective ears.

Doing anything above or below deck in those conditions is a major production. Dave said, "one hand for you and one hand for the boat." In other words: hang on or you're going flying. The wind was blowing at nearly gale force and coming from 75°, exactly the east northeast course to get us home. The closest we were able to steer to our intended direction was either 35° towards Alaska and the Aleutian Islands or 120° towards the South Pacific, neither option anywhere near where we wanted to go!

Unable to steer the course which would get us to San Francisco, we had to constantly tack back and forth making little headway against a fierce easterly wind. Unable to sail directly into the eye of the wind and not being able to sail anywhere near the direction of our ultimate destination, we decided to turn around. We ran back toward the Luzon Strait.

The seas were still rough, but at least our point of sail was much more tolerable. The second night after turning around, I spotted a large boat in the distance, heading our direction. As it got closer, looking at it through the binoculars, I saw it was a large rusted-looking tramp steamer laden with containers, plowing into the wind with waves breaking over its bow and on a collision course with us.

"I hope that fucker sees us," I called to Killian.

"Let's not take any chances. They're probably on autopilot or asleep in the bridge," Killian said. "Fall off to port thirty degrees."

"It's still coming," I yelled, fifteen minutes later. "I don't think they see us."

Dave turned on the engine, gunned it and barked, "Fall off another twenty."

I did and it narrowly missed us, passing to starboard at no more than fifty feet. The rusted scow towered over us like a giant blind leviathan. They never saw us, never changed course, barely missed us, disappeared to the east and never even knew we were there. If it had hit us, it would be like a Peterbilt eighteen wheel semi-tractor-trailer running over a toothpick. It would have cut us in two, we'd have gone down and nobody would have ever known.

I consulted *Ocean Passages For The World*,[2] a mariner's reference book I'd brought along showing worldwide sailing routes, to find another route which might be more favorable. I found the normal passage was to follow the Great Circle route from the South China Sea north to the East China Sea through the Bonin Island chain south of Japan into the North Pacific. The book said that at 35° to 45° north latitude, the prevailing winds would be westerly and *Nepenthe* could run home downwind. What I failed to realize was that *Ocean Passages* is a publication widely used by navies and shipping companies, giving them the most direct ocean routes from point A to point B, at any time of the year. However, we soon found out that for a forty-one-foot sailboat

---

2 Referenced Books, Item 8, Page 532.

attempting to follow such a recommended crossing of the North Pacific in mid-winter, it's a totally different story.

It was now December and the weather got colder the farther north we went. *Nepenthe* passed within sight of the partially cloud covered green hills of the east coast of Taiwan. We were now in the Formosa Strait. Northward, we crossed into the East China Sea past the Ryukyu Islands. At about 28° north, the winds turned bitterly cold and the seas began building. The sea looked like a mountain landscape in motion with the average wave size between twenty and thirty feet. An occasional forty footer rolled by that made *Nepenthe* seem insignificant.

Yours truly on the ocean crossing in December of 1973. The weather was starting to get bitterly cold and we had to shed our tropical attire for the cold north Pacific crossing as seen here.

Taking out my volume of *Bowditch*, the sailor's bible, I saw it included photographs of sea conditions relative to a scale known as the Beaufort Scale. I matched the current wind and sea conditions to a photograph in the book labeled 'Beaufort Force 10'. Even Killian with twenty years of sailing and four years in the Coast Guard had never experienced anything like it.

"Looks like a clip from the opening scene of the television series *Victory At Sea*,"[3] I said, coming on deck for my two hour watch, relieving an exhausted Willie in the driver's seat. The scene, from the early 1950's TV series, depicts a U.S. Navy battleship plowing headlong into huge ocean waves breaking over its bow coupled with the show's awe-inspiring symphonic musical score playing in the background.

Nepenthe was on a beam reach with the storm jib up and a double reefed mainsail sheeted out to maximize speed. As I surveyed the wind and sea, I was filled with awe and at least a little bit of fear. The ocean was in a state of exaggerated motion. One

3 Referenced TV & Movies, Item 19, Page 533.

moment *Nepenthe* was riding the crest of a thirty foot wave and I could see for miles. Within seconds the boat tobogganed down the steep wave face into a trough almost as deep as the mast was tall.

"Yeah, but *Nepenthe* ain't no battleship, Rick. Course to steer is 50 degrees. Once in a while a wave will sneak up on you from over the stern quarter, so be real careful," Willie cautioned.

From my orange float coat pocket, I took out a ten foot length of light gauge Samson braided line with snap shackles spliced on either end. Hooking one of the shackles through the two 'D' rings on the front of my day-glow orange float coat and the other end through the starboard lifeline, I was now tied to the boat.

"OK. I've got her," I said grasping the tiller. I tucked myself under the canvas dodger on the starboard weather side, huddling next to the bulkhead.

Willie threw open the companionway hatch, stepped over the hatch boards and went below to begin the process of drying himself off. He smiled, remembering that Joe had included a tape of the Richard Rodgers musical score of *Victory at Sea*, popped it into the stereo and turned the setting on the outside speakers up to maximum volume to play the most recognizable track *Song of the High Seas*.[4] The music blared in the cockpit.

"Very funny," I murmured as I adjusted myself to the boat's radical pitching and yawing motion.

Within twenty minutes I was totally absorbed and focused, maintaining the desired easterly course. I was beginning to have fun steering the boat down the big roller coaster waves, when out of nowhere, a rogue thirty foot monster crested and crashed down behind me, on the starboard quarter just forward of the stern. I didn't even know what hit me. Next thing, I felt myself being lifted up, hurled over the tiller by a wall of water instantly sweeping me across the cockpit, through the port lifelines and overboard, in less time than it takes to bat an eyelash.

The last thing I did, perhaps by instinct, was to give the tiller a push with my foot to keep the boat on course as I sailed over it and out through the lifelines. The next moment, I was dangling over the side, attached to the boat only by my safety line as tons of water cascaded over me.

There was nothing I could do but laugh hysterically. Down below, the force of the breaking wave was felt as an explosive crash. "Is everything all right up there?" thundered Killian.

"Yeah. Everything's just great!" I replied through my laughter. "I'm over the side, the cockpit's full of water and there's nothing left up here. Get up here right now!"

With the extra thousand pounds of freezing salt water now filling *Nepenthe*'s cockpit coupled with the weight of the majority of the weed stored in the aft sail lockers, *Nepenthe* instantly became dangerously unbalanced. Her bow rose to a desperate thirty degree pitch, which in turn caused the stern deck rail to drop to within inches of the ocean's wild surface, potentially scuttling us from behind.

Killian practically flew up on deck and took in the scene: the cockpit was full of

---

4 Referenced Songs & Music, Item 8, Page 530.

water, the custom canvas dodger was torn and its 3/4-inch stainless steel tubing support system was bent like overcooked linguine. The cockpit cushions were pasted against the port lifelines and I was suspended over the port side of the boat in the water banging against the hull, trying vainly to clamber back aboard.

"Joe, get two buckets and start helping me bail," Killian ordered. "If another wave hits us now we're going down! Willie, get up here and take the helm!" He then reached down and grabbed my outstretched hand and heaved me back onboard like a sack of potatoes.

Willie jumped out of his bunk, in a valium-induced haze, where he had just fallen asleep. In his underwear, he scrambled up into the freezing water in the bathtub-like cockpit and grabbed the tiller. Joe rushed on deck with two buckets and along with Killian began bailing. Within a couple of minutes much of the water was out of the cockpit and *Nepenthe* began to stabilize. Killian put the remnants of the dodger below.

Adrenaline coursed through my soaking and thoroughly drenched body. I felt no cold, nor fear. Looking forward, I saw the lapper, the sail which had been tied to the spinnaker pole on the foredeck, had come undone and was now trailing in the water along the port side of the hull. Carefully, I worked my way forward, attaching my safety line to the port lifeline, and with all my strength began struggling to pull the sail back aboard.

On the bow, the boat's motion was twice as exaggerated as I'd experienced sitting in the cockpit. My stomach felt like it was at the back of my throat as *Nepenthe* surfed down a thirty foot wave and hit the trough. The 'G' force slammed me to the deck as another wall of water washed over me as the boat went up and over the next giant. After securing the sail, I worked my way aft and for the second time in half an hour relieved Willie at the helm.

Willie, thoroughly soaked, nearly frozen and wearing only his boxer shorts turned to me and said, "Do you mind letting me get some sleep now, Jerk?"

I flashed him a broad smile as I went back to work steering the boat.

For the next forty-eight hours *Nepenthe* continued to run through the huge seas with only the storm jib and the reefed mizzensail. At one point, when the seas rose to an average of forty feet, Killian decided to take all the sails down and run with the waves.

I could see, while Killian was steering the boat, he was a man completely at one within his element. Peering out the unzipped hatchway cover, I saw a Mt. Everest of water bearing down upon *Nepenthe*'s stern. Killian, grinning from ear to ear, with a relaxed grip on the helm, nonchalantly pulled the tiller six inches toward him and caught the wave as the boat took off to the right, sliding down the forty foot face like a big wave surfer at Hawaii's Makaha Beach.

I quickly closed the canvas cover and left Killian on watch. I went forward to a stash compartment in the forepeak where I had hidden a couple bottles of Myers Rum. I fixed a hot buttered rum on the galley stove and passed it to Killian through the open canvas. Elated, Killian took the drink and downed it in three swallows. I made another and fed him two Dexedrine capsules from the ship's medical kit. Killian remained at the helm for the rest of the day, standing three consecutive watches, grooving on the waves while the rest of us stayed warm below, smoking joints and listening to music.

At one point when the waves were at their biggest and the seas at their angriest, I took some pictures to try and capture it for the record. I went on deck and snapped a few of Dave at the helm with forty to fifty foot monsters bearing down on us and Dave calmly surfing the boat down them like 'a walk in the park.' At sea and with the enormity of it all, it was hard to capture the ferocity in all its magnitude, but I felt pretty sure I got it. I used up an entire roll of 35 mm film.

Later in the day, I finally got up enough nerve to take the helm when my turn at watch came up. I took over and Willie got the bright idea to put another roll of film in the camera, but for some reason the rewind mechanism in the camera jammed. I saw it all happening right before my eyes and envisioned a catastrophe in the making, but because I was at the helm, I was helpless do do anything about it. I literally begged him to wait until at least I got off watch to attempt to open the camera and change the film, but in his stubbornness he just couldn't. I pleaded with him to wait until dark when we could safely open the camera and save the roll, but in his idiocy he just had to open it 'right now.' All I could do was sit there and watch helplessly as he opened the camera in broad daylight and, guess what? He ruined the precious roll of film… as predicted.

"You fucking moron. Now look what you've done. In our lifetimes we'll never see anything like this again and you've gone and ruined it. What a fucking jerk!" I wailed.

He just stood there with a stupid guilty look on his face. The exposed and now destroyed roll of film in his hand. "Oops," was all he could muster.

Of course I didn't leave it there and had to rub it in, just as he did to me whenever the tables were turned. "How could you be so fucking stupid? You just couldn't wait till dark. Now look what you've done, you asshole!" It went on and on until I'd thoroughly exhausted the issue. Such was our normal banter, but I relished the fact that it was nice to be on the delivering end for a change, and not in my usual role as Willie's punching bag.

The fact, however, remains today: I don't have those pictures which would have been included in this book to show just how hairy the situation really was. Oh well! The best example I've seen to compare with it is portrayed in the movie *The Perfect Storm*[5] in the scene where the fishing boat was capsized. The waves and sea conditions we experienced in those couple of days were every bit as huge and outrageous as depicted in that movie.

We passed the Bonin Island chain, south of Japan, sailing by an erupting volcano. We marveled at the nighttime sight of brilliant reddish gold lava flowing into the ocean. Approaching our northerly apex of 48° north latitude, the same latitude as Vancouver, B.C., the northern Canadian province of Newfoundland, and Budapest, Hungary, places which routinely experience very harsh winter conditions, the weather got much colder and it became a challenge to stay warm and dry. In an attempt to mitigate it, when it was extremely cold, which was now most of the time, I would raid the medical chest and take an Empirin #4 tablet with codeine before my watch, hoping to

5 Referenced Television & Movies, Item 11, Page 533.

somehow dull the cold. I would also wrap each foot and leg with plastic saran wrap for added warmth before putting on my foul weather gear bottoms and sea boots.

It was not unusual for Willie, before he came on watch, to grab any pair of sea boots within reach, no matter who they belonged to, and they usually belonged to Joe, as my foot was smaller than his. For God only knows why, maybe to make some sort of fashion statement, Willie would tuck his foul weather pants into his sea boots possibly trying to look like the movie star Alan Ladd in the movie classic *Two Years Before The Mast*.[6] This resulted in sea water dripping down his pants and into what might otherwise be dry boots. Not wanting to wear wet sea boots, he would grab the first pair of dry boots within reach, Joe's. Willie also had a physiological and anatomical issue which was a constant problem for him, and the rest of us. He had a small bladder and whenever he had to urinate, it was an immediate issue. He too had to bundle up, saran wrap his legs and don long underwear and foul weather gear, the bottoms of which had no zipper and slipped on over pants and long underwear underneath. When he came on watch and frequently when he had the urge to go, which he referred to as 'uncontrollable pissing', he didn't have time to undo all the layers so he simply pissed in his pants. It would invariably drip down his saran covered legs and flow directly into Joe's sea boots. Swabbing out the sea boots as would normally happen presented another problem. They were always wet by the time Joe would use them for his watch. Joe wore three pairs of socks so the boots would dry in time for Willie to sour them a few hours later. They began to stink of urine which added to the cacophony of the stale air now reeking in the cabin.

The crew's mood became as oppressive and brittle as the cold metallic gray skies. For over a month we had not seen the sun and there was an edgy uptight atmosphere aboard the boat.

I was always fastidious about my personal appearance and hygiene and while in the tropical and more temperate climates, I would bathe daily on the stern deck, soaping down with Prell Shampoo and Dr. Bronner's Castile Soap. I would rinse off with a couple of buckets of salt water, sponge off with precious fresh water, then towel myself dry. Now, unable to perform such a hygienic regimen because it was so cold, I had to resort to the briefest of sponge baths every couple of days and a wipedown with moist towelettes. It was virtually impossible to completely get rid of the stickiness and salt residue that accumulated on our bodies.

The 'grunge factor', as we referred to it, seemed to be affecting me more than the other crew members. Willie had appropriately named the combination of dirt, dried salt, sweat and body odor 'grunge'. My narrow port side pipe berth above Willie's bunk was my personal space, my place of refuge where I could sleep, read, relax or just insert earplugs and tune out the world. I tried to maintain a 'grunge-less' area, keeping my sleeping bag clean and neat, and toweling off the salt water and sponging with fresh following my watch, before climbing into my bunk. My clothes and personal gear were meticulously organized, folded and stowed in a three foot long net hammock that hung next to my pipe berth.

6 Referenced Television & Movies, Item 13, Page 533.

Willie, on the other hand, was a complete slob. His sleeping bag and bunk, littered with food crumbs, dried salt and an assortment of dirty clothes, were about as clean as a sheep's pen. His hammock was jammed full—bulging with balled up t-shirts, dirty socks, dirty underwear, blue jeans, magazines, his toiletries and an extra blanket—sagged, stretched and slumped so low that even though it was suspended above his bunk with plenty of clearance, it now rested only inches from his head and body when he was lying flat on his bunk. It reeked worse than a gym locker. After cooking a meal on the stove, he would leave the dirty pots in the sink and unwashed dishes scattered throughout the boat and usually on his bed, which doubled for his dining room table as well.

"Automatic dishwasher on the fritz again?" I asked sarcastically, nodding toward the remnants of the previous night's spaghetti dinner piled haphazardly upon the narrow galley counter.

"Say what?" Willie said, pouring his morning coffee into a dirty cup. He had just awakened and his matted curly hair looked like Medusa's ringlets.

"Do you think these dirty dishes are going to get up and wash themselves?" I added harshly.

"If they're bothering you, why don't you wash them?"

I rose from the stool behind the chart table, brushed past Willie and started tossing the crusty plastic plates and coffee mugs into Willie's bunk.

"Just what the fuck do you think you're doing?" Willie said, his voice rising.

"Look, Professor," I replied as reasonably as I could. "This is a small space and we all have to live together, which is impossible to do with all your shit strewn all over this boat and your slovenly habits of not cleaning up after yourself. Tell you what, I'm going on watch now and I expect your area to be clean and neat and all the dishes done by the time I get off. If not, I will take all your shit and throw it over the side!"

I remember when I was growing up. We lived in a four-story home in San Francisco and my room was on the top floor along with my father's home office. From the fourth floor, my dad's office had a spectacular view of the Golden Gate Bridge and my room across the hall, which he had to pass by, overlooked the neighbor's house and their landscaping three stories below. One morning he came upstairs as I was just leaving for school and told me to clean up my room. I responded that I'd do it when I got home later in the day. When I returned home, I went upstairs and, to my surprise, my room was picked up and devoid of the messy condition in which I had left it. Upon further examination, looking out my window I happened to look down and there were all my clothes, books, magazines and whatnot lying atop the neighbor's bushes. He'd thrown everything out the window. I had to go over to the neighbors, confess to what had happened and ask permission to go into their fenced yard and retrieve my clothes from atop their bushes. I was very embarrassed, but never did it again. I now envisioned doing the same thing, although with more permanent consequences, to Willie, *Nepenthe*'s petulant and defiant little child.

Surprisingly enough, when I got off watch the boat was immaculate, all the dishes had been cleaned and put away and Willie's area was spotless. Nothing needed to be said and nothing was.

Early one morning before dawn it snowed, then as the weather cleared it became bitterly cold and the temperature dropped to below freezing. We all pitched in and bent to the task of chipping ice off the deck and rigging. Killian said that the added weight of the ice might prove too heavy for the already overburdened *Nepenthe*. I got out *Bowditch* and read the section on 'Deck Ice'. It was clear. It was a common reason for boats to break apart and sink due to the added weight. There were pictures of the damage this had caused to other vessels which hastened us to get rid of it immediately.

"We've got to have some heat," said Willie, rubbing his hands together after an hour of prying up the last chunks of the deck ice. He, Joe and I were huddled in the main cabin drinking hot coffee and Swiss Miss hot chocolate and attempting vainly to try and get warm again. Killian was at the helm.

"God, I'd love to be in front of a fireplace right now with a hot brandy and a big fire blazing," Joe said. His breath was visible as he spoke.

"Don't forget my Swedish blonde!" Willie added.

It was then that Willie came up with a novel idea to heat the boat. He grabbed a cooking pot and climbed the companionway ladder. Squeezing by Killian, he went to the lazarette hatch, opened it and retrieved a one gallon fuel can of diesel fuel out of the storage area. He unscrewed the cap and poured about three inches of the oily liquid into the pot.

"What's that for?" Killian asked.

"Oh, nuthin," Willie answered, basically ignoring him and went below, leaving the canvas hatchway cover unzipped. He added a couple of tablespoons of stove alcohol to the diesel fuel and to Joe's and my astonishment, lit a match and dropped it into the pot as if he were in the process of creating a flambé.

A fire burned upon the surface of the diesel fuel. There was indeed a very small amount of heat produced from Willie's concoction, but most of all there was thick black smoke filling the cabin.

"You imbecile! Now look at what you've done!" I cried as Willie wiped the black smudges from his face.

"Jesus Christ!" exclaimed Killian. "What did you do?"

With black smoke billowing out of the open hatchway cover, it looked like a World War II newsreel of a torpedoed tanker. Killian could hear violent coughing down below as I hurriedly emerged from the smoke and threw the burning smudge pot over the side. Both Joe and Willie were laughing and coughing simultaneously as they hurried topside to fresh air, both in virtually mime-like, smudged blackface like in a Three Stooges slapstick-like comedy scene.

Mid-winter storms continued to batter *Nepenthe* as she progressed across the North Pacific, sometimes as slowly as two or three knots. We were forced to crawl along the ocean's surface due to the fierce winds we were experiencing. If we had been on land it would be like being on our stomachs and low crawling from China to the U.S. Even though the wind was constantly howling, we could only sail with the reefed storm jib, about the size of a pocket handkerchief, and reefed mizzensail, so as not to put any more pressure on the already over-burdened yacht. The wind never let up and was always between twenty five and thirty five knots. Many nights the wind would gust and blow with such ferocity that the stainless steel hanks, shackle-like fasteners sewn into the sail's leading edge, would tear out, leaving the sail only barely attached to the forestay. The sail would then only be held on at the top and bottom, with all the middle hanks gone and in a pile on deck at the bottom of the forestay. It seemed like every other morning, I would have to sew the hanks back onto the sail's luff. The weather was constantly so bad during this period of time that each night when we would finally crawl into bed, we were never sure if we'd live to see the light of day again.

Each night as I fell asleep I could hear myself say: "just think good thoughts… " Hopefully I'd be alive the next morning to be able to 'think more good thoughts'!

We had been at sea for nearly two months and still had almost fifteen hundred miles to go. Having grossly miscalculated the amount of time for the return passage, food and water soon were in short supply and we were forced to ration. Killian prepared the food in single one-pot meals; beans, potatoes and canned vegetables were thrown together and when cooked, appeared like a thick brown mush. The only way to choke it down was to put on a heaping Tabasco sauce topping. Luckily we'd brought along three large, 12 oz. bottles and wouldn't run out, unless we were forced to eat only that.

Our skin had become wrinkled like prunes and our once beautiful golden bronze tans had faded to a pasty white pallor. Each of us had lost considerable weight. Killian, at 6'4" and normally weighing two hundred forty pounds, now weighed one eighty. Willie, tall and gangly at 6', went from one seventy to one thirty five. Joe, who had begun the voyage at one hundred eighty, now weighed one forty five, and I had gone from one forty five to a scant and gaunt-looking one fifteen. We all had the concentration camp look with sunken cheeks and hollow looking eye sockets.

Finally after two and a half months of nearly freezing temperatures, precipitated by cold, arctic born storms and without sun, the wind and sea conditions changed as we approached the California coast. By this time, the food and water had run out and we were eating lifeboat 'C' rations and drinking our ten gallon store of bottled water from our emergency supply. I plotted a course to the Farallon Islands, and after seventy three days out of the sight land, we saw the bare rocky islands twenty six miles west of the Golden Gate.

Being a self taught navigator and having learned the art by the seat of my pants always gave me self doubts. It was referred to in the Army as OJT (on-the-job training). It really wasn't until the end of the voyage that I realized I'd sort of mastered it. After 73 days out of the sight of land, I had actually successfully plotted our course and hit the Farallon Islands dead on. Although there wasn't really time to bask in the glow of that achievement, as there was still a lot to do in preparation for our arrival, inwardly I knew, and so did my guru and sailing master Dave Killian. To me it was all the accolades I needed.

I'd used every navigational tool available plus every instinctual and natural sense I possessed, and had actually been successful in pinpointing our location from the vast nothingness of the open ocean, as Dave had instructed me—it seemed so long ago.

The first thing we did after sighting land was to make *Nepenthe* appear as if she had only been out for a day sail. The fifty-five gallon diesel tanks were jettisoned overboard along with all the weapons, the ship's log and all the Far East charts. Lines were coiled neatly and everything up on deck was scrubbed down and squared away. We tidied ourselves up as best we could by cutting our beards and shaving our faces clean. The return trip had taken a total of one hundred and six days and the entire round trip voyage had lasted nearly eight months. It took over a year and a half to put the trip together from our first vision of it in the summer of 1973 until now, but there were still many more questions to answer.

March 5, 1975
San Francisco, California

For the past two months, I had fantasized about sailing beneath the Golden Gate Bridge at dawn, smoking a giant joint, while listening to the Rolling Stones turned up to maximum volume.

Now, on a crisp, clear late winter morning as the sun rose over the Berkeley Hills, a red eyed, Dexedrine wired Joe popped in the tape of Mick Jagger's 1969 *Performance* album and cued up the song entitled *Memo to Turner*.[7]

'… Come now, gentlemen, I know there's some mistake
How forgetful I'm become, now you fixed your business straight…'

Two hundred and fifty eight feet above the heeling picturesque white yawl, the morning traffic was getting started. It seemed to be an endless procession of headlights and tail lights carrying commuters across the bridge from Marin County into San Francisco. If everything went as planned, many of those commuters on their way to work, right above our heads at this very minute, would be enjoying the fruits of our labor in the very near future.

'… Come now, gentlemen, your love is all I crave.
You'll still be in the circus when I'm laughing in my grave…'

Puffing on a joint of our precious cargo, wearing my personal talisman, the lucky blue shirt, underneath a turtleneck sweater and my float coat, I felt full, as complete with myself as I had ever been.

In future years I frequently reflected on this particular moment and relished it.

'… The baby is dead, my lady said, "You gentlemen, why you all work for me."

It was decided to drop me off at the Sausalito Yacht Club in Sausalito. I was to call Phil from a phone booth and catch a taxicab to San Francisco to retrieve my pickup truck which was stored in a Twin Peaks garage. Meanwhile, *Nepenthe* would proceed to the Richmond Yacht Club, where Killian was a regular member, and tie up at the guest dock.

Once *Nepenthe* was safely at the yacht club in Richmond, the stash compartments

---

7 Referenced Songs & Music, Item 9, Page 530.

would be unsealed. I would arrive at the yacht club and Phil would be on his way from the valley in his truck. The marijuana would then be unloaded, put into sail bags and wheeled to the trucks in dock carts. Phil and I would drive the trucks over to the Twin Peaks garage while the rest of the crew cleaned up the boat in preparation for the Customs inspection.

Phil was overjoyed to hear from me. *Nepenthe* was more than one month overdue, and Phil had been anxiously waiting and very worried something disastrous had happened to us. Part of the plan had always been for no communication while at sea unless it was a dire emergency. This meant no ship-to-shore telephone calls and no shortwave or CB radio communication. Wait until it was possible to use a pay phone. We always carried rolls of quarters with us everywhere just for that purpose. It really wasn't necessary for anyone to meet us as we'd done before, since the crew of the boat could virtually unload everything themselves. I always felt that if we didn't tip our hand and give any information over the airwaves, anyone trying to intercept us or figure out what we were doing would have a much more difficult time of it. We all had our jobs to do and unless anything went horribly wrong, just let it happen the way it's supposed to. Think good thoughts…

When he arrived at the dock, Phil was shocked at the change in our appearance. "Shit! What happened to you guys," Phil said when he arrived at the boat. "You run out of food?" he added jokingly.

"That's about it, Phil. I'll tell you about it later," I replied. "Now let's get the boat unloaded and cleaned up for Customs.

The load was transported to the garage in two trucks, as planned. After the boat had been cleaned, Killian called Customs and *Nepenthe* was cleared over the phone with no physical inspection. Killian reported that *Nepenthe* had left the United States and visited some military bases and World War II battle sites in the Pacific and had nothing to declare.

After an hour long shower and a good night's sleep in a comfortable bed, I was ready to inspect the load and prepare it for sale. Phil and I went to the garage and drove the trucks down to Joe's Belmont stash house. The process of inspecting the load was begun, the weighing, labeling and inventorying of each package for sale. Not one of the packages had gotten wet or had mildewed during the voyage home.

Within two days the entire ton was labeled and ready for sale. 'Yorktown' Billy had been advised of my arrival. Up to now, only small amounts of Thai stick had been available, at the most, in ten and twenty pound lots. Would Billy be able to sell the load, and would his clients be willing to pay upwards of $1,650 per pound? These were questions in my mind when I telephoned 'Yorktown' Billy and spoke to him for the first time in ten months to arrange a meeting.

"My God!" a stunned Billy exclaimed in a hushed whisper, as he reverently held the package of Thai sticks I had brought to his Mission Street flat. There were eighty sticks, each weighing about ten grams, in a thick plastic bag which was vacuum sealed shut. Ten sticks laid side-by-side in two rows, one on top of the other, made up a bundle which was tied together by a fine piece of twine. There were four bundles to a package.

This package weighed 925 grams or a little over two pounds.

Billy slit the package with a knife. At once, the characteristic potent Thai stick smell, which had been inert for the past four-plus months, suddenly came alive and permeated the small living room.

"It's so fresh, Rick!" Billy said, amazed like a child on Christmas morning.

"We vacuum sealed it."

Billy snipped the twine on one bundle and carefully separated a few sticks. The sticks were about six inches long. They were the diameter of a nickel, while some of the larger ones were as round as a quarter. One of the larger sticks weighed 17 grams, over half-an-ounce.

"How much of this do you have?" Billy asked. His voice was still in a whisper, as if he were speaking to somebody sitting next to him during a church service.

"We brought back a ton. Do you think we can get $1,650 a pound?"

"Oh, yeah, most definitely, but I'm not sure the public will be ready for this."

At first, it was slow moving. Everybody bitched about the price, but absolutely nobody complained about the quality. For two weeks, the marijuana sold in only one and two pound lots.

"At this rate, it will all go stale before it is sold," I said.

"'Don't worry. I feel that all of a sudden it will start flying out the door. Just be patient, Rick," Billy said.

After almost three weeks, Billy got his first one hundred pound order, then another and another. The same thing happened with JQ, the red haired mustachioed giant who was also brokering weed for me. One month later, the load was completely gone and the marijuana-smoking public all over the country was craving more.

In the process, we had sold a load of the finest marijuana in the world, in a quantity never seen before. All the crew received handsome six figure payouts and as investors Phil, Pat and I were able to put away tenfold of what we'd been making on each of our Mexican scams, which was now buried beneath Phil's valley home. The three of us were now in a league of our own, having transcended from the world of average everyday large volume pot smugglers into the rarefied stratosphere of elite pioneers, at the very forefront of a whole new cadre of marijuana entrepreneurs that were to follow our lead.

Section 4

Contract Loads (1976–1977)

Chapter 22

Cindy

The tall, brown-eyed, long-haired brunette beauty emerged from the passenger side of Phil's new tan Mercedes Benz 450 SL Roadster. Together they entered the neo-Frank Lloyd Wright-style home in the affluent Peninsula suburb of Woodside which Phil, Pat and I had recently leased. The hide-a-way home, tucked into the dry brown hills, featured a panoramic view of the Bay Area and was accessed by a remote controlled gate at the top of a long steep driveway.

Papi bounded, half slid across the sunken living room's hardwood floor and greeted the pair in the vestibule.

"Down boy!" Phil said, pushing the Golden Retriever aside. "Rick, I'd like you to meet Wendy Carmichael."

"Hi Wendy. Phil's told me all about you and I can see why."

"Hello, Rick," Wendy said in a soft friendly voice, extending her hand to me. She had a firm yet soft handshake.

We moved into the living room. The 5'9" tall woman with a model's sculpted hourglass figure and waist-length braid sat on a couch next to Phil. I sat opposite them in a comfortable leather-covered armchair. I opened an exquisitely lacquered antique Chinese box and withdrew a baggie containing half an ounce of cocaine. I laid out a small amount of the powder on the glass coffee table's surface and proceeded to chop the crystalline white flake with a razor blade, carving out a number of lines.

"Phil said you've been sailing around the world on a large yacht for the past couple of years. Tell me about it," I said passing Wendy a rolled up Franklin.

Wendy inhaled two of the lines and passed the rolled up bill to Phil.

"Well, Rick," Wendy began, "when I was in my senior year at college in Southern California, one of my classmates bought a beautiful 75-foot John Alden design classic wooden ketch, *Kalahari*, with his inheritance money. First launched in 1929, the boat had a storied past and was once owned by one of Hollywood's movie legends. After graduating, our friend who now owned *Kalahari* invited eight of us, all couples, to sail around the world with him. We left from Los Angeles and sailed to Hawaii, then through the Marquesas, the Tuamotos, and Society Islands, through the South Pacific down to New Zealand and Australia. It took us about four years. Along the way we stopped, got jobs and rented houses. I was with my former boyfriend from college and after four years with him I got tired of the lifestyle and left the boat. I came back home to the Central Valley where I am living now."

"I'd sure like to meet someone adventurous like you one of these days. Any ideas?" I asked.

"Well, since you mention it, one of my friends from the yacht is coming home in a month or so for a short vacation. She might be interested. There's only one catch… she's married."

"Really… sounds kind of interesting," I replied. Silently I thought, 'I think I've seen this movie before.'

Mid-Spring 1975
Los Angeles, California

Tires screeched as the China Airlines flight from Hong Kong touched down at Los Angeles International Airport. Sitting in the plane's tail section in economy class was Cindy Walker. It had been five years since she and her husband Glen Walker, along with her close friend and classmate, Wendy Carmichael, and five others had left the States on a round-the-world sailing odyssey, the kind most people only dream about.

Cindy was about 5'2", slender, attractive and very bubbly. Her curly hair was auburn with a silver streak in front. She had a lighthearted disposition and was very funny. Her most striking physical feature though was her sparkling blue eyes which glowed like lanterns, creating a beautiful contrast to the golden suntan she acquired from years spent sailing in the tropics.

She was glad to be back in her native California. Cooking for a crew of eight for five years, combined with Glen becoming so completely self-absorbed in his position as first mate aboard *Kalahari*, was bringing stark reality to Cindy's dream of sailing off into the sunset. It was becoming drudgery and she knew it, and, at the very least, she needed a break from it all, just to clear her head, if for nothing else.

Cindy was looking forward to spending a week or two with Wendy in the valley before returning to Los Angeles where she would spend a final week picking up supplies for the yacht before returning to Singapore. Wendy had written her and casually mentioned her new boyfriend Phil Erikson and his business associate, me.

She spent the first few days with her father and stepmother who lived in the suburbs of Los Angeles. Cindy's father George Smythe had divorced her mother, Louise, years before while Cindy was still in high school. George was a public servant working for a southern California school district. He was marking time until his retirement when he met another school administration employee, Ginger, whom he later married. Both George and Louise were alcoholics and had abused Cindy both emotionally and physically. Louise Smythe used to tell her young daughter that she had never meant to have her and that she was the accident which ruined her life. In retribution, Louise used to spank Cindy with a wooden spoon and occasionally burn her with cigarettes as punishment for crying. Besides being an alcoholic, she was also a chain smoker. Cindy's most fond memories of her mother were… well, she didn't have any fond memories of her mother at all. In fact, she hated her! She could never understand what her father saw in the bitch in the first place.

On the other hand, she rather liked her father and his new wife Ginger. She was also close to her aunt Mildred, George's older sister, and her husband General Aston Crunchworth, a retired one-star Air Force general. Cindy also had a 95-year-old grandmother, Gramma Mabell, who she adored. She was looking forward to a visit with them all, except her mother who she vowed never to see again. She had planned to see them when she first arrived back in LA and again, before she left to return to *Kalahari*.

Cindy had excelled in public school and entered college on a full academic scholarship. She had married Glen Walker in her senior year, a man she had been casually dating, more for the opportunity of sailing around the world than for love. She was also dreading the prospect of returning to LA and living alone. In her sophomore year she had had a dream: even with her fine education, the only job that she would be able to find was working the graveyard shift as a waitress at Perko's Coffee Cup restaurant, for minimum wage or less. The vision haunted Cindy for years and she vowed to do anything to keep it from becoming a reality.

Cindy sensed she needed a change. She was at a point in her life when a break from Glen was necessary if their relationship was to continue. Cindy desired a better lifestyle than the one she had been living. Cruising around the world was fun, but not very much fun anymore. Every time they pulled into a new port, their main concern had to be getting a job rather than enjoying the sights and relaxing.

The week she had spent with Wendy had been entertaining, although California's Central Valley didn't hold much allure for a woman who had traveled around the world. Wendy suggested they drive up to the Bay Area, cruise around San Francisco first, then visit her new boyfriend Phil at the fabulous hillside home he shared with his friend Rick. On the three hour drive up to Woodside, Wendy told Cindy about Phil and me and that we were in the marijuana business and had made lots and lots of money.

It was more of a surprise to herself than to Wendy when Cindy asked, "What's Rick like?"

"I really think you'll like him. He's cute, athletic, Jewish and has a great sense of humor. Also, he's rich which I know won't put you off. He's a little shy though," Wendy said.

'Not a problem,' Cindy thought.

Wendy's Volvo reached the top of the long driveway. The remote controlled gate had admitted them to the fenced property after they rang the bell and had spoken with me over the intercom. Cindy was wearing a brightly colored ankle length Batik skirt that she had made herself, an airy white blouse and no bra. She was an excellent seamstress and made most of her own clothes. Wendy was dressed in white tennis shorts and a red Izod tennis shirt and white tennis shoes, no socks.

An overexcited Papi greeted them at the front door. Cindy fell in love with the golden retriever at first sight. She got down on the floor and clutched Papi in her arms while he passionately licked her face. She rose slightly embarrassed, when Wendy introduced her to me.

"I love this dog," were the first words out of Cindy's mouth. "Hi I'm Cindy, you must be Rick. Wendy never told me you had a dog."

"At this point, I wish I were Papi," I blurted out. "That was quite a scene."

"Does he act like this with all women?"

"Actually, I've never seen anything quite like this performance. I know this is going to sound funny, but are you using Canine perfume or did you roll in dog-doo or something? I'm not trying to embarrass you but I've never seen this animal act like that before. I mean, look at him. He seems like he wants to get it on with you. Hey, that's enough, boy. Calm down!" I said petting his beautiful rust-colored back.

"Did I hear you correctly? You actually asked me if I had rolled in shit? That's a lovely thing to say to somebody you've just met," Cindy said pretending to be offended.

"I'm sorry. I didn't mean to offend you." I said, slightly embarrassed. "I was just trying to be funny. You know, 'the joke lamp was lit'. Guess that went over like a lead balloon."

"Because of your wonderful dog, you're forgiven," she said. It sounded like a royal dispensation.

The tension eased out of me like air escaping from a balloon and before I knew it we were sitting in the living room swapping sailing stories. I took an instant liking to Cindy. I enjoyed her humor and relaxed manner and could tell right from the beginning she was very intelligent and witty. This was confirmed when she told me she had been valedictorian of her graduating class.

I questioned the fact she was married, but Cindy simply shrugged as if to say it wasn't important to her. Later, we went out to dinner at Julius' Castle, my favorite and one of San Francisco's most elegant restaurants. We dined at a special corner table which had a spectacular view of downtown San Francisco, the Golden Gate and Bay Bridges, with the East Bay hills in the distance.

To begin, I requested an estate bottle of white French Montrachet wine, imported Beluga caviar and Scottish smoked salmon. We shared the house Caesar salad and the Chateaubriand for two topped with Bearnaise sauce. To complement the meat, I had the waiter bring us a bottle of red Bordeaux wine. It was a 1964 Chateau Lafite Rothschild. For dessert, I ordered a chocolate soufflé and rounded off the dinner with two snifters of the finest Napoleon brandy. Cindy was flabbergasted. It was the most magnificent meal she had ever eaten. The bill came to five hundred fifty dollars and with a fifty dollar tip, I left six crisp one hundred bills.

The evening flowed with careless ease. I sensed that this was going to be more than a casual two-week fling. Everything seemed right. My life was working, colored with adventure, risk and money, but there was no one beside me to share it. At one level, I knew, my success in the smuggling business was just a distraction, a futile attempt to avoid dealing with the hollowness that I felt at my center, a sense of incompleteness which had dogged my life for the past six years, since the death of my childhood sweetheart, Sally. Maybe Cindy would be the one to fill that void, I thought.

Cindy knew the situation presented unlimited possibilities and my wealth and stability could provide the finished polished frame on the picture of her life. She saw the dynamics had the potential for being completely reciprocal.

Driving back to Woodside in my new silver Mercedes Benz 280 sedan, listening to the Rolling Stones, the cocaine from my vial only fueled our mutual anticipation. We couldn't make it to the bedroom fast enough. Our passion was like another drug, giving both of us the feeling there might be much more to this relationship.

"You know, none of this would have happened if I hadn't fallen in love with your dog," Cindy said in mock seriousness.

As we lay there in each other's arms we both suddenly became aware of another noise in the bedroom, a thumping sound on the floor next to the bed. It was Papi's wagging tail thumping on the hardwood floor.

"I think he approves," I said laughing.

Cindy and I spent the next couple of weeks getting to know each other, just hanging out in Woodside by ourselves after Wendy and Phil had returned to the valley. Pat was due to arrive from Hawaii and I had told Cindy all about him.

Upon his arrival he went to the BMW dealership and bought a new 1975 3.0 CSI coupe. It was metallic blue and his new pride and joy. The three of us were inseparable and went everywhere together, mostly in Pat's new car. Unlike my car, which had a Pendleton blanket covering the back seat for the dog, Pat's car was pristine... no dogs allowed.

One morning Pat and I had to leave and go to Hillsdale Shopping Center to run some errands. We took my Mercedes. Cindy, nearly a genius wordsmith, stayed behind finishing up the *New York Times* crossword puzzle she'd been working on and relaxing in the sun with Papi.

An hour later, returning home I saw smoke coming from the hills behind the house.

"Pat, check it out. It looks like a fire up there," I said pointing to the hills above the where we lived.

I turned the sedan up the hill as Pat was saying, "I think it coming from the house! My car! Step on it, Rick!"

As we rounded the corner and came to the steep driveway leading to the house, we saw Cindy leading Papi up the street, away from the area. Flames had engulfed the hillside behind the property and had gotten as far as a large oak tree in the backyard. Its limbs overhung the house.

I ran from the car, got the garden hose and climbed a retaining wall next to the house and got onto the roof. I began to hose the backyard and roof down. Pat leaped into his new BMW, which had less than five hundred miles on it, and drove it out the carport.

We heard the sirens as fire trucks came up the hill. Within minutes, the fire department had the situation under control. The three of us were standing at the top of the long driveway.

"What happened?" I asked.

"I was on the back deck sunbathing with Papi when I smelled smoke. I went over to the fence and a fire was burning up the hill toward the house. I called 9-1-1 to report the fire, but when they asked me the address, well, uh, I didn't know the address, only it was somewhere in the town of Woodside. I stayed on the phone while they traced the number."

I put my arm around her. Papi licked my other hand.

"I knew the only thing I could do was take Papi and get away from the fire. So we left and came up here. That's when you and Pat drove up."

"So you left my new car to burn?" asked Pat.

"Oh Pat, insurance would have bought you another car, but I don't think it covers Papi! Isn't that right, boy?" she said bending down and hugging the dog.

Another funny incident, which wasn't too funny at the time, occurred at the Woodside house one afternoon. Although the home was secluded on a quiet street with a long driveway, it did have a neighbor across the street whose house overlooked our driveway and was located up on an embankment with a large picture window positioned for the spectacular view over our house and beyond to the South Bay in the distance. It also looked directly down onto our driveway and was usually occupied by an elderly woman who sat in an old rocking chair seemingly all day long observing anything beyond or below which caught her attention.

On his bicycle, one afternoon, the paperboy was making his home deliveries and for some reason our gate was open and I was babysitting Willie's dog, Sunshine, who was visiting and playing in the yard with Papi. Both dogs heard the paperboy toss his paper and came barking up the driveway, through the open gate and into the street, pinning the boy up against the embankment. The woman in the window above immediately called the police who arrived a few minutes later. The young cop jumped out of his patrol car just as Joe came up the driveway, at which point, the cop with a clipboard in his hand, turned towards the dogs and pointing at Papi with his clipboard yelled, "Whose dog is this?" At this point, Papi lunged at the officer and bit him in the upper thigh. The cop screamed and reached for his holstered semi-automatic weapon. Quick thinking Joe jumped between Papi and the cop, restraining an angered Papi who was now growling and angling for another hit.

"Put that away, before you hurt someone!" Joe ordered to the stunned officer, who rather sheepishly re-holstered his gun. It really wasn't too funny at the time, but we had a good laugh about it later. Papi could have been shot, but instead was quarantined at home for two weeks and I had to go to the police station and present his rabies certificate and apologize to the officer, who declined to file formal charges.

* * *

Almost three years earlier, in November of 1972, following my arrest for cocaine possession in Chicago, I had double-crossed my father by returning to Mexico rather than going to work for him in Cleveland. My decision to continue smuggling marijuana broke the signed agreement I had with my father. As a result, my father had disowned me.

Dick saw the situation in black and white, while my mother Helen's love colored her actions. Helen was torn between her husband's decisions and her love for me, her son. Although Dick would have nothing to do with me, Helen frequently talked to me and occasionally I'd meet her for lunch. It was a never-ending argument between Helen and Dick which seemed to dominate almost every dinner conversation and it was affecting their marriage. Helen was constantly coming to my defense while Dick adamantly stuck to his contractual agreement. In Dick's mind, there was right and wrong and nothing in between. I was wrong to have broken the written agreement and was reaping the consequences of my defiant actions.

It was such a constant sore point, Dick finally issued my mother a written ultimatum, as only he could.

My dearest Helen,

… You are my wife and I love you with all my heart. This continual aggravation cannot continue. I implore you to make a decision based upon moral principles rather than blind motherly love. At this point, you will have to choose because it is driving us apart. Either you stop seeing our son, or I will have to move out…

Helen sent a copy of the letter, along with a letter of her own to me.

Dear Rick,

… I love both you and your father but I cannot allow this situation to break up my marriage. We are going to have to reach a common ground. I don't want to lose either of you, so our relationship has to be very low profile. I want you to never doubt, both your father and I love you; each of us in our own way…

For the next two years Helen's relationship with me was conducted clandestinely, while she chipped away at Dick's dogmatic position. It was only after my astounding financial success from the first Thai smuggling trip, Helen finally began scoring points.

"You should meet Rick's girlfriend, Cindy, dear. She's such a lovely girl," Helen said, refilling her wine glass.

"Mumm…" Dick grunted. At least it was a step up from tossing down his fork and storming away from the dinner table.

"She was valedictorian of her graduating class in college."

"Mumm… Pass the butter please, Helen."

Another time it was "Rick just bought a new Mercedes, dear, and you should see the house down in Woodside he's renting. It look's like he'll have made more money by the time he's thirty than it took you twenty-five years to make." The remark was not made to disparage Dick's business acumen, but rather to show him I'd finally one-upped my father within my father's own value system: cold hard cash and lots of it.

Finally, begrudgingly, Dick moved off his inflexible position. He rationalized that his son was no worse than old Joseph P. Kennedy, rum-runner and former U.S. Ambassador to the Court of St. James, a man who had made a fortune smuggling whiskey down from Canada during Prohibition. Dick ceased his war against me and nothing more was ever said about me breaking the agreement and my father's trust.

* * *

I was devastated when Cindy made the decision to return to Singapore. It was eleven thirty at night after a late dinner at the chic San Francisco restaurant, Trader Vic's, with Cindy and my parents. It was the first time I had been with Dick in nearly three years, although I had briefly talked with my father on the telephone. On the drive back to Woodside, Cindy broke the news.

"I am going back to Singapore."

The bottom suddenly dropped out of my world. The past two months with Cindy had been timeless. I guess, though, in reality I knew this day would come, but when it did, I wasn't prepared for it.

"Have I done anything wrong?" I asked, stunned.

"No, Rick. It's not about you. It's about me. I think you know how I feel. Do you trust me?"

"Yes," I said, putting on a brave face and trying not to show my emotions.

"Look, I promise to come back. I have to take care of some stuff with Glen, and it's going to take a little while. I need a little space to sort everything out. This is all happening too fast. Please give me a little time. You understand, don't you?"

"Yes, I understand. I'll write you," I said swallowing the knot in my throat.

So, Cindy left for LA, then two days later caught a flight to Singapore, the boat and her husband. A week later, the 75-foot yacht *Kalahari* departed for the Seychelles, an archipelago of 115 islands located in the middle of the Indian Ocean.

August – September 1975

The preparations for the next smuggling venture began. It had been decided to streamline the operation for efficiency. We started by making the packing and sealing operations in Thailand more like an assembly line. Joe and I began researching ways to better seal the bags. We located a firm which manufactured vacuum sealing machines in San Francisco.

We made an appointment to see the equipment, using the story that we would be packaging ginseng root and dried fruit in the Orient for shipment to the U.S. and worldwide. We were shown portable machines which weighed about 150 pounds, had wheels and could be powered by 220 DC, common in the Orient, or with a generator if no other power source was available. We were also told that to seal, store and transport the perishable merchandise of our business proposal, we would need oxygen moisture-barrier bags made of poly-mylar and not plastic. The salesman further explained that a regular plastic bag would eventually leak and lose its vacuum seal, while a poly-mylar bag would hold its seal and preserve the freshness of the contents within the bag almost indefinitely. Joe found a source in the East Bay and submitted a start-up order for one hundred thousand bags. Although the poly-mylar bags were three or four times as expensive as regular plastic bags, it would certainly be worth it if there was no deterioration of the weed during shipment; also the new bags were crystal clear, unlike common plastic bags which were slightly hazy. This would show off the Thai sticks in the best presentation possible for sale, after the long overseas journey. Three sealing machines were purchased. Two of the 220 DC version were to be shipped to Thailand and the third, a 110 AC model, was to be kept at the stash house to seal any bags which might get ruptured in transit. Joe suggested that other things could be sealed: stores for the upcoming sea voyage and also money. Now money could be vacuum sealed and buried directly in the ground, without the ammo boxes which might otherwise mildew, and would no longer be subject to discovery with a metal detector.

Willie proposed, to save time, why not ship the boat on a freighter to the Orient? Killian and I did the legwork and found out, indeed, *Nepenthe* could be shipped to Singapore aboard a container-carrying freighter. It would save time, wear and tear on the yacht and minimize the risk of another possible encounter with pirates, at least on the voyage over. The shipping cost was ten thousand dollars and *Nepenthe* could be loaded at Long Beach. We discovered it wasn't unusual to ship yachts overseas in this manner and that it was done virtually all the time, as yachts being built at various shipyards worldwide were usually shipped to customers located overseas from the construction yard. The cover story was that *Nepenthe* would be racing in the Southern Ocean Racing Circuit and was going on a shakedown cruise in preparation for the racing series. The shipping line's branch manager accepted the story at face value, not even raising an eyebrow.

Willie had a hidden agenda. He was basically hedonistic and lazy. He would rather spend the two months required to sail the boat to the Orient indulging himself in his usual pursuits of women, drugs, alcohol and gambling, rather than being sequestered in close quarters aboard a sailboat with a bisexual sea captain. The following year, the decision to again ship the boat to Singapore would prove a costly error. I remembered saying to my cousin Marty, "Never let the trip get out of your hands."

Nepenthe on the cradle in Long Beach shipyard in preparation
to ship her to Singapore aboard a container ship in 1975.

Nepenthe was fitted with the latest satellite navigation system, SATNAV. The old LORAN system was in the process of being fazed out, but was still operable and would be kept as a backup. Killian, Joe, Phil and I sailed her down the coast from San Francisco to Long Beach. Again, Phil got horribly seasick and had to be let off, this time 100 miles down the coast in Monterey. At Long Beach, a sturdy wooden cradle was constructed, upon which the boat would be set for its shipboard journey across the Pacific. Both the main mast and mizzen masts were taken down and stored on *Nepenthe*'s deck. Phil went back to Adobe House and dug up half a million dollars. The money was wrapped in neat bundles which we secreted into the hollow of the eight-foot-long spinnaker pole which we inconspicuously stowed down below with the rest of the sails and gear.

It was decided that I would not sail on this trip. Willie was offered the chance to be navigator. Knowing Willie's propensity to blame others for his mistakes, I made it clear to him that this was unacceptable and I would not tolerate it.

"Now if you're going to be navigator, then you are going to be the one who'll get the proper charts and all of the navigation aids," I told him. "I'm not gonna do it for you."

"Yeah, yeah, yeah, I understand."

"Hey screwball, don't give me that 'yeah, yeah, yeah' shit. You sound like a Beatles record. Listen Willie, and I want you to hear this loud and clear. You will be responsible for any miscalculations or bad judgement. I will not take the blame for any missing charts or poor decisions you make as navigator. This part of the trip is resting on you and you alone. If you fuck up, it's on you. I accepted that when I was navigator and when I screwed up, you sure let me know about it. Well I won't be there this time, but nevertheless I'll hear you from thousands of miles away, if you blame me for anything. Got it? You have to give me your word, you will assume the consequences for your actions. Do you understand what I am saying?"

There was a pause as Willie digested all of this.

"OK, Rick. I understand what you are saying and I accept."

Willie spent days at the chart store in downtown San Francisco gathering the material required for the voyage. He vowed not to take the same route home we had taken last time, and he would do his part to streamline the return passage. Willie reasoned that if the load was completely sealed and hidden from sight, as on the prior trip, they could cross the Pacific in tropical latitudes, stopping wherever they liked.

I proposed that *Nepenthe* should be shipped to Singapore sometime between October and November, which would give the crew plenty of time to refit the boat for the voyage home. Pat determined that the best time to procure the load would be in December or January, in order to get the best quality marijuana. It would be the height of the growing season, when the flower tops would be at the pinnacle of maturity. The Thai crew would have ample time to acquire the weed from the growers and plenty of time to package and store it for a mid-March loading aboard *Nepenthe*. Also during this time of year, typhoons in the western Pacific were usually rare. The container ship would be taking a much more southerly route to avoid being in most known storm tracks and therefore we, as well wouldn't risk going through another one like last time.

August 1975
Mahe Island, the Republic of the Seychelles

Cindy set her empty wine glass down and bleakly looked at the dirty dishes piled in the sink, the remains of a spectacular lamb curry she had cooked for dinner. The rest of the crew were in *Kalahari's* salon finishing the tropical fruit salad and their fourth bottle of wine.

"Cindy," Glen called from the salon, "can you bring another bottle of wine?"

Even with the two galley fans going, it was still very hot and humid down below. Glancing out of the porthole, she could see that dusk was still an hour away.

'Screw this,' she thought, untying the kitchen apron from around her waist and hanging it up on a hook. She felt angry. Then she remembered that my latest letter was in her apron pocket.

'If I were with Rick, I wouldn't be cooking for eight people every goddamn day,' she thought, retrieving the letter and going up on deck. It was slightly cooler and the late afternoon breeze dried the sweat which trickled down the cleavage between her two petite breasts.

She walked aft to the stern and sat in a canvas-covered deck chair. Finally able to relax a bit, she put her feet up on the rail and took the letter from her pocket and began to read it. She had already read the letter at least five times.

My dearest Cindy,

Life without you is dull and boring. Your spirit and humor are really missing in my soul. I sure wish you were here in my arms...

"What the hell is going on here? I thought I told you to get us some more wine. Have you suddenly been struck deaf?" snarled Glen.

"Yes, sah! I'll get right on it, bwana."

"Hey, what are you reading there?" asked an agitated Glen. "Looks like a letter from home. Here, gimme that!"

Glen grabbed the letter and started to read... *My dearest Cindy...* "What the fuck is going on here. I think somebody is screwing my wife!"

Cindy lunged at Glen and snatched the letter back. Glen reached out to grab it back and accidentally hit Cindy with a glancing blow on her chin.

"You bastard!" she cried. "That's my letter."

"Give it to me, you slut!"

They were both shouting now, Cindy tore the letter from his hands. She balled it up in her fists and the last thing she screamed before diving overboard was: "I'm through with you, asshole!"

Reaching the shore, she sat in the sand, buried her face between her hands and began sobbing.

* * *

Somewhere in my subconscious I could hear a persistent ringing and, as I came up out of a deep sleep, I realized it was coming from my bedside telephone. I woke with a start. The digital clock showed 2:12 AM. I fumbled for the light switch on the night table.

"Hello?"

There was nothing but the sound of static for a second or two, then a tinny distant female voice came on the line.

"This is the international operator. I have a collect call from Cindy Walker, in Mahi in the Seychelle Islands. Will you accept the call?"

"Yes," I said as my heart leapt into my throat.

"Rick, I've left the boat and Glen. It's over."

"What do you want to do, Cindy?" I said. I could feel my chest pounding as if I had just run the hundred yard dash.

"I want to come back to California."

"Shall I send you a ticket? No strings attached."

"Yes, please."

The most direct flight to San Francisco involved a change of planes in Bangkok with further connections in Hong Kong. Cindy arrived in Bangkok at the same time as the political unrest reached its peak in South Viet Nam, Laos and Cambodia with refugees flooding into Thailand. The situation was chaos as telephone communication was disrupted and flights out of the country were temporarily suspended. Cindy, having little money, was stranded at the Opera Hotel, a cheap, third rate dive near the red light district of Bangkok, off Patpong Road.

For five frantic days she was marooned there while she tried to get a flight out of the country. On the fifth day, she decided to take a chance and go to Don Muang Airport and try to somehow get out.

The Bangkok traffic was a mess, worse than usual, but she finally hailed a three wheeled open-air 'tuck tuck' and with her one tattered suitcase climbed aboard. She was nearly asphyxiated during the hour long ride to the airport, breathing the smog-filled air. When she arrived she was drenched with sweat and her eyes stung from the direct exposure to vehicle exhaust fumes, which had billowed into her face for the past hour. She managed to get the last seat aboard a Garuda Airlines flight to Hong Kong, where she then was able to catch the Korean Airlines puddle jumper that stopped in Seoul, Tokyo, Guam, Honolulu, Los Angeles, and finally San Francisco. The trip took nearly twenty-six hours.

Totally exhausted, Cindy arrived in San Francisco and decided to recuperate at our Woodside house for a couple of weeks, then figure out what to do next. What came next was, she moved in permanently. I was thrilled. I had already been looking to buy a house and now with Cindy here, the situation couldn't have been more perfect. I found a nice house in a quiet neighborhood in Menlo Park on three quarters of an acre for $80,000.

I knew, even though I had the money, plunking down $80,000 in cash would be extremely stupid, and leave me vulnerable to anyone questioning such a blatant display of a cash outlay. Instead, I went to my father who agreed to cosign a loan with Bank of America. This was a very important move for me, as I was able to make my monthly payments like clockwork, thus establishing both my credit and financial credibility.

Escrow closed within ten days, and the following week, Cindy and I moved into the Menlo Park house. Together, we bought furniture and Cindy did the decorating. Her favorite color was blue which she tastefully wove into all the furnishings and appointments.

The 1800-square-foot main house and detached garage and storage room were encompassed by a large yard offering complete privacy. Set back from the street, the little compound was surrounded by a six-foot wooden-grape-stake fence in front of which, on the street, was a six-foot-thick row of mature ten-foot-tall, thorny bottle-brush plants with red flowers. There was a long driveway with an electrically con-trolled gate. The landscaping was so inconspicuous and natural looking, unless you really looked for the house while driving down the quiet street, you would never notice it was even there. It would be a great place for Papi to roam, and the storage room in the detached garage building was perfect for the forthcoming load.

Cindy had no trouble adjusting to my wealth and the excitement of my way of life. I was very generous. She took to her new lifestyle like the proverbial duck to water. I liked to drive my pickup truck, so Cindy used the Mercedes to do her errands. It soon became 'her car'. I gave her money, whatever she needed. It was not unusual for Cindy to spend a thousand dollars on jewelry and designer clothes, which she looked great in. She would often lunch at fashionable Palo Alto restaurants and always had a supply of cocaine within reach. There was a vial in her purse, one in her sewing basket and a quarter ounce in a kitchen drawer. It was seemingly a bottomless supply, which I regu-larly indulged in as well.

Her favorite song without question was, appropriately entitled: *Dear Mr. Fantasy*,[1] by the British rock group Traffic, and indeed she certainly fantasized about a future life with me.

> 'Dear Mr. Fantasy play us a tune, something to make us all happy
> Do anything take us out of this gloom, Sing a song, play guitar, Make it snappy…'

For Cindy, the outside world she had held in her mind's eye was beginning to take shape. It was to become an attractive web from which to entice, control and manipulate those around her, especially me. Money was not an end in itself, but for someone like Cindy, her stunted inner life still remained that of a shamed and fearful 14-year-old abused girl, unable to trust or love anybody other than animals.

---

1 Referenced Songs & Music, Item 10, Page 530.

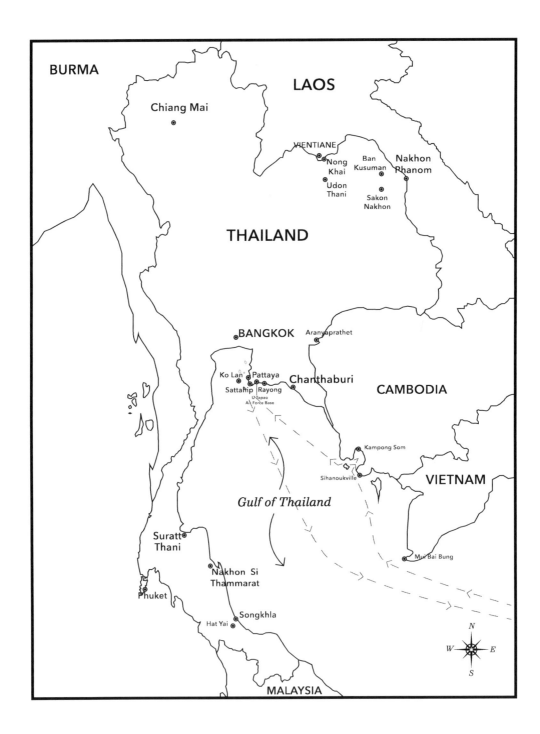

Chapter 23

Christmas Tree Farm

November 1975

Preparations continued for *Nepenthe*'s second Thai smuggle. I flew to Los Angeles to help Killian ready the boat for shipment to Singapore. *Nepenthe* was carefully secured to a wooden cradle, her two masts lashed tightly to her deck. A crane then picked up the cradle and deposited it upon the freighter's deck among hundreds of shipping containers. Three weeks later, *Nepenthe* safely arrived in Singapore with Killian and Joe present to supervise the unloading and to help clear the yacht through customs.

Killian looked very official dressed in his starched white duck trousers and white polo with 'Yacht *Nepenthe*' monogrammed above the pocket in blue lettering. He carried himself with a sophisticated air, reserved for yachting types everywhere in the world. Although I pleaded with him not to wear his ridiculous looking captain's hat, he wore it anyway and along with his 'dress whites' and snobbish attitude, he sashayed through his meetings with customs officials without any unusual questions. In reality Killian was the perfect smuggler as he didn't look or act like any of the rest of us. With his clean-cut looks, dressed in his spiffy, clean captain's outfit and with his unmistakable confident attitude he was never questioned by authorities who always assumed him to be on the up-and-up. Conversely none of the rest of us could pull that off as easily, as we all pretty much looked like what we were… smugglers!

Pat was already in Thailand scoring the thousand kilos which were to make up the next load. I flew to Singapore and checked into the Raffles Hotel where I met Joe. We took the half million dollars stashed in the spinnaker pole and caught a flight to Songkhla in southern Thailand where customs was virtually nonexistent. Joe returned to Singapore the same afternoon while I, with half a mil in a flight bag, took a domestic flight to Bangkok, since there were no customs whatsoever on flights within the country. I put the money in our safe deposit box.

Two vacuum sealing machines and fifty boxes of special poly-mylar bags which had been sent to Pat's uncle's import/export business two months earlier were being stored at his Bangkok office, having routinely cleared Thai customs. The machines, bags and a series of roller tables were transported to the Chanthaburi ranch. The tables had been acquired to speed up the packaging operation much like a conveyer belt. With the machines in the middle of the assembly line and two rolling tables on each side, it was set up so the packages could be efficiently fed from where the Thai crew carefully put the individual Thai stick bundles into the bags, to the sealing machine station, and then after sealing, onward down the line to where the sealed packages were put into gunnysacks. The ranch's buildings had been completely repaired, re-roofed and wired for both 220 and generator operation complete with a transfer switch in case we lost power, which could happen frequently in the Thai outback. It took a week to set up the assembly line and perfect its smooth running operation. Often in the hot and humid afternoons, Pat and I would break from work and ride our motorcycles through the jungle surrounding the ranch.

"I think it time to show you where ganja is grown. It good idea for farmers to meet you. They get great 'face' if you go to them," said Pat. We were sitting on the same rock by the waterfall where we had first discussed getting into the Thai marijuana business two years earlier and smoking a Thai doobie. This time, though, the weed was much more potent and far superior to the outstanding average Thai weed we smoked back then, which was the best I'd ever had, until now. The waterfall's fine mist cut through the late afternoon's thick heat.

"How long will it take to get there?" I asked.

"Mabbe day and a half to get up country to Sakon Nakhon in Northeast Thailand. We drive by Cambodian border, then along Mekong River up by Lao border."

I nodded and took another hit.

Pat continued, "It important for you to make growers understand, you want only best quality. They see you as 'big boss' from America."

I agreed, it would have a great impact on the villagers at the grass roots level if they knew that anything less than the finest quality would be rejected. Showing the growers exactly the quality I wanted would establish a standard of excellence for them to meet, now and for future loads.

Two days later, Pat and I left the ranch and drove north on the main road paralleling the Thai-Cambodian border. We had been warned by a service station owner when we filled up in Chanthaburi not to venture off the highway, even to take a piss, as the trenches beside the road had been strewn with claymore and anti-personnel mines. Refugees were streaming across the Cambodian frontier, to avoid being slaughtered by the Khmer Rouge. The horror inside Cambodia still remained unknown outside this little corner of South East Asia. The Khmer Rouge were systematically exterminating much of the Cambodian population. Before the 1979 Vietnamese invasion, upwards of two million Cambodian people, mostly upper and middle class citizens, intellectuals and property owners, had been butchered in what later became immortalized in the book[1] and Academy Award-winning movie, *The Killing Fields*.[2]

Every fifteen or twenty miles we had to stop at Thai military checkpoints. Heavily

1 Referenced Books, Item 13, Page 532.
2 Referenced Television & Movies, Item 12, Page 533..

armed Thai soldiers manned the checkpoints, intensely scrutinizing us as we passed through. Before coming over to Thailand, I had made a quick trip to New York to go to the United Nations Headquarters souvenir store where I bought a couple of dozen UN stickers, t-shirts, windbreakers and baseball caps emblazoned with the UN insignia. The stickers were pasted onto the bumper of Pat's BMW 530 and all over our brief-cases and camera bags. We wore the t-shirts and baseball caps and Pat told the army officers at the checkpoints that we were photographing for the United Nations. We were summarily waved through and usually given a sharp military salute.

We passed the largest Cambodian refugee camp located a few miles north of the border town, Aranyaparathet. Driving by, we gazed at the hoards of listless dull-eyed people standing behind the barbed wire encampment staring back at us. In this camp there were thousands of refugees who had escaped with only the clothes on their backs and now lived in a run down, disease infested tent city behind guarded gates and razor sharp concertina wire hoping to someday return to their once beautiful country, now being run by one of the most despicable characters in modern history, Pol Pot. It was sad, beyond belief.

Farther north, the road paralleled the Mekong River. Laos lay across the coffee-colored water to the north. Hours later we arrived in the dusty northeastern Thai town of Nakhon Phanom. We turned off the north-south road and headed west some fifty miles to Sakon Nakhon where, after twelve hours on the road, we spent the night in the town's best hotel, what would generally be regarded as one step above a 'flea-bag' motel, but at least it was clean. Next morning we traveled an hour down a bumpy dirt road to a remote jungle village called Ban Ku Su Man. Fine red dust and mud covered the BMW.

Thirty or forty thatched huts stood on stilts in a clearing which had been cut from the dense green jungle. Pat parked the car in front of the village's longhouse, a sort of town meeting hall. The other huts were individual family dwellings. The village was very primitive and there was no electricity or running water. Pat and I climbed up a set of wooden stairs and entered the main building.

Pat introduced me to the village Chief. He was an old man and with his two sons, both in their late twenties, ran the marijuana growing operation. The Chief, his sons and a number of important village elders, already gathered in the longhouse, placed their palms together in a Thai gesture known as a 'wai' and bowed deeply, as a sign of great respect.

I gave a short speech which Pat translated into the northeast Thai dialect and again the village elders 'waied'. I now suddenly understood why I was so highly respected. I was their ultimate benefactor, directly responsible for their livelihood.

"I'd like to see the fields," I said to Pat.

Pat spoke with the Chief's sons.

"OK, we go with these two," Pat continued, gesturing toward the two youths standing in front of the longhouse with M-16 automatic rifles carelessly slung over their shoulders.

The group including the Chief's two sons, the guards, Pat and I walked about a mile on a dirt path through the jungle. We came to a clearing where in front of us appeared to be a five-acre Christmas tree farm, only the Christmas trees were eight to ten foot tall marijuana plants at the height of maturation. The flower tops sparkling with potent resin glistened in the sunlight. I had never seen such a beautiful sight.

At the field's far end were drying sheds where row upon row of freshly cut flower tops hung upside down to dry. I took out a pack of Zig-Zag wheat straw rolling papers from my pocket, plucked a top from the most beautiful plant I could find, and proceeded to roll a four-paper zeppelin-shaped joint. I lit it and inhaled deeply. It was the most potent weed I'd ever smoked. I passed the joint to Pat. The marijuana was so fresh, it wouldn't stay lit and I had to re-light the joint after every hit. By the time we'd each had three tokes, both Pat and I were supremely stoned. I took a few photographs of the plants. The Chief's sons proudly posed for pictures of themselves, with M-16's slung over their shoulders and dwarfed by the towering plants with sparkling buds, heavy laden with pollen and resin, drooping over their heads.

We returned to the village where we were introduced to a typical Thai family. Pat and I climbed up the steps into the thatched hut. There was one main room, where the entire family ate and slept. Sitting upon bamboo mats were the grandmother, the mother and two young girls. In front of the women was a large thirty-three-gallon plastic bag, filled with freshly dried marijuana flower tops. The women and girls were meticulously manicuring each individual top with cuticle scissors then breaking off the flower tops from the main stem and fastening each one to a thin bamboo stick, and securing them with a fine piece of twine. The combination of sticky resin and twine held the tops securely to the stick. Each twenty sticks were then secured together in two rows of ten stacked one on top of the other then secured together with another piece of twine and held in a bundle.

Each woman had a stack of bundles at her feet. I picked up a particularly nice looking bundle from Grandma's pile and using one of the few Thai phrases I knew, I spoke directly to her, "Suay, mak, mak," meaning very beautiful. The old woman put her palms together in a 'wai' and bowed. Her tan and wrinkled face broke into a wide toothless ear-to-ear grin.

I turned to Pat. "The quality must all look like this. Only the freshest, lime-green to gold color is what we want. All of the sticks should be fat like this, so the buds are not too compressed." As an example I picked up a particularly gorgeous one, a half inch in diameter stick showing it to the group of women workers. I produced a small hand held gram scale from my briefcase and weighed the stick. It weighed 18 grams. Then I weighed a particularly fat bundle containing twenty sticks. It weighed 285 grams.

"Nobody in the United States has ever seen anything like this and it will blow their minds! This is exactly what we want and only this, Pat. Make it clear to the Chief, we will accept nothing less and please impress upon him, if they send anything other than this down to the ranch we will throw it away and not pay them for it. If they have anything of lesser quality, please ask them to sell it to someone else. We will not accept it. Period. I can't stress the importance of this concept enough. If we accept anything less, then that's what we will get. Not to be trite, but 'water seeks its own level, the lowest level.' If we set the bar as high as it will go, we can dominate the market and anyone else who brings it in will have lesser quality and won't be able to compete."

I continued: "You know, Pat, others are going to follow us and right now we are the only ones doing this kind of quantity and quality. It can't last. Probably Ciro will get involved as well. It's only a matter of time. We both know that."

"I never want to work with him again. He fuck me over. First time shame on you, second time shame on me!"

"Well, you know how close Phil is with him and I can't guarantee he won't spill the beans and put pressure on us to include him," I said.

"No way!"

"Well, I don't want to say 'I told you so', but it's coming. We have to keep this part of the trip really quiet. There's a lot at stake here and not just the money. If we can keep this to just our small group, we can do it for many years to come. If we allow others in it will spiral out of control and it will change, just like Mexico and Columbia. Others will be coming to us, I guarantee it. There's nobody who can get the quality we can, because we have the right of refusal. It's not like we're scoring in Bangkok or Pattaya, like most other smugglers. We're up here at the source. If it's not up to our standard, we're not going to pay for it. They know it and the Chief agreed to it."

We left the village hut and returned to the longhouse, the Chief's domain, where he sat as we had first found him. Pat explained everything to him and he agreed. I didn't understand exactly what Pat was saying, but I got the gist of it as the Chief was nodding approvingly to Pat at the end of each request.

Pat then reached into his briefcase and handed the Chief twenty stacks of purple 500 baht notes. Five hundred baht was about $25 U.S. Each stack contained one hundred notes, or twenty five hundred dollars. The entire amount handed to the Chief was one million baht, the equivalent of $50,000. This represented the down payment for the entire load.

"Please tell him, we will pay the balance upon delivery to the ranch," I said.

The Chief was very happy and told Pat the first half-ton would be delivered to the ranch in five days. As a token of the village's gratitude, the Chief's wife gave me a sacred piece of religious cloth which had been in their family for a number of generations. We said goodbye and returned to Bangkok to pick up more money and rendezvous with the Thai team.

Between last year and this, the Thai team had gone through a complete internal reorganization. Suay really couldn't handle the responsibility and logistics Pat required. Another Thai figure emerged who could, Soomchart, or just plain Chart. I Americanized it and called him Charley. Charley, through his family, was well connected with members of the Thai government and the Thai military police. His father, Charley Sr., whom we called 'Papa', was a former ranking officer in the Thai Army whose military connections ran deep. He had spent years providing U.S. soldiers with anything they wanted when in Thailand and on leave or R & R from Viet Nam. Charley, the son, was a fast-talking, good-looking, fun-loving Thai about the same age as Pat and me. He was also a very accomplished race car driver and had spent many years racing Asian stock cars, mainly Toyotas and Hondas, in races throughout Asia. He was becoming well known on the racing circuit and was developing quite a following. Although quite hot tempered, Charley had great organizational skills and a very loyal group of close associates who now comprised our Thai team. Charley came from Bangkok, but now lived in Pattaya. He also spoke and understood very good English, which was a welcome change from Suay, whose command of the English language was about the same as a kindergartner in most American schools. Although there was a 'slick' side to Charley, I took an instant liking to him and because of 'Papa', I knew we were well protected in case of any trouble.

It was decided that Charley would send one of his team north to Ban Ku Su Man in a ten wheeled truck on a weekend, when the highway traffic would be heaviest and passing through the checkpoints much easier. 'Papa' would be riding shotgun and would be carrying a briefcase full of baht in case of any problems. In Thailand, money talks and bribes are commonplace, especially at the military checkpoints, where a couple of 'purples', 500 baht notes, would usually get you waved through without any inspection and just a snapped military salute.

The following Sunday, a crew of five Thais arrived at the ranch to join Pat and me. The next afternoon a brightly colored ten-wheeler pulled up. It was loaded with fresh manure and the stench was overpowering. The Thais shoveled the manure off the truck and onto a large pile. It would be used as fertilizer for the ranch's banana and rambutan trees, which were now back in production and producing fruit after many years of lying fallow, as Pat's grandfather's interests now lay in running his Bangkok service station. Beneath the shit, on the truck's flatbed, carefully placed under multiple layers of plastic sheeting and quadruple bagged in large garbage bags, was 2500 twenty stick bundles, half-a-ton of Thai stick marijuana. The remaining half-ton was due in exactly one week. The Chief's eldest son had accompanied the truck down from the Northeast. Pat gave him another million baht for the remaining half-ton.

Next morning, the assembly line went into action. One man carefully unloaded the Thai stick bundles and placed them at the end of one of the roller tables. Another man placed four 20 stick bundles weighing between 800 to 1000 grams (one kilogram) into one of the special oxygen moisture barrier bags. He then placed a brand new crisp five baht note (25¢ in U.S.) inside the bag. I had decided to enclose a bank note depicting a likeness of the King of Thailand, King Bumibol Adulyadej, also known as Rama IX. It gave the package a distinctive polished look and would be our trademark. I had picked up several thousand brand new five baht notes from the bank in Bangkok before coming to the ranch.

A third man took the weed-filled bag and placed the bag's open end into the vacuum sealing machine. He depressed the foot pedal, whereupon the jaws of the machine closed on the bag, leaving two flat metal suction tubes inside the bag to suck out all of the air. When the air had been extracted, the tubes were automatically withdrawn and the bag was sealed between two heat strips located between the machine's jaws. It was decided not to use the second machine in the assembly line, but to keep it in reserve in case anything happened to the first one.

Great care had to be taken so as not to seal the bag too tightly, just enough to draw out all of the air without compressing or crushing the beautiful Thai sticks. After a little trial and error, the settings were perfected and each bag was completely sealed. The process was again repeated with two more bags to ensure against punctures. Consequently each package was triple bagged, as was done in Mexico. The sealed packages were then sent down the opposite roller tables to a fourth man who placed the packages into a gunnysack. Each gunnysack had a green stripe running down the length of it, serving as a guide for filling the sack evenly.

When the gunnysack was filled with thirty packages, the top was sewn together with red plastic twine by the fifth man and then weighed. The twenty gunnysacks making up a half-ton took two days to package and were stored in a separate room. Another half-ton remained. The Thai crew left for their respective homes after being told to return to the ranch in one week.

It was now December 1975. I flew home to spend the Christmas holidays with Cindy. Pat remained in Thailand to oversee the packaging of the remaining half-ton.

Nepenthe was still in Singapore with Killian, Joe, and Willie who recently arrived with Pete Newman. Willie had come equipped with all his charts and updated sailing directions, ready to assume his position as navigator. Killian had moved the boat from the commercial wharf to the Changi Yacht Club. Killian quickly became a fixture at the yacht club bar, where he spent six hours a day drinking Singapore slings.

One night Joe, Willie and Pete decided to arrange a little surprise for Killian. They went down to Bugis Street, a raucous street in downtown Singapore where during the day it is a famous bazaar for shopping for Indonesian batiks and all sorts of local treasures, but at night it is transformed into a virtual walkway and parade of transvestites. At considerable cost, they hired one of Singapore's most beautiful transvestites for the entire evening. Joe was completely dumbfounded. The 'woman' who went by the name of Tam was absolutely stunning, about nineteen years old and an Asian beauty. She had high cheekbones, a gorgeous hourglass figure and long raven colored hair. Her makeup was done to perfection and she wore a high necked blue silk Chinese cheung som dress, slit up the side, and black stiletto high heel shoes.

"She's beautiful," Joe exclaimed. "I just can't believe, Tam's actually a man! Doesn't seem possible."

"Do you want to make sure?" challenged Willie.

"Not on your life!" said Joe, shuddering.

"When Dave lifts up that dress, he'll be in for the shock of his life," remarked Pete.

"And I'm not sure he'll mind!" said Willie.

Killian was aboard *Nepenthe* sitting behind the chart table, drinking gin and going through a list of supplies when Willie summoned him on deck.

"Hey, Dave." Willie called loudly from the dock. "We've brought a little company for you."

Killian came up on deck. When he saw Tam, his mouth dropped open; he was speechless. Killian had always fancied Asian women, but Tam was by far the most beautiful 'creature' he'd ever seen.

"Everything's been taken care of Dave. Why don't you two get acquainted and we'll see you tomorrow?" said Joe.

As the three crewmen walked down the dock toward the yacht club bar they were shaking with laughter.

The following morning Joe, Willie and Pete returned to the boat. Killian, bare chested, wearing parrot green Bermuda shorts, was lounging in the cockpit, smoking a cigarette and splicing a line. Nothing was said as the three causally boarded the boat, but the captain looked very relaxed. When Joe surreptitiously shot a glance at him, Killian was grinning like the cat who had just swallowed the canary.

* * *

Phil and I decided to bring Cindy and Wendy to Thailand for a vacation while we made final preparations for loading *Nepenthe*. This was probably one of the stupidest decisions we ever made. We must have blindly succumbed to their requests to again visit Asia as they'd done aboard *Kalahari* years before. Previously on the boat they were forced to work whenever in port. This time however, in their minds, this trip would be first class, all expenses paid for, exotic shopping holiday fun. Somehow, we conveniently overlooked the fact that what we were doing was very serious and dangerous, to say the least. Our lives and freedom were always at risk. This was a business and not just a carefree vacation. What Killian had once said about ocean sailing still applied, now, even on land. "This job requires one hundred percent of our attention, one hundred percent of the time," if we wanted to be successful. Not that we didn't love girlfriends, but injecting them into our smuggling team dynamics was, at minimum, a huge distraction and potentially a recipe for disaster.

Anyway… The four of us plus Pat stayed at the Pattaya beach bungalow.

After the first day, tension began to develop like approaching storm clouds. Phil was the first to be affected. Wendy demanded his constant attention, interrupting the planning sessions with the three of us.

"I've squeezed you a fresh glass of orange juice," said Wendy, coming into the rattan furnished 'war room'.

"Thanks Wendy. That's one beer and two glasses of orange juice you've brought me in the past hour," Phil replied. "Please don't take this the wrong way. I really appreciate you're trying to help, but can you just let us work alone for a while, hon? We're pretty busy. Why not go to the beach with Cindy?"

"I'm already sunburned!"

Phil sighed. He rose from the table. "We need to talk. Let's go outside."

I purposefully shuffled my notes while Pat just looked very annoyed.

They walked out onto the porch. "Look Wen. Pat, Rick and I have a lot of work to do and we can't be distracted. We're under a real tight deadline."

"You aren't spending any time with me, Phil. Don't you want to be with me?" Wendy pouted.

Phil sighed again. He knew a hook when he saw one. "Wendy, my first priority in being over here is this project with Pat and Rick. It's business. Would you rather Rick and I had left you and Cindy back in the States?"

"No." She sounded like a little girl.

"Then please leave us alone. We need to work," he said in a slightly raised voice. He turned and walked back into the bungalow leaving Wendy alone on the porch.

I was also stressed. Cindy, who had had little trouble entertaining herself by reading for hours on end, was finally getting bored.

"Rick, why don't you take a break. Let's go shopping," Cindy said breezing into a midmorning planning session we were having out on the bungalow deck.

Pat had a sour expression on his face as if he had heartburn. Phil impatiently drummed the tabletop with the fingertips of his right hand.

"Look, sweetheart," I said. "I have to concentrate on business right now. Can't you read for just a while longer or go to the beach with Wendy while we wrap this up. I promise to join you soon."

The look in her eyes was as hard as Solingen steel.

"Honey, please," I pleaded, trying to head off an argument. Instead, I unwittingly added kerosene to the fire.

"Promises, promises," Cindy shot back. "This is what you always say, but it never happens. I didn't come here to play second fiddle."

"I'll be just a few more minutes, honey..."

"Look, don't patronize me with this 'sweetheart' and 'honey' bullshit!" said Cindy suddenly erupting. "I've had it, Rick! All you three do is work. I need some attention too. You just ignore me and expect me to be there at night to spread my legs for you when you're finished with your secret deals. The next morning you run off and forget I even exist. You really don't love me, Rick. I just know it. You only love me when it's convenient for you. Well, screw you, lover boy!" she yelled, picking up a bottle of Stolichnaya vodka from the liquor cabinet and storming out of the room.

The room was electrified with tension. I arose from the table, visibly shaken, and excused myself. "Don't go anywhere, guys. I'll be right back. I'm sorry for this," I apologized.

I walked through the adjacent living room, out the front door and hurried down the bungalow's exterior staircase where I caught up to Cindy and Wendy just outside the carport. "Cindy, please wait. Let's talk about this. I want to explain something to you... please," I implored.

"Talk, talk, talk. That's all you do. I just want outta here. Get me a plane ticket back to the States, now," Cindy demanded.

"Cindy, please..."

"Come on Cindy, please talk to Rick," Wendy said, trying to interject some calm into the situation. "We need to stick this out together till they're finished. It'll only be a few more days, and then I'm sure they'll make it up to us somehow. Anyway, I don't want to stay here without you for company, and I can't leave Phil."

A cold, calculating look drifted across Cindy's face and then it was gone as quickly as a passing ocean squall. She theatrically set the bottle of liquor down on the polished hood of Pat's BMW sitting in the carport. "Rick," she purred coyly. "I might feel better if I had that ruby necklace and earrings we saw at the gift shop at the Pattaya Palace yesterday."

"Oh, honey, you'd look great wearing that jewelry. I promise you when we're finished here I'll take you to Bali. Just you and me alone, and we can shop for all of the neat things we find there. I promise," I continued, blindly allowing myself to be sucked deeper into her web. "Here's enough baht for that neckless and earrings. I love you, sweetheart." I said handing her a wad of purple 500 baht notes.

"Thank you, sweetie," Cindy said. She kissed me affectionately on the cheek and left with Wendy in tow. It was almost as if she'd completely forgotten about her outburst just a few moments prior.

I picked up the whiskey bottle, returned upstairs to the meeting and replaced the bottle in the liquor cabinet.

"Well, well. If it isn't the spineless worm," spouted Phil. "Why don't you crawl back up into your chair so we can get back to business?"

"Thanks, I really appreciate that," I said sarcastically, trying in vain to quell the deep humiliation I felt.

Now it was Pat's turn. "Here, women respect men and don't cause man to lose face in front of friends. I hope tonight you give her good beating with stick."

Pat did not escape the strain. He was grumpy. His happy go lucky, carefree attitude was gone. He would burst into a rage for no apparent reason shouting in Thai at Charley or any of the Thai crew who happened to be within range.

Pat and I were driving back from the ranch to Pattaya in Pat's BMW.

"What the hell is wrong with you?" I demanded. "Why are you acting so pissed off?"

"Nothing wrong."

"Come on Pat, something's eating at you. You've been this way since the girls arrived." Suddenly a lightbulb went on in my head.

"Has it anything to do with Cindy and Wendy being here?"

"No."

"You're not a very good liar, my friend. Tell me what's going on. I promise you, it won't leave this car."

Then it all spilled out, like a faucet you couldn't turn off. "It all changing Rick. You know how we used to go to massage parlors, you, me and sometimes Phil? Sit up late at night, drink, laugh, have fun. It different now. You not have freedom. I not have 'fan', like you guys," Pat said, using the Thai word for girlfriend.

"I don't know what to say Pat. There's nothing to feel threatened about. Yeah, things are changing for everybody, but our feelings for each other as friends and business partners remains the same, khao jai?" I said using one of the few Thai phrases I knew the meaning of, 'do you understand?'

"Khao jai kop, I understand." Pat said.

The load was ready to be moved from the ranch to the bungalow. The women moved into two suites at the luxurious Pattaya Palace Beach Hotel.

Nepenthe was scheduled to leave Singapore in the middle of February. This time, the boat would not check in at Pattaya, but rather stage from the southern coastal Thai town of Songkhla, where she would fuel up and take on final provisions before the three day sail north to the loading site at Ko Lan Island.

Phil and I flew from Bangkok to Songkhla and met *Nepenthe* where the projected timetable for the night rendezvous with the Thai fishing boat at Ko Lan was finalized. I had hoped that Phil and I could return to Bangkok on a flight out of Songkhla, but a plane crash had closed the small airport. Also, the train which ran the entire length of the Malay Peninsula from Singapore to Bangkok had already left the station on its route north from the nearby town of Hat Yai. So, with our last viable option of the day, I hired a local taxi to take us five hundred miles north to Bangkok.

The taxi was a battered '69 Chevy Impala with no muffler, bald tires, worn suspension, a broken front windshield, and an air conditioner seemingly only working intermittently or not at all. The chain smoking taxi driver was a sullen character with a black pirate-like patch over his left eye who never stopped talking.

It was the most miserable trip Phil or I had ever made. The drive north was hot and sticky and we both stuck to the plastic seat covers in the taxi which made the trip even more unbearable. The trip took a horrific thirty six hours and ran through some of the most dangerous provinces in Thailand, areas notorious for Communist insurgency, where fierce fighting broke out on a regular basis. On roads leading into major provincial towns, there seemed to be military checkpoints every ten miles. We passed through Nakorn Si Thammarat where the driver pointed out, like a tour guide for the damned, that a 'hit man' could be hired for as little as 100 baht ($5.00 U.S.). We passed the menacing town of Surratthani. To me it seemed that the entire southern part of Thailand was populated with rude, scowling people who radiated nothing but terminally bad vibes. We both tried to sleep, but it was impossible. It seemed that as soon as either of us fell asleep, the driver would awaken us with some nonsensical bit of local trivia delivered in such broken English, neither of us had any idea of what he was spewing on about or we'd hit a pothole and be bounced awake.

We finally arrived in Bangkok, dog tired, where we picked up Pat's second car, a Toyota, and drove back down to Pattaya to tell him *Nepenthe* was already on the way. She was due at Ko Lan within the next forty eight hours. Pat and Charley had already made sure the load was prepared to move from Chanthaburi to the beach house at a moment's notice. *Nepenthe* arrived on the lee side of Ko Lan the following evening. Next morning, Pat, Phil and I drove a speedboat five miles to Ko Lan, met *Nepenthe* and confirmed she was ready to take on the cargo.

That afternoon, Charley and 'Papa' brought the load to the Pattaya beach house and met the rest of the Thai crew. After dark, they took the load, consisting of forty gunnysacks, to the beach in a Toyota van with the rear seats removed. The entire load took two trips in the van.

Each weed-filled gunnysack measured three feet tall by two feet wide by one foot deep and weighed between 55 and 60 pounds. The forty gunnysacks amounted to 240 cubic feet, and if placed side by side in four rows,(stacked two gunnies high) it would consume a space 12 feet long by 5 feet wide and 4 feet high or about the size of the interior space of a completely stripped Volkswagen bus.

It took the four Thai crew members thirty minutes to hump the gunnies, one at a time, across twenty yards of sand and place the sacks aboard the waiting fishing boat, whose bow was beached on shore. Pat, Phil and I boarded the fishing boat which crossed to Ko Lan where *Nepenthe* rested at anchor.

With the vessels rafted together the crew transferred the load to *Nepenthe* where the gunnies were opened and the load stashed into the concealed compartments. Stashing the weed, sealing the compartments, and repainting the stash covers took the rest of the night, and at dawn, *Nepenthe* raised anchor and headed south out of the Gulf of Siam.

Phil, Wendy, Cindy and I left Thailand and flew to Hong Kong for some rest and shopping before returning home. While Phil and Wendy returned directly to California, true to my promise, I took Cindy for a weeklong 'real' vacation in the tropical resort island of Bali. There we relaxed and enjoyed each other's company by spending time on the beach and leisurely shopping for some of the unique Balinese artwork which characterized the colorful Indonesian island. A week later, we returned home to await *Nepenthe*'s arrival.

* * *

As navigator, Willie had a completely different idea how *Nepenthe* was going to make the trans-Pacific crossing. He had plotted a course through the tropics and he planned to motor as much as possible, hopping from island to island. Their last stop was Saipan in the Mariana Islands. The 'island hopping' concept was great, so long as there were islands in their general direction. Unfortunately, after Saipan, unless they veered north toward Wake, some 700 miles out of their way, there was nothing but blue water between *Nepenthe* and the North American continent, about 5,000 miles somewhere to the east.

It soon became apparent that Willie's navigational skills left something to be desired. After fueling twice in the Philippines and again in Saipan, unless they got more diesel somewhere, they might have to, in Willie's words, "do the unthinkable and actually sail."

Somewhere out in the middle of nowhere, Joe spotted a large boat on the horizon.

"Hey, guys," Joe called from his position at the helm. "Maybe we should try and contact that boat and see if they can fuel us up and give us an accurate position, since 'the Professor' can't seem to pinpoint us."

The crew came on deck and Joe handed Willie the binoculars.

"Looks like a freighter, but I can't tell what flag they're flying," Willie said.

"I'll try and reach them on the radio," Killian answered.

"Little boat to big boat. Little boat to big boat. Come in big boat," barked Killian over *Nepenthe*'s radio. He held the mic in his right hand and depressed the 'talk' button again.

"Hello, big boat, this is little boat 50° off your starboard bow. We are approximately two miles east northeast of your present position. Do you copy?"

In a heavy Russian accent came the reply, "Da, little boat. Ve see you. Are you in distress? Over"

"Little boat to big boat. No. We are not in distress. I am an American private yacht, *Nepenthe*. We have a slight navigational problem. Can you give us your exact position? Over."

"Da, our current position is 16° 20' 19.37" North latitude, 169° 33' 41.22" East longitude. Can ve help you? Over"

"*Nepenthe* to big boat. Thank you. We could use some diesel, if you could spare a hundred gallons or so. Over"

"Russian vessel to *Nepenthe*. Ve can help you. Ve vill slow and come to you in fifteen minutes. Hold your position. It takes time for us to slow and turn. Over."

On a glassy sea, fifteen minutes later the huge 500-foot Russian freighter loomed over the 41-foot sailboat like a dinosaur compared to a mouse. The freighter lowered a skiff into the water, carrying three Russian crewman, two fifty-five gallon barrels of fuel and two liters of Russian vodka in bottles capped with Coca Cola bottle tops. Killian put the fenders over the side and soon the two were rafted together. Joe got out the hand pump and transferred the diesel to *Nepenthe*'s blue deck barrels. Killian worked out a suitable barter for the transaction by offering three bottles of California Pinot Noir and four recent issues of *Penthouse* magazine he had brought along. An hour later, they said their goodbyes and *Nepenthe* resumed heading eastward.

Their course took them no higher than 30° North latitude where the weather was balmy and pleasant for the most part of the voyage. At about one thousand miles off the California coast they turned northeast up to 38° North, San Francisco's latitude, and on one of the last days of April 1976, a little after 3:30 AM, *Nepenthe* sailed underneath the Golden Gate Bridge. The entire trip took 57 days, almost half the time as the first smuggle.

Willie called me from the Sausalito Yacht Club in Sausalito, before motoring over to the Richmond Yacht Club. Accompanied by Papi and in my lucky shirt, I drove over from Menlo Park to meet the boat. Phil came down from the valley with his truck. The weed was put into sail bags and ferried in dock carts to our trucks and driven back to my house. The boat was sanitized and Customs was called. At 7:30 in the morning, a sleepy Customs inspector came to the boat.

"Where's this vessel been?" queried the Customs inspector, as he swung his legs over *Nepenthe*'s lifelines onto the boat.

"We campaigned her down in Australia during the Southern Ocean Racing Series," Killian replied.

"Uh, huh. How'd you do?" the inspector asked as he followed Killian down the companionway ladder.

"Not as good as I had hoped."

"What was your last port of call?"

"The island of Saipan. How about a cup of coffee. I make it the Navy way, strong with a little salt."

"Thanks," the inspector said looking around the main cabin.

Killian suddenly paled. Sitting in the spice rack was a sealed glass mason jar containing several golden Thai sticks. It was part of their smoking stash. He casually slid the plastic partition closed and poured two cups of coffee.

"How do you take it?" Killian asked, trying to maintain his composure. His hands were rock steady as he poured the coffee.

"Black," he answered coming out of the forepeak.

Killian handed him the cup. "I'm going topside. I've had enough of this boat for awhile. Meet you there when you're done," Killian said. He prayed the man would not slide the spice cabinet open.

The inspector took a couple of swallows, set the cup down and followed Killian up the ladder.

"Thanks for the coffee," the Customs inspector said, getting off the boat. "Everything's in order. I hope you fellows have better luck in your next races."

Willie, Joe and Pete patiently waited on the dock standing by their duffel bags as the inspector left. He casually checked Pete's bags and ignored the other two and said goodbye.

"Cheers," the man said as he left.

The load was driven to my Menlo Park home and put into the storeroom. The weed was inventoried, weighed, and readied for distribution. The load had arrived in perfect condition and was the best quality ever to reach the U.S. This time Ciro's partner Walter Brugger was given a share of the load to broker as well as 'Yorktown' Billy and John 'JQ' Quinn. The ton of Thai stick was sold in three weeks and bonuses were paid all around to the sailboat crew. Again we pocketed ten times what we would have made on the Mexican trip and a month later Pat and Joe flew back to Thailand with a quarter mil for the Thai crew's share.

I was right in my premonition, others would come. I later learned that while we were doing our second boatload smuggle, Ciro and Walter had shipped a converted Airstream trailer to Singapore and had scored a three hundred pound load of Thai sticks. The load had been scored by one of Ciro's acquaintances named Joe-the-German who had frequented Thailand as a tourist and was a regular at the various massage parlors on Bangkok's Patpong Road. There Joe had contacted a local Thai who was able to score the three-hundred-pound load. The drivers, a couple in their 50s, drove the loaded trailer back to Singapore where it was shipped to Los Angeles and made it through customs without a hassle. The load was second or third quality and couldn't hold a candle to what we were bringing in. But the door was now opened and I knew we hadn't heard the last of it.

Chapter 24

Going Galactic

Late August 1976
Homewood, Lake Tahoe, California

Ciro Mancuso, extremely competitive by nature, was green with envy over Phil's, Pat's and my success. The thought of his former associates, especially Pat, who had once been a subservient gofer, now making so much more money than him, rankled Ciro to the core of his being. The curly haired, olive skinned marijuana entrepreneur was still running loads from his avocado ranch in Tlaquepaque with the trailers Pat had outfitted years before. However, he was not making nearly the kind of money his old friend Phil Erikson was burying beneath Adobe House. Even the three-hundred-pound Airstream load from Thailand with mediocre Thai weed couldn't compare to the loads Phil, Pat and I were bringing in, and the rewards for his efforts paled in comparison. He was furious and extremely jealous.

Over the course of the summer Phil saw Ciro quite frequently. Phil had just bought a chalet at North Shore and Ciro was just completing construction of his new million-dollar lakefront house on the West Shore, not ten miles away from each other. Ciro would invite Phil to his house for a drink or whatever to enjoy an afternoon at the shores of Lake Tahoe, sitting in the sun out on his dock. They'd smoke joints, sniff coke, drink beer and talk. The discussions would always be centered around our Thai trip. Over time, Ciro would ask questions and Phil couldn't lie to his longtime friend and business associate and would let bits-and-pieces of information out. Finally after about the third dockside session, Ciro just came right out and offered to partner with us if we would load his boat. By then, Phil had told him all of the details and our 'trade secrets' and now he wanted to copy what we were doing, as well as score from us and load his boat. Ciro assured Phil it would be 'a piece of cake' and he would not try to 'reinvent the wheel', as he put it, and since we had already worked together successfully, we could do it again. He had enticed Phil to do what he could, to convince Pat and me to work with him, promising him that if we did, it would mean wealth beyond belief.

I was astounded when Phil proposed this joint venture to me and that he 'sort of' told him how we did it.

"I can't believe you told him everything," I said. I was livid. "Ciro will fuck us. I promise you, he will fuck us. I'm totally against this, Phil. I don't want to bring any more people into the trip. It'll start getting way out of control. You mark my words."

"Calm down, Rick! We stand to make a lot of money. Ciro told me, he's planning to buy a boat which can handle about a ton and a half. We'd get 40 percent of the load just for scoring the weed and loading his boat. Think about it. That's almost another three million split between, you, Pat and me."

"I'm sure, Pat will be dead set against it. He really hates Ciro and you know it," I said.

"I've already talked to him, and the amount of money we'd be making convinced him to put aside his personal feelings. Pat's behind this one hundred percent, if Ciro pays him the fifty plus interest he owes him."

"You what? Phil, goddammit!" I exploded. "I can't believe you went behind my back. What are you, working for Ciro now? Fuck! I can't believe any of this shit! You promised not to and now you're going to be responsible for fucking up our whole gig! You're fucked!"

"Settle down, Rick. Everything will be all right."

"Well, I can see from all of this you've stacked the deck and the vote is already two to one, so what choice do I have? If we go ahead with this, Phil, I guarantee you, with more people, the trip will spin out of control and somewhere down the line, and I don't want to be an 'I told you so' but, believe me, somebody is gonna fuck up big time, and we'll all wind up in jail. Mark my words!"

* * *

Ciro Mancuso and his partner Walter Brugger purchased a 50-foot ketch named *Drifter*. They planned to ship it to Singapore late in the fall aboard an APL container ship, exactly as Phil had told Ciro we'd done the previous year and were planning to do again next month.

Meanwhile, Ciro had another run-in with the law. He was arrested south of San Francisco near the small coastal town of Half Moon Bay for possession of half an ounce of cocaine. He hired one of San Francisco's best defense attorneys, Patrick 'Butch' Hallinan, who got the charges reduced to a misdemeanor. Hallinan's fee was $25,000 which Ciro gladly paid. Ciro's relationship with Hallinan was to last another fifteen years.

There were other smugglers who now wanted in on the action. Mexican pot smugglers and hashish smugglers who brought in hash from Morocco and Lebanon were now aware of our Thai scam and wanted to be able to score loads from us. The prospect of doing contract loads was becoming overwhelming. Including Ciro, three different smuggling groups approached us and wanted Pat to score for them. The only reason the wiry Thai even considered doing contract loads was the prospect of making a phenomenal amount of money. Like Phil, Pat's pursuit of money began to outweigh his judgment and predictably I was outvoted two to one.

Pat negotiated a 60/40 split with Jonathan Jacoby who proposed a one and a half ton load. Jacoby, a friend of Pat's old friend Mike Stallings, who had sailed with Killian and Woz on the second Mexican boat trip, was from Hawaii. Jonathan, an avid surfer, was in the rarefied ranks of those who surfed the big 30 to 40 footers at Makaha, Waimea Bay and the Pipeline. He had been running hash smuggling scams from Lebanon and Morocco to Maine aboard sailboats. A recent incident on his last run brought 'heat' and a desire to forgo any more East Coast offloading operations. During offloading two-tons of Moroccan hash on the rugged coast of Maine near the town of Machias, Jacoby unexpectedly encountered a park ranger on patrol in the state park where the nighttime clandestine operation was taking place. He summarily planted a smashing left hook into the side of the stunned ranger's face, knocking him out cold. The ranger's last words as his knees buckled and he hit the soft Maine beach sand were "Lordy, Lordy, Lordy." He eventually came to, but the load was long gone by then. However, he reported the incident and a BOLO (Be On the Look Out) was circulated on the East Coast. Nothing ever came of it, but Jacoby was thoroughly spooked and was in search of greener pastures. Jacoby, the six feet tall, sun-bleached-blonde surfer with an athletic body and a smile that women found irresistible, had a 55-foot ketch motorsailer named *Kona Wind*.

Another 60/40 deal was negotiated by Pat who was introduced to a group of San Diego area smugglers also through contacts of Mike Stallings and Jonathan Jacoby. The group called themselves the Coronado Company and were said to run their smuggling operation like a military combat team.

Pat and I were first introduced to only Bob Lahodny who was initially the face of the group. Bob was from the north San Diego county beach community of Encinitas. The 5'11" dark haired, smooth talking, former member of the Coronado High School swim team had the slick, flashy personality which matched his Hollywood good looks. Bob's idea of dressing up was wearing a Hawaiian shirt unbuttoned halfway to his waist, khaki slacks, loafers with no socks and more than one gold chain around his neck. His flashiness and outgoing personality got him the nickname 'Lights'.

Later we met Ed Otero, the 'commander' of their beach unloading crew. Ed was a roly-poly six-foot-tall cigar smoking surfer from Oceanside, California, with long curly blonde hair, a pencil thin mustache and loud mouth. He always exuded an infectious and very confident enthusiasm, an old 'slap you on the back' and 'let's get 'er done' kind of guy.

The real leader of The Company was a shadowy, seldom seen figure, who was only referred to in whispers and always went by an alias. He was actually Louis Henry Villar, the former Coronado High School Spanish teacher and coach of the high school swim team. Originally from Cuba, Villar was tall, thin, wore glasses and drove a '66 Corvette. Not your typical high school teacher, Villar was 'cool' and a favorite among his students. Villar had migrated to San Diego several years earlier from New York. Spanish being his native language, he was able to secure employment teaching Spanish at Coronado High School. He had medium-length graying hair which he wore slicked straight back. Usually quiet and reserved, Villar played tennis and dressed conservatively. Back in the late 1960s a couple of his pupils were members of the swim team and were also small time smugglers, bringing in a few kilos from across the border in Tijuana. Since they didn't speak Spanish, they invited Villar to come along and translate for them and together, Otero and another student by the name of Lance Webber formed what became known as the Coronado Company.

Ed Otero had started smuggling while still a student at Coronado High. He and Webber would buy a few kilos of weed in Tijuana and paddle them across the border in San Diego Bay on their surfboards. They graduated to Zodiac inflatables and finally to fishing boats and their entourage of smuggling participants grew as well. As the amounts they smuggled grew larger, they recruited their former high school Spanish teacher Lou Villar, who negotiated their deals in Spanish. Villar remained virtually a shadow figure, mainly negotiating with the suppliers and staying in the background while Webber and Otero ran The Company's operation. They called Villar 'Pops' because of his age and sophistication and he soon ascended to the top of the organization.

Bob Lahodny, now a student and marijuana dealer at San Jose State College up in Northern California, had a circle of friends and customers in nearby Santa Cruz which included Jonathan Jacoby, Mike Stallings and his partner Dennis Moronsky. It was Mike Stallings who then introduced Bob to Pat Suraghoomkol. Bob owned a 60-foot ketch named the *Pai Nui* and did one Mexican sailboat smuggle to build up capital for Coronado's first Thai trip. Because of Bob's connection to Pat, the Thai connection, Bob was granted a full one-third partnership in the Coronado Company. He replaced Lance Webber who was reluctantly bought out of the organization, a move which would later come back to haunt them in spades.

Pat envisioned the upcoming year would be a banner year: another ton aboard *Nepenthe*, 1½ tons for Ciro and Walter aboard *Drifter*, 1½ tons for Jonathan Jacoby aboard *Kona Wind*, and 2 tons for the Coronado Company on *Pai Nui*. He predicted the gross returns could possibly top the eight figure mark.

Pat began to view himself as if looking through a camera's fish-eye lens, spotlighted in the picture's center, having the primary role, while the others, namely Phil and me, were only peripheral, and thus viewed distorted and of minimal importance, at the edge of the lens' image. Pat saw himself as the more important partner. He thought of himself as doing more work than Phil or me and demanded a greater share of the profits. Pat claimed his job was the operation's pivotal point: scoring the weed, packaging the product and loading the boat. Pat did not consider Phil or my roles in the operation as being so important. After all, we were only responsible for unloading, storing and selling the weed and transporting the funds and equipment to Thailand and managing the stash house. There was also trouble brewing in paradise, as the Thai crew, especially Charley and 'Papa', began to resent Pat's newly acquired 'farang' or Westerner's attitudes and affectations. They saw him change from one of their own to a snobbish elitist who looked down upon them as if he was a king sitting on his throne and they were mere subservient peasants who should jump to his every beck and call.

Pat threatened to break up the partnership with Phil and me, and it was only due to a great amount of persuasion, conciliation and kowtowing on my part that our little group remained intact.

"When it comes down to it, I not need you guys. I'm paying two of you to do one man's work," Pat said. He had dropped by my Menlo Park home late one morning for coffee. Cindy was out shopping.

"Wait a minute," I interjected. "You're paying me? I think you're missing the point, Pat. Aren't we all in this together? Have you forgotten how this all got started? Wasn't it Phil's and my capital which got this whole thing off the ground?"

"Yeah, but things are changing. I'm doing all the work."

"That's bullshit! We do the unloading, and run the stash houses. We provide you with the supplies and funds, and we're responsible for holding the money."

"So what? The people I've negotiated new deals with can do all that stuff. What I need you and Phil for?" Pat said. He was getting a little agitated.

"Are you sure you can trust those people? Didn't Ciro fuck you over once before? This time it will be on a much grander scale, and you can bet on it!"

"Tell you what I do. I give you guys twenty fi percent of my share on contract loads, but we keep same deal on *Nepenthe* trip, OK?" Pat offered.

"No, not OK!" I responded. "The trip is falling apart. Everybody is starting to think of themselves as being the most important and downplaying other people's roles. The trip has worked so far because of trust and fairness. This is not fair. We don't work for you. We work with you. Remember, Pat this is not your trip alone."

"I still feel, on contract job, what I'm doing is half the work and one of you could do what both of you are doing. Mabbe we split the share on these loads. I get half and you guys split the other half."

Both Phil and I reluctantly agreed to Pat's proposed division on the contract work; otherwise, we feared, Pat would cut us out completely. I felt like this was a deja vu event, just like when Woz met Ciro to try and negotiate the terms of the second Mexican boat trip, except this time Pat was in the role of Ciro and Phil and I were Woz. I guess nothing ever changes. After all those years of watching their 'holier than thou' attitudes from the position of being Ciro's coolie and Walt's gofer, some of it must have rubbed off on Pat. He was now becoming like them, always trying to gain the upper hand at someone else's expense.

I can't say I wasn't changing as well. A person could not make the kind of money I was making at such a young age or live the kind of lifestyle I was living with the nice cars, exotic vacations, ounces of cocaine within reach, the best pot in the world to smoke whenever I wanted, and with the power a major league drug smuggler commands, without a basic change in attitude. Indeed I was confident, probably cocky at times as well, and occasionally maybe a bit arrogant. As with most drug smugglers, it comes with the territory.

It seemed like everyone I knew was driving exotic cars, so I thought if I got one and tried to tone it down a bit, so as not to make it 'over the top' conspicuous, it wouldn't attract too much attention, especially where I lived in Menlo Park where affluence abounded. Just up the street on El Camino lived one of the Saudi royal princes who was attending Menlo Junior College, the so-called stepping stone to Stanford. He always had the flashiest cars around, Ferraris, Lamborghinis, Porsches and I even saw a Bentley pull into his gated driveway one afternoon. So I didn't think it would look out of place if there was just another nice car in the neighborhood. I really wasn't into sports cars very much, so I decided to find a Mercedes Benz 450 SEL 6.9 sedan. I wanted one in metallic silver blue, so I set about to find a dealer who carried this particular model and color. After calling nearly every Mercedes dealer in the country, I found exactly the car I was looking for in New Orleans.

After speaking with the dealership's manager, I negotiated the price to $55,000. With cash in our briefcases, Joe and I split up and went to six different banks in the Bay Area and got cashiers' checks in $9,000 amounts. You could get any amount under $10,000 without having to fill out any paperwork, just give them a name, any name, like 'Joe Schmo' and tell them who to make it out to. So with $55,000 in cashier's checks we flew first class to New Orleans where we were met by a driver from the Mercedes dealership in a new 500 Limo. We were escorted into the manager's office who took us to a huge warehouse loaded with three floors of new Mercedes Benzes in every make, model and color. He led us straight to the car I had requested. It had 18 miles on it. After a great dinner in the French Quarter, Joe and I set off for the West Coast, with a library of Rolling Stones tapes, an ounce of cocaine and, of course, I'd rolled several joints of Thai stick for the road, of which Joe was forbidden to have any due to his 'limitations' dating way back.

The 6.9 had an adjustable ride height knob which hydraulically could raise and lower the vehicle several inches for a smoother ride. Six hours later, after the odometer read 501 miles, one mile over the required 500 mile break-in period, on a lonely stretch of Interstate-10 somewhere in Texas, I lowered the vehicle to its lowest setting and floored it. It seemed like, in the blink of an eye, the speedometer was pegged at over 140 mph and yet it felt as if we were hardly moving.

My plan was, when I got home I would have the 450 SEL and 6.9 silver emblems removed from the trunk lid and replace it with the more common and much less expensive 280 SE label. Not nearly as outrageous looking as driving the very expensive 6.9. I'm not sure it fooled anyone, but I felt much better about it.

"Has it been five minutes, yet?" Joe asked, referring to the amount of time which had elapsed since he had his last blast of coke off a gold coke spoon he had acquired at a gold jewelry shop in Kota Kinabalu on the first boat trip. Willie and I also each had one.

"I think it has, better give me a sniff too," I said.

"Um… do you think it might look odd, if a cop stopped us doing 140 in the wee hours of the morning, sniffing an ounce of cocaine and listening to the Stones at full blast?"

"Oh, sorry." I said. "I'll turn the music down!"

* * *

Phil and Wendy were married in late September. Phil purchased a piece of property near his family's ranch in California's Central Valley and had designs drawn for
a custom house to be built on a bluff overlooking the San Joaquin valley. The construction cost was estimated to be north of three quarters of a million dollars. He had
also recently purchased a quaint small old time Lake Tahoe chalet overlooking Tahoe's
north shore.

Phil was starting to take more of a back seat role in the partnership, taking fewer
risks now, since he was married and hoping to raise a family. This was upsetting to me
as it looked as if I was going to have to take up Phil's slack.

It seemed as if Pat had assessed the situation correctly.

"Look, Rick, my main priority right now is getting the house built. Things change
when you get married. I have to play it a little safer now. You'll understand when you
get married," Phil said knowingly.

"Oh, sure. Great cop-out!" I replied. This couldn't have come at a worse time. "You
know, we actually have at least three times more work to do now, since we're going to
be scoring weed and loading boats for other groups, and you're easing up. If you recall,
this was your idea. Now, I'm beginning to feel like Pat, doing the majority of the work,
taking the major risks and turning over half the money."

"Look at it another way, Rick. One of us has to be clean and in the background if
things turn ugly and someone gets arrested."

"Just so long as it's not you who gets popped, eh, Phil?" I sarcastically said.

Phil ignored me. "Things will go easier if you think of the extra work as three times
more money."

"That's fine for you to say when you're hanging out at your new place, or, should
I say, places, and I'm running around the world like a chicken with my head cut off;
turning all these loads and running back and forth to the Far East like a yo-yo. I guarantee Cindy is not gonna be real happy about this, Phil."

My words couldn't have been more true. Not only was Cindy upset because I was
going to be away more often, picking up Phil's share of the work, she also found it
nearly impossible to run our household now, since we'd started an extensive remodeling
project on our Menlo Park home.

Construction had begun on a new garage, with an adjoining party and game room
and sauna. Beneath the sauna's removable grated floor a hidden safe was installed and
in the attic, above the game room, a false wall was built which could completely conceal
over a ton of weed. A guest cottage and office were also built. In addition, termite and
dry rot damage had to be repaired in and under the main house. The grounds were re-
landscaped around a new kidney shaped swimming pool and spa, creating an exclusive
country estate setting.

For the first time in my smuggling career, the drudgery of work was getting to me.
The adventure was becoming stale, mundane and the rush was ebbing.

"Goddam it! Screw it all!" I swore, as I worked my way through the telephone book.
I found the number I wanted, picked up the telephone and dialed Air France. "Cindy,"

I yelled above the sound of hammering, the shrill whine of electric saws and popping of pneumatic nail guns. "We're going to Tahiti!"

September 1976
Bora Bora, the Society Islands

The island of Bora Bora was a forty minute flight from Tahiti. The view from the small prop driven airplane evoked romance with a capital 'R' and an almost mystical feeling. Jagged volcanic peaks loomed above the green island whose color was so brilliant, it almost made the eyes sore. The scent of tropical flowers wafted in on the humid afternoon breeze.

"Wow!" I exclaimed, stepping off the plane. "This place is Bali Hai!" I said, referring to *Bali Hai*,[1] the song about the fictional magical island of Rogers and Hammerstein's 1949 musical *South Pacific*.[2] It was as if everything on the island, the colors, the smells and the emotions were somehow magnified.

> '… Bali Hai will whisper in the wind of the sea:
> "Here I am, your special island! Come to me, come to me"…'

We stayed at the Hotel Bora Bora in one of the thatched beach huts on the sparkling white sand. During the days we went snorkeling on the reef lying beneath the turquoise water, or we bicycled around the island buying paintings, wood carvings and trinkets. Enjoying the simplicity of just being together, we contentedly spent each sunset lying in the Pawley's Island hammock, strung between two palm trees in front of our hut.

"I can't think of anything better than this. Why can't life be like this all the time?" I said wistfully.

"That's because we're rarely alone, sweetie," replied Cindy. "There's always somebody at the house or else you're gone. It's not like you have a nine-to-five job you can leave at the office."

"You're right, you are absolutely right, and it's getting to me. I'm toying with the idea of retiring. Pat's getting greedy, Phil's pulling a lame number and I'm the one stuck doing a lot more work. It's not that much fun anymore."

After a blissful week spent alone for the first time in our relationship, Cindy and I returned to Menlo Park, to reality, construction, and to prepare for the upcoming smuggling season.

The week was filled with wonderful memories and I wished it could have lasted longer.

> '… Bali Hai may call you, any night, any day.
> In your heart, you'll hear it call you: "Come away… come away"…'

* * *

---

1 Referenced Songs & Music, Item 11, Page 530.
2 Referenced Television & Movies, Item 14, Page 533.

Joe's role was changing too. He and Jenny had rented a house in affluent Atherton. His cocaine use had risen dramatically and he was never without a minimum of at least half an ounce. Driving down the road in his pickup truck, steering wheel held steady between his knees, Joe would hold the baggie in one hand and with the other hand he would shovel cocaine into his nose using a Swiss Army knife. Sometimes he wore a cowboy hat and, with his huge drooping mustache, he looked like the cartoon character 'Yosemite Sam'. He referred to himself as the *Magic Christian*[3] recalling the 1969 movie title whose main character, Sir Guy Grand, played by the actor Peter Sellers, generously doled out money to whoever happened to be around. In Joe's case however, it was cocaine, doled like he had a bottomless supply of it.

He was constantly congested and had frequent nosebleeds. His cocaine abuse actually eroded a one-half-inch diameter hole through his nasal septum. One afternoon at dusk, he and I were headed north across the Golden Gate Bridge. Joe was driving and I was in the passenger seat. Joe said something funny, as was his nature, and I turned my head to the left to look him. Looking west beyond him at the setting sun, and as I glanced at Joe, I could actually see the sun drop below the horizon through the hole in Joe's nose, as if it was a tiny window to the world.

Joe was becoming the center of the party. In wanting to take on greater responsibilities, he began to align himself socially with people who were virtually in competition with Pat, Phil and me. He was becoming quite friendly with Ciro, Walter, Jonathan Jacoby and some of his 'Colorado' connections and most recently Bob Lahodny, one of the Coronado Company's three leaders.

In his perpetually wired state, Joe, like Phil, was giving away some of the trade secrets Pat, Phil and I had worked so hard to develop over the past few years. In his mind, Joe didn't think he was doing anything wrong and was just being helpful with the knowledge he'd gleaned; however, in reality he was unknowingly becoming similar to a counter espionage agent by compromising nearly every aspect of our Thai scam.

I was unaware that Joe was also hanging out with Ciro and his entourage. In his spare time when he had nothing else to do, Joe was taking money to Thailand or Hong Kong for Ciro, making between $10,000 and $50,000 for his services. He just couldn't sit still and always had to be doing something, especially if it involved socializing and/ or increasing his net worth.

Even the steadfast captain, Dave Killian, was changing. He had purchased some land in the Sierra Nevada foothills near Grass Valley where he planned to build a fancy A-frame house whose interior was to be laid out like a boat. Since he didn't have enough money to start construction, Killian bought a trailer and had it moved onto the property. He also rented a home in the East Bay hills near Richmond.

It wasn't so much the cocaine with Killian, but marijuana and liquor which made him the center of a group of adolescent boys. I had heard about Killian's eccentric propensities but had not personally witnessed them, until the day I came to his home to drive him down to the Richmond Yacht Club while his truck was in the shop. When I knocked on the door I found it ajar. Entering the smoke-filled hallway, I saw Killian

---

3 Referenced Television & Movies, Item 15, Page 533.

in the living room surrounded by a group of five teenage boys watching a gay porno-graphic movie. They were smoking joints and Killian was wearing only a G-string bikini. To me, Killian's homosexuality was one thing, but it was another matter when it involved under-aged youths. 'Marvelous' I thought as I retreated outside and closed the door. 'Next voyage he'll have an eight-year-old as cabin boy performing unnatural acts aboard *Nepenthe*.' I rang the bell until Killian answered. Killian was bare-chested, but had put on a Polynesian lava lava. I decided the wisest policy was to keep my mouth shut. I never said a word about it.

October 1976

Killian, Joe and Pete Newman sailed *Nepenthe* down to Long Beach in preparation for shipping the boat to Singapore. Ciro and Walter had their vessel, *Drifter*, prepared by a German boat captain Herman Schmidt, who was an acquaintance of Joe-the-German who had arranged for their Airstream load the year before. Like *Nepenthe*, *Drifter* was also shipped to Singapore using American Presidents Line (APL), the same carrier we'd used last year. The two boats were transported within a month of each other.

Joe, accompanied by either Phil or me, made several trips to the Orient with bun-dles of money hidden in his boots and briefcase. The most each of us would carry was $250,000 and one million-plus was needed for the upcoming loads. Joe also took care of ordering more poly-mylar bags to be sent to Pat's uncle in Bangkok.

The scheme was to acquire two-and-a-half tons from Ban Ku Su Man and load both *Nepenthe* and *Drifter* by February or March and at the same time, while the weed was at its freshest, acquire, seal and stockpile the additional three and-a-half tons for a May or June loading of *Kona Wind* and *Pai Nui*. We all felt it would be best to stagger the two sets of loads in case of any problems and so we wouldn't flood the market. Pat would set about to construct hidden stashes to conceal the loads while waiting a couple of months to load, remembering what had happened to Ciro in Mexico with the load exposed in the basement of his ranch. He constructed two storage sheds in the remotest part of the jungle property and built a false walled hidden stash room in each.

February, 1977
Pattaya, Thailand

Pat had rounded up the Thai crew and began organizing his end in December. The first two-and-a-half tons for *Nepenthe* and *Drifter* had been harvested and cured up north in the village. Both sailboats were currently in Singapore, awaiting a phone call from Pattaya confirming everything was ready. Killian, Joe, and Willie, making his second trip as navigator, were completing final preparations at the Changi Yacht Club while the *Drifter* remained offshore at anchor in Singapore Harbor. Pete Newman couldn't make the trip this year so he was replaced by our old friend Nape from the 'Boraxo' adventure in Nogales seven years ago.

The Pattaya beach bungalow was again the command post. Phil, Pat and I, as usual, were staying there. This year we decided to leave Wendy and Cindy back in the states, but Ciro and Walter had just flown down from Hong Kong en-route to check on *Drifter* in Singapore and would be staying at the bungalow as well.

I still felt very uncomfortable about letting Ciro into the operation. Ciro had been to the Chanthaburi farm and had seen the assembly line with the roller tables and the vacuum sealing machines and the entire ranch setup. If Pat was leery about reconnecting with Ciro, he kept it to himself. Pat had told Phil and me that Ciro had made a big show of repaying him the fifty thousand plus interest. Now they were all buddy-buddy, like nothing ever happened. It seemed to me that Pat's rekindled relationship with Ciro was now manifesting itself in his attempt to show off to Ciro by trying to one-up and prove to him just how far he'd come from worker to kingpin, far surpassing the Mexican trip Ciro had prided himself in. It was obvious Pat's ego was getting the better of him.

"We should keep both boat trips completely separate. *Drifter* should be loaded at least two weeks after *Nepenthe* and she should take a separate route home," I proposed, pouring myself a glass of lemonade from the pitcher on the polished mahogany table.

"I agree, the boats should be loaded at different times, but I think you're wrong about separate routes. It doesn't mean a thing if *Drifter* pulls into the same ports *Nepenthe* does. They won't be sailing together. So, what's the big deal?" Ciro asked. His heavy hooded dark eyes roamed the rattan furnished room looking for agreement. Phil was noncommittal, Pat doodled on a scratch pad, avoiding eye contact. Only Walter nodded his head in assent.

"I don't believe in coincidences, Ciro," I said. "I recommend that *Drifter* take a different route home. There's no need to jeopardize the whole scam just for the sake of conveniences." I felt, Ciro, as usual, was trying to usurp control. Somehow I knew that if Ciro got his way, things were bound to go wrong.

On an overcast mid-March night, *Nepenthe* was loaded with a ton of weed from the little cove on Ko Lan's lee side, exactly as had been done twice before.

During the two weeks between *Nepenthe's* loading and when *Drifter* was to take on her ton-and-a-half, Ciro, Phil and I flew to Nepal for a week to view the Himalayas and kick back. Walter and Pat remained in Thailand as troubleshooters in case problems arose on the assembly line during the rest of the packaging.

We flew to Kathmandu, then on to the mountain landing strip in Namche Bazar, the stepping off point for Mt. Everest expeditions. The three of us stayed at the Hotel Everest View located halfway between Namche and Mt. Everest base camp. At nearly 14,000 feet, the hotel stood in the shadow of the majestic 22,000 foot Mt. Ama Dablam, which towered over the hotel setting.

Each room in the old hotel had a balcony and a panoramic view of Mt. Everest. The quaint rooms were heated with coal burning fireplaces. Due to overbooking, only two rooms were available for the three of us, so we tossed a coin to see who got the single room and who doubled up. Phil won, so Ciro and I became roommates for the next couple of days.

We hiked up to the Tangboche Monastery, a place where all Everest climbers stop and pay reverence to the 'mountain gods' for a safe climb. At nearly 15, 000 feet the air was thin and we all had to rest every few hundred feet to catch our breath. We had intended to hike up to Everest base camp at 17,000 feet, but the altitude and ten-mile hike was too much for us flatlanders. We were warned that unless you spend at least two weeks getting acclimatized to the altitude, hiking for more than an hour was very dangerous and could lead to severe mountain sickness or worse yet, pulmonary edema or even death. Indeed, the Monastery was very enlightening and you could feel the presence of many famous mountaineers who'd come there before us.

"I never really told you how much I appreciated what you did for me while I was in prison in Mexico, Rick," Ciro said. It was the night before we returned to Thailand. "I count you as a real friend, and to me trust and friendship are everything."

The three-quarter moon bathed the mountains in a ghostly, spectral light. I turned from the window, walked back to the fireplace and threw in more coal.

"I agree. They are my bottom line values. I wouldn't work with anybody unless he was a friend, or at least a friend of a friend," I responded. "I know I can always count on you Ciro. You understand about loyalty."

Ciro paused and took a hit from the hash pipe. He held the pungent smoke deep in his lungs and then exhaled.

"You bet I do, Rick. Friendship and loyalty are the glue which holds our business together. It's all about honor. The cops don't know anything unless you tell them. Remember, I was sweated by professionals and I held my mud. I know you'd do the same for me. I would never give up a friend."

* * *

Meanwhile, out at sea, *Nepenthe* cruised slowly eastward following the same path as the year before. Making her final port-of-call in Saipan, she was fueled up and provisioned for the 5,000 mile trans-Pacific crossing which lay ahead.

Once again 2,500 miles from nowhere, the crew was able to hail a passing freighter to re-fuel out at sea. This time it was a Panamanian freighter whose crew was more than happy to oblige. They put a small dinghy over the side with three men and two barrels of diesel. After the fueling was complete, the Professor came up with another 'brilliant' hare-brained scheme.

"Hey, why don't you guys give us a tow. We could make it home much faster that way."

"Si, Señor, no problema," answered the Panamanian officer.

The freighter's crew returned to the towering 350-foot vessel with one of *Nepenthe's* extra ropes and tied it to a giant rusted deck cleat on the stern while the other end was secured to the shiny stainless cleat on *Nepenthe's* bow. With Joe at the helm, Willie gave the thumbs-up signal and the freighter began to slowly move ahead at four knots. Willie gave another thumbs-up signal, indicating 'more speed'. The freighter increased to eight knots.

Sailboats are designed to attain a maximum speed under sail which is determined by a mathematical formula combining the length of the boat at the waterline by a square root factor. The resulting number from this calculation is called the 'hull speed'. Sailboats can go faster than hull speed when surfing down a wave, but control becomes an issue and one false move when exceeding hull speed can spell instant disaster. *Nepenthe*'s hull speed was about seven to seven and-a-half knots.

"I can't really control this. The helm feels like it weighs a ton!" Joe exclaimed, as the freighter increased its speed to twelve knots. *Nepenthe*'s bow came out of the water like a breaching whale.

"Holy fuck, Professor! Cut the line or we'll be dragged under. I have no control of the boat. One more knot and we're going to be pulled under!" Joe yelled.

Dave joined the fray and rushed to the bow with a fisherman's knife and cut the line just as a wall of water washed over *Nepenthe*'s bow and she was saved in the nick of time. The freighter's crew stood on the stern in stunned disbelief. Some were laughing and others were pointing with the look of horror on their faces as *Nepenthe* settled back in the water.

"Any more bright ideas, Professor?" Killian said. "Why didn't you just ask them to hoist us on deck, rather than trying to sink us, you idiot."

"Hmmm. Good idea. Maybe next time we should carry a spare cradle. I'll have Rick build us a collapsible one for next trip," Willie replied.

"Let's just stick to sailing," Killian answered wiping the sweat from his face.

Chapter 25

Narrow Escape

May 15, 1977
Richmond Yacht Club, Richmond, CA

"Hey, Rick. Got a minute? I've got something I want to talk to you about," said Rich McKenzie, owner and manager of Richmond Yacht Service, the local chandlery at Richmond Yacht Club.

Papi, my trusty sidekick and constant companion, and I had driven over to the Richmond Yacht Club to reconnoiter the marina. *Nepenthe* was due to arrive from Thailand within a couple of weeks, if this voyage was anything like last year's.

"Sure, Rich. Great to see you. Been awhile," I said, extending my hand to the trim, rather short man in his forties with thinning blonde hair and stocky build. Rich was an old friend of Dave Killian, who Dave had introduced me to when Pat and I were working on *Nepenthe*. I had frequented the chandlery to buy parts and came to know Rich casually myself. Rich had known Dave for over twenty-five years, going all the way back to the summers when Killian, as a teenager, gave dinghy sailing lessons at the yacht club.

"Good to see you, Rick," said Rich. We walked along the seawall bordering the yacht basin. The low layer of morning fog was lifting, the temperature in the low 80s.

"Come on boy," I said to Papi.

"Look, Rick. I don't know what you and Dave are up to and I don't care. Dave and I go way back."

"Yeah, I know, Rich," I replied. Suddenly, there were butterflies in my stomach.

"Well, for the past two weeks agents from the F.B.I., the D.E.A. and the U.S. Customs have been hanging around the yacht club asking questions about Dave and your boat, *Nepenthe*. They wanted to know where the boat was and when she's expected to arrive. They are also asking questions about another boat by the name *Drifter*. They've had an unmarked car posted near the yacht club's entrance. It's not there now. Probably gone to lunch. Anyway, that's about as much as I can tell you. Just thought I'd let you know."

"Thanks Rich. I really appreciate your concern," I said, trying my best to conceal the rising anxiety.

I was perspiring heavily as I left the yacht club, and it wasn't only the warm day. The adrenaline rush had drastically changed. It was no longer the excitement of pulling off another smuggling scam. It had shifted suddenly to just not getting busted.

On the drive across the Bay Bridge I considered the possibilities. Who could have blown the whistle? Two months later, after the dust had settled, I realized that *Drifter* had not only booked passage for shipment to Singapore on the same transport carrier, APL, as *Nepenthe*, but had stopped in all the same ports as *Nepenthe* on the return voyage. It was exactly as I had cautioned against at the Pattaya meeting. Somewhere, either from the Singapore Customs House or along the passage home, somebody must have thought it strange, two sailboats were shipped to and from the same ports by the identical shipping method and/or were following exactly the same route. I suspected the information had come from Singapore or the island of Saipan where someone must have alerted the authorities.

I called Walter from a telephone booth to warn him that the Feds were also looking for *Drifter*. From the moment I knew the heat was on, I decided, all business calls would be made from phone booths and I was never without several rolls of quarters in my pickup truck.

The current problem was how to let *Nepenthe* know they were sailing into a trap when they showed up, as planned, to unload at Richmond Yacht Club. I had long avoided the use of the radio, since I felt that confidential conversations, even in code, could easily be monitored. I thought, 'There must be some other way I can warn *Nepenthe* to steer clear of the yacht club'.

May 19, 1977

The small single engine Cessna 182 took off from San Carlos Airport. At the controls was Steve Stallings, brother of Mike Stallings who had previously crewed for us aboard *Frankly Scarlett* back in '71. In the co-pilot right seat was Rico Fromriko, also a crew member on *Frankly Scarlett*. I was in the back. Steve took the plane up to an altitude of ten thousand feet and gently banked left and set a course for the coast. The plan was to try and locate *Nepenthe*, even though the odds of finding her were, at best, slim to none.

The early afternoon sun warmed the cockpit as the plane headed out over the open ocean. I had brought along several sealed bottles in which I had stuffed the message: "Do not come into San Francisco Bay. There is heat all over. Sail down to Del Rey like we did in the old days... R.B."

Hoping to find *Nepenthe* and drop the message bottles, we flew sweeping search patterns from the Farallon Islands, west fifty miles out to sea, and north to Ft. Bragg, and back down the coast. It was a cloudless day and we could see for miles in all directions. We saw no boats resembling *Nepenthe*. For four days, we repeated the procedure, alternating our search patterns either farther north or south. I purchased two walkie-talkies and sealed one in plastic which I planned to drop instead of the bottles if we sighted *Nepenthe*. We saw nothing.

One morning, I drove by the yacht club and saw a dark green Plymouth sedan with two men in the front seat parked by the entrance. The unmarked vehicle had 'Fed' written all over it. The agents had a clear view of the yacht harbor and the Bay. Undoubtedly, there were other men and more cars positioned elsewhere waiting to swoop down on *Nepenthe* and her unsuspecting crew.

With each passing day, I became more tense and would snap at Cindy for the least little thing.

"If it goes down bad, I want you to get as far away from here as you can," I said to Cindy.

"Where can I go?" she asked.

"I don't know. You figure it out," I growled. "Go stay with your dad in LA, go stay with Wendy, just make sure you get out of here if the shit hits the fan."

I made sure I had an emergency stash of money hidden in the safe beneath the sauna's floor. I went through and thoroughly cleaned up my office and set anything suspicious aside in a pile to burn. Cindy and I went through the house frantically adding to the burn pile, such items as phone records and old plane tickets.

"What do you think we should do with these?" Cindy said holding up the photographs I had taken the year before of the Thai 'Christmas tree-like' pot farm.

"If the Feds found those, our goose would be cooked for sure," I replied. "I hate to get rid of them; they might be useful someday. But, we just can't take a chance. Burn 'em!"

We tossed all of the incriminating evidence, including my cherished photos, into the fireplace at our Menlo Park home and burned all of it until there was nothing left but a pile of smoldering ashes. There was no sense in leaving a trail in case agents came to the house.

Finally, there was nothing left to do but sit and wait… and pray. Think good thoughts….

Memorial Day, 1977

The telephone was ringing in my dream, but it wasn't a dream. I fumbled for the receiver. The digital clock on the nightstand read 4:21 AM.

"Hello," I said groggily.

"Herr Admiral, this is Herr Navigator. We're here," came the familiar voice over the phone.

I was instantly awake. "Oh, my God!" I said to Willie. "Don't go to the Richmond Yacht Club. There's heat everywhere waiting for you! Can you make it back out the Bay and down south to the Del Rey Yacht Club where we used to pull in?"

"No way," answered Willie. "We'll just go the small boat harbor in Richmond where we used to berth. Meet us there. I know we can pull this off."

'Right," I replied. I knew, the argument was over and the trip was now in the hands of the 'smuggling gods'.

By this time, Cindy was wide awake and frantically dressing, assisted by several lines on the bedside mirror. I turned to her and said, "Cindy, I love you. Now please get the hell out of here. Go up to Sacramento and visit your friends and wait for me to call. There's no sense in 'all of us dying in the war' and you getting in trouble if I get busted."

I gave her some cash and she packed and left in the Mercedes. I quickly got dressed and nearly forgot to put on my lucky shirt, but managed to remember it at the last minute. I thought, 'maybe this shirt will come through again.'

"Come on, boy," I said to Papi. "We've got work to do." He was alert and ready for anything. It was now 5:02 AM and we were on the road. I felt like David heading into the arena against Goliath.

Willie had made the phone call from the Sausalito Yacht Club in Sausalito. He told Killian about the change in plans. Nape, the fourth crew member, became overwhelmed with paranoia. Willie recognized it and saw that in his mental state he would be a liability, and probably attract attention. He told Nape to leave the boat, take a cab into The City and check into the Holiday Inn on Van Ness Avenue; they'd be in touch with him later. While Joe and Killian powered the boat to Richmond, Willie took a cab to the Twin Peaks garage and picked up the covered pickup truck I'd left there for him.

Forty five minutes later, Willie arrived at the small boat harbor. A few minutes later, *Nepenthe* and I arrived there almost simultaneously. Killian maneuvered *Nepenthe* into the same slip where Pat and I, nearly three years earlier, had first fashioned the stash compartments. It was now a little after six in the morning on Memorial Day weekend, and things were beginning to stir. People began arriving with ice chests and duffle bags ready to cruise on the Bay on the long holiday weekend. With trusty Papi on a leash, I casually strolled the area looking just like a boy out for a morning walk with his dog. It was crystal clear, no fog and a gentle prevailing breeze from the northwest. My heart was pounding a mile a minute. Still, no sign of the Feds.

Joe and Willie began unloading, carrying the filled sail bags up the dock to the waiting trucks. There were no dock carts like there had been at the marinas and yacht clubs where *Nepenthe* had previously unloaded. Killian was aboard putting kilos into sail bags which were then humped up the dock to the trucks parked in the adjacent parking lot. No more than thirty or forty pounds were put into a sail bag, so it would simply look like the normal dockside activity of each of them carrying a sail bag stuffed with a sail to be cleaned or repaired. It was nothing unusual or out of the ordinary for a sailboat returning to the harbor. I had gotten into the back of my pickup truck and was unloading the sail bags, stacking the packages neatly so they would fit. One truck was filled and then the other in the same manner.

Killian made a quick phone call to Pete Newman and asked him if he could accompany him aboard *Nepenthe* for a trip to Los Angeles. If he could meet the boat within an hour then I would pay him one thousand dollars. Pete gladly agreed. Within two hours of arriving, *Nepenthe*, now totally sanitized, backed out of the slip and headed toward the Golden Gate. Willie, Joe, and I drove back to the Twin Peaks garage and left the trucks. We took the second vehicle which had been parked there, the Goon, the trusty old Chrysler station wagon, and we all drove out to Land's End below the Palace of the Legion Honor, the exact site where my parents had once threatened to dispose of our first sailboat load. We stood on the cliffs watching as *Nepenthe* passed beneath the Golden Gate Bridge and out of San Francisco Bay. As she passed our position beyond Mile Rock Lighthouse, I knew that this was probably the last time I would ever see *Nepenthe*.

I just stood there and silently shed a tear. Looking through my binoculars at *Nepenthe* heading out to sea on the ebb tide, Genoa and mainsail flying, set to a beam reach in the prevailing northwest breeze, I could clearly see Dave at the helm in his orange float coat sitting on the port side of the cockpit, appearing as calm as ever in his natural element and usual pose, drink and cigarette in one hand and tiller in the other. It was clear as a bell and *Nepenthe* was the only vessel in my entire field of vision from the Golden Gate to the Farallones. I was truly comforted by the fact that she appeared to be all alone out there and wasn't being tailed by a Coast Guard cutter, police patrol boat or Navy cruiser. Nothing but open ocean and blue sky. Not even a helicopter or spotter plane was visible. We sadly watched until she disappeared from view.

I was not in a rush to get rid of the load. Quite the opposite. I felt the load could just sit while the situation cooled down. During the following week, with the load still in the pickup trucks garaged up in Twin Peaks, Willie and I set out to find a new stash house which could be used for the entire summer. Three additional loads besides the one sitting in the garage were expected to arrive between June and early September.

After considering different places in the Bay Area, we decided on a vacation rental in an upscale resort, where our comings and goings at any hour of the day or night would not look out of place. Willie had volunteered to manage the stash house while the loads were being distributed. The search led us to the North Bay, to Silverado Country Club, in the heart of the famous Napa Valley. Within the gated community, most of the houses had swimming pools and were located around one of the two championship 18-hole golf courses, which were the Club's main attraction.

Willie, acting as a wealthy San Francisco retailer, contacted a real estate agent in the Napa Valley, and within two days she located a rental for him which seemed tailor-made to his particular requirements. It was a sprawling four-bedroom ranch style house with a long driveway and three-car garage. The house was completely furnished and had a spa and swimming pool with a blue circular waterslide at one end. The fenced property, a great place for Willie's dog Sunshine to roam, had a gate behind the pool which opened directly onto the fairway of the picturesque Par 4, 12th hole on the North Course. He relished the thought of being able to play a few holes in the evenings, when the course was empty, to sharpen his game. He played to a 10 handicap.

The rent was $3,000 per month. Willie gave the agent two cashier's checks, one for $9,000 for three month's rent and the other for $3,000 for security deposit. Remember: no paperwork at the bank if the cash amount is under $10,000, so two checks were necessary for the $12,000 total. He took occupancy immediately. A few days later Joe drove the first of the two loaded trucks to the new stash house, where the load was inventoried and readied for sale.

Two weeks later, *Drifter* arrived. After passing under the Golden Gate Bridge she motored up the North Bay, near the mouth of the Petaluma River where the ton-and-a-half of Thai stick was unloaded onto a trailerable fishing boat late one foggy night. The load was driven up to a Sierra foothill ranch near Placerville occupied by Brad, Ciro's lieutenant from the Mexico trips. *Drifter* stayed at the guest berth at the small yacht harbor at the mouth of the Petaluma River for two days before motoring down to a boatyard near Richmond for repairs.

Drifter left the small yacht harbor under power bound for Richmond with only two of the crewmen from the Pacific crossing aboard. As they passed the Brothers, two islands in the North Bay near the Richmond-San Rafael Bridge, they noticed a forty-foot Coast Guard port security patrol boat closing rapidly from astern.

"Vessel *Drifter*! This is the United States Coast Guard. Heave to and stop your engines. Prepare to be boarded," came the metallic voice over the patrol boat's loud speaker. The fifty-foot ketch stopped dead in the water, while the patrol boat came alongside. Four armed Coast Guardsmen and three U.S. Customs agents boarded *Drifter*. Six of the officers swarmed below and searched the boat, while the seventh held the two crew members on deck with the barrel of an M-16 pointed at their heads. Under the floorboards in the bilge located in the main cabin, one of the Customs agents found ten vacuum-sealed Thai stick marijuana packages each weighing about two to two-and-a-half pounds. One of the two crew members had stashed the weed as a sailing bonus to himself, thinking Ciro and Walter would never notice. He had rationalized they were going to make enough money anyway and the twenty-five pounds of Thai weed was worth more than what he made in a whole year at his 'day job', in his other life as a carpenter. The two crew members were summarily arrested and the boat was seized by authorities and taken to the Coast Guard pier at the Treasure Island Navy Base, on Yerba Buena Island located in the middle of the San Francisco Bay Bridge.

One week later, on my way up to Placerville to collect our share of the load, I took the mid-span offramp to Treasure Island and from the 'Vista Point' parking lot, I took out my binoculars and spotted *Drifter* in the distance, tied up to the Coast Guard dock.

When I arrived at the ranch, I was met with another surprise. Instead of the 1,320 pounds I expected to pick up, representing our 40% agreed upon share of the ton-and-a-half load, there was only 500 pounds.

"Hey, Brad, what's going on?" I asked.

"I dunno," replied the cowboy through his drooping mustache. "Ciro jes tol me to giv y'all fi hundert pounds. Thas all."

"What the hell do you mean? Our share of the load comes to 1,320 pounds?"

"Lizzen, Rick. Why don y'all talk wi Ciro when everthang cools down?"

"Wait a minute. I just want our full share now. What was agreed upon. Our thirteen hundred and twenty pounds! That's all."

Brad's face turned hard and through pursed lips said: "Ciro tol me to tell y'all that if ya got upset, and if ya wanna walk outta here, jes take the fi hundert pounds 'n go. Yew got that amigo?"

Twenty minutes later, I was in a phone booth fuming at Phil, blaming him for the whole turn of events.

"Phil, I told you your slimeball friend would screw us! I told both you and Pat, but neither of you listened. Pat is gonna go into orbit when he hears about this. Do you realize your friend, Ciro, just fucked us out of a million dollars or more? Hello! If you opened your eyes, you could see this coming from a million miles out. Maybe you should be responsible for the loss, after all it was your OTO (original turn on)."

"Come on Rick, I'm sure we will sort this out. There's a lot of heat on those guys right now. Let's wait and see what happens. I don't think we want to hassle him right now with *Drifter* tied up at Treasure Island and two of their crew in jail. At least we got something to tide us over."

"OK. We'll wait, but I've got a real bad feeling about this, Phil. The way Brad threatened me, I'll guarantee you, we ain't gettin' more from that prick, Ciro. This is beginning to sound like a broken record: I don't wanna be an 'I told you so', but…"

June 18, 1977

Nepenthe was still on the Coast Guard and D.E.A. 'stop and detain' list in the Bay Area. Dave Killian had sailed the boat down to the Del Rey Yacht Club, then returned to his Richmond apartment. Through several of his yachting friends, he found out there was still an active search for *Nepenthe* going on throughout the Bay Area.

I met Dave at the Sausalito Food Company, a bar and restaurant near one of Sausalito's many marinas. At eleven in the morning, Killian ordered his first double Beefeaters on the rocks of the day while I requested coffee.

"We've got to get rid of the *Nepenthe*, Rick. Sell her. Maybe we can find a buyer, somebody who will take real good care of her," said Killian. "We can list her through one of the LA brokerages."

"Yeah, I know, Dave. She's a hot item, but I don't think selling her would cover our tracks. There's still a paper trail leading to your dummy company. She needs to just disappear. What if we took her out to sea and sank her?"

"Sink *Nepenthe*?" Killian recoiled. He was incredulous. "Are you heartless? Jesus Rick! She's like a real person to me."

"I know how you feel, Dave. I feel the same way too, but it's the only way we can be sure she won't be found. Don't you think?"

Killian flew to LA two days later to make preparations to dispose of *Nepenthe*. His plan was to dismantle her of all equipment, then charter a fishing boat, and rendezvous with Joe and me aboard *Nepenthe* at a location at least fifty miles offshore and 'pull the plug' there.

I took him to the airport and I've never seen him so depressed. He told me this was going to be the hardest thing he ever does in his life and maybe, as captain, he should just 'go down with the ship'.

Killian went immediately to the Del Rey Yacht Club bar where he ran into *Nepenthe*'s previous owner who just happened to mention if he, Dave, ever wanted to sell *Nepenthe*, a friend of his would buy her immediately and was bummed he couldn't afford her when he had originally sold her. Killian told him, indeed he was down in LA, for that very reason, to sell the boat and if it could be arranged, he really didn't need a broker and would sell it to his friend directly. Again, I guess, the 'smuggling gods' were looking out for us, as Dave consummated the deal, survey and all, and in two days, *Nepenthe* was sold for $48,000, nearly double what we had paid for her. Actually from all the upgrades we'd done over the past four years, we'd put much more money into her than we realized from the sale price and she was in far better condition than when we'd first acquired her. She had, in turn, been responsible for us reaping outrageous rewards from her service to the cause!

At the last minute, miraculously, *Nepenthe* was saved from what would have been her final voyage… to Davy Jones' Locker at the bottom of the ocean!

* * *

Nepenthe's third load was sold without a problem. 'Yorktown' Billy's operation was now working like a well-oiled machine. He had regular customers in the Bay Area as well as people who came from as far away as New York. A few of his local customers were respected businessmen who supplemented their legitimate income by selling Thai marijuana to their friends. Billy moved the weed in one hundred to three hundred pound lots, and it was always cash on the barrelhead. Each sale amounted to between $150,000 and $500,000. The money Billy delivered to me was always correct, neatly stacked and banded together. I did not have to double check it; I counted it later. In all the years I did business with Billy, there was never so much as a penny missing.

John 'JQ' Quinn also helped me move the Thai stick. JQ had sizable markets in both Colorado and Texas as well as customers in the Bay Area. Between 'Yorktown' Billy and JQ, I could move a ton within two weeks and have all the net proceeds safely buried in the ground.

All of the crew's pay was doubled from the past year, except Nape who was still at a respectable five figure 'entry level'. Pat, Phil and I raked in about the same as the previous year, plus what we made from our 'shorted' Ciro deal. Not bad and we still had two loads ahead of us. However, the fact remained that Ciro had seriously 'ripped' us for over sixty percent.

* * *

Pat was back in Thailand. He had been accumulating, sealing and storing the remaining three-and-a-half tons through the height of the growing season for the freshest, best, 'num-bah-one' Thai stick for the last two loads, one-and-half tons for Jonathan Jacoby and two tons for 'Lights' and company. Pat pretty much lived at the ranch in Chanthaburi overseeing the production line and storing the loads in his cleverly concealed outbuildings, ready to load.

In late April, I made a trip to Thailand to help Pat with the loading. On April 26th, Jonathan Jacoby's fifty-five foot ketch, *Kona Wind*, was loaded in the lee of Ko Lan Island. On the evening of loading, Pat had come up with a cockamamie plan to have me take the Zodiac alone, from the north end of Pattaya Beach out the nearly five miles to Ko Lan. There I was to rendezvous with Pat and the load in the lee cove site of the loading, then Pat and I would return together and the fishing boat could go on its way and out to the fishing grounds in the Gulf. Well, I launched at dusk which, after a mile or two in the Gulf, became dark and then pitch black, in what seemed like mere minutes, at which point I became hopelessly disoriented. The reference lights I had used from the north towards the city of Chon Buri melded into the lights of the offshore fishing boats as did the lights on Ko Lan. For at least a half hour I was heading out into the unknown waters of the Gulf of Thailand with no compass and in the black of night. I was nearly feeling the effects of vertigo as the lights of the stars, the boats and shore lights seemed to form a planetarium-like ball with pinpoints of light everywhere and me in the center. Somehow, I guess I managed to fixate on one particular pinpoint and nearly forty-five minutes later, I came into the Ko Lan cove. For a brief moment I had the sinking feeling and fear of being lost at sea. I was never so happy as to find Pat and the loading boat.

Two weeks later, we loaded *Pai Nui*, the 60-foot motorsailer, in the same Ko Lan cove. As Ron, the captain of *Pai Nui*, Pat and I orchestrated the loading scene from the stern of the yacht, I talked to Ron about his sailing experiences. His most memorable comment from the brief meeting with me was, "I've sailed so much, I could sail this rig, backwards, through the eye of a needle."

Kona Wind arrived off the southern California coast in the third week of June. Jacoby had a surfing buddy who was the caretaker of a five hundred acre ranch on the coast north of Santa Barbara, near Goleta. The ranch had a private gated road extending westward off the Pacific Coast Highway for a couple of miles, disappearing in the scrub dunes and terminating all the way to water's edge on a desolated beach. The ton-and-a-half was brought ashore in Zodiacs by offloaders, Mike Stallings, Dennis Moronsky, Rico Fromriko, Joe and Jonathan, who then used four-wheel-drive pickup trucks fitted with special tires which could be driven on the sand and taillights with cutoff switches installed, so the brake lights could be disengaged and not seen at night, so any passerby on the main highway wouldn't see anything happening on the beach, even in the distance. The unloading went like clockwork and two days later, Joe drove our 40% share to the Silverado stash house.

Willie had turned the stash pad into his personal love nest. His girlfriend, Melinda, was also in residence. When I bought my Menlo Park house, Willie had purchased a house in the same neighborhood around the corner, and moved in with the short-haired blue-eyed brunette with the great smile and, as Willie put it, boobs like casaba melons. He continued to have at least two other girlfriends on the side, and sometimes stayed out all night.

Willie's activities at the stash house consisted of watching sports on the widescreen TV, screwing, eating, screwing, playing golf, swimming, tanning and screwing. Several times Joe would arrive at the house and catch Willie in the throes of his most popular activity. Willie and Melinda would just continue grunting and groaning, hardly noticing Joe was present.

"When I walked into the living room, Willie was back in the saddle, as if coming out of 'bucking chute number one' at the rodeo. He just looked up and said 'Hi', never missing a stroke," an amazed Joe told me. Joe could not believe how nonchalant Willie and Melinda were about their sexual activity in front of an innocent passerby. While Joe went about the house weighing and inventorying packages, Willie and Melinda would walk about scantily clad, all sweaty and reeking with the characteristic odiferous smell from their latest exertion. Sometimes Joe would lay out lines of cocaine for the three of them. Willie took it in stride and maintained that this was his way of 'watching' and staying on top of the load appearing as if what was going on was completely normal; and in his mind, that's exactly what it was.

The year's final trip was the Coronado Company's two ton load aboard *Pai Nui*. In the beginning of May, 'Lights' had leased a farm in Northern California near the town of Leggett, north of Fort Bragg. The 'Company' had purchased a surplus U.S. Army amphibious vehicle known as a DUKW, commonly called a Duck, which had been used in WWII to unload troops and supplies from boats offshore to the beaches of northern France. An isolated beach was located off the rugged Northern California coast adjacent to Highway One where the Company's 'army' would unload *Pai Nui* onto the Duck and transport the load through the surf, across the beach, up onto the highway, and three miles north east to the ranch. The Duck was transported to the farmhouse on a big rig trailer and kept in the barn. 'Lights' and Eddie arranged for a crew of about 12 Southern California surfer types to carry out the unloading operation.

Pai Nui arrived at the end of June. Two of the crew donned California State Park Ranger uniforms and blocked off Highway One, north and south of the intersection leading to the farmhouse. The bogus 'rangers' were equipped with walkie-talkies so that they could communicate with each other if any vehicles showed up; in which case, they were well rehearsed to say: "There's been a chemical spill 'up-a-ways' which is almost cleaned up. You'll be on your way in no time. Thanks for your patience."

With ten men aboard, the Duck was driven out of the barn and south on Highway One a couple of miles, where it was driven off the road, down an embankment, and across the beach into the water. The amphibious vehicle easily negotiated its way through the surf line out to where *Pai Nui* lay at anchor, same as she had done over three decades ago on France's Normandy beaches. The entire two tons were offloaded into the Duck. The vehicle then chugged back across the water, through the surf line, over the beach, up the embankment, onto Highway One and up the couple of miles back to the barn. The procedure took a little over an hour. Fortunately, the unloading took place early in the morning and no cars came on that lonely stretch of Highway One to the makeshift barricades.

Next morning Phil and Joe showed up to claim the roughly three quarters of a ton making up our share of the load. They drove the weed to the Silverado lust pad and stash house. Within two and a half weeks, Billy had sold our share of the weed from both boat trips. Joe and Willie each received healthy six-figure amounts for their delivery and baby sitting roles. Pat, Phil and my shares were divided accordingly and buried along with the rest of the booty from our previous Thai trips.

July 30, 1977
Central Valley, California

By the time Pat returned to the United States in July, the weed from all the contract loads had been sold and the money collected. The year had been a complete success with the exception of the *Drifter* bust, coupled with the fact that Ciro had shorted us over 800 pounds.

Pat then made a rather surprising announcement: "I am retiring from smuggling business. Close the books. I want to divide the money we've collected and call it quits. It getting too dangerous."

So, three days later Pat, Phil and I, each of us about thirty years old, officially retired from the marijuana smuggling business. We met at Phil's Adobe House to divide the money accumulated during the past three years, which had been buried beneath Phil's tan adobe house. Phil and I had been burying money beneath the house since the Fall of 1971, shortly after Phil had acquired his valley home. Money had been routinely dug up as needed to finance smuggling trips, or to purchase homes and automobiles. Some of it had been banked in the U.S. or taken to Switzerland and converted to gold Krugerrands or one-ounce gold bars and put into safe deposit boxes.

Wearing coveralls, we set up construction lights beneath the house's foundation and began digging up the boxes which had been marked on three treasure maps. Ammo box after ammo box all filled with money were dug up, cleaned and brought into the house.

"Who says crime doesn't pay?" joked Phil as he opened the ammo boxes and removed the stacks of banded bills. "I told you this would be a much better idea than putting it in safe deposit boxes."

"I must admit it was a good idea. There's no way we could have put this amount of money into safe deposit boxes in the U.S. without attracting attention to ourselves. We couldn't have even taken this amount to Europe without making lots of trips," I said, as I separated the stacks of bills by denomination. I ran the bills through a money counting machine I had borrowed from 'Yorktown' Billy. There were separate piles for hundreds, fifties, twenties and anything smaller, of which there were tens, fives and even a surprising number of one dollar bills.

Phil's living room was about fifteen feet wide by eighteen feet long or roughly two hundred and fifty square feet. Pat carpeted the entire rustic wood-planked floor with all the stacks of bills I had counted and separated by denomination. Not one speck of wood was visible from beneath the piles of cash. After dividing it all up, each of us netted a sizable mound of cash with Pat taking the largest share because of the larger percentage he had negotiated on the contract loads.

I had brought the vacuum sealing machine, which Joe kept in his Atherton home, with me to the valley. The money was put into $50,000 and $100,000 bundles and vacuum sealed in poly-mylar bags to prevent mildewing. I later buried my share beneath my Menlo Park home and under my parents' Tahoe vacation home while they were traveling in Europe. I also kept a couple of hundred thousand on hand in the hidden safe beneath the sauna floor.

"Here's the fifty grand you lent me three years ago when I quit working for Ciro," Pat said smiling as he handed me a sealed $50,000 package.

"Thanks for remembering, Pat," I said taking the money. "Since you brought him up, I don't want to rain on our parade, here, but… in case either of you forgot, there's still over a million dollars which—your buddy Phil—that asshole Ciro still owes us."

"I'm sure there's good reason why he shorted us," Phil broke in. "Don't worry, we'll get it settled. We'll get together with him and clear this thing up. Remember, he finally paid Pat what he owed him." Phil didn't want to spoil the moment.

"Oh, bullshit!" I said vehemently. "Ciro is a ripoff artist to the core. That's his style. He talks honor and friendship, but I'd never turn my back on him. Didn't I warn both of you he'd do something like this?"

Anger colored Pat's face. "He pay me back because it was only way he could get into our Thai trip. I'm not giving that shit stick a chance to screw me again. The heat has cooled down enough! Phil, you set up meeting with him, just you and Ciro, but all three of us will show up!"

Late August 1977
Homewood, California, on the west shore of Lake Tahoe

The lazy Indian summer was slowly winding down. The cool hint of approaching autumn seemed to lengthen the late afternoon shadows. The wind's soft hum played through the tall tamarack and pine trees adorning Tahoe's west shore.

Pat and I had driven up to Phil's new north shore property in Pat's BMW. In addition to the Adobe House and the new valley home under construction, Phil had recently purchased a quaint old Tahoe style two bedroom wood and stone vacation cottage on a bluff near Carnelian Bay overlooking Tahoe's north shore.

"I spoke with Ciro this morning. He has no idea you two are coming over," Phil said as we drove through the small west shore community of Homewood in Phil's Mercedes Benz. We were approaching Ciro's recently constructed lakefront villa located behind a high wooden fence and gated entry.

"I'm really curious to see how he dances out of this one. I'll bet he has no intention of paying us," I said.

"If he screws us, I will get even with him, no matter how long it takes," Pat said.

"Settle down, both of you," ordered Phil. "You two are mind fucking this thing to death. Let's at least hear what he has to say!"

Ciro met us at the front door. He was visibly surprised at Pat's and my presence but handled it well. He wore tan trousers, a light blue Lacoste polo shirt, Topsider boat moccasins, without socks, and a gold Rolex on his wrist.

"Great! Good to see you guys. Come on in. Why didn't you tell me Pat and Rick were coming over?" Ciro said to Phil. There was an undercurrent of displeasure in his voice.

"Didn't know they were coming up, Ciro. Took me by surprise too," Phil said deftly.

"Andy, see who's come to visit," Ciro called to his longtime girlfriend, Andrea.

"Andrea and I finally got married," Ciro said for Pat's and my benefit.

"I heard. Congratulations Ciro," I replied.

"I hope you have many healthy sons," Pat interjected.

"That's what it's all about, friendship and family. Right Pat? Ah! Here she is now," Ciro said.

"Well, Hello, Phil!" Andrea said. She kissed him affectionately on the cheek. "Rick, Pat. How nice to see you." She nodded at both of us. Andrea was clad in white tennis shorts and a blue halter top and wore a pair of baby blue Keds tennis shoes. Her long brunette hair was tied back in a pony tail. She had on gardening gloves.

"We've got some things to talk about, hon. Why don't you go back to your gardening?" Ciro said.

"Sure, honey. Maybe they could stay for dinner? We could barbecue the Mackinaw you caught yesterday. Should be delicious."

"We'll see, dear. Now run along," Ciro said, dismissively shooing her out like a disobedient child with a waving backhand motion.

We moved into the large mahogany paneled den. Ciro gestured toward a round poker table where Pat, Phil and I took seats. Ciro moved in behind a large ornate early American antique oak bar.

"Beer, all around?"

"Sure, that's fine," Phil answered.

I took it upon myself to open the conversation. 'Why beat around the bush?' I thought. I laid my cards on the table. "We came here for the balance of the money you owe us, Ciro." I paused, letting the sentence hang in the air for a long moment. "I'm sure you haven't forgotten, we all had an agreement; the three of us would get forty percent of *Drifter*'s load. That comes to 1,320 pounds. I picked up 500 pounds from Brad. That leaves a balance of 820 pounds or the equivalent in money. Either way, you owe us."

Ciro came around the bar and set three green bottles of Heineken down on the table.

"Well, Rick," Ciro said, walking back to the bar and getting one for himself. "With so much shit happening after *Drifter*'s bust, it seemed like a good idea to lie low for awhile."

"Everybody laid low. Now is time for money accounting," Pat said. He seemed impatient.

"All right," Ciro said. His facial features seemed to harden. "Let's get to it. The bottom line is, both you and Phil stole Pat from me," he said, pointing an accusing forefinger at me. "The eight hundred and twenty pounds which, if sold for $1,500 per pound, is…," he did the quick math in his head, "$1,230,000. That's the compensation you owe me for the business I figure I lost on my Mexican trailer scam because you stole Pat."

"What? Are you fucking crazy or something?" I exclaimed incredulously. "We didn't steal Pat. No way!"

"You certainly did, Rick! He was working for me, and you stole him away for your Thai scheme," Ciro said.

"Ciro, wait a minute," Pat broke in. "I quit when you not pay me fitty thousand you owed me. Nobody stole me. I not a piece of furniture or a coolie slave or baseball player you can buy, trade or steal." His English became much more stilted whenever he got excited.

"Hey, come on guys! Let's not get heated," Phil said trying to interject some calm.

"You owe us the money, Ciro," I insisted.

"Bullshit. I owe you nothing!"

"Well now. I guess welshing on our deal sheds light on what you're really made of, eh Ciro? Remember the pretty little speech you gave me up in the Himalayas about trust, friendship and honor? You don't have a fucking clue what honor is all about. You're a fucking phony; a greedy flimflam man who's at his best when he's scamming his friends," I said with disgust.

"How dare you insult my integrity!" Ciro exploded.

"This is going nowhere, guys. Cool it down right now before things get outta hand. Come on," pleaded Phil.

"Oh, shut up Phil!," I snarled. "This fucking thief has about as much integrity as something unpleasant my shoe picks up in the gutter."

Ciro flew out of his chair and made a quick lunge to get around the table and onto me. Pat and Phil were up instantly and held Ciro back with difficulty.

"Your life has as much value as a pissant, you little shit! I got even with that greaser informant in Mexico once before, and I can easily do it again. How'd you like to find out how really deep Lake Tahoe is, asshole," raged Ciro. He was trembling. His black eyes were flat and menacing like a cobra's. "You'd better watch your back, Rick."

"That's just your style, Ciro. You're a back shooter!" I said, just as Andrea entered the room, alarmed by the screaming she heard from the garden.

Now she chimed in the screaming as well, "Get the fuck outta my house, you asshole. Nobody talks to my husband like that!"

I turned abruptly on my heel and left out the front door with Pat and Phil following me like ducklings, dutifully following the mother duck across the street.

I later tried to analyze the whole situation, but only came up with more unanswered questions. Phil made me a promise, the day I returned home from my first visit to Thailand back in '73, agreeing he wouldn't ever let Ciro in and, based on that agreement, we formed the three-way partnership. I guess now, making nearly a million a year wasn't enough for Phil.

What in the world could have possibly possessed Phil to let Ciro into our trip? To tell him exactly what we were doing and how we did it? To reveal our trade secrets, when he knew how much Pat and I were against it from the get-go? I certainly wasn't aware that any part of our original agreement wasn't still in effect.

'Why?' I wondered.

In the back of my mind I just couldn't help but think that maybe there could have been a back room deal, an OTO commission payment to Phil from Ciro if Phil could convince Pat and me to let him in. And, if so, maybe the payoff came from what Ciro had shorted us in weed.

Could it have been the reason for Phil's calm demeanor at the meeting, while Pat and I fumed? More unanswered questions.

Whatever the reason was, I never found out; however, greed certainly played into it.

Phil knew I wanted us to keep the trip to ourselves and I felt that bringing others into it would jeopardize everything. Regardless of his promise to me, I think he felt bringing others in would increase the amount of money we'd make and, using that logic, he was able to convince Pat as well, regardless of what I felt.

I guess in a way, we were both right.

I'm pretty sure in Phil's mind, the saying 'make hay while the sun shines' was the motivating factor in his convincing Pat to work with other groups. As Phil saw it, we sure made more money in the short term, but, as I predicted, it brought our trip down, got heat on us and doomed our partnership to an early and untimely end.

Who knows what the future might have been had we stayed small and kept the trip to ourselves. We might have been able to continue on for years, but times were changing and people's lives were changing as well. In retrospect it's impossible to know what might have been. What actually happened might have happened anyway, but this sure sped up the process.

We escaped by the skin of our teeth, but our anonymity was gone and there was no doubt the feds were looking for us.

Section 5

Early Retirement (1977–1979)

Chapter 26

Life Is Good

Late October 1977
Menlo Park, California

"Hey, Rick! How ya doin?," said a raspy, barely intelligible voice.

"What? Speak up. I can't hear you. Who is this?" I said into the telephone.

"This is your cousin Marty," said the voice, sounding as if the speaker had gargled with gravel and grain alcohol. "I must see you. I'm staying in San Francisco, in a cheap hotel. Can you come and visit me?"

"Sure," I replied. "I'll be up in a couple of hours, after dinner. What's the matter with your voice? Sounds like you have laryngitis or a terrible cold."

"I'll explain everything when I see you. I'm at the Mars Hotel. You'll probably recognize it from the cover on the Grateful Dead album, *From the Mars Hotel*. It's nothing glamorous, but at least it's a clean bed. It's south of Market Street at 192 Fourth Street. I'm in room 321."

I set down the phone and walked into the kitchen. Cindy was cutting mushrooms for Veal Scallopini. I opened a bottle of Chianti and poured two glasses.

"That was quite a surprise. It was Marty. I've told you about him. He's been in a Mexican prison for the past five years. My grandmother recently told me he was released a few months ago. I said I would be up after dinner. He's staying in a skid row dive, south of Market."

"Please be careful," cautioned Cindy. "That's a rough neighborhood, especially at night… and be careful of Marty. It might be a setup."

"Oh, you worry too much," I said.

"Just keep your eyes and ears open, and for God's sakes, don't tell him what you've been up to since he's been gone. People change when they've been through what he's been through," she said.

"OK."

"Promise me?"

"I promise," I said, giving her a reassuring kiss.

Following dinner, I put one thousand dollars into an envelope, stuffed it into the inside pocket of my windbreaker and left for The City in my pickup truck.

South of Market Street was the low end of San Francisco's skid row Tenderloin District. It was an area dotted with cheap bars, pawn shops, flop houses and tattoo parlors. Winos stood in alleys or slumped on stoops, drinking from bottles in brown paper bags. This area was a wretched dismal abyss which hungrily devoured lost souls, where hopelessness and despair were the price of admission. It was also littered with runny nosed, shifty eyed junkies, hanging out on street corners with the onset of withdrawal, anxiously awaiting the return of their dealers and their next fix. It was even too dismal a place for the local hookers to ply their trade. They stayed away and 'tricked' a few blocks north of Market Street amid the sanctity of the porno shops and sex theaters.

The Mars Hotel was an older, rather dilapidated looking building, located near the intersection of Fourth and Brannan Streets. It had fallen into a state of nearly complete disrepair and probably couldn't withstand even the slightest earthquake. I found a parking space right in front and entered the hotel through the swinging double doors. Warily, I climbed the narrow staircase to the third floor. The dimly lit hallway smelled of vomit and stale urine. The paint was faded and peeling from the walls as I squinted at the room numbers.

I knocked on the door to room 321. I heard a shuffling sound approach from the other side of the door. It opened and before me stood a gaunt, sunken eyed, almost hunch-backed man who I barely recognized. It had been five years since I last had seen him in the yard at Lecumberri Prison in Mexico City.

An emotional riptide surged within me as I felt a wave of compassion while at the same time was equally repelled by the dirty, unkempt, vile smelling man standing before me. I looked deep into my cousin's face. Marty's brown eyes appeared lifeless and dull, as if the spark behind them had been permanently extinguished. The blank eyes, devoid of feeling, stared back at me through hollow cheekbones of his death's head, lifeless face. The left side of Marty's face seemed frozen in a sardonic grin, as if he found life to be an extremely bad joke. He was a man who had experienced the worst of life and had no illusions left. There was a strong odor of alcohol and stale sweat in the small dingy room. I noticed, on the table there were a couple of vials of pills, a syringe resting in a half-filled water glass and a bent spoon, blackened on the bottom.

'Oh, God,' I thought.

"Marty, I'm glad to see you," I said. "You made it out alive."

"Alive? Well, that's rather questionable, depending upon your point of view," Marty said in a sandpaper sounding voice. "Let me tell you about it." Marty motioned me to a chair, while he sat upon the bed.

Over the next hour, Marty told me of his five years in the circle of hell in Lecumberri Prison, of the beatings, both by fellow prisoners and guards, the rapes, the humiliation, the deprivation and the awful loneliness and isolation. To be sure, his girlfriend Carol had supported Marty the best she could. However, the gradual weakening of her body from multiple sclerosis was taking its toll and she was physically unable to visit him on a regular basis. She was finally only able to come and see him every other week, and sometimes only once a month.

In 1977, after serving five years of his thirty-year sentence, Marty, along with other Americans imprisoned throughout Mexico, was released in an amnesty and prisoner exchange program arranged by President Jimmy Carter.

When the timeless horror appeared to be over, it was while he and Carol were safely back in the U.S. and in Florida staying with Carol's mother, Marty noticed a lump on the side of his neck. A biopsy revealed cancer. He underwent a dangerous ten-hour surgery. The cancer had metastasized around the cervical portion of his spinal cord and lower brain stem, but miraculously, the doctors had got it all. However, the operation left one side of his face paralyzed, his vocal cords severely damaged, and him completely deaf in one ear. The doctors told him, the cancer was probably due to numerous severe blows to the head, similar to those experienced by prize fighters taking too many hits to the head in the boxing ring.

Marty became addicted to painkillers, tranquilizers, sleeping pills and alcohol during the months of his painful physical rehabilitation. He 'mainlined' the morphine-derivative potent painkiller Dilaudid, tablets of which he crushed up, dissolved in water and shot into his black-and-blue severely tracked-up arm. He regularly popped Percodan, Valium and Seconal sleeping pills like candy, which he washed down with whatever, mostly rot-gut alcohol was available. Carol, unable to deal with his alcoholism and drug addiction, finally couldn't take it any more and walked out on him. Marty was devastated. Carol had been his sole emotional support throughout the five years of his imprisonment and during his lengthy rehabilitation following his cancer surgery.

He returned to California alone. He optimistically dreamed of reuniting with his father, Donald. Donald's only support during Marty's incarceration had been to send an American missionary, a Catholic priest, to visit him in Lecumberri. But at the start of the prison visit, Marty only laughed at the man and told him to get out and leave him alone. He told the clergyman that money was the only thing which could save him, not some spiritual mumbo jumbo. In a brief meeting with his father in Los Angeles, Marty's misguided and optimistic hopes of a reconciliation were quickly dashed. Donald disowned him, virtually spat on him with disgust and told him to change his last name as he was a slur and blight upon the family name and reputation. He relayed the conversation, verbatim, to me.

"You are a shame and a pox on our family. Change your name so I won't have to be related to you. I don't want you to screw up my professorship at Pepperdine. Stay away from your grandparents. Don't ever call me again. I want nothing to do with you. You rejected the spiritual help I sent you. Your body may have been released from prison, but your soul has been damned for all eternity, since you have failed to accept our Lord Jesus Christ as your personal savior. Now, get out."

"Guess you must have slept through the sermon on love and compassion, eh Dad? Well, fuck you, your self righteousness, and your coveted position at Pepperdine. Thanks for nothing!" Marty said, as he had somehow managed to blurt out to his astonished father, through the veil of tequila and Dilaudid.

I fought back tears as Marty concluded his story.

"So you see, Rick, I have nobody, nothing, just a needle to take my pain away."

"You know, Marty, maybe you can turn this whole thing around. Try to make a positive experience out of the whole situation. Perhaps you could write about it, while it's still fresh in your mind; maybe a book or a screenplay? It would be a very compelling story. Check out a new movie called *Midnight Express*.[1] Possibly it'll give you some ideas. You're a smart guy with a college education. Why don't you give it a try? Here's a little money to tide you over," I said, withdrawing the envelope from the inside of my jacket and handing it to him.

"Thanks for the encouragement. Maybe I will give it a try," Marty replied setting the envelope down on the table next the syringe and blackened spoon.

I returned home emotionally drained. Cindy lay in bed reading. I related the evening's events to her.

"I'm glad for once you listened to me and didn't tell him what's been going on in your life, the money you've made and how you've been living," she said, propping her reading glasses up on her forehead. "Even though I've never met him, I don't trust him. He's not the same person you once loved. Stay away from him, Rick. He's nothing but trouble. He will look at you and then at himself and try to get even with you for all the suffering he's been through."

I tossed and turned all night, snared in a nightmare's web. Shaving before the bathroom mirror next morning, a sudden realization shook me. I saw my cousin's fall as a progression of logical events, predicated by foolish decisions. Marty was not some poor schmuck, struck by bolts of idiotic and whimsical karmic forces. 'Shit,' I shuddered, 'Given some bad choices on my part, it could have easily been me!'

December 1977

"Let's go skiing in Europe for a few months and really air it out. We need a real vacation after the past three years, plus we need to move some of our assets," I said, sitting in the kitchen having my morning coffee.

"What about Papi?" replied Cindy, brushing her hair. "We can't just dump him in a kennel for two or three months."

"He's not staying. We're taking him with us. In Europe, dogs can go anywhere people can go."

We packed lightly as we planned to buy whatever we needed in Europe. I purchased a large dog kennel to accommodate Papi for the flight from San Francisco to New York and the connecting flight to Geneva. I fashioned an inner liner for the kennel by 're-customizing' a custom car mat so it fit the bottom of the kennel perfectly, under which I could comfortably conceal a hundred grand. So with Cindy and I each carrying an equal amount in our carry-on baggage and in her large Balinese purse, the three of us couriers and European vacationers departed SFO International, Cindy and I in first class and Papi in his first class dog kennel with food and water and sitting atop a new large comfy forest-green flannel L.L.Bean dog bed.

---

1 Referenced Television & Movies, Item 21, Page 533.

The beautiful and friendly golden retriever served as our emissary of goodwill throughout the European vacation. Papi expedited our way past Swiss Customs at the Geneva Airport when the otherwise stern-looking inspector flashed a smile at the sight of the happy dog and waved us through with hardly a second glance. At the luxurious Richmond Hotel, one of Geneva's finest, Papi was greeted warmly and treated like royalty as we stood at the reception desk, Papi between Cindy and me standing on his hind legs with his paws on the counter and tail wagging. The concierge, Gianni, laughed and wanted to know if we desired special meals for the dog which would be prepared in the hotel's five-star kitchen. Gianni seemed genuinely disappointed when I declined the offer, saying Papi only ate dry dog food. He would however accompany Cindy and me into the hotel's dining room where he would lie quietly under the table, occasionally savoring some of Geneva's finest cuisine table scraps.

We kept about fifty grand out for spending money and converted it into Swiss Francs and, with the remainder, bought gold bars which I put in the bank safe deposit box.

The winter was characterized by an unusually heavy snowfall and excellent skiing conditions. I bought a new Volkswagen Passat station wagon, equipped it with snow tires, a ski rack and the best Blaupunkt stereo and we set off crisscrossing Switzerland, France and Austria, skiing our way from one chic ski resort to the next. First, we drove west to the classic French alpine resort of Chamonix nestled at the foot of the Alps' tallest mountain, 14,000-foot Mt. Blanc. There we outfitted ourselves with the latest ski equipment including fashionable ski and apres ski clothes. The skiing was fantastic as we hopscotched from Chamonix through the Northern French Alps, back through the Swiss Alps then into Austria.

During the next two months, I think, we hit most every major ski resort in those areas: Alpe d'Huez, Courchevel, Les Arcs, Megève, Tignes, Val d'Isère, Val Thorens, then back into Switzerland to Verbier, Zermatt, Gstaad, Davos, St. Moritz, and Interlakken, then into Austria and the Arlberg and Kitzbuhl.

In St. Moritz we stayed in the Palace Hotel in the same suite as was reserved for the Shah of Iran. It was in Gstaad where I almost killed Papi. I took him up the gondola with me and for two runs down the mountain he chased me down through the powder. By the end of the second run he was so exhausted, I had to carry him back to the hotel room. When Cindy saw me carrying him she yelled in anguish, "You killed him!"

"No," I replied, "He's totally exhausted." She filled the bathtub with hot water and massaged him and lay him on the bed, where he didn't move for two days.

Cindy took lessons wherever we went and I was usually left to ski alone. Never wanting to be without music when I skied, I had brought along one of the latest innovations with me, Astraltunes. It was the world's first portable tape deck and was scarcely known about in Europe. It predated the Walkman by five years and was designed in the Sierras primarily for use in freestyle skiing in the mid-1970s. Astraltunes was actually a rechargeable battery-powered eight-track cassette player fitted in a padded pack with Sennheiser headphones. The entire contraption, measuring 10 inches tall by 6 inches wide and 3 inches thick, was strapped to a skier's chest and buckled tight with 3/4 inch wide webbing material. Nearly every skier I ran into in Europe was flabbergasted to see me skiing to music and a day never went by without someone asking if they could buy it from me. I could have sold as many as I could have gotten my hands on. The song *Terrapin Station* by the Grateful Dead was my favorite music to ski to. In Europe the ski runs are usually several miles long and I could listen to the entire 16 minute song from beginning to end on just one run without interruption. I was in heaven!

Cindy was now divorced from her husband Glen, so we decided to get married and made plans to tie the knot in Europe. On the first day of spring, March 21, 1978, with my parents, Joe the best man, and his girlfriend Jennifer in attendance and with Papi, the best dog carrying the ring down the aisle, Cindy and I were married in a 12th century castle in a small Swiss village above the shores of Lake Geneva. After the wedding, with my parents in tow, we left for Vienna, Austria, where we stayed at the famous Hotel Sacher, site of the invention of the famous confectionary known as the Sacher Torte, a chocolate cake with apricot filling. You could buy a six pack of mini-Sacher Tortes, like a six pack of beer, from the pastry shop on the first floor.

Our suite at the stately old hotel was on the third floor and after checking in and being escorted up the elevator and to our room and my parents to the room next door, I turned to Cindy. "Where's Papi?" I said after the bellboy set our bags down.

"I thought he was with you," Cindy said. "Or was he with your parents?"

I dashed into their room. No Papi. I turned and saw a wide set of stairs leading down two flights to the lobby. I raced down the stairs, two or three at a time and as I arrived at the foot I saw two bellboys running down the street. I went out through the two sets of automatic doors and onto the main street of Vienna, where I saw the bellboys chasing Papi, now almost two blocks away.

"Oh shit!" They caught up to him and held him until I got there a minute later. I guess he'd had enough and decided to abandon us in downtown Vienna. What was he thinking? I brought him back and we had a good laugh. Cindy cried and was overjoyed. She thought he was gone for good. I said, "No, he was just living up to his namesake, Papillon, the escape artist from Devil's Island."

It was now spring and we decided to go up to Germany and check out the famous mineral baths at Baden-Baden, located in Bavaria in Southern Germany at the foot of the Black Forest. We arrived in the late afternoon and checked into the exclusive Brenners Park Hotel and Spa. I wanted to take a swim before dinner, so I went to the mineral pool and just before diving in I looked at my 'waterproof' white gold Rolex President watch which I just had serviced in Geneva. It was 7:15 in the evening when I dove in. I swam laps for about fifteen minutes and when I checked the time, it was still 7:15. 'What, the hell…' I thought. 'Am I in some sort of time warp, where time stands still?' Then I looked closer and saw water halfway filling the inside of my ten thousand dollar watch.

"Aw shit!" I exclaimed to Cindy as I hurried back to the room. "My watch is filled with water."

"How can that be? You just had it serviced?" she asked.

"Maybe you have to pay extra for the waterproofing?" I joked.

The nearest service center was a day's drive to Frankfurt, where we went the following day. By the time we arrived at the Rolex service center in Frankfurt, the insides were completely rusted and frozen. It took about a month, but a few weeks after we returned home a new watch was sent from Rolex headquarters in Switzerland with apologies for the inconvenience. The whole episode would have been a great advertisement for Rolex. As it turned out the service center had misaligned the crystal when they serviced it and it had leaked. But they stood behind it and replaced it, free of charge.

We returned to Menlo Park to a beautiful California spring, refreshed and looking forward to life as a married couple.

It seemed like everyone was settling into retirement as well. Pat was courting a new girlfriend, Rebecca, who had moved in with him at his Woodside house. Willie had married his latest girlfriend, Melinda, on the 18th hole at Pebble Beach Golf Course in a lavish event hosted by Melinda's wealthy parents. Joe and Jennifer were living in the posh town of Atherton. Killian had earlier bought land in Grass Valley and was building a boat-like A-frame house, and Phil and Wendy were expecting their first child.

This is Willie, myself and Papi up at Lake Tahoe in 1977. It appears in this shot that our 'early retirement' agreed with us as we had both gained back the weight we'd lost on the first Thai trip.

'Yorktown' Billy had one of the most interesting transitions of lifestyle following our early retirement. Although not really retired, Billy still had other well-established contacts for whom he could act as a middleman. With his longstanding and very reliable network in place in San Francisco, he could now turn loads for an easy five figure return with only a phone call and without lifting a finger. With his longtime girlfriend, Mary Jane, Billy relocated from his flat in the middle of the Mission District in San Francisco to a small house he bought in the forest not far from the northern California coastal town of Fort Bragg. He bought a 38-foot salmon fishing boat and became a Pacific

Ocean fisherman. He lost nearly fifty pounds and became a muscle-bound physical specimen of health. He fished every day and discovered he had a rare gift of knowing exactly where the fish were. He would catch the limit daily even when his fishing buddies in nearby waters were getting skunked. Mary Jane, a retired botanist, became an expert in mushrooms. In the fall, wild chanterelle mushrooms grow in the dark forest around Fort Bragg. They are a prized component on the menus of numerous high-end San Francisco restaurants. The ever resourceful Billy and Mary Jane would harvest hundreds of pounds of chanterelles off the forest floor, their only investment being the 'sweat equity' of picking, packing and transporting them to San Francisco, then selling them for top dollar to some of Billy's pot customers who were also restaurant owners. During the late fall, it wasn't unusual for Billy to sell one hundred pounds of pot and one hundred pounds of mushrooms to the same person.

Life was good.

May 1, 1978
Menlo Park, California

"Go get the paper, Boy," commanded Cindy.

Papi bounded down the long landscaped driveway of our newly renovated home. Just on the inside of the gate lay the Monday edition of the *San Francisco Chronicle*[2] wrapped in plastic. The lovable golden retriever returned to the back door carrying the morning edition in his mouth and wagging his tail.

"Good boy!" Cindy said taking the paper from Papi and giving the furry red dog a big hug.

She went into the kitchen, poured herself a cup of coffee and returned to bed to read the paper, while I continued to sleep peacefully. It was a beautiful lazy spring morning.

"Holy shit, Rick! Wake up and take a look at this," exclaimed Cindy.

I bolted upright in bed, "Huh? What's happened?" I mumbled.

Cindy handed me the newspaper. Right there, in the front section on page 4 was a full page article detailing the *Drifter* bust, and an exposé of both the *Drifter* and *Nepenthe* smuggling trips. There were photographs of the impounded *Drifter* and the twenty-five pounds of seized Thai stick. *Nepenthe* was referred to as the 'Fruit Boat,' in a not-so-veiled reference to her captain. The article suggested a floating homosexual palace, complete with an all gay crew romping and frolicking their way across the Pacific amid bales of high grade Thai marijuana.

I winced as if slapped in the face. "Son of a bitch!" My facial expression transitioned from total disbelief to abject horror, as I pored through the journalistic nightmare spread before me on the bed.

There it was. The feature length article laid out the whole scam for the world to see in black and white. Everything from how the load was scored and loaded, to how the marijuana was distributed in the United States. Mercifully, the only items missing were names: mine, Pat and Phil's names, the names of *Nepenthe*'s crew, the names of towns

2 Referenced Newspaper Articles, Item 1, Page 529.

and villages and connections in Thailand.

The phone rang. It was 'Yorktown' Billy.

"Did you see it?" he asked.

"Yeah, just now." I replied.

"I think it's time to be cool before our goose gets cooked," said Billy.

"Right. I've got to think about this. Talk to you later," I said, then hung up the phone.

"It looks like somebody on *Drifter* spilled their guts to both the cops and the newspapers. Well," I said turning to Cindy, "it's definitely early retirement."

"They didn't mention any names. Do you think they know about you and the others?" Cindy asked.

"I don't think so. *Drifter*'s crew only knew us by our first names. Hopefully, the guys who got popped kept their mouths shut. Ciro has always made it real clear what he does to rats," I answered.

"This sure puts the spotlight on Willie and Joe," Cindy said pouring me a cup of black coffee. "I wonder if they got a little too lonely out there?"

"I doubt that, but whatever was or wasn't going on out there, the name 'The Fruit Boat' in print, for all to see, sure doesn't bode well for Willie and Joe and I'm sure they'll never be able to live this one down," I said.

"Well," Cindy replied, "the name 'Fruit Boat' does have a nice ring to it, although in this context I can't really picture a yacht laden with bananas bound for the San Francisco produce market, unless they've moved it to Castro Street!"

Chapter 27

Blackmail

Menlo Park, California
June 1978

While in Europe, following our wedding, my parents accompanied Cindy and me to the Hotel Sacher in Vienna, Austria. For the first time in years we thoroughly enjoyed each other's company, going to the world famous Vienna Symphony and museums in the city steeped with tradition. Dick took the opportunity of our time together to renew his relationship with me. It carried over when we returned home.

At our home, on a beautiful spring evening following an exquisitely prepared five course dinner Cindy had made for my parents, my father Dick and I strolled our secluded park-like grounds. As we neared the new greenhouse I had recently built for Cindy, Dick steered the conversation towards my future.

"I know, it's futile to talk about you joining me in the family business, so why not let me help you start a business of your own?" Dick suggested. "You know, I'm licensed in real estate, insurance and securities and although I am not active in those fields, my licenses are current. We could form an investment company and you could sit for the license exams and have your own investment business. Son, since you're retired from 'that' business and by the grace of God you haven't been arrested, you need some legitimate business interest. If you've learned anything from me over the years, you should remember, I've always said: 'let your money work for you; never dip into your capital'."

I suddenly realized, for the first time I could recall, my father was actually talking 'with me' and not 'at me'.

"Sounds like a great idea, Dad. What exactly do I have to do to get started?"

Helen was in the kitchen helping Cindy load the dishwasher. The distinctive looking gray-haired woman felt a new sense of family togetherness and was more content than she had been in a long time.

During the years of Dick's and my estrangement, she had never given up hope that one day her family would be emotionally reunited. Helen had secretly defied Dick's requests; she had kept the channels of communication open with me throughout the five years of family turmoil, despite the fact that her own marriage seemed to be deteriorating. Now, it appeared, her dream of a united family seemed to be coming true.

"Cindy, I am so proud of you for turning Rick's life around. Just look at him with his father talking man-to-man without yelling at each other. I'm really proud to have you as a daughter-in-law. I feel blessed that you've come into his life."

"Thanks Mom," Cindy replied. It was the first time she had called my mother, 'Mom'.

"You'll never know how hard it has been for us to stay together knowing Rick was risking his life and freedom doing what he has been doing for the past ten years," Helen continued. "Dick and I have been talking about Rick's future and how we can help you both. Dick is going to offer Rick an opportunity to start a business of his own. I hope you will help convince him; this would be a good way to really get his life back together and be legitimate. It would certainly make us very proud of him."

My youngest sister had recently graduated from law school and along with her husband was looking to buy a house and start raising a family. She had asked my father for a loan to make the down payment. My father, in his usual compassionless business mode, agreed but wanted to tie her up 'six ways to Sunday'. She refused and came to me with her problem. I was only too happy to help and offered to comply with her request with 'no strings attached'. Explaining this to my father, he cautioned, "Don't do it that way, because if you loan them the money and do it my way, you'll have them where you want them."

I responded that this was my decision and that I would do it my way, unencumbered, regardless of his warning. I said, "My only interest is in helping my sister out and I don't care about making money off of her or putting her in an uncomfortable position, no matter what. It's not always about business. Isn't that what families are all about, for Christ sakes?"

I went on to help her my way. In years to come, my cavalier and rather bullheaded decision to help her was one I'd come to question and wonder about, when the tables had turned. Maybe good ole Dad had a point... again!

Following my father's suggestions about my future, I proceeded to get licensed, first as a securities broker, then as a real-estate and insurance broker and finally as an investment advisor licensed by the U.S. Securities and Exchange Commission. Armed with these licenses, Dick and I formed an international investment company called Med-Dent Investment Company, although Dick's involvement was in name only. I leased an office on the twenty-second floor of the newly constructed Fox Plaza Office Complex in San Francisco's financial district.

The office was small but had a panoramic view of San Francisco Bay. It had a New England flavor with classic paintings of 19th century windjammers charging for Cape Horn or anchored in the bays off Singapore and Hong Kong. The office had been furnished in early American oak furniture with tall bookcases and an antique oak rolltop desk. Sitting comfortably behind the desk in a black leather swivel chair, with my licenses displayed prominently behind me, I surveyed my little domain. I felt like a big-shot, Taipan executive ready to do business.

My grandfather, Herb Salinger, a rather stodgy old-time San Francisco corporate lawyer, was able to get me a connection with the head of the bond department in the Bank of America's International and Finance Division. I could now purchase tax free municipal bonds directly from the underwriter issuing the securities. My first clients were my grandparents who were large bond purchasers and kept a stock of municipal bonds in their investment portfolio. They were happy to assist in getting me started in business.

My next clients were my parents. It soon became evident to me that my associates in the marijuana smuggling business would be the perfect clientele. They could turn their cash into above-board investments and I could start legitimizing myself.

So the first order of business was to develop and perfect a safe way to get their cash money into the system.

As I already knew, getting a cashier's check from virtually any bank involving a cash transaction below $10,000 is not reported, there is no paperwork other than signing the draft and it is not necessary to show any identification; therefore any name can be used. This seemed to be a good way to get large amounts of cash money into the system without causing suspicion. The checks then could be run through my commercial banking business trust account, the same type of account large investment companies routinely run millions through daily and are required to maintain for their clients. I could then purchase the bonds through regular banking channels.

I made a list of banks in the south Bay Area around Palo Alto and south to San Jose. Dressed in one of my Hong Kong tailored business suits and with a dozen envelopes each containing between $9,500 and $9,900 in my slim black Halliburton attache case, I set off for twelve different banks and bought twelve cashier's checks. Occasionally a bank teller would question such a cash transaction and I would simply say, I sold a boat or car over the weekend and didn't want to accept a check, so I always insisted on cash. That always seemed to do the trick and I just printed and signed with any fictitious name I made up on the spot.

I deposited the cashier's checks in the business trust account I'd set up for my clients. I now had the money in the system and I secured a list of municipal bonds which were available directly from the underwriters from my banking connection. It was amazingly similar to how I was able to work directly with the source in my marijuana smuggling business and how I was able to get only the best; now I was able to get the best, 'Triple A' rated top quality municipal bonds and at the lowest wholesale price. These bonds are sometimes called 'bearer bonds', because the bearer of the bond is the one who physically keeps the bonds in his/her possession. Interest is paid quarterly in the form of coupons which are clipped off the actual bond itself. Most any bank will accept the coupons without question and will pay the interest, in cash or check, to the bearer of the coupon. An additional feature of the bonds is, they are tax-free and do not require reporting the income or paying tax on it. The interest paid was from 8% to 10% and was tax-free as well.

After seeing my own trial run worked flawlessly, I asked Pat, Phil and Jonathan

Jacoby if they'd be interested in buying bonds. They repeated the process and now my little business was off and rolling. After my first few months in the bond business I'd sold over a million dollars in municipal bonds.

I attended monetary conventions and learned about diversification of assets, about offshore banking and how to move money globally without using the U.S. banking system. I researched the countries where offshore accounts are routinely held and found out the preferred countries were Switzerland, Lichtenstein, Grand Cayman Island, Costa Rica and Panama. It was also known that these countries prided themselves on banking secrecy and made it known not only to blue-blooded wealthy individuals, but also to international arms dealers and to drug smugglers. I chose Costa Rica and decided the small Central American country would be the ideal place to form an international corporation.

"You want in?" I had asked Pat one night on our way to a movie.

"Why not? I need way of getting money out of U.S. to Hong Kong," Pat replied.

Four days later, Pat and I flew to Costa Rica with our briefcases and boots stuffed with cash. With Pat and me again together it was reminiscent of our first trip to South East Asia five years earlier, with no hassles and the carefree attitudes we shared previously. Through my banking connections in San Francisco, I was able to secure the name of a Costa Rican corporate attorney, Juan de Mendoza-Lopez. For a nominal fee, Mendoza-Lopez was able to form two international corporations, one for me and one for Pat.

The slim, slightly graying, green-eyed dapper Costa Rican advised us that the Banco Nacional was the best bank with which to do business, so we deposited our cash into an account which had the ability to facilitate funds being transferred anywhere in the world. The possibilities were endless. I could now transfer funds to Switzerland and Pat could do likewise to Hong Kong. I could even charter a private plane and fly it directly to Costa Rica with cash, where it could be transferred to Switzerland or anywhere else. Customs in Costa Rica was almost nonexistent and bringing cash into the country had very little risk even on commercial flights.

Menlo Park, California
June 1979

The renovation of our Menlo Park house was finally completed. The house was accessed by a long driveway which had at its end a six-foot-tall grape stake electric gate with remote control access. A high redwood fence encompassed the grounds. The house itself was set back among a stand of majestic white oaks. Behind the house was a 20 foot by 50 foot kidney-shaped swimming pool with a built-in jacuzzi spa attached on one side. There was a two-car garage attached to a party and game room, which featured a sauna, beneath which was my hidden safe. A guest cottage bordering the pool opposite the house served as my home office.

Cindy relished reading by the swimming pool and spa with Papi and our new puppy named Bubba without the distracting noise of hammering and power tools. Papi had been bred to another Golden Retriever and we got to choose pick-of-the-litter, Bubba, who officially became Cindy's dog and followed her everywhere. Bubba, although a gorgeous retriever in his own right, was not nearly as smart as Papi and lived as the underling and second dog behind his stately sire. To round out the family, we also had a beautiful long haired Himalayan cat named Mr. T. The animals served as children for Cindy and me and provided good company for Cindy during my absences.

Wendy and Phil had also finished their new home on a bluff overlooking rich valley farmland. Their first child, Jake, had been born in January of 1979. Phil and Wendy had joined an exclusive valley golf and country club where they hobnobbed with the large landholding farmers and ranchers, the Central Valley's elite. There were occasionally subtle rumors and whispered questions about Phil's past and where he had acquired his wealth, but they were dismissed as idle gossip since Phil had been managing his parents' extensive fruit orchards. Before the birth of Jake, Wendy had become a born again Christian and was involved in church work and local charities. People in the valley often said Phil and Wendy, both with quick smiles, friendly personalities and All-American good looks, were such a charming couple.

Willie and Melinda and their dog Sunshine were living in the same Menlo Park neighborhood as Cindy and me. Cindy and Melinda had become good friends during the time I was in Costa Rica or away at international monetary conventions. Cindy was the dominant partner in the two women's relationship. They would sunbathe by the pool or have lunch and go shopping. Once in a while, after the two had snorted half a gram of cocaine, or so, and had quaffed a couple of Long Island iced teas in the sun by the pool, Cindy would launch into a diatribe, condemning others involved in the scams, such as Phil.

"Rick's done all the work while Phil has been back peddling in the shadows trying to do as little as possible. Wendy's 'born again', devoting all her time to her baby and her church. Rick's always wanted children, but everything has to take a backseat while he holds everything together for all of us," Cindy said. She neglected to say, however, that though Rick wanted children, she was much happier without them.

Melinda would bemoan the fact that Willie was still up to his old tricks.

"I love him dearly, Cindy, but I don't trust him anymore. He comes home about three in the morning at least once a month, all wobbly and drunk, coked to his eyebrows, smelling of another woman. Then he lies through his teeth, giving me some stupid excuse. Next morning he goes out and purchases something to buy me off. What can I do?"

"I'd make him really pay for his screwing around, Melinda. Demand something expensive, and if that doesn't work, remember, honey, 'what's good for the goose is good for the gander'."

Joe lived in the nearby chic upscale town of Atherton with his new girlfriend Donna Stevenson. The long-haired blonde was the former girlfriend of Bob Lahodny. She had met Joe the previous year, around the time when he had transported our portion of the Coronado Company's load from the *Pai Nui*, which came ashore via the amphibious Duck. Joe had socialized with Bob on several occasions and had been quite friendly with Donna. She hailed from La Jolla and Newport Beach. Trim and athletic, Donna finally had enough of Bob and the Southern California flash and trash scene. Joe was pleased with himself, having lured Donna away from 'Lights', as Bob was called. Bob, however held no grudge as women always flocked around his good looks and generosity, especially when it came to his seemingly endless pile of cocaine. Joe still loved to socialize with anybody in 'the business'. He would frequently fly to Southern California to party with Donna's friends and the other members of the Coronado Company. He also frequented Tahoe where he hung out with Ciro Mancuso and his crew of Walter Brugger and his trusted lieutenants Jeff and Brad.

Although Pat, Phil and I were unaware of it at the time, Ciro was still doing smuggles from Thailand, even after the *Drifter*'s bust. He continued to work with Pat's old Thai connection, Charley, whom he had recruited on a secret trip back to Thailand, where he found him at his usual hangout, the bar at the Pattaya Palace Hotel. It was just like Ciro to rip us off for nearly a million dollars for allegedly stealing his man, Pat, then go and reconnect with our people and use our equipment behind our backs and conveniently overlook compensating us in any way. Typical!

Joe was jockeying to integrate himself into Ciro's operation. Unbeknownst to me, Joe was taking Ciro's money over to Thailand, and was helping Ciro refine his offloading operations with Mike Stallings and his new partner Dennis Moronsky, a former hippie turned smuggler-businessman. Joe further compromised our operation by telling Ciro exactly where the vacuum sealing machines and special poly-mylar bags were purchased. Joe had actually purchased several sealing machines and one hundred thousand bags under his own name and had shipped the gear to Thailand. He rationalized his actions not as betrayal, but as upgrading Ciro's operations, since Pat, Phil and I had retired.

Dave Killian was also putting together a life for himself with the proceeds from the last couple of marijuana trips. He now had enough money to start construction on the ten acre lot he had acquired in the Sierra Foothills. It was a custom A-frame home, complete with a recording studio at ground level. The house's insides were designed after a boat's interior, hand crafted with custom redwood and teak woodwork. The home was finished in 1979. Killian spent most of his time there, occasionally entertaining groups of young gay men up from San Francisco's notorious Castro District. The liquor flowed like the small creek below the house. Marijuana, 'poppers' (amylnitrate) and gin were consumed in large quantities during Killian's soirees. Once in a while, he came down from the hills only to disappear for days in the Castro District bathhouses and bars.

Late Summer 1979

I was swimming laps in our pool late one afternoon. The temperature was in the mid-'80s following a long hot day. The poolside phone began ringing. I lifted myself out of the water, toweled off my face and picked up the receiver. I immediately recognized my cousin Marty's barbed wire scratchy voice.

"Hi Marty. What's up?" I said.

"Rick, I'm living down in Santa Barbara with Bruce and we're getting along real well," rasped Marty. Bruce Bibbero was Marty's brother, some thirteen years younger.

"Last time I heard, Bruce didn't want to ever see you again, dead or alive. Did a number on you just like your dad."

"That's a used to be, Rick. It's history. Listen, I've got something I'd like you to see and I'd like you to fly down here and check it out."

"Well, I can make it down day after tomorrow. Can you give me a clue?" I questioned.

"All I'll tell you now is, I've been doing what you once suggested and I think you'll be quite surprised at my progress," Marty replied.

"Sounds good. See you soon." I hung up the phone and thought for a minute. 'Something didn't seem right. Marty pals with Bruce?'

Bruce and his brother Marty had never been close. By the time Bruce was a teenager, Marty was a small-time dealer in San Francisco's drug scene. Their mother had died of cancer and Bruce had been raised by his father Donald, who rarely had time for his youngest son, or his other children, two daughters, for that matter. While his wife was dying, Don was dating other women and the care for his dying wife fell onto the hands of his youngest daughter. Bruce had to fend for himself, so, following the example set by his father, it was not long before he learned how to lie, scheme and run petty scams for money. Only his grandfather, Herb, kept an interest for him. Herb offered to pay for Bruce's schooling at the prestigious Menlo Junior College, known as the stepping stone to Stanford University. One semester's tuition fee was $10,000, so Bruce convinced his trusting grandfather to fund his education. He enrolled as a part-time summer school student for $1,500 and pocketed the rest of the money.

Menlo College was not far from Menlo Park where Cindy and I lived. Bruce visited us a couple of times and was always attempting to connive me with some scheme for me to buy him liquor since he was underage or to loan him money. I refused on both counts and didn't trust him any further than I could throw him. I had also been very distressed at his attitude towards his brother. It had been clear to me that Bruce hated Marty's guts. His father, Donald, had brainwashed Bruce into believing Marty was no good and had no business being in the family following his cocaine bust and incarceration in Mexico. Donald's conversion to his newly discovered self-righteous Catholicism completely soured Bruce on a brother he hardly knew.

I went inside and told Cindy about the call.

"Rick, I'm telling you again, like I said two years ago, stay away from Marty. He's a no good son of a bitch and Bruce is as slimy as they come. I'm telling you, Rick, it's trouble. You go down to Santa Barbara and, as sure as I'm sitting here, you're going to get screwed by those two. I'll even put money on it. Five thousand says they've got a scheme cooked up which will land you in more trouble than you can handle. Whaddya say?"

"Oh, come on Cindy, you're always being so paranoid. Last time I saw Marty, I gave him a challenge to write something about his experiences and it seems like he's risen to the occasion. I'm actually pleased. Maybe he's really turning his life around with Bruce's help."

"Five grand. Put your money where your mouth is, Big Shot!"

"Alright! You're on!" I said.

"Oh, boy! I just can't wait. Hmmm… let's see, what do I need? Maybe a new Rolex would be nice. Or perhaps I'd better rathole the five grand for your bail? If you get mixed up with those two you'll probably land in jail."

"OK, OK. You've made your point, but I have to see him. I'm going down day after tomorrow and I'll be home the same day. I don't plan to dilly-dally or waste time there. I do thank you for one thing. I'm sure glad I took your advice and never said a word about any of the Thai trips," I said.

Cindy purred. "I just can't wait for my new Rolex. I kind of like the one with the diamond bezel. Don't you, sweetie?"

Santa Barbara, California
Two Days Later

A big blue Bentley pulled up in front of the airport's passenger pickup zone and stopped at the curb. Bruce Bibbero was at the wheel of the right-hand-drive vehicle. He was wearing a tennis outfit which accentuated his tall muscular body.

"I see you're still a big shot, Bruce. Where'd you steal the car?" I inquired.

"I borrowed it from a movie producer friend of mine who might be interested in doing Marty's story. Hop in. I'll let Marty tell you all about it. I don't want to steal his thunder."

"That'd be out of character, but I promised not to pre-judge, so let's go."

I got into the Bentley's left-hand side. Bruce pulled away and began the leisurely drive to the cottage he shared with his brother. It was located in the ritzy section of Santa Barbara known as Montecito, home to many of Hollywood's rich and famous.

"Tell me something, Bruce. How come you and Marty are so tight? Last time I saw you, you wanted nothing to do with him. As a matter of fact, you were ashamed he was your brother and, as I recall, you said you hoped he would just die. Why the turnaround, Bruce? Brotherly love or what?" I asked.

"No, Rick. It's different now. I've really gotten to know Marty. I never really knew him before and my father bad rapped him so much, I simply hated him on my father's word. By the way, he's much better than when you saw him last, down in that San Francisco flophouse."

We pulled up to a set of sculpted iron gates which Bruce opened from a remote control clicker on the visor above his head. The gates swung open to a long curved driveway lined with palm trees leading to a palatial estate, highlighted by tall white columns and a domed entry complete with a porte-cochere. The grounds resembled the television set on the TV show *Magnum P.I.*

Bruce parked the Bentley. "We stay out back, in the guest house. Follow me."

He led me down a pathway along the side of the mansion. At the rear of the house, the path opened up onto a huge lawn the size of a football field. On the far side was a guest house, a smaller version of the main house. Beyond was the tennis court and

Olympic-sized pool. There, on a chaise lounge, sitting by the pool, was Marty.

He was wearing Ray-Ban sunglasses and a bathing suit and was working on improving his already golden brown suntanned body. He appeared to have gained some weight and seemed in better spirits, if you discounted his *Phantom of the Opera* frozen grimace.

"Bruce, why don't you get us a couple of Coronas and we can relax and tell cousin Rick what we've been up to," Marty said.

"What do you mean 'we', Marty?" I said. "I thought you were writing the story?" In the back of my mind, I began to think I might owe Cindy five grand.

"Well, Rick. You see Bruce is assisting me with the storyline. He's giving me some direction with the plot. He thinks one of his producer friends might be interested in reading the script. It's really happening."

Bruce returned with a cooler filled with Coronas and opened one for each of us. Taking a chair next to his brother, he brought out a tape recorder, plugged in a cassette and gave it to Marty.

"This is what we have so far," said Marty, as he pushed the 'play' button.

The tape began to play. It was Marty's voice, but to my stunned amazement, it was my own story. The tape's gravel voice told about me and Willie Sherman and how we started smuggling marijuana across the Mexican border, with kilos on our backs. It told about how Del Carlucci got into the picture and about Phil Erikson and how things escalated through Phil's friend, Ciro Mancuso.

I listened dumbfounded about Dave Killian and Mark Wozenberg and the numerous smuggles aboard racing yachts returning from Mexico. For an hour the tape played on, as the recorded hacksaw voice recounted everything he knew about my smuggling career. There was no mention of Marty or his bungled smuggle or his experience in a Mexican prison. There were veiled references to Dick Bibbero and his helping me launder money through a legitimate business enterprise. Mercifully, there was no mention of any of the Thai trips.

"We want you to take over the direction of this project, Rick," commented Bruce.

"You see, Rick," said Marty picking up on his brother's well rehearsed cue. "Your story is much more interesting and salable than mine. You pay us and you take control of the project. We want you to buy us out. We've got it this far and through Bruce's connection, we have a Hollywood producer who might be interested in making a movie out of the story. It's pretty interesting, don't you think?"

"What do I think? If this is the fantasy and make believe story you have, I'm not really interested. You might have at least considered letting me know in advance what you were up to and saved all of us, especially you, from wasting time with this nonsense. As far as I know, there's not a shred of truth to it. It's all made up bullshit and a concocted fairy tale. I would think any legitimate Hollywood producer is not going to take this garbage seriously or at face value, and there's no one I'm aware of who'd corroborate this nonsense."

"The price is $300,000, Rick," answered Bruce. "You pay us three hundred grand and you can do whatever you want with it."

"Bruce, are you so stupid or deaf as to not have heard what I just said? I didn't think Marty's deafness was contagious, but obviously I was wrong on that score, because you seem to have the same problem with your hearing. But, for your benefit, I will say it again so even someone with your apparent dim-witted intelligence can understand. I'm not interested in any participation with this bullshit which obviously was cooked up in the deranged mind of a heroin addict needing money to support his habit. You're a fool to have bought into this, but what else could I have expected from someone who hood-winked, lied and took advantage his own grandfather's generosity. You're scum, Bruce, and so are you Marty."

"Rick, you know it's all true," rasped Marty, "and we're going forward with it, with or without you. We also think the authorities might be pretty interested in it as well, but we just wanted to give you the opportunity to control your own destiny."

"Sounds like a threat to me. I always knew that nothing, not even extortion or blackmail, was below something your fucked up brother wouldn't stoop to, but I never thought you could be conned into something like this. Oh, I guess I forgot, you're nothing but a heroin addict who will do anything to support your wretched habit. Good luck with that. Don't bother to get me back to the airport, I'll manage on my own. And by the way, I've taped this entire meeting for posterity, so in the event you pursue this preposterous fabrication, be assured, you will hear from my attorney," I said, taking my Olympus voice-activated mini tape recorder from my pocket and flashing it in their direction. Trying my best not to show my anger, I abruptly turned on my heels and headed towards the gate.

Upon my return to Menlo Park, I went immediately to my safe hidden beneath the sauna's floor and withdrew one stack of neatly bound one hundred dollar bills. I then went inside and without saying a word, handed Cindy $5,000. As I poured myself a glass of Cabernet, I couldn't help but think: 'I don't think I've heard the last from those two assholes!'

* * *

During this same time period of 1978 and 1979, the Coronado Company was con-tinuing to work in Thailand, but they were having trouble acquiring high-quality loads like they'd once gotten from us. Currently, the Coronado Company was using the ser-vices of a successful Thai marijuana smuggler nicknamed Abdul Blackie. Abdul had his own organization and would do his own smuggles and would also score loads for others. He worked closely with Stan Yamamoto, a Japanese American, also in the busi-ness. Ab and Stan had a system of transferring money through legitimate banking channels in Hawaii, directly to Thailand. Ab had the ability to score large loads, but the quality was substandard, far below the quality Pat and I had been able to get.

As we found out in Mexico, there is only so much high quality marijuana in Thailand. I set the bar as high as possible by telling the growers we would only accept the best and would refuse anything less. Between 1976 and 1979 many other smug-glers who'd had success in places like Morocco, Lebanon, Columbia and Mexico saw the opportunity we had opened in Thailand and jumped in. Names like Brian Daniels, the Shaffer Brothers, Bob Leitzman, and Michael Forwell[1] appeared on the horizon and started smuggling larger and larger multi-ton loads from Thailand. It soon became a general free-for-all and there just wasn't enough high-quality marijuana to go around, so the quality declined, as the demand for larger loads increased.

The growers quickly realized they could sell larger loads without nearly as much work on their part. Even for many of these large loads, they could sell it loose at virtually the same price as they were currently getting and not waste the time and manpower (or rather woman-and-child-power) putting the marijuana on sticks, which was probably the most unique feature of Thai weed itself. Since there was only a finite amount of the highest potency flower tops produced by each marijuana plant, the rest of the plant had to be sold as well. Since there was a larger quantity of this lower-quality part of the plant, it could be sold in larger amounts to the greedy 'johnny-come-lately' new arrivals into the Thai smuggling scene who, operating through Thai middlemen, didn't care or couldn't get top quality. They only relied on the name 'Thai weed' and literally ruined the mystique, uniqueness and high price it had formerly commanded. This disillusioned the U.S. market and once-satisfied and content customers now routinely bad-mouthed and virtually boycotted shipments of Thai weed and refused to continue to pay premium prices for everyday-quality weed, even though it was falsely billed as top-quality.

'You can fool some of the people some of the time, but not all of the people all of the time.' The market was wising up.

The Coronado Company had done two smuggles with Stan and Abdul, one in 1978 and another in '79, both in the four-ton range, but the quality seemed to get worse and worse with each successive load. It had been difficult for anyone in The Company to sell these low quality loads, and the only price they could get was never above $500 per pound. It was a far cry from the $1,650 they got from the sale of the 1977 *Pai Nui* load they got from us.

Late in the Summer of 1979, Bob Lahodny, Eddie Otero, and Lou Villar had a meeting at Bob's million dollar Montecito estate to explore the possibilities of acquiring better quality merchandise. They decided they'd attempt to lure Pat out of retirement by enticing him to return to Thailand with a proposition for a ten-ton load which would entail an extremely unusual offloading procedure.

---

1 Referenced Books, Item 2, Page 532.

Section 6

Back To Work (1979–1980)

Chapter 28

The Coronado Company[1][2][3]

Fall 1979
Woodside, California

Pat received a phone call late in the afternoon at his home in the fashionable Peninsula suburb of Woodside Hills. He was out in the greenhouse manicuring his prize roses when he heard the phone ringing. He rushed inside to catch it on the fourth ring. He was dripping with sweat and out of breath, as the ambient temperature was well into the 90s. The Bay Area was experiencing an unusual fall heat wave.

"Hurro."

"Hey Pat, this is your old friend 'Lights' down in Santa Barbara. How ya doin', buddy? Haven't seen you in a blue moon."

"What goin' on wit you guys? How you been?"

"Listen Pat, the reason I'm calling you is, I'd like to invite you and Rick down here for a little powwow. I've got a proposal for you and before you say a word, just come here and listen to what I've got to say. I can send for you and have a plane pick you up at Butler Aviation at San Francisco Airport in, say, the next couple of days."

"Lights, you know how I feel about working again. You might as well save your money and your breath. I don't think I'll be interested," answered Pat, his brow beginning to furrow.

"Please Pat. I don't want to discuss anything now on the phone and I'm just asking you to listen to what I have to say. It won't cost you guys a penny and you can walk away from here and we'll still be friends. Why don't you ask Rick, if the two of you would just agree to meet me and hear me out?"

"OK Lights… but don't count your chickens."

Pat called me to come up to his house and later the two of us met and decided to

---

1 Referenced Books, Item 16, Page 532.
2 Referenced Magazine Articles, Item 4, Page 533.
3 Referenced Television & Movies, Item 7, Page 533.

go to Santa Barbara to at least hear what Bob Lahodny aka 'Lights' had to say. It was decided that we would fly to Santa Barbara the following Thursday at noon.

* * *

The pilot was waiting for us in the airport lounge at Butler. It was exactly noon, as scheduled.

"I'm Skip and I'm taking you to Santa Barbara. Follow me, gentlemen," said the pilot as he put down his cup of coffee and led Pat and me out of the building. To our surprise, waiting for us was a shiny new Lear Jet 24 parked in the guest parking spot on the edge of the tarmac.

"Buckle up, gentlemen. We're about to take off. Flying time to Santa Barbara will be about an hour, give or take. Relax and enjoy the flight. There's some snacks and drinks in the cabinet."

The Lear taxied and took off like a rocket out of SFO, climbing steeply to a cruising altitude of 30,000 feet.

"This is impressive," I said. "They must have something awfully important to discuss to give us this treatment."

"I tell you what, Rick. I'm not impressed. I know they want us to go back to work and I don't want to. I told everybody, I close the book. I finished and not work again. I have enough money. I don't want risk and I don't want headache."

I decided not to push it with Pat, but just enjoy the flight and see what Bob had to say. It was a beautiful sunny day and as we cruised over California at 30,000 feet, languishing in the Lear's plush leather seats, we were also occasionally snorting lines of coke I had brought along in a one hundred dollar bill specially folded into a small envelope-like bindle.

We arrived at the private section of Santa Barbara Airport where we were met at the foot of the stairs by Bob Lahodny and his partner Ed Otero. Having not seen each other in two years, we were greeted by the two with hugs and warm handshakes. Bob was dressed in his Hollywood casual outfit consisting of tan slacks, woven slip-on leather shoes with no socks and a colorful Hawaiian shirt open to the third button. He sported a large Thai gold chain around his neck, a yellow gold Rolex President watch on his wrist and topped it off with his usual Ray-Ban sunglasses. With his good looks, chestnut wavy hair and broad movie-star-like smile, it looked as if he just stepped off the set of *Hawaii 5-0*. Eddie, on the other hand, appeared rather disheveled as a typical California surf bum. He had on baggy cargo shorts, a tattered old Hawaiian shirt and well worn shower thongs. Both had golden suntans which obviously came from long days spent on the Southern California beaches surfing or, as we found out later, playing polo with the scions of the richest of the rich, in Montecito's famed polo grounds.

Bob's jet black Mercedes Benz 450 SEL sedan awaited just off the tarmac, about twenty feet from where the Lear parked outside the private terminal. We got into the Benz and departed the airport, whereupon Bob immediately produced a large joint of Thai weed, lit it and passed it around. Within minutes the car was engulfed in a cloud of the pungent smoke. He cracked the sunroof which let the smoke out and generally cleared the air.

"We'll be at the hacienda in a few minutes," said Bob. "I have something to show you which I think you'll find pretty interesting."

We headed just south of Santa Barbara to the posh enclave of Montecito. Weaving up through the eucalyptus covered canyons, we came to a large wrought iron gate at the end of a cul-de-sac. With a touch of an automatic gate opener, Bob opened the gate from the remote access control panel inside of the Benz. The majestic gates swung open and Bob negotiated the quarter mile curved driveway lined with palm trees. The driveway ended in a circular courtyard at the front of a large white hacienda style mansion, complete with curved archways, huge entry columns of marble and a red tile roof. The home was open and airy with Saltillo tile floors in warm earth tone colors everywhere. The rooms and hallways were littered with large Persian and old American Indian carpets as area rugs. On the walls were a gallery collection of framed Tibetan Thangkas. The villa oozed of money and here 'Lights' was king. He had several Mexican housekeepers and groundskeepers. In back was a large swimming pool and adjacent tennis court with lights for playing at night. Bob led us off to the south wing of the house, where we entered a large paneled conference room with a huge walnut conference table in the center.

"Rick and Pat, I'd like to introduce you to Stan Yamamoto and our old partner Richard Sheldon," gestured Bob. Both men stood and shook hands with us. Stan, of Japanese descent, had a warm smile and a casual, friendly demeanor. It seemed like we 'clicked' immediately. Richard was tall and slim with a pencil thin mustache, thinning curly sandy colored hair and tortoise shell glasses. In reality Richard Sheldon was actually an alias for Lou Villar, but since neither Pat nor I had ever met him and never knew his name, we never knew the difference and simply took him at face value. We would find out much later just who Richard Sheldon really was, but by then it would all be academic.

All six of us were seated at the table and two large pitchers of ice tea were brought in by one of the servants, who delivered them on a silver platter with a round of glasses and placed one by each of us. The weather was hot and balmy, but a slight westerly ocean breeze took the otherwise steamy edge off the room.

Bob started with his proposal. "Pat, I know you have been retired and have said you weren't interested in ever going back to work. Rick, I assume you and Pat are in agreement. Correct?"

"I think you could safely say that," I answered.

"Pat?" queried Bob.

"Yes, I already told you on the phone that was my position. Nothing's changed."

Bob continued as if well rehearsed, "Gentlemen, I respect that, but I would like to tell you what we have been doing for the past two years and at least get your opinion on what to do. Stan here, along with his partner Abdul, has been scoring loads for us for the past two years. We've had no trouble getting the amounts we wanted. We've done two, four and five ton loads. The problem is the quality. Ever since we worked with you, we haven't been able to get the quality which makes this trip worth doing. You guys really spoiled us. But, since then… hell, we were getting better stuff out of Mexico."

"Well, like I said before…" said Pat.

"Please Pat, let me finish. I already know what you're going to say." Pat was silent. Bob continued. "We are going to do another trip this year and we've revolutionized or really streamlined every aspect of it and we'd like to run it by you guys and see if there's any interest. So before you say anything, let me tell you what this is all about."

"Show them the pictures," said Eddie.

Richard Sheldon reached into his leather briefcase and pulled out an envelope which contained several 8 x 10 photographs. Now it was Richard's turn. "This first shot is of the boat we just bought. It's a 175-foot oil rig supply boat. She'll do 15 knots all day and has a range of at least 10,000 miles or more. We figure she can carry a load of probably 15 to 20 tons of weed without any problem. We also figured, with a load of ten tons, it could almost all be concealed."

Richard proffered the second and third pictures from the large envelope which even added more intrigue. They were of two giant military Chinook helicopters flying low over the water. One was almost touching the water itself. "This is how we intend to offload," Richard continued. "We have contracted with two reserve Washington State National Guard helicopter pilots and their crews. We are going to upload the weed with the Chinooks. They will rendezvous with our ship about three to ten miles off-shore somewhere off the coast of Washington and lift the load off of the deck of the ship in specially constructed steel nets, and deliver it several miles onshore in a heavily forested area, the drop zone, where our semi truck will be waiting. We've calculated the entire load can be unloaded and on the road in under an hour in a paramilitary-style operation. We have purchased a load of cedar roofing shingles to be used as a prop to cover the load once we have loaded it into the semi. The highly aromatic cedar shingles will mask any marijuana smell in case we have to open the truck at any weigh station along the route. We've driven the route several times from Washington to California and have never been asked to open the truck, but just in case… we've actually been practicing making dry runs with the helicopters and our best time is 47 minutes for the entire unloading operation. Each helicopter can carry about three, three and a half tons per load."

The last 8 x 10 picture was of a large ranch and barn somewhere in what appeared to be foothill country. "This is our ranch in Central California around Bakersfield, where we will bring the load by semi tractor/trailer after we have unloaded and driven it down from the Northwest. The farm is completely safe, remote, and out of the way. Stan has been hanging out there and can attest to it." Stan silently nodded as Richard continued. "This is where we will bring the load in a semi and divide it up. We have several large electronic scales, so the weighing and dividing of the load will be easy, fast and very accurate. Naturally we will have lookouts posted at strategic points in the area to monitor any unauthorized activity. You know, we always do that. It will be com-pletely cool for you to take your share out in pickup trucks."

At this point, Eddie, with a cigar in hand, chimed in. "One more thing we have is state-of-the-art communication during every phase of the operation. One of our most trusted lieutenants is stationed at a specially designated listening post out in the high California desert near Borrego Springs with the most sophisticated HAM radio equipment available on the market today. He has rigged a huge antenna nearly fifty feet tall, and he is a completely licensed radio operator and can communicate anywhere in the world. This guy has all the top secret military codes, he can even listen to NASA when they communicate with the astronauts in space. We will maintain constant communication with the ship at sea every day at specific times. And we've developed a unique code so we can speak with confidence, not giving away our position, if we are being monitored. Once the load is on the ground and in the semi, we have lead and follow vehicles which are radio equipped to communicate with the semi, should any problems occur on the road."

Like a wrestling tag-team, Bob took over at this point. "We've got this whole thing completely wired, except for the quality of the weed. If you guys score the load and get the quality you are famous for and if we split it with you 60/40 as before; according to my calculations at $1,600 per pound, your share would amount to about 14 or 15 million dollars. Of course you would pay for your share of the score and we would pay for ours, but I figure that after expenses and investor payoffs and whatever, you should be able to net at least 10 to 12 million off of this load."

"Do you guys think you might have any interest in this plan?" Richard added, with a sort of sheepish grin on his face.

Eddie cut in, "I don't think it's fair to put them on the spot like that, Richard. Maybe you guys need some time to think it over. What do you say, Rick, Pat?"

"Well," I said trying to conceal my excitement and trying to act very cool, "Do you mind if Pat and I take a walk around and talk this over for awhile?"

"Not at all," answered Bob. "Why don't you go out by the pool or walk on the grounds if you want. We're in no hurry. Maybe you need to think it over and get back to us later. Whatever you want."

Pat and I got up from the large conference table and left the room. We went for a walk on the spacious grounds which were landscaped and manicured to perfection.

"I don't know," I said first. "A load of this size could be a little out of our league. What, the largest we've ever done is two tons, and they want to do ten. Do you think we could even get ten tons of the good quality?"

"I think it's possible, but we'll have to find out," said Pat.

"Another thing which is bothering me," I continued. "This plan of theirs is so high tech, I wonder if it's totally under control. We've had so much success in the past and these trips have been low key, grassroots ventures. Now we're thinking of contracting with others who in turn are contracting with still others who we don't really know and who they don't really know. I think if the shit hits the fan there will be no loyalty. It will be everyone for himself. No real team spirit like we've pretty much had in the past."

"Rick, we need to go back to the Bay Area and think about this. There is no way we can answer this proposal right now. It will take some time and figuring just to see what actually has to be done. I am still not sure I even want to think about going back to work. I'm retired, for Christ sakes, and I like my life just fine. I've just met Rebecca and I don't know whether I want to subject her to all this stress. I really can't decide now."

"Let's tell them we need some time to think it over. OK, Pat?"

We continued walking through the gardens. The pink and purple bougainvilleas gently rustled in the afternoon breeze. We went back into the hacienda. The atmosphere was casual when Pat told Bob of our decision. We agreed to meet the following week and would give them our answer then. Bob asked Stan to give us a ride back to the airport where the Lear was waiting.

On the way back I asked Stan what he thought about the scheme and his answer sort of surprised me. "Well, Rick, if anyone can pull this thing off it's the Coronado Company. But there's so much equipment and so many people required for this scam. We've always kept things more simple, but these guys have always thought big. I don't know. What I do know is, Abdul and I haven't been able to get the quality merchandise you guys can get, so all this effort isn't really worth it, if the profit isn't there. Abdul doesn't have the right of refusal with the growers. He has to take what they give him. You guys are different. That's what 'Lights' said. You can get the quality because you set the standard and would accept nothing but the best. He also told me that you told the growers if they sent you anything but the top quality weed, you would throw it away and not pay them. If Abdul told them that, he wouldn't be able to do any business in Thailand. He simply doesn't have the relationship with the growers and the people like you do. You guys are a legend. I hope you decide to go back to work because my people would love to have that quality to smoke again, like before. I can turn multi-ton loads in a matter of hours if it's top quality. I can also turn low-grade loads fast, but the price has to be real cheap. But if the price is cheap for such low grade crap, it's really not worth going to all this effort because nobody makes enough money. You have to watch The Company real close too, Rick. They don't pay their people very well. They want to make it all themselves. It doesn't build loyalty. That's why I deal with them independently. I negotiate every deal with them. Well, you guys think about it. Here we are at your plane. You know, I arranged this whole thing with the Lear, too. These are my people and Skip is my pilot. I just let Bob and the boys use him so they could look good for you. Have a nice flight."

Stan dropped us off on the tarmac at the stairs of the Lear. Within minutes we were airborne and headed back to the Bay Area.

At 30,000 feet in the night we jetted back north up the California coast.

"Boy that was sure an interesting ride back to the airport, Pat. Sounds like Stan really doesn't trust these guys. I don't know; it was almost like a warning. Whaddya think?" I said gazing down at the lights of Monterey.

"Let's just sleep on it and work on it in the morning. Lot to think about," Pat replied.

Well, I continued to think about the whole situation for the remainder of the flight. One point Stan had made or let slip out was the name of their Thai contact, Lec. I remembered one of our original Thai crew from back in '74 and '75 was a character named Lec, who I later confirmed with Stan was indeed the same Lec as we had previously employed. He was part of the team our original Thai connection Suay had put together. He was about my height but had a slight build and was very thin, even rather bony. He was very light skinned and exuded a rather effeminate pulchritude about his nature. Most male Thais are usually masculine and macho and the others on the crew would constantly tease Lec and call him 'kathoey', the Thai word for effeminate gay male. Although friendly with me and the rest of the Thai crew, I always felt he was very nosy about the inner workings of our trip. He was hired as a driver and laborer and because of his nosiness I never trusted him and we let him go after our second *Nepenthe* trip. However, since he had driven loads to Pat's Chanthaburi ranch from Ban Ku Su Man, the village where the marijuana was grown, he was now emboldened with the location of our source and struck out on his own, as someone who could supply loads to other smugglers.

As it was, Lec made the connection with Abdul Blackie and became his main source after we had retired. The only problem was he didn't have the 'right of refusal' and had to take what was left over after the limited amount of top quality weed was already gone. Yes, he could get quantity but not the connoisseur quality which we, and our successors as we later found out, had demanded from the village. As the Coronado Company soon discovered the hard way, as Stan told us, this lower quality was only salable at a much lower price and thus made their continuation of the Thai trip barely a lackluster success, with profits less than one third of what they had originally realized working with us. Indeed, it seemed like Mexico was a better option unless they could somehow convince us to go back to work.

It had taken Pat and me a year and a half to cultivate and cement the relationship with the growers which obviously didn't extend to Lec, who was forced to take whatever 'garbage' was left over. Take it or leave it! They, along with other large-volume smugglers, took it in huge quantities hoping to make up for the diminished profits by dramatically increasing the quantity. To an extent, it worked, but eventually the 'smoking public' got wise to this folderol. It seemed like the once mythical 'Thai weed' would soon be relegated to the ash heap of history and pot lore.

During the next week Pat and I met daily, analyzing the proposal and trying to figure out what would be required to pull this trip off and whether we really wanted to do it. Slowly Pat's reluctance to go back to work began to fade as he considered the possibility of making such a great amount of money on just one trip.

From the beginning, meaning 'this new beginning', starting now and going forward, Pat made it clear, things would be different if we were to reconnoiter and do it again. Pat was now going to be solely in charge of the operation and there would be no equal split with Phil and me, as before. This trip would be his and he was only willing to split it two thirds for himself and one third to me. Phil would just be an investor and it would be solely my responsibility to handle distribution. Pat would handle everything in Thailand and my presence would not be required. Joe could be responsible for transportation of the money.

'Well', I thought, 'as much as I like being in Thailand, the reality is that it has to be getting crowded with smugglers', as I'd heard tell of other groups getting in the game. This was like a sports figure who retires at the peak of his career, then tries to make a comeback a few years later, but the game had significantly changed during his absence. Maybe being relegated to the back seat with Pat in control wouldn't be a bad place to be, since I wouldn't have to spend time away, wouldn't be taking nearly the risk and wouldn't have all of the responsibility heaped on my shoulders. Anyway, if things worked out as planned my share would be well into seven figures, which was fine with me. Let Pat have the lion's share.

We figured the upfront cost for Pat's part of this project would easily exceed a million dollars, so we agreed to solicit other investors so the investment burden would be shared and in case anything went wrong, one person wouldn't be ruined financially. Plus, other people in the business were always asking if there was any room to invest. I was happy to include Phil, JQ and one of his business partners at a three to one return on their investment. Along with what Pat and I would invest, I had no trouble raising the balance of what was needed.

One week later a meeting took place at Pat's Woodside home where we met with Bob and Lou Villar, a.k.a. Richard Sheldon. Pat told the leaders of the Coronado Company of his decision to participate in the plan to score ten tons of high quality Thai weed. He agreed to their proposed 60/40 split and would need their $600,000 in Thailand by the end of December. It was agreed and the wheels were set in motion.

Chapter 29

The Concorde

Late Fall 1979

Cindy and I had been planning a trip to Europe to move more money out of the U.S. and into the Swiss bank. This seemed like the perfect time for a quick trip, and what could make it quicker than to fly on the fastest commercial plane in the sky, the Concorde, the newly commissioned British/French supersonic commercial airliner. I had heard that aboard the Concorde, the customers were treated like royalty during the three hour flight from either New York to London or Washington to Paris, so Cindy and I decided to try the experience for ourselves.

We would fly first class to New York, transfer to the Concorde then go to London where we would transfer to a Swissair flight, again first class, and on to Geneva where we would make the deposit, stay for a few days, and finally return home first class via Swissair non-stop to San Francisco. This would be the first of many flights I would take on the supersonic transport which had been inaugurated into service two months prior.

I loved to indulge Cindy and myself on travel and despite the fact that tickets on the Concorde were 40% more expensive than regular first class fares, it was of little consequence to me, plus just the experience of supersonic travel far outweighed the cost.

I confirmed the reservations by phone then purchased tickets in person at the British Airways ticket office in downtown San Francisco with a cashier's check. The round trip fare for the two of us was about seventy-five hundred dollars. I simply considered this the cost of doing business as in fact we would be transporting a pile of money to Europe on this trip and I reasoned, it would be nice to indulge ourselves a little. I also knew the risk of transporting the money internationally would be minimal, as first-class passengers were usually whisked through European customs in a special line. I surmised correctly; customs for Concorde passengers would be almost non-existent.

For Cindy, who just four years previous had flown back to the United States from the Far East in only one section above steerage on both the Garuda then Korean Airlines flights from Bangkok to come and live with me, this was heaven. She was now fully entrenched in the jet-set high-life style and to her flying aboard the Concorde was simply a natural progression in her ascent from poverty to wealth. The two of us carried off the lifestyle flawlessly in first class without even a hint of nervousness one might expect when each was carrying six figures in cash secreted on our bodies and in our hand-carry luggage.

We deplaned in New York and exited to a special Concorde lounge to await preferred boarding. When time came we were ushered to a private section of Kennedy Airport where we boarded the sleek, needle nosed British Airways pride and joy. Upon boarding the Concorde, I was amazed at how small it was compared to the 747's I was used to flying. It was very narrow, but adorned with plush Corinthian leather seats two to an aisle. I also noticed the windows were very small, only about twelve by eighteen inches. Our seats were in a forward section just aft of the forward bulkhead. Directly in front of us high on the bulkhead was what appeared to be an LED screen about two feet square in size trimmed with a gold bezel. The stewardess told me this was a machmeter so the passengers could see how fast the Concorde was actually traveling.

Mach indicated the speed of sound or approximately 740 miles per hour. Cruising speed for the Concorde was mach 2 or nearly 1400 miles per hour. These speeds could only be attained by the Concorde over open ocean because of the sonic boom which would be created when breaking the sound barrier.

The taxi to takeoff was pretty normal, but as soon as flight was attained, the climb to altitude was incredibly steep. It felt like the plane was going nearly straight up. The angle of attack was probably between 60 and 75 degrees (90 degrees being straight up). Regular subsonic commercial aircraft ascent was at about 30 degrees to a cruising altitude of about 33,000 to 37,000 feet. The normal flight from New York to London took approximately eight hours. Three to five minutes after takeoff, the Concorde was out over open ocean cruising at nearly 70,000 feet above sea level and traveling at a speed of nearly 1400 miles per hour. In three hours we would land in London. Interestingly, going in the other direction, from London to New York, flying aboard the Concorde seems to defy the laws of time itself. Because of the five-hour time difference, going from east to west, the three hour Concorde flight would actually arrive in New York two hours before it took off from London.

As soon as the plane leveled off, complimentary Dom Perignon champagne was served in fine crystal champagne glasses with the Concorde British Airways logo etched in the glass. This was soon followed by several rounds of hors d'oeuvres consisting of Russian beluga caviar, Scottish smoked salmon and French pate fois gras. More Dom, then the main course of Australian lobster tails, beautifully adorned with glazed vegetables, more Dom and a specially prepared caramel custard for dessert. For those who didn't care for the lobster, Chateaubriand was offered as a substitute. The meal was followed with complimentary snifters of Remy Martin cognac or Courvoisier. The meal was superb and the service excellent, by far the finest I had ever experienced in flight.

After lunch, I asked the stewardess if I could take a tour of the cockpit. The beautiful British stewardess replied that she would check with the Captain to see if it would be OK. She returned momentarily and told me to follow her. She led me forward through a curtain into the cockpit. To me it appeared as though I'd stepped into a space capsule. The co-pilot gave me his seat at the right hand controls. I sat in the co-pilot seat for about five minutes and listened to the pilot explain how the controls worked then he gave me a tour of the instrument panel. I was amazed at the comfort of the plush leather pilot and co-pilot seats. The seats were so soft, I barely noticed the bulge in the small of my back from the money belt strapped around my waist containing $50,000 in crisp new hundred dollar bills.

I returned to my seat, where Cindy was finishing her second snifter of brandy. The machmeter, up on the bulkhead directly in front of us illuminated in blue LED lights, showed we were traveling at twice the speed of sound or mach 2. As I pressed my nose to the undersized window, I noticed the sky was much darker than usual and the Earth below seemed much smaller. The horizon in the distance was characterized with a noticeable view of the curvature of the Earth. From this altitude it was easy to confirm that the world was not flat!.

In under three hours I saw land in the distance and then felt the sensation of the aircraft slowing down as we approached. The machmeter soon indicated slowing to a speed just under mach 1, and as the plane began to descend I saw in the distance the city of London. The sleek aircraft then made a sweeping turn as London's Heathrow Airport came into view.

We were soon on the ground and deplaned. Again we were escorted into a special Concorde lounge where we awaited transfer to our Swissair flight. The hour-long Swissair flight in the first class section was wonderful, although a far cry from the royal treatment we had just received on our transatlantic supersonic flight. We landed in Geneva and were waved through Swiss customs without incident using the green 'Nothing to Declare' lane. Cindy and I took a taxi directly to the Richmond Hotel, dropped our bags and walked across the bridge at the mouth of Lake Geneva directly to the bank where we changed the U.S. currency into gold South African Krugerrands. We then took the gold downstairs to the safe deposit box storage area and retrieved our safe deposit key from the guard, who accompanied us to the box. We took the box to a private room, closed the door and added the new load of gold coins to our already burgeoning stash.

With all of the gold and assorted paper currency stored neatly and safely in the safe deposit box, I was suddenly aware of the sheer weight of the box. One box would never be sufficient. The weight alone was well over one hundred pounds. I left Cindy and went to get the guard to get another box so I could split the load between the two. Each box weighed between 70 and 75 pounds. I wanted it to appear, for the guard's sake, the boxes merely contained papers for safe keeping and were not laden with so much weight. I struggled with the first one and placed it into its slot at chest level. The second box was at just above head height and I had to hoist it up and into its slot. I felt my back strain, but was able to get it securely into its place. We returned to the hotel and I soaked in a tub of hot water for the better part of an hour to try to relax my strained back. We stayed in Europe for a few days, but I was uncomfortable and had to take painkillers to ease the pain from the injury I had suffered from putting the gold into my safe deposit boxes. It actually took a couple of weeks and three trips to the chiropractor to get back to normal.

The flight home aboard Swissair's non-stop flight from Geneva to San Francisco took about twelve hours most of which I slept behind several Seconal capsules, taken strictly for medicinal purposes, to be able to travel with such back pain. Two weeks later, with my back pain relieved, I was ready to start putting together the upcoming smuggling venture with Pat.

Being introduced to the opulence and flamboyant lifestyle of the Coronado boys and specifically the flashiness of Bob Lahodny made Pat and me realize how naive and uneducated we'd been regarding the hiding of the vast amounts of cash money we'd accumulated in the past few years. Bob had suggested that we consider buying investment grade diamonds as a way to accomplish this. As a matter of fact he told Pat that he had a contact who sold these diamonds and would be happy to introduce us if we were interested. I was a little reluctant, but Pat was definitely interested and asked if a meeting could be arranged.

Since transporting the sum of money required to make such a purchase would be risky using commercial transportation, Bob arranged for the Lear to pick up Pat and take him to Santa Barbara for the transaction. Pat invited me along for the ride.

The Lear picked us up at the San Carlos private airport and delivered us to Santa Barbara where we were met by Bob who again took us to his Montecito villa. There we met his diamond connection, a tall balding gentleman dressed in a dark business suit by the name of Brad Ferrar. Pat had brought along a million dollars in neatly stacked hundred dollar bundles in a black tennis equipment athletic bag with the name HEAD emblazoned on the outside in bright yellow letters.

At the same conference table that we had sat around a couple of months earlier discussing the upcoming load, Brad proffered a cache of sparkling diamonds ranging from .5 carats to over 2 carats of VS1 to VVS1 high quality stones. Each stone was individually wrapped in a small paper bindle ranging in value from around $15,000 to $50,000 each. Both Brad and Bob assured Pat that these stones were of the highest quality and were acquired from Brad's connection directly from De Beers, the world's premier diamond source. Each stone had a detailed certificate of authenticity from De Beers and Brad assured us that he was selling them to Pat at a wholesale price which amounted to about 50% of what they would go for retail. In all Pat bought nearly everything Brad had to offer which amounted to thirty of the most beautiful stones I'd ever seen. He gave Brad the tennis bag in exchange for a black alligator skin covered box that contained the diamonds. He also gave Pat an envelope of De Beers certificates identifying each stone in precise detail. Pat cradled the box like he was holding a newborn baby. Brad assured him of the highest confidentiality regarding the transaction, confiding in Pat words to the effect, "You don't have to worry about a thing. This transaction is totally confidential and off the books. I've done this plenty of times for your friends here. Your secret is safe with me." And of course Bob vouched for Brad completely.

As we flew back to the Bay Area, Pat beamed with pride over his new acquisition.

Little did any of us know that Brad's reassuring words would one day come back to bite both Pat and our Coronado Company 'friends' in all of their collective asses.

Chapter 30

"It's My Trip"

Pat had made it clear to me that if he was to return to Thailand to reorganize the Thai smuggling trip, he was in charge. He told me my responsibility would be to act as support to him by making sure the money was in Thailand when it was supposed to be, making sure he had enough poly-mylar bags, sealing machines and machine parts to operate the assembly line and finally to sell our share of the load. Pat said it would not be necessary for me to be in Thailand. As a matter of fact, Pat told me, he specifically did not want me there.

Over coffee one morning, Pat said, under no uncertain circumstances, "It's my trip. I handle everything in Thailand. You not needed over there and Phil not needed at all."

Although I loved it in Thailand and relished the action of actually scoring the weed and being on that end of it, it was not to be. After all, I was the one who actually set the quality bar high and since we hadn't been there for the past two years, I wanted to make sure we could still get the same quality as before. I couldn't impress that fact on Pat enough, but finally I acquiesced to his wishes. He assured me over and over that quality would be his main focus and that he would do his part to maintain that standard and I didn't have to 'ride herd' on him. 'Well', I thought, 'if he can keep up those standards, the trip would be worth enough to me without the added risk and exposure.'

I also noticed a significant change in Pat's nature. He was not very much fun to be around anymore. His 'happy-go-lucky' spirit was gone. Before, having traveled the world with him, Pat had been one of the most fun people to be around, always very animated and joking. But now he was always sullen and serious. He carried a big chip on his shoulder about Ciro and could never get it out of his craw. He blamed Phil and me for the significant loss of his share of Ciro's load. He said it was our responsibility to make sure he would get paid the negotiated fee. He had even suggested we compensate him for the loss. However, Phil assured him, in no uncertain terms, we were all in this together and any loss would be shared equally.

One afternoon at my house, a rather agitated Phil told Pat, point blank: "There's no way in hell Rick and I will make up for the difference to you for the money Ciro didn't pay us."

In a warped sense of reality, I could kind of see where Pat was coming from. But, on the other hand, I had to remind Pat, I sided with Phil. I reminded him the decision to work with Ciro again was based on a vote and I was the only one of the three of us who voted against it, so in fairness, I should be the only one who could legitimately make such an argument, being against it from the get-go. As a matter of fact the split on the loss should have been commensurate with the anticipated split on the gain, with Pat absorbing the lion's share as he had demanded on the contract loads. However, I saw no point in pressing it and going down that road as, in reality, it was a waste of time and would only further serve to 'throw gasoline on the fire' and antagonize an already irritated Pat on the subject. Anyway, Ciro, being who he was, would never repay us per our agreement for, in his words, 'stealing Pat'.

Additionally and consistent with his character, as I would later find out, when the tables were turned, Ciro would never reimburse us for continuing to work with the Thai team we'd set up plus using our equipment, methods and our team members we had worked so hard to put in place. With him, it was always a one-way street… his way!

Also, I was never 100% clear in my mind of the possibility that Phil might have negotiated a side deal with Ciro to 'let him back into the fold' and, if true, this subterfuge with his old longtime childhood friend did not include Pat or me. At any rate, Pat never forgot the conversation and quickly ruled Phil out of any future involvement.

It almost seemed to me that as my punishment for the Ciro affair, Pat would only give me a rather minor role in *His* new trip with the Coronado Company.

* * *

In the late fall of 1979, Pat left to return to Thailand for the first time in more than two years. Of significant importance, and unbeknownst to me, was the fact that Pat had not paid Charlie and the rest of the Thai crew their bonus money for their work from the previous trips. I knew he'd not gone back to Thailand, but was unaware, in not doing so, he had forsaken his responsibility of the promise he'd made to Charlie two years previous. Although he kept their three quarters of a million dollars in bonus money in safe keeping, buried in the foundation of his new Woodside Hills home, and knew he'd return 'someday' to pay them, it turned out he had just got caught up in the American lifestyle and felt they could wait. In fact, he had rudely and irresponsibly not even made contact with them and left them wondering and angry if, indeed, they'd been hoodwinked and ripped off.

Pat had been busy in the past couple of years building two homes for speculation in the Palo Alto area and never had the time to return to Thailand to take care of his obligation.

Aside from his new home in the swank Woodside Hills, Pat was courting a new lady friend named Rebecca Cromwell. Becky was from nearby San Mateo. She had a college education and was working as the manager of an organic farm in the coastal town of Half Moon Bay. She was introduced to Pat by the foreman of one of his construction projects. Becky was sweet and comely, but not strikingly beautiful like Wendy or Melinda. At five-foot-five with a nice figure and long brown hair, Becky had a good sense of humor and a light carefree attitude. Pat was extremely proud to finally have a girlfriend. With his friends Phil and me and to a lesser extent Willie, all seemingly happily married, Pat felt left out not having a lady in his life. Rebecca filled the missing space in Pat's life and she was becoming very attached to him.

Although Becky was not Pat's first Caucasian girlfriend, she definitely had possibilities for their future together. Ten years previously Pat had arranged a marriage of convenience with a former high school girlfriend named Constance Beldon.

Connie and Pat had been close in high school and when Pat graduated, his American visa extension would be over and he would not be allowed to remain legally in the United States. Connie agreed to a marriage of convenience with Pat so he could legally stay in the States, if he would support her with a monthly stipend. Pat agreed. Since it only amounted to a few hundred a month, Pat was only too happy to pay her so he could stay in the U.S., as the legally married spouse of an American citizen. They were friends and would always remain so, plus the relationship was casual and not a hassle to Pat. Connie was a hippie and only too happy to get the few hundred a month from Pat, plus he would always give her marijuana or LSD whenever she wanted it.

Now, Pat was finally in love and very busy with his life and this added to his reluctance to return to his homeland, even to pay off Charlie. In Pat's mind, Charlie had plenty of money and could just wait 'til Pat got there, whenever that was and whenever the spirit moved him. Pat also sported a new chocolate brown turbocharged 911 Porsche Carrera that he was extremely proud of. He loved the car, almost more than Rebecca. He was always taking pictures of it or having me take pictures of him driving it around and in those pictures he always had a cocky, holier-than-thou smirk on his face. This newly displayed arrogant attitude would soon come back to haunt him and 'bite him in the ass' in a big way.

Pat and Joe transported the money over to Thailand so, first of all, Pat could pay Charlie and the Thai team from their previous year's work, and secondly to have enough to get started on the new project.

On the outside Charlie was very happy to see Pat and even more happy to finally get paid for the work he had done two years ago. On the inside, however, he loathed and hated Pat for not showing up with the money for two years and for not at least having had the courtesy to communicate his intentions, basically leaving him in the lurch and in limbo and letting his anger fester like an open wound.

Charlie also despised Pat's attitude. In Charlie's eyes, Pat had become the 'ugly American'. He would place himself on a pedestal when around other Thais. There was a great deal of animosity and jealousy because Pat seemed to have everything and flaunted it in front of Charlie and the other members of the Thai team. He would show them pictures of his home complete with gardens and swimming pool, of his new shining Porsche sports car and his 'farang' (Caucasian) girlfriend.

Now, finally, after all this time, here was Pat with all of his 'things' and all of his money and his arrogant attitude, looking down his nose at his Thai compatriots and

suggesting to them that they again work together on this huge ten-ton load and everything would be fine. Right!

Meanwhile, I began to solicit funds from other people as investors. I offered a three
or four to one return on investment and had no trouble acquiring the funds from
Willie, Phil, Joe, JQ and two other investors who were also in the marijuana business.
Pat and I each put up equal amounts of the lion's share and it was not long before I had
raised what would be needed for our share of the venture. The money was to be used
for not only our share of the load itself, but for support equipment and any payoffs necessary to accomplish the scoring, packaging, storing and loading of the ten-ton load of
Thai sticks.

Additionally, the Coronado Company was collecting and transporting their agreed-
upon six hundred thousand dollars. Stan Yamamoto was in charge of the transportation
of the money overseas. Unlike us, Stan transported funds through banking channels.
He had a banker in Hawaii who would transfer funds to a Hong Kong bank then to
a Thai bank. It was all done under the guise of a legitimate jewelry and gem business.

On the other hand, Joe and I transported money the old fashioned way, on our
bodies, secreted in money belts, in our boots and in our business-like leather briefcases.

On one such trip we decided to leave from San Francisco and travel to Thailand
laden with money, then continue around the world, instead of returning back the way
we'd come, as was usually the case. Our four-day journey took us from San Francisco
to Hong Kong then on to Bangkok. From there we went to Bombay, Athens, Geneva,
and London where we had a whirlwind taxi tour of the city then direct on to Seattle.
Upon our arrival in Seattle, I guess somehow we had been followed on our journey and
monitored by U.S. customs, because I didn't even make it out of the jetway before being
surrounded by four armed Customs agents. They ushered me directly into the back
room for a thorough search and interrogation. I only had a carry-on bag and took a
rather indignant stance in response to their questioning. Of course they found nothing
and twenty minutes later let me go to catch my connecting flight back to SF. I could
only imagine my travels had caught the attention of Customs as a result of my Chicago
bust several years previous. I guess the tail from that incident follows you until death!

Also unbeknownst to Pat or me, Charlie had not been sitting idle during our two-
year hiatus, but had been continuing to work in the marijuana business. His main customer was none other than Ciro Mancuso who had gone back to Thailand following
the *Drifter* debacle and found Charlie in Pattaya and re-organized the Thai trip on his
own.

Charlie was now only partially in charge and had taken on a new partner who was
more business-like and level-headed than himself. Recognizing his own foibles as a
playboy, race car driver and hot-headed marijuana trader who had trouble keeping
the other members of the Thai crew in line and not fighting amongst themselves,
Charlie had let a new figure emerge as co-leader of the Thai organization. Soonthorn
Kraithamjitkul, nicknamed 'Thai', was a smooth talking, very good looking, classy
former car dealer who was respected by all of the Thai team including Charlie and
'Papa'.

During the Viet Nam War, 'Thai' had many U.S. military friends stationed in Thailand who he would do favors for, such as get them 'mia Thai', the Thai expression for a Thai wife. He also could get guns, helicopters or any other military equipment. His connections ran deep into the Thai government, all the way up to the prime minister. 'Thai' had connections in both the Thai government and the Thai military and he was just the asset the trip needed. It was clear to Ciro that the Thai trip could not continue to grow if it continued to operate totally in a clandestine, grassroots manner. Sooner or later too many people would find out and it would get busted, just like what had happened to him in Mexico. 'Thai' was the perfect liaison between the marijuana smuggling trip and the military/government complex, fully entrenched and now running Thailand.

At first Charlie seemed eager to work with Pat, but after consultation with 'Thai' and the other members of the Thai crew, it became clear that the main problem was Pat himself. Pat tried to assume control of the Thais, but with 'Thai' at the helm this was not possible, plus there was too much resentment from Pat's failure to pay the Thais in a timely manner. 'Thai' told Pat that he would not work with him and, if he wanted to work and score this load, he would have to re-organize with someone else or pay twice the going price for the load. Pat blew up and told the Thais he didn't need them and he really didn't want to do the trip anyway. He just couldn't understand their attitude, but at the time, he didn't realize the fact that they had been working successfully for the past two years and didn't need him either.

* * *

In early January of 1980 Pat called me at four in the morning at my Menlo Park home to tell me that the trip was off. He was closing the book and coming home. He said he was unable to perform his function and would not be able to get the merchandise as he had contracted with the Coronado Company.

Meanwhile, I had gotten my end of the trip together and all of the necessary equipment was now in Thailand as well was all of the money, as planned. Over a million and a half dollars had been transported to Thailand both by human ferry and through normal banking channels.

In the wee hours of the morning phone call, Pat flatly told me that if there was any chance to salvage the trip, I had better get over to Thailand at once. He said, in no uncertain terms, that if I was not over there by mid-January, he would leave and he didn't care what happened.

"If you're not here in ten days… Fuck it all," were his parting words as he slammed the phone down in my ear. All that I was left with was the static of the now disconnected overseas call.

Chapter 31

Taking The Reins

My mind raced as I began to consider the ramifications of the four-in-the-morning phone call from Pat. I was now wide awake and telling Cindy what had happened. Cindy reached to the nightstand and first blew her nose and tossed the used tissue into the wastebasket on the floor next to her side of the bed. The basket was almost half full of used Kleenex. She immediately opened the drawer of the nightstand and removed a mirror she had carefully placed there before and brought it on the bed. It had a large pile of white powder on it and a glistening gold razor blade and a neatly rolled up $100 bill rolling around at the edge of the mirror.

"Please Rick, be still. I don't want to wake the gang," Cindy said nodding at Papi who was peacefully sleeping on his back stretched out on the bed between the two of us and 'Mr. T', who was curled over one of Papi's front paws, now awake and gently purring at the activity on the bed.

Cindy carefully separated the pile of cocaine on the mirror with the razor blade and created six perfect lines measuring five inches long by a quarter inch wide and a quarter inch high. She placed the wide end of the $100 bill in her crusted left nasal passage and carefully inhaled. Half of the first line disappeared from the mirror. The same procedure was repeated in the right nostril. She then handed the mirror to me and I did the same.

"So, what's going on?" asked Cindy, who was now wide awake and alert as the coke hit the mark.

"Well, that was Pat. Guess he's all freaked out over in Thailand. Seems like he's having trouble scoring the load. Things aren't the same over there anymore."

"Doesn't surprise me one bit," replied Cindy taking the mirror and having another sniff. "You know, he's really changed lately. The way he treats you is terrible. And you let him get away with it. He's turned into an arrogant asshole, kind of like your old buddy Ciro. He's always on his high horse, making demands and you just jump to his tune like some marionette on a string."

"Hold on a minute, honey. This is the last time we're going to do this. We'll probably make a small fortune and then we should be set for life. We won't have to take shit from anybody. Not that we do now. This is his trip and up to this point it has been pretty easy. We really don't have the risk we had before, because we now have the money to do this trip right. We don't have to be around the load or the money, like the old days."

"Well, get to the point, Rick. So what's his problem now. I mean he's calling you at this ungodly hour. Tell me what's going on… No, first let me guess. The Thais probably hate his guts. He probably treats them like shit, the way he treats everyone else, and they're telling him 'Fuck you.' I can just see it now. He probably wants you to drop everything, jump to his 'beck and call' and come over there and fix everything. You're just too nice, Rick. You let that fucker just push you around. When he says jump, you say 'how high'. Am I right or what?"

"Well, once again Cindy, you hit the nail on the head. He wants me to get my butt over there immediately or else he's leaving, come what may. That asshole will just leave the trip high and dry. Seems like he just doesn't give a shit about all the people who've invested in this venture. He just wants to close the book and come home to Rebecca. That's what this is all about. A few years ago he would have stuck it out and made it work. All of his big talk about how this was *His* trip and how he didn't need anybody else was just a bunch of bullshit. Now I have to get into the middle of it. I'll tell you one thing. When I go over there, the first thing I'm going to do is renegotiate our deal. I'll be damned if I am going to lift a finger over there without a major increase in my percentage of the load. He can't just drop the ball on me without considering that first."

"Well, I hope you do. You better not get wishy-washy on that issue. If you have to leave me here to hold down the fort, while you chase your ass all over the world, you had better be awfully nice to me when this is over. A new 450 SL might make me feel better about it," Cindy purred as she nuzzled close to me. "You know what we haven't done in a while?" she said huskily as she returned the mirror to the nightstand.

"It's kind of crowded up here. Go on Papi. Take a hike. We've got business to attend to," I said.

The huge golden retriever slowly got up and lumbered off of the bed, turning to the two of us with a look of disgust. 'Mr. T' repositioned himself to the corner of the bed and quickly fell back asleep. Nothing bothered him and he was oblivious to the activity taking place next to him. Papi's puppy, Bubba, could be heard howling outside the bedroom window.

* * *

The one thing I still had to accomplish before leaving for Thailand was to secure a safe stash house and find somebody responsible to guard the load as the housesitter. Willie was the natural choice, since this had been his forte in the past, but he was working in The City at his family's mercantile store. Joe, my second choice, was just too busy to house sit and plus he was the type who always had to be in motion. A job of simply housesitting for Joe just wasn't in the cards either. Not wanting to go outside of my inner circle, I had to find somebody who I knew very well and who could be trusted and responsible, plus it had to be someone who really didn't have anything else going on. The only name I could come up with who fit the bill was an old friend of mine who I had grown up with, Carl J. Peakman, known in his high school days as CJ. However, along the way he had picked up another nickname, the result of the large quantities of drugs he consumed by the shovelful and with an occasional freak-out: he became known as Shoveler Freakman. The name stuck. Although I hadn't seen him in a couple of years, I remembered he had once remarked that if I ever needed anybody to do anything, please give him a call.

I had actually followed Shov from high school to the University of Colorado, where we had once been roommates. He had been a year ahead of me and, like me, was rather short and very outgoing. He was known as a ladies' man and was very popular, but after an old high school football injury he became addicted to painkillers. This transitioned to cocaine and finally heroin. He had always been keenly interested in my smuggling operation and had tried a hand in it himself.

After college he found a position in the Peace Corps and wound up being sent to Thailand to teach English. On one of his trips back home he brought back a large stat-uette of a hollowed out wooden fish which was packed solidly with what he thought was pure heroin. It turned out that his connection had burned him and put baking soda inside of the statuette. Having a diplomatic passport issued to him by the Foreign Service made his passage through U.S. customs merely a formality. However, after his failure at this bungled smuggling attempt, his nerves were shot and he never tried it again. The fiasco did, however go down in local smuggling lore as 'The Maltese Flounder', reminiscent of the old Humphrey Bogart movie, *The Maltese Falcon*.[1] It was an inside joke which Shoveler laughed at on the outside but never found very funny himself.

As I pondered memories of Shoveler Freakman, he seemed to emerge as the per-fect candidate to watch over the load, plus he was always fiercely loyal to me. Shov had always wanted more than anything to be part of my successful smuggling opera-tion. So I gave him the opportunity and called him. He agreed to meet me at a local San Francisco coffeehouse. Shoveler jumped at the idea and was excited to finally be included in the operation; he said he could commence immediately to find a place suit-able to my needs. I gave him the criteria to begin his search for a secure stash house. The place had to be in a location of easy access with some seclusion and privacy, two or three car garage accessible day or night without suspicion and in a nice neighborhood, etc. Shov preferred the coast and said he would start his search in the Half Moon Bay area. I guaranteed him fifty grand for his services and gave him a couple of thousand to begin the search and for a deposit, if he found anything suitable.

It seemed like I had found the right man for the job. The one thing I was unaware of at the time was just how advanced Shoveler's drug habit had become.

---

1 Referenced Television & Movies, Item 16, Page 533.

Mid-January 1980

I arrived in Thailand where I was met by Pat at Bangkok's Don Muang Airport. After the twenty-two hour flight, I would have normally been exhausted and suffering from jet lag, but now I was energized with anticipation of what was in store for me. I had always wanted to return to Thailand and was very disappointed when Pat had first told me I wasn't needed over here. Now there was an excitement building within me. I could only dream of what the future held for me and how the situation would evolve.

Pat was living with his aunt and uncle in Bangkok and on the drive to their house, Pat relayed to me what the situation was. After having not been in Thailand for two years, I immediately noticed a change in the landscape. There was certainly more traffic and congestion and it appeared as if the city was booming with new construction and new industry. I noticed all of the bright colored ten-wheel trucks carrying building materials seemingly everywhere. Bangkok was a hubbub of activity.

Pat seemed very depressed about the situation. He just couldn't get anything going with Charlie and the Thai team. They really didn't want to work with him anymore and he just couldn't see going out and finding new people to start the whole trip over again at this point. It was also getting very dangerous to work in the marijuana business in Thailand without significant connections into both the police and military. The two-year hiatus and his lack of communication with the Thais had left Pat in no position to be able to just jump back into the business, dictate the terms and run the show as before, without significant risk to freedom and the security of the trip. He also had learned that the DEA was a significant presence now and there were many undercover agents lurking in the local hangouts where one might look for a new connection.

The past couple of months had been very frustrating for Pat and his patience was at an end. He saw the writing on the wall and knew he could no longer function as the 'head honcho' in Thailand. He no longer had the respect of the Thais. With 'Thai' as the new leader of the Thai crew, Pat no longer had the power he had previously commanded. He realized it was still possible to do the trip, but he would have to remain in the background. Since I had been there before and had gotten along so well with Charlie and the other members of the Thai crew, Pat felt if I could assume the reins of the trip in Thailand, he could return home to be with Rebecca. Thus he would still reap significant benefits and not have the risk or the hassle of being in charge, which he now realized wasn't even an option. This seemed to be the best of all worlds to Pat, who really didn't want to be there in the first place.

'What the hell,' thought Pat. 'If I only make two or three million and just let Rick make the rest, that wouldn't be so bad and I won't have the risk or all the headaches.'

As soon as we arrived at Pat's uncle's house, Pat made arrangements to have a meeting with 'Thai' and Charlie to discuss what was going to happen next. Actually, Pat couldn't wait to get out of there and back to Becky. He scheduled a flight back to San Francisco two days later. In the next two days he made all of the introductions and got me set up at the bank with all of the signatures so I could access the money in the safe deposit box.

As Pat was packing his bags at his uncle's house and making preparations to leave and return to the States he turned to me and said: "If this trip works out and you make the millions you will, I hope you give me a bonus for setting you up here. I sure wouldn't mind a new Ferrari."

"We'll see," I said. "It sounds reasonable, if we are as successful as we have planned to be. I'll do my best. Anyway, guess you're probably tired of your Porsche by now and need a new toy, eh, Pat."

By January 20th Pat had departed from Thailand and left me alone and in control of the trip. We had renegotiated and I would stand to make something in the realm of an eight figure return, depending on how much weed I could finally score. Pat would make about two mil for turning the trip over to me and he would be virtually out of it, awaiting his payoff from the plush surroundings of his Woodside Hills retreat. Pat had closed the book on, or at least ended this chapter of, his involvement in the smuggling trade in Thailand.

Now it was my turn.

Chapter 32

Tony The Thai

I was now alone in Thailand for the first time. Pat had left to return to the United States and left me alone and in charge of the largest smuggling operation our organization had ever attempted. For me it was 'showtime'. The entire responsibility of the smuggling operation rested squarely on my shoulders.

The first order of business was to set up a place to stay at least temporarily, until I really got my feet on the ground and was able to meet 'Thai' and move forward with a plan. I chose the Oriental Hotel, one of Bangkok's finest. My corner room on the 14th floor had a balcony overlooking the Chao Phraya River. From my suite I could see Bangkok's skyline and the Royal Palace in the distance to the north. The gold spires glistened in the afternoon sun. The river was the center of activity. Brightly colored longboats with large engines zoomed up and down the river carrying both cargo and tourists. The air was hot and steamy, but the hotel itself was beautiful and the room service was among the best I had ever experienced.

Next was to set up a meeting with 'Thai', the leader of the Thai team whom Pat had introduced me to the day before he left. 'Thai' received my telephone call at the number that Pat had left for me. He told me he would come to the Oriental within the hour. The next call I made was to Stan Yamamoto who lived in Vista, California, located east of the coastal city of Oceanside in North San Diego county. Bob Lahodny had asked me to contact Stan when I arrived in Thailand and Stan would be standing by if I needed anything and would be coming to Thailand soon to help and oversee their interests. Stan also had connections in the gem industry and was always traveling to the Far East on legitimate gem business as well as any smuggling ventures he was involved in. I told Stan I would be in touch in the next week or so and would advise him of the situation and update him then. Stan reassured me he would be available and ready whenever I needed him. Bob also told me it would be Stan's responsibility to inspect the load as his representative, whenever it was ready.

There was a knock on the door. I answered it and invited 'Thai' into the room. We sat at the table on the balcony overlooking the river for awhile and room service brought a pitcher of Thai iced tea. One thing I noticed immediately was that I felt very comfortable in the presence of 'Thai'. He had a warm smile and kind eyes. It was apparent that he too took an immediate liking to me.

"I am very happy to be here and I love being in Thailand," I started a bit nervously.

"I know, Rick," 'Thai' said. "Pat tell me all about you. We cannot work with Pat. He not treat us right and Chart, who you call Charlie, no want to work with him no more. Charlie say, he only work with you, no Pat. Pat come back here like big guy, you know. He show us pictures of big house in America and new Porsche, but he no pay us for years. What he thinking? Now he have 'farang' woman. He not like Thai people anymore. He think he too good for us. Well, I tell him, he cannot work with us. If he want to work again in this country, he work by himself. I don't care. One ton, five ton, ten ton, fifty ton I can get. The best, just like you like. Pat cannot work here. We work with you. What you say?"

"Well, Pat called me and told me he was having trouble putting anything together and I guessed exactly what the problem was. Actually, my wife knew this would happen. She's very smart about people and she could see, Pat has changed in the past few years. Since he now has money, he treats people differently than he did before… even me, for God sakes; and he and I, just the two of us, started this whole thing over here. My wife and I knew he might have trouble coming back over here. What I didn't know was, he did not pay the Thai crew until now. I would be pissed off too. Anyway, 'Thai', I am glad to be here and I want to work. I have the whole responsibility now on my shoulders and I want to do a good job. When can we get started?"

"We start today. First, you not stay here at the Oriental Hotel. Too many people see you and it not good. You not want to have too many 'farang' see you. Too many questions. Maybe DEA or CIA notice you if you stay here. Maybe start asking questions. We no want trouble. You must keep low. You come with me and check out of here. You stay my house. I have plenty room. No problem for me. You like Thai food, 'Gin cow', that means we eat now."

"Thai food is my favorite in the whole world," I answered.

"I have many places for eat Thai food. I have special cook at my house. She cook anything. Any Thai food she cook for you. My wife sister is schoolteacher for children. She teach you Thai language like Thai children learn from book. You learn to speak Thai like Thai people, not 'farang'. Maybe few months you can read Thai too. You stay with me, Rick. No worry. I take care of everything."

I checked out of the Oriental and accompanied 'Thai' in his BMW. Together we went to a typical Thai restaurant and ate and got to know each other. I could sense this was going to be a very special relationship. 'Thai' told me, he had connections in the government, the military and with the local police. He told me that in order to work in Thailand you needed connections and money with you at all times in case there was any trouble.

"Work in Thailand today, not like before," 'Thai' continued. "No same as before. Without connections maybe get big trouble. Have money, maybe one million baht with me all the time, for payoff. No get trouble."

'Thai' said that he had the trip completely covered and could get whatever I wanted. I told 'Thai' that the most important thing for me was quality rather than quantity. I only wanted the best and would settle for nothing less. My mission was to score ten tons of top quality Thai stick marijuana, if at all possible.

We began to strategize as to how we would put the whole trip together. All of the details needed to be worked out. It was now the end of January and in order to have everything ready by mid to late spring we would have to get busy. 'Thai' told me he had never scored a load of this size of this quality before and would have to see what quantity of the 'number one' was available. I told 'Thai' the group I was working with, who we had scored for and loaded two years ago, had used a guy named Lec to score the last two loads since Pat had left.

Thai laughed. "Now I know why these guys want to work with you again. Lec is bullshit. I know him. Charlie said he work with you guys long time ago, but now go on his own. He have no connections and can get no good quality. He only take what the growers give him. Low quality. No same like before. Maybe all work for little money in America. No good. Lec no good. And no can trust. Maybe he not happy and turn 'farang' into police for money. He not good people. You can trust our Thai team. If trouble come, no talking to police. Government people on our side and can help if have trouble. No worry. Our team all good people."

Later the same day, I moved into a small house 'Thai' owned located across the street from his own house. He lived with his wife, daughter and his wife's sister in a rather nice home in a modest Bangkok neighborhood. I felt more comfortable in the house than at the hotel after what 'Thai' had told me about staying in Bangkok hotels for any extended periods of time. I certainly did not want to draw attention to my presence in Thailand, given the rather clandestine nature of my business. The house where I lived was a two-story white stucco house, as most were in Bangkok, due to the potential of flooding during the rainy monsoon season. Pat had left all of the equipment for sealing the loads in a storeroom at 'Thai's' home, including both machines and polymylar bags. After I inventoried everything, it was apparent we would need more bags.

To fulfill my need for more oxygen barrier bags, I felt that a new supplier outside the United States would be preferable, because fewer questions and less of a paper trail would be better. In countries other than the U.S., vendors could be paid in cash without drawing suspicion, which a large cash purchase of any kind for anything would in the States. I then sent Joe to Japan in search of bags and within a couple of weeks Joe located a vendor in Tokyo and had a shipment of bags en-route to Bangkok. In Japan, the same bags were one third of the U.S. price. An order for one hundred thousand bags could be filled in less than one week and they were only too happy to receive payment in cash with no questions asked... a far cry from the paranoia of ordering bags in the U.S., then shipping them to Thailand.

'Thai' had also streamlined the money transferring procedure. Now it was only necessary to bring the money as far as Hong Kong rather than take it all the way to Bangkok. Bringing money to Thailand was much riskier than to Hong Kong. Hong Kong is the world banking center and it is not illegal to transport cash to Hong Kong... or if it is no one pays attention, whereas it was always a risk to bring cash directly into Thailand. 'Thai' had a cousin who lived in Hong Kong named Boonsak who had a jewelry store in Kowloon. The jewelry store was only a front for a large black market money-transferring operation. Millions of U.S. dollars were transferred through Boonsak's jewelry store and were picked up in Bangkok in the form of Thai Bahts at the most favorable exchange rates, which were much better than the exchange rates given through banks or even through local money changers.

A secure stash house was next on the agenda, wherein 'Thai' had leased a ten acre farm from a military friend of his, located near the town of Rayong on the Gulf of Siam, about twenty miles east of the U.S. airbase at Utapao. The location would be perfect for receiving the loads from up north plus packaging and storing the load while awaiting for the arrival of the boat to bring the load to the U.S. Although the farm was only ten acres in size, much smaller than Pat's 100 acre farm used in the past, in many ways this was a much more preferable situation to carry out the operation.

A few days later 'Thai' took me to see the farm. I relished the countryside and looked forward to getting out of Bangkok, even if only for a short period of time. The smog, smoke, congestion, pollution and generally all of the humanity concentrated in Bangkok seemed to have grown dramatically in my two-year absence and I couldn't wait to get out of there.

The main road between Sattahip and Chanthaburi along Thailand's southern coastline bordering Cambodia to the east and the Gulf of Siam to the west is densely forested with jungle, rubber plantations and small farming operations, where native tropical fruit are grown commercially. Several small fishing villages sporadically dot the highway and a sizable Thai Navy base is located just west of the town of Rayong. The main highway serves as the primary route of commerce along the coast in southeastern Thailand and ultimately leads east to Cambodia. There are numerous military checkpoints in the area, but none close to the farm.

The farm itself is located in a very secluded spot and is accessed by a non-distinguishable dirt road off the main highway. The jungle is very thick in the area and one must know exactly where the road is or it can be easily missed, and it would never be noticed by the casual passerby. The dirt road quickly disappears into the jungle after meandering for about a mile off the highway, whereupon we encountered what 'Thai' explained is 'our first line of defense and early warning system of any unauthorized visitors', a guarded gate. The gate itself is a large log suspended three feet above the roadway on a metal tripod with a weighted block of concrete attached to one end. Seated next to the gate is a sleepy looking but smartly dressed uniformed soldier sitting on a metal folding chair under a brightly colored umbrella, a holstered .45 Colt 1911 on one side of his web belt and a holstered high tech black Motorola walkie-talkie on the other side. His stern looking face broke into a wide, gold grilled grin as he recognized 'Thai's' BMW. He placed his hands together in the traditional 'Wai' and bowed graciously, then raised the gate to let us through. 'Thai' returned the bow.

"Sa Wat De, Kop," 'Thai' said in the traditional Thai greeting to the soldier.

"Kop," replied the soldier in acknowledgement.

We proceeded and the dense jungle opened up into rows and rows of planted trees. The trees were covered with green colored fruit about the size of a football, but covered with foreboding looking pyramid shaped spikes.

"This number one food in all of Thailand, Rick," said 'Thai'. "This fruit called durian, but this variety called 'monthong'... the best. Number one in all the world. I know you gonna like."

"What is that awful smell, 'Thai'? Are we close to a garbage dump?" I asked pinching my nostrils closed with my fingers.

"That monthong! It smell so sweet. Number one in all the world," laughed 'Thai'.

We continued on and came to a clearing where the house was located. The house was up on stilts in the traditional way so the living space would not get wet or flooded during the monsoon and flood season. Underneath was a large carport where a truck could easily pull in. Around the house was parking space for many other vehicles and the entire area was surrounded by durian trees laden with ripe fruit and the whole farm was buried deep into the jungle and only ten miles from the Naval dock where the loading would take place... the perfect setup for our operation.

We parked and went into the house. Upstairs were two large rooms and a smaller storeroom and a bathroom with a typical country-style Thai toilet, which is a porcelain hole set directly into the floor with a place for each foot on either side of the hole and next to it a large water filled urn with an aluminum pot floating on the water which is used to flush and swab out the toilet. It is rather primitive, but after a couple of uses it became rather routine in living 'the Thai way.' Also upstairs was a small but seldom used kitchen. Since the Navy base and many food vendors were only a few minutes away, we could easily send someone for food without having to mess up the kitchen and further permeate the constant durian smell with kitchen cooking odors. 'Thai' had already moved the sealing machines, equipment and poly mylar bags to the farm and they were set up, production-line-style as before, in the main room and ready to go. The farm was powered by a generator located in a small building outside the main farmhouse. 'Thai' had insulated the generator room so it wouldn't make much noise if it were run at night and although there were no neighbors, we wanted everything to be as quiet and unnoticed as possible.

"This place is perfect, 'Thai'. How did you find something like this?" I asked.

"My friend in Thai military is Chief Colonel Police. His father have durian farm here for many years. I use before for business. Same like this business, but now can use for you and your business. Now have another farm too. Can use for another guy so not have same merchandise together. No good that way, you know. Many confusion possible. Now have two farms so no have confusions."

"Thai, you have other clients who are working now and you are supplying them at the same time?" I asked.

"Yes, but you must keep very quiet about it. Nobody know. I think you know him too. He just like you Rick and from California. Work before with Pat. His name Ciro. He very good guy. Work with him before. He no like Pat, too."

"I've known him for a long time, 'Thai', since college days. Pat used to work for him in Mexico, but he treated Pat like some coolie and didn't pay him $50,000 he owed. So Pat quit working for him and came home to Thailand where he and I started this business back in 1973. Pat introduced Ciro to Charlie, but we thought he had stopped working a couple of years ago, but I guess not. So, he's been working with you all this time. It's just like him to work with our people and not pay us for the connection. When Pat and I loaded his boat back in '77 he kept a million dollars of our share of that load and never paid us the contract amount. He said I stole Pat from his team in Mexico, which was total bullshit. Pat quit Ciro's team because Ciro stiffed him. I got into a big fight with him at his house in Lake Tahoe and he threw me and Pat out. He probably doesn't like me too," I said, as I began to boil with anger at the thought of what had been going on for the past two years.

"Rick, please, no say nothing about this to no one. We do big business for you and you make big money. We all make big money. You have best merchandise, I guarantee. Better than Ciro. He no care too much anyway, not like you. I know you want only top quality… number one. No want problem. I do both trips. Rick, you no worry. You make plenty money for your team. Now, Rick we eat monthong… and you forget all about Ciro. Best fruit in whole world!"

Even at Thai's suggestion and no matter how hard I tried, I just couldn't forget about Ciro and how everything had evolved since Phil had 'spilled the beans' and broken our agreement by confiding in Ciro and opening the door to letting him into our trip. It now became crystal clear to me that Ciro had been given the trade secrets to our trip, the keys to the castle, and basically had been handed our Thai scam 'on a silver platter.' That's not to say that he couldn't have built it on his own, starting from scratch with contacts that he had developed on his own and without the 'insider information' given to him. But that's not what happened. He had built his organization on, at least as far as I was concerned, free goodwill. In exchange for giving him an introduction to our Thai contacts, use of our stored equipment and an avenue to pursue his own Thai venture, and although I was never sure if any compensation, i.e., OTO (original turn-on), was given to my former 'partners', I was personally rewarded with absolutely nothing on that score and had even been ripped off by him for my share of the *Drifter* load two years ago. It became obvious to me, at that point, the old concept of OTO only worked, as far as Ciro was concerned, when it benefitted him. He certainly used the OTO logic in not paying the balance due on the *Drifter* scam, but conveniently neglected it, at least as far as I ever knew, when the shoe was on the other foot. So much for fairness and 'quid pro quo'. But, in reality, what else could I have expected?

I settled down and decided to follow 'Thai's' suggestion and not think about Ciro for now, but just do a good job and get this trip done and prove to myself I could handle a trip of this size. If this scam worked out as planned, I knew I would revolutionize the entire marijuana industry with a load of this size and quality. Nothing like this had ever been done before on such a grand scale with such a high tech offloading plan.

With the groundwork completed, the operation was ready to commence. 'Thai' ordered the first load of Thai sticks and within ten days the first thousand pound delivery arrived at the durian farm. It was exactly as ordered. The sticks were beautiful.

Huge, fresh, glistening, brilliant green, panatela-like, zeppelin-sized Thai sticks were delivered to the durian farm, as promised and on schedule. The Thai team of about ten men methodically packaged the load, inventoried and stored it in about one day's time. Within a week the next delivery came as scheduled. The operation was repeated. Then again and again, flawlessly.

Back in Bangkok, I contacted Stan and told him to come over to Thailand and inspect what had been done to date, so he could report back to the Coronado Company exactly what was going on. Within four days, Stan arrived in Bangkok where 'Thai' and I met him at the Oriental Hotel.

Stan and 'Thai' seemed to hit it off right from the get-go.

"The first thing I'd like to do is to change your name," Stan said to 'Thai'. "From now on, we will call you Tony. I don't want any others to know who you are. OK?"

"Sound good to me," 'Thai'—now Tony—replied. And from then on, he became known as 'Tony the Thai' or just plain Tony.

Two days later we were at the durian farm just in time for the next delivery. Stan completely blew his mind when he saw the operation—the quality, the quantity, and the efficiency of how the whole operation was running. To date we had scored over five tons. Over 200 gunnysacks were sealed and ready to go. It was now the first week of March 1980 and within a month, Stan and I estimated, the entire ten-ton load would be ready. The operation was running like a fine-tuned Swiss watch.

As we sat around the farm, the three of us began to fantasize about the future. Stan wanted to try to streamline the operation by using airplanes instead of boats for smuggling.

"Just think of the time you would save. You could have a load back to the U.S. in a couple of days instead of a couple of months," said Stan.

"I have friend who is big general in Thai Air Force and we can get to use Utapao Airbase to load big airplane," said Tony.

"I still like boats. It's an awfully big ocean out there and so few controls. Airplanes have many more regulations and systems to cross," I argued. "Slow and steady, like the old Tortoise and the Hare fable. Anything this good takes time, and boats are easy to lose track of, even if the other side knows you are coming… like what happened to us a couple of years ago."

"Oh come on, Rick," said Stan. "You never thought you'd be unloading with helicopters. I bet we could get the use of a military airbase in the States to unload a military jet with, say, five tons a week. You figure it out. What's that, about 15 mil a week. Think you could handle that?"

"I don't know, you guys. Let's just get this done safely then we can go Walter Mitty ourselves to death. OK?" I said.

A week later and after another two tons had been scored, bringing the total up to about seven tons, Stan and I went back to Bangkok for a few days. Stan liked to stay at the Oriental in a corner suite on the twelfth floor overlooking the river. Since he only stayed for a few days, and he was in Thailand on legitimate gem business, I felt relaxed and comfortable being there with him. While back at the Oriental, Stan was frequently visited by his gem contacts and he began to acquire several beautiful high-quality rubies and sapphires for his gem business.

"Stan, have you ever tried durian?" I asked.

"Are you nuts? That's the most god-awful stuff I've ever tasted," answered Stan. "To me, it smells like a combination of rotting onions, rotten potatoes and dirty gym socks. Yuk!"

"For something smelling like that," I said, "I'm starting to like it."

Section 7

The Ides of March (1980–1981)

Chapter 33

The Ides, March 15, 1980

March 15—'The Ides of March'
Palo Alto, California, 9 AM Local Time

Cindy filled her portable water bottle, secured it in her fanny pack and exited the Menlo Park home through the rear door. She was wearing her black flowered running tights and blue Kapalua visor as she prepared for her morning hour-long jog with Papi at her side. Each morning at about nine she would run with the beautiful golden retriever throughout the quiet rural neighborhood. She came to the gate at the end of the driveway and pushed the button for the gate to open. The street was not busy with traffic and she and Papi carefully exited the property and suddenly as the gate began to close an unusual concerned look came over Papi's face. At once he whimpered and fell over on his side. Stunned, Cindy rushed to him and cradled his head in her arms. All at once he sighed, looked directly into her eyes, stopped breathing and closed his eyes for the last time. She at once smelled a putrefying odor as the dog's sphincter muscle relaxed and he involuntarily defecated on her running outfit. He died in her arms at that moment.

Cindy screamed. "Oh no. Papi you can't die on me. Not now. Please to God. No! No! No!"

Cindy dragged Papi's limp body back through the gate and left him by the side of the driveway at the far end. She ran back to the house and stumbled inside. She went directly to the nightstand in the master bedroom, opened the drawer and grabbed the baggie containing an ounce of Peruvian flake cocaine and the eighteen bladed red Swiss Army camping knife lying next to it. She then proceeded to open the large knife blade, plunge it into the white powder, extract a miniature mountain of coke which took up nearly one third of the three inch blade and without chopping it up put the blade next to her left nostril and inhaled. She repeated the process again on the right side, then with a white powdery ring residue circling both nostrils and tears streaming down her face, she blindly found her way to the liquor cabinet and gulped several mouthfuls of

Stolichnaya vodka straight from the open bottle. Terrified to be alone and while crying and screaming hysterically, and already feeling the numbing effects of the alcohol and cocaine, five minutes later Cindy picked up the phone and called Willie and Melinda who lived around the block.

"Hello, everyone. You have reached Willie and Melinda. Sorry we can't come to the phone right now. Please leave your message at the sound of the tone and we'll call you back soon. Have a beautiful day," the cheerful sound of Melinda's sing-song voice intoned on the answering machine.

"He's dead. He's dead. Oh my god, Mel. Please help me. I don't know what to do," screamed and sobbed Cindy as she blubbered into the phone.

March 15 – The Ides of March
Bangkok, Thailand, Oriental Hotel, 11:30 PM Local Time

Stan and I had just returned to Stan's suite. We had just finished a wonderful lobster served in the hotel's riverfront restaurant and I was just about to leave when the phone rang. Stan answered.

"Just a moment please. Rick, it's for you. Long distance."

A momentary chill overcame me as I reached for the phone. I wondered out loud. "This must be trouble. Who could be calling from overseas at this hour?"

"Hello."

"Rick, it's Melinda. I don't know how to tell you this. But… Papi's dead."

I felt as if my heart had been torn from my chest. I gasped as my eyes began to fill with tears. "What happened? Where's Cindy?"

"She's out cold. I got a hysterical message on the machine this morning and rushed over. I found the gate open. Papi's body alongside the driveway. When I came to the house, the back door was open and Cindy was curled in the fetal position on the living room floor, drunk and babbling incoherently. Her nose was covered in white powder and Bubba was whimpering in the corner. This number was by the phone and I called you immediately. What would you like me to do with Papi's body? I'll stay with Cindy. Please come as soon as you can," she pleaded.

"Call the vet and ask him what to do. He'll know. I'll be there first flight I can get out. And Mel, please don't leave Cindy there alone," I replied, sobbing and stunned.

"Rick, what the hell is going on?" asked Stan, who had been listening to my end of the conversation. "Who died? How can I help?"

"Oh, Stan. This is the worst day of my life. My dog died. He was my best friend in the whole world."

"Whew," breathed Stan with a sigh of relief. "I thought it might have been a child or parent. At least you can always get another dog, Rick."

"Stan, you don't understand. This dog was very special. He can never be replaced. I have to go home for a while and deal with this situation. You'll have to stay here till I get back. I have to leave immediately, my wife has gone to pieces," I said wiping back the tears.

"What the hell are you talking about, Rick? Let's get real here. This was a dog! You can't just leave in the middle of this operation. We still have three more tons to score and you're the guy who's responsible. I understand what you're going through, but you've got to get a grip. This trip is worth millions to all of us. I've seen how Tony and the rest of the Thai team are around you. They respect you. This operation is going like clockwork because of you and if you just leave, because your dog died… it won't be the same with me in your place."

"Listen Stan, I'm outta here in the morning on the first flight. This is an emergency in my life and I've got to deal with it. The millions won't be worth shit to me if I lose everything else in my life. My wife is hysterical and I've got to go to her now. I'll be back in a week, ten days max. You can stay on top of this thing til I return. Tony will take care of everything. You just have to monitor the situation… no sweat. I think there's a flight out of Don Muang in a couple of hours. I'm going to put a few things together for the flight and catch a cab. Please tell Tony what's going on… I'm sure he'll understand."

I turned and left the room.

March 17

After the twenty-two hour flight I was tired and stricken with grief over the loss of my friend and the apprehension about the mental state of my wife. I arrived at our Menlo Park home to find it in a state of disaster. The place was a mess and Cindy was beside herself.

"Oh Rick," cried Cindy. "You're never here when I need you. You never have time for me. You're always running all over the world doing your dope trips, and never taking care of us. Now look what's happened."

I surveyed the scene. Cindy was sitting in the living room drinking Stoli at 10:30 in the morning. She looked like she'd been on a months-long bender. There were deep circles under her puffy, bloodshot eyes. Her hair hadn't been combed and she was still dressed in her bright blue flowery nightgown. Bubba was outside on his dog bed but had not been fed. Our bedroom was a mess with clothes strewn everywhere. Dishes sat in the kitchen sink unwashed for days with food caked on, and newspapers were stacked up in the driveway and at the front door, all unopened.

"Cindy, you've got to pull yourself together. Here let me help you," I said reaching to help her to her feet. "We've got to be strong."

"Stay away from me, Rick. Don't touch me!" shrieked Cindy as she burst into tears. "This is all your fault. If you'd been here, none of this would have happened. Papi loved you and you abandoned him. You abandoned us. He died of a broken heart. Damn you, Rick."

"Look, Cindy… this isn't any easier on me than you. Sure, I loved him and I love you. I didn't abandon anyone. You know, I'm just trying to do this so we'll have a good life. I'm doing what I'm doing for us. Don't you understand that? What I'm doing isn't like a regular job. It's something special. It's what people dream about and fantasize about, but I'm doing it. I don't like being away for so long, but I have to be responsible. My job is not going to get done by itself. I have to do it. But, remember, this is for us… not just me alone. Even my leaving now and coming back here could jeopardize the whole trip."

"You see… it's always the goddamned trip. You just never have time for me any-more. You don't care about me. And now my only real true friend in the whole world is gone. Papi cared. You don't!!"

"Please Cindy. Don't make this any harder on us than it already is. I feel just as bad about Papi as you do. Where is he anyway?"

"The vet suggested we cremate his body. He took care of it. We can go and pick up the ashes later today." Tears welled up in Cindy's eyes. "Oh, Rick… I'm so sorry about this… what are we going to do?" Cindy relented as the hardness in her tone melted away.

"Let's deal with this for a few days," I said. "I've got to get back to Thailand as soon as possible. Then in a couple of weeks you can come over and we'll travel around the Far East. Maybe go to China. I think I can arrange it through one of my contacts in Hong Kong."

What I somehow neglected to tell Cindy was that I had already been offered to tour China in the company of a young Chinese actress I had previously met on a Swissair flight from New York to Geneva. The gorgeous actress named Tina Leung, who went by her stage name, Tina Ti, was the first Chinese actress to act in, what was considered at the time, a risqué film. I had visited with her on numerous occasions while traveling through Hong Kong, where she was also a frequent visitor at the chic Peninsula Hotel in Kowloon. It turned out she had contacts high within the Chinese government and had previously offered to take me through China on a diplomatic tour, only afforded to high government officials. When I told her about the death of my beloved dog and about how distraught my wife was, she suggested to invite her along as well. Even though I thought it might be somewhat awkward, I agreed.

"Another thing too, Cindy, we still have Bubba. He's Papi's son. A part of Papi lives on. And he's your dog, not mine. You've got to give him the attention he needs now." I let the puppy in the house. I noticed he was no longer a puppy but nearly a full grown dog now and had a striking resemblance to his father. I smiled as the dog bounded past me and nuzzled up against Cindy. Cindy wrapped her arms around Bubba and cried into his neck.

* * *

A week later after things had calmed down a bit with Cindy, I returned to Thailand, but things were different. "We've had a few problems," Stan said. "Tony will tell you what's been going on while you were gone."

"We try to bring two thousand down from north when you gone, but get caught at checkpoint. Now have hassle. Lose two drivers. Now in jail up country. Lose one ton merchandise. Now can get no more merchandise. Maybe drivers talk and lose village too. Situation not good now."

"Come on, Tony," I said. "You have friends in government. Can't you just pay and get them out and we can continue. No problem."

"I think I can get them out, but can get no more merchandise. Too much risk for village. Anyway you have seven tons good quality. That enough. No want more trouble."

At that point, the gravity of the situation began to sink in. In my mind, the events of the past week were a reflection of the death of my beloved friend Papi, and coincidentally the day he had died—March 15—foretold a bad sign in the annals of history. It was maybe a premonition of things to come.

March 15th is a date in history known as the Ides of March. On March 15th in the year 44 BC, Roman Emperor Julius Caesar was assassinated. He was stabbed to death on the floor of the Roman senate on that date following a warning and premonition by a soothsayer, who implored him to "beware the Ides of March." Caesar had scoffed at such a notion; however, as a student of history, I reflected on these thoughts with an uneasy sense of foreboding.

Now, since there was not going to be any more marijuana procured for this load, there was nothing more for me to do but wait for the loading of the oil supply boat. It had been scheduled to load in April; however, due to repairs on the boat, it would not happen until June.

Meanwhile, both Thai drivers were released from jail. Tony had secured their release by paying a fine of 50,000 Baht for each of them and by making arrangements to send the chief colonel of the provincial police and his wife on an all-expenses-paid shopping trip to Hong Kong.

I decided to have Cindy come over and felt it would be a good time to do some traveling. Cindy arrived in Hong Kong in mid-April. I had already arranged with Tina for a diplomatic tour of the Peoples Republic of China and for the next month Cindy and I, accompanied by Tina and her two brothers Henry and Eddie, toured China.

China had only recently opened for tourism and the travel conditions were quite primitive and substandard to what we were used to. There were very few automobiles and most of the people rode bicycles and were dressed in traditional Mao-style blue uniforms and most wore berets with a red star embroidered on the front. In 1980, it was rather an unusual sight to see Westerners traveling in China and it seemed like all of the people were always staring at us. Cindy coined a name for these gawkers and called them 'blue coat watchers.' They were everywhere, like ants!

Even the best hotels were quite utilitarian and the room service left much to be desired. We had been warned by Tina that it was possible the hotel rooms were bugged with listening devices put there by government agents who were always very paranoid of Western ideas and conversations. Cindy and I decided to test it, so as we arrived in our room in Beijing at the five star Beijing Hotel, Cindy started to complain loudly and in a rather upset tone of voice, to the only other person in the room, me, saying that the 'idiot maid service' had left us only one bath towel and no soap. We were tired from the flight in from Hong Kong and only wanted a warm shower… she was pissed! Within less than one minute, there was a knock on the door and a uniformed maid, dressed as all of the other 'blue coat watchers', appeared with fresh towels, several bars of soap and a broad smile. That pretty much confirmed Tina's warning, so from then on we held most conversations either outside or if in the room made notes to each other.

During our trip we visited Beijing and the Great Wall of China, Canton, Shanghai, Guilin and Shouzhou. The trip served as a sort of recovery from the devastation of Papi's death and we enjoyed ourselves, relishing the wonders of China. While visiting the city of Shouzhou, Tina took us to the Chinese National Research Embroidery Institute where, upon entering the building, one is awed by a 20 foot by 20 foot embroidery painting of Chairman Mao Tse Tung in his glory days. While visiting the Institute, I had the idea to commission a silk embroidery painting of Papi. For good luck, I always carried a photograph of Papi, looking his regal best, in my leather passport wallet. I negotiated a price of $2800 to have a two foot by three foot embroidery painting done in the likeness of the photograph. I gave the commissar of the Institute $1400 as a down payment and was told that it could take between six months and one year to complete the project.

We toured China for about one month and then returned to Hong Kong and proceeded on to Bangkok in preparation for the loading of the Coronado Company's boat, named the *Jonathan Winter*. The *Winter* had arrived in Singapore to take on fuel and supplies and to receive the final rendezvous instructions from Stan. They were given maps indicating the location of the Thai Navy base near Rayong and the radio frequencies and codes for contact with me and Tony to coordinate the loading.

On a moonless June evening the *Jonathan Winter* arrived at the Rayong naval base and the loading itself came off without a hitch. All 335 gunnies, totaling seven tons of the highest-quality Thai stick marijuana, were transferred aboard the oil supply boat at the Royal Thai Navy base by the Thai crew. The Naval base was secured by officers of the Royal Thai Navy who were paid off handsomely by Tony. Several Navy seamen assisted with the loading of gunnies from the trucks to the boat docked at the end of the Navy pier. The entire loading operation was completed in 45 minutes. I met and was with the boat captain for a few minutes that dark evening, who introduced himself as Captain Don, and I wished him luck on the voyage home. This would not be the last time I was to have the pleasure of meeting boat captain Donald McMichaels. I was there to make sure everything was OK and so I could report to Stan and The Company that the load was safely aboard and on its way.

Captain Don escorted me aboard and into the ship's hold to observe the stashing operation. It was in there that I saw, to my astonishment, one of the other crew members who was stacking the gunnies was puncturing some of the bales with a knife.

"What the fuck is he doing?, I asked Don, in utter amazement as I could hear the whooshing noise of air escaping and now started smelling the sweet characteristic Thai stick smell oozing from the punctured packages.

The weed inside the mylar bags was so fresh and voluminous, apparently not all of the air had been sucked out during the sealing process. It was a fine line to preserve the product as much as possible, while at the same time not ruin it by sealing it too tight. Obviously, some air still remained in the sealed packages and I saw, some of the bales had sort of pillowed and ballooned from their normal shape and wouldn't stack neatly one on top of the other, but instead teeter-tottered on the cushion of air trapped inside the packages.

"I told him to pop those bales, so the whole load would fit here in the hold. We need all of the space in here to be able to completely conceal the load on the trip home," Don replied.

"Have you fucking lost your mind? Our team over here just spent the last four months handling this load with kid gloves. We triple sealed each package for the maximum return when the load gets sold and so the packages won't leak and the weed won't mildew during the voyage. And now, in an instant, you're compromising all of our work," I said, as I was beginning to lose my temper. "This is the best load of this size that's ever been scored over here and now, like a bunch of fucking monkeys, you're ruining it."

"What did you just call us, you little punk?" Don yelled, shoving me backwards into an already stacked pile. "I don't take that shit from anyone aboard my boat."

"Fuck you, asshole," I barked, regaining my balance and starting towards him. "Maybe I should have my guys take the load back ashore and you can go home empty handed. We've worked our asses off for this and obviously you don't care, you piece of shit!" I could feel the adrenaline pumping now as I approached the captain, contemplating, in an instant, if I should just haul off and kick him in the nuts.

Hearing the commotion coming from below the deck, I turned and saw another crew member jump down the companionway ladder. He immediately got between us and broke up what could have turned ugly in a heartbeat. I looked directly at him and right away recognized him as Captain Ron, the friendly guy who'd captained Bob Lahodny's yacht, the *Pai Nui*, back in '77.

"What the fuck is going on down here?"

"This fucking moron," I said, pointing an accusing finger at Don, "told this other brainless wonder, here, to pop these bales 'cause they wouldn't stack just right. They're all perfectly sealed, and these idiots are ruining all of our work. Are you all this stupid?" Ron's hand was now extended on Don's chest as he restrained the captain from inching towards me.

"Just calm down. Everybody take a deep breath. Rick, why don't you just get outta here right now? And I'll take care of it," Ron said, handing a roll of gray tape to the other crew member, who was standing there with his mouth agape at the potential altercation. "Here, tape up those holes and let's all just do our jobs and settle down. We've got a long trip ahead of us."

"OK," I said retreating back up on deck with Ron right behind me. I stepped off the boat, but made a mental note to report the incident back to Bob and Ed when I got back to the States. I was livid at their stupidity, and told myself I'd carefully inspect those compromised gunnies and any of the punctured bags would be part of Coronado's share, not mine.

Other than that, everything else went smoothly, and a half hour later, the *Jonathan Winter*, and my future, departed the Royal Thai Navy Base at Rayong, bound for the West Coast and the planned revolutionary offloading procedure.

Meanwhile Cindy was waiting for me to return to our suite at the Oriental Hotel. The following morning after loading the *Jonathan Winter*, we departed Thailand and headed for home by way of a tropical paradise, the Indonesian island of Bali. We spent a week relaxing in the tropical sun with seemingly not a care in the world. Everything seemed to be in order for the biggest score in my eleven-year career as a marijuana smuggler and entrepreneur.

All I had to do now was wait.

Chapter 34

Shoveler

Menlo Park
Early June 1980

"Rick, Rick," cried the frantic voice on the other end of the phone. "Ya gotta get over here right away. The cops have the place surrounded. I'm holding them off, but I can't last much longer. They know all about the trip. We're doomed."

"Shoveler, is that you? It's three o'clock in the morning. What the hell's going on?" Then I heard the staccato sound of gunfire over the phone.

"Rick, they're in the bushes. All over the place. Get over here right away."

"Whoa. Just calm down, Shov. Sounds like there's a war going on. And you want me to come and get into the middle of it?" I replied, startled and now wide awake.

"Now!" screamed Shoveler. The phone went dead.

For the next ten minutes, I tried repeatedly to call Shoveler back at the newly rented stash house in Half Moon Bay, but all I got was a busy signal. Cindy had gone to Sacramento with Bubba to visit a friend, so I was all alone except for 'Mr. T', who was now awake, purring and nuzzling up to me for attention.

"Guess I'd better go and find out what's going on with Shov," I said to the cat. "If you were Papi, I'd take you with me, but you'd better stay here and hold down the fort." I hurriedly dressed and left in my truck at 3:30 AM and headed to the coast... not knowing what to expect, but fearing Shoveler had somehow gone off the deep end.

An hour later I arrived at the secluded stash house in Half Moon Bay. All seemed to be quiet, but just to be safe I passed the house and parked around the corner. The lights in the house were off and everything seemed normal. I went to the front door and knocked, then called in as quiet a voice as possible but loud enough to be heard, "Shoveler, it's me, Rick... open the door." The door opened about one foot and, unseen from behind the door an arm reached out from the darkness, grabbed me by the sleeve of my jacket and pulled me inside. I stood motionless in the entryway as Shoveler turned on the hall light. There was Shoveler dressed in military camouflage pants, black paratrooper boots with no shirt, his face was covered with black grease paint. He had a black bandana wrapped around his head, a cigarette was dangling from his mouth and over his shoulder was an AR-15 military assault rifle loaded with a thirty round banana clip. There were two more clips taped end-to-end, for rapid reloading, on his ammunition web belt along with a military canteen and military-style olive drab goose-necked flashlight. He appeared ready for guerrilla warfare in a scene straight out of a Rambo movie. His eyes were wide and appeared to be spinning in their sockets with what seemed to be sparks emanating from the center of his dilated pupils. My immediate thought was, Shoveler was on a bad acid trip, characterized by his pungent smell of body odor and fear. As my gaze panned from Shoveler to the immediate scene of the stash house, my initial amazement turned to despair. The house was a total disaster. Furniture was overturned, windows were barricaded and a kitchen window in the rear of the house was broken out. It appeared as if a tornado had struck from the inside.

"The cops know everything. They're waiting out there. I'm amazed you made it through the enemy lines," panted Shoveler. "They know about the load and the trip. We're going to be busted for sure. Rick, you've got to call the trip off. We're finished! I may have shot one of 'em earlier who was trying to come in through the rear window. Here take this and keep down for god sakes," said Shoveler as he thrust a 9mm Baretta into my hand.

"Please, Shov, try to calm down. I don't need this gun right now. I think we're safe for the moment. I didn't see anyone and I surveyed the entire area before coming to the house," I said as calmly as I could while trying not to be too sarcastic and send him further into the abyss. "Don't worry. I'll call off the trip. It's not too late. No problem. Maybe we should go for a ride, which hopefully might settle you down. Why don't you put the gun away, wash your face, get a shirt on and let's go out for awhile and get some fresh air… you look like you could use a little."

We drove around for an hour or so until Shoveler was relaxed, then we stopped in Redwood City at Denny's for coffee and breakfast.

"Rick, I really appreciate you coming over and rescuing me. I never told you this, but when I was in Thailand I developed this weird stomach disorder, upset stomach and diarrhea all the time. The doctors over there couldn't figure out exactly what the problem was, but medicated me for it anyway. They gave me massive doses of the steroid Prednisone to try and cure my problem, but instead they made it worse for me… mentally, I mean. I sometimes have these incidents where I feel like I'm losing my mind. I later found out, there can be adverse reactions to Prednisone and one of them is temporary psychosis. Rick, sometimes I just lose it… then in a while I'm OK. In all honesty, Rick, I'm not really sure I'm the right person for this job. We've been friends forever and I wouldn't want to do anything to jeopardize what's going on."

"I really appreciate your honesty, Shov, but don't worry. I've already called the trip off," I said assuring Shoveler the trip had been called off and we wouldn't have anything to worry about, because we hadn't done anything wrong. After all, it wasn't against the law to rent a house. I told Shoveler to clean up the mess, have the broken window replaced and to terminate the lease on the stash house, using the excuse that he had just been offered a position on the East Coast and would have to move out right away. I felt bad about having to lie to Shoveler. It wasn't my nature, but I just couldn't risk the possibility of such 'a loose cannon' with such unpredictable tendencies to be responsible for my future. Being as loyal as he was, I was pretty sure the Shovel man would understand and not hold it against me. I couldn't afford a repeat of what had just happened at the Half Moon Bay stash house, especially with the load there. I gave Shoveler $1,000 for his relocation and trouble and set about to find a replacement housesitter and a new stash house. The load was due to arrive in the next six weeks or thereabouts, therefore time to reorganize was at a premium.

I decided I would once again appeal to Willie Sherman for his services of sitting on the load. He was really the only person I could trust to housesit and had proven very successful in the past. The only problem was, Willie had promised his family he would now settle down and work diligently in their San Francisco retail business. I thought, if I 'sweetened the pie' enough, it would be an offer he wouldn't be able to refuse; one hundred grand for a couple of months' work… which, in the Professor's mind, amounted to manning a sex palace, while watching sports 24/7 on a widescreen. He told his family he had to take a sabbatical from the rigors of the daily j-o-b. He claimed stress and, although his family didn't wholly buy the excuse, he left anyway.

After an exhaustive search, Willie found a suitable rental house in the foothills north of Santa Rosa. It was a Victorian-style house with a swimming pool located on five secluded acres accessed by a long curving quarter-mile driveway. Willie figured he could hole up there for as long as was necessary in the comfort he was used to, while serving the cause, and the load would be secure under his watchful eye.

For our purposes of securely storing and concealing the load, the house had a unique feature. In the ceiling of the closet in one of the second story bedrooms was a drop down staircase which accessed the unfinished attic space. The staircase folded in the center and had a wooden panel concealing it in the closet's ceiling. A rope hung down from the panel allowing the stairway to be pulled downward into the open position. I pushed the rope all the way into the panel and secured it with a piece of tape and unless anyone knew it was there, no one would notice it just by chance The rent was $2,500 per month and Willie paid for three months in advance. Again Willie was in his element. However, the house was listed for sale with a 24-hour advance notice required if a real estate agent was to show it to a prospective buyer.

Two months previously Willie and Melinda had separated. Melinda just could not take Willie's propensity to chase other women and still be married to her. Frequently he wouldn't come home at night or would return smelling like he had been with someone else. Melinda would confide in Cindy about this situation and Cindy would advise Melinda to dump Willie and not take any more of his shit. Willie resented Cindy for putting such ideas in Melinda's head, but by the summer of 1980 it was too late for the relationship. Furthermore, Willie felt that Cindy was advising Melinda to divorce him and 'take him to the cleaners'. He told me of this and warned me that she might someday do this to me as well. I, of course, in my naiveté, pooh-poohed the notion.

Melinda had, by now, moved out and into an apartment with her sister, and Willie, letting no moss grow under his feet, was already courting his next 'victim.' This time it was Debbie Caldwell, a cute rather innocent little pixie who had worked for one of his clients at the family store.

The Professor had a 'no-lose' formula for reeling in his women. First he'd wine and dine them at the best restaurants and/or take them on short vacations up to the wine country, but the coup de grace was always a two-week vacation to Maui to 'seal the deal.' Of course, plying them with copious amounts of marijuana and cocaine made them 'ripe for the pickins'. Debbie fell right into his trap and in less than a month had moved in with him. Seemed like all the nice ones fell for him and Deb was no exception. Everyone loved her, but somehow Willie ended up with her falling head over heals for him following the Hawaii trip. She was a natural to accompany him to the Santa Rosa stash house, so she quit her job, convinced by Willie that the two of them had a future together. I was always surprised at how easily these women could be 'wooed' with his bullshit, but the process was repeated over and over and over again with startling success. At any rate, Willie figured that he and Debbie could sit on the load up in Santa Rosa in relative bliss. Debbie would be there for plenty of sex and to take care of his other nutritional needs. He had his wide screen TV brought in and hooked up to the ten foot in diameter satellite dish located at the edge of the property, which was operated remotely. He also had a 'black box' for the TV where he was able to pirate over 150 channels ranging from sports to X-rated movies for free. Additionally, Willie had saved an extensive stash of Thai weed from our previous trips to go along with a seemingly endless supply of coke. The two of them could stay constantly stoned while he was on duty round-the-clock in his role of housesitter.

With the stash house now once again secure, I had only to wait for the load to arrive. I was in constant touch with my 'new best friends', Bob 'Lights' Lahodny and Eddie Otero, for status reports on the progress of the load. I even made several trips to Santa Barbara to see 'Lights' and tell him of the successful loading and to establish a closer friendship and fantasize about future endeavors with his organization. Lights' only complaint was that the load was only seven tons, instead of the contracted amount of ten… but then he understood that this was one of the variables in the business. His complaint was easily mitigated by both my and Stan's report of the quality of the load.

Never had a load of this size and quality been scored in the past. The quality of this load was the finest I had ever done… even better than the previous years' efforts. I told Bob and Eddie that I felt asking a couple of hundred dollars more a pound, if they wanted to, would go a long way to making up the difference they might have realized if the load were ten tons instead of seven. They were both placated with this information and they also realized that if they pulled this off, the following year they might be able to do 20 tons or more.

Indeed, we'd all be set for life.

Chapter 35

Neah Bay

August 1980

It seemed to me like the Coronado Company had thought of everything and they were the most sophisticated and professional group of smugglers in the business. One of the things they were most concerned about was phone security and the possibility telephones might be 'bugged'. Although I didn't fully understand the need for such high security measures at the time, I nevertheless went along with it and accepted their strict communication policy without questioning it. It was only later that I found out the real reason for their paranoia, but by then it was too late. They had strict communication rules, among which was that no telephone conversations or communication was to take place on private telephone lines. The only telephone connections between me and any members of the Coronado Company would be on public telephones. Bob always stressed to me and Pat, when he was involved, that one of the first things the cops investigated in their pursuit of busting smuggling outfits was telephone records of suspected smugglers. He told me that private telephones were routinely bugged by the DEA and conversations could be intercepted very easily. This happened very frequently, both legally by court order and illegally, at the whim of some overzealous DEA agent. To mitigate this, the Coronado Company had devised a method for communication, to attempt to elude detection by anyone listening to phone conversations: it was known as 'Code 73.'

I was instructed to obtain the numbers of at least five public telephone booths in the area where I lived and both Bob and Eddie did likewise for themselves in their area. If we wanted to talk to each other, the call from the initiating party would be done from a public telephone… never from the home telephone, so it would never appear on a telephone bill. If I wanted to call Bob in Santa Barbara, I would go to a pay telephone booth near my house and jot down the number on a piece of paper. I would then encode the number by multiplying each digit by seven, but only noting the second digit if the result was a two digit number. On the other end of the line, Bob would write down the encoded number given over the phone by me, then he would decode it by multiplying it by three, again only noting the last digit and for further security the area code was never encoded… it was given in its true form or simply one would say, "You know the area code." It was felt that if someone was listening to the conversation and knew the area codes from which the calls were being made, encoding the area code would be a sure way to compromise the code.

For example, I would go out to a pay phone located in nearby Palo Alto whose number was (415) 323-9462. I would perform the following calculation, writing down only the last number of a two digit integer. In this example, 7 x 2 = 14, only noting the 4, then 7 x 6 = 42, only noting the 2, etc:

$$\begin{array}{r} 323 - 9462 \\ \times\,7 \\ \hline 141 - 3824 \end{array}$$

I would then call Bob from the pay phone and tell him, "Call me at the field office. I'm in the usual area code. The number is 141 - 3824." Bob would write down the number, then decode it in the following manner, again only noting the last number, if the calculation yielded a two digit integer:

$$\begin{array}{r} 141 - 3824 \\ \times\,3 \\ \hline 323 - 9462 \end{array}$$

Bob would know the area code was 415, because it was my usual area code for the Menlo Park area, then he would call me back at (415) 323-9462, where I would be waiting for the call. It would usually come within five to ten minutes, if a further delay in the return call was anticipated, one would say, "I'll get back to you in 45 minutes," or whatever.

Up until now, I had not been too security conscious; however Bob and Eddie opened my eyes and changed my thinking regarding security. I had come from the position of virtually no communication for security, and had always thought that minimal communication was preferable. The size of previous loads and the unloading process had always been manageable with only a few people. However, now with the size of this load and the sophistication and complexity of the proposed offloading, it became obvious that the coordination and manpower required to pull it off would necessitate constant communication and an acute awareness of the security necessary to avoid the possibility of the load being compromised by a phone tap. The 'Code 73' method seemed to me to be an ingenious solution.

We communicated regularly on this basis, so it came as no surprise when I got a call from Bob in the early afternoon on August 22, 1980, telling me to call him back at his field office at 682-3855 in 15 minutes. I wrote down the number as Bob had given it to me then decoded it by multiplying by 3. I then left for the nearest pay phone located at the Shell gas station on University Avenue in Palo Alto. I knew the area code for Santa Barbara was 805. Fifteen minutes later I dialed (805) 846-9455.

"Hey, Bob. How's it going? What's up?" I asked.

"Well, we've had word from the rig; they've had some problems. They can't unload because there's been a continuous fog bank off the Washington Coast. The choppers have been unable to pull off the unloading. They have been trying to unload for the past three days, but it's been like pea soup, the fog is so thick. The boat has been coming in to the pre-arranged spot as planned for the past three days. They have taken the load up on deck and put it into the steel cages in preparation for the helicopter unloading, three times now, but each time they have only been able to hear the choppers above them, and each time with the fog right down to water level, they have not been able to make visual contact and the offloading is too dangerous. They are going to try again this afternoon, but it doesn't look too good. The fog just doesn't seem to be lifting. The pilots now tell us the duty rosters have been changed and they might not be able to get the choppers again after today. We might have to go to 'Plan B'. We've sent Dave, our top lieutenant, up to survey the situation. I'll keep you posted."

"Wait a minute, Bob," I responded. "I thought all of you, or at least Eddie, your beach commander, would be on location and in charge of the unloading operation… just like the old days. I didn't expect to contract with armchair quarterbacks. Just who's in charge up there, and what is 'Plan B' anyway?"

"Rick, everything's been in place. The drop zone has been totally secure. The National Guard pilots and choppers have been ready and flying as scheduled, but this fog has really fucked things up. Dave is surveying an alternative unloading spot and we think he's found a good one. It's on an Olympic Peninsula Indian Reservation. It's completely secure and the Indians will assist in the operation itself by using their fishing boats to transfer the load from the rig to shore. We will then put the load in the truck and transport it as planned to the ranch."

"What? You mean, you are going to let a bunch of fucking people who have no experience in this sort of thing unload this multi-million dollar cargo. You are actually considering putting all of our futures in their hands. Have you lost your mind? Listen, Bob, I have five four-wheel drive pickups ready to go right now. I want to go up there and help. We can be on the road in half an hour and be up there by morning. I want someone who is responsible and who has a significant vested interest in this load to be on location, the same as you required Stan to be in Thailand monitoring me. If you and Eddie aren't going to be there, I want at least Joe and myself there. We want to take our share right from the beach and, I'm sorry Bob, but I just don't trust the Indians with my future,"

"Listen, Rick. That's not possible. This is our part of the venture and we intend to take care of it. It's what we contracted for and that's our agreement."

"Fuck the agreement, Bob. I have a bad feeling about this and I want to get our share as soon as it hits the beach. I want to help with this to protect our investment. Now, tell me where to go… right now!"

"I'll tell you where to go, Rick. You can go to hell. We've got this end of it covered. You just stay put and I'll let you know when the load has arrived at the ranch, as planned. Just calm down… everything will be OK. You know, we've handled this kind of thing before. We're professionals… best in the business and we don't need a bunch of your people up there getting in the way. This is under control. Trust me, will you, Rick?"

"Who the fuck do you think you're dealing with, a bunch of amateurs? We're not just some people getting in the way. We're very experienced in our own right and, unlike you and Ed, are willing to be on scene and have had 100% success in the past even in the face of serious adversity. These Indians, your new unloading crew, are the ones with no experience and absolutely no stake in all of our futures. Now, come on. Get real. Where exactly is this operation all going down?"

"Two dollars and fifty cents more please," the operator interjected. I could hear the sound of quarters being inserted into the phone on the other end of the line. "Thank you."

Bob continued after depositing the additional $2.50 into the phone. "Just settle down, Rick. I'll phone you this evening and let you know the status. Maybe the choppers will have a window this afternoon. Just stay calm and stay put, but keep your trucks and drivers ready. OK."

"No, Bob. It's not really OK. I want to be closer in case of emergency. We're at least 15 to 20 hours away from the unloading. We could get into the area if we left now. Please, just tell me where the reservation is and we can at least be close if you need us. If not, what's the harm? If all goes well, we can at least act as escorts in getting the load back to the ranch and if you need us, we're there to help."

"Rick, let's see what happens this afternoon, then I'll have a clearer picture from Dave as to the exact status and we can go from there. I'll call you this evening. OK?"

"I'm not happy about this, Bob. I want to be there, but I'll wait until tonight for your call. We're gassed up and ready to go on a moment's notice," I said. "I'll speak to you this evening."

For the next two days, I heard nothing from Bob. I tried repeatedly to call both Bob and Eddie's houses, but got no answer anywhere. My anxiety began to build. Finally on the morning of the third day, August 27, the call came from Bob. I hurried to the phone booth.

"Rick, we blew it. The bad weather and surf got us. We lost most of the load, but salvaged a pickup load or two and they're on their way back. We're abandoning the ranch and the load will go directly to Stan's place in North San Diego county."

"What the hell happened?" I asked.

"Look, Rick. There's nothing else that can be done now. I don't want to get into it right this minute. Please meet me tomorrow at Stan's and I'll tell you everything." The phone went dead and I was left standing there with my stomach in my throat.

I assembled my drivers, Joe and Rico, for the trip down to Southern California. I then called Stan to see if he could find out anything more about the situation.

"Rick, I don't know much more than you. I think it was a fiasco on the beach with the Indians and all. My report is, they got a ton or more but the rest was lost in the surf. Some was left in a truck which went off a muddy road in the rain. That's all I know. I'll see you down here tomorrow," said Stan.

"Stan, I had a weird feeling about this. What the hell are we going to do?"

"There's nothing we can do. We just have to move on from here, and see what we can salvage. All we can do, at this point, is wait and see," said Stan.

"What about the heat?" I asked. "If most of the load was left on the beach or in a truck left stuck in the mud, I can imagine the cops will be all over it sooner or later. How do we know it's safe?"

"They told me everything was cool, but they had to get away and salvage what they could," Stan replied.

"I just don't believe it. I'll see you tomorrow," I said.

The following morning, on my way to Stan's house in North San Diego county, I stopped at the Los Angeles International Airport and went into the United Airlines terminal. I went over to the big screen on the wall which informed passengers about arrival and departure information. I saw where a flight was just landing from Seattle and proceeded to the gate of the incoming flight. As the passengers disembarked from the plane, I boarded the plane like I was a passenger who had just forgotten something. I found a *Seattle Times* newspaper sitting on a first class seat and took it, then deplaned with the last of the passengers. As I opened the paper, right there on the front page was the article which I had most feared. The headlines read: 'Riptide Foils Plot, 290 Bales of Marijuana Found Near Neah Bay Worth Millions.'[1]

The article went on to say that nearly five tons of high grade 'stick' marijuana, most likely from Thailand, was recovered by Customs and DEA agents from the Makah Indian Reservation at the northwestern tip of the Olympic Peninsula at Neah Bay. Acting on an anonymous tip, the agents swarmed on the area and arrested several members of the Makah tribe, who were now being held pending further investigation. Included in the article were pictures of gunnysacks littering the beach and the picture of a Ryder truck clearly stuck in the mud. The back door of the truck was open and several agents were unloading gunnies. It was reported that 60 gunnies were recovered from the beach and another 230 were recovered from the truck. It was also reported that various pieces of military equipment were recovered from the scene, among them were two infrared 'starlight' night vision scopes plus several canteens and flashlights. Other suspects were being sought.

I cringed as I read the article. I then departed for my truck where Joe and Rico were waiting in the parking lot. The part about 'other suspects being sought' definitely had all of us worried.

"I'll bet we could have saved at least our share, Rick," Joe said.

"I know. You're probably right," I responded. "This article says that they didn't find the load until the afternoon. For Christ sakes, it just sat there for ten or twelve hours. It seems like the sun came up, as it always does, and these yellow bellied cocksuckers just chickened out and ran. I know we'd have done what it takes to save the load. I just can't figure out why they ran."

"I'm sure we'll find out, but they really fucked us," said Joe. "I just wish you would have required we have our people with them to protect our interests, like Ciro did with Wozenberg, way back when."

"Well, if wishes were fishes, we'd have a fish fry until we were sick and throwing up fish," I joked. "Remember, it was Pat who made this deal with the Coronado Company

---

1 Referenced Newspaper Articles, Item 2, Page 529.

and I only took over when he bailed and threatened to leave everyone in the lurch. Seems like both of us were so mesmerized by such a high tech proposal, we neglected to question such things like 'Plan B' or requiring our people to accompany the load when it was in their possession. Maybe if we were in charge from the get-go, we could have insisted on that. I guess, for now, we'll just have to deal with what we get and figure out where to go from here. What else can we do?"

When we arrived in the North San Diego area I called Stan who told me the coast was clear and the load had just arrived. Upon arriving at Stan's house in the hills outside the town of Vista, we were met by Bob, Eddie, Dave, Stan and the two drivers who drove the pickups down from Washington. Dave, who we later found out to be David Vaughn, seemed to be out of place as a drug trafficker. He appeared to be more like a wannabe businessman than a marijuana smuggler. He was tall with dark hair which was perfectly combed and neatly parted on his right side. He had on a Brooks-Brothers button down collar long sleeved white dress shirt and a pair of new Levi's perfectly pressed with a creases running down the front of his legs. His dark socks and shiny slip-on loafers didn't quite exude one who had just spent the previous night in the rain trying to save the load on the beach. He had a clipboard in his left hand which had a sheaf of notes attached to it and a thin gold Cross pen in his right.

We went into Stan's garage where the load, or what was left of it, was stacked neatly against the wall. Dave began to explain and report exactly what had happened. He glanced down at his notes, then recited his spiel:

"The ship stood off the unloading zone for five days. For three days, she came inside the twelve mile limit with all the weed up on deck loaded in the steel cages, ready for the chopper pick up. But the fog just hung there, like a thick blanket. The choppers never sighted the ship, and on the ship even though they could hear the whoomp, whoomp, whoomp sound of the helicopters somewhere above them, they never sighted the choppers. They were in radio communication with each other. Believe me, the helicopter crew wanted to make the pick up as badly as the boat crew wanted the shit off the boat, but with the fog right on the deck it just wasn't possible without risking the lives of everyone involved. The helicopter pilots even attempted a blind pick up, by lowering the hook towards the boat without actually making visual contact, and came so close to the water trying to see the boat they nearly put one of the Chinooks in the drink. After the third day, the helicopter crew informed us that the Chinooks were no longer available due to a change of orders in the duty roster, something the helicopter crew had no control over. It came from upstairs in the military ranks and took us completely by surprise.

"However, that wasn't our only problem.

"With each passing day of failed unloading attempts, the boat crew began to get more and more paranoid and anxious of being sighted and busted. You see, they had to come into the pick up zone at around three miles off the coast, bring the load up on deck, put it into the steel cages and wait there basically with their pants down for all the world to see for a couple of hours while the helicopters hovered, then had to abort each day and re-stow the load and return to back outside the twelve mile limit. After the third day of this routine, the ship's crew were at their wit's end and were threat-ening mutiny. We were in daily contact with them, twice a day as a matter of fact, from our station out in Borrego Springs, and our radio operator reported that the boat crew was going to jettison the load overboard if there was another failed attempt, as they felt sure they had been sighted and reported. I told them, through our radio operator, to just go out and hover for a few days as I had already arranged an alternate plan. To that request, I was given an ultimatum: 'Get this shit off the boat immediately or it goes over the side.'

"Meanwhile, I had already surveyed the entire Olympic Peninsula coast and had found a suitable alternative unloading spot up at the tip at Neah Bay. I then negotiated with the Makah Indians to unload on their Neah Bay reservation with our help. They were willing to do it, but only had longboats used for fishing. Each of their boats were only able to carry about 6 or 7 gunnies, so the unloading with their boats would take all night or longer. We had, however, brought our portable raft and Zodiac with us which was able to transport the bulk of the load from the ship to the beach. The situation seemed, at that point, to be under control, but the weather just wouldn't cooperate. It had deteriorated from dense fog to a steady rain. I told them the weather was supposed to break in the next couple of days, but the crew demanded we proceed with the offload that night, regardless of the weather… so we did. What choice did we have?"

At that point in the story, I just couldn't contain myself any longer and I interrupted, directing my attention fully to Bob and Eddie rather than Dave, the storyteller. "What choice? If you had balls or were in a real position of authority, like Ed used to be, the boat crew might have respected you and listened to your request. I just wish you had let us be there and I'm particularly disturbed that the rest of you weren't on location. I never envisioned that either of you would have had the gall to turn over all of our futures to your flunkies, or even worse to a bunch of inexperienced Indians who you just met. No one who had any real serious financial stake in the operation was even there. What the fuck? I just assumed you guys would always be there, like before… as you required me to be there and personally take responsibility on my end, which 'Stan the man' right here will attest to."

"Hold on a sec, Rick," said Bob rather defensively. "Dave here isn't just some flunky. He's been one of our most trusted lieutenants almost since we started in this business."

"Yeah, maybe so, but he sure ain't no Ed Otero," I said. Looking at Ed, I continued, "You're the beach commander and I can't imagine you'd just run at the first sign of day-light and leave a goddamned mess like this. You'd fight to the death to get this done and not just run like a fucking coward, like Dave here did."

"What did you just say?" Dave said with an agitated look on his face.

"I said, you're a fucking coward!"

At those words, Dave Vaughn jumped to his feet and approached me with fists clenched, at which point Joe, a few inches shorter than Dave but much more stocky, and Rico at nearly 6'6" tall and 275 pounds, sprang up and intercepted Dave's approach.

"Whoa boys, let's settle down. This isn't going to get us anywhere," Stan said, in his mellow way, trying to calm everyone down. "Let's let Dave finish the report. OK?"

"Well, what's happened has happened and there's nothing to be done further at this point, except to pick up the pieces and go on from here," Dave said. "But let me finish telling you what happened."

"Sorry, continue." I said.

"OK. Now, where was I? Oh yeah, the crew demanded we offload that night, regardless of the weather, so we did. The surf was huge and there was a riptide in the cove where we were going to unload. It was raining and very dark. The Indians in their long-boats managed to get some of the bales safely ashore. Fuzzy here took our raft towed by the Zodiac out to the mother ship," Dave said pointing with his clipboard at the curly haired giant of a man who had been silently standing against the garage wall. "The boat crew then transferred about 250 gunnies onto the raft and, with Fuzzy manning the Zodiac with the raft in tow, they started for shore. Several of the longboats were loaded as well and as the raft got to about a hundred feet from shore, it got caught in the rip-tide just as an eight foot wave closed out underneath the raft. Fuzzy and the load went crashing onto the beach and the rocks at the south end of the cove. It's lucky Fuzzy wasn't crushed or killed."

Dave paused, took off his tortoiseshell glasses and rubbed the bridge of his nose. He took a long sip from a green Perrier bottle. The room was as silent as Tutankhamen's tomb.

He put his glasses back on and continued. "The rest of the load was successfully brought ashore in the longboats and loaded into waiting pickup trucks at the water's edge. Two of our people were posted at lookout points with night scopes overlooking the beach and saw the whole mess happen before their eyes. There were gunnies strewn all over the south end of the beach and on the rocks and some floating in the surf. Our guys and the Indians scrambled to salvage most of the gunnies and dragged them ashore. We couldn't see all of them and some must have just been left on the rocks and on the beach, but most of them were put into the large Ryder rental truck waiting at the end of the beach on the dirt road. As the truck pulled away loaded with about 200 or so gunnies, it skidded off of the slick rain soaked dirt road and into a ditch. The driver, Fuzzy here, got out and tried to open the large cargo door in the back of the truck to attempt to transfer the load, but the entire back of the truck tweaked and wouldn't allow the cargo door to open because of the weird angle of the truck stuck in the mud. By this time it was about six in the morning and getting light and I realized there was nothing more we could do, so we split the scene and at least got what we already had into the first two pickups. They left everything else on the beach and just got away with the ton and a half we have here," said Dave pointing at the 55 gunnies stacked next to him.

"On my way down here, I stopped by the LA Airport and picked up this morning's edition of the Seattle newspaper," I said. "This story and these pictures tell what happened. From what appears in this paper, it looks like the cops didn't find the load until about three in the afternoon. You say you left the scene at around six, so I'd say you had at least nine hours to bail this situation out, but for the life of me, I can't understand why you guys just ran away."

"I guess it's like this," said Bob. "In 1978 we did a scam and got popped. That's why none of us were on location in Washington when this happened. Most of us were on probation from that bust and some of us are still fugitives and couldn't risk getting caught at the scene."

"Son of a bitch! I can't believe what I'm hearing, Bob," I said, my face turning red with anger. "You mean to tell me you guys were hot and didn't tell me, plus you wouldn't let me take some of my 'responsible' people up to assist in the unloading. You were supposed to be responsible… professionals, as you put it… the best in the business, to quote you. You lied to me. The truth of the matter is, you guys operated like a bunch of armchair quarterbacks. It's like you were running the scam by remote control… from your nice cozy mansions. You got too high-tech and forgot about the basics and your people just turned tail and ran at the first sign of danger. It all makes sense now. There wasn't anybody responsible on location to bail out the unloading and get the boat crew under control. Lemme tell you all something. We might not be as sophisticated as you guys, but five years ago when we had our backs against the wall, we hung in there and bailed it. The cops were everywhere, but we had the balls and determination to take a chance and we pulled it off. You guys weren't there and your flunkies ran at the first sign of trouble and nobody was there to even try and save the load… at least no one who was responsible. You guys are fucked. You and your high-tech bullshit," I said, sneering in disgust.

Nobody moved. In the silence which followed, I could sense the other men's embarrassment. Bob finally spoke.

"All right, Rick. You've spoken and I acknowledge that we blew it, but please, calm down," Bob said. "But listen. Usually when a load goes down, all is lost and everybody goes to the slammer. You guys haven't experienced it… yet. Look at it that way."

"The newspaper said two of the Makah Indians have been arrested. I'm not real comfortable about that. I'm sure they'll talk, so I doubt we've heard the end of this," I said, now trying to calm down a bit.

"Well, I don't think they can tell the cops too much. They really didn't know anything about us, where we're from or what our names are. So we're pretty safe. We still managed to save about 2800 pounds, so it's not a total loss. At 40%, that gives you about 1100 or so pounds. It's better than nothing," Dave said.

"Wait a minute!" I snapped. "Since my people did their jobs by acquiring, packaging and storing the load and successfully loaded your boat, and since your people lost most of the load, I think the percentages should be reversed. I think we deserve the 60% and you guys get the 40%. We've still got the Thais to deal with."

"Hold on a second, Rick. Give us a minute to confer about this," Bob responded as he, Ed and Dave left the room. They returned momentarily.

"How about if we just split it 50/50? That's about 1400 pounds apiece. The weed is so good we can probably sell if for two grand a pound, which comes to about 2.8 mil. That's better than a poke in the eye with a sharp stick," Bob said.

"Well, I feel like I just got poked in the stomach with a dull one, but I guess that's fair. Right now, I need to take our share and get outta here. I don't know what I'll tell our investors or the Thais. I'm probably finished as far as future loads go," I said.

"Rick, I'm sure the Thais understand, loads are sometimes lost. It's part of the nature of this business. Shit, they even lost one load over in Thailand this year. It happens. You are a good man, Rick. You know how to score the highest quality loads. And from what Stan told us, the Thais greatly respect you. We'd sure like to work again with you," Eddie finally said.

"There's no way in hell I'd work with you guys again, unless you get up off your collective asses and actually participated in the front trenches. I will only work with people who are totally involved on their end. Right now, I can't think about the future. I want to get our share safely home and regroup to see where we are. I'll get back to you in a week or so, when I've had a chance to settle down and digest the situation." Now I fully understood why the Coronado boys were so paranoid about everything… they were hot fugitives and had been so for at least two years. I felt like a mushroom, kept in the dark and fed a load of shit!

The 1400 pounds was loaded into Joe's truck with Rico riding shotgun. I followed in my truck on the long drive north to the Santa Rosa stash house. The following morning the load arrived and was inventoried, weighed and readied for sale. Even Willie came up for air and helped with the process. I then contacted 'Yorktown' Billy. The formerly pudgy bearded man with the Fedora hat had retired and moved up to the Fort Bragg area on California's Mendocino Coast. He now appeared as a mere shadow of his former self. He was now cleanshaven, fit, trim and muscular. He'd lost nearly fifty pounds, bought a fishing boat and had become a commercial salmon fisherman. Through much finesse, I was able to lure Billy back into the business to sell this particular load. In addition, I was able to up the price to $1,750 per pound, a $100 increase from before. Billy understood that I had to try and max out the price in order to be able to pay back the investors and the Thais. He grumbled as did his customers who really didn't care about my problems, but given the quality, he and his customers reluctantly agreed. The load was sold within two weeks.

It was during this two week time period that a crazy coincidence occurred at the Santa Rosa stash house. With the load safely stored in the attic, Willie received a call from the real estate agent requesting a house showing for the following day. The agent and his clients showed up at two the following afternoon and Willie answered the door to let them in.

"What a surprise. What are you doing here?" said an astonished and bewildered Willie, as he stood face-to-face with the eldest of my two younger sisters and her husband standing next to her along with the Century 21 real estate agent.

"We're out house hunting and this house is on our list. Question is, what are you doing here? This is just like old home week. Isn't it?" she answered, referring to the fact that our families had grown up across the street from each other in San Francisco.

"Um… well," said Willie, caught off guard, but regaining his composure. "I rented this vacation house for a couple of months. I needed a break from working fifteen hour days at the store. This is the perfect getaway. Come on in and have a look around."

My sister called me and told me about the surprise visit.

"I'll check it out," I said. "Knowing Willie, I'm surprised there weren't naked women swinging from the chandeliers."

"Well, if there were, we didn't see any. But, it was a beautiful place, out in the country. Maybe we'll buy it. He's a lucky guy to get so much time off."

"Right!" I said, thinking, 'hopefully we'll have the load out of there by then.'

* * *

I still owed Tony and the Thai crew about two million dollars, which I couldn't pay. Everybody including the investors would have to take a severe cut in their anticipated profits. Even with over two and a half million dollars of my share of the load, there just wouldn't be enough money to make everybody happy. Nobody would make nearly what they had anticipated, but I rationalized using Bob Lahodny's logic that at least it would be better than what usually happened when a load was lost.

On the phone with Tony who was in Thailand, I explained as best I could in code exactly what had happened. Tony already knew, as the story had already hit the newspapers in Thailand. He was very understanding and said that he would be coming to the States shortly and then we could settle everything.

"No worry, Rick. Everything be OK. At least you no have big problems. You not in jail. No worry. We fix everything when I get there," Tony said enthusiastically and upbeat as usual.

In the end, I was able to pay back all of the investors their principal plus a 50% profit, Willie and Joe got their salaries as promised and the Thais received about 35% of what they were expecting. No one was really happy about the results as they were much less than expected, but, then again, no one really complained as they all understood the risks associated with such a venture and that the alternative could have been much worse. The only one who really came out on the short end of the stick was me, for all the effort I had personally put into the trip. I had spent nearly six months in Thailand putting together the entire load and expected a very handsome seven figure return for my efforts and investment. Instead, I netted a mere fraction of that, barely covering my up front costs. I rationalized that I could have just as easily come out without anything, but it left me with an empty and unfulfilled feeling. I really wanted now more than anything to try again… only this time I was determined not to fail and the only way to do that was, in my opinion, to do it all myself and only with my own trusted people. Failure was not an option!

Chapter 36

Vegas

September 1980

Tony the Thai called me and said he was in Hawaii and he'd be in California the following week. He said he was vacationing there… in fact he was meeting with Ciro on the Island of Maui where Ciro had a waterfront home. Ciro was paying Tony for his share of the load which they had done earlier in the year. Ciro met with Tony then sent his two main gofers, Jeff and Brad, to Hong Kong with Tony's share plus enough for another load the following year. Tony then proceeded to California to meet with me.

Following the debacle in Washington, life on the home front was changing for me. Cindy's dependence on alcohol and drugs was manifesting itself in ways that were affecting both her attitude and character as well as our relationship. The funny, witty and carefree demeanor that originally attracted me to Cindy were gone and were replaced with a caustic, moody, angry, bitter, paranoid and hyper-critical bent that was driving me away from her. Even her appearance was being affected. The once cute, bubbly, loving and radiant personality that used to personify her being had now morphed into something totally alien and unrecognizable to me and with each passing day I couldn't help but feeling increasingly rejected, isolated and pushed away. It was becoming as clear as the nose on my face that something had to change and it was seemingly quite obvious that the feeling was mutual. She was also becoming less tolerant of my further forays and escapades into the world of international drug smuggling. Apparently, since the death of Papi, she was finding more solace in her use of drugs to escape the loneliness she felt due to my travels and my neglect of her needs. Sure, I would shower her with expensive gifts like cars and jewelry, but she felt it was more of an attempt to buy her off rather than share my life with her. She became more and more resentful and more abusive in her criticism of me, my methods, my friends and my business. I also noticed that my friends and associates saw it as well and became less frequent visitors to our home.

In my determination to be successful, I was guilty of neglect as well. Often, I felt the need to just get away from Cindy's barrage of attacks on me. I would regularly travel down to Vista to visit with Stan, whose mellow personality and commonality of purpose with mine was becoming the basis of a longstanding friendship, as well as a refuge away from Cindy and her rants.

One particular event exemplifying her changed behavior occurred one evening while at a friend's party where Cindy had been seemingly enjoying herself while drinking glass after glass of wine. Suddenly without warning she erratically went off on me. "I wanna leave right now," she angrily demanded. So we left. However once we had departed and were in the small confines of her new 450 SL Mercedes, her drunken abuse continued and devolved into her screaming into my face. "You bastard. You ignored me the whole time we were at the party. You never pay any attention to me anymore. I hate what you've become," she raged.

In my typical, without thinking, sarcastic response I retorted, "Jeez Cindy, what's your problem? Can't you just mellow out, relax and have fun like we used to?" This only exacerbated the situation and was like pouring gasoline on an already raging bonfire whereupon Cindy commenced flailing at me with fists clenched into my face. I would never retaliate in such a way towards any woman. It's not in my nature. However in an attempt to defend myself from her physical onslaught in the cramped space where we were sitting I accidentally, while trying to block a punch aimed at my nose, tore her favorite Balinese blouse she was wearing.

"Sorry, I didn't mean to do that," I sheepishly blurted realizing what I had just done and seeing a piece of the torn fabric now resting in my outstretched hand just as we started to drive home. She burst into tears and relented but I was shaken to the core of my being and knew that this was probably the beginning of the end of our relationship. To me the baffling paradox in all this was that she was benefitting greatly in her lifestyle from what I was doing while at the same time she was constantly putting me down and raging at me for actually doing it. At that point I just had to get away.

Visiting Stan's house in Vista, I couldn't help but notice all the Buddhist religious artifacts adorning every room of the ranch-style house. There were numerous statues of Buddha, as well as Tibetan thangkas, Oriental carpets and shrines seemingly everywhere surrounded by votive candles and burning incense sticks, giving off the sweet pungent smell of either patchouli or lavender.

Often there were visitors in residence wearing traditional Buddhist saffron robes who could frequently be heard chanting monotone Tibetan chants. One of his frequent guests, Stan told me, was a Tibetan high priest known as The Karmapa. Stan said he was the leader of one of the four major schools of Tibetan Buddhism and on a parallel religious hierarchy as the famed Dalai Lama. I was often curious about the monks who seemed to always be hanging around Stan's house and wondered if the whole scene was a true religious experience or if these 'holy' people were just more 'hangers-on' for the financial ride and, like others, gravitated to Stan's good nature, generosity, and his always 'footing the bill'.

It was on one of these visits that I was introduced to Stan's older sister, Tanya. We hit it off immediately and a torrid love affair soon followed.

Tanya was a pleasant change from Cindy. First with Tina, the Chinese actress, and now with Tanya, it seemed to be a fact: I had developed an affinity for Asian women, since I had spent a great deal of time in the Orient during the past seven years. Tanya was very mellow and easygoing. She was about 5'1" tall, very petite, had a beautifully proportioned hourglass figure and long raven colored hair. She had dark alluring eyes and a quick sense of humor. She was very spiritual in nature and often intensely preoccupied with Buddhist religiosity. She had many books about the eastern religious teachings from such famous spiritual gurus as Baba Ram Das and Paramahansa Yogananda. As an outsider, I never totally bought into it but was enthralled with the calming, happy and carefree effect it seemed to have on Tanya. It was a relief and welcome change from what I was used to at home and I liked it.

I soon found myself making excuses to Cindy. I would tell her that I had to go to San Diego for one reason or another to visit and strategize with Stan, when in actuality I was going to be with Tanya. Maybe I was just trying to get away from Cindy's verbal and mental abuse. In addition to his house in the hills in North San Diego County, Stan also had a condominium at LaCosta, the world-class chic resort and spa located some 35 miles north of San Diego in the coastal town of Carlsbad. Tanya and I would stay in Stan's condo whenever we were together. It was like staying in a fashionable hotel with 24-hour room service.

Tanya was very open and I found it very easy to talk to her about anything; as a matter of fact, I had never met anyone who I could converse with so openly. Soon, I found myself growing closer and closer to Tanya and I began to wonder if this was something which would last. Unlike my old friend Willie, I was starting to feel guilty about having an affair behind Cindy's back. I could feel that at some point, I might have to make a decision as to who I wanted to be with, my girlfriend Tanya or my wife Cindy. The only thing which sort of scared me was that Tanya was flighty. Stan had warned me that she might have more than one boyfriend at the same time.

When Tony arrived in Menlo Park, I decided, it would be best to travel to San Diego with him to visit our friend Stan. It would be a more conducive setting for Tony and the weather was warmer down south. Tony liked Hawaii and the warmer climates more like Thailand, rather than Tahoe or other parts of Northern California. On the way to San Diego, I explained to Tony exactly what had happened and about the fiasco in Washington. Tony didn't seem too bothered about the mishap and said we would try again next year… maybe without the Coronado Company. I could do it again myself, like the old days. Tony said he would guarantee another load for me next year in which I should be able to make up what was lost at Neah Bay, if I agreed to pay the Thais an additional million to cover the loss they had incurred this year.

In his usual upbeat way, Tony said, "No worry, Rick. You make plenty money next year. You work with Stan. No work with Coronado people. You two guys make big money. No problem."

* * *

Tony and I arrived at Stan's house at about 9:00 on a late September evening. The weather was clear and balmy as it was normally in the late summer. We were warmly greeted on our arrival by Stan and Joe, who happened to be in San Diego at the time and who Stan had invited along.

"I've got a surprise for you," said Stan. "We're going to Vegas to have some fun. I have connections there and we can get anything we want."

At Stan's direction, the Lear 35 was standing by at the Palomar Airport in North San Diego County. At about 11:30 in the evening, Stan, Joe, Tony and I boarded the Lear for the half hour flight to Las Vegas. Although Tony had been to the United States before to visit Ciro, private jets were a new experience to him and right away I could tell that Tony was thoroughly enjoying himself and really looking forward to visiting Las Vegas… in Tony's eyes, the mecca of gambling and women. A dream of Asian men the world over.

The flight across Southern California was over in a heartbeat and upon our arrival we were greeted by a stretch limousine waiting at the foot of the stairs as we disembarked from the Lear. There was a bar in the limo and Tony poured himself a snifter of cognac en-route to Caesar's Palace. This was the first time I'd ever seen Tony drink any alcohol whatsoever. Tony had once explained to me that he couldn't drink anymore because he had been quite indulgent as a young man and the alcohol had damaged his esophagus and stomach. He said he had had many surgeries to correct the problem, but it left him with a virtual roadmap of scars on his torso from just below his throat down to his waistline.

"Tony," I said. "You told me that you couldn't drink. Are you sure it's OK?"

"Oh, Rick. You worry too much," Tony replied. "Just a little cognac. OK for me. Have problem many years ago. Now OK. No worry. No problem for me."

"Well, just go easy on it. You're a good friend and I don't want anything bad to happen to you."

Tony just shrugged it off nonchalantly. "Rick, you like a mother hen. I told you, it no problem for me. Just a little cognac. No hurt no one. Just relax. Now we gonna have fun in Las Vegas."

Now Stan was really in his element and had everything covered. After departing the private terminal at the Las Vegas airport we were then chauffeured for the ten minute drive down the Las Vegas strip and over to Caesar's, one of the most fashionable mega-resorts in 'Sin City'. There was no check-in at the registration counter as normally was the case; our quartet was merely greeted at curbside by the concierge who took our luggage and whisked us to the top floor penthouse.

The setting was palatial; neither Joe or myself or Tony had ever seen anything like it before. This was no typical hotel room or suite. I'd stayed in some of the finest hotels in Europe and Asia, but nothing compared to this. As we entered I had the feeling I was in the foyer of a mansion. Marble floors, gold fixtures everywhere and a grand spiral staircase leading upstairs.

"I hope everything is in order and to your liking, Mr. Yamamoto," said the concierge with a noticeable British accent.

"Splendid, as usual Manchester," replied Stan. "I think some room service would be in order. My friends are hungry… we haven't eaten dinner yet. What can we get at this hour?"

"I'll prepare anything you like, Mr. Yamamoto. Why don't you have a look at the menu here while I make up the dinner table in your dining room."

The concierge went through a door to the left in the penthouse and set up the table while the four of us selected orders of lobster and Chateaubriand, a bottle of Dom Perignon, a bottle of Chateau Lafitte Rothschild, a caesar salad for four and a special dessert of baked white cake topped with ice cream and meringue known as Baked Alaska.

"Dinner will be served in 15 minutes, gentlemen. Why don't you just make yourselves at home. I'll return shortly," said Manchester. As he departed, Stan shook his hand and surreptitiously give him a one hundred dollar bill which was folded and transferred upon the handshake.

"Let's have a look around. This place is outrageous," I said in amazement. I went upstairs where there were two huge staterooms, each with a king sized bed and mirrors on the walls and ceilings. Each had a widescreen television and VCR and each had adjoining marble laden bathrooms complete with jacuzzi spas and gold fixtures including toilet, bidet, glass walled showers and heated towel warmers. The two staterooms were connected by a large common living room which separated them from each other for complete privacy. The living room was decorated with the finest leather furniture and marble tables. There was a bar in one corner of the living room. The view was magnificent. I opened the sliding glass door and went out onto the balcony, where I stood transfixed at the splendor of the Las Vegas strip with its brilliant lights extending away from my feet and into the distance. Downstairs, there were two more staterooms located off either side of the dining room just like the ones upstairs. By simply rearranging a few chairs and adding a leaf to the mahogany side table, Manchester had converted the living room into a dining room fit for a king, complete with sterling silverware and fine crystal stemware.

"First we'll eat then get some ladies up here in an hour or so. Will that be OK with you Tony?" asked Stan with kind of a shit-eating grin on his face.

"OK for me. Maybe can get nice blonde for me… would like one who have 'moitong'," laughed Tony referring to the Thai word for blonde pubic hair.

"How many would you like?" queried Stan. "Two, three, four… whatever you want. Maybe one blonde with blonde pubic hair, one redhead with red pubic hair and one green head with green pubic hair."

"No like green pubic hair… only want natural color," answered Tony. He then got a rather quizzical sort of serious look on his face. "They have natural green hair here in Vegas? I never see that before."

"No problem. Anything!" answered Stan. "I can get anything for you. You can do anything you like. You're gonna have a good time, Tony. Live your fantasy here… you too Rick. What kind of women do you want?"

"Oh, let's see. I think I'd like to start with one at a time. You know, kind of ease into it. Let me start with a real tall one, long legs, beautiful and really nice are my only requirements for the moment."

Then Joe chimed in, "Stan, I'm not too particular, but I'd like something real exotic and different."

"No problem. I can handle it all," answered Stan. "Joe, I've got something real special for you in mind. Exotic, eh!"

"Let's see… it's about midnight now. I think I'll have the ladies up here at about 1 or 1:15. That should give us plenty of time to eat and relax a bit. From then on we'll play it by ear," said Stan as he picked up the phone to place his order.

"Hello, Francis… Stan Y. here. We need about six of your finest here in an hour or hour and half. Remember the blonde and redhead from the dance show going on at the MGM last time I was here. The real beauties doing the special dance in the cage… are they available this evening? That would sure make my friend Tony very happy. He's visiting us from the Orient and wants to be treated to a real nice time on his visit here. Think you can handle that? Great. And the tall raven haired girl, I think her name is Chrissy. You know who I mean. She works at the front desk at the Stardust. I think my friend Rick would go crazy with her. I better tell him to be careful. He might fall in love. Great. And for me… let's see. Fran, why don't you just surprise me. If there's one person I can trust in this department, it's you. You've never let me down. Great. One more thing Fran. Remember the lead singer of that hot new rock group in town? I think they're called 'The Soul Sisters' or something like that. Yeah, that's the one. She still in town? Fantastic. I've got a real special friend here, Joe. He'd love to rock and roll with her. Right on. We'll see them at 1:15 or so, if that works for you? Great. We're in my usual penthouse at Caesar's. If we need more or others, I'll let you know in a while. Thanks a million, honey." Stan hung up the phone.

There was a soft knock on the door. "That's Manchester. Let's eat now, so we'll be ready for later," laughed Stan.

The food arrived and was served on silver platters. First we drank the champagne and toasted to the upcoming year and to a new partnership in business. Stan, Tony and I were joining forces for the upcoming smuggle. This year would be a good year and, having learned from the previous year's debacle, we vowed to keep it simple and not make the same mistakes again. We ate dinner and talked of the future.

Manchester had turned on the stereo and the sound of soft rock music filled the room. Appropriately, the music of the Eagles' hit *Hotel California*[1] was playing:

> '…Welcome to the Hotel California, such a lovely place
> They livin' it up at the Hotel California, what a nice surprise, bring your alibis…'

After we finished dinner and Manchester had cleared the table and departed, Stan went to his briefcase and proffered an envelope which bulged curiously in the center. He opened it and deposited a glistening rock of cocaine on the glass top coffee table. As he broke off a flake and started to meticulously chop it into long slender lines, a soft knock was heard at the door to the suite. Stan looked at his gold Rolex… it was exactly 1:15 AM.

---

1 Referenced Songs & Music, Item 12, Page 531.

"Right on time," Stan said. "Why don't you let them in, Tony?"

"Me? OK," said Tony, slightly blushing.

"Well, hello. You must be Tony," said the gorgeous redhead standing closest to the door. I'm Crystal and this is Celeste," she said introducing the ravishing blonde to her right. "Mind if we join you… we just happened to be in the neighborhood and thought you guys might need some company. This is Chrissy, April and Stormy," she said motioning to the three beauties standing right behind her.

"Oh, come in. Nice to meet you," said Tony haltingly, while trying to use his best, non-broken English extending his hand to Crystal. She shook his hand, pulled herself gently towards him and lightly planted an affectionate kiss on his lips.

From the table in the background Stan said, "Hi, ladies. Look what we've got for you. Come on in and have a seat. Rick this is Chrissy. What do you think? And Joe, I'd like you to meet Sugar. Sugar this is my good friend Joe." Sugar appeared to be half black and half Asian. Indeed she was the most exotic fox Joe had ever laid eyes on… virtually panting in anticipation, he just couldn't wait.

"Sugar, lets adjourn to the room next door. I've got some serious business to attend to with you. It just can't wait," Joe said, his eyes almost popping out of their sockets and tiny bubbles of spittle appearing at the corners of his mouth.

"Sure baby… let's do it," replied Sugar, as Joe grabbed her hand and led her to the first bedroom to the right off the living room, which Manchester had just converted back from the dining room setting. Joe grabbed a quick snort, but Sugar declined, saying she didn't do drugs because of her singing voice.

I immediately blushed, turning six shades of red, and was caught off guard for a moment and at a loss for words. I quickly regained my composure and looked up at the raven-haired beauty towering over me, at nearly 6'4" tall. She was slender with a great evenly proportioned figure with waist-length jet black hair pulled back and braided down her back. She had high cheekbones and was almost surely a professional model, I thought. She was dressed to the nines, in all black with a leather skirt which stopped just above the knees. She wore black high heeled shoes with pointed toes, black sheer stockings and completed the ensemble with a rather tight fitting black crocheted knit sweater open at the neckline to reveal the top inch or so of a well defined cleavage. She had a pair of ruby earrings which perfectly matched her red lipstick, accentuating her rather pouty lips. She was the most gorgeous creature I had ever laid eyes on.

"Hi Rick," she said. Her voice was warm, friendly and very sexy. She took a seat next to me and spied the pile of coke on the table. "May I?" she coquettishly asked.

"By all means. That's what it's there for. Help yourself," I said handing Chrissy a rolled up one hundred dollar bill. Each of the ladies took turns at the neat lines of cocaine. We all did likewise. Stan chipped another flake off the rock and chopped new lines, replacing the ones which had just vanished.

"So, let's see, why don't you and Tony take the rooms upstairs," said Stan, gesturing to Tony and me. "I'll just hang out down here with April and Stormy."

"Sounds good to me," said Celeste as she took Tony's hand and led him up the grand staircase towards the right of the two upstairs penthouse suites. Crystal followed.

"What are we waiting for, Chrissy?" I asked.

"One more toot and we're off. OK, Rick?" said Chrissy as she bent to sniff one more line of coke.

"No problema... sweetheart... OK, let's go," I said. Hand in hand we ascended the staircase and disappeared into the suite on the left. I felt kind of embarrassed at first as the two of us looked like the comic book characters Mutt and Jeff as Chrissy towered nearly a foot above me. However, inside the suite, my embarrassment quickly melted away as I found Chrissy relaxed and very easy to talk to. She unbraided her beautiful raven hair, shook it out and let it cascade down her back. In a few minutes I too was relaxed, back to my usual animated self, letting the moment and our passions follow their natural course. After what seemed like an eternity of ecstasy, but in reality was probably only twenty minutes, the two of us lay in each other's arms bathed in each other's sweat.

"You know, Chrissy, I have a question for you. I hope you won't be angry with me for being so personal."

"No, go ahead Rick and fire away. You'll find I'm very open and honest."

"I know this sounds kind of trite, but I just can't understand why a beautiful woman like you would be, um... working like this, here in Vegas?"

"Rick, I rarely do this... only for special friends of Fran's. I normally do modeling part time and I have a full time position as the receptionist at the Stardust. Sometimes, I guess, I just get bored and like to have fun. This was just one of those times. Actually, Fran told me a week or so ago you guys might be coming and asked me if I'd be interested. I said 'sure'. So here I am. By the way, I'm ready to go again, if you are? Making love is sure a lot of fun with you."

The next hour was spent in bliss and later capped off with the two of us frolicking in the jacuzzi. At about 4:00 in the morning we emerged and, arm in arm, came downstairs. With a 'shit-eating' grin on my face, there was no question about it... I'm sure I looked like the cat who ate the canary.

"Rick, would you like to switch?" asked Stan who was sitting comfortably on the living room couch with the two remaining women snuggled up to him on either side. "April and Stormy here are 'the real deal.' Take my word for it, together they'll really knock your socks off. I guarantee it."

"No thanks, Stan. Although I appreciate the offer, I'll just stick with Chrissy here. She's all I can handle for the moment. Have you seen either Joe or Tony?"

"Yeah, Tony's down in the casino with Crystal," said Stan. "Turned out, he liked her much more than the blonde, Celeste. As for Joe, I haven't seen hide nor hair of him... although I did hear some rather loud moans coming from the room next door... they're probably sleeping it off now... I can only imagine he's exhausted by now. Sugar's a real ball of fire."

"I'll think we'll wander down to the casino and see if we can find Tony. Make sure he's not getting into any trouble," I said. "Come on Chrissy, let's go find Tony and Crystal."

"OK, sweetie... whatever you like." She took my hand and led me to the glass elevator at the end of the hallway. We rode the twenty-two floors down in silence gazing into each other's eyes. My neck was starting to ache from looking up into her hazel colored eyes as the door opened to reveal the ground floor casino awake amid a hubbub of activity. The smoke filled casino, awash with rows and rows of one-armed bandits and all night gamblers, seemed a blur to me as I walked through it with the gorgeous Chrissy on my arm and towering over me. I felt like a king and was sure all eyes in the casino were looking in my direction with awe at the sight of me, at an optimistic height of almost 5'5" tall with this giant of a woman on my arm. I couldn't care less what they thought, but it made me feel good. I hardly noticed the crowds and only had eyes for this tall beauty on my arm.

Soon we found Tony and Crystal at the roulette table. Tony had a stack of chips in front of him and was directing Crystal to put chips on his lucky numbers.

"I've only lost about $2000. Not bad, eh Rick. I love to gamble. No matter, win or lose. I love this," exclaimed Tony. "Crystal very good in bed, but no like 'moitong'," he said referring to the blonde pubic hair of Celeste. "She not gentle like Crystal. She play too rough. I send her away and stay with Crystal. Like red hair, better than 'moitong'. Crystal have red hair everywhere," Tony laughed as his number came up on the roulette wheel. He won back all he'd lost… and gave half his earnings to Crystal, who clung tighter to Tony's arm in her excitement.

We all returned to the penthouse for more coke and to continue where we'd left off.

We slept all day until three in the afternoon, whereupon the girls left as they had other pressing engagements. Chrissy told me she had to model for the next few days and wouldn't be available till the weekend if I wanted to see her again. I said I'd see what was on my schedule, but I'd try.

Joe finally emerged from the lower suite with Sugar and promptly sent her home. He looked completely drained. "She was great, but I'm bushed. I just can't take it anymore. She's an animal. That should last me for awhile."

"Don't we have to pay them?" I asked.

"Don't worry, I've taken care of everything. I put it on my charge account," laughed Stan.

* * *

The following evening Stan called the Palomar Airport and his Lear was waiting for us at Las Vegas for the return flight home. Once back at Stan's we strategized on the future trip and planned to start to work to organize it in the next two weeks. It was none too soon to get started. We had a lot of work to do to get ready. It was already the end of September and we had to be ready to load in February or March. This would be the optimum time to do the next scam.

Now I had to re-focus and begrudgingly with trepidation look forward to my return to Menlo Park and Cindy's anger, tirades and general bitchiness compounded by alcohol and drugs. It seemed to me like she was going through a steady diet of PMS every day of the year. I just couldn't wait to get back to the Far East and immerse myself in the future. I fantasized, 'Why couldn't I have someone like Tanya or even Chrissy in my life, instead of Cindy. Cindy's just not mellow anymore, like she used to be. I still love her, but with her drugs and alcohol, she's just out there and becoming an albatross around my neck. The drugs and alcohol are taking their toll on her. I just wish I could help her, but all I get is bitched at and badgered continually... no matter what I do.' I felt trapped as the words of *Hotel California* just kept running through my head:

'... Last thing I remember, I was running for the door
"You can check-out any time you like, but you can never leave!"

I thought, 'If Cindy had something to do, other than just sit around, maybe it might give her a purpose and she could use her creative talent to revive her and get back to her old self.'

Cindy and I discussed what she might like to do and we came upon the idea of a home remodeling project where she could be in charge of interior design. We searched and found an old home in disrepair located in the fashionable section of Woodside Hills, a few blocks away from where Pat lived, and bought the rundown mansion for what I considered a steal. I financed the purchase and project entirely through my company, save for a small cash down payment. We soon acquired possession and began the interior demolition. To oversee the demolition, I hired Cindy's younger brother Tad, who had relocated from Southern California and who was currently living in our guest house. It was a big job and I felt Cindy could use the help and some company during my anticipated absence.

With a renewed sense of confidence, bolstered by Tony the Thai's positive outlook toward the future, I set forth on a mission to accomplish the upcoming smuggling venture with a vengeance.

Chapter 37

Stone Cold Junkie

The first item of business was to locate a transport vehicle to carry the load back from Thailand to the States. Although Stan preferred to attempt a smuggle by air, Tony and I felt we should go again by sea and if it was successful we would research the possibility of a flight.

I was in Marin one evening having dinner with my old friend John 'JQ' Quinn, who had been doing coke trips from Colombia for the past two years and was looking for a change. I told him all about the fiasco in Washington and how I wasn't going to work again with the Coronado Company. JQ told me he had an old sailing buddy who had been sailing in the Far East for the past several years. He had a 54 foot motor sailer which was equipped for smuggling and had expressed an interest to JQ. Just three weeks prior, this boat captain had told JQ he wanted to sail a load of weed from Thailand and he was pretty much ready to go. His name was Michael Barrington. He was Canadian… a bit out there, but a hell of a sailor. His boat was presently in Singapore for some repairs, but he could be ready to sail within a month or two. I said I was very interested and asked JQ to contact him and set up a meeting.

Three days later, JQ contacted Barrington who was in Hawaii at the time. He said he would return to San Francisco in the next two days to meet with me, and he was definitely interested and would be ready to leave for the Far East immediately. This was great news. The only problem was, he was broke. This was not such great news.

I was reluctant to front any money to Michael. I didn't know this guy from Adam and certainly wasn't willing to just hand him a pile of money with no strings attached. So in order to facilitate the venture, JQ was hired on to manage any repairs to Michael's boat and to be part of the return sailing crew. In essence, JQ's role would be to watch over Michael and act as my direct representative for this part of the venture. I knew that at 6'5" tall and 230 pounds of pure muscle from the past two years of sailing the eastern Pacific, he could physically handle generally any situation which might arise. I'd known JQ for over a decade and had worked closely with him for years. He was very honest, responsible and loyal and despite what had happened to my cousin Marty,

I couldn't blame JQ for Marty's irresponsibility which had brought his world crashing down upon himself. JQ could be trusted and counted on and I felt secure having him on board. So, I gave him $50,000 which was to be used to acquire supplies and make repairs on the boat. JQ gave Michael $7,500 to get started and two days later Michael left for Singapore to begin to prepare his boat for the smuggling venture. JQ would be coming to Singapore to help within two weeks.

Meanwhile, I had spoken to 'Yorktown' Billy about the possibility of offloading a load onto his fishing boat if we worked again. Billy said it would be possible as he had been fishing the North Coast for the past several years and nobody up there knew of his past dealings in the drug business. It would be natural for him to handle the unloading as he was a regular at all the harbors in the area and nobody would think him out of place wherever he was fishing there. Also his honesty and loyalty were without question.

A few days later, with the wheels already set in motion and Michael off to Singapore to prepare the boat, Stan, JQ and I traveled north to the Mendocino Coast to visit 'Yorktown' Billy, see his setup and negotiate the offloading. Both Stan and JQ were impressed with Billy, his fishing situation and his boat. Offloading to a known fishing boat and going to a small secluded cove to bring the load ashore would be ideal. As opposed to what had happened last year at Neah Bay, we all agreed, this was what 'keeping it simple and going back to the basics' was all about. We could pull this off with a minimum of trusted people, and with the exception of Michael Barrington, I had known and had previously successfully worked with everyone who was to be involved. However, with JQ 'riding herd' on Michael, the only wild card in the equation, I felt pretty secure we could pull this off.

A strategy meeting was held to set up contact points with radio frequencies for ship to ship communication. JQ wanted to see the offloading and rendezvous points as he would be the person on the sailboat who would be contacting Billy to do the offloading. For his part of the scam, Billy would get one million dollars. Following the meeting, all seemed to be in order and now JQ could go to Singapore and facilitate getting the sailboat ready. Soon, Stan and I would go to Thailand and Singapore to make sure all was ready and to oversee the scoring of the load.

Back in Thailand, the rest of the Thai crew, other than Tony, was not too pleased with my performance the previous year. Charlie had argued with Tony; they had a very comfortable cushion of cash from Ciro's previously successful loads, so why should they take another chance with me, considering my less than favorable previous results. Tony argued that they should hedge their bets and not put all their eggs in one basket, and anything could happen. It would be better to have two different groups to work with, if something bad happened to either one. He further stressed that if they were both successful they would be all the richer. So Charlie acquiesced to Tony's logic and they prepared to do both smuggles. Additionally, on his last trip to the States, Tony had met with Mike Stallings at Ciro's request and had, at least preliminarily, agreed to do a trip with him in addition to the other two ventures already scheduled. As it turned out and unbeknownst to me at the time, since I didn't want to take another chance with the Coronado boys, Mike Stallings had negotiated with his old friend Bob Lahodny to procure a load for them... the third load of the upcoming '81 season. In addition to his own load, Ciro would also have a share of this third load. If all went as planned for Tony, each group would do four tons apiece. 1981 would be a twelve ton year for the Thai crew; indeed a banner year was forecast as the Thai and Laotian marijuana crop was at its all-time best. There was plenty of the top quality to be had and quite enough to go around.

The only problem Tony envisioned would be the increasing presence of the DEA in Southeast Asia to try and stem the prolific flow of drugs from the area back to the United States. Additional Thai military checkpoints were set up along all the main routes to Bangkok from the Golden Triangle area of Northwest Thailand, Northeast Burma and Southern Laos for the heroin traffic, and to Bangkok from the North Central and Northeast Thai regions around Sakon Nakhorn, Nong Khai and Udon Thani, the main marijuana growing areas of Thailand, and along the main transport route from Southern Laos into Northern Thailand across the Mekong River. The new U.S. policy of drug interdiction was primarily geared for this region, which was one of the main sources for illegal narcotics trafficking in the entire world.

To address this issue, Tony foresaw additional payoffs being required with more help needed from the military and provisional police units. Since he had close ties with the government, Tony put out calls for help to make sure the loads arrived safely down south to be packaged and stored at the durian farm and ready for loading. Tony decided a military convoy would be used, and larger shipments could be moved all at once, which would eliminate the need for many small trips, thereby reducing the exposure of the loads on the routes of transportation within Thailand.

November 1980

JQ arrived in Singapore about three weeks behind schedule, due to the fact he wanted to tie up some loose ends before departing for the Far East. He had planned to be gone for several months and expected to find Michael Barrington well under way in preparation for the sailing journey. Michael had already been in Singapore for nearly six weeks. JQ's arrival and immediate assessment of the situation in Singapore was much different from what he expected to find.

After checking into the Raffles Hotel, JQ went to Changi Yacht Club where he was to meet Michael. Not finding Michael at the Yacht Club bar where he expected him to be, JQ hired a skiff and had the boat driver deliver him to Michael's motor sailer which was moored at anchorage, adjacent to the club located at the mouth of the Johore Strait. The boat was only occupied by a cabin boy named Timor, hired by Michael to watch over the boat.

The boy was Asian, appeared to be about 15 years old, very dark complected and wearing only a pair of faded cut-off blue jeans, designer sunglasses and a New York Yankees baseball cap. JQ said, "Hi, I'm Michael's friend JQ from America... where's Michael?"

"Me Timor. I watch boat for Michael. Michael no here. He stay in Hotel Singapore not far from here. I no see Michael for five days."

JQ looked around the boat and it appeared as if nothing had been accomplished in preparation for the voyage. The boat was nowhere near ready. 'What the hell had he been doing for the past six weeks,' thought JQ to himself.

"I'll take a taxi to see Michael in the hotel. See you later, Timor."

JQ found the Hotel Singapore in what surely was the most sleazy part of town, and sure enough, Michael was registered there in room 461. It was 3:25 in the afternoon when he knocked on the door to room 461.

"Who da hell's zehr?" slurred a groggy voice from the other side of the door.

"Hey Michael, it's me JQ. Open up."

The door opened and there was Michael Barrington clad only in his white boxer undershorts which appeared to have been soiled with several yellowish colored urine stains in front. He was hardly recognizable and had deep circles under his eyes and appeared completely disheveled and unkempt. The room was dark as all the shades were drawn, and it was a minute before JQ's eyes adjusted to the darkness. He finally found the light switch and flipped it on. The bare fluorescent light in the center of the room flickered then came on. JQ was aghast at the sight before him.

On the nightstand was a needle, a spoon in a glass of brownish colored water, a hand-held portable torch and a bag of what appeared to be brown crystalline powder. JQ recoiled as the full realization of what he was seeing began to register in his mind. Michael was a stone cold heroin junkie and was completely strung out and in no shape for anything… much less to captain a ship across the ocean on a smuggling venture worth millions of dollars halfway around the world. This was somebody who was supposed to be responsible. Lives would be at stake and here was our trusted ship captain: a fucking mess! JQ had completely misjudged Michael and how the hell was he going to explain it to me? And what was his next move? The trip was already in motion on his representation of Michael… and now this. 'Holy shit', thought JQ. Rick and Stan would be arriving in Singapore in the next couple of weeks… maybe he could get things together before we arrived… these thoughts flashed in JQ's mind in the next few seconds, as he surveyed the situation in stunned silence.

Right then, the bathroom door opened and a woman covered only by a Hotel Singapore towel emerged. She had stringy dirty blonde matted hair which looked like it hadn't been washed in weeks and deep purple circles around her eyes appearing as if she'd been the recipient of a couple of jabs planted squarely into each eye socket.

"JQ, this is my wife, Lacy. I wanted her to come over and help me get the boat ready." Lacy stared blankly at JQ, as if looking right through him, then without a word, sat on the edge of the bed and lit a cigarette. No 'Hello'. No acknowledgment of JQ's presence in the room. No nothing. The cigarette just seemed to be stuck to her lower lip as she puffed on it and gazed in a stupefied trance into the black nothingness of the squalid room. Obviously, she was past the point of any speech or cognizant conversation and appeared to be in much worse shape than Michael himself.

"How the hell is she going to help you get the boat ready in her condition. For that matter, how are you going to get the boat ready. I was just at the boat and it looks like nothing has been done." JQ was on a tirade. "I'd say from the looks of it, you've spent the money I fronted you on junk. Now look at you. I trusted you to come over here and get started. You've really blown it, Michael. I don't see how we can go on from here. You expect me to put my life in your hands or entrust you with a load in your condition. You're nothing but a fucking junkie! I'll give you exactly one hour to meet me back at the boat or you're fired."

"But, JQ, please. I can explain… ," started Michael.

"Not another word, Michael. One hour at the boat, or you're history," said JQ, as he turned and stormed out of the room, slamming the door behind him as he left. The flimsy doorframe shook and the door nearly shattered.

In exactly one hour, they met on the boat and JQ had calmed down. Michael had miraculously recovered from his stupor and was cognizant of the situation and very lucid, showing no signs of his condition one hour previous. And to show JQ just how good a shape he was in, he did ten pull-ups on an overhead bar which was attached to the cabin top inside of the companionway.

"See, JQ, I can handle it, no problem. Lacy came over and we just partied for a few days that's all. I'm ready for work, right now," said Michael.

"Hold on a minute, Michael. It's great you can do pull-ups, but just what have you accomplished towards getting this boat ready since you've gotten here? And how much money is left of the $7,500 I gave you in San Francisco?"

"Well, I ordered some new sails, a new steering wheel for the helm, a new bin-nacle compass for the cockpit and a couple of new Lewmar self-tailing winches to be installed here in the cockpit for the jib sheets. All of the gear should be here this week. Had to put about a five grand deposit on all the stuff, plus about a couple of grand for plane tickets for Lacy and me and about $500 to party on… which wasn't really in the budget, but I'll pay you back, I promise."

Placated for the time being, JQ developed a 'wait and see' attitude towards Michael Barrington… but he didn't have to wait long to see Michael's true colors. JQ began to work in earnest on the boat; sanding and oiling the teak decks and making the many repairs to the rigging and hardware which were necessary to make the motor sailor sea-worthy for the upcoming transoceanic journey. Ten days into his work regimen, he was again hit with the reality: Michael was indeed very unreliable and untrustworthy. JQ found Michael had not used the money for down payments on sails, winches, etc. as he had represented to JQ on the day he arrived in Singapore; but instead had bought drugs, specifically heroin, with the funds.

While away from the boat to get a few supplies at the local ship chandlery, JQ returned earlier than expected to the boat and from the shore, viewing through his bin-oculars, he saw an unsavory local character aboard the yacht, shake Michael's hand and proceed to leave the boat. Very curious and suspicious as to what he had just witnessed, JQ waited for an opportunity to search the boat. It didn't take him long; later in the day he found, secreted at the bottom of the forepeak chain locker, what he feared most—a bag of heroin, a can of crystalline baby formula to cut the heroin, a scale and a stack of local currency. Michael had been dealing heroin from aboard the yacht.

The laws for such action in Singapore were the most severe in the world: death to drug dealers. At this point, JQ realized, not only was the trip in jeopardy, but indeed his very own freedom was at risk. This was the final straw. With Stan and me to arrive two days later, JQ had only one option left: to fire Michael, sever the relationship with him and preserve all of the remaining cash.

Upon our arrival in Singapore, JQ informed Stan and me of the situation with regard to Michael Barrington, but left the final decision up to me as to whether to fire Michael or try the best we could to work with him and salvage the trip. I saw no alternative but to let Michael go and try to seek other means of transportation for the load. I knew we just couldn't risk the trip with a liar and heroin addict, and I also realized we still had a few months to reconnoiter and regroup.

I warned JQ to be careful, so as not to leave Michael with any information which could later be used against us, should he try to tip off the DEA as to our plans after being jilted. Together we came up with a plan to tell Michael which would easily allow us to get out of the contract, without making him suspicious as to our true motives. It was decided that I would call a meeting to inform all of them that everybody had been busted in Thailand and the trip was called off indefinitely.

The following day, the meeting was held aboard Michael's yacht and Michael was informed there would be no trip this year, but next year was still possible to use his boat and his services. I said I was sorry, but with no possibility of scoring a load, his services weren't needed now. I gave Michael $2,500 for his trouble which gracefully and regrettably ended Michael Barrington's involvement.

As we departed the boat via the local water taxi, JQ turned around and looked at Michael Barrington's boat for the last time. What he saw was a fitting end to our involvement with this irresponsible drug addict. There in the distance was Michael's 54-foot motor sailer at anchor in the Singapore Straits, appearing naked and without a steering wheel, which, JQ found out, had been bartered off in trade for a few grams of heroin. It was a fitting final image to the Michael Barrington debacle.

What to do next?

There was still time for us to find another boat and get it ready for the trip. Meanwhile, everything was going like a finely tuned engine up in Thailand. It was now the middle of December and already two of the scheduled twelve tons had been scored, warehoused and readied for shipment. Tony was right on schedule. When I informed him of the problem in Singapore with Michael, Tony was his usual upbeat self.

"You have plenty time to find another boat… no problem. Rick you go to Hong Kong. Have plenty boats. You can find one. No worry," said Tony.

Stan, on the other hand, was becoming frustrated, and he was one to become easily sidetracked. In his quest to become a legitimate entrepreneur, he found himself 'easy pickins' for scam and con artists seeking investments for less than scrupulous characters. He was exemplary of the old adage, 'A fool and his money are soon parted'.

Stan had set up an investment company called International and Worldwide Investments, with its headquarters in Carlsbad, California, near his condominium at

LaCosta. He answered all kinds of solicitations appearing in the want ad sections of various financial magazines and newspapers. One such ad which he answered sought investors with a deposed former so-called strongman of the burgeoning Central African nation of Cameroon, located on the West Coast of Central Africa. Answering the ad, Stan was solicited by representatives who claimed they were acting on behalf of the deposed strongman Dr. Jeremy Chiumbo Dada. It was said, 'the good doctor' had contracts to riches beyond belief in Cameroon, which included natural resources such as gold, platinum, diamonds, gypsum and oil. Stan was soon to get sucked into a scheme which elicited millions of dollars from would-be investors guaranteeing them a percentage of the anticipated wealth derived from the contracts.

It was a complete sham, dragging Stan from Singapore, where he left JQ and me to find a new boat, to London, where he wined and dined Dr. Dada and his entourage for several months, to the tune of one and a half million dollars. He was promised over fifty million dollars when the 'phony' contracts came due, six months hence. They never did, but the ever optimistic wannabe entrepreneur never gave up hope the scam was real. Stan tried to get me to join him, but I refused, stating I would rather do one job well than spread myself too thin. I tried to get Stan to listen to reason by pleading with him that he was being scammed, but it fell on deaf ears... the same as when the actor Strother Martin said in a southern drawl to Paul Newman in the infamous line from a scene in the classic movie *Cool Hand Luke*:[1] "Wot we have he-yah, is fail-ya to commun-cate. Some men ya just cain't reach... !"

So, JQ and I sought to pursue a new sailing vessel and continue with the trip. Meanwhile, Stan said he would be available if we needed him, but for now, he said, he was going to follow through with the Africans to its conclusion, which he believed was just around the corner, and to 'riches beyond belief'.

* * *

JQ and I arrived in Hong Kong and checked into the prestigious Peninsula Hotel on the waterfront in Kowloon and set up headquarters. We procured yachting magazines for all of the Far East. We visited the Choy Lee Shipyards in Hong Kong and finally got a local yacht broker, Sir Malcolm Penwick, to help us in our search. We told him we were looking for a racing yacht we could campaign in both local and international ocean yacht races. Penwick was a ruddy-complected, old salt yachtsman from England who had migrated to the British Crown Colony of Hong Kong after serving with the British in India and Singapore during World War II. He was heavily decorated and knighted at the end of the War, but had been wounded as a POW and walked with a noticeable limp and with the aid of an ivory handled cane. He sported a clipped mustache and wore a black beret.

"I think I found you one, mates," Penwick said, calling me on the phone while I was in the middle of a nap on the afternoon of January 10th.

"That's great," I answered. "What is it?"

---

1 Referenced Television & Movies, Item 17, Page 533.

"She's a real beauty. Been raced both here and in Australia by her owner who's just ordered a new yacht. She's a Camper Nicholson 55 foot sloop. Built in the early '70s, she needs a bit of sprucing up and TLC, but she's still competitive. The boat's a winner. Won several races a few years back. You chaps might 'ave 'erd of her. She's named *Mamamouchi*. Pretty famous 'round these parts. We call 'er *Mama* for short. Owner's a real big shot here in the colony and wants a quarter mil for 'er, but I think we can get 'im down."

"When can we see her?" I asked.

"Morrow at 1300 hours. Righto blokes. Already set it up for you mates. She's berthed at the Royal Hong Kong Yacht Club. Meet me at my office here in Kowloon at noon tomorrow and we'll go together," said Penwick.

* * *

"I've never seen a more beautiful boat," I exclaimed.

"Righto. She's a bit tired but a real winner," Malcolm Penwick agreed. "She placed among the leaders in a couple of Manila to Hong Kong races as well as the Sidney to Hobart race in the mid-'70s. She's been cruised for the past couple of years. She has an extensive racing sail inventory and is complete with an aft cabin; the works."

"We'd like to take her for a test ride," added JQ. "Then pull her for an inspection of her hull and schedule a marine survey."

SV (Sailing Vessel) *Mamamouchi* when I first saw her berthed
at the Royal Hong Kong Yacht Club in early January 1981.

"Will do. I'll set it up," answered Penwick.

Later, back at the hotel, I said, "You know JQ, I know you've had quite a bit of sailing experience and I have personally as well, but if I'm going to make a purchase like this, there's one person whose opinion I respect above anyone else's and I'd like to get him involved at this point… that's Dave Killian. I know he's kind of a weirdo, but when it comes to his knowledge of sailing and boats, there's nobody I know of who has more experience than Killian."

JQ began to get defensive. "Well, maybe you need him more than me, Rick."

"Look, I didn't say that. I think I need you both. When I sailed with him he needed to be kept in control. I won't be sailing this time, so it can be your responsibility. Please, don't get so defensive here. I'm the one who has to make the decision whether to spend a quarter of a million dollars here, and I'd sure value Killian's opinion. I've personally done this before with him. That's my decision and I'm going to get in touch with him before this goes any further. Knowing Killian as I do, I probably can have him here within a week."

SV *Mamamouchi* in 1981 as we took her out for a survey and sea trial in Victoria Harbor and eastward out into the adjacent South China Sea.

* * *

Five days later Killian arrived in Hong Kong and in his usual fashion, took charge of the evaluation of *Mamamouchi*. Killian and Sir Malcom hit it off immediately and became quite close friends. Both had a love for the sea and had plenty of 'war' stories to share with each other at the bar of the Royal Hong Kong Yacht Club, where Killian was definitely in his most comfortable element and fit in perfectly. He was a natural at the yacht club setting and picked up a lot of information and history about the Sailing Vessel *Mamamouchi*.

Despite JQ's reservations it became immediately apparent that having Killian on location was a great benefit for both JQ and me. We could now fade more into the background, where both of us were more comfortable, leaving Killian as 'point man' for the trip. Furthermore, Killian had the image of being the more responsible person, an image which I bolstered to the public, specifically to Sir Malcolm Penwick. Killian just inherently looked the part, whereas JQ and I looked more like smugglers rather than the 'yachty type'. Upon survey and a test run out through Hong Kong Harbor and into the South China Sea, *Mama* proved sound and in fairly good condition. Killian recommended I make the purchase.

I then instructed Killian to set up a Hong Kong 'nominee' corporation to take title of the boat, as we had done in the past with *Nepenthe*. The procedure for setting up a corporation took one day and cost about $1,000. I negotiated a purchase price of $220,000. I had the money in my Swiss safe deposit box, so it was no problem for me to make a quick three day round trip flight to Geneva and back, change some of my gold into cash and have the funds wire-transferred from Geneva to the Hong Kong branch of the Hong Kong Shanghai Bank.

Killian recommended several things be accomplished on *Mama* before attempting an ocean crossing: a new set of sails, several new winches, a new diesel engine and to convert her from a sloop to a split rig yawl configuration to make her safer in heavy weather, like we had done before to *Nepenthe*. He estimated the repairs and upgrades would take approximately two to three months. If all went well, we could be under way around the first of April. Another feature aboard *Mama* which Killian was unaccustomed to was its solid rod rigging. Normally, the standing rigging was wound stainless steel which could be adjusted or repaired (jury rigged) if necessary, but with this particular rigging, the forestay, shrouds and backstay were all made of one-piece solid stainless steel rods which worried Killian, but Malcolm reassured him it was customary for this particular boat. Still, in the back of his mind, Killian was uneasy about it, but let it slide as there were much more pressing issues to deal with to get the boat seaworthy for an ocean passage in two months. Anyway, the condition of the rod rigging passed the survey, so Killian moved on to other seemingly more pressing issues in getting the boat ready for sea.

The first order of business was to commence the conversion from a sloop to a yawl. A mizzen mast and all of its standing rigging was measured and ordered. This alone would take about three weeks. New sails were also ordered to replace the tired old ones. The engine also had to be replaced. I went about to find another one locally, but to no avail. I was told it would take about two months and a new engine would take at least a week or two just to install and test out. After making a few telephone calls, I decided the best way to expedite the procuring of a new engine for *Mama* was to travel to England, where Perkins diesels were made, and see if I could find one there and have it air freighted out to Hong Kong.

I caught the red-eye late night Cathay Pacific 747 flight direct from Hong Kong to London. I boarded and quickly fell asleep. I awoke at dawn to a beautiful panorama just as the sun was coming up over the Himalayas and strolled up the aisle from my first-class seat and through a curtain separating the main cabin from the cockpit area. I wanted to see if I could get a better view and take some pictures from the cockpit, as I had done several times in the past. It was now 1981 and obviously airline security had gotten much stricter, because I somewhat startled the captain who told me that I had just entered a restricted area and ordered me, under no uncertain terms, to leave the cockpit immediately. I tried to explain, but to no avail and summarily complied with his request, returning to my seat somewhat stunned, dejected and disappointed as it would have been a spectacular photo opportunity. Consequently, I never tried that again.

The following day I met Stan Yamamoto, who was staying at the fashionable Manchester Arms Hotel located right near London's Piccadilly Circus. Being with Stan in London would give me a chance to see how his venture with the Africans was progressing and report to him on the progress of the smuggling scam.

Stan really knew how to roll-high and hob-nob with the big shots. Even though he was not particularly flashy himself, Stan was always surrounded by an entourage of people along for the ride; this time it was the group of eight Africans, whom he was supporting financially in his pursuit of 'real big money', as he put it. I was very cautious and rather uncomfortable around these unfamiliar people. I felt sure they were just simply scamming Stan and I was much more comfortable away from the entourage and out trying to find my engine so I could return to Hong Kong as soon as possible. In my mind I was convinced Stan would surely be ripped off by these African scammers, but Stan felt sure the deal was real and he was going to pursue it, no matter what.

In Southern England near the harbor of Portsmouth I was able to locate and buy a Perkins 4-271 diesel engine, have it crated and air freighted directly to Hong Kong. The engine would arrive in Hong Kong in ten days, a far cry from the two months I was told it would take otherwise.

Mid-January 1981

Mama was in good hands and Killian could pretty much deal with anything in my absence, so there was no need for me to rush back to Hong Kong. Instead, with a week or two to spare, I had plenty of time to go back to California to be with Cindy and check on the progress of our remodeling project on the Woodside house. The demolition part of the project was running smoothly, with Tad doing most of the heavy lifting and Cindy assisting and working on the design and construction plans.

A couple of days after my return I received a call from my father, who was basking in the glow of Ronald Reagan's November election victory. Dick had previously served on one of his committees when Reagan was governor of California and was looking forward to a national appointment now that Reagan would become the 40th president of the United States.

"I have a couple of extra VIP tickets to the Inaugural Ball in Washington DC next week. Would you and Cindy like to join us?"

"Sure Dad. That would be great. We'd love to join you and Mom. I just got back from Hong Kong and have some new investment clients I've been cultivating," I replied.

"I'll tell you about it when we get together."

Cindy and I flew to Washington, where on January 20th we witnessed Reagan's inauguration. It was a clear and cold day, and a drastic change from the tropics I had grown used to. It was also an unusual dichotomy. I was standing in the crowd of thousands watching the swearing in of one of the most law-and-order presidents in recent history, and at the same time, I was in the middle of preparing another Thai stick marijuana smuggling operation. The new president was definitely not on the same page as me. Plus, as I would later come to learn, Nancy Reagan's pet project, 'Just Say No' to drugs, directly flew in the face of what I was currently doing. This might not be a good sign of things to come! That evening we accompanied my parents to one of several inaugural balls, where Dick proudly had his picture taken with the newly sworn-in president.

Here I am in Washington DC on January 20, 1981, where I accompanied my parents to witness the inauguration of Ronald Reagan. Even though I was politically ambivalent, I simply couldn't pass up this once-in-a-lifetime opportunity.

* * *

A few weeks later, I was back in the Far East with Cindy, who agreed to join me as she was ready for a vacation from the remodeling project she had been working on for the past two months. She left Tad in charge and accompanied me to Hong Kong where we checked into a suite at the Peninsula. For the next couple of weeks, I worked on the boat and Cindy shopped and toured Hong Kong, Kowloon, Macao and the new Territories.

The new engine had safely arrived and by the time I returned, Killian already had it installed and was diligently working on the remaining list of items necessary to get the boat ready for the upcoming voyage.

By April the boat was ready and preparations for loading were finalized. Cindy had returned home a few weeks earlier, then Tony came to Hong Kong to assess the yacht, pinpoint the loading spot and set up radio frequencies for communication. It was felt that the trip could be handled with a crew of three, as we had equipped *Mama* with a state-of-the-art self-steering autopilot. Being a sailing purist, Killian didn't like auto-pilots or self-steering devices, but acquiesced to avoid yet another argument with JQ.

The boat crew consisted of Killian as captain, and JQ and Davey Bartholomew as crew. Davey was an old and trusted friend of JQ's from his college days who was between jobs and looking for a new adventure. From my experience of sailing and generally being around Killian for the past ten years, I gave JQ a piece of advice, 'never let him off the boat' in addition to keeping an eye on him, especially on his drinking.

The next evening I decided to break my own rule of 'never letting Killian off the boat'. I thought it appropriate to take him to one of the finest restaurants in Hong Kong as sort of a going away present.

We took the Star Ferry across the harbor from Kowloon to Hong Kong where we caught a taxi which took us to the base of the highest promontory in Hong Kong. At the top of this mountain is located the Peak Restaurant, one of Hong Kong's finest accessed by a tram which takes dinner guests up the mountain to the restaurant featuring the most spectacular views anywhere in the Colony. Our reserved table at the window gave us the unparalleled view of Hong Kong, Victoria Harbor, Kowloon, the New Territories and mainland China in the distance to the north. Aberdeen and the gambling mecca of the Far East, Macau, were clearly visible far to the west as dusk gave way to night. Killian, dressed for the occasion in his white duck sailor's outfit, was in rare form as he commandeered the waiter, embarrassingly giving him orders and instructing him on how to do his job.

Without even looking at the wine list, Killian commanded, "Bring us a bottle of 1966 Chateau Haute Brion. That's a French Premier Cru Classe. Two glasses, if you will. Open it and let it breathe." The waiter did as he was told, glancing at me for some assurance and waiting for his next order from this buffoon.

Killian then perused the menu as if he were a connoisseur of fine dining. His next command was even more embarrassing as he motioned to the waiter with a beckoning finger gesture to report to our table instantly. Pointing to his choice on the menu he said, "rack of lamb for two… all for me," loudly snapping the menu closed in a theatrical gesture resounding throughout the restaurant like the pop of a gunshot. The poor Asian waiter jumped back in astonishment as if to say, 'this guy is really the ugly American.'

For his final act, he ordered the now bewildered waiter: "Garçon, bring us the dessert menu and a list of after dinner-aperitifs." After glancing at it he bellowed, "Creme caramel for two and two water glasses of your most expensive Courvoisier XO cognac. On the double!"

I've never been so embarrassed as I paid the bill and tried to slink outta there. For the two of us, the bill was nearly $500. I tipped the waiter $100 for his having to put up with Killian's buffoonery. I was never so happy to dump him back aboard *Mama* and retreat back to the Peninsula Hotel reaffirming my previous mantra: 'never let him off the boat.'

The boat was in perfect shape as she sailed east out of Victoria Harbor through Kowloon Bay before turning south and entering the South China Sea on the crystal clear morning of April 5th. The anticipated loading was to take place in one week… ten days at the outside. I left for Thailand to await the loading.

Tony met me at Don Muang and after stopping by his house in Bangkok for a quick bite to eat and to pick up a few things, we drove south down the coast to the stash house at the durian farm near Rayong. This would be our 'home away from home' until we loaded. I set up the radio equipment I had brought from Hong Kong and settled in to wait for the call from the boat, expected in the next few days. At exactly 12 noon and at 6 in the evening each day, as previously arranged, I waited by the radio for the call from JQ aboard *Mama*… first a week went by then ten days and still nothing was heard from the boat. Finally, on the 19th of April I received a message from JQ who had called Tony's house in Bangkok. The message was to call JQ at the Royal Hong Kong Yacht Club immediately.

"JQ, what the hell is going on. Man, I've been really worried about you guys," I said.

"Rick, you wouldn't believe it. We were cruising. Six days out of Hong Kong and right on schedule when we got hit by a tropical squall around the tip of Viet Nam and all of a sudden there was this loud crack. A kind of 'boinging' noise. It was the sound of the forestay snapping. That fucking solid rod rigging, there was no way to jury rig it. I'm really sorry, man… but what the hell could we do? We couldn't continue with the boat messed up like this so, we decided there was no other choice, but to limp back to Hong Kong and get it fixed."

"Fuck!" I replied, in shock at this turn of events. "I'll come to Hong Kong as soon as I can get there and reconnoiter the situation. Everybody is OK, right?"

"Yeah, we're all OK," JQ answered. "Our spirits are down, but we're fine. See you when you get here. Ciao."

Chapter 38

Fate Brought Us Together

In Thailand things weren't going exactly as Tony had planned.

Tony had managed to score two four-ton loads, one for Ciro and one for me, and while attempting to score the last load earmarked for Mike Stallings, the village of Ban Ku Su Man and the surrounding villages had been raided by the Thai Army while searching for Communist insurgency in Northeast Thailand. All of the marijuana crops were destroyed. In each village all the beautiful ripe plants, dripping with resin and ready to be harvested, were hacked down, dumped into huge piles, set afire and burned to ashes. There would not be any more marijuana available for the remainder of the season.

Tony had scored and safely stashed eight tons of high-grade Thai sticks but would be unable to get any more. Shortly thereafter, Tony had successfully loaded one of the four-ton loads on a motor sailer contracted by Ciro. The load was bound for the U.S. where the plan was to bring it into San Francisco Bay and continue up the San Joaquin Delta to an island near Stockton, where it would be unloaded by his regular unloading team run by Mike Stallings and his partner Dennis Moronsky.

Meanwhile, Mike and Dennis had contracted with Bob Lahodny and Coronado to smuggle the third and final of Tony's anticipated three four-ton loads. Coronado then contracted with Captain Dan and his 80-ft. fishing trawler to do the smuggle and had directed the boat to travel to the northern Borneo town of Kudat, located at the northern tip of Borneo in Malaysia's Sabah state, a virtual hop, skip and jump across the South China Sea, and await loading instructions.

* * *

Mama was a mess. Since the forestay was broken, no real pressure could be put on any of the standing rigging. They had sailed south from Hong Kong and had rounded the tip of Viet Nam when the forestay had snapped during a tropical squall. Rather than try and continue on, both Killian and JQ, who generally disagreed about most everything, both agreed to return to Hong Kong for repairs. The return trip was dismal in both spirits and weather and took twice as long as expected because they had to go slowly so as not to further stress the boat and possibly lose the mast.

The anticipated repair time for *Mama* was estimated to be approximately two months as new rigging would have to be custom-made in England, and even if air freighted to Hong Kong would take six weeks to prepare. This put a new loading date around the first of July, which was deemed unsatisfactory for two reasons. First, it was getting close to the local typhoon season and the weather could be unpredictable in the South China Sea and surrounding waters, and secondly, the Thais were getting nervous at the prospect of keeping the load stashed for an additional two months, given the additional DEA manpower now in Thailand, coupled with recent busts of rival marijuana smuggling groups. Tony also worried about the possibility that with the increased drug interdiction task force manpower in Thailand, one of his own Thai crew might get busted and if enough pressure was brought to bear, as in torture, even the most loyal of his team might succumb and reveal to the authorities the location of the durian farm stash house.

Tony considered the situation and made the following suggestion, or rather request, to me: "Rick you have load with no boat. Mike Stallings have boat with no load. Maybe you can work together. Share load this year, still make plenty money. Next year you have plenty time to fix boat and work on your own load."

"I don't know, Tony," I said. "Mike is working with Coronado. I really don't want to work again with them. When they have problems, who's in charge? I'll tell you who. Some piece-of-shit flunky who has no stake in the load and who will run at the first sign of danger, like at Neah Bay. Another thing, Tony, the FBI and DEA are actively looking for all of the main Coronado honchos who ran from them two years ago. When they get caught... and they will one of these days when they least expect it. In America the police don't give up and can't be bought off like here. When that happens, I don't want to be anywhere around them."

"Well, maybe you can work it out with them. It no good for me to keep load for another two months. Might have big problem for me. I can no wait for you to fix boat... maybe July or August no good for weather. Maybe get big storm too. Please, Rick, try to work it out."

Reluctantly, but faced with the reality of what Tony was suggesting, I sucked up my worries and called the only one of the three Coronado guys who I thought I could trust, Eddie Otero, and arranged a meeting with him for one week later at my Menlo Park home.

* * *

I left Killian on the boat in Hong Kong to supervise repairs. JQ and Davey Bartholomew both returned to the States as there was nothing more left for them to do. The plan was to repair *Mama* and wait until the following year and then put together another trip. We would then have plenty of time to get the boat ready without the pressure of trying to hurry.

Killian was quite content to stay in Hong Kong and he had already prepared himself to be gone from the home he had built in the Sierra foothills with the money from his previous smuggling ventures. He had arranged for an old sailing buddy, Jimmy Tillman, to housesit for him during his absence. However, Killian made one big mistake. Jimmy Tillman was broke and before coming to stay at his house for the anticipated extended period of time, he had convinced Killian to secure a loan for him. Killian secured a deed of trust on his house for $25,000 and gave the funds to Jimmy so he would have plenty of money to survive on and to service the debt during his absence. Tillman figured he could actually make money with the loan by selling marijuana and then be able to pay off the deed of trust in a few months.

Things did not go as Tillman planned and he ended up getting ripped off for the entire twenty-five grand in a bungled money transaction with several unsavory characters whom he barely knew. Unable to pay the debt service for the loan, the house was soon foreclosed on and the bank ended up with it. Killian could do nothing about it, but figured that as long as he had the boat to live on, he didn't care.

Killian often said, "Why worry, it doesn't do any good." So, he was quite content living aboard *Mama* and waiting until next season to do the trip. He figured, by then he would have enough money to either re-purchase the house from the bank or buy another piece of land and build a new one. Hong Kong would be an ideal place for him to hang out. He soon became a fixture at the Royal Hong Kong Yacht Club bar and could always be found there at happy hour, which for him was generally any time after sunrise, seated comfortably on his specially reserved stool overlooking Kowloon Bay.

June 5th
Menlo Park

"Seems like fate has brought us together again to do this trip, Eddie," I said. "After what happened last year, I really didn't want to work with you guys again, but it seems like now we both have a problem: me with no boat and you with no load, and here we are. I am willing to try again with you guys, but I have two requirements: first of all, you must personally be there and in charge of the offloading, plus I want a couple of my guys and their trucks with you on the beach. Secondly, whatever arrangement you have with Mike Stallings, you have to deal with it. In other words, you have to square up with him and whatever new arrangement you make with him must come out of your share of the load. The percentage will be the same as before, 60/40, and you pay for your share of the merchandise up front."

"Sounds fair, Rick. The only problem is, we've already spent a fortune so far this year and I would like to reimburse you for the cost of our share out of the load itself, but everything else is OK. Whaddya say, Rick?"

"Ed, you've got yourself a deal. I just want to make sure we have a clear understanding, you take care of Stallings. I don't want any hassles from him or especially his partner, Dennis Moronsky. You have to take care of them out of your share, or no deal. Agreed?"

"OK, it's a deal then and we'll take care of Mike and Dennis out of our share," replied Eddie.

"OK. Then, we'd better get this show on the road. Tony's beginning to freak out and wants to get the shit outta his stash and loaded as soon as possible. If we hurry, we should be able to do it in the next couple of weeks. I'll make arrangements to leave either tomorrow or the next day. I'll meet the boat in Borneo and brief them on the loading, then I'll go to Thailand and load them as soon as they can get there."

The following day, I left for the Far East. I caught a Singapore Airlines flight direct to Singapore then a Malaysian Airlines puddle jumper over to Kota Kinabalu and the short hop finally to Kudat. My arrival was expected by the boat skipper. 'Captain Dan' as he was called, who had skippered several previous boat trips for the Coronado Company. He was about 5'10" tall, had a stocky build and a noticeable beer belly. He was ruddy-complected and had a weather-beaten look from having spent the past ten years of his life captaining ocean-going fishing boats… when not smuggling. The one comment I had heard repeatedly about Captain Dan was, he had a gorgeous tall blonde wife, a real knockout, as Eddie put it.

Up til now, Captain Dan had become increasingly frustrated at the prospect of waiting in Borneo til the next marijuana season before being able to bring home a load. My arrival was indeed a welcome event for Captain Dan and the boat crew. Dan told me Kudat was the ideal spot to stage the loading from, and it was a very mellow place to hang out. One of the main people who lived in Kudat was a friend of Dan's, a man by the name of Paul Lo. Dan introduced me to Paul upon my arrival in Kudat.

Paul was an short spry-looking Asian man in his mid-sixties who looked about twenty years younger. He was a local hero who had saved many of the local villagers in World War II during the Japanese occupation of Malaysia and Indonesia. During the war, Paul had been a guerrilla fighter who, it was said, on one occasion single-handedly killed an entire Japanese squadron and saved Kudat from almost certain annihilation. For the entire period of the three-year Japanese occupation, Paul Lo lived in the dense jungle around Kudat and became the most deadly sniper and guerrilla fighter of the region. It earned him legendary, larger-than-life status, but to me he just seemed to be a very quiet, respectful, unassuming, rather diminutive gentleman, who sported a perpetual smile and a warm, friendly demeanor.

"Paul can and will do anything for you," Dan said. "If you ever have any trouble in any part of Indonesia or Malaysia, Paul can fix it. Anything at all. He is one of the most powerful men in the whole area. We have been stopping here for years and Paul is like family to us. Probably one of the finest people you'll ever meet."

Paul supplied fuel and supplies to the boat and was ready to procure guns and ammunition, of any make, model and caliber necessary, and with any other support which might be needed for the trip.

A few days later the boat was ready. I had coordinated the radio frequencies and loading spot with Captain Dan and the loading was set for June 16th. With everything secure, I returned to Thailand to wait with Tony and the Thai crew. As scheduled, the loading took place at the Royal Thai Navy Base near Rayong and everything went like clockwork.

Now with the load finally on its way, I thought I could now just go home and relax and wait for it to arrive in about six weeks. It was sure an optimistic dream. Working with these guys again… what was I thinking?

Chapter 39

Yakuza

July 4, 1981

I had just returned home from the 4th of July fireworks display in San Francisco, which Cindy and I viewed from our dinner table at the five-star restaurant called the Carnelian Room, atop the 52-story Bank of America building in San Francisco's financial district. We were just commenting on the lovely evening we had spent together when the phone rang. It was Eddie Otero calling from Southern California. Using the code 73, he instructed me to call him back immediately.

"We've just received word, the boat has broken the tail shaft at sea and has been adrift in the northern Philippine Sea about 450 to 500 miles east northeast of the island of Luzon. The load is safe. They radioed for help and had just been towed by a U.S. Navy destroyer to the Island of Iwo Jima, where they were in port awaiting help," Eddie said. "They told me explicitly, they had been through customs on Iwo Jima and the load was safe… at least for the time being. They have to make repairs if they are to continue. But we have a plan. Problem is, it will cost plenty. I think we need to have a meeting."

"Eddie, why don't you just have it fixed? I don't have to remind you, this part of the trip is your responsibility," I said.

"Rick, you don't understand," said Eddie. "This isn't some little thing you can just fix on the fly. It's a major repair. The boat has to be pulled out of the water and a new tail shaft must be installed. Without it the boat ain't moving under its own power. I think we're going to have to raise some money. We might even have to buy another boat to put the load onto. What is the current shape of your boat in Hong Kong? Is it ready? I wonder if it could be used, if necessary."

"Not a chance, Ed," I replied. "If it was ready, we'd be doing the trip ourselves and you'd be suckin' soup waiting until next year for a load, but it won't be ready for at least another month. Why don't you have a meeting with Mike Stallings? He might be able to help."

"OK, I'll get in touch with him and get back to you," Eddie said.

I returned home completely bummed out. "Looks like they've fucked up again," I said to Cindy. "This is our last chance. If we can't bail this one out, we're finished in this business. Tony will never work with us again, nor will any of the other Thais."

"Wouldn't bother me a bit if you were finished in the business," Cindy said. "I really am tired of all the hassles and what it's doing to our marriage."

"Well, don't expect to live in the lifestyle you've grown accustomed to, if this trip goes down."

A meeting was arranged by Ed Otero at Dennis' house in San Mateo to try to raise some additional funds to salvage the trip. Three days later the meeting was held. Tony was in the States visiting Ciro to collect his share of the first load, which had recently arrived and had been successfully unloaded in the Delta. Both he and Ciro were present as were Mike, Dennis, myself and Bob Lahodny. From the start of the meeting, it became quickly apparent to me that Eddie Otero had not dealt with Mike Stallings as he had promised me he would do. Instead, he had simply abandoned Mike and Dennis in favor of me, when they no longer had a load. Mike and Dennis were very pissed off and as the meeting progressed Bob Lahodny seemed to side with Mike and Dennis leaving me by myself. Eddie was not present and Bob claimed to know nothing about the arrangement I had made with Eddie. I felt alone and abandoned with nobody except Tony to try and mediate the situation. Mike and Dennis claimed the load should be theirs and I should be out of it, and if it weren't for Tony I would have been.

But Tony interceded and suggested I pay Mike and Dennis to keep things from getting out of control. Ciro's load had just arrived and had been successfully unloaded by Mike and Dennis' team up the Delta, so all of them were in good shape financially. All of them were flush, except for me. Everyone else in the room except Bob and I had made money this year and now I felt like I was being forced to acquiesce or possibly lose the load entirely. With little other choice, I reluctantly agreed to give Mike and Dennis a substantial seven figure sum out of the proceeds of the load to settle the dispute. Bob had argued it couldn't come out of their share because he was going to have additional expenses to repair the boat and then bail the trip out. When I queried Bob as to why Eddie either hadn't been present now or explained the deal to him, he said Ed had left for Japan and they simply hadn't had time to go over it in detail.

I felt fucked over, backstabbed and generally miserable, but was backed into a corner and didn't have much of a choice in the matter. It was extortion, plain and simple… either I agreed to pay or I lost the load and make nothing for all my effort.

* * *

Several years before meeting and marrying Captain Dan, his wife Georgina, who everyone called Gina, originally from New Orleans, had worked as a high-class escort in Japan. The six-foot-tall blonde with electric blue eyes and a fabulous body lived in Tokyo and among her clients were several members of the Japanese Mafia known as the Yakuza. She became friendly with some of the leaders of the Yakuza, and while she no longer worked as an escort, she had maintained contact with several of them through letters and occasional visits to Japan. Now, even though she was married to Captain Dan, Gina maintained a friendly relationship with the Yakuza heavyweights.

Captain Dan had an idea; Gina's relationship with the Yakuza might help them out of their jam. Gina was only too glad to help and with a few short phone calls to set up meetings, she and Eddie Otero were on the first flight to Japan.

Gina made the introductions and Eddie negotiated the deal to repair the boat and save the load. He had carried $50,000 with him for boat repairs.

The plan was to tow the boat from Iwo Jima to Yokohama for repairs. The tow boat was a fishing boat used by the Yakuza. While en route to Yokohama, the load would be transferred to the Yakuza boat which would then 'hover' in the area while repairs were made. After repairs were completed, the smuggling boat would then rendezvous with the Yakuza boat, the load would be transferred back and the smuggle would continue on to the United States as originally planned. The fee for the Yakuza services would be $250,000 and could be paid from the proceeds of the trip. It was agreed, the first two-hundred and fifty grand received from selling the load was to go to the Yakuza. The only catch was that Gina would remain in Japan as hostage until the $250,000 ransom was paid. Her surroundings would be most comfortable and luxurious, but nevertheless she could not leave unless and until the money was paid.

While in Yokohama, Captain Dan relaxed on the beach with Gina, but always under the supervision and watchful eye of a sinister-looking character who bore the classic mark of the Yakuza: the tips of his ring fingers on both hands were missing.

The boat repair to replace the broken tail shaft took six weeks and by mid-August the boat left dry dock in Yokohama and was once again at sea. In the lee of Kozu Shima, one of the least populated islands in the Izu Shichito island chain located about 100 miles south of Yokohama, the smuggling boat rendezvoused with the hovering Yakuza boat and re-transferred the load and Captain Dan was on his way home with the load safe and sound and secured in the ship's hold; his beautiful wife was left as a hostage, held for ransom in the hands of the Yakuza.

The trip from Japan to the proposed offloading site at Bear Harbor on the rugged Mendocino Coast, south of Eureka, was anticipated to take about a month.

Chapter 40

SFO Airport

Early September 1981
Menlo Park

Tony the Thai had returned to Thailand after the early July meeting, then returned to the States and had been vacationing in Hawaii with Ciro while Ciro's partner Walter Brugger sold his four-ton load.

I received a call from Tony who told me he was in Hawaii and was leaving the next day, bound first for Tahoe then to come and see me on his way back to Thailand.

On September 4th, Tony arrived at my house in Menlo Park and then booked a flight the following day to Thailand. He was carrying two hand-carry bags with him when he arrived. One, an over-the-shoulder folded black fabric clothes bag, containing the few clothes he had bought with him and the other was a silver metal Halliburton suitcase which could be hand carried aboard the flight and would fit under the seat. The metal suitcase contained $1.2 million in cash which he had just received from Ciro as part of his share of Ciro's load. Ciro held the final one million dollar payment he owed Tony, saying he would pay him later.

The two of us were sitting in the cottage behind the main house as Tony laid the suitcase on the floor and opened it. "Shit!" I exclaimed as he opened the suitcase and revealed the $1.2 million which had been squeezed tightly into it in, banded stacks of $5000 in each stack.

"You mean to tell me, you intend to carry this suitcase full of money onto the plane with you. Are you fucking nuts? It's really a huge risk, Tony," I said. "I can't let you carry this money by yourself. It's just too dangerous. Please, Tony," I begged, "why don't you let Joe and a few of my people help you carry the money, in smaller amounts?"

"No problem for me. I businessman. I do many times before. No trouble. Put in suitcase. Get on plane. Go Hong Kong then give money to my cousin Boonsak who in jewelry business. Money transferred to Thailand in black market. Get good rate. Better than bank. Now money in Thailand. Work next year. No problem, Rick."

"Look, Tony. I can't believe your supposed friend Ciro would let you take a risk like this. You won't believe me when I tell you, Ciro doesn't give a shit about you or anyone else other than himself. He's a selfish, self-centered son of a bitch, and the fact he'd let you take a chance like this only underscores what I am trying to tell you."

"No, Rick. You wrong about Ciro. He a good guy. Do big business with me and Thai crew."

"Thai, you just don't get it. Maybe someday you'll understand what I'm saying. I've known this guy for over ten years and believe me, he's a ruthless, arrogant prick who'd probably sell his own mother down the river if it was to his advantage. I just can't believe he'd let you take this risk and wouldn't get his flunkies Jeff and Brad to take this money to Hong Kong for you. Don't you understand, you are the big boss of the Thai crew and of this whole smuggling operation, and if anything happens to you we're all fucked," I emphatically said.

"This no problem for me. I do many times before. You worry too much, Rick."

"Look, Tony. I'm your friend and I don't want anything to happen to you. I insist, Joe goes with you and helps you carry the money, OK?"

"OK. OK, Rick. You like Joe to go. Fine by me," answered Tony. "No worry."

"Thai, you're just too stubborn about this. At least Joe can help out some, so let's just get on with reorganizing this money. You win, but I still don't like it," I responded.

Tony and I packed a couple of carry-on bags for Joe, which included a folding garment bag and leather briefcase. I was able to pack about $400,000 into Joe's bags. Tony insisted on putting about $800,000 into his silver Halliburton case and filling the leftover space with dirty clothes.

However, as we repacked his money, I continued to carp at Tony, but as much as I tried to dissuade him from personally carrying the money, he continued to insist on doing it himself, until I finally told him, "God dammit 'Thai', it's your money. Do what the hell you want… it's late and I'm tired of arguing with you. I'm going to bed. Joe will be here in the morning and I will take you two to the airport."

Bob Lahodny happened to be in the Bay Area. He called first and I invited him over to my house for an early breakfast, then he accompanied Tony, Joe and me to the airport. I dropped Joe, Tony and Bob off at the curbside and went to park the car. Bob followed Joe and Tony at a discreet distance as they neared the security checkpoint. Joe passed through security without a problem and headed for the boarding area.

Tony placed his two carry-on bags onto the conveyer belt. The security man observed a suspicious dark mass as the metal Halliburton case passed through the X-ray machine.

"Pleas open de bag, sor," the Filipino security officer requested in a thick accent.

Tony's mouth went dry. He spun the numbers on the combination lock and lifted the lid. The security man pushed aside the dirty clothes to find the case was filled with neatly banded stacks of one hundred dollar bills. His eyes widened. A gasp of astonishment came from the people standing in line behind Tony. The man reached down under the counter and swiftly pressed a button. In less than a minute, three agents from U.S. Customs appeared, crowding around Tony like wasps whose nest had been struck by a stick.

Joe had witnessed the fracas just twenty-five feet away as the agents grabbed and quickly handcuffed Tony with his hands behind his back and, with an agent on each side of him, their hands under his armpits, Tony disappeared through a side door. Nonchalantly, Joe picked up his bags, turned and walked back to the main terminal. Bob and I were waiting at a newspaper stand.

"Tony's been busted!" Joe whispered. "Security opened his bag and found the money."

"Aw, fuck!" I exclaimed.

Immediately, Bob went to a phone booth and telephoned his Los Angeles attorney Phil DeMassa. The attorney told Bob he would represent Tony. He said he would catch a flight up to San Francisco later in the day.

"Here, Rick. You take the money," Joe said. He put his two bags down in front of me. "I guess I'd better catch that plane. My passport and ticket are under my name and I think it might arouse suspicion if I decided at the last minute not to go."

"Good idea. They'd surely connect you with Tony if you didn't. Take care Joe and get back here in a few days," I said.

Meanwhile, in the U.S. Customs interrogation room, Tony spoke to the agents. "I bring money to America to buy house. I no find house. This country too cold for me. I go home with my money. No problem."

"It's a big problem, pal. Where's your customs declaration for this money?" asked one of the agents. "Can't you read the sign which says: it is illegal to travel with more than five thousand dollars in cash without a customs declaration?"

"I see no sign. No problem. I businessman. Have plenty money," Tony said, his confidence beginning to wane.

"Soonthorn Kraithamjitkul, you are under arrest. You have the right to remain silent. Anything you say can and will be held against you in a court of law…"

Although Tony didn't understand everything the Customs agent was saying to him, he knew full well what the word 'arrest' meant and he knew he was going to jail. Tony also knew he should keep his mouth shut.

Later the same afternoon, Phil DeMassa visited him in San Francisco County Jail. DeMassa was able to reassure the Thai that he would be able to get him out of jail in the next couple of weeks.

Tony spent the next week and a half in jail before he was taken before a federal grand jury and subsequently indicted for his failure to declare the $831,000 in cash and for perjury for his lying to a federal agent. On September 14th, Tony was released on bail. I had given DeMassa $200,000. One hundred thousand dollars for ten percent of Tony's million dollar bail and another hundred grand as a retainer and for expenses for DeMassa's services.

Tony decided to fly to Los Angeles to await his hearing which was scheduled for six weeks from now. The Bay Area was too cold for him. Plus, Tony had a friend who lived in the downtown area of LA off of Vermont Street, which was the largest Thai community in the United States and had plenty of Thai restaurants, the only food Tony really liked. I gave Tony the rest of his money which Joe had returned to me following the airport debacle. Tony figured he'd need it as he expected a lengthy stay in the U.S.

in order to resolve his legal troubles. We met briefly for lunch at a Thai restaurant in San Francisco prior to his departure for LA. As we dined on fresh lemongrass and shrimp soup, called Tom Yam Goong in the Thai language, Tony told me of his fearful premonition.

"Rick. I afraid I never going home to Thailand again. I'm going to die in America and never see my family again."

"Don't be ridiculous, Tony," I said. "Phil will get you out of this mess in no time and you'll be back home before you know it. It will cost, but, what the hell. It's only money. I've given Phil plenty for your defense and he thinks he'll be able to clear it up with a fine and probation. We'll just put an extra half-ton on next year's load and no big deal."

"No, Rick. I have sick stomach. I am not well and need my doctor in Thailand. I want to see my wife and little girl. Think I maybe die in America."

* * *

Following the repairs in Yokohama and with the load safely back aboard, Captain Dan's fishing boat was now plowing full-speed-ahead towards the rugged Northern California coast and due to arrive in less than a week.

Eddie was the first one to get the call from the HAM radio operator in Borrego Springs letting him know, he'd just received word from Captain Dan and the load was due to arrive on the North Coast in the next couple of days. It was time to mobilize.

Eddie called me to assure me that this time there would be nothing left to chance and he would be in charge and on the scene at the offloading. There would not be any 'armchair quarterbacking' this year and, just like in the past, he would be the full hands-on 'beach commander' to assure everything went as planned. Nevertheless, I was skeptical and insisted that I and my team be on scene in case we would be needed or at least to claim our share of the load at the beach.

The planned offload was to take place in Bear Harbor on the California Coast north of Fort Bragg. Bear Harbor is an isolated bay in the Sinkyone Wilderness State Park accessible only by a little-used dirt road ideal for the clandestine offloading operation. It would be my job to check into the Eureka Inn overlooking Eureka's scenic harbor and specifically to keep an eye on the 82-foot Coast Guard cutter docked at the Coast Guard station located in the harbor and in plain sight of my hotel room. Eddie would orchestrate the offloading at Bear Harbor using the old tried-and-true method of ferrying the load from the trawler to the isolated beach in Zodiac rubber boats, then to pickup trucks and finally to a secure rented stash house in Arcadia, ten miles north of Eureka, to divide up the booty.

"No fancy high-tech shit this year," Eddie said. "Just back to doing what we do best and have been doing for years."

I agreed and felt more confident that finally there was a good chance for success. I had planned to have Joe and Rico accompany me with their pickup trucks to assist with the offload, if necessary, and then transport my share back to Silverado Country Club Estates where Willie had again rented a beautiful high-end estate adjacent to the lush fairways of the exclusive Silverado golf course in Napa.

October 17
Eureka

As planned, Joe, Rico and I arrived in Eureka and checked into the famous old Eureka Inn. Naively, I signed the hotel register for two rooms using my own name, stating to the hotel clerk that I was a professional photographer and two of my assistants would be joining me later. My use of my own name at check-in would come back to haunt me, but my professional photographer cover along with the camera cases I carried over my shoulder gave me a false sense of confidence; plus I was not comfortable lying, even to an unassuming hotel clerk. I requested a corner room overlooking the harbor so I could photograph it at different times of the day and night. Since the hotel was virtually empty, my request was granted.

Upon entering the room and crossing it to the picture window, I stood there with an unobstructed view of the white Coast Guard cutter with its emblematic red bow stripe, resting and docked at the Eureka Coast Guard station in the harbor below my window observation post.

Eddie had instructed me to be on the lookout and keep an eye on the cutter. I was to report to him every few hours on a pre-arranged time schedule, telephone booth to telephone booth. We set up a code to use for our communication with each other. If the cutter left its mooring the following day or night, I would inform Eddie that a 'red' tide might affect his fishing grounds. If the Coast Guard boat remained at rest in the calm harbor and no unusual activity was observed, then I would report to Eddie that no weather was expected and his large catch would make other fisherman 'green' with envy. Or any use of the word 'red' would mean danger and any use of the word 'green' meant the coast was clear.

As it was, the Coast Guard cutter remained at rest for the next two days and I reported regularly to Eddie that 'all was green' and the sailors came and went and appeared to be performing their usual duties of swabbing the decks and keeping the vessel pristine and white. I patiently observed that all activity aboard seemed routine and normal... 'green'.

On the morning of October 19th, Eddie called me to report that the load had been successfully offloaded the previous night with no mishaps and was now at the stash house in Arcadia awaiting me and my crew's arrival for weighing and distribution. Ed had assured me my crew was not needed on the beach, so the three of us arrived at the Arcadia stash house an hour later and were greeted by several members of the Coronado Company's unloading crew including Eddie. I recognized 'Mr. Beancounter', David Vaughn, who as usual had a clipboard in hand, and the tall curly haired behemoth named Fuzzy from last year's load dividing at Stan's house. Handshakes and congratulatory praises were circulated among all and the job of weighing and dividing up the load was then accomplished.

Joe, Rico and I had each brought our pickup trucks with camper shells covering the truck beds. In each truck bed were various construction and landscape tools: ladders, hoses, chain saws and other items including plywood boards the loads could be stored beneath to conceal what was actually being transported back to the stash house. To the casual observer glancing in the camper shell's windows, it appeared that the three trucks were just loaded with construction equipment and the drivers were going to another job down the road, in case any of us were spotted or questioned. Nothing out of the ordinary happened on the trip back to Silverado and the load was again weighed, put into boxes, tabulated and prepared for sale.

'Yorktown' Billy, JQ and Stan each got the shares promised and the load was sold within two weeks. Stan got the lion's share of my half, plus a portion of Coronado's load and was able to sell it and receive the money back in one week. Stan had an efficient network to distributors who could handle over 1000 pounds at a time. JQ and Billy also had networks as well, but could only handle around 100 to 500 pounds at once, however, both were effective sellers in their own right and not one pound was ever lost or went unpaid for.

We Northern California smugglers were not the only ones who favored burying money rather than putting it into banks. Stan did likewise on his rural property in Vista, although on one occasion with a very different end result. He and I buried one hundred grand out behind his house for safekeeping with the intention of retrieving it later if we needed it. Late one night with shovels, flashlights, and paper to make a treasure map we put the cash in a watertight ammunition box and buried it three feet underground in his landscaping. We carefully plotted its location using three points of triangulation. Many months later, when we went to reacquire it, we went to the spot but never found it. We hypothesized that one of his gofers, probably the one nicknamed the Mole, found out about it and dug it up. Maybe Stan told him in one of his coked out stupors; I never knew. At any rate, the bottom line was: burying money was not the panacea it was cracked up to be, especially if anyone else knew of its location. No honor among thieves!

At the same time there were several loose ends which needed to be tied up, including and most important, getting Georgina, Captain Dan's wife, released as the Yakuza hostage in Japan. Eddie flew back to Japan and saw to it that the $250,000 ransom was paid and Gina was released. She had enjoyed her captivity, not being mistreated in any way, renewing old friendships, and being lavished with fine Japanese meals in a guarded hotel suite with two Yakuza thugs outside her room 24/7. I later found out that this was not the first time the Coronado Company had left a hostage behind for a ransom to be paid after a load was safely landed, albeit with much a different outcome.

The money from Tony's share was transported to Hong Kong by Joe, Rico and a new member of our crew, Ed Lehmer. Ed, a builder by trade, an avid sailor and a former neighborhood little league baseball buddy of Rico's, was anxious to help us wherever he could. Ed seemed to be a good fit, was eager to participate and with a seemingly endless supply of energy, was a welcome addition to the future of our operation. While in Hong Kong, they stopped by the Royal Hong Kong Yacht Club to visit Killian who was entrenched there and overseeing the repairs to *Mama* in preparation for the next year's operation. Ed seemed to be a natural for next year's crew and he and Dave appeared to be much more in tune with each other than Davey and JQ. Since we would have to wait until next fall, we decided to move *Mama* to a more favorable location which would be out of next year's predictable typhoon tracks. The majority of cyclonic storms in the Western Pacific usually occur in the late summer and fall, originate in the island chains south of the Philippines and track northwesterly mostly through the Philippines, into the South China Sea and towards Hong Kong and mainland China. Therefore the next few months would be ideal to move into the South Pacific and wait it out down there in relative calm weather. Dave, Ed and another newcomer to our operation, Dennis Hathaway, a second cousin of Phil Erikson, would be available not only to move the boat to Tahiti now, but possibly would also be the crew for another boat trip next year.

Now, for once, I was pretty flush after the last trip, however there was still the issue of what to do about the deal I was forced to make regarding compensating Mike and Dennis. I wasn't too happy about the prospect of paying them anything and was looking forward to having it out with Ed Otero when I would have a chance to meet with him in the next couple of weeks. In the back of my mind, I also knew that Ciro had an investment in the last load, or at least in the load which would have been Mike and Dennis' and this might be my opportunity to get back at least some of what he stole from me from the *Drifter* load. It would be interesting to see how it would all play out, but somehow I knew, it probably wouldn't be pretty.

Chapter 41

The Other Side

Early Spring 1981
San Diego, California

Special Agent James Conklin sat behind one of a dozen utilitarian gray metal desks which adorned the Drug Enforcement Administration's San Diego office. The DEA had rented office space in an industrial complex located in the San Diego suburb of National City. Ten other agents in the room likewise sat behind their gray metal desks researching cases and following up on leads. The shuffling of papers, clicking of typewriters and occasional phone conversations could be heard as a cacophony of office noises permeated the smoke-filled 20- by 40-foot room. After about ten cups of coffee and sitting all day in an uncomfortable gray metal folding chair, Jim Conklin was ready to call it quits for the day. His back was sore and the long legs of his six-foot frame were starting to cramp as he looked up at the wall clock and noted the time. It was 6:30 in the late afternoon. He had been sitting in the same position for nearly twelve hours.

'Another half hour,' he thought, 'then I can wrap it up for the day. I can almost taste those Miller Lites already.'

Jim had been assigned to the fugitive detail and was trying to locate anyone on his long list of federal fugitives who had absconded from justice, but was having little luck today as leads had gone cold and these guys seemed to have vanished into thin air. The black phone on his desk started ringing.

'I wonder who could be calling at this hour,' Jim thought as he picked up the receiver.

"Hello. Jim Conklin."

On the other end of the line, Jim immediately recognized the squeaky voice of one of his informants, Dave Martin. Dave was a small-time cocaine dealer who lived on Coronado Island and had been busted several times and finally saw the writing on the wall: another bust and he'd be going down for a long time, so he decided to become a government informant. He was one of many who Jim had convinced that his only avenue to avoid spending years in prison was to cooperate and give Jim information on anyone else he knew to be dealing drugs.

"Hey Jim. Dave Martin here. I just got popped again and they told me I could have one phone call. I'm in a holding cell at the Coronado Police Station and I've got some news I think you'd be interested in."

"I'm listening," said Conklin. "This better be good or I'm done with you. I told you last time, if you fucked up again, I might not be able to help you out. So, what is it?"

"I promise this is the last time. My wife is going to kill me if she finds out I've been busted again. Come and get me and, if you're interested, I will tell you about a guy I know who's a big time scammer from Coronado. I think I know where he lives. His name is Ed Otero and he's living up in Santa Barbara."

"You know this guy? How'd you come by this information? And, yes I'm very interested. I'll be by to get you in about an hour and you can tell me all about it."

Two hours later Special Agent Jim Conklin and his confidential informant Dave Martin were seated at a table at a local Coronado Island deli having coffee. Jim was still wishing for that Miller Lite, but now was not the time. He needed to be clear-headed and focused on what Dave had to say.

"Yeah, I heard he was a high roller now living up in Montecito, driving a fancy car and living the high life. I knew him back in high school in '71 when he was swimming kilos across the Mexican border. Now I heard he's become a big time smuggler."

"I've been looking for Otero. He got indicted back in '79 and he fled to avoid prosecution. He's on my list. So, tell me all you know about him."

Dave Martin told Agent Conklin that Ed Otero had become sort of a clandestine folk hero around Coronado and he was one of the leaders of a huge marijuana smuggling operation, known around these parts as the Coronado Company. Martin said he'd previously heard of the indictment through the grapevine. It was big news on little Coronado Island.

Lighting a cigarette, Martin continued, saying he'd attended a party in Santa Barbara a few weeks ago, and there he had heard Otero was living in Santa Barbara on the lam, as he put it, living under the assumed name of Ed Morgan.

Jim Conklin did his best to conceal his excitement at this startling bit of information. Otero was at the top of his list of federal fugitives and this might be a big break, if this low-life Dave Martin was telling the truth. Maybe today wasn't such a bad day after all.

It was now after 10 o'clock when Jim Conklin arrived home to his small house on the outskirts of San Diego where his wife Nancy, already on her fourth or fifth carafe of cheap white wine, was getting tired of waiting up and listening to Jim's war stories of the day, about making busts and chasing drug dealers. She had already put the three kids to bed an hour ago and was relaxing, drink in hand, as Jim strode through the door.

"Hi babe. Sorry I'm late but, I think I may have just gotten a big break in one of the fugitive cases I've been working on," Jim said enthusiastically.

"Listen, Jimmy. I'm not really interested. It's always about what you're doing. What in the hell do you think I've been doing all day, sitting around eating bonbons? And waiting for his royal highness to come home and tell me stories of you chasing drug-gies all over hell-and-gone! Who do you think takes care of these kids? Gets them up. Feeds them breakfast. Gets them off to school. Picks them up. Takes them home. Feeds them dinner. Reads them stories before bedtime and finally puts them to bed. Me, that's who! Now it's nearly midnight and I'm supposed to get excited about what you've been doing all day. Forget it. I'm going to bed and you can heat up the leftovers in the fridge. Good night."

"Listen, honey. I wasn't trying to downplay your job of taking care of the kids and everything, I was just excited about what happened today. Sure you don't want to hear about it?"

"No, I'm exhausted. I'm sure your buddies at the office would be more interested anyway. Like I said already, good night!"

Deflated but still amped up Jim finally sat down alone and cracked open the Miller Lite he'd been longing for and contemplated his next move on the federal fugitive, Edward R. Otero.

The next day, Jim Conklin set the wheels in motion to find Otero in Santa Barbara. The first order of business was to requisition funds for travel, investigation, surveil-lance and whatever else was needed. This was no easy matter as the DEA budget was almost non-existent and trying to appropriate funds to pursue marijuana cases was of low priority. What little money there was in the DEA budget was earmarked for hard drug cases with heroin, cocaine, and other dangerous drugs taking precedent over mari-juana cases. However, he might be able to convince the higher-ups of the importance of this particular case, since there might be considerable assets to be seized which could bolster the dwindling DEA financial reserves. Jim was reluctantly given a modicum of funding to start the investigation and along with it he was also assigned a new partner, a special agent from the Internal Revenue Service named James Nielsen. It was felt an IRS agent could assist the DEA in matters involving the seizure of property and tracing and tracking the movement of money and Nielsen, a young, brilliant, experi-enced IRS investigator was the perfect agent for this task.

The tall, rather gangly Jim Nielsen had developed a reputation around the IRS as a smart and savvy investigator, who had discovered a better way to seize assets than simply taking them as ill-gotten gains. Nielsen developed what he called the 'Net Worth Theory', wherein a drug criminal's net worth would be ascertained from work records or tax information or any other source, then anything over this amount would be deemed illegal and subject to seizure and forfeiture through provisions of the Controlled Substances Act. Nielsen was excited, as this case would be the first test of his newly developed theory. A team of agents headed by Conklin and Nielsen was assembled to pursue Otero and was given a rather funny and unusual acronym, F.A.R.T., which stood for Financial Asset Removal Team, and this would be their first case.

Jim Conklin knew that successful investigations are not only the result of dogged and tedious police work, but are often successful due to sheer luck and being at the right place at the right time. Conklin also knew, through his ten years of experience as an investigator, first for the Bureau of Narcotics and Dangerous Drugs (BNDD), then the DEA, and now having attained the high government ranking grade of GS-13, that persistence and patience were the keys which nearly always led to his most successful busts. Not all of his cases resulted in immediate arrests. A hot lead could turn cold in a heartbeat, leaving even the most determined investigator, like Conklin, with nowhere to turn. He simply had to be patient and wait for a break or new lead, which may or may not come.

As luck would have it, a new lead did indeed come shortly thereafter.

* * *

The team of 'Two Jims' seemed to be the perfect marriage between the DEA and the IRS, two government agencies competing for attention in the war against drugs. Not only were they competing for attention, but their organizations were very protective of sharing information with each other. Basically, both agencies were fighting the same battle, but until now, the right hand didn't know what the left hand was doing. The 'Two Jims' were about to change all of that and set a precedent which would carry forward for decades to come. The bottom line was: the DEA was all about catching drug criminals and putting them out of business and the IRS was all about chasing the money derived from criminal activity via seizures and forfeitures.

Historically, the prosecution of the case of Chicago gangster Al Capone in 1931 was only successful because of the fact that he was prosecuted on tax evasion. Because of mutually profitable relationships with Chicago's mayor and with the police department, Capone was virtually immune from law enforcement and prosecution for his criminal activity, which included murder, bootlegging, prostitution and violence. He also gained local favor and notoriety by contributing to charities and appearing at sporting events. Some even called him a modern day Robin Hood. However, on February 14, 1929, the St. Valentines Day Massacre changed everything, with Capone's South Side Italian gang's murder of six rival North Side Irish American gang members. Following this violent event and pressure from local influential citizens whose businesses and Chicago's reputation were now being adversely affected by the violence, the federal government stepped in and devised a theory to bring down Al Capone once and for all. Thus, Capone was finally successfully charged, convicted and sent to federal prison for tax evasion. The 'Two Jims' were about to use generally the same model to prosecute drug cases now 50 years later, in the 1980s, and would set a precedence for the same procedures to be used going forward.

At six feet tall, trim, athletic, muscular and showing early signs of male-pattern baldness, Jim Conklin exemplified the image of a dedicated, focused and bulldog drug investigator. Born in Boston in 1943, Jim was the second of five children whose middle class parents personified the American dream. His father was an FBI agent who was transferred to the Detroit office in 1945, where Jim grew up. His stay-at-home mom raised their five children in a happy family setting; Jim remembered his parents as never speaking harsh words with each other. Graduating high school in 1961, Jim went on to college at St. Bonaventure University in Allegany, New York, where he majored in philosophy. Following the Cuban missile crisis and the start of the U.S. involvement in Viet Nam, a now 'gung-ho' Jim Conklin graduated college and immediately enlisted in Marine Officer Candidate School in Quantico, Virginia, where he became a 2nd Lieutenant in the Marine Infantry and was summarily shipped to Viet Nam as an infantry platoon leader. Commanding a unit of nearly fifty marines on his first mission into the Vietnamese jungle, the young 'scared shitless' lieutenant and his squad were ambushed by the Viet Cong. They took heavy casualties and were forced to beat a hasty retreat and had to leave their dead behind. The next thirteen months were a real eye opener of total combat and luckily Jim rotated out of the war zone with only a shrapnel wound in his left arm. He was awarded a purple heart and in 1968 left the service to try and figure out what to do with the rest of his life.

He found a job as a management trainee for a trucking outfit but soon became bored and wondered if this was 'as good as it gets'. If it was adventure he was looking for, a friend suggested he apply for a position as a narcotics agent with the Bureau of Narcotics and Dangerous Drugs, a newly created agency within the Department of Justice which merged the Bureau of Narcotics from Treasury and the Bureau of Drug Abuse Control from Health, Education and Welfare into one agency. Conklin became one of a thousand or more BNDD agents and was assigned to the New York office where, as a 'Narc', his focus was on busting heroin, usually supplied by the Mafia.

Nearly all of the agents in the New York office were beer drinkers and would meet for drinks for many hours after work and it was joked around the office that BNDD stood for Bureau of Neurotics and Dangerous Drunks.

In one incident, lacking funds for private transportation, Jim had to carry a cardboard box filled with confiscated heroin and $150,000 in cash through the streets of downtown New York from his office to the courthouse. This was typical for the underfunded agency and in 1973 the BNDD became the Drug Enforcement Administration (DEA) which was created during the Nixon administration to federally consolidate and control drug activities both in the United States and abroad.

Jim Conklin became a DEA special agent and in 1974 requested and was given a transfer to the San Diego office. Jim loved Southern California and was happy to be out of the East and looked forward to raising his family in the warm California sun. With a wife and three young kids, he lived in a modest three bedroom home in the San Diego suburbs. He was assigned mostly to border cases which involved seizing drugs crossing the Mexican border. After several years and numerous drug busts at the U.S./ Mexican border, Jim was given a new assignment: to track down and arrest federal fugitives. It was now 1979 and at the top of his list were the names of members of the Coronado Company who had fled to avoid prosecution resulting from an indictment in San Diego, California. Jim knew tracking fugitives was a long and arduous process which involved patience and the tedious task of following leads, which most often led to dead ends; but he also knew that with dogged determination, one day hopefully in the not-too-distant future he would come face-to-face with fugitives Lou Villar, Ed Otero and Bob Lahodny, the kingpins of the Coronado Company.

Jim Nielsen, the tall, quiet, reserved special agent for the Internal Revenue Service was pretty much the polar opposite of his partner Jim Conklin. Nielsen was a brilliant numbers guy, and not at all what one would expect to be on the front lines in the War on Drugs. Nielsen appeared as the gawky, bookworm type with a large nose, black Buddy Holly style horned rim glasses and trousers cut about an inch or so too short. He was constantly ridiculed, because he looked like he was a plastic pocket protector carrying, nerdy geek, waiting for the flood. But, his rather comical appearance was soon overshadowed by his brilliance and savvy approach to nailing drug offenders by using the old IRS adage—follow the money.

Although both men were considered equal in the team of Two Jims, the more macho Jim Conklin was clearly the leader and outspoken voice of the two agents. Nielsen loved cars and his hobby was to collect and restore '60s muscle cars, but when teamed with Conklin, Nielsen always occupied the 'shotgun' or passenger seat in Conklin's 4 door green '79 Chevy, when the two were together on assignment. This was kind of disappointing to Nielsen, but his mellow demeanor just allowed him to roll with it without a fuss. Both carried .38 Smith and Wesson snub-nosed revolvers, but neither was considered a 'gun-guy'.

Jim Nielsen was born in 1945, a California native who grew up in Long Beach and attended Long Beach State University where he majored in accounting. After college Jim went to work for the Internal Revenue Service, where after ten years he became a seasoned agent and auditor. After a stint on the East Coast with the IRS, Jim returned to California. He was now married with two young daughters and looking for more adventure. He found it by requesting a position in the field, away from his mundane desk job, working on the front lines in the War on Drugs with Customs and DEA.

Now really in his element, Jim was able to parlay his expertise and experience at being a 'numbers guy' into revolutionizing a more effective method of catching drug dealers and seizing their assets. Jim loved his work in the field and it was only by a random stroke of luck he was paired with DEA Special Agent Jim Conklin.

They say opposites attract, and this couldn't be more true than with the pairing of the Two Jims to pursue the Coronado Company. Where Conklin was the more aggressive, 'bull in a China shop' type, Nielsen had the more reserved, cerebral and contemplative personality, making for a unique and very successful partnership. Nielsen loved the action of being on the scene at surveillance and drug busts, but was never 'first through the door' when the action was actually taking place. His speciality was really 'following the money' and, to that end, F.A.R.T. was assembled to pursue the Coronado Company and seize their assets. The documentation required to complete the forfeiture process was formidable and required patience, diligence and a virtual mountain of paperwork, just what Jim Nielsen had been doing for the past ten years at the IRS. He felt like a baseball player who had just come up to the major leagues from a ten year career in the minors, where he thought he'd never make it to play with the big boys and now, here he was. Finally, he was in his element and ready to 'play ball'.

* * *

Following informant Dave Martin's revelation that Ed Otero was living in Santa Barbara under the assumed name of Ed Morgan, a second piece of the puzzle came to Jim Conklin's attention.

After returning from lunch one afternoon in the late spring of '81, Jim was given a message from his assistant Emma. She was a tall, gangly woman in her mid-30s with dark blonde hair pulled straight back, wore glasses too big for her thin face and was a spitting image of Olive Oyl from the *Popeye* comic strip. The hard working, dedicated assistant Emma reported to Jim that she had taken a call from a DEA agent in the Richmond, Virginia, office named Dexter Tidewater who asked that Agent Conklin get back to him right away. He said he had received an interesting call from a Hilton Head, South Carolina, contractor who said he'd been ripped off by a guy who was a Thai pot smuggler from Southern California.

"Hello, Dexter. This is Jim Conklin from the San Diego DEA office. What have you got for me?"

"Thanks for getting back to me. I was just about ready to wrap it up for the day. It's almost five o'clock our time and I was about to head to the local pub. But, let me fill you in. I got a call today from a disgruntled contractor named Jerry Agnor from Hilton Head, South Carolina. He said he and his brother Mike were contractors and they had been working on building a mansion for some guy at an exclusive seaside setting in Hilton Head. The place even had a clay tennis court, the only privately owned one in the area. He said the guy, known to him as Richard Sheldon, had stiffed him for fifty grand, claiming he was known in Southern California as Mr. Thai Pot and had recently lost a big load of Thai weed and was broke and couldn't pay for the work they'd done. He told the Agnor brothers he'd double their pay next year after another load came in. They pleaded with Sheldon that they had to pay their workers and suppliers out of their own pockets and couldn't float him for another year, but Sheldon still cried 'poor mouth' and left town paying them nothing. They were really pissed off. Jim, I checked the address of the property under construction and it's registered to a Hong Kong company, and I think Richard Sheldon is an alias. Maybe you can follow up on this from your end, since Southern California is in your bailiwick."

"Thanks Dex. I'll contact this Jerry Agnor in the morning and see what's what. I've got a sneaking suspicion this Richard Sheldon might be an alias for one of the guys I've been looking for on a fugitive warrant. I owe you one, buddy."

Now, with these two pieces of information, the wheels were set in motion for Conklin and Nielsen, the team of Two Jims, to actively pursue these leads. However, this would prove not to be an easy task, since they soon discovered both of the leads they were pursuing were fake names, used to conceal the real identities of the suspects they were trying to find.

The trip up to Santa Barbara to try and locate Ed Otero yielded another piece of the puzzle. The house rented to an Ed Morgan was empty, so the team of Two Jims did what all good investigators do in this situation: follow any of their suspicions which might pick up a trail gone cold. First of all they checked with all of the utility companies which had serviced the home. All of these leads also proved to be dead ends, as the utility accounts were initiated in fake names leading to post office boxes also in fake names, set up by people using fake identification. The bills and statements were always paid in cash and no one at the utility company could remember the payee or having ever seen anyone at the location in question. Their final stop to try and figure out just who this Ed Morgan really could be was at the Montecito branch of the U.S. Post Office. The discussion with the local postmaster, however, did yield a new name where Ed Morgan had forwarded his mail. The name Bambi Merryweather surfaced as the recipient of Ed Morgan's forwarded mail. Further investigation yielded that indeed Ms. Merryweather was a real name, and she was employed as a secretary for a nominee company which was owned by another individual also using a fake name.

"Well, at least we have a real person to lean on now," said Jim Conklin as they drove back to the San Diego office. "Maybe these jokers are not as smart at concealing their tracks as they thought."

"They never are," replied Jim Nielsen. "It's the paper trail which will eventually sink them. At IRS, we worked these kinds of cases routinely and, trust me, it's always the money which eventually brings them down. These fuckers think they're so damn smart but it's almost always a small slip-up like this that brings their world crashing down."

"Yeah, you're right, Conklin responded. "Somehow, my gut tells me the tip I got from Agent Tidewater in Richmond is related to this investigation. I have arranged a meeting with the Agnor brothers in the next couple of days and, 'dollars to donuts' I bet we find more chinks in the armor."

Actually, it took several weeks to requisition the funds necessary to fly the Agnor brothers out to San Diego from Hilton Head. With weed cases taking a low priority at DEA, the process to secure the financing necessary to pursue those in the marijuana business involved practically reams of paperwork, in triplicate, and a dogged determination by government agents to overcome all obstacles.

The Two Jims rose to the task and by mid-summer of 1981, Jerry and Mike Agnor were sitting in Jim Conklin's San Diego office. They explained they had been hired by a man they knew as Richard Sheldon to do fine woodworking in a magnificent seaside home he was building in Hilton Head. Sheldon was so pleased with their work, he flew them out to California to do some work for his friends on their houses. Mike Agnor told Conklin he had met two of Sheldon's associates on the trip to California: Bob Hill and Ed Morgan. Then, Jim pulled out his file of fugitives and proceeded to show the Agnor brothers pictures of the people on his list. Conklin was able to pull both California and South Carolina driver license applications for all three and, even though their appearances had changed in the several years since the licenses had been applied for, Agnor was able to positively identify all three.

Mike went on to tell them the same story he had told Agent Tidewater, saying that Sheldon had told him that he was broke and they would just have to fend for themselves for awhile until he could bring in another load the following year. Frustrated, unable to meet their promised obligations and with nowhere else to turn, they called the local IRS office and told their story, hoping if the government busted this Mr. Thai Pot, they might somehow get reimbursed for their losses. Jim Conklin assured the

Agnor brothers that if he was able to seize assets from this Richard Sheldon, he would do his best to make sure they were made whole again.

So now with the discovery of Bambi Merryweather and with the testimony of the Agnor brothers, the Two Jims were able to make the identities of Lou Villar a.k.a. Richard Sheldon, Ed Otero a.k.a. Ed Morgan, and Bob Lahodny a.k.a. Bob Hill. Like a tag team of professional wrestlers, the Agnor brothers took turns in telling the two agents everything they knew about the Coronado Company and anyone who they knew to be involved with them, including the name of Villar's accountant, Andy Willis. Another piece of the ever-growing puzzle.

"Who said our job description included being a dumpster diver and rummaging through garbage?" Nielsen, dressed in a coat and tie, said to the more casually dressed Jim Conklin as they collected the garbage and other refuse from the dumpster behind Andy Willis' San Diego office.

"I guess they fooled this guy Willis too, because obviously he didn't think he had anything to hide and thank God he didn't use a shredder," Conklin said extracting copies of deeds to houses, receipts for several Ferraris, Mercedes Benzes and even for a mouth watering Shelby 427 Cobra from the trash.

"Boy I'd sure love to have that car," drooled Nielsen, green with envy.

"If you play your cards right, you might be able to buy it and add it to your car collection, for pennies on the dollar at the government auction, after we seize it," Conklin joked.

So now with an expanding file nearly four inches thick on the Coronado Company, entitled CorCo, the team of Two Jims set a date for the upcoming bust in Santa Barbara. It was decided by almost as random a method as picking numbers out of a hat. Thursday, November 5, 1981, would be the day to make the simultaneous arrests of Lou Villar and Bob Lahodny in Santa Barbara, and Ed Otero, who was now living up on the Central California coast on the Monterey Peninsula.

As luck would have it, November 5, 1981, would coincidentally prove to be one of the most successful days of search and seizure in DEA history to date. Still, with the DEA budget almost nonexistent for marijuana cases, again requisitioning the money for such an ambitious endeavor would be a challenge. Reports and requests had to go through headquarters in Washington, D.C., and down through the ranks of the DEA to even be considered for such action. A Mobile Task Force (MTF) team of more than a dozen agents had to be organized to travel north from San Diego.

Around the first of November, with still hardly any funds available, an exasperated Jim Conklin told the higher-ups at DEA he would personally pay for gas and food for all of the agents, if the funds could not be allocated for the upcoming bust. DEA finally relented and gave them a few shekels, as Conklin put it, although they still had to sleep in their cars and eat hot dogs during the following five days of surveillance and related activities which they were facing in their pursuit of these multi-million dollar drug dealers. The real Easter egg hunt, to find and arrest these three fugitives and to seize CorCo's assets, was on.

If music and sound effects were being played as this scene unfolded, one could almost hear the foreboding nightmarish, suspense-laden musical score from Alfred Hitchcock's classic movie *Psycho* [1][2] as heard in the famous final shower murder scene.

1 Referenced Television & Movies, Item 1, Page 533.
2 Referenced Songs & Music, Item 16, Page 531.

Chapter 42

Humpty Dumpty

November 5, 1981
Santa Barbara, California

It was a typical day in early November in Southern California. The sky was unusually clear and the weather crisp in the mid-60s. The winds were calm and there was little surf breaking down along the running and bike path which meandered to the beach by the fashionable pink beach palace otherwise called the Biltmore Hotel and Beach Resort, the closest beach to Bob Lahodny's Montecito Spanish style rancho. It was 7:00 in the morning.

Bob felt great as he awoke from a peaceful night's sleep. His latest girlfriend, nicknamed Bootsy, brought him his usual glass of fresh squeezed California orange juice and a cup of hot, freshly brewed Special Reserve Jamaica Blue Mountain Coffee, a pound of which cost nearly $100, delivered in bed as was his daily custom. She also had under her arm the morning edition of the *Los Angeles Times*, which she had gone down the long driveway to retrieve. She silently tiptoed into the master suite and gently placed a kiss on Bob's lips. Yes, Bob felt great as he opened his eyes to the gorgeous creature delivering his morning breakfast. That's the way he liked it… customary juice, coffee and paper. No surprises.

'Boy, am I lucky,' Bob thought. 'Bootsy is the most beautiful and sweetest woman I've ever been with. Gonna marry her one of these days.'

"Morning, beautiful," said Bob, rubbing the sleep from his sparkling blue eyes. "I sure love you and the way you treat me. What a great day. Are you ready to go for a morning run?" he asked. Bob and Bootsy were both in great physical condition, 'hard bodies' in the most pure Southern California sense of the phrase.

"Sure, just let me get my shorts and a tank top on, and I'll be ready in a sec," answered Bootsy.

"Got a meeting over at Pops' house at 10 this morning so we'll have to get right to it," said Bob, referring to Lou Villar who at 43 was considered the 'elder statesman' of the Coronado Company and who everyone affectionately called 'Pops'. "We want to have enough time for a 'roll in the hay' after our run and before Ed gets over here to pick me up."

Bob slipped on a pair of San Diego Charger workout shorts, donned his Vuarnets and put on his gold headband which perfectly matched the emblematic gold lightning bolt Charger insignia embroidered on the right leg of his running shorts. They both had brand new sparkling white Nike running shoes, hers with a trademarked pink Swoosh and his with day-glow orange.

Their usual path took them down the driveway, out the gate and down the hill. They'd go past the famous lush gardens and the sweet smelling pink bougainvillea vines climbing the adobe walls of the old San Ysidro Ranch, the romantic hideaway site of John and Jackie Kennedy's honeymoon. From there it took them across Highway 101, to the grounds of the palatial Biltmore and onto the beach below. There they'd run for a couple of miles on the deserted pristine white sand beach at water's edge, then circle back towards home along the same route. All told the run usually took about an hour. It was a daily ritual for Bob and Bootsy.

The couple looked fabulous as they departed the gate, Bob bare chested with his muscles bulging and Bootsy with her long blonde hair tied in a ponytail and sinewy body taking long antelope-like strides. They both sported beautiful golden brown Southern California suntans glistening on their perfect bodies accentuated by a freshly applied coat of Johnson's Baby Oil.

Upon their return, Bob glanced at the gold Rolex on his left wrist. "It's 8:15 sweetheart. Looks like we just have time for some real exercise now, before the boys get here."

"Sounds great, hon. Just what the doctor ordered," Bootsy purred seductively as she playfully patted Bob's sweaty behind as they passed through the gate and hurried towards the waiting bedroom.

At 9:40 a silver Mercedes Benz 450 SEL 6.9 pulled up to the gate. Ed Otero reached out of the driver's window and punched in the four digit code. Both majestic wrought iron gates swung open and Ed, along with his passenger David Vaughn, proceeded down the long curved driveway, parking under the porte-cochere at the entrance to the hacienda. Ed lightly tapped the horn and Bob appeared a second later at the front door with Bootsy clinging to his arm. Bob waved a friendly 'hello' to the car parked a few feet away from him, gently kissed Bootsy on the lips and said, "Hey, babe. Hold that thought and I'll be back in a couple of hours. We can take up where we just left off. I sure love you, beautiful."

"Me too. I'll be waiting," Bootsy answered suggestively.

Bob climbed into the back seat and the three of them left for the scheduled 10 o'clock meeting at Lou Villar's house, located a few minutes up the hill in the most exclusive section of Montecito. Bob pulled a cigar sized joint out of his Hawaiian shirt pocket and lit it, drawing the pungent smoke deep into his lungs as he passed it forward to David sitting in the 'shotgun' seat. As they turned on to Lou's street, Ed noticed one rather out of place looking vehicle parked just down from Lou's house. It was a dark green 1979 four door Chevy with two men both wearing Ray-Ban-style sunglasses sitting in the front seat, just sitting there.

"That car doesn't look right, in this neighborhood," said Ed as they passed it approaching the gated entrance to Lou's compound. "I'm going to take a loop around the block, just to be safe. Let me have a hit on that joint, Dave."

* * *

For the past three days, the team of 'Two Jims' along with ten agents in a total of five vehicles sat surveillance in the posh neighborhood of Montecito in the vicinity of the multi-million dollar home belonging to Lou Villar. They had arrived on about the 1st of November basically on a wing and a prayer, with virtually no funds to back them up. The agents had slept in their cars and had taken turns on watch. They waited in vain for any signs of activity coming from the gated mansion. The inside of the cars reeked of manly sweat, cigarette smoke and stale air and were littered with hot dog wrappers and empty drink cups from the food they'd purchased from Der Wienerschnitzel, the hot dog fast food joint. With the ashtrays full and their patience running thin, Jim Conklin and his partner Jim Nielsen sat in Conklin's Chevy and waited. The otherwise musty air inside the unmarked car was now thick with tension and anticipation.

From the information gleaned from Andy Willis' office and in his dumpster, the team of Two Jims also learned the location of the current residence of Ed Morgan, a.k.a. Ed Otero. A scrap of paper in the dumpster revealed that Otero was living up on the Monterey Peninsula; therefore Conklin had to coordinate and synchronize the November 5th busts to occur simultaneously not only in Santa Barbara but also 250 miles up the California coast on the Monterey Peninsula. To accomplish this, Conklin put one of his senior agents, a real no-nonsense 'hard-ass' named Larry McKinney, in charge of busting Otero's house up on the Monterey Peninsula.

At almost exactly 10 AM a silver Mercedes 6.9 pulled around the corner and slowed as it approached Villar's gated entrance. The three men in the smoke filled Mercedes, all wearing sunglasses, looked over at the parked Chevy simultaneously. The 6.9 slowed, then accelerated past the entrance.

"Hey Jim. Get a load of that. Another 6.9 in front of Villar's house," said Conklin.

"Yeah. Only movie actors and drug dealers have those cars. I checked with DMV and there are only about 100 of them in California. Clint Eastwood has one and so does Lou Villar, a black one. I wonder who this one belongs to. Looks to me like Ed Otero was driving."

Conklin reached for his walkie talkie and depressed the talk button. "Wing Man, this is Red Leader, follow that silver Mercedes and await my orders."

Immediately a nondescript white Chevy with two burly agents both wearing sunglasses whipped around the corner and began to tail the silver Mercedes. A couple of minutes later, the gate to the mansion opened and a black 6.9 appeared in the driveway as it was preparing to leave. Conklin nudged his Chevy forward, blocking the driveway and the exit of the black Mercedes, and the two Jims jumped out of the car, guns drawn. Conklin still had his walkie talkie in his hand and again depressed the talk button, "Now! Take 'em down! Go! Go! Go!"

* * *

Ed was now down the hill and turning south onto Highway 101 and was just taking a hit off the joint when all of a sudden, as if out of nowhere, a white Chevy sedan with two occupants passed him and got in front of the Mercedes. Ed looked into his rear-view mirror and saw another white Ford on his tail, then looking to his left a white late model Chevy next to him. The man in the passenger seat was waving a badge at Eddie and motioning him over to the side of the road. The car in front of him was slowing and the car to his rear, now only inches from his bumper, had a red portable light mounted on the roof now flashing incessantly at Ed's Mercedes. He hurriedly passed the joint to Bob in the back seat.

"What the fuck is going on?" said Ed turning slowly to Dave sitting in the passenger seat. Ed looked at Bob in the rearview mirror and noticed beads of sweat appearing on his brow. "Get rid of that joint. I think we're being busted."

Bob cracked the window as the car was slowing and flipped the joint onto the road. The car was still filled with smoke as the Benz rolled to a stop on the shoulder of Highway 101 just south of Santa Barbara.

A tall blonde Aryan-looking DEA agent, somewhat resembling the muscular Swedish actor Dolph Lundgren, stuck a .45 up to the driver's closed window, pointed it directly between Ed's eyes an inch or two from his face and yelled, "Open the door and get out. All of you… slowly. Hands where I can see them. You're under arrest!"

Badges and guns appeared from everywhere. Within seconds the three were hand-cuffed and lying face down on the side of the highway with half a dozen FBI and DEA agents hovering over them.

"Finally gotcha, Otero. It only took two years. We're your worst nightmare," the agent said. "Let's head back to Villar's house in Montecito. We'll start the circus there. This is going to be fun."

The agents forced the three smugglers into the back seat of Eddie's Mercedes Benz and drove back to Villar's mansion. The gates were already open and there were four cars in the driveway. Agents swarmed around the vehicles as they arrived in the portico. The three were herded into the living room where Lou Villar was handcuffed and sitting on the sofa looking bewildered and in a state of shock.

Conklin began, "Looks like we've finally rounded you guys up. You could have gotten off easy last time, but you chose to run and become fugitives from the indictment back in '79. The way I see it, you boys are going to be looking at the same scenery for the next 20 to 30 years, unless we get a little cooperation from you."

"I haven't got the slightest idea what you're talking about," said a bedraggled looking Bob Lahodny. "I don't know what's going on, but I believe I'm allowed to call my lawyer."

"You'll do what I tell you, when I tell you, Bobby, my boy," said Conklin. "First we're going to have a little chit-chat, man-to-man. Tell me where the dope is stashed."

"Like I said, officer, I don't know what you're talking about. I think you've got the wrong people."

"Well, Mr. Hill, we'll just see about that. That is who you are today? Right? Bob Hill, that is… or is it Robert Kent Lahodny? Well…" replied Jim Conklin.

"I ain't saying nothin' till I see my lawyer. I got nothing to say to you, Dickhead," Bob answered.

Normally, Jim Conklin would have dropped Bob Lahodny to his knees with a roundhouse punch to the solar plexus for making such an inflammatory comment to his face and in front of his colleagues, but mustering up all of his restraint, he withheld his anger, not wanting to jeopardize the two-year investigation and the biggest bust of his career with a sudden outburst of his violent temper. "We'll see just how cocky you are after a couple of decades or so in the slammer Mister Hill or whoever the fuck you are today, Dickhead! Now we'll see what your compadres have to say. So, as for the two of you… Villar and Otero, and I presume as well Mr. Clean over here, we can do this the easy way or the hard way. Up to you"

"I got nothing to say," answered Ed Otero.

"Me neither," whimpered Villar in a voice barely audible, while removing his glasses and wiping a tear away from his eye.

"Well, Mr. Thai Pot, guess you're not such a big shot after all," interjected IRS agent Jim Nielsen. "I've gone through all of your tax returns, the ones you actually filed, anyway, and since you stopped filing back in '74, the way I see it is that, your net worth from teaching is only about $23,000. Therefore, all these houses here, in Tahoe and in Hilton Head, plus all of these vehicles and all of your other assets seem to come to a scant bit more than $23,000 and will be forfeited pursuant to federal law. Now what do you have to say for yourself, Mr. Thai Pot?"

"I jus wan my lawyer!" Villar sniveled.

Meanwhile, at Ed Otero's home was a different scene completely.

Ed lived up in Pacific Grove on the Monterey Peninsula with his common-law wife Vicky. They lived in a modest home on the bluffs overlooking the ocean just north of Pebble Beach and the swank Spanish Bay Hotel and Resort.

For the past week while Ed and Vicky were down in Santa Barbara, Vicky's parents were visiting and staying in the detached guest house at their Pacific Grove residence.

At exactly 10:30 on the foggy quiet morning of November 5th a team of ten DEA, FBI, IRS and U.S. Customs agents out of the San Jose and San Francisco offices led by Special Agent Larry McKinney broke down the door and surprised Vicky's parents, who were in their late 70s. They handcuffed them and proceeded, with a search warrant, to tear the place apart. All they found at Eddie's house was $25,000 in cash and five pounds of Thai sticks. In Conklin's quest for more booty, he instructed McKinney and the other officers to tear apart the sheetrock walls. He felt sure that since he had found so much treasure in Santa Barbara, there was more dope or money stashed in secreted hollow spaces behind the walls. They found nothing in the walls, but left the house appearing as though it had been struck by a cyclone from within. The interior was completely demolished and Vicky's parents were left in a state of shock and were virtually terrorized by the incident. They had been handcuffed for nearly six hours while the officers searched Ed's home.

At around 3:00 in the afternoon, while the officers were searching Ed's home, the phone rang.

In the most light, cheerful and sing-song voice he could muster, given his normally gruff, brusk and rather rude nature, Larry McKinney answered.

"Hello, Eddie's place."

* * *

I was looking forward to going down to Southern California to finally meet with Eddie Otero to straighten out the 'deal' we'd made with each other. I couldn't wait to remind him of our agreement. It was to have been his responsibility to make arrangements to cover Mike and Dennis, and because of his negligence I'd gotten screwed at the summer meeting. Ed had already assured me we'd fix everything when we were scheduled to meet the following day at La Costa.

Cindy and I were on our way south, headed down to Carlsbad for a few days of R&R and golf and the meeting with Ed the following day. En route at around three in the afternoon I stopped in Oxnard to fill up and call Eddie to confirm tomorrow's meeting. He was living up in Monterey at the time which was the only contact number I had for him.

I went to the pay phone, deposited the coins and waited for the phone to ring.

"Hello, Eddie's place," answered a friendly male voice on the other end of the line.

"Hi, is Ed there?" I asked.

"No, I'm sorry, he's out right now. Can I take a message?" the congenial voice answered.

"Oh, just tell him Rick called and I'll meet him at LC tomorrow as planned," I said, referring to La Costa Resort and Spa where Cindy and Ed's girlfriend Vicky were planning a day of massages and facials while Eddie and I played the renowned La Costa Golf Course, which had recently hosted the PGA Tournament of Champions.

"OK, Rick. By the way, what's your last name? So I can tell Eddie which Rick called," the cheerful voice on the other end politely asked.

"Huh?" I mumbled, as I recoiled. My mind raced. I thought, 'this is a rather unusual question. Nobody at Ed's would ask such a question. Nobody in Ed's world would dare ask such a question. It was definitely out of the realm of questions which would ever be asked from a smuggler or a smuggler's friend.' My guard immediately went up.

"Who is this, anyway?" I queried.

"Oh, I'm just a friend of the family and am staying here while Eddie is out for awhile," answered the voice, which was now not quite as friendly, but seemingly more matter-of-fact-like at this point. "OK," the voice continued, "Rick, I'll tell him you'll meet him at LC's tomorrow. And, it's Rick who?"

Another alarm went off in my ears. 'LC's? I didn't say LC's, I said LC,' I thought. 'For some reason, this person is really prying me for information and trying to find out what my last name is. I don't like the feel of this at all.' I continued pondering.

I decided to take the offensive and see what happens. "Look, I don't like the sound of your questions. What's your name anyway and exactly who are you. Let me speak to

Vicky then. Right now," I demanded.

At this point, the voice on the other end became noticeably agitated, "Look, Rick. Just tell me what your last name is. Vicky is not available."

At this point, I guessed what was going on and angrily responded, "Go fuck yourself, whoever you are," and hung up the phone. I returned from the pay phone to Cindy who was waiting in the car. "Cindy, there's definitely trouble at Ed's house. I just got off the phone with somebody who was there and he was asking me the weirdest questions, like what my last name was, which he asked twice. I'm almost positive I just spoke to the cops who were in his house. I got very strange vibes from the person on the other end of the line. I'm not sure what's going on, but I know it was a cop on the phone."

"Well, let's go to La Costa, have dinner and at least stay the night and find out what's going on," Cindy said. "If things look weird we can leave in the morning."

Cindy and I proceeded to La Costa, arriving at about 7:00 PM. I was still worried about the phone call to Eddie's and couldn't get it out of my mind. We had reserved a suite in one of the 'casitas' located on the golf course. Upon settling into our suite, we began to relax and unpack. We decided to order dinner from room service which was served directly from La Costa's five-star restaurant. At 7:30 we ordered dinner to be delivered to our room. From the menu we ordered a Caesar salad, rack of lamb for two, baby potatoes, steamed asparagus with hollandaise sauce and for dessert crepes Suzette with caramel sauce, on the side. We also ordered a particularly nice bottle of French bordeaux red wine, a 1970 Chateaux Margaux. Dinner arrived promptly at 8:00 and was set up in the suite on a portable dining room table. The salad was served and the remainder of the dinner kept in a special warming cart under domed silver food warmers. The setting was exquisite.

Just as I opened the wine the telephone rang. The time was 8:05.

"Rick, this is Phil DeMassa. I'm Ed Otero and Bob Lahodny's attorney. This morning the two of them along with Louis Villar and David Vaughn were arrested and charged with conspiracy to smuggle marijuana into the United States. They are all now being held in the Federal Jail in Los Angeles. I just came from visiting them. Eddie told me that in the middle of the bust of his Pacific Grove home, you called and had a conversation with one of the agents searching the house. He told me that you told the agent who you were and that you planned to meet Eddie tomorrow at La Costa. He only hoped I wouldn't be too late in telling you. My advice to you is: leave immediately. Don't waste another minute."

"Thanks for the heads-up, Phil," I said as I quickly hung up the receiver.

"Cindy, get your things packed, we're leaving right now. Not in five minutes, but right this instant!" I exclaimed.

"What? Who was that?" asked Cindy. "What's going on?"

"No time to explain now, just get your shit into the car… we're outta here," I repeated.

Within two minutes we had gathered our belongings, loaded the car outside in the carport and were on the road.

We went to the nearest pay phone where I called Stan Yamamoto, who lived close by, on a ranch just east of the town of Oceanside.

"Stan, mind if Cindy and I stop by. I must talk to you right now," I said.

"Sure, come on over."

We proceeded to Stan's house and told him what had happened. Stan thought it best if Cindy and I stay the night at his house then return to the Bay Area first thing in the morning.

Half an hour later, an unmarked green 1979 Chevy pulled into La Costa, found the night manager and barged into the suite we had rented. The room was empty except for the feast which lay untouched on the table. Jim Conklin poured himself a glass of the 1970 Chateaux Margaux and helped himself to the rack of lamb which was still nice and warm under the silver warming dome. He turned to Jim Nielsen who was with him. "Here, Jim, have a glass of wine and some dinner. This sure beats hot dogs and soft drinks. Looks like we just missed Rick. It's been a long day. I'm tired and hungry. Don't worry, I'm sure Rick Bibbero will surface sooner or later and when he does you can bet I'll be waitin' for that scum bag. We just put the Coronado Company outta business and Rick's a marked man, Jim. Cheers."

* * *

On November 5, 1981, the team of Two Jims indeed put the Coronado Company out of business. They arrested and charged Coronado's three principals with conspiracy to import, possess and distribute marijuana. They also arrested David Vaughn and charged him likewise. The real booty however was in the form of what they were able to seize. November 5th had been chosen at random as the day of the bust. The 'arresting Gods' must have been smiling on the two Jims that day, because it just so happened that since the Bear Harbor load had only landed a couple of weeks prior, Lou Villar, who was never comfortable fronting his share out to be sold, still had a considerable quantity of his sizable share of Thai sticks stashed at his house. In the wine cellar of Mr. Thai Pot's home, they found 700 pounds of the most gorgeous Thai sticks any of the agents had ever seen. They also recovered thousands of dollars of jewelry, $200,000 in cash and a safe deposit box key, which they soon discovered opened a box at a local bank. There, with a court order, they opened the box and found over $100,000 worth of South African Kruggerrands, nearly $1 million worth of investment grade diamonds, another $450,000 in cash and deeds to homes in Santa Barbara, Lake Tahoe's Incline Village and one in Hilton Head, South Carolina. In the garage of Villar's home were two of his Ferraris, a Shelby Cobra, and a new GMC pickup, all of which were confiscated. They also confiscated Villar's black 6.9 Mercedes Benz in the driveway. Jim Nielsen also discovered Louis Villar had a total of 18 exotic cars in his stable of vehicles. Ultimately, however, they were only able to confiscate nine as the Feds ran into a sympathetic 9th Circuit Court Judge, who threatened Conklin with a jail sentence if the seizures didn't immediately cease, based on the Feds usurping their authority from the state level.

At Ed Otero's home they recovered five pounds of Thai weed and $25,000 in cash, which was seized as well as the home itself plus his silver Mercedes 6.9. Bob Lahodny likewise lost a sizable stash of diamonds, his palatial Montecito rancho, thousands of dollars of jewelry and artwork, an unspecified amount of cash and his Mercedes 450 SEL.

All told, the random choice of November 5th proved to be one of the largest seizures in DEA history to date. Larger busts would occur in the future, but this event set the precedent as the first test of Jim Nielsen's F.A.R.T. program. It would earn Nielsen legendary status among his peers for decades to come.

From that fateful day in early November 1981, Ed Otero never saw the light of day and was incarcerated until 1997. Bob, however did get released for a short time on bail, but served a total of six years and was finally released from custody in 1996. Bootsy, Bob Lahodny's girlfriend, stuck around for the better part of two months, before calling it quits. She was questioned by the authorities but knew virtually nothing of the Coronado operation and was summarily dismissed. The love of his life and potential wife soon realized the party was over, and like most of the significant others, the girlfriends and wives of drug smugglers, vanished when the party was over and the shit hit the fan.

I can't think of more appropriate or truer words to describe this, than those sung by Rick Springfield in his 1983 hit and record album by the same name, *Living In Oz*.[1] It couldn't have been more clear in this situation and many others like it:

'… All the people that protect and serve, would disappear if the well dried up…'

The Coronado Company itself was effectively destroyed and put out of business forever, as of that fateful date. It was sadly reminiscent of the old eighteenth century English nursery rhyme *Humpty Dumpty*.[2]

'Humpty Dumpty sat on a wall, Humpty Dumpty had a great fall
All the king's horses and all the king's men couldn't put Humpty together again!'

However, Lou Villar, along with several other Coronado Company conspirators chose a very different path.

---

1 Referenced Songs & Music, Item 13, Page 531.
2 Referenced Songs & Music, Item 17, Page 531.

Section 8

Rats Leave The Sinking Ship
(1982–1993)

Chapter 43

Tony Bites The Dust

Early Spring 1982

Bit-by-bit my world was crumbling before my own eyes. As I thought back, since the death of my beloved dog Papi, everything which had gone so right previously was now disintegrating into an uncontrolled maelstrom and I feared the worst was yet to come.

Papi had died on the day known as The Ides of March, the same date in history Julius Caesar was assassinated. While Caesar mocked his soothsayer's premonition to 'beware the Ides of March', the quote made famous in Shakespeare's play *Julius Caesar*, I felt a sense of dismay and impending doom at such a coincidence. With the bust of the three principal players in Coronado's organization, I felt it was only a matter of time before the Feds would be knocking on my door.

With that in mind, I proceeded to put our Menlo Park home on the market. It sold within a month. Cindy and I moved to the Monterey Peninsula and again felt a rather false sense of security now that we were out of Menlo Park and the Bay Area. We also sold the Woodside home which was still under construction, so we could move lock, stock and barrel out of the Bay Area.

It seemed for a while that things had quieted down, until one morning in mid-March when I got a call from Tony the Thai who was staying in Los Angeles, out on bail and awaiting trial.

"Rick, I very sick and in hospital. Maybe need surgery. Stomach bleeding. Can you come see me?" said Tony. His once strong voice now seemed weak and whispery.

"What? Sure, 'Thai'. I will try and get down there tomorrow, but in any case I will be there in two days at the latest," I replied. "You just hang in there."

Tony, trying to be as upbeat as usual said, "No worry too much. I probably be OK by time you get here."

Two days later, at 3:15 in the afternoon I arrived at Cedar Sinai Hospital in Los Angeles and went directly to the third floor nurses station. "What room is Mr.

Kraithamjitkul in? I am a friend of his here to visit him," I asked.

The nurse blanched and replied, "I'm so sorry. Mr. Kraithamjitkul passed away an hour ago. I'm so sorry."

I just stood there, stunned, not knowing what to do or say. Then weakly and on the verge of tears I asked the nurse: "What happened?"

"In surgery, we just couldn't stop the bleeding," said the nurse now also in tears. "The walls of his esophagus and stomach had deteriorated and were so thin and damaged, we just couldn't get them to hold closed. Mr. Kraithamjitkul was a very sick man and we did all we could to save him. Again, I'm awfully sorry. He seemed to be such an upbeat person when we saw him in pre-op."

"Well, thank you. I know you did your best," I said. "And, yes, he was the most upbeat and positive person you'll ever meet."

I was crushed and in kind of a state of surrealistic shock as I headed back to the elevator. While waiting for the elevator I noticed a bank of pay phones on the opposite wall. The only phone which was being used at that moment was by a blonde lady who was laughing into the phone and speaking rather obnoxiously loud given the quiet hospital setting. As she turned around I saw that it was a very well-known Hollywood actress whom I instantly recognized. She seemed so happy and animated on the phone across the hall from me whereas I was devastated and in the depths of depression. The elevator came and I stepped on and pressed the 'down' button and the doors closed. Right then, I came to the realization that when you die, no one except your family and close friends care. The world goes on. Nevertheless I was a wreck.

I could never really think of him as Tony. To me he was and would always be 'Thai.' Aside from my childhood sweetheart, Sally, who was killed in a car accident fourteen years earlier, 'Thai' was the second really close person in my life and of my peers to die. I'm not sure how old he was, maybe thirty-five, but he was one of those people who had an infectious personality, one who you always wanted to be around. He had a great sense of humor, but commanded great respect from not only his family and friends, but from every single other member of the Thai crew as well as from various members of the Thai military and Thai police whom he knew and who had helped him with our operation. I always felt very safe in Thailand when he was around, although he always packed a Colt 1911 with him in his briefcase. We had great times together, from the time in Vegas to times in Hong Kong, Bangkok and 'up country' in Thailand. He had introduced me to disco music, his favorite being a German disco group named Boney M. Being a rock-and-roll aficionado, I hated disco, but Thai gave me a new appreciation of it. In turn I introduced him to the rock-and-roll music of Pat Benatar. He couldn't get enough of her voice and Grammy award winning songs. We played music of both artists constantly as we cruised around Thailand. I think it was one of the highlights of his life when I took him to see Pat Benatar live at a show in San Francisco. We sat in the front row and it totally blew his mind. His wife's sister, a schoolteacher for young children, taught me to speak, read and write the Thai language and 'Thai' himself, maybe most importantly, finally got me to appreciate and even really like to eat one of the most revered of the many Thai delicacies, the monthong variety of durian…

as 'Thai' used to say: "Number One fruit in whole world!"

It was just unbelievably sad, he had to die so young. Over the years I think of him often and have come to miss him greatly. He was indeed a true friend.

It seemed I could hardly focus on anything for the next few days as 'Thai's' death weighed on me heavily, but as the numbness began to wear off, I slowly came to the realization that without 'Thai', I had also lost any hope of being able to stay in the marijuana business in Thailand. I knew that without 'Thai' it wouldn't be possible for me to be able to work with Charlie or any other of the Thai crew. They already had Ciro and others in his group and had done several successful trips with them and it was only through 'Thai's' persistent cajolement that the Thai crew had even agreed to do the Bear Harbor load with me. Now, with 'Thai' gone, I was done, pure and simple, unless I wanted to start over from scratch, the same as 'Thai' had suggested to Pat several years back. Pat declined back then and I could see the writing on the wall; I would soon be following the same path, only this time my retirement might not be of my own choosing.

* * *

Although the move to the Big Sur coast seemed to temporarily mollify Cindy's growing contemptuous attitude towards me, with each new revelation of my world coming undone, Cindy would again hit the bottle and bag. With each successive swig and snort, she would become more out of control and abusive. I found the only way I could contend with her was to get away. I found more frequent excuses to have to go to Southern California to assist Stan with something or other. In reality, it was to spend more time with Stan's sister, Tanya, as our relationship deepened. On the other hand, Cindy was not sitting idle during my frequent forays out of town. Cindy was likewise being 'comforted' by another new member of my crew, Kevin Masters, one of my helpers who had moved up to the Monterey Peninsula from Southern California. Masters, who had been a great help in getting us moved to the South Coast, was a friendly giant of a man. At 6'6" tall with curly black hair and tipping the scale at nearly 265 pounds, Kevin couldn't have been more helpful to me, doing odd jobs and getting ready to help wherever he could in preparation for possibly another trip later in the year. He was a great guy and Cindy found herself leaning on him for support and 'comfort' and, as I later found out, practically threw herself at him numerous times, until he just couldn't resist her advances. In reality, we were indeed a busy pair as each of us sought solace in the company of others to satisfy our needs and growing desire to get away from each other.

A few weeks later, I received two phone calls which really disturbed me. The first was from Ed Otero's girlfriend, Vicky. She told me she was relaying a message from Eddie, who was now sequestered in the Federal Prison at Terminal Island in Long Beach, California. Eddie had told Vicky I owed the Coronado Company $350,000. Eddie told her that it was an old debt that the Coronado Company had paid on my behalf to Dennis and Mike for my share of the payoff to them from the Bear Harbor load. She told me that I needed to give her the money as Eddie, Bob and Lou really needed it, as nearly all of their assets had been confiscated when they were busted. I told her I'd think about it, but she need not worry as the money was safe with me and I would return it to them when they got out. Vicky wasn't particularly happy with my response but said she would relay the message to Eddie and get back to me. The second call a few days later was of a much more sinister and disturbing nature to me and one I would learn a bitter lesson from. It was from Phil DeMassa, Coronado Company's lawyer, the same attorney who had warned me to vacate the La Costa suite after their bust and who had represented Tony after his bust at the San Francisco Airport. DeMassa told me, under no uncertain terms, that if I didn't immediately return the money I owed them, he (DeMassa) couldn't guarantee that they wouldn't implicate me. Although Phil didn't say it directly to me, he certainly implied the possibility of one or all of them cooperating with the government and that if I wasn't forthcoming with the money right now... well?

To me it was extortion, pure and simple. My intention was to hold the funds for safekeeping until their release from prison as well as to have some leverage against them in case they ratted me out and I had to defend myself. In that case I'd planned to use the money for my defense. Phil also implied that possibly physical harm might come to me as well if I didn't pay up. He even intimated that even though 'the boys' were locked up, they had friends on the outside who could still do their bidding.

This was actually the third time in my involvement in the marijuana business that I had been threatened with bodily harm. The first was when Willie and I got ripped off by George at gunpoint in the Nogales quarry in the early days and the second was back in 1977 when I was threatened by Ciro at his house at Lake Tahoe following the *Drifter* episode. It took awhile but I was now beginning to realize that there indeed was a darker side to the so called 'mellow' marijuana business, and it wasn't pretty or 'groovy' as I'd once imagined.

Against my better judgement, I called Vicky and arranged for a meeting with her where I would give her the money. Big mistake!

The bitter lesson which would soon become apparent to me was: if someone threatens something they will follow through with their threat.

Following my return of the money, in the early spring of 1982 Lou Villar decided to cooperate with federal investigators. He had called Jim Conklin from the pay phone at Terminal Island and indicated he wanted to cooperate. As a matter of fact, Villar told Conklin, he had wanted to cooperate all along but couldn't because of his attorney Phil DeMassa. DeMassa had advised him that if he cooperated fully he would have to implicate DeMassa himself which would cause a conflict of interest, therefore he couldn't do it.

Conklin, however, had another plan. He arranged for Villar to fire DeMassa and hire an attorney from Incline Village, Kevin McInerney, to represent him. Through a series of protracted negotiations, between McInerney, Villar, Conklin and IRS agent Jim Nielsen, Villar was able to work out a 'sweet' deal.[1]

In exchange for not only his freedom but a new identity in the Witness Protection

---

1 Referenced Newspaper Articles, Item 8, Page 529.

Program plus the return of substantial assets and cash which had been seized, Villar agreed to tell the Feds everything about the Coronado Company's smuggling operation from the beginning.[2]

During two and a half weeks of intense debriefing during February and into March, Villar told Jim Conklin and Jim Nielsen everything. He told them who was involved in every trip, the amount of money realized and exactly what had happened from the beginning, starting with the first forays into the dope business back in the late 1960s. It was all laid bare. Villar had a keen memory for even the minutest details of the organization's history and activities and not lost in his regurgitation of everything was the incident of Pat's trip to Santa Barbara to purchase one million dollars of wholesale diamonds from his diamond connection Brad Ferrar. When confronted with this revelation, Brad Ferrar sang like a bird. So much for his promise of confidentiality. Even though retired, Pat was now caught in Villar's web and would be doomed with Brad Ferrar's corroboration and his magically produced confidential records of all diamond purchases. The team of Two Jims practically had to beat Villar to shut him up. However he wasn't alone. That summer both Alan 'Fuzzy' Logie and David Vaughn also agreed to cooperate along with several others including boat captain Donald McMichaels.

Conklin now had a very clear picture of all of Coronado's activities and could actively pursue anyone and everyone who was involved or had ever been involved. In exchange for a complete and truthful debriefing and with the promise of his honest testimony as a government witness in any future trials, Louis Henry Villar would be released from federal prison. He would then be set up in a secure location, with a new identity. In addition, he was returned a huge seven figure settlement plus the remaining nine exotic sports cars which had previously not been seized pursuant to the Ninth Circuit Court's earlier ruling and directive against such action. Logie, Vaughn and McMichaels were subsequently released from custody and given probation.

Meanwhile, at Terminal Island, one day Villar was there in a nearby prison cell close to Bob Lahodny and Ed Otero, and the next day he was mysteriously gone. Bob immediately called Phil DeMassa who confirmed that Lou had 'rolled over' and they had better get word out to everyone who had ever been involved with Lou or who he had ever met in the course of the Company's marijuana business and advise them that their days were probably numbered. Vicky relayed the news to me and I passed the word along to my crew, including Pat and Joe who could actually be identified by Lou Villar, of the situation and impending doom.

It was felt that Phil, Willie, and others would be pretty safe as they had been kept in the background and most likely Villar didn't even know of their existence, much less their names or identities. However, Joe Schroder and Jeremy 'Rico' Fromriko were another matter. Since they both had been at Coronado's distribution houses on the Neah Bay load at Stan's house in Vista, and in the Bear Harbor load stash house in Arcadia, and had met and shaken hands with Coronado snitches, Alan 'Fuzzy' Logie and David Vaughn, they both could be positively identified. It was only due to Stan's

2 Referenced Legal Research, Item 2, Page 532.

quick, on-the-spot and almost reflexive thinking that Rico was saved from being ID'd. When Rico entered the garage at Stan's house to start loading our share of what was left of the Neah Bay load, David Vaughn inquired as to who he was. Stan introduced him by the name of 'Harold'.

A subsequent Report of Investigation (ROI) of Alan Logie's debriefing[3] identified him as Harold LNU (Last Name Unknown) and from then on Rico became known in our circle as Harold L'New, spoken with a rather French accent, making a last name of the letters L-N-U. Rico would forever be indebted to Stan for that ingenious quick response. Joe, on the other hand, was not so lucky as he was well known in those circles, had attended some of their Southern California beach parties and had dated Bob Lahodny's former girlfriend, Donna Stevenson, all in his own real name and he could easily be ID'd.

Pat, as well, even though he had retired and quit before the Neah Bay episode, would certainly be implicated. Pat got an attorney and was advised that being a Thai citizen, if he were to get busted he would be incarcerated in the U.S. for however long his sentence might be, then deported back to Thailand and probably never allowed to return. With this news, he sold everything—his Woodside home, his Porsche, his other vehicles, his spec homes—and along with his new wife, Rebecca, he left the country to relocate back to Thailand. With him the only thing of value he took was his $2,000,000 in cash and his $1,000,000 in diamonds, whose value had significantly increased. He was able to transfer another $2,000,000 through his Swiss bank account so, in his mind, he was pretty set and safe. But not being able to stay or return to the U.S. again and lead the life he'd grown accustomed to left him a bitter man.

Jim Conklin, however, was able to have a chat with him prior to his departure. Conklin served a search warrant on Pat's Woodside house. He found nothing, but Pat actually tried to bribe him by offering him his investment grade diamonds, now having a retail value of nearly $4,000,000. Conklin refused and sought to confiscate them, but at that point Pat disappeared with his cash, diamonds and wife.

Conklin would have an opportunity to speak with Pat years later in Thailand and tried to convince him to cooperate, but since Pat had been out of the loop for so many years, he had nothing to offer and his case was dropped. However, the mellow guy who I had spent so much time with, traveling the world and originally setting up the whole Thai stick operation with, was gone. He was now stuck in Thailand forever with a huge chip on his shoulder because he was forced to leave the country and lifestyle he'd grown accustomed to. Even though he was able to sell all of his assets and take the proceeds out of the country, marry his sweetheart and leave the country virtually unscathed and wealthier than he ever could have imagined, he suffered from a perpetual temper tantrum and was always mad at the world and would try to take it out on anyone he could… including me!

---

3 Referenced Legal Research, Item 3, Page 532.

Chapter 44

Patrick 'Butch' Hallinan

End of July 1982

Cindy and I took a vacation and went to Lake Powell to relax and water ski in the sun and remoteness of the Southern Utah scenic wonder. We rented a 50-foot houseboat and a ski boat and stayed for ten days totally out of communication. We became lost in a haze of marijuana smoke, alcohol, cocaine, blistering 100° temperatures and plenty of sunshine.

Upon leaving Powell in my 6.9 Mercedes Benz, I headed west back across Utah's scenic red canyon lands. There was virtually no other traffic on the road and I decided I'd open her up. In what seemed to be out in the middle of nowhere and with the speedometer nearly pegged at 140 miles per hour, the radar detector mounted on my sun visor started beeping. I let off on the gas pedal and as I came over a rise, I saw a red light shining at me in the distance ahead. I slowed to 65, but it was too late.

The Utah highway patrolman, in his Ray-Bans and Smokey the Bear hat, was now out of his car and standing in the middle of the road up ahead and motioning me to pull over. I complied and the cop sidled up to the driver's window and looked inside. He said: "I see you have a radar detector, well, let me show you what I have." He instructed me to get out and check out the new equipment in his cruiser. I sheepishly did as I was told. Mounted inside on the floor underneath his radio was a large electronic looking box the cop called 'the latest high tech device to catch speeders.' He said it was a lock-out device blocking his radar signal until he had line-of-sight visibility. Obviously this was why my state-of-the-art radar detector failed to pick up his signal… he'd blocked it and had caught me 'dead-to-rights'. He further told me that he could sit upon the rise we were currently standing on and look into the distance on the isolated straightaway from where I had just come and, with binoculars, spot speeders two miles away. As soon as he saw a car speeding towards him in the distance, he would release the lock-out, instantly recording the speed of the oncoming vehicle and wait to nail them. He told me I was just one of many he'd cited that day, and he had clocked me at 110 miles per hour, the number blinking repeatedly in flashing red lights on his digital readout. This was serious and I was shitting bullets, not only because of my speed, but because of my stash of marijuana and cocaine sitting in the console.

Then the most amazing thing happened: the cop told me he would radio ahead to the small town of Kanab, Utah, where I would be in exactly 25 minutes, if I traveled at 60 miles per hour. A local sheriff would meet me there and escort me to the courthouse and, if I wanted to have the incident 'forgotten' about, I could simply put $250 in an envelope and slide it under the judge's door, otherwise I could spend a couple of days in the local jail in the scorching 100° heat with an air conditioning system that only worked intermittently. I breathed a sigh of relief and complied. At the time, I didn't realize just how lucky I had been, but I was soon to find out.

A few hours later Cindy and I arrived in Las Vegas where we had planned to spend a couple of days, then return home to the coast. We checked into a suite at the MGM Grand Hotel on the Las Vegas strip. After being escorted to our room, I telephoned my friend Stan in San Diego. Stan told me my name had been in the newspapers and I, along with 26 others, had been indicted in Federal Court in San Diego[1] and was wanted by the authorities. Stan advised me not to go back to my home, because certainly the Feds would have a BOLO (Be On the Look-Out) for me in and around the Carmel area as well as in Menlo Park at my former residence. Right then, I realized neither the Utah highway patrolman who had stopped me for speeding nor the local Kanab sheriff's deputy who had escorted me to the courthouse had run my name in the database and obviously weren't aware of my 'Wanted' status. Otherwise, I'd have been arrested on the spot. It was really a quick payola scam which the Utah cops had going, but it worked in my favor. I had truly dodged a bullet… for the moment!

"Don't panic, don't panic," I told myself and Cindy as we departed Vegas later that night. I had again checked into the MGM under my own name and I figured it was only a matter of time before the net would close around me, so we left and headed for my parents' vacation home in Lake Tahoe.

"I'm going to have to figure something out and face the music," I said. "I need a lawyer," I continued. "I've heard that it's better to surrender to the authorities on your own terms with a lawyer at your side rather than be arrested. That way you can maintain a degree of control in your situation, rather than have the cops cuff you, ransack your home and haul you off to the slammer in the back of a squad car. It also helps to 'self-surrender' when it comes to getting released on bail, as it shows that one is not a flight risk." I also knew that, once arrested and hauled away, the three principals of the Coronado Company were held without bail and considered flight risks. Lou Villar was only released after his complete cooperation with authorities. Ultimately, Eddie Otero and Bob Lahodny had pled guilty and served nearly seven years in federal prison before being released. They were also given ten years on parole and lifetime probation.

Every year thereafter on November 5th, the anniversary of the biggest bust of their careers, Jim Conklin and Jim Nielsen met at a local bar in San Diego and toasted each other with Miller Lites and congratulated each other on the success of having put away

---

1 Referenced Legal Research, Item 4, Page 532.

one of the largest smuggling operations to date on the West Coast. However, their work was now just getting started.

Lou Villar and Alan 'Fuzzy' Logie had great memories for all of the details and every one of the participants of each load the Coronado 'boys' had ever done and provided the team of Two Jims with over one hundred names. Lou was indeed 'the goose that had laid the golden egg' right on Jim Conklin's lap. Conklin now had the names of not only direct participants in each load, i.e., beach crews, boat crews, and distributors, but also the names of investors and indirect participants, such as the name of the jeweler who had sold diamonds to the Coronado principals and to Pat Suraghoomkol and others.

Conklin and Nielsen aimed to put everyone away who had anything to do with Coronado or any other participants in any other smuggling groups which Villar knew of. It would prove to be a virtual smorgasbord for the U.S. judicial system to feast on.

* * *

Upon our arrival at Lake Tahoe, Cindy and I had time to discuss the future and make plans, hopefully without the threat of agents showing up at the front door to arrest me.

Cindy had heard the name of a well-known San Francisco criminal attorney who she thought might be able to help. His name was Ephraim Margolin. I contacted him and arranged for a meeting with him in the next few days.

In an earlier life, before becoming a lawyer, Margolin had emigrated to the United States from Israel. As a young man Margolin was an Israeli freedom fighter and part of group whose activities led to Israel's becoming an independent state in 1948. Subsequently, Margolin left Israel, was educated in the United States and went on to a successful career as an attorney in San Francisco, earning many awards during a 40-plus-year career.

We met at his office whereupon I hired him to represent me and arrange for my surrender to authorities in San Diego. The two of us flew to San Diego where I was booked, fingerprinted, arraigned and immediately released on bail. My parents collateralized their home for my bail. Following my self-surrender, Margolin and I began to prepare for my upcoming trial, which was scheduled to take place early in 1983. I liked Ephraim very much, but during our trial preparation it became clear to me he had all but conceded any chance of my winning at trial. To me it seemed like he was preparing for my appeal rather than the upcoming trial. The evidence seemed pretty thin and was based almost exclusively on the statements of Villar and Logie, two individuals of rather dubious backgrounds and who themselves had made deals with the government to avoid their own prosecutions.

Something my father had once said to me started to ring in my ears. He said: "If you ever hire a lawyer, you had better know your own case inside and out." He went on to say: "How many cases does your lawyer have and how many do you have? If it ever gets complicated, he can always go on to another case... you, on the other hand, have only one case and it's your life, not his."

During this time period my parents seemed to circle the wagons and try to help me as much as possible. My father agreed to put up the money for my defense, which was actually my money in the first place, but his help was certainly a much appreciated turnaround from his previous position of wanting nothing to do with me. When it comes down to it, I guess that's what families are all about. My mother also continued to be supportive. As it turned out, her nephew, one of my first cousins, Peter Feldstein, was an Assistant United States Attorney in New York City. She contacted him and relayed my situation to him. His response was: "Tell Rick to tell the government everything he knows. It's his only chance." These words and his advice to my mother would haunt and piss me off constantly for the next five years.

I felt I could be better represented at trial by another attorney, and didn't want to go down without a good fight. After less than one month, I fired Ephraim Margolin. He told me it was the first time in his career he had ever been fired, but I told him I was not comfortable with the direction my case was headed. I was facing ten to twenty years in prison and wanted my best chance in court and not concede it to an appeal, as Margolin had suggested. Too bad… but I wanted a real fighter with a proven track record in trial court.

I met with my old friend John 'JQ' Quinn one evening and told him of my dilemma regarding my legal representation. JQ had spent many years working as a bartender at one of the most popular San Francisco bars located near the Financial District. His knowledge of 'who's who' in the legal profession was virtually unparalleled. He'd either personally met or had heard stories about all the top lawyers in The City. He suggested that without question the best trial lawyer in San Francisco was Patrick Hallinan. He had the reputation of 'living and dying' with his clients and was one of the best attorneys for drug cases in the entire country. After the meeting, there was no doubt, Hallinan was my man.

Patrick Hallinan was the eldest son of one of San Francisco's most notable firebrand lawyers, Vincent Hallinan, who actually had run for president of the United States in 1952. Vincent and his wife Vivian lived in Marin County and had six boys. Patrick was the de facto leader of his younger siblings. All six were given nicknames by their father and were trained as fighters in their youth. Butch and younger brothers Kayo, Ringo, Dynamite, Tuffy and Danny were known to terrorize Marin County in the 1950s, getting into fights where they acted like a 'tag team', which earned them legendary status. You don't mess with the Hallinans… you get one, you get all six. Patrick went on to the University of California at Berkeley where he majored in anthropology. He was also on the college boxing team where, as a middleweight, he competed and was a finalist for the NCAA boxing championships in the mid-'50s. After earning his undergraduate degree, he went on to Hastings Law School and finally, following in his father's footsteps, became the second firebrand Hallinan to be admitted to the California Bar Association.

I had originally heard of Patrick, known to his friends as 'Butch', from Ciro Mancuso, who had been represented by him back in the days of the *Drifter* debacle and also when he had been busted in Half Moon Bay for cocaine possession. He had managed to get

Ciro off on both occasions.

I met him later in the week and we immediately hit it off. I could tell at once, no matter the outcome, we would be friends for life. He was just that kind of person and I hired him on the spot. We got right to it and prepared for my trial. He thought it would be an uphill battle, but we had a good chance of actually winning at trial.

In my indictment alone, there were a total of 27 defendants and I would be the first to go to trial. Butch viewed it as a significant advantage because, as he explained it, the prosecution would not be as prepared for the legal onslaught he would deliver out of the gate as they would be for later cases. This impressed me. Patrick also told me he wouldn't represent anyone who cooperated with the government. Of course we also discussed my history in the marijuana business. I was very frank and open with him about it and pretty much told Butch the complete tale from the beginning. I told him of my long-time involvement with one of his other clients, Ciro Mancuso, from the days of Mexico and up through the *Drifter* incident. Patrick acknowledged that and then informed me he'd had some real estate dealings with Ciro who had arranged for the sale of his mother's Squaw Valley home and Ciro had even done work on his Marin home. He went on to say he was really happy with Ciro's transition from the marijuana business to his being a legitimate contractor and real estate developer and that he'd put all of his dealings in the 'business' behind him.

I sat there stunned.

"You mean to tell me, he told you he was out of the marijuana business?" I asked, completely dumbfounded.

"Yup. That's exactly what I mean," answered Patrick.

"Well, I don't mean to rain on your parade, but that's total bullshit," I said. "I know it for a fact. He stole our Thai connection and, believe me, he's still very actively involved. Believe what you want. It's none of my business. Trust me. He'll say anything or tell any lie to anyone if it's to his advantage. He doesn't give a shit about you or me or anyone else. I've known him for over fifteen years and for Ciro, the bottom line is, it's always all about him. If you want to trust him, I guess, that is your business. But from where I sit, he's about as ruthless as they come. Believe me, I know from personal experience. Do whatever you want… but it's the truth. Let's move on."

Reflecting on this conversation years later, Butch wanted to trust and believe in Ciro. I have always considered Patrick to be very smart and very intuitive about people, but in this instance, he just put blinders on and wouldn't listen. I don't think he believed me or, if he did, didn't want to believe me. This intransigence and gullibility would come back to haunt him, even as astute as he was, in ways he couldn't foresee or ever imagine in his wildest dreams.

During the months of our preparation for trial, I was repeatedly called to come to San Diego to have a 'discussion' with DEA agents. I was offered all kinds of leniency deals in exchange for my cooperation. I basically told them, in so many words to 'go fuck themselves', and Patrick added, "We're going to trial. Bring on your witnesses. C'est la guerre."

Preparing for trial was an exciting time and a real learning experience for me, one which would follow me to this day. I became totally immersed in my defense and with Patrick's help, built up a substantial degree of confidence. Patrick's sage advice on legal and procedural issues continually got me to reexamine my thinking and change my perspective regarding subjects which, under my father's tutelage, I'd grown up with. I would harken back to my father's counseling principle in which he would say: "What's your plan son?" If I actually did have a plan, it would always be followed by, "OK, but what if 'Plan A' fails, then you must have a 'Plan B'… and what if 'Plan B' fails… then you must have 'Plan C'," and so on. Well, Patrick put a stop to that type of thinking, right then. He explained to me that we cannot play the 'what if' game. He said, "We only deal with what's on our plate. If we play the 'what if' game, and deal with what may or may not happen, you will waste all your money on hypotheticals and we won't get anywhere on the reality in front of us." He emphatically told me, "Don't do that! It's not productive. I don't care what your father says. My Daddy taught me that at a very young age, and I'm telling you… Stop it, right now!"

"OK, OK. I get it!"

We held mock trials with me on the witness stand answering rapid-fire questions until I was totally comfortable in that situation. We were also back and forth to San Diego like a couple of yo-yo's for the various pre-trial hearings and motions, most of which were denied by the sitting trial judge, Judith M. Keep, federal district judge for the Southern District of California.

I later found out that the team of Two Jims were not sitting idly by during this time period but were diligently building a case against me. They flew to San Francisco and staked out my parents' home in Sea Cliff and my father's office building in downtown San Francisco, hoping to find any evidence that I might be financially involved in either. They had hoped to seize property which might have been the ill gotten gains of my involvement in the marijuana business.

They stayed several nights in a cheap motel on Lombard Street where, during the day, they rummaged through my parents' household garbage and through the dumpster located outside of my dad's building. They found nothing but useless paperwork and half-eaten Chinese food containers, which they brought back to their motel room and scoured through. Their room stank of spoiled food and was a god-awful mess which yielded nothing for all their efforts.

Previously they'd gotten lucky dumpster diving outside Andy Willis' San Diego office and hoped for a repeat performance now in San Francisco. However on this occasion, it was a total waste of time which resulted in discovering only typical waste from a printing business plus the spoiled remnants of several Chinese take-out meals that had spilled out of their white Chinese food cartons. The mess on the floor included rotting chow mein, moldy white rice, opened and partially used soy sauce and hot mustard packets, discarded cheap wooden chopsticks, used toothpicks and crumpled bits of paper revealing nothing more than unfulfilled fortunes from previously consumed Chinese fortune cookies.

Late that evening an exhausted Jim Nielsen stood up from where he'd been seated on the floor of the small motel room at the foot of one of the twin beds after sorting through the printing waste and stinking mess of spoiled food strewn about and laughed almost uncontrollably as he handed Conklin one uncrumpled fortune cookie fortune that read: "Today is your lucky day."

Chapter 45

Remanded

January 18, 1983
San Diego, California

My trial date finally arrived.

Our little entourage left the plush comforts of the posh Westin Hotel located in downtown San Diego's famous Gaslamp Quarter, and we walked over to the courthouse, about a block away. The weather in San Diego was overcast and rather cool, and not the usual sunny and warm winter day one expects in Southern California.

It's a foreboding experience to go on trial in Federal Court. It seemed like the entire weight of the U.S. Government was looming over little me, as the clerk of the court looked at her court docket calendar and read aloud: "Case number 82-0572, the United States of America versus Richard Virgil Bibbero, Jr. and James Paul Marshall. Please, all rise for the presiding judge in this case, the Honorable Judith M. Keep."[1]

My co-defendant, Jim Marshall, was allegedly a member of the Coronado beach crew who chose to go to trial rather than plead guilty like the rest of the beach crew. Marshall's court appointed attorney was Eugene Iredale, a noted and highly respected San Diego criminal defense attorney who routinely took on cases like Marshall's pro bono. The two defense attorneys, Patrick Hallinan and Eugene Iredale, would be formidable opponents to the government prosecutor, and the case was shaping up to be a long and complicated battle. Nothing is assured when a case goes to trial, and this one would be no different.

A jury of eight women and four men were seated. They were made up of mostly what seemed to be twenty and thirty year olds with a few who appeared to be in their mid-forties. Butch viewed it as a good sign as probably most of them had at least been exposed to marijuana and might not view it personally as bad as the government might make it seem. So the stage was now set. My wife and parents chose seats in the audience right behind the defendant's table on the right side of the courtroom. I sat down between Butch and my local attorney Rick Barnett. Across from us on the left side of

---

1 Referenced Legal Research, Item 5, Page 532.

the courtroom was the enemy. The lead prosecutor was Stephen Peterson, an Assistant U.S. Attorney for the Southern District of California.

If anyone could have chosen the perfect employment for his looks and personality, it was Steve Peterson. Peterson was a rather large and paunchy man, about 6'2" tall with reddish brown hair, a beard and wire rimmed glasses. His fair complexion and a rather rumpled cheap suit typified a government employee. Seated next to him was Special Agent for the Drug Enforcement Administration, Jim Conklin. They were leaned into each other whispering, probably discussing Peterson's opening statement due in a few minutes. As Peterson started to speak and then drone on about the government's case against me, I could tell right away he was a monotone plodder, about as interesting and captivating as watching paint dry. He kind of reminded me of the plodding flat footed professional boxer Jerry Quarry when he fought Mohammad Ali in 1972. Quarry was no match for the much more agile Ali and it seemed like Butch might do the same to Peterson, although the odds were in favor of the prosecution, like always, in most any federal case. The burden of proof is always on the government and my case was no different, although Patrick and his legendary courtroom presence, quick rapier wit and a reputation as a fierce cross examiner, was the wild card.

Peterson fired the opening salvo across our bow by trying to have my local attorney, Rick Barnett, thrown off the case because he'd acted as local counsel for several other defendants, including Bob Lahodny. Patrick's smooth rebuttal quickly overcame Peterson's objection and the trial moved forward. The first few seemingly inconsequential witnesses took and departed the witness stand as the government commenced its prosecution of me. Peterson meticulously slogged along, weaving in all kinds of evidence against me including some of the marijuana which had been seized at Neah Bay. I nearly burst into tears at the sight of the beautiful Thai sticks that were entered into evidence as Government Exhibits number 8 and 9. Right in front of me, less than 10 feet away, was one of the burlap gunnysacks that my Thai crew had packaged three years ago. And next to it was one of the clear mylar wrapped packages from inside of one of the gunnies. If only I could open that package and roll a joint, right now, maybe this whole scene would just evaporate into a bad dream.

Next, the first government snitch was called to the witness stand. He was Allen 'Fuzzy' Logie, one of the beach crew and the equipment manager for Coronado. It was everything I could do to keep from falling asleep as Peterson trudged his way through the direct examination of Logie, laying foundation after foundation of all of his activities working for Coronado since 1975. After the second day, it was Patrick's turn. The entire courtroom including the twelve members of the jury were on the edge of their seats, as Butch jabbed relentlessly at Logie as if he was a virtual punching bag. By the time he was done on the stand, Butch had Logie contradicting his own statements, admitting that he had lied to everyone including the government agents, his own lawyer, his probation officer and even the senior trial judge for the Southern District, Judge Thompson. With his sharp, saber-like wit and with the skill of a professional butcher, Patrick made mincemeat out of Allen Logie and we felt certain there was no way the jury could have possibly believed this serial liar. Patrick made him look like the fool he was and destroyed whatever credibility he might have had. As Patrick pummeled Logie, I had a chance to glance over at the prosecution table. Peterson was red faced and flustered, interrupting Patrick whenever he could with objection after objection, trying to stop the onslaught and browbeating Logie was taking. Patrick countered each objection, and by the end of Logie's time on the witness stand, one of the government's star witnesses looked like the beaten and dejected liar he actually was. I could tell that Patrick was truly in his element and like Ali, he was indeed 'floating like a butterfly and stinging like a bee.' In short order, Logie was demolished.

Logie was followed on the stand by Donald McMichaels, the boat captain of the Neah Bay debacle. This was even more of a circus and made the government appear even more on the ropes than it was during Logie's testimony. It was now Friday afternoon, and Peterson was doing his best to walk McMichaels through all of the steps to be able to identify me as having come aboard his boat when the loading took place back in 1980. It was a moment of suspense as Peterson asked the boat captain if he could identify me as the day in court came to a close at 4:00. His response—after staring right at me for what seemed like an eternity, but in reality was no more than 15 seconds, from his position right in front of me on the witness stand—was a clear and unmistakable "No." Peterson went berserk as the judge called for a recess until Monday and summarily dismissed the jury for the weekend. At that point, an angry red faced Jim Conklin jumped up from the prosecution table and in a loud and agitated voice, as if almost to the point of yelling, said: "McMichaels, get the fuck up to my office immediately!" We sat there dumbfounded as McMichaels lowered his head and, like a scolded puppy, slunk out through the side door with Conklin seemingly nipping at his heels and frothing at the mouth in anger and rage.

"What a break," Butch said to me, as he gathered up his papers and put them into his briefcase. "I can't believe one of their star witnesses couldn't even identify you. You can bet Peterson and Conklin will be taking that boat captain to the woodshed over the weekend. I assure you, it will be very different on Monday, but we'll be ready, don't worry. I can't wait to take a piece out of this idiot's ass on Monday when, out of the blue, his memory suddenly returns and he ID's you. I know I'm right on this. Rick, you just wait and see. This is going to be fun!"

"Believe me," Butch continued. "The jury is going to have a hard time with anything Logie has alleged to be true, given he's admittedly lied to everyone, basically stole money from his employer, and ratted out over 50 of his best friends, in order to save his sorry ass. But let's not get ahead of ourselves. I can destroy all of the government informants, but it's the independent and disinterested third parties, like the hotel clerks and utility company workers who testified earlier and have nothing to gain, that the jury is going to believe, and that's where the real problem for you is going to be. Like I said, I can make any of their informants look like the liars and scumbags they are, and prove they will do and say anything to get themselves off the hook. It's these others I'm worried about. I think we can justify your being at LaCosta. You were going to meet Otero there and play golf. But you and Joe in Eureka at the same time the load was being landed, that's another story. Why the hell would you two stay in a hotel during this operation under your own names? It's always these little things which come back to bite you in the ass. Well, we can't worry about that now, we'll just plug along and see what's next."

"I guess we just weren't thinking," I replied. "Plus, if we were just up there as observers and friends of Otero, like we're going to claim, we had nothing to hide so we used our own names. It seems kind of lame, but what else can we say? Also, I can't believe Judge Keep is denying almost all of our objections and motions. How can the government get away with that? It's not fair."

"Look Rick," said Butch. "Nobody said it was going to be fair. It isn't. Remember, the judge and the government attorneys have the same paymaster and the deck is stacked against us from the start. But the law is on our side. That's what we really have going for us. My objections to the judge allowing hearsay statements in against you and to the government withholding statements made by their informants and only providing us with expurgated copies, where names or lines in the document have been blacked out, claiming 'an ongoing investigation', is reversible error. I can almost guarantee, if you get convicted, it will almost certainly be reversed on appeal. We'll win that argument for sure, because according to the rules of discovery, we must be provided with all of the government witnesses' statements in order to be able to broadly cross examine them. So the government has to decide, either give us everything and go to trial, or withhold evidence and continue their investigation. They can't have it both ways. That's the law."

"I guess that's where Ephriam Margolin was originally headed," I responded. "He was preparing for my appeal, not winning at trial."

"Well Rick, you made the right choice," Patrick said. "We are going to put on an aggressive defense here at trial. We are not going to just blindly follow other defendants over the cliff, like a bunch of lemmings. If we build a strong defense and lose the trial, we will have a great appeal which, I'm confident, will reverse a conviction, if that's what happens. Remember there is an ebb and flow in all trials and you have to be patient through the entire process, including the appeal. Never give up hope. The government never plays fair. That's why we have the appeals process. You'll see! But I don't think they are going to make these stupid mistakes again, especially when Villar takes the stand. But right now we're looking good."

Just as Butch predicted, Donald McMichaels took the stand as the trial reconvened on Monday morning. And, as predicted, he ID'd me this time. Butch went nuts as McMichaels denied having been coached by either the U.S. Attorney or federal agents between the time he left the stand on Friday and now, on Monday. Under the fire of Butch's probative questioning, McMichaels lost his temper and became argumentative. This reaction unmistakably showed the jury McMichaels was lying. You could see the disbelief in their faces.

The next key witness for the government was none other than Louis Villar himself.

When he took the stand, I barely recognized him. He appeared to be a rather contrite man, probably in his late 40s. His light brown hair was short and curly. He wore a brown business-style suit, had on tortoise shell glasses and sported a Boston Blackie style, pencil thin mustache.

He was first questioned by Assistant U.S. Attorney Peterson who boringly plowed through his questions, laying foundation after foundation as to Villar's smuggling activities and to his implicating of both Marshall and myself as being participants. It was all a very clean, neat and pat picture of my involvement, that is until the cross examination commenced. The cross examination was a brutal onslaught, wherein it became unmistakably clear that Villar was, like his compatriot in 'snitchdom' Alan Logie, a serial liar, had lied to everyone he'd come into contact with over the past decade, had lived continuously under fake names and had corrupted everyone he knew.

Furthermore, Villar admitted, in one of Coronado's previous hashish smuggling escapades to Morocco, they had left one of their people, a former student of Villar's, as hostage for payment due. The hostage, a man by the name of Fred Stocker, the brother of Villar's wife, was held in a Moroccan prison cell, chained to a bed for five months and subsequently went insane from the experience and has never been the same since. Our defense was also able to show that Coronado's ruthless practice of leaving a hostage for payment was not unusual for them, as they did it again with Captain Dan's wife left as hostage in Japan for payment of boat repairs in the Bear Harbor load.

Under the barrage of Butch's grilling, Villar went from the contrite and soft spoken witness he had portrayed himself to be during the government's questioning to an arrogant, argumentative, evasive and very hostile witness during the browbeating he was taking under the glare and probative questioning of both defense attorneys. He would question the questions being asked of him, while trying to turn the questions back on the attorneys. He told them his education included a year and a half of attending law school and now he was trying to act like a lawyer on the witness stand. After two days of intense interrogation by the defense, in my wildest imagination, I just couldn't see the jury believing much of what he'd testified to. Would someone who'd lied for the past decade in everything he did and to everyone who he'd come into contact with now be believable and telling the truth, when it was obvious his cooperation and future sentencing was based on the quantity and quality of the number of people he 'rolled' on? Both Butch and Gene Iredale also made it unmistakably clear that as a result of Villar's cooperation, he stood to get millions of his ill-gotten gains returned to him by the government in exchange for his testimony. However, even though Villar was the consummate liar, he did implicate me through corroboration of other conspirators' notes, specifically those of the copious notetaker, fellow traveler and government informant David Vaughn, and in backing up the testimony of such disinterested third parties as hotel clerks and phone company employees.

In one of the most bizarre scenes during the trial, a small blond-headed boy of about five years old appeared in the courtroom audience and somehow, when no one was looking, he sauntered up to Villar on the witness stand and hopped up on his lap. This was a pathetic attempt either by Villar or by Villar in concert with the government to try and make this asshole, Villar, look human. The little boy was hugging Villar and Villar was patting him on the head in front of the jury. The whole incident seemed to me to be a staged event to try and elicit sympathy from the jury for poor Lou Villar, now the victim of relentless interrogation by the mean bad guys, the defense lawyers!

Well after a few more government witnesses, the government rested its case and it was now our turn. First, my co-defendant Marshall's counsel put on a couple of character witnesses stating Jim Marshall was just an abalone diver and it would have been totally out of character for him to have participated in smuggling activities.

Finally, I was called to the witness stand. During Patrick's direct examination, we talked about everything we'd been preparing for during the past several months of pre-trial preparation. I denied all of the prosecution's allegations, claiming I was just a businessman trying to do business in the Far East and had no connection to the Coronado Company except socially. I admitted that I'd been to the places the government and their witnesses said I'd been, but I stated that I was doing other legitimate business or I'd been invited by Otero to observe his smuggling activities, but I was only an invited guest and observer, and never a participant in any way.

On cross examination, U.S. Attorney Peterson was flummoxed as I continued denying all of his accusations. His face seemed contorted and bright red as his exasperation and frustration grew with each question he asked, which I summarily countered and contradicted. Finally after three days on the witness stand, it was over.

With that, the defense rested. All that was left was closing arguments and jury instructions.

As expected Patrick, with his silver tongue, carefully explained away all of my actions in his smooth and convincing style. He further told the jury that Lou Villar was like the character Fagin, the leader of a group of children whom he teaches to engage in criminal activities to make a living as portrayed in Charles Dickens' famous novel *Oliver Twist*.[2] He said that all the government witnesses were given their freedom in exchange for their testimony and would say anything to that end. It was an artful and convincing dance, but unfortunately would not be the last word the jury heard. As in all trials, the defense lawyer's closing argument is followed by the prosecution lawyers who have the last say to the jury, as the burden of proof rests with the prosecution.

I really never looked at myself as a bad person, and still don't by the way, however as Steve Peterson plowed through his closing argument, if they believed him, the jury was presented with a picture of me almost rivaling the Devil himself. He said I was an investor and owner of the Coronado Company's loads of Thai marijuana in smuggling trips 8 and 9. He told the jury that I was, in effect, actually worse than a worker and real participant in the smuggling ventures because I did nothing but sit back and greedily collect my money on someone else's efforts. Maybe if he'd really known the true extent of my involvement, he wouldn't have come down on me with such vehemence. Right!

However in all fairness, what else could I have expected, having gone to trial and testified in my own defense. It was a high-stakes gamble in which I'd played out my best hand. All of my chips were now on the table and I was only left with the judge's jury instructions and the rest was up to the 12 jurors sitting only a few feet away from me.

'Think good thoughts',and maybe the Lucky Shirt I was wearing beneath my dark business suit had one more bit of good fortune left in it for me. It was, however, at this

2 Referenced Books, Item 14, Page 532.

point virtually threadbare and frayed so thin after thirteen years of use that there was almost nothing left of it. Reality told me, like Julius Caesar two millennia ago, 'beware the Ides of March' and that my luck had probably run out the day Papi died. Funny, how history repeats itself.

With the trial concluded and the jury given its final instructions from Judge Keep, the jury deliberations began. Butch and all of our entourage, including my parents, Cindy and I departed back to our hotel room at the Westin to wait.

We weren't back in the hotel room twenty minutes when the phone rang. My dad, who was sitting on the bed next to the phone, answered it. "Hello."

"Hello, Uncle Richard, this is your nephew Bruce," replied Bruce Bibbero on the other end of the line.

"Well, hello Bruce. How are you and how'd you get this number?" asked Dick.

"That's not important now. But let me get right to the point," answered Bruce.

"OK. What's your point?" Dick questioned, his brow beginning to furrow.

"Well, you see Uncle Richard, it's like this. The DEA came and visited Marty and me the other day and started asking questions about your son, Rick. I told them nothing but said I'd get back to them. So, here's my proposal. Marty and I won't say anything if you'll agree to pay us $300,000 in exchange for our silence. If not, we are prepared to tell them everything we know about Rick's involvement in the marijuana business from the beginning, back in 1969. We are also prepared to tell them how you and Aunt Helen and Grandma and Grandpa also helped Rick launder his marijuana profits through Grandpa's banking connections and through your business."

"What? Are you crazy? Look, you little son-of-a-bitch. You can go fuck yourself. You're nothing but a piece of shit. The next time I see you will be in hell," Dick responded. "Just a minute there's someone here who'd like to speak with you," Dick said as he put his hand over the mouthpiece and quickly told Patrick what was going on; then handed the phone to him.

"Bruce, this is Pat Hallinan, Rick's attorney. What you are suggesting is extortion which, if you don't already know, is against the law. If you know what's good for you, you will crawl back into the hole you just came out of, because as soon as this call is over, I am going to call the U.S. Attorney here in San Diego and file a formal criminal complaint against you. Also, I'm letting you know right now, I've taped this conversation and will turn over this tape to U.S. Attorney Steve Peterson as evidence. I do, however, have a piece of free advice for you. I suggest you get yourself an attorney to defend you right away, because the shitstorm you're unleashing on yourself is way above your pay grade. Have a nice day."

"But… but…" could be heard on the other end of the line as Pat slowly placed the receiver back in its cradle.

"Well, that was interesting," Patrick said. "You know, I was bluffing about taping the conversation, but I'm pretty sure it scared the piss outta him. Hearing from me really caught him off guard. I don't think they thought this through very well and I don't think you'll hear from him again. Anyway, there's nothing they can do… the trial's over and the jury's out, for Christ sakes. This is an idle threat and I don't think you have anything to worry about."

"As if we don't have enough to worry about. Well, you can bet your bottom dollar that when their grandparents hear about this, these two little pipsqueaks will live to regret what they've just done. I guarantee it!" Dick said. His face was beet red and he was visibly shaken.

"You know, they tried to extort me as well, a while back," I said. "After Marty got out of prison, which was a brutal experience for him, I suggested he turn his experience into something positive. Maybe write a book about his experiences. He said he would. He called me a year or so later from Santa Barbara where he was living with his brother Bruce. He told me he had taken up my suggestion and I should come down there and he'd show me what he had. I went to Santa Barbara and he and Bruce showed me all right. What he'd done, probably convinced to do by his conniving brother, was to tape record my story, not his, because he said my story was much more interesting. He suggested that I take over the project, which he said also had some interest from a Hollywood movie producer and they were willing to let me do so for... guess what?... $300,000. I told them that I had no idea what they were talking about and basically said they could kiss my ass."

Cindy had just come out of the bathroom. I noticed a speck of white dust just on the inside of her left nostril. I'm not sure anyone else noticed. Then she chimed in: "I knew we hadn't heard the last of these two. I should have upped the ante to ten grand."

"Huh? What are you talking about?" asked Butch.

"Before Rick went to Santa Barbara to listen to their nonsense, I told him that they were up to no good. He pooh-poohed me and I told him to put his money where his mouth was. I said, 'five grand says I'm right.' And when he returned, I collected. What I meant is that I should have bet him ten grand," she said pouring herself a second glass of chardonnay.

Day after day, we sat in our hotel room awaiting a call from the courthouse. At the end of the first day, we received word that the jury had requested some clarification on certain of the prosecution's exhibits. On day two, more clarification with Patrick going over to the courthouse to assist... no verdict. Patrick told me that this was a good sign and that the jury must be deliberating on some of the finer points made during the trial. He said the longer they take to reach a verdict, historically, usually works in favor of the defense.

Right after lunch on day three, the call came in that the jury had reached a verdict. Patrick gathered up all of his paperwork, I put on my coat and tie and underneath I wore my lucky blue T-shirt, which for thirteen years of marijuana smuggling had brought me luck and good fortune. We proceeded to the courthouse.

"All rise for the Honorable Judge Keep," the clerk of the court said.

"Be seated," responded Judge Keep. "Ladies and gentlemen of the jury. Have you reached a verdict?"

"We have, your honor," replied the jury foreman.

"Mr. Bibbero, please rise and face the jury," the judge instructed.

"We find the defendant guilty as charged, on all three counts."[3]

I felt my knees weaken and the blood drain from my face and neck. I quickly looked for the exit and sort of made a move in that direction, when I felt a hand grab my arm followed by a stern instruction, "Don't even think about bolting," Patrick said. His grip getting firmer on my arm.

"You are hereby remanded to custody of the U.S. Marshals," replied the judge. "Sentencing will be set for March 14th. Court is adjourned."

"What does that mean?" I asked.

"It means, we're going to the bucket," Pat said.

"We? What do you mean 'we'? Can't you get me out on bail?" I frantically asked.

"We are going to appeal and you will be released on bail pending appeal, but that won't happen until you're sentenced," Patrick said. "You can only get bail at that time, so just relax and try to make the best of it. You'll be at the Metropolitan Correction Center (MCC) for about six weeks. I guarantee you it won't be that bad. Just read and exercise and, for god's sake, don't say anything to anybody about your case. The place is loaded with snitches, but you'll be fine. Just keep your nose clean, your mouth shut and don't do anything stupid."

Just then I noticed four uniformed U.S. Marshals moving in to surround me. I glanced back into the audience and saw both my mother and Cindy in tears. My father sat there stoically, just shaking his head. Within seconds I was handcuffed and led out the side door, down a flight of stairs and into a long tunnel connecting the courthouse to the MCC where I was booked, fingerprinted, photographed and given a set of prison clothes and a pair of size 11 blue Keds, slip-on tennis shoes. My shoe size is seven and a half and they felt like clown shoes left over from the circus. I put all of my street clothes including my lucky shirt, whose luck seemed to be on the wane, into a paper bag and gave it to the guard for safekeeping. I was then escorted up to the 9th floor, which would be my home for the next six weeks.

OK. There I was, now convicted, awaiting sentencing, remanded to the custody of the U.S. Government and a bit bewildered, to say the least. The trial phase was over but we still had to prepare to try and convince the judge to go easy on me when she was to hand out my sentence on March 14th… Two chances. Slim and none, and 'slim' had left when I took the witness stand!

Butch had advised my parents that it could be helpful if longtime friends of mine and theirs write letters to the judge on my behalf. My dad jumped into action and composed a letter asking friends of both him and my mother to write letters of support.

As my father would have it, the letter opened in rather dramatic fashion almost making it sound as if I was dead.

> *Dear So and So:*
> *A terrible tragedy has befallen our family. Our son, Richard Jr. …*

The letter went to doctors, lawyers, politicians and friends. Over 75 people wrote in response to my father's request. They were largely very supportive, saying wonderful

---

3 Referenced Legal Research, Items 5 & 6, Page 532.

things about me as a youngster, a young adult and student with a great future, etc.

Meanwhile the government had other ideas about me and, to that end, sent one of their stooges over to MCC to interview me and to write a pre-sentence report. This would also be presented to the judge, along with all the letters my dad had solicited. It would present a very different picture of me and would most certainly juxtapose any argument Butch could make to her Honor.

At MCC I was then assigned a roommate, by the name of Tony DeMarco who was a roly-poly jovial fellow in on a crack cocaine bust.

MCC San Diego is a 20-story tan, rather nondescript building located in downtown San Diego. It kind of looks like an office building, but it is characterized by long narrow windows. Depending which side you are on and what floor, the view is magnificent. My room was on the western side where I had a great view of San Diego harbor and Coronado Island in the distance.

Even with the breathtaking view, it was, however, a stark contrast from my previous night's accommodations at the Westin. At the Westin I had a two-room suite with living room and bedroom exquisitely appointed with Louis XIV furniture and veined marble bathroom with gold fixtures. My suite was on the fifteenth floor with a balcony accessed by a large sliding glass door, magnificent harbor view, two televisions and a fully stocked mini-bar. My bed was a king-sized plush pillow-top mattress. At MCC San Diego I, likewise, had a splendid harbor view, however the similarities stopped there. I was now in a six- by twelve-foot room with a metal bunk bed on top of which was an Army surplus two-inch -thick mattress that felt like it was filled with straw, a stainless steel toilet and sink and a narrow one-foot by four-foot double-thick security window. There was definitely no balcony, only a two-hundred-foot straight drop down to a busy San Diego boulevard… pretty much thwarting any escape ideas. There were about one hundred other inmates on my floor of all races, colors and creeds. There were gang members there as well, among whom were several members of the Hell's Angels motorcycle club.

Upon my arrival to the 9th floor, I was warmly greeted by one particular Hell's Angel, named Tim, who told me that he and his friends had been following my trial in the newspaper for the past three weeks. It turned out that Tim and several of his Hell's Angel buddies were also drug dealers in the San Diego area and had dealt significantly in Thai weed and were de facto customers of mine, who had been dealing my weed for several years. Also, because I hadn't cooperated with the government, I instantly became a sort of cult hero. Tim told me that if I ever needed anything or required any help during my stay at MCC, just don't hesitate to ask. I really didn't want anything but was glad to have someone watching my back… just in case.

As an adolescent and during my youth, I had become quite an accomplished ping pong player. I won several medals at camp and was one of the better players in my neighborhood. Here at MCC there was a ping pong table in the middle of the recreation area, so I decided to have a go at it. In a matter of days, I was the champion of the 9th floor and was beating all comers. Within a few days a tournament was organized and other inmates were betting heavily during each match. A lot of money was bet on me winning and there were even veiled threats that I'd be 'fucked' if so-and-so lost money.

One day I was minding my own business watching television alone when a couple of 'brothers' came in and switched the station. Immediately, Tim and two other Angels came in and threw the blacks out and returned the TV to my station. 'Great!' I thought, 'now I'll have the blacks wanting revenge.' Nothing ever came of it, but I was always on my guard and usually was never without an Angel close by.

A week or so after I arrived at MCC, I got a call to report to the visiting room. Seated at a table was a rather nice looking thirty-something brunette dressed casually wearing designer glasses. She had a briefcase lying in front of her on the table and greeted me, introducing herself as Miss Thompson from the San Diego Federal Probation Department. She said she had been assigned to interview me and write my pre-sentence report. First she asked me background information: my upbringing, family life, education, military service and the like. It started as a pleasant conversation of questions and answers. She had kind of a cute smile and seemed quite relaxed, that is until she got to the heart of the issue and wanted basically a confession and explanation of the activities which I'd been convicted of… Right! After I'd just spent three days on the witness stand denying everything, now this lady wants me to admit that I was lying the whole time. Admit I'd committed perjury, which would essentially mean I was stepping on my own dick. A new crime punishable by five years in prison. 'I don't think so!' Plus Butch told me not to say anything to anyone about my case since he was preparing my appeal.

This really pissed off Miss Thompson whose friendly demeanor now took a turn for the serious. She wrote in her pre-sentence report that even though I was very cordial and friendly, I was extremely uncooperative and not forthcoming or remorseful regarding the events leading to my conviction. She recommended I serve seven years in prison and pay the maximum fine. Butch had warned me this would happen, but ever the optimist had also said that we had a 'winning' appeal, so keep my mouth shut and admit nothing. I did as he instructed… throwing caution to the wind.

"On advice of my counsel, I can't discuss my case which is pending appeal."

Oh well.

Days slowly came and went until on the 40th day, I was hauled back into court for sentencing and my bail hearing. In another bizarre twist, U.S. Attorney Peterson stood up before Judge Keep and now claimed that both he and Agent Conklin had just received an anonymous phone call from someone claiming to know all about my past smuggling activities dating back to the late 1960s and early '70s in Mexico. This anonymous person also claimed I had multiple passports and I would flee if I ever got caught. Peterson stated he was going to be getting back in touch with this anonymous caller in the next few days to try and verify his claims, thus he requested I be held in custody until he could sort it out.

Again Patrick went crazy, questioning Peterson as to how in the world, if the call was indeed anonymous, he could get back in touch with someone who hadn't even identified themselves. He argued vehemently that this was nonsense, was never brought up at trial and I should be allowed to have my sentencing and bail pending appeal hearing right now. Taking note of this discussion, the judge agreed to allow Peterson time to investigate all of this new information and agreed to postpone today's hearing for a few days. I was summarily escorted back to MCC for another four days.

All of a sudden, the lightbulb went on inside my head... unless Peterson was making the whole thing up, the only one who could have made the anonymous call was my cousin, Bruce Bibbero. I guess the fucker was making good on his extortion threat he'd made to me in Santa Barbara years ago, as well as to Patrick and my father six weeks ago. Cindy was again right. We hadn't heard the last of these two scoundrels.

Another four days elapsed and again I was brought back into court. No further information had been gleaned by the agents and now on the 44th day, the judge agreed the hearing would commence today, because enough time had passed with no further viable communication coming forth from the 'anonymous' informant. Peterson argued for more time, but this time his request was denied and the hearing went forward.

In another strange twist, a couple of days into my stay at MCC I was approached by another inmate named Jim McCann, who by now knew my name and who I was. He asked me if I was related to someone named Bruce Bibbero. I told him he was a cousin. Jim told me that he was from Santa Barbara and the reason he was in here was that Bruce had ratted him out to the local sheriffs as a cocaine dealer, and they had turned him over to the Feds. He told me Bruce had been busted in Santa Barbara for selling cocaine and he'd become a rat or government informant in order to save his own miserable ass. I told Jim he'd ratted me out as well, and I was his cousin, for Christ's sakes. As far as I was concerned, the next time I'd see him would be, like my father told him six weeks ago... in hell! Later I found an article in the Santa Barbara local newspaper confirming Jim McCann's story about Bruce, his cocaine dealings, his bust and his cooperation with authorities that implicated others, guaranteeing his own freedom and exoneration. The title of the 1985 article in the *Santa Barbara News-Press*, "How Beneficial Is Letting A Suspect Go To Catch Another Wrongdoer?",[4] says it all and confirmed what I already knew: Bruce had no integrity whatsoever and was truly the scoundrel and deceitful punk that I always knew he was. Nice family, eh!

Given this series of events surrounding my cousins, especially Bruce and his nefarious, snitch-laden, double-dealing history, I soon began to suspect that there might have been more to both of his attempts to extort me than I'd originally thought. He possibly could have been working with the Feds all along in order to mitigate his bust by trying to set me up. His whole Santa Barbara scene at the Montecito mansion could have been a possible sting operation in an attempt to get me to admit to some criminal activity in such palatial surroundings. The whole thing could have been tape recorded. The mansion could have been rented and staged all in an attempt by the government to use an eager and willing snitch like Bruce to ensnare me and to build a case against me, just as was reported in the referenced newspaper article in the *Santa Barbara News-Press*. Its strictly conjecture on my part, but I wouldn't put it past a rat and scumbag like him.

4 Referenced Newspaper Articles, Item 9, Page 529.

So, four days after my scheduled sentencing, I appeared before the judge.

"I received nearly 75 letters from all these nice people, singing your praises," Judge Keep began. "Well, Mr. Bibbero, you might have fooled all of them, but you didn't fool me. I am going to follow the recommendation of the probation department. You are hereby sentenced to seven years in custody[5] and I'm ordering you to pay the maximum fine allowed by law, plus five years' probation to follow upon your release."

Well, so much for any leniency. As stated earlier, I thought my prospects of leniency were 'slim and none'. 'Slim' had already departed, and now 'none' like Elvis, had definitely just left the building!

We immediately appealed and I was released on bail pending appeal. Patrick reiterated I had a very strong appeal on several issues which had come up during my trial. The government had withheld critical evidence claiming releasing it to me would compromise their ongoing investigation. Also we appealed the actual indictment claiming the government had indicted the case as a single ongoing conspiracy of the Coronado Company, when actually each load of marijuana smuggled was a separate conspiracy with different participants, different agreements, different locations and smuggling several different illegal commodities. The idea behind this argument was that if we could prove multiple conspiracies on appeal, instead of the single conspiracy as was alleged in the indictment, then we could show I had no connection with all of the earlier Coronado smuggling activities, thus the indictment was fatally flawed and I was irreparably prejudiced with testimony of conspiracies which I had nothing to do with. The law is clear that if an individual joins an ongoing conspiracy, in this case the single conspiracy alleged in the indictment, he is liable for all of the previous acts of the conspiracy even though he presumably had nothing to do with the earlier conspiratorial acts. Therefore our argument of multiple conspiracies was the crucial component of our most important appellate issue.

The bottom line of this argument would be to show that my conviction was based not on evidence of my guilt, but on the substantial evidence submitted in connection with conspiracies which I had absolutely no connection with, and probably so inflamed the jury they could not fairly and dispassionately evaluate and separate the evidence against me from the ruthless and heinous activities of Coronado and specifically Villar himself. Technically, it was a complicated legal theory, but if we were to win the argument, my conviction would be overturned and I would walk free. In any case, Patrick was confident my conviction would be overturned and reversed on appeal. He said the appeal process could take years to resolve. He advised me to get on with my life, keep myself busy, stay out of trouble and leave the worrying about my case to him.

So, I did just that.

---

5 Referenced Newspaper Articles, Item 7, Page 529.

Chapter 46

Kick 'Em When They're Down

Late Spring 1983
Carmel, California

Patrick had advised me during my 44 days of incarceration to prepare bail so that at the moment I was sentenced, all the necessary paperwork would be in order and I could summarily be released from custody on bail pending appeal. In his experience and in discussing my situation with Rick Barnett and other local lawyers, he felt my bail would be set at one million dollars.

I knew that posting such an amount in cash would be stupid and foolhardy; therefore I went to my father, instead of a bail bondsman, to see if he could arrange for properties to be used as collateral for my bail, which the court agreed to as an option. I assured him that under no circumstances would I ever consider jumping bail, thus forfeiting these collateralized properties. He agreed and said he would arrange it by putting up their home as collateral. This would amount to two thirds of the required amount. He told me the other one third could be made up of two properties he had recently given to each of my sisters. The older of my two sisters eagerly agreed to do whatever was necessary, however to my amazement, my youngest sister refused to allow her property to be used for my bail. When told of this, I couldn't help thinking back to when the shoe was on the other foot and she had come to me for help to be able to purchase her house. At the time, I was only too happy to help her with no strings attached despite my father's warnings against it. I was shocked and deeply disappointed in her response; however being incarcerated and virtually at everyone else's mercy, there was nothing I could do about it. I guess now, with our roles reversed, I came to the obvious conclusion: this is what families are really all about, contrary to my originally thinking otherwise. As the saying goes: 'No good deed goes unpunished!' My father then scrambled around and came up with the remainder from another source and all of the necessary paperwork was in order at my sentencing.

Butch was right and the judge set my bail at one million dollars which was immediately posted and I was released.

I subsequently returned to Carmel where I was in for yet another surprise.

Cindy and I had moved to Carmel Highlands the previous year and by all outward appearances things seemed pretty normal. However, in our life it was anything but normal. The tension at home, following my trial and my having spent 44 days in prison, with the prospect of a long and drawn-out appeal process, was starting to wear on our relationship. We were constantly bickering with each other and as the days wore on, I would dream of the life I'd lived for over a decade. I would fantasize about just running away and living a life on the lam. These discussions, even though they were just a fantasy, began to wear on Cindy. As it turned out, Cindy had other plans for our relationship, which would soon become all too evident to me.

Our house in Carmel was a beautiful two-story Monterey colonial style home set on two acres with a long curving driveway, gated entrance and a spectacular view of Point Lobos and the rugged California coastline. Most of the living quarters were on the upper floor, with the lower floor having an office and two spare bedrooms each having its own entrance door. Access to the property was gained by a combination code at a call box on the quiet street where the home was located.

It was about 8:30 in the morning as the fog had just lifted and I had awakened to the sun shining in our bedroom window. Just then, I heard a knock on one of the downstairs doors. I turned to Cindy lying next to me in bed and said, "I wonder who could be at the door and how someone has gotten in through the gated entrance."

"I haven't the slightest idea," she said. "Why don't you go and see who it is."

I got up and went downstairs and saw a man casually dressed with a briefcase in his hand at the door to the first bedroom.

"Yes? Can I help you?" I asked, opening the door slightly.

"Richard Bibbero?" asked the man.

"Yes," I answered.

He reached into his briefcase and thrust some paperwork into my hand through the open door. "You've been served. Have a nice day."

"Huh?"

As the man departed down the driveway, I turned and started upstairs glancing at the divorce papers I was now holding in my hand. I went back to the bedroom where Cindy was now sitting up in bed. "So, you have no idea who was just at the door?" I asked.

"Well…"

"You knew exactly who was at the door," I responded throwing the papers I had in my hand at her. "As a matter of fact, you gave that man the combination to the gate. Cindy, you're a fucking coward and a liar. I thought that even though our relationship was rocky at times, we could at least discuss things. You never said a word and just had me served with divorce papers. You dropped a bomb on my head out of the blue, and then had the gall to deny knowing what was going on when, in fact, you set it up. We could have, at least, discussed this and maybe worked it out… but, you sneaky little bitch, you just did this to me without any warning. Willie saw right through you years ago and tried to warn me about you back then, when you advised Melinda to run and take him to the cleaners. He said you were nothing but an opportunist, a real bitch and a gold digger, but I was too blinded by your bullshit to believe him. He was right. You've been nothing but a gold digger all along. You loved the high life, but when things got tough, you jumped ship on me, same as you literally did to Glen eight years ago. Some things never change. You're still the same piece of shit you always were and I was just too stupid to see it."

"Look, Rick. You said you were going to run and leave me holding the bag with nothing," Cindy said as she burst into tears.

"Aw, come on Cindy. It was just idle chatter and you know it. For christ sakes, my parents put up their house for my bail. You think I'd run and forfeit their house? You know me better than that. You're just using it as an excuse. You've been planning this for a long time. Right? Why would you be so upset? You knew this was coming! You know what I really think? Look at you. You've become a paranoid drunk and coke addict. In your paranoia, you've concocted all of this in your head and none of it's true. Have another sniff, I'm sure that'll clear it all up. Go ahead. The bag is right in your night-stand drawer. And when you're done with that, maybe you could have a few glasses of wine. That should right the ship. You're addicted to this crap and that's the long and short of it—as long as you have the bag and bottle within reach. And now with the real possibility of it all coming to an end, you throw in the towel and file for divorce. No trying to work it out, no nothing. You were always just along for the ride and the good times, but when it's not looking so good… just 'adios amigo'! I am going up to the Bay Area for a couple of days and when I get back I expect you to be gone. I don't care where you go. Question is: did you ever really love me or just the lifestyle? You know what I think, you're not capable of loving anyone but animals. Just get the fuck outta my life."

All I could think of was the song by Don Henley which had just hit the charts the previous fall called *Dirty Laundry*.[1]

'Kick 'em when they're up, kick 'em when they're down, kick 'em all around
You don't really need to find out what's going on… Just leave well enough alone'

When I returned from the Bay Area, Cindy was indeed gone. She had left a note on her desk saying she had gone to Hawaii and would be staying with some friends of hers who she had sailed with and who had moved to the beach in Maui. As I was sitting at her desk, I noticed an envelope sticking out of one of the cubbyholes of her roll-top. I saw that it was addressed to her and was from her aunt who lived in the Phoenix area with her retired military general husband. It was dated a month previous and apparently Cindy had confided her paranoia to her Aunt Mildred, her father's sister, and told her everything I'd been up to for the past decade and made it seem as if she didn't know anything about what had been going on. In the letter, Auntie Mil, as she called her, instructed Cindy, under no uncertain terms: "take him for all you can and get away as quickly as possible." It was just as I suspected… the woman I'd confided in and given my heart to for the past eight years was only along for the ride and good times and had most likely been conniving like a rat leaving the sinking ship and to take me for every-

---

1 Referenced Songs & Music, Item 14, Page 531.

thing she could from the moment we found out about my indictment. She had a track record for this kind of behavior and literally did jump ship on Glen eight years previous. I should have seen it coming a million miles out, but she was a very good actress and played me like a Stradivarius.

It seemed like all the women, of everyone I knew who got busted, split when the going got tough. So much for loyalty!

A couple of other realities also became apparent following my bust.

First, I became a pariah to most all of my so-called friends. It was like I had leprosy. Most of those who I'd been close to for ten years or more suddenly wanted nothing to do with me, such as Willie and Phil and to an extent, even Joe.

Secondly, after you've been busted it seems like all debts are suddenly absolved. Anyone who owes you money, all of a sudden, owes you nothing and even though some of your compatriots are still working in the business, you are not invited to participate, even as an investor. No one ever offered to help me or give me an opportunity to participate in any way in any future Thai scam, even though I started it all and kept my mouth shut when the chips were down. That was really disappointing to me, because I'd gone through most of my savings in the legal defense of my case, paying the fine plus handling all the costs of my deteriorating marriage, subsequent divorce and settlement as well as paying the attorney's fees on both sides. As a matter of fact, the continuing Thai trip and its investment opportunities were all kept very hush-hush and secret from me and I only found out what was really going on much later and by then it was all academic. The Thai trip was continuing and most of my so-called close friends whom I'd worked with were continuing to make money hand over fist.

I guess in retrospect, my non-involvement was a good thing because surely I would have been implicated and re-indicted when it all came down years later. In my case, when I went down I felt like I was abandoned on an island all alone, and it seemed like I'd just joined the NFL… No Friends Left!

There's an old jailhouse saying: 'You've got nothing coming.' Between cousins Marty and Bruce, my sister, Cindy, and most of my lifelong friends, this saying couldn't have been more appropriate.

'Kick 'em when they're up, kick 'em when they're down… kick 'em all around'

But this is not the end of the story. As sad as it was for me at that point, from my perspective, I just had to move forward and under Patrick's tutelage I regained some of my confidence.

I knew I had to do something positive and not dwell on the negative. I put the house up for sale and moved up to Marin County. My father also came to my rescue and offered me a position in his company where I could work while my case was on appeal. This would not only look good for me when I came back before the court, but it would also give me something to do to occupy my time and keep my mind off of the negative. Patrick told me it could be two to three years before I would have to face the music, even if we lost on appeal, so I just needed to stay positive.

So with the Sword of Damocles hanging over my head, I moved on with a positive attitude. I knew there was nothing I could do about what had happened in the past and I also knew there was little I could do about my legal issues. It would have to follow whatever course it would lead to. I just had to move on.

Something my old MCC cellie (roommate) Tony DeMarco had once said stuck in my mind and was a saying I would have to live with for the foreseeable future. He said, "the wheels of justice grind slowly, but exceedingly fine." I knew, in time, I would probably be ground up by the justice system, but it was something I couldn't dwell on without going crazy.

I moved on.

Chapter 47

Music Biz

Summer of 1983

I left Carmel and moved up to the small Marin County town of Fairfax. I lived in a small bungalow-style two-bedroom, one-bathroom home which was owned by my sister, and went to work at my father's company now located in nearby Petaluma. Incidentally, this was the house I had helped her purchase years ago. Maybe she felt some sense of remorse or guilt for not assisting with my bail as it was rent-free. Anyway, I was way down financially and really appreciated it.

The job was boring but at least it was a job; however it didn't take me long to get distracted with something much more to my liking. One of the other employees, Don Martinez, was the bass player of a local rock and roll band who had quite a following in the Bay Area. He invited me to one of the band's performances at a local Marin County nightclub. I was surprised at how together and tight the band was and at how big a following they had. The place was packed and everyone in the audience seemed to know the words to all of the original songs and music the band played. I thought, 'boy, these guys are really good. I wonder why they don't have a record contract. They are certainly as good as many of the acts whose music is heard regularly on the radio and whose records are topping the music charts.' Don introduced me to the other members of the band who were led by their lead guitarist and vocalist, Dave Jones (not the same Davy Jones of the Monkees fame). Dave was a young guitar player who had moved to Marin from Des Moines, Iowa. He was a fantastic musician and as accomplished a guitar player as many of the big name guitarists in the industry.

Soon I was going to all of their rehearsals and shows. It was blowing my mind that they didn't have a record contract and I asked their manager why? He really didn't have a good answer. He said he was trying to get the group more appearances as an opening act to other major groups appearing locally but wasn't having much luck. The band was also getting frustrated and someone suggested that I possibly take over as manager. Mostly for the love of their music, I agreed.

It turned out that one of Butch Hallinan's best friends was one of the most renowned and colorful entertainment attorneys in the entire music industry. His name was Brian Rohan. Brian had represented many of the biggest musical acts in the world such as Santana, The Grateful Dead, Journey, and the Jefferson Airplane. Butch introduced me and I could tell right away that Brian was indeed a piece of work.[1]

We met at a local Marin hangout, a restaurant and bar named Marin Joe's. I found Brian there, sitting on a bar stool nursing his second water glass full of Jack Daniels on the rocks. It soon led to a third, fourth and fifth as we sat and discussed the music industry in general and the prospects of my band getting a record contract. Even after slogging down five Jack Daniels, I was amazed at how coherent Brian still was. I was still sipping my first gin and tonic and noting that if I drank even half of what Brian had just consumed I'd be on the floor.

He agreed to come and see the band and would let me know what he thought. I certainly had my reservations, but Butch told me Brian was indeed the real deal, and if anyone could get a record contract for my band, Brian could.

My amazement continued as we left the bar an hour or so later. As I escorted Brian to his car which he sort of stumbled over to, I saw his battered Japanese sedan looked like it doubled as his crash pad. It was littered with food wrappers, wadded up assorted receipts and other scraps of paper. There was a Big Gulp drinking cup with a dislodged plastic lid partially covering the top sitting in the cup holder between the two front bucket seats. Beneath the lid I noticed there was still about two inches of dark colored liquid remaining in the cup. There was even a pillow encased in a soiled pillowcase on the back seat. He had a legal file in his hand and fumbled in his pocket for his trunk key, which he produced and opened the trunk. The trunk was even more of a disaster than the car's interior. It was strewn with legal paperwork, boxes of legal files and more of what appeared to be a vast collection of bits of paper. In the corner were the remainder of what I assumed to be the rest of his wardrobe: crumpled up dirty t-shirts, dirty underwear and a pair of muddy and grass stained tennis shoes appearing as if he'd recently walked or stumbled across a wet soccer field and muddy track. I surmised they were the result of his trundling through the rain earlier in the day. He jammed the file into the box of other legal files and closed the trunk.

I wondered how in the hell this famous entertainment attorney was ever going to drive home and offered to drive or at least escort him home. He waved me off dismissively and I said a silent prayer for him as he got in and drove off. At least, I noticed, he put on his seatbelt. Maybe that would save him.

This guy was a mess, to put it mildly... but a very likable mess with an extremely quirky sense of humor. He was rude and loud and definitely the center of attention. How he could command the respect of such musical idols was a mystery to me, but nevertheless he was a legend in the industry with a phenomenal track record. I took an immediate liking to Brian who would become another colorful character in my life.

Right at about this time, I met a nice cute little Jewish gal and we started dating. This was the first time I'd dated another Jew. Kathy Markowitz was a petite, very pro-

1 Referenced Newspaper Articles, Item 10, Page 529.

fessional marketing specialist in the electronics and computer industry. She was also a very loyal, no-nonsense kind of person with a great sense of humor, but also extremely jealous and possessive of both my time and of who I might meet in the music business. She was also very good for me at a time when I had fallen from grace, from the pinnacle of the marijuana business to a convicted felon whose future prospects included a healthy stint in federal prison.

Although Kathy loved music, she was less than enthused about my foray into the music business. She cautioned me as to the ruthlessness of the music industry… but, of course, I wouldn't listen and proceeded forward as the manager of the band and in pursuit of the elusive record contract. As usual, I threw caution to the wind and jumped in with both feet… much to Kathy's dismay and consternation. It proved to be a constant source of irritation to her, fomenting her jealousy as various female groupies always surrounded the band and even though I pretty much ignored them, she was always annoyed and on alert about it.

At any rate, for the next year and a half I managed the band. Through Brian's introductions and connections, I hired two very well known music and recording producers to put together several demo tapes of our best songs. Brian then arranged for our music to be presented to some of his major connections in the music industry. All of our efforts failed and the recurrent major comment voiced by every major music industry player was: we didn't have strong enough vocals.

* * *

At the same time my legal case was proceeding through the appellate courts. Patrick was right. I had very strong appellate issues and, in early 1985, my conviction was overturned by a ruling of the Ninth Circuit of Appeals.[2] As Patrick predicted, the Ninth Circuit ruled that the government had withheld information critical to my defense and had used hearsay evidence, among other things, to get their conviction. However, the remedy of their ruling to overturn my conviction was that the case be remanded back to the same court and judge for a re-trial. The one issue the Ninth Circuit denied was the one which would throw out my case entirely and set me free. This was the Single/Multiple Conspiracy argument which Patrick had first proffered at my trial. Obviously, this was the biggest issue and one we had to pursue to the highest level: the United States Supreme Court. Of course, to pursue any appellate issue was expensive and double or triple the cost of the trial itself. The amount of paperwork required to appeal a case is staggering. Volumes of motions and legal arguments had to be researched, created and presented. Months of legal research had to be expended by Patrick as well as his legal assistants and private investigators, all of which was at the 'reduced' going rate of nearly $200 per hour. It seemed like I was hemorrhaging money. The faucet was on and gushing cash and there was no way for me to turn it off.

In addition to my case, Cindy was over in Hawaii spending money on my credit cards like there was no tomorrow. Also Dave Killian was sitting in Tahiti aboard *Mamamouchi* barely surviving on the modicum of money I was sending him. The small

2 Referenced Legal Research, Items 6 & 7, Page 532.

fortune I had left was dwindling before my own eyes and I was still facing a divorce settlement, paying a substantial fine as part of my sentence, paying for my legal services of which there was virtually no end in sight, and I was still looking forward to spending an indeterminate amount of time behind bars.

I was truly in a descending maelstrom, but at least I had the band and the support of Kathy to take my mind off of the reality of my situation, which, I knew, had to come to a head in the very near future. And I was right.

In the summer of 1985, the Supreme Court[3] decided not to hear my case. The case was therefore remanded back to the District Court for re-trial. Patrick and I flew to San Diego in September for a pre-trial meeting with Judge Keep. In the judge's chambers, Patrick told the judge we were prepared for another trial, unless she could offer us an attractive deal to avoid a re-trial. He reiterated the fact that we had come close to winning, based upon his polling and interviewing the jury at the first trial, and there were no assurances we wouldn't win, if tried again. Judge Keep agreed.

In order to prevent the government from spending a fortune and taking a chance of losing by re-trying me, she consented to a reduced sentence. In exchange for my guilty plea to the charges of conspiracy to import and possession of over 1000 pounds of marijuana, I would not spend more than 30 months in prison. Her proposal was I be given a sentence of five years and after 30 months she would modify my sentence through a Sentence Modification procedure known as a Rule 35 and release me on time served. She also proposed that I would pay the maximum allowable fine as stipulated to the charges I pled to. We agreed.

On September 25, 1985, I pled guilty under the terms of our agreement and agreed to self-surrender to MCC San Diego at the end of December to start serving my sentence. I now had three months to get my shit and my head together to face the music. I had to mentally prepare myself to spend the next two and a half years in prison as well as clear the decks of all other distractions: the band, my job at my father's business, my dwindling finances, the divorce, my relationship with Kathy, and what to do with all of my stuff… well, whatever was left of it after the divorce settlement. I had a lot on my plate and not much time left.

The walls were closing in.

* * *

I was not the only one of our group to have legal troubles as a result of Villar's cooperation. Earlier in the year a second wave of indictments were handed out in San Diego. Among those swept up in the dragnet were Joe Schroder and Stan Yamamoto. They along with all but one of the remaining defendants in my indictment, and the 20-plus newly indicted defendants, all pled guilty and were left to negotiate the best deals they could in front of Judge Keep. Joe, who was viewed as merely a helper, was given a six-month sentence, while Stan, who was seen as a major Southern California marijuana distributor, was given five years. Joe was in and out before I even started my sentence. He was sent to the Federal Prison Camp at Lompoc, California, where he did

---

3 Referenced Legal Research, Item 8, Page 532.

his time working on the prison fire crew. He was released and given five years' probation. He came out virtually unscathed but seemingly didn't learn his lesson. I guess he
suffered from the clinical definition of insanity: doing the same thing over and over and
expecting a different result. Stan, on the other hand, surrendered to Terminal Island
Federal Prison where he spent six months before being transferred to Lompoc Prison
Camp where he spent the next three years working on the coveted prison cowboy crew,
a position which, although I didn't know it at the time, would greatly help me out in
the future.

Stan's arrest at his home in Vista didn't quite come off as planned and was highlighted by a rather comical incident. The agent in charge of the arrest was none other
than Jim Conklin. In preparation for the following morning's arrest, the evening before
in his garage, Jim took apart and cleaned his .38 revolver, reassembling it in what he
thought was his usual and customary manner as he'd done countless times in the past.
Not being a real 'gun guy', this time however he unknowingly reassembled it incor-
rectly, somehow forgetting to securely re-latch all of the parts correctly. The arresting
party led by Jim Conklin consisted of eight young gung-ho agents from the DEA, U.S.
Customs, the FBI and a member of the local Vista Sheriff's office. One of the FBI
agents was a beautiful 5'4" newly commissioned young woman with long brunette hair
and a gorgeous slender body. It seemed like all of the other agents, including Jim, had
an eye for her and were trying to impress her as they assembled in preparation for the
pre-dawn raid. As the moment approached Jim ordered everybody outside Stan's front
door to draw their weapons. Jim, standing next to the beautiful FBI agent, likewise
drew his out of his concealed belt holster and as he raised the weapon in an upward arc,
the gun summarily fell apart with all of the loose unsecured parts dropping in a pile
at his feet and only the grips remained in his outstretched hand. Dumbfounded and
now thoroughly embarrassed, macho Jim Conklin stooped and sheepishly picked up
the scattered gun parts and had to give a 'stand down' order while he took the next five
minutes to reassemble his weapon amid the quiet snickers and guffaws from the rest
of the group now standing idly by waiting for him to get his shit together. The woman
simply rolled her eyes and 'cool' Jim probably lost any chance he might have had to woo
her at that moment. The rest of the raid came off without a hitch, however Jim was left
with a minorly tarnished legacy which he was never quite able to live down in the storied annals of DEA arresting lore.

The only other defendant aside from James Marshall and myself to go to trial in
either indictment was Abdul Blackie, the procurer of the two Coronado loads of bad
quality Thai weed they scored after our early retirement in 1977. Butch was again right
about my going to trial first and the fact that the prosecution would be much better
prepared for subsequent trials. Abdul's trial was nearly a slam-dunk for the government. They had definitely tightened up their case and Ab was convicted and sentenced
to the same seven-year sentence I was originally given by the same judge. He had virtually no appeal and served five years in prison.

* * *

Cindy had indeed done her homework. She had retained the legal services of one of the most aggressive and feared divorce attorneys on the Monterey Peninsula. I had originally hoped for an amicable settlement, but her lawyer had the reputation of going for the throat, and mine would be no exception. She was demanding nearly everything of value I had acquired, even from before we were married. This was going to be a fight and one which had to be over in the next two months, if I were to have any sanity left. I could not go to prison with an unsettled divorce hanging over my head. I knew I had to go to prison with no unresolved issues in order to make my time pass as quickly as possible. I knew I'd go nuts in prison, as I'd seen happen to others at MCC San Diego in the same situation, if the divorce wasn't settled first. I hired a local attorney to represent me in the divorce. We haggled back and forth for the next month and a half and finally agreed to most of her demands, as I had little choice unless I wanted to continue to fight her from prison, a very unsettling prospect to deal with.

Following my bust, I'd asked Cindy to go to Switzerland and close out the safe deposit box. We'd been invited to invest in a development project in Palm Springs and this would be a good opportunity to use some of those remaining assets. She went and was able to transfer some of the funds into the developer's account, however she took what remained for herself, leaving me nothing. I was powerless to do anything about it because, first of all, the government had seized my passport upon my original surrender in San Diego in 1983, so I could not travel internationally and secondly, Cindy knew there was nothing I could do about it, since the assets in Switzerland were the result of my illegal smuggling activities and she knew I couldn't make a legal argument regarding it. So, she followed her Aunt Mildred's instructions and took from me everything she could while she had the chance, which was in addition to what she and her lawyer could squeeze me for, including his legal fees, given the short time frame of my continued freedom. She was indeed proving herself to be the gold digger I'd accused her of being, in my rant to her back when she first had me served divorce papers at the house. Well, I guess the good news is, I wouldn't have to worry about what to do with all my stuff for the next two and a half years… it could all pretty much be stored in a small closet, and not in a large rented garage which I had originally envisioned. I was left with virtually nothing.

* * *

The disappointment of not getting a record deal left the band in a state of disarray. I felt the only way to salvage it was to look for a new singer. The music was there, but with no outstanding voice to deliver it, it was dead. One of the people whom I'd met in the music business had heard of a young female singer in Texas who was not only beautiful but had a great voice and was looking for an opportunity to perform with a rock and roll band. Her name was Denise Sullivan. I heard a demo tape of her singing and immediately played it for the band, who agreed to give her a tryout. I flew Denise out to Marin for an audition. She sang the parts Dave had originally sung and the band sounded phenomenal with Denise singing lead. The problem was, they also looked fantastic. Denise was more beautiful in person than in the pictures I had of her. She was about 5'2" tall, long flowing blonde hair, electric blue eyes, a gorgeous petite body and a fantastic voice, somewhat reminiscent of my deceased friend Thai's favorite singer, Pat Benatar, who happened to be one of the most successful female singers of that time period and who also fronted for a very talented all male band. It would be a totally new look for the band and one that I thought might play off of Pat Benatar's success and possibly could turn things around for them. Boy, was I in for a surprise!

The presence of a beautiful female singer in our group proved to be too much for the wives of the band members as well as for my girlfriend, Kathy. The jealousy in the air was unbelievable. The women went into panic mode as they feared their husbands running off with Denise, the beautiful blonde-bombshell singer. It was disaster from the get-go. Kathy went crazy as did the wives of the other band members who collectively convinced their husbands not to go in that direction, for whatever reason. The band subsequently broke up a few weeks later. At least I didn't have the band and its future to worry about. Dave, the only outstandingly talented member of the group, left Marin and relocated to Austin, Texas, where he went on to make a name for himself in the local music scene there with a new group and finally to a successful future in the music business.

* * *

Denise's tryout for the band was the final straw for Kathy's and my relationship. Her jealousy finally caught up with her, imagining I had had a relationship with Denise. I hadn't. With my surrendering date looming, I had little choice but to break it off with her. I rationalized that 'I did the crime and now it's time for me to do the time', and it wasn't fair to make Kathy do the time as well. She needed to get on with life and not be stuck with my sentence to deal with for the next two and a half years. We broke up, but being as loyal as she was, she agreed to keep whatever stuff I had left in safekeeping until I got out. It was a great relief to me, even though I had little left to salvage from Cindy and the divorce.

I was now free to do my time without any of the previous encumbrances to make it harder. I was also getting into shape both mentally and physically in preparation for my stint in federal custody. I worked out fanatically at a local gym and counseled with both Patrick and my friendly probation officer, Fred Cheverria, about going to prison and doing time. Their advice was to read, keep my nose clean, stay positive, stay healthy and fit, and don't do anything stupid to make my time longer or harder.

I spent Christmas 1985 at my parents' home and it was as pleasant as it could be given the prospect of my impending prison term looming, which kind of put a damper on the evening's festivities.

I spent the night of December 29th at Joe's home up on Skyline Drive above the town of Woodside on the San Francisco Peninsula. We snorted coke and smoked joints until the wee hours. It was right then that I made a resolution to myself: no more drugs. No weed. No coke. I already knew drugs were plentiful and easy to come by in prison but was determined not to do anything which could jeopardize me in prison or make my time any longer than it had to be by doing something stupid. It was an agreement with myself that I stuck to religiously. I had to change my ways and this would be the perfect opportunity.

The next morning, Joe gave me a ride to SFO airport where I caught a flight to San Diego to start what I considered to be a new adventure.

Chapter 48

Home: MCC, FCI, FPC

1986 and 1987

So, this was it. I had cleared the decks of all baggage. The divorce was finalized. I got fucked, but was moving on. The relationship with Kathy was over; sad, but necessary in order to clear all attachments and enter prison with as little 'street' baggage as possible. The band had broken up; an unfortunate situation, but probably better in the long run for their careers to move on. The Carmel house finally got sold. I was sorry to see it go, but at a $5000 per month debt service, it just wasn't sustainable. Killian finally returned home and left the boat in Tahiti; not a great situation, but one of the crew members, Ed Lehmer, agreed to take over possession of it with the prospect of putting together another smuggling venture with Jonathan Jacoby. At least there was the dim hope of possibly getting reimbursed for the original cost of it; if not, at least I didn't have to worry about it for the time being. The well had virtually run dry. What little was left of my financial resources was at least stabilized and the uncontrolled hemorrhage of money mostly stopped. Lawyers had been paid off, and most of my other loose ends were tied up. It all amounted to my being nearly broke, but free and unencumbered, so I could spend the next two and a half years with as few outside or street hassles as possible and could focus on the next adventure at hand, doing time in federal prison and doing it with as positive an attitude as I could.

After Joe dropped me off at SFO, I caught an early morning flight to San Diego and took a cab from the airport to downtown and was dropped off in front of MCC (Metropolitan Correctional Center) San Diego. The building itself looked like a foreboding skyscraper looming above me, but I wasn't scared or apprehensive as I was almost three years ago. I was actually kind of looking forward to this new experience. I wouldn't have any of the headaches or worries I had in the past, trying to run a business operation. I was done with using drugs and was looking ahead to doing some reading and getting into a positive mindset to be able to face an unknown future, whatever it might bring.

At a stroke before 10 AM, my scheduled time for arrival, I entered MCC and went through the same rigamarole as I had done previously: booked, fingerprinted, photographed and given a set of prison duds in exchange for my street clothes. This time I was actually given a pair of shoes which fit. I was then escorted back up to my old surroundings on the 9th floor where I was assigned a room. I was hoping for a cell or room by myself... not gonna happen! I entered the room I was assigned to and it was empty... for the moment. There was obviously someone else living in the room, as it was neatly cleaned with someone's stuff laid on the lower bunk. There was a bible placed on the pillow. I put my few things on the upper bunk and settled in to wait and see who my roommate was. I didn't have to wait long.

About 15 minutes later, the door opened and before me stood an African-American man who was at least 6'6" tall with rippling muscles hidden behind a gray wife beater tank top. He had a short crew cut and a rather menacing persona about him.

He stuck out his hand and said: "Hi. I'm Robert Johnson, your new cellmate."

"Uh, OK," I replied in the most courageous voice I could muster. I shook his huge black hand rather apprehensively. Now I was truly scared. "I'm Rick. Pleased to meet you," I managed, trying not to show my inner nervousness.

Robert picked up on it immediately. "Rick, I know this must look strange and scary to you, but don't worry. I'm one of the good guys. You're gonna be just fine."

"Uh, OK," I squeaked. Robert must have noticed my rapid breathing.

"Rick, calm down. Look, I'm big and black," he said with a wide grin. "I'm also an ordained Baptist minister. I have a congregation here in San Diego and nothing is going to happen to you."

"Well, if you're a man of the cloth, what are you doing in here?" I asked, relaxing a bit.

"I got caught up in a robbery scheme. I'm sure I'll be cleared, but it's gonna take some time. So here we are. And what's your 'beef'?"

"Marijuana," I answered. "Conspiracy to import and sell pot."

"It's a stupid law, but there's a lot of you folks in here. I see a lot of drugs in my congregation, kids mostly. I don't like to see them using, but I understand it. Anyway, we're going to be roommates for probably a month, so I'd like to get to know you better. I can show you how to do time and how to stay healthy in here and wherever you get transferred to. You play cribbage?"

"I do, Robert," I answered.

"OK then. I'll show you how we do it in here. You see, we play for points and the points represent push-ups. The more points you get, the more push-ups your opponent has to do. It's fun and you get a good workout as well. I can see you need to build up your body strength. So, let's get to work."

So my fear of being cooped up with a huge black man went away with each hand of cribbage and each set of push-ups we both had to do. It turned out that Robert Johnson was one of the best people I met during my entire period of incarceration. His attitude was very motivational and uplifting and it seemed he wanted nothing more than to make sure I was well prepared both physically and mentally for the next two years in prison. I followed his lead, and by the end of the month there was a noticeable improvement in my physique and the positive attitude.

On the morning of January 28th, as I was sitting watching TV and drinking my morning coffee, I witnessed aghast as the pictures came streaming in of the Space Shuttle Challenger disintegrating over the Atlantic Ocean some 73 seconds after takeoff. The TV room was silent as other prisoners and myself stared in stunned disbelief at the disaster appearing in front of our collective eyes. The room was so silent, for a change, you could hear a pin drop.

It seemed a rather strange coincidence: two historic events in NASA's space program, the moon landing back in 1969 and now the Challenger disaster, would immediately precede my destiny.

Three days later I was transferred to my next home, FCI (Federal Correctional Institution) Tucson. This was a medium security facility and also my punishment for going to trial and testifying. Normally, I would have been sent directly to a low security prison camp, as were others in my case who pled guilty. But since I went to trial and testified in my own defense and was convicted, the court must have thought I lied (can you imagine that?), so the justice system found it necessary to mete out some more punishment to me. I later found out that this is a common occurrence.

The all-day trip from San Diego to Tucson was an experience unto itself. I was transported in a late-model white Chevy van. It was like being in a cage. I was with six other prisoners, three in the back and three in the way back of the van. All of us were shackled with chains around our wrists and ankles and were chained to the bench seats as well. We were separated from the U.S. Marshals, one driving and the other riding shotgun, by a thick black metal wire mesh. We'd be fucked if we were in a rollover accident. 'Just think good thoughts,' I told myself.

The trip across Arizona's Sonoran desert was uneventful except for two issues. First of all it was a fairly warm day, around the high 70s, and for some reason the marshals didn't turn on the air conditioning. Whether it just didn't work or was a little more punishment, I never found out. In any case, the smell inside the van was rank and overpowering with the rancid sweat stench of six manly men cooped up in the back of the van. The reeking smell alone almost made me hurl. But the second issue, an even more crucial one, was that the marshals refused to stop for any reason during the long 400 mile trip and I really had to take a piss. They kept saying "We'll be there soon… just hold it." Well, by the time we arrived, it was all I could do to keep from peeing in my pants. I had to go so bad when we got there, I actually couldn't go. It was like my urethral sphincter just wouldn't relax. It took an extra ten minutes in the lavatory for the pee to finally come and I was never so relieved… whew!

At FCI Tucson we had to go through the same booking procedure as at MCC San Diego, after which I was assigned a room. My cellmate turned out to be another good guy. He was originally from Cuba and was in on a coke beef stemming out of Southern California. His name was Armando Salcido-Cortez. For some reason he was nicknamed 'Big Jungle' or 'The B' (the king bee), as he put it. We got along great and 'The B' showed me some tricks of the trade, such as how to heat soup or coffee with a homemade heating element, called a stinger in prison slang, which is crudely fashioned from a bed spring and two wires plugged into the wall socket. There were all kinds of other similar illegal devices which ingenious inmates created in their cells to make life on the inside easier. I was however cautioned by 'The B': one must not get too carried away with things like this because it was possible to have a shakedown inspection at any time and if you were caught with anything like a stinger or even a homemade knife, called a shiv or a shank, you'd be sent directly to solitary confinement, known as the hole, and the good time you'd earned might be compromised, reduced or even eliminated entirely. Any infraction of the rules would be noted in your official records, also known as your jacket, which would follow you wherever you went in the prison system and particularly would not bode well for you when you went before the parole board.

So this was life at FCI Tucson. The facility was located on South Wilmot Road on the outskirts of the city of Tucson, not too far from Davis-Monthan Air Force Base. FCI Tucson is located on about ten acres enclosed in a double-fenced perimeter housing several hundred inmates in low, air conditioned pueblo-style buildings. There was a track circling the facility as well as a weight pile. There was some grass, but mostly it was a fenced in barren desert setting. The all-male population was considered to be non-violent offenders of minimal to moderate security risk.

While incarcerated in federal prison, it is mandatory that all inmates have jobs. These range from working in sanctioned prison industries such as the clothing shop, laundry or kitchen to working on the water or fire crew. Some inmates even have jobs allowing for some degree of freedom outside of the facility, usually when accompanied by a prison staff officer. So I began searching for a job. I found out there was a possibility of an opening as a clerk for the prison's Catholic priest. Nothing says a Jew can't work for a Catholic priest, so I went to the office of Father John Sorce, the prison chaplain, to apply for a job.

"Come on in and let's talk," said Fr. Sorce as I stood at the door. "What the heck is a Jew doing in a priest's office, anyway?"

"Well, I came here because I had heard your office needs help. I have a college degree and I can type as well as organize this office," I said looking around at numerous file boxes piled on the floor and papers strewn all over his desk. "Looks to me like this place is a mess. Father, you could use my help, believe me."

"Why should I? Look, I've never been in a place with so many innocent people. And I suppose you're one of them," he responded with a smile on his face.

"Well, I didn't say that, but still, I can see at just a cursory glance, this office needs me… badly, I might add. Look at this mess. How can you find anything in this pigsty?"

"Oh, so now you see this holy sanctuary as a pigsty?" he questioned.

"Well, maybe not quite that and if it were really, I'd have to decline… you know… Jews and pork don't mix."

Father laughed and hired me on the spot. I later learned many others had applied for the same coveted position with the chaplain and all but two were turned down. It was one of the most sought-after jobs at FCI Tucson. Those two were two other inmate clerks who worked for the Father, and whom I would soon meet. My job was to straighten up the office, something apparently his other two clerks were incapable of. So I went to work right away. The first order of business was to requisition several file cabinets and get the floor cleared of the boxes which seemed to be littered everywhere and stacked one on top of the other in the small 15' x 15' office. Within a couple of weeks I had the office cleared of all debris and it began to look like an actual office, instead of a dumping ground.

I met the other two clerks who were both in for marijuana offenses. They both seemed like nice fellows, Steve Gallardo and Alberico Bellicosta. Steve was a major pot dealer from Los Angeles and Al was a small time marijuana dealer from Arizona. I liked both of them and soon came to discover some of the benefits of working for the priest. First of all, we were sequestered away from the general prison population for most of the day and much of the time were left to our own devices alone in the office. It seemed 'while the cat's away the mice will play,' and we did. The Father kept his communion wine and wafers secreted away, underneath a pile of papers in one of his desk drawers. Nearly every afternoon while the chaplain was busy tending to other religious chores, we would party in his office; drinking the wine and putting Cheese Whiz on the communion wafers and watching our favorite TV shows we'd recorded on the priest's VCR. I'm sure Fr. Sorce knew what was going on but overlooked it. I mean, how could he not know, when his communion wine bottle was suddenly only one quarter full and his stash of communion wafers (crackers) were now almost always down to a few left. It was indeed good times for the situation I was in.

As it was, Steve and I became pretty close friends, but Al and I soon discovered we had a strange coincidence in our past. One day when we were reminiscing about the past and Al had mentioned he attended Arizona State University, somehow we got onto the subject of skiing. Al told me of the time he had gone to Aspen with his friend back in his college days. As the conversation went on, I told him I used to live in Aspen and had a close friend who had also attended ASU roughly at the same time as Al had. He told me about the trip to Aspen and how he'd stayed with a friend of his ASU pal who had lived there and this friend had gotten beaten up by his roommate right after they arrived, because his friend's dog had shit on the floor.

"Oh my God," I said. "Guess whose apartment you stayed at? Mine. I was the guy who had gotten his ass kicked by my roommate and your friend from ASU was none other than Willie Sherman, one of my oldest and best friends. Right?"

We both couldn't believe in the coincidence. But it was true. Of course when I finally told Willie of it, he wanted nothing to do with Al and said knowing him as he did and when he did, he was certain he'd wind up in jail someday. Well, it was one of those strange coincidences you'd never expect… and it wouldn't be the last time this would happen to me in these circumstances.

So, I passed my time in Tucson reading voraciously, working for the chaplain, working out daily, running the track and generally minding my own business. I did have several visitors during my stay. Among them was Dave Jones and his wife Annie who stopped to see me on their way from Marin to Austin, Texas. Kathy also came to visit as did both of my sisters with their young children as well as my mother. My father chose not to come, which didn't surprise me. Also my old friend Shoveler came. His was the most memorable visit as he brought me an item which I really needed. Since we both had the same shoe size, he brought me a new pair of Nike running shoes, which I surreptitiously exchanged with him under the table in the visitor's room, giving him my institution tennis shoes to throw away.

I was also able to spend considerable time in the prison law library, where I picked up some valuable information regarding post-conviction issues. I began researching cases regarding the Rule 35 Sentence Modification and what had happened to others in the same situation as mine. I soon discovered there were many instances where a Rule 35, although granted by the presiding judge, could be overturned by the U.S. Attorney's office if it wasn't acted on within one year of its issuance. In several cases I researched, the presiding judge lost jurisdiction of the case and the Rule 35 was disregarded by the U.S. Attorney. In my case, I was sentenced to 5 years with the provision; Judge Keep would modify my sentence to 30 months, at which time she would release me on time served. However if she lost jurisdiction of my case for failing to modify within one year, I had no such agreement with the U.S. Attorney, who hated me for supposedly lying on the witness stand. I was advised by one of the best jailhouse lawyers I knew that I had better somehow force the judge to rule before the year after I was sentenced was up. I did the research and wrote Patrick a letter explaining all of this to him and citing the relevant case law. I further instructed him that unless Judge Keep ruled on my Rule 35 in the next month, which would be the year anniversary date from my sentencing, I would withdraw my plea and go back to trial. It was a bold move, but a necessary one given the circumstances and the peril I was facing.

Butch wrote the letter to the judge explaining the circumstances and citing the relevant cases I'd brought to his attention and to my amazement, the judge agreed and modified my sentence. This really worked to my advantage, because if the judge got her original wish, I would have had to do every day of the 30 month sentence with no 'good time' applied. Now, with the 'good time' I'd accumulated and would continue to accumulate, as long as I didn't have any negative incidents, I would only have to do two thirds of my sentence… or about 20 months. I had saved myself nearly a year in prison. I can't fault Butch for this oversight, because most criminal attorneys don't really know post-conviction law. The best source for information on the issue is usually found through 'jailhouse lawyers', and there were a couple of great ones incarcerated at FCI Tucson. I was indeed fortunate to meet them. They taught me how do legal research and how to write legal briefs. I became very good at it and soon others were asking me for legal advice and to do legal research for them. It turned out to be a good source for additional goodies at the prison commissary.

Finally, some ten months later my transfer to camp finally came through. It was a time filled with mixed emotions. I was sad to be leaving Father Sorce, but on the other hand, it was time to get out of a level 2 prison and into a camp. I think I left Tucson for the better than when I arrived. One of the assignments I'd been working on at Tucson was the requisitioning of a new chapel. Everything was in the works when I left and I later got word from the Father, a few weeks after my departure, that indeed the new chapel arrived in the form of a new manufactured building. I had completed all of the paperwork and through a series of letters and interviews, I convinced the Bureau of Prisons to spend over $100,000 to purchase the new chapel. It was to be a new and separate sanctuary and place of worship to conduct all religious services and, I believe, is still in use at FCI Tucson to this day.

I was given a bus ticket and a couple of days to go unescorted (no marshals) to Lompoc to complete my sentence. My brother-in-law came to Tucson to accompany me on the bus back to Central California. Usually, the justice system gives you virtually free rein to travel unaccompanied from a medium security facility to a low security prison camp. They figure that if you are stupid enough to run away and face an additional five years for trying to escape, you don't deserve to go to camp in the first place.

During my time in Tucson, I had been communicating through letters with Stan's sister, Tanya, who told Stan I would be coming to Lompoc soon. When I arrived Stan, who by now knew all the ropes, greeted me and had a job waiting for me on the cowboy crew… the most sought after job at camp. I was 'in like Flynn'.

I was actually quite relieved to finally get to camp. The atmosphere was so different from Tucson, I almost expected to wake up in the morning to the cheerful voice of Uncle Ernie from the song entitled *Tommy's Holiday Camp*[1] played by The Who in their 1969 rock opera *Tommy*:

> 'Good morning campers! I'm your Uncle Ernie,
> and welcome to Tommy's Holiday Camp!
> The camp with a difference, never mind the weather,
> When you come to Tommy's the holiday's forever!…'

FPC (Federal Prison Camp) Lompoc was completely different from FCI Tucson. First of all, there were no fences or bars. Lompoc had once been an Army base and had been converted to a prison camp years earlier. At camp it is said that the bars and fences are in your mind only. One could easily walk away, although it rarely happens because the consequences are very severe if you get caught… and you surely will, sooner or later. They never stop looking! I was assigned to a dormitory room with Stan and six other inmates, five of whom were also on the cowboy crew.

One of the functions at FPC Lompoc is to provide the other federal prisons with steaks, hamburger and other assorted meat products. FPC Lompoc has a herd of 2,500 cattle, a slaughterhouse and meat packing plant. The cattle, like on any other cattle ranch, roam the adjacent pastures which, in this instance, are located on the 40,000 acres comprising Vandenberg Air Force Base, right next to the prison facility at Lompoc. The prison cowboy crew is made up of roughly 20 inmates who are given horses, trucks and all of the equipment necessary to manage the herd. The crew is responsible for keeping track of the herd, rounding them up, inoculating and castrating the young steers, and providing the slaughterhouse with cattle to slaughter and package the meat for distribution to the other prisons. My function was to be the clerk of the cowboy crew. I had to keep track of the herds, account for each animal, and assist wher-

1 Referenced Songs & Music, Item 15, Page 529.

ever needed. We were also responsible for mending and building fences and for making sure there was always adequate water for the herds to drink.

The crew itself consisted of 20 inmate cowboys from various walks of life. They were mostly run-of-the-mill smugglers, like Stan, Bob Lahodny and myself. Ed Otero, who was also at camp, was blackballed from the crew because of his boisterous attitude which might jeopardize the rest of the crew. Ed had tried to get on the crew, however he had a reputation around camp of being a drunken loudmouth and none of the other cowboys wanted him around. Some of the other crew members were: a couple of Klamath River Indians in for poaching salmon offseason, several real cowboys on the outside in for drugs, a border patrol agent gone bad and even a graduate of the Air Force Academy who'd flown F-4 fighter jets in Viet Nam busted for flying cocaine into the U.S. from Colombia. Most all had been ratted out by someone else, so everyone was truly 'rat sensitive'.

There was an unsaid hierarchy on the crew based on a combination of seniority and overall macho-ness. On this particular cowboy crew it was not all 'Kumbaya' with cowboys sitting around the campfire roasting marshmallows and reciting cowboy poetry. Like all issues in prison, mountains can quickly be made out of molehills and disagreements of what would normally be considered trivial and overlooked on the outside could quickly devolve into knock-down, dragout fights at the drop of a hat.

One such incident occurred while six of us were in a pickup truck out to repair a broken water line in one of the pastures on Vandenberg. It involved a rather macho, arrogant heroin dealer from one of the United States' Pacific Island territories who considered himself to be a real badass and thought another of the truck's occupants, a rather short, stocky, unassuming Rocky Mountain cowboy, should get out and open the cattle gate, when it was the Pacific Islander's job in the first place. He was trying to intimidate and throw his weight around and pretty much assumed everyone should give him the wide berth he thought he deserved.

The ensuing conversation went something like this:

"Hey, Rocky, you gate hoob!" barked the well tanned islander, referring to the job of opening and closing gates which is always reserved for the lowest crew member. "Get the fuck out and open the gate, if you know what's good for you."

"Fuck you. Get it yourself. It's your job."

"I told you what to do. Now get on with it, punk," said the Islander as the veins in his neck started to bulge and his left eye began to twitch in anticipation.

Right then, Rocky, the cowboy and former rodeo bronc rider, sitting in the middle of the back seat, reached across the erstwhile heroin dealer, opened the door and pushed him out and onto the ground. Then he immediately jumped out, landing on top of him, and proceeded to go totally Western, beating the crap out of the stunned and bewildered Pacific Islander. Needless to say, nobody messed with Rocky after that and the Islander's status on the crew dropped significantly.

This is me as a cowboy at FPC Lompoc in 1987. All of my cowboy ensemble from hat to boots had to be clandestinely dropped off at Vandenberg and then smuggled into camp.

I really never had problems with any of the crew because I was the clerk and not a threat to the cowboy crew hierarchy and was generally left alone. I pretty much did what I wanted. I could go out with any of the crew on the water or fence detail, or if I had nothing better to do I could just take my horse and wander any of the thousands of acres of pastureland adjacent to the corrals. Aside from the Idaho cowboy, Rocky, who was pretty much my size, I was the smallest cowboy but tried my best to always pull my weight. I dogged young 250-pound steers, wrestling them to the ground and tying off their feet like any of the other cowboys. Rocky took me under his wing and showed me the proper cowboy technique so as not to get hurt.

I was always teased about being a Jewish cowboy and felt like I was acting in the crazy scenes as depicted by the fictional movie character Avram Belinski, played by Gene Wilder in the 1979 movie entitled *The Frisco Kid*.[2] In the movie, set in the late 1800s, Belinski, an innocent and trusting rabbi, arrives from Europe, fresh off the boat, in Philadelphia with a Torah in hand looking to travel to a synagogue in San Francisco.

2 Referenced Television & Movies, Item 5, Page 533.

The inexperienced and gullible traveler hooks up with a group of con men and bank robbers and the crazy journey begins from there, as a series of wild and goofy episodes of the naive Jewish cowboy in the Wild West. That was me on the cowboy crew.

This photo is a spoof photo of me on the weight pile at Lompoc
holding up 200 pounds with one hand... Right!

On the crew, however, it was for the most part pretty mellow, with everyone getting along with each other and quietly doing their time. But occasionally, shit happened.

Being on the cowboy crew was the most coveted and envied job at camp and I was extremely lucky I had Stan to pave the way for me to be included. The job was also one which required trust and secrecy, because of all the opportunities to roam free and take advantage of the freedom. There was one cop or jailer to manage all twenty of us smugglers and drug dealers. We were basically given free rein to roam at any time, day or night, on Vandenberg, the top secret military base which was also NASA's Western Space Shuttle Launch Facility. It was a common occurrence for us to be called in the middle of the night to find cattle that had gotten out of the fenced pastures and were roaming on the base roads, the airport tarmac, the Shuttle launch pad or down on the adjacent beach.

It was loosely controlled chaos at all times, and it was a dangerous job constantly fraught with peril.

The danger reared its head on my first day as a cowboy. The 20-man cowboy crew was herding cattle down one of the many steep hills on Vandenberg when one of the cowboys lost control of his horse while chasing after a loose steer. The horse shied and the rider, one of the inmate cowboys, was thrown into the air and landed upside down, snapping his neck like a twig. He was pronounced DOA when his body was delivered by ambulance to the military base hospital. We were cowboys like any other cowboys in America, both past and present, and the dangers associated with that line of work were constant. It quickly became apparent to me that when you play around on horses, you are going to get hurt... it's only a matter of when and how bad.

During my time as a cowboy I was thrown or fell off my horse several times. Once my horse bolted forward and I went sailing off backwards like a rodeo circus clown, luckily landing on soft dirt, but with my foot caught in the stirrup and I was dragged for several yards before my boot came off, freeing me from what could have been a serious disaster. The other time I was thrown and landed on my right hand, compressing and breaking two of my knuckles. The soreness and stiffness I still feel from the incident serves as a constant reminder of my life as a cowboy.

Many of the crew would have their girlfriends or wives come and clandestinely meet them for what we called 'bush furloughs' or romp in the bushes, when no one else (the cop specifically) would be looking. Someone always had to stand guard... just in case the cop or an MP would unexpectedly come by. Then there were the drop-offs. We would arrange for our friends on the outside to drive through a designated road open to public traffic on Vandenberg and drop off whatever we requested. It included drugs, clothing, food, equipment, booze and anything else we needed. We would then go find the dropped off goodies in the bush and smuggle them back to the corral area then sneak it back into camp.

We rarely ate with the other inmates, because as clerk, I could resurrect dead cows by substituting their ear tags with live ones and then we would lead one of these 'resurrected dead cows' into the slaughterhouse and have the inmates who worked there secretly give us the meat, which we could then barbecue at the corrals or in the field on Vandenberg. It was merely a matter of juggling the numbers so I'd always make sure the accounting for the total number cattle in the herd always balanced. We also ate other delicacies we caught in the field. We trapped and grilled wild quail that had wandered into the corrals, but a favorite was rattlesnake. Several of us would go up into the hills and hunt rattlesnakes hanging out on the rocks above the pastures sunning themselves in the warm SoCal sun. It seemed like there were hundreds of them in this one area and we'd whittle a forked tree branch into a snake-stick allowing us to trap the snake's head then cut it off with a knife... yes, it was rather brutal, but it was survival of the fittest and we were hungry! We'd then skin the snake and preserve the beautiful skin with glycerine and barbecue the meat. It was a delicacy taught to us by the two native Americans on the crew. It was great and tasted somewhat like chicken. The two Indians also taught us how to tan and fashion the skins onto leather belts and wallets to take home as souvenirs.

The whole cowboy crew operation was built on trust and any inmate who wanted to be on the crew, if there was an opening (which rarely occurred), was carefully scrutinized by the other crew members. We wanted to make sure no rats were allowed on the crew, who might tell the cops of all the shenanigans we were up to, maybe for some reward or sentence reduction, thus jeopardizing the whole scene for everyone else.

If it ever came to light, the mischief we were getting away with, we'd all probably get a quick trip across the street to the USP (United States Penitentiary) which loomed adjacent to the camp, hidden from view by groves of eucalyptus trees like some foreboding concrete monster ready to gobble you up. It was the place for the most hardened criminals in the country and one where you absolutely didn't want to go.

One of the crew members was tight with one of the prison counselors and could find out about anyone's jacket, which is how we knew if someone was a rat or not. On the door to the corrals was a picture of a rat in a red circle with a red diagonal through it… No Rats Allowed!

This picture is of the actual drawing that was posted on the door to the cowboy office located at the Lompoc corrals, which I secretly lifted as a souvenir just prior to my departure from camp. It was a serious issue on the cowboy crew where trust between inmates was paramount and this photo is pretty self explanatory!

Being a cowboy was fun as well as challenging. With the freedom we were afforded, we got to be away from camp most every day. If we weren't at the corrals, hanging out or doing any menial work like cleaning stalls or policing the area, we were off on adventures, like the daily checking and patrolling of the pastures, to make sure the 2500 head of cattle roaming on the 44,000 acres of Vandenberg always had water and feed and the hundreds of miles of fencing were maintained and repaired whenever needed. Occasionally, one of the crew would find an abandoned calf and bring it back to the corrals where it could be bottle-fed until old enough to join the rest of the herd. If we had any idle time, we always managed to find something interesting to do, such as trapping quail or hunting rattlesnakes for an afternoon BBQ, out in the field.

Even with all the contraband available, I stuck to my own admonition and stayed away from the drugs and alcohol which were readily available. My friend C.J. Peakman, a.k.a. Shoveler, made two trips to Lompoc to visit me. Each time he brought a garbage bag full of goodies for me including new blue jeans, cowboy boots, my own special pillow, beef jerky, licorice and other assorted items of food and sundries to share with the other cowboys. He'd leave it hidden in a manzanita bush just off the main road on the base at a pre-arranged spot and later one of us would drive by in a prison pickup truck and retrieve it and return it to the corral area. Then later I could sneak it back to camp when I returned, usually for the four o'clock count, when we all had to be back and in our bunks. It was truly an amazing situation and was nothing like the image of prison one usually imagines. Coincidentally there have been several shows aired on TV in the past twenty years on the subject of inmate cowboys, and although quite revealing on the subject in general, none of them exposed the extent of the antics I experienced as one.

One day when I had just come back to camp from the corrals, I saw a familiar face entering my dormitory. Although he now had short hair, it was unmistakably Woodacre 'Woody' Bob, the Marin County marijuana dealer and former customer of 'Yorktown' Billy's whom I'd met fifteen years ago, who had the psychedelic painted VW bus and had stripped naked atop the Marin hills to do the weed deal with us.

"Hey Woody Bob," I called. "What a coincidence seeing you here. How ya doin'? What was your beef?"

"Rick. Great to see you buddy. Sure is a small world. I got busted up in San Rafael with 750,000 hits of acid and picked up a nickel," he said, referring to a five-year sentence. "Billy told me you'd gotten 'ratted out' by the schoolteacher in the Coronado gang. Sorry to hear about it, man."

"Yeah, I guess that's the way it goes. Seems like all the good guys get ratted out."

"I sure miss that great weed you had back then. There's never been anything like it since you went down," Woody Bob replied. "Boy, I sure miss that. Well, I've got to boogie. Got a camp baseball game to play in ten minutes. I'm starting in left field. Great to see you, man. Sorry it had to be in here, but maybe we'll meet again on the outside."

"Well, I'm done with 'the biz', but maybe we will. See ya round," I replied. 'Jeez, you just never know who you'll run into in a nice place like this,' I thought.

My time in prison was finally over after spending a year at camp and I was released back to a halfway house in San Francisco, where I would spend the next three months transitioning back into society. On the bus ride back to San Francisco, I happened to sit next to a pretty lady who was traveling by bus from SoCal and going to The City as well. I told her of my past two years in prison and how it was a pretty interesting time for me. The news didn't bother her in the slightest. She was a schoolteacher who was visiting from New York. We hit it off immediately and the relationship carried on for several months following my release.

The halfway house was actually an experience unto itself. It was located in San Francisco's Tenderloin District, not far from the Mars Hotel, where I had met my cousin Marty following his release from the Mexican prison. The three-story building had seen its better days and although in a state of disrepair it was clean and livable with private rooms and one step closer for inmates to reintegrate back into society. It was occupied by others who had been released from prison or jail, many of whom were drug addicts. The halfway house was staffed by contract employees who were given the authority to conduct drug tests and random inspections of inmates, their property and living quarters. During my three months there, never did one day go by when one of the other residents wasn't 'rolled up' for a violation and sent back to prison. But I survived without incident and in December of 1987 I was released from federal custody and was again a free man, although with five years of probation to look forward to.

***

All in all, my time in prison was a positive time of my life and although I would have rather not been in prison, it changed my life and made me realize the importance of my freedom. It also served to teach me the importance of personal integrity. Although I had been offered sweet deals to cooperate with the government, I remained true to my own ideals and held my mud, the prison expression for keeping your mouth shut and not being a rat.

My grandfather used to scold me for never reading. He was an immigrant who had taught himself English and to read when he first came to America in the late 1800s. Well, in prison I read every day and managed to read nearly 100 books during my stay. I am never without a book to read to this day. 'Thanks Pop', which is what I called him. Even though he passed away in 1969, I know he would have been pleased about that... even if he otherwise would have been totally bummed out about the circumstances that forced me to acquire such a passion.

So, after 13 years as a smuggler in the marijuana business and two years in prison, I was once again a reasonably free man; however I still had a 'five year tail' following me on probation to complete to really be free. Although I had little money left of the fortune I'd made, I learned, through Father Sorce's tutelage, that I could never go back into the drug business. He said: "Once you've been caught, if you ever go back, the chances are nearly 100% that you'll be caught again. And next time you'll be lucky to get out in 20 years." Such was the case of Alberico, the other chaplain's clerk in Tucson, who even though he was considered a 'small time dealer', was a three-time offender and served nearly 25 years. Some people never learn. The recidivism rate, the average number of repeat offenders who go back to jail, nationally, is about 85%.

After my release, I still had a score to settle with my cousin, Pete Feldstein, for the advice he'd given my mother five years ago. He had told her to tell me to "tell the government everything I knew and save myself." This would have put me in the perilous position of being a rat in prison. I did the crime and was willing to do the time and I could now look myself in the mirror and not see the whiskers and pointy-nosed face of a rat looking back at me, like all the other government informants. I felt that at least I had taken the honorable path and held my mud. I still had the 'burr under my saddle' for the past five years and knew I had to confront my cousin about it. I then asked and received permission from my probation officer to travel to New York to see some of my family I hadn't seen since the '70s. I arranged a meeting with my cousin Pete and subsequently flew to New York. Pete had retired from the U.S. Attorney's office and was now in private practice. Many of his defendant clients were from organized crime organizations, whom he'd prosecuted as an assistant U.S. attorney. He invited me to join him for lunch at the revered New York Athletic Club. We sat in a secluded corner whereupon I unloaded on him.

In a voice which most likely could be overheard by other patrons, I said, "Pete, how the fuck could you have told my mother to tell me to cooperate with the government, when you didn't know me or the circumstances. You were condemning me to being a rat in prison or fear of those repercussions for the rest of my life. You were suggesting the easy and cowardly path. Well, that's not me and you were an asshole for even suggesting it to my mother. Is that what you advise all of your clients now since you're in private practice? Don't you know by giving them that advice, if they follow it, you are basically condemning them to life as a rat and possibly retribution of future violence or worse. What kind of perverted motherfucker are you? It was an irresponsible and cowardly suggestion and you owe me an apology." My rant lasted for about one minute and certainly drew the attention of others in the room. Pete stammered and was dumbfounded. He profusely apologized and the incident was never mentioned again. At least I'd finally gotten it off my chest.

So with my life as a smuggler behind me once and for all, I was able to reconcile with my father who supported and backed me as a real estate developer. But the best news of all is, I met a wonderful lady whom I fell in love with and who kept me on the straight and narrow. She too had a storied history, and as we later discovered, our paths had crossed several times in the past, but somehow we never knew each other until now.

In early 1988 we were married.

I looked forward to a bright new future with a beautiful new lady in my life and both parents who now supported me in a new profession.

But, what I didn't know at the time was, there was big trouble brewing on the horizon and my legal troubles were far from over.

Chapter 49

It's Never Over

1988 to 1993

I t's not what you know that can hurt you. It's what you don't know!
What I knew for sure was that I was completely out of the marijuana business and had been so ever since the Bear Harbor load back in '81. I also knew, after my release from prison in 1987, I had an additional five-year tail following me and that I had to report to the Federal Probation Office once a month and any violation would send me straight back to the bucket, a place I knew I didn't want to go, no matter what… so long as it didn't involve being a rat. Then all bets are off.

What I didn't know was that Ciro's Thai operation had grown dramatically during the past seven years while I was going through all of my legal hassles. 'Tony the Thai' had told me he had loaded a couple of boats for Ciro back in the years of '79 through '81. But then Tony had died and I didn't realize his death was merely a 'speed bump' in Ciro's operation. Following 'Thai's' death, Charlie reassumed control of the Thai crew and began to load boats exclusively for Ciro, sometimes two or three a year. Those loads ranged from the smallest one aboard my old yacht *Mamamouchi*, now owned by Ed Lehmer, with over three tons to the largest being a load to Alaska of nearly 15 tons in 1989 also skippered by Ed. During this time period Ciro and his partner Walter in concert with his Thai procurer, Charlie, had smuggled an estimated 70 tons of Thai weed into the U.S. worth somewhere in the neighborhood of $200 million. Indeed, as they had once envisioned back in the old days, their operation was now in the *Fortune 500* league.

As it also turned out, Joe, my old confidant and main helper, was right in the middle of Ciro's operation, ferrying money overseas, procuring equipment like additional sealing machines and poly-mylar bags from our source in Japan and shipping them to Thailand as well as assisting in the unloading of numerous loads and sailing some of the loads across the ocean, personally, himself. He was a busy boy and so were several others who had formerly worked with me, like Phil's cousin Dennis Hathaway, Kevin

Masters, Ed Lehmer as well as Jonathan Jacoby, Mike Stallings and Dennis Moronsky. Although I wasn't too happy about the fact that Joe had divulged the trade secrets of our operation to Ciro as well as assisted him in his further smuggling ventures in Thailand, I couldn't bemoan the fact that he was simply using the skills that he'd gleaned and helped to develop for our smuggling trip. He had to work to support his habits and lifestyle and since we'd retired he had to find something else to do and was only trying to do the best job he could. I don't fault him or his loyalty for that. However it would have been nice for Ciro to have compensated us for the use of our 'main man', Joe with all of his experience and knowledge to further Ciro's own smuggling operation. Like he forced me to do regarding my use of 'his main man' Pat. Obviously, that would never happen! It always seemed to be a one-way street for Ciro and anybody who got in his way better 'watch out' and watch his back.

As clandestine and as careful as they all tried to be, the operation didn't go smoothly at all times and, more significantly, didn't go unnoticed by the authorities. Several of Ciro's organization literally were caught with their pants down while trying to carry cash in Europe. Wearing specially designed stash vests, three members of the organization were transiting Germany and while at a train station, wads of money began falling out of one of the group's pants legs and onto the departure platform in a Keystone Cops-like comedy. They were all arrested. One of their boats carrying nearly ten tons of Thai weed was busted off the Oregon Coast, another carrying three tons was seized in Australia. At least one load of three tons was jettisoned by a paranoid crew following the Australia bust.[1]

With each bust, each arrest and each mishap, things began to unravel at various levels of the Mancuso organization. Pressure was being applied to those in trouble and people began to cooperate with authorities.

One particular U.S. Customs agent named Richard 'Rick' Pierce found himself on a personal quest to try and bring down the organization. He had become aware of Ciro's illegal activities shortly following the *Drifter* bust and had been investigating bits and pieces of it for nearly ten years. Aided by several individuals who'd 'rolled', Pierce began to assemble a mountain of evidence against Ciro and his band of cohorts. It wasn't long into the mid-'80s before the Reno, Nevada, DEA office and Reno U.S. Attorney's office became involved and began to assemble a task force specifically targeting Ciro and all others involved with him, both past and present. Soon Pierce's path and mine would cross and I would be unwittingly dragged into their investigation as if swimming in the ocean and being caught in an unseen undertow and now fighting for my life.

It was now the spring of 1988 and I was newly married and living in Point Richmond, California, coincidentally in a condominium on a hill overlooking the Richmond Yacht Club, where some 15 years previous I had sailed *Nepenthe* back from Thailand and unloaded it with our first load of Thai weed. I would wake up each morning and look directly at the yacht club and listen to the halyards slapping against sailboat masts rocking gently in the harbor breezes and dream about the good old days.

While stirring a hot cup of coffee and sitting on our deck with my wife, Lu, one

---

1 Referenced Magazine Articles, Item 1, Page 533.

beautiful spring morning, just relaxing and enjoying each other's company, we were startled at 7 AM by the phone ringing.

"I wonder who could be calling at this hour?" I said in a rather curious tone.

"I'll get it, honey," said Lu, as she was sitting closest to the kitchen wall phone. She picked it up on the third ring.

"Hello," she answered. On the other end of the line, she heard the unmistakable static and crackling noise coming from an overseas call.

"Hello, this is the international operator. I have a person-to-person call for Rick Bibbero from Thailand. Is Mr. Bibbero there?"

"Yes. Just a minute and I'll get him." I noticed a quizzical look cross her face.

"Hello," I answered.

"Rick, it's Pat," said Pat Suraghoomkol.

"Hey, Pat! It's been, what, six, seven years. How's it going?"

"Not too good Rick. I'm stuck here in Thailand. You know. I can't come back to States and live like you."

"Well, at least you didn't have to go to prison, like I did. I can't travel, like you. My passport was confiscated. So you aren't the only one with problems. Plus I have five years of probation, where the man can look up my ass anytime he wants and there's nothing I can do about it. So don't tell me your life is so bad. At least you're free and don't have that to deal with," I said, now getting rather annoyed at the direction of the conversation.

"Well, speaking of the man, that's what I want to talk to you about."

"Whaddya mean?" I asked.

"I had visit the other day by DEA man. He say he want to know everything, especially about you. I know that you still been working. I heard rumors over here," Pat answered, now in a rather accusatory tone.

"Are you outta your fucking mind, and what the hell are you talking about? I haven't been doing anything, since before you left. I told you, I'm on probation, and believe me, I don't want to go back to prison. I'm out of it all together."

"Not from what I heard. I know you still working. Tell you what Rick. If you want me to keep my mouth shut and not tell DEA man everything, you better consider paying me to keep quiet."

"Listen Pat because I'm only going to say this once. You're way over the line here. You don't know what you're talking about. I don't know what you've heard or from whom, but whatever it is you're talking about, it's bullshit and I don't like the direction of this conversation. You have the nerve to call me up after all these years and accuse me of something I haven't done and now are trying to extort or blackmail me. Well fuck you, and one more thing. I don't know how you got this number because it's unlisted. Undoubtedly you got it from the man, who's probably standing next to you right now recording this whole conversation. The two of you can kiss my ass and, by the way, don't ever call me again. Fuck off!"

I hung up the phone and just sat there in stunned disbelief. Lu was listening to my end of the conversation and was equally disturbed as well.

"I don't know how he got this number," I said. "But you can bet the DEA gave it to him. I'd bet the conversation was taped as well. This is really bullshit and I think they're trying to set me up."

This would be the first of several incidents which occurred in the next few years which would really open my eyes to see just how vulnerable you are and how thin the ice is underneath you when the government has its hooks into you and you're in their sights.

I decided to put my life back together and become a builder and my parents agreed to back me financially in this new endeavor. We moved to Carmel to start a building project on the Big Sur coast on a piece of property owned by my mother. I partnered with a designer/builder named Jared Arbuckle who lived up in Tahoe and had built Phil's house in the valley several years ago. Of course anything I did had to be approved by my probation officer who was out of the San Francisco office and wouldn't cut me much slack, no matter how much I tried to convince him I'd reformed and learned my lesson. I was glad to relocate and get out from under his clutches.

After the relocation I was assigned a new probation officer out of the Monterey office and, much to my dismay, I found that this new guy was as bad as the one I'd just been released from. I was reminded of a famous line in a song by The Who entitled: *Won't Get Fooled Again.*[2]

'Meet the new boss, same as the old boss.'

Well, fortunately for me he retired about two months later and his replacement turned out to be the nicest and most encouraging government person I'd met since my release from prison. Jose Guerrero was much more trusting and understanding and indeed a breath of fresh air from the suffocating and tight-reined men, whose thumbs I'd been under since getting released from the halfway house nearly a year earlier. I still needed permission to leave the Monterey area, which I had to secure from Jose in order to travel up to Lake Tahoe to work on the plans with Jared.

Jared was a big burly guy about 6'2" tall and probably tipped the scales at 230 pounds. He was a rugged mountain man type of individual with a friendly attitude and a rather loud voice. He was renting a beautiful home on Tahoe's west shore where we set up to design and draw the plans for the Big Sur project. I would travel to Tahoe numerous times during the fall and into the winter to assist Jared and give my input on the project.

In early December of 1988 on one of my trips to Tahoe, Jared and I were working on the plans, which were spread out on the pool table in Jared's living room, when there was a knock on the front door. Jared answered it and introduced me to a 6' tall rather husky man with shaggy brown hair which kind of fell into his eyes, who had apparently worked for him on one of his previous construction projects. His name was Phillip Byron and I was immediately taken aback by his rather prying questions about who I was and what we were doing. I was further blown away when Byron asked Jared if he knew where he could get some cocaine. Jared answered "no" but added, if he located

---

2 Referenced Songs & Music, Item 18, Page 531.

some he might be interested in getting a gram or two. Upon hearing that exchange, I left the house immediately, to the point of being very rude, blowing past both of them in a huff, to take a walk down on the pier to wait until this idiot left the house. When I returned about 15 minutes later, I exploded on Jared, threatening to end our partnership instantly if anything like this ever happened again. I reminded him again of my situation and he was jeopardizing my freedom by having contact with anyone like this.

What I didn't know (but found out later) was that this was a DEA setup and Phil's cousin, Dennis Hathaway, who'd previously worked for Jared, had been busted along with this Phil Byron, who had agreed to become an informant rather than face the music. Phil was attempting to snare Jared and anyone else Jared was connected to. Byron reported back to his DEA 'snitch master': he'd met me and noted my license plate number from my car parked in Jared's driveway. This information quickly shifted the focus of their investigation from Dennis to me. At this point, I was a known major drug trafficker who'd been convicted of smuggling, had spent two years in the slammer, was now out on probation and, in their eyes, must be back up to my old tricks again.

What I didn't know was that in light of this incident, I now became a major target of the DEA who, by this point, were intensely focused on Ciro Mancuso and, through information gleaned from other informants' debriefings, knew I was associated with Ciro. Again, I was guilty by association, which was exactly what Father Sorce had warned me about before I left FCI Tucson, but it didn't stop there.

A month or so later, sometime in late January or early February 1989, while Lu and I were having a peaceful evening at our newly rented home in Carmel, enjoying the company of Lu's grandchildren, at about 5 PM there was a knock on the door. Lu answered it and stood face-to-face with two men dressed in dark suits.

"May we come in?" said the friendly, blonde, tall good looking agent, extending in his outstretched hand his black government issued wallet with the gold U.S. Customs badge on one side and his picture ID displayed in plastic on the billfold's other side. "My name is Rick Pierce and we'd like to speak with your husband, Rick Bibbero."

Her 18-month-old grandson was hanging on her leg and our golden retriever, Burt, was at her side wagging his tail as Pierce petted the friendly dog's head.

Pierce, now the lead investigator in the Mancuso case, had apparently connected the dots and figured I was still active in the 'business', most likely from both discussions with the DEA agent in Thailand who had interviewed and tried to set me up through Pat Suraghoomkol, and now with the DEA agent in Tahoe who'd ID'd me in connection with the investigation of Dennis Hathaway through the debriefing of the rat Phil Byron.

"Just a minute. Please wait here," Lu politely replied. "Rick," she called to me while I was in the kitchen fixing a cup of hot chocolate for her grandson. "There are some men here at the door who want to speak with you."

"Really?" I replied, now coming to her side. "Who are you and what do you want?"

"Like I said to your wife, I'm Rick Pierce from the U.S. Customs office and this is Special Agent Smith from the DEA. We'd like to come in and ask you a few questions. Is that OK?"

"No, not really. Do you have a warrant? Am I under arrest or something? What's the problem here?" I asked.

"I don't have a warrant and you're not under arrest. We'd just like to have a friendly discussion with you. Mind if we come in out of the cold?" Pierce asked. His tone was friendly and his demeanor relaxed.

"It wouldn't be my first choice, but I can see it's freezing out there. So sure, come on in. Would you like some coffee or something?" I replied. My guard was immediately up as they came inside whereupon I threw down a friendly gauntlet. "If you'd like to talk about the weather or have me give you some sightseeing information about Carmel, that'd be fine. By the way, have you seen the new aquarium in Monterey? It's spectacular. You don't want to miss it. However, if you want to discuss anything else, I'd rather have my lawyer present. If that's OK with you?"

"Um… that's fine. I guess we'll take that coffee," he said rather taken aback. "And, yes. We'd like to talk to you about another matter. We can meet at your lawyer's office, say, next week. And that would be who and where?"

"My lawyer is Patrick Hallinan and his office is in San Francisco. Why don't you give me your card and I'll call him and set it up."

They left and first thing the next morning I called Butch. I was surprised when he told me he could no longer represent me, because of a conflict of interest. He said he had another client who was the subject of an ongoing investigation, who I undoubtedly knew, but whose identity he didn't reveal to me at the time. I certainly knew exactly who he was talking about.

I explained to Butch what was going on and he recommended I speak with a former associate of his, Dale Kovac, who was now in private practice for himself and working in Sacramento. Dale had also done some work for me on my case, while he was still working for Patrick. I knew him to be both a smart and savvy lawyer as well as a great guy.

It's a small and incestuous world in the legal field of very competent drug lawyers, which Dale certainly was, and coincidentally Dale was also representing Dennis Hathaway on his coke bust. Dennis had now moved from Tahoe back to his home in the Central Valley. It was also Patrick who had recommended Dennis to Dale.

I contacted Dale and asked him to give Agent Pierce a call and set up an appointment to meet whenever it was convenient for all of us to get together at his office in Sacramento.

During our conversation Dale said, "Rick, it's funny that you should contact me, because your name came up just the other day in another seemingly unrelated case of another client of mine, Dennis Hathaway. I think you know him. I have a Report of Investigation (ROI)[3] sitting here on my desk that I think you should see. I can fax it over to you. You'd better take a look at it. Seems like you are the center of attention."

"What are you talking about?" I asked, now really concerned.

"What's your fax number?"

"Give me a minute and let me switch it over to the fax machine. Use this number."

---

3 Referenced Legal Research, Item 10, Page 532.

I said and waited for the fax to arrive.

Holding the curling fax paper in my hand, I read the ROI in a state of suspended disbelief. Time seemed to stand still for both Lu and me as I read aloud a report made by a DEA Agent named Rick Wiley of the Incline Village's DEA office entitled 'Debriefing of SRA-X008 and Related Surveillance' that detailed exactly what I had witnessed which had occurred at Jared's house on the evening of December 1, 1988. But what really got my attention were the details of a subsequent one page 'Status Report' which was included as the last page of the fax. This later ROI dated Feb. 12, 1989, stated that a Special DEA Task Force Agent by the name of Jack Bax of the North Lake Tahoe DEA office had directed the informant, only identified as SRA-88-X008, to "continue his efforts directed at developing a viable criminal case against Bibbero." It was now a foregone conclusion: SRA-88-X008 was indeed the snitch Phillip Byron.

I subsequently called Jared and gave him the information and told him, in no uncertain terms, if he ever had contact with this low-life degenerate again, we were through.

I also read in the report that my probation officer, Jose Guerrero, had been contacted regarding all of this. I felt certain his trust in me was now beginning to wane and he was certainly having his doubts about my insistence of having nothing more to do with the drug business. Only time would tell if I could regain his confidence. I thought it might be a good first step to be open and honest with him regarding the events as described in the ROI. Also I needed to meet with him anyway to obtain a travel pass to go Sacramento to meet with my new attorney and Agent Pierce.

As I sat with him in his Monterey office, I relayed the events which had happened up at Lake Tahoe last December then handed him the ROI. He read it carefully, as if he'd never seen it before, then looked up at me askance.

"Jose, this is complete bullshit," I started. "I was only doing exactly what I told you I would be doing when I asked you for the travel permit in the first place. This is not the first time the DEA has tried to set me up." I told him of the call from Pat when I still lived up in Point Richmond. "I know the DEA believes that, as with most people who've been caught in the drug business, once a criminal, always a criminal. I don't know what I can do to convince you that, although it might be the case with others, that's not me. I'm out of it completely and for good. Believe me, I've learned my lesson. There isn't a day goes by that my wife doesn't keep reminding me to stay on the straight and narrow and to be very careful of whom I associate with. It's like a broken record around our house. I had no idea what was going on at Jared's house that evening and, you can see it yourself in the report, as soon as the conversation drifted in that direction, I left immediately and later told Jared, that if he ever saw this individual again, our partnership was over."

"Rick, I believe you," Jose said. "But guilt by association is a very dangerous spot for you to be in given your past and present situation. Look, I really only want the best for you and I appreciate your honesty and forthrightness regarding this. Just be very careful and keep me posted as to what's going on with this. Maybe we can head it off at the pass. Just keep your nose clean," he said with a smile.

"Believe me, I'm not into that shit anyway," I laughed.

"OK, then, here's your travel pass and let me know what happens."

"You got it."

* * *

A week later, I went up to Sacramento with Lu and we waited in Dale's office foyer for Agent Pierce to show up at the appointed time. It was an unusually warm late spring day in Sacramento and we worried about leaving our dog Burt out in the car in the hot sun, so we took him inside. I went inside to the conference room and Lu waited, reading a book sitting on the leather couch outside in the waiting room, with Burt resting comfortably at her feet. Agent Pierce came and warmly greeted her in his usual friendly manner, as if the two of them were old friends. Seeming to remember him from his Carmel visit to our home, Burt nuzzled him affectionately at his pants leg, his tail wagging like a metronome. However, as soon as he entered the conference room all his friendliness quickly disappeared and he was all business. It soon became apparent that Agent Pierce was a zealot on a mission to rid the world of illegal drugs and marijuana was at the top of his list. His friendly manner disappeared and was replaced by a very direct and confrontational attitude. The questioning quickly went from his rant about marijuana to the Ciro Mancuso investigation.

I told him that I had only known Ciro briefly years back but had no idea what he was up to now. I said I hadn't seen him in at least a decade and probably wouldn't even recognize him if I did.

He then asked me if I knew his partner Walter Brugger. He said in a very accusing tone that surely I must have had dealings with Brugger, who he believed was Mancuso's outlet in the sales of his marijuana.

Several weeks earlier I had met Phil Erikson for lunch in Carmel. During our conversation Phil said, "Oh Rick, I almost forgot to tell you, I saw Walter the other day and he told me that his main old 'casino nugget' and trusted gofer Jimmy Lee Phelps was dead. Walter said that he'd found him one morning in the driveway of his house, lying underneath the front bumper of his car with a needle in his arm and 'deader than a doornail'. I always liked Jimmy, but we all knew he was a junkie and it was bound to happen sooner or later." The news saddened me as well, and although I didn't realize it at the time, this bit of information would prove very useful to me in the not-too-distant future… Dead men tell no tales.

I told Pierce I really hadn't dealt with Brugger, at least not face-to-face, but had only worked with Jimmy Phelps and it was a long time ago. I told him that I wasn't sure who the marijuana actually came from and didn't know if Walter Brugger was the source or not. I said I hadn't seen Jimmy in many years and had no idea where he was now. "Sorry I can't help you," I said rather apologetically.

Pierce exploded, screaming at me and accusing me of lying and threatening me with perjury as well as being an active part of his ongoing investigation of the Mancuso smuggling operation. He said, now nearly frothing at the mouth in anger, that as a second time offender, if I didn't come clean with him immediately, I'd be facing 20 years.

At that point, Dale feared for the worst and told the agent he'd like some time to confer with me and asked him if we could adjourn and schedule another meeting for maybe later in the month or next month if possible. Frustrated, but at the same time aware of my rights to have counsel present, Pierce agreed, with a stern warning directed right into my face. "Go ahead and take all the time you need to confer with Dale here, but the next time I see you I want the truth and no bullshit. Or I guarantee, you're going down. Mark my words."

He stormed out of the office, but the instant he left he morphed from the evil Mr. Hyde back to the kindly Dr. Jekyll, as described in Robert Louis Stevenson's famous novella entitled *The Strange Tale of Dr. Jekyll and Mr. Hyde*,[4] as Pierce once again returned to his friendly and good natured 'other self' warmly bidding adieu to Lu and Burt. He was really a psycho and I thought a good candidate for a heart attack.

Later in the day I met with Dale to come up with a plan as to how to deal with Pierce. I still had my principles and was determined not to rat on anyone. I was determined to continue to be as evasive as possible with this nutcase, Agent Pierce, but knew in the back of my mind that I might have to suffer serious consequences for this approach. I thought if we could come up with excuses to delay another meeting with Pierce for as long as possible, he might lose interest or whatever. We managed to put off the second meeting until late summer for one reason or another, until Pierce had had enough and demanded my presence or he'd subpoena me.

Meanwhile the surveillance at Jared's house continued.

* * *

That summer, Jared moved from the lakefront house on Tahoe's west shore up to another house at Squaw Valley, the site of the 1960 Winter Olympics. His house was located right on the ski slope at the foot of the famed Mountain Run. It was the last house up the mountain and with only three houses below him was isolated by itself with a spectacular view of the ski runs up the mountains to the west and the entire Squaw Valley laid out seemingly at his feet to the east. There was an adjacent paved parking area for all four houses and guests just to the north, where at the far end was a utility pole with telephone, utility wires and a transformer at the top of the pole.

One morning as Jared was leaving he noticed a couple of telephone utility trucks parked in the parking lot. When he returned later in the day, he saw a small tent had been erected at the top of the pole. He thought nothing of it and assumed it was there to service either the transformer or maybe to replace the old wires providing telephone service, power and cable TV to the four houses.

Day after day the tent remained in place and the trucks appeared each morning and left later in the evening. The tent had a direct and unobstructed view into his house where I came and went on occasion to work on the plans. Jared also had several lady friends who'd frequently spend the night with him and it wasn't unusual for them to run around naked at the secluded house or sit nude in the hot tub on the deck. The house was so isolated there was no need for curtains or shades in any of the rooms and

---

4 Referenced Books, Item 15, Page 532.

privacy on the deck wasn't an issue since no one else was usually around. This went on for about three weeks until Jared finally became suspicious and wondered what the hell was going on, why was the tent still there and what in the world could these utility workers and their vehicles be doing spending all this time parked in his parking lot when nothing seemed to be wrong with his power, cable TV or phone service.

The next morning while having a cup of coffee before going to work at a job he was completing at Lake Tahoe, he squinted at the tent atop the utility pole and suddenly realized the tent had a slit-like opening that looked directly into the north-side picture windows located both in his living room and up in the loft bedroom.

That evening after the trucks had departed, Jared thought he'd climb the pole and see just what was going on in the tent. Atop the 50-foot wooden pole, which he ascended step-by-step using the metal pins attached to the side of the pole as makeshift ladder, he peered into the tent. What he found shocked him to the core of his being. His loud voice could probably be heard echoing over the valley below. "Holy fuck," he screamed.

There in the tent was a small school desk chair and a set of binoculars in their case attached to the wall of the tent on a hook. He also now saw that the slit opening he'd observed from the ground was indeed an opening in the tent's south facing wall with two drawstrings to close and conceal it when the tent was unoccupied. It was obvious to him from the position of the chair directly adjacent to the slit and from the fact that the binoculars were right next to it that someone had been staring directly into his house.

It all came back now, like a wave washing over him… he was being surveilled as a result of Phil Byron's continuing effort to set him or me up. He phoned me immediately to report what was going on.

The next morning he irately confronted the 'workmen', accusing them of spying on him, and told them he was going to report them to the Squaw Valley Sheriff's Department as soon as he left. By evening the tent and trucks were gone and never appeared again. Obviously, the DEA had not given up in trying to link either of us into their web of drug dealing investigations which were continuing in the Tahoe area.

Of note, the tent also had a commanding view in the other direction towards Ciro Mancuso's spectacular 10,000-square-foot concrete and glass mountain retreat, which stood out like a sore thumb with its copper roof and indoor swimming pool. Its construction had been completed a few years previously and had been built for all to see, almost as an arrogant monument to himself, basically flaunting his newly acquired wealth to anyone who looked up in the northerly direction from the valley floor below.

* * *

The second meeting with Agent Pierce went about as well as the first one, with Pierce finally serving me a subpoena to appear before a Federal Grand Jury in Reno scheduled for late October. Dale and I prepared for it and he counseled me on how to answer their questions, if I chose not to cooperate. He advised me on exactly how to invoke the 5th and 14th Amendments to the United States Constitution, but said a contempt charge would likely be the result of my stance. I was prepared to sit in jail rather than become a rat, even if that cooperation meant 'dropping a dime' on Ciro.

However, on October 29, 1989, I was saved by the bell, as the Grand Jury disbanded by handing down a 125-page, 49-count indictment[5] charging Ciro Mancuso and 17 of his associates with charges of violations of United States laws ranging from operating a continuing criminal enterprise to possessing and distributing controlled substances, as well as providing for criminal forfeiture. This indictment, compared to mine seven years ago, made mine look like a child's coloring book contrasted to Leonardo da Vinci's famous painting of the Mona Lisa.

The culmination of a 12-year investigation had resulted in a thoroughly detailed indictment which not only included all of the overt acts and criminal activity of Ciro and his compatriots but also listed all assets and bank accounts worldwide. Pierce and company had really done their homework this time and no stone was left unturned.

Ciro was dragged naked from the shower in the early morning raid on his Squaw Valley hilltop mansion and in the blink of an eye he went from riches to rags as the feds swooped in on him, seizing everything they could lay their hands on including numerous properties, bank accounts around the world, vehicles, and even down to the last sticks of furniture in his spectacular home. Among others caught up in the ten-year investigation and subsequent raids were his two main gofers and longtime friends Brad Stockman and Jeff Welch. Walter Brugger had meanwhile relocated to his native Switzerland, but was arrested over there as well.

Unlike the former so-called plush surroundings he'd bribed his way into in Guadalajara prison 17 years previous, the Washoe County jail in Reno, Nevada, was just a bare cell where Ciro languished for more than a year. He was dragged out routinely every week thereafter for intense interrogation by DEA, FBI, IRS and U.S. Customs agents. Rick Pierce who had spearheaded the ten-year investigation had finally got his man and it looked like the former entrepreneur and real estate developer, who was actually one of the most successful marijuana smugglers in U.S. history, would be going away for a very long time, maybe even life in prison.

I thought finally I'd be left alone since the feds had gotten the one who they'd really wanted and all of his organization had finally been brought to its knees. They'd even indicted Charlie in Thailand, but like Pat, extradition of a Thai citizen was out of the question.

But as baseball great Yogi Berra famously once said: "It ain't over till it's over."

* * *

The U.S. Attorney's Office in Reno, spearheaded by another drug-hating zealot, Assistant U.S. Attorney L. Anthony White, just couldn't be satisfied with only busting Ciro. He smelled blood in the water and wanted a still bigger fish to fry. Backed by U.S. Attorney Dorothy Nash Holmes and the U.S. Justice Department, White wanted San Francisco's most famous drug attorney, Patrick Hallinan, whom he'd accused of being the 'consigliere' to the Mancuso organization.

With the aid of Mancuso, White sought to bring down Hallinan.

---

5 Referenced Legal Research, Items 9 & 11, Page 532.

For more than a year Ciro refused to cooperate with federal authorities, so they did what they always do, they brought extreme pressure to bear. They put Ciro between a rock and a hard place, by arresting his wife and threatening to indict his sister and parents. He was told his daughters would never see their parents again and would be forced to live in foster homes. Even his wise and trusted counsel, Pat Hallinan, couldn't save him this time, so he agreed to cooperate, claiming Butch had sold him down the river by trying to negotiate a ten-year sentence under the old federal sentencing guidelines. This would have been a real sweet deal considering he was facing life behind bars; moreover with this proposed negotiation he would only have to serve six years on a ten year sentence. But it wasn't good enough for Ciro, who figured Butch could again get him completely off the hook as he had done in the past. This time that wasn't going to happen. So Ciro conned his lawyer, one of the young associate lawyers in Butch's office who'd helped Butch on his case, named Kate Alfieri, to quit Hallinan's office and represent him as a government witness, promising to pay her far more than she could make as a mere associate attorney. Then, with Kate at his side, Ciro finally capitulated, telling the agents everything he knew. There's an old jailhouse saying: 'there's no such thing as half a rat.' Either one talks or he doesn't. They virtually had to, like Lou Villar ten years earlier, beat him to shut him up.

Ciro meticulously told the feds everything he'd ever done and laid his entire empire to bare in the hopes of leniency. However with the cajoling of U.S. Attorney Anthony White, Ciro saw an opening which he might be able to crawl through and secure his freedom.

In exchange for his complete cooperation, with Kate Alfieri's assistance he was able to negotiate a super deal for himself in order to minimize his own sentence, keep his own family out of prison and have millions of dollars of his fortune returned. To Ciro, Kate was now worth her weight in gold, having negotiated his freedom and the return of some of his fortune and screwing Butch for failing him. In essence, Kate stabbed her former employer, Patrick Hallinan, in the back. Butch had naively been blindsided. He never saw it coming. However the deal not only involved giving up all of his lifelong friends and business associates, but now centered around implicating and testifying in court against his longtime attorney, Patrick Hallinan, claiming Butch was the 'consigliere' for Ciro's smuggling schemes, reminiscent of the role played by Robert Duval in the movie *The Godfather*.[6]

White was so taken in by Ciro's tall tales of Hallinan's involvement in his smuggling operation, he became 'gut hooked' and bought into his fish story, hook, line and sinker. He was summarily released from the Washoe County Jail and sent on a 'fishing expedition' to convince others to help him in his quest to put Hallinan away and satisfy White's voracious appetite to nail a real big shot in the legal community. It would be a huge feather in White's cap.

Ciro told others in his organization: "Don't be the last to roll over." Following his reinvented sage advice, like dominos or lemmings, Ciro's top lieutenants Brad Stockman and Jeff Welsh soon followed suit as did trusted others in his organization. It seemed

6 Referenced Television & Movies, Item 18, Page 533.

like no one in his former organization wanted to be the last in line with nothing left to bargain for.

Ciro's scheme to extricate himself set up a feeding frenzy for him and his former smuggling buddies to try and devour Hallinan, and in so doing set himself free along with his friends who joined him to 'get Butch.' With White's help, anyone who wouldn't cooperate would be thrown to the wolves.

Ciro was out to get anyone he thought he could to try and get an even better deal for himself. One evening, shortly after his release, Ciro showed up at Phil's valley house wearing a wire trying to convince Phil to rat me out, even though I had done nothing I hadn't already paid the price for. In addition to that, Phil later told me he'd also met Ciro's father at a local market one day who said to him: "Rick better confess, if he knows what's good for him." Obviously, Ciro Sr. was out to do all he could to help his son in implicating others. Two peas in a pod! Phil balked at all of both Ciro's and his father's machinations and cajoling in trying to convince him to join their merry band of rats.

In the fall of 1992 I had served my five-year probationary sentence and Jose Guerrero bid me goodbye and gave me a letter saying I had successfully completed probation and would not have to report to his office anymore. I was, at last, a free man and could do anything and go anywhere I wanted without the tail of the government behind me.

This, however, was not the end of it for me.

* * *

Based on Ciro's cooperation[7] two more indictments were handed out, one in November of 1992[8] and another in July of 1993[9] rounding up another twenty-three of Ciro's former organization. It was almost all over except for the final piece of the puzzle.

Again in July of 1993 I received another subpoena to appear before Tony White, who was directing the Reno Grand Jury in pursuit of his prize target, Patrick Hallinan. It was rather a curious but typical way of White's intimidation tactics of how I was to be served with the subpoena.

While getting ready to go horseback riding at our newly constructed Big Sur home, Lu was suddenly startled by two men who had our housekeeper by the scruff of the collar and were at the open sliding glass back door screaming at her: "Where's Rick Bibbero?"

Lu said nothing as they barged into our home, whereupon I appeared from the bedroom just after putting on my cowboy boots and wondering what all the commotion was about.

The agents repeated their question and I answered that I was who they were looking for, but by now I had really lost my temper and ordered them to "Get the fuck out of my home," and if they wanted to speak with me we could do it outside.

7 Referenced Television & Movies, Item 8, Page 533.
8 Referenced Legal Research, Item 12, Page 532.
9 Referenced Legal Research, Items 13 & 15, Page 532.

Out in the driveway they served me with a subpoena to appear before the Reno Federal Grand Jury. I requested their business cards and badge numbers and told them that they were assholes and could just as easily have called Jose Guerrero and arranged for a meeting at his office. I told them it would have been the human thing to do rather than using such strong-arm, storm trooper tactics. Our maid was so shaken up she summarily quit our employ, which was a real bummer because she was the best house-keeper we'd ever had and I was sorry to lose her, but on the other hand, I really couldn't blame her. She had been terrified by these two jerks who, it turned out, were only doing as the fanatic Tony White had instructed.

Again I called Dale Kovac and asked him to accompany me to Reno. The rules were that you couldn't have an attorney present in the actual grand jury room. Your attorney had to wait outside and you could go out and confer with him after each and every question put to you. Again, he'd counseled me on exactly how to invoke the 5th and 14 Amendments, as was my constitutional right, and that's precisely what I did. I was prepared to sit in jail on a contempt charge, rather than agree to testify against my old friend and former attorney Patrick Hallinan. White said he'd grant me immunity, but that I'd have to wait for it to come down from the Justice Department in Washington, D.C. I agreed to wait which seemed like a good opportunity to stall as long as possible, knowing full well that I had no intention of cooperating whatsoever, immunity or not. Now the real prospect of doing time on a contempt charge loomed over me like a dark and foreboding thunderhead of an approaching storm.

Again, fortunately for me, on August 3, 1993, the grand jury disbanded, indicting Patrick Hallinan[10][11] and I wasn't called again.

Ultimately Hallinan was tried in Federal Court based on Ciro's testimony. It turned out Ciro had convinced several of his former associates to testify against Hallinan[12]. Ciro was even sent by the U.S. Attorney's office to Mexico and successfully convinced his old Mexican strongman friend and connection, Heriberto Torres, to come and tes-tify against Hallinan. As I later read in the January 1994 edition of the *California Lawyer*[13] magazine, it really didn't bode well for the prosecution when, on the witness stand, Torres was asked by Patrick's attorney about his possible nefarious activities, such as drug trafficking and murder. Torres replied candidly in a rather cryptic manner: "In Mexico many things just happen." He continued in front of the jury telling them with a rather cocky smile on his face, "If, in Mexico you're, for example an elephant and the police say you're a rabbit, well, then you're a rabbit."

Hallinan was acquitted by the jury after they deliberated for only about four short hours. Immediately following the acquittal U.S. Attorney L. Anthony White flew into a rage and then threw the book at Ciro, stating that he had concocted and fabricated the story in order to try and shift some of the blame and minimize his own culpability. Ciro was sentenced to nine years in prison,[14] but in exchange for his cooperation was

---

10 Referenced Legal Research, Item 14, Page 532.
11 Referenced Newspaper Articles, Items 15–20, Page 529.
12 Referenced Newspaper Articles, Item 22, Page 529.
13 Referenced Magazine Articles, Item 2, Page 533.
14 Referenced Newspaper Articles, Item 24, Page 529.

returned much of his seized property and millions of dollars of his illegally gotten gains.

Ciro was sent to the Federal Prison Camp at Lompoc where one night he was rewarded with an inmate 'blanket party'. It was common knowledge that Ciro was a rat and this would be his just deserts. While asleep in his dormitory bunk, he was surrounded by several other inmates, rolled up in his Army surplus blanket and summarily and literally had the shit kicked out of him. He was immediately 'rolled up' and for his own safety put into isolated protective custody. He was then finally sent to what was known as 'the rat camp' in Yankton, South Dakota, where he served the remainder of his shortened sentence and was released in 2000.

On the face of it, one might have thought that with his Sicilian heritage and purported family ties to the Italian mafia, Ciro would have bitten the bullet and kept his mouth shut, respecting the principle of Omertà, the long standing deep-rooted family sense of the code of silence. Ciro preached it for many years, however when the chips were down and when he saw an opportunity to extricate himself at the expense of others, he simply let the chips fall where they may, completely ignoring his former long standing principles. He could certainly talk the talk, however it was a different story when it came to walking the walk. His Sicilian ancestors would probably roll over in their graves!

Father Sorce always used to preach to me by saying: "You don't have to go to the electric chair to know that's a place where you don't want to go." Using that same logic in regards to cooperating with the government in order to save yourself at the expense of your friends and associates and live forever with a sense of shame, no matter how you try and justify it, I say likewise: "You don't have to be a rat to know that's a place where you don't want to go."

Not that it really mattered to anyone but me, but in the end, I couldn't help but recall Ciro's sage admonition to me long ago in the view of Mt. Everest, where he pontificated: "You must never say anything and the authorities don't know anything, unless you tell them." In his own perverted guru-like egocentric view of himself in the world according to Ciro, his reinvented sage advice now seemed to be: 'Fuck everyone and save yourself.'

For better or worse, this was one piece of Ciro's advice I chose not to follow.

Epilogue

So, as I look back on these two decades and reflect, I have to ask myself: 'What did I learn from all of this? Am I sorry and remorseful for my activities? Would I do it again? Additionally, I am confronted as to the moral issues regarding the War on Drugs and specifically regarding the legalized use of marijuana in today's society.

Of course, smuggling of anything is an illegal activity. However, illegal or not, it is not an activity for the faint of heart. In some respects smuggling has even become a glorified profession and an accepted part of the lexicon in today's world, as exemplified in one of the most successful movies of all time, *Star Wars,* and its glorification of the character Han Solo, the professional smuggler and outlaw who has been revered by most of the millions of theatergoers who have seen the movie. People always say, "Oh, dealing drugs is easy money... the easy way out." In some cases maybe it's true, but I can say categorically, it wasn't true in my case. I took the life very seriously and shouldered the responsibility of trying to do the best job I could. I was, and am, very detail oriented and of the philosophy that 'if you can't do a job right, then don't do it at all.' Also, I had a problem delegating responsibility to others. This inevitably led to my downfall. I just had to be everywhere to assist in getting the job done right and to perfection. I accomplished that. I always held myself to the highest standard, even in the marijuana business. My quality was always the best. I always tried, even though unsuccessful in the end, to keep us at a small manageable grassroots level. That idea worked for nearly ten years and was most likely the reason for our success, but ultimately greed won out and our little organization grew to be out of control, which was the source of our downfall.

I must say, I did act naively; unlike the leaders and employees of the Coronado Company, I traveled and stayed in places in my own name. That was stupid! Had I not stayed in Eureka under my own name, I might have walked. Would-a, should-a, could-a. That was not to be.

I will say, I had more fun and more adventure in my thirteen years as a smuggler than most people do in a lifetime. I wouldn't trade those adventures for anything, but I did pay the price. I learned and lived with those consequences.

Was it worth it? Yes!

Would I do it again? No!

During the 1960s, '70s and to a large extent, the '80s, the world was much less sophisticated in terms of technology and surveillance. With the onset of global terrorism and overt acts of piracy on the high seas in the '90s and beyond, governments, for their own security have become much more aware and have taken serious measures to act for their own safety and well being. With the internet and the technological advances of the past decade, governments have become much more vigilant of smuggling operations. Additionally, mandatory sentencing laws have become much harsher and more severe for even first time offenders. It went from a virtual 'slap-on-the-wrist', probationary or minimal incarceration sentences handed down in the '70s and early '80s, even for large quantity marijuana smugglers, to a 10-year minimum sentence for a first time offender and double or triple that for repeat offenses… and in some cases, life in prison.

I always felt, and still think, marijuana should be legal… the same as alcohol. I was just 40 years too early. I looked upon myself and others in the marijuana smuggling business as being the same as Joe Kennedy during prohibition. He got away with it, controlled the market and eventually became a wealthy and respected citizen. We were just way ahead of our time, pioneers so to speak. The problem is: what happens to pioneers?… They sometimes end up with arrows in their backs!

The so-called War on Drugs has been a miserable failure and one of the worst, most deadly and costly U.S. policies ever undertaken by our government. It has resulted in hundreds of thousands of otherwise innocent and non-violent people being incarcerated and has directly resulted in many thousands of murders by drug cartels and gangs that would not have even existed if it weren't for this misguided policy. The agencies and agents employed to fight the War on Drugs have cost taxpayers an astronomical amount of wasted dollars and, for the most part, have become virtually lawless entities using basically as ruthless and brutal tactics as the jackbooted thugs and 'brownshirts' of the Nazi regime in Europe in the 1930s. It also seems as inherently wrong, perverted and depraved as Hitler's Youth Movement, where children informed on their 'subversive' parents for kudos and rewards, for a system to reward kingpins and informants at the top and at mid-levels of marijuana groups, with millions of dollars and reduced prison sentences for their cooperation, at the expense of underlings, family members and lifelong friends in their own organizations.

Anyone who has studied history knows how crazy things got during the Prohibition Era in the United States with the passage of the 18th Amendment to the U.S. Constitution in 1919. They also know how that insanity pretty much all stopped following its repeal by passage of the 21st Amendment in 1933. It took nearly 15 years for society to come to its senses and realize the fact that Prohibition was a failure. The War on Drugs and specifically the prohibition of marijuana in today's society has gone on for nearly 50 years. What's different from the prohibition of alcohol segment of history compared to marijuana in today's society? Nothing. Those who continue to replay the mistakes of history are doomed to repeat the same failures of the past… again!

As I write this, 26 states and the District of Columbia have now enacted laws broadly legalizing the use of marijuana in some form and many others are soon to follow. It seems to now be only a matter of a very short time before the U.S. government legalizes it on a federal level. There is just too much money and future taxation revenue involved, plus it is such a waste of time and manpower to effectively pursue it anymore. The domestic cultivation of marijuana is a multi-billion dollar business, which has virtually eliminated the need to smuggle it from other countries. In many colleges, there are now courses teaching students how to grow marijuana and the techniques and technologies for cultivation have far surpassed those of the past.

There are still those arguments surrounding the health of marijuana use, the use of it by children and whether marijuana is a 'gateway' drug leading to the use of harder drugs and the like. However, there are estimated to be millions of both recreational and medical users in the United States alone, and no matter how much the government tries to curtail its use, marijuana use can never be stopped in a free country. Science and research are continually discovering new benefits related to marijuana use. So why waste all the time, energy and manpower to try and stop it? It's pointless… Let's just legalize it once and for all and move on.

Of note, everyone whom I encountered in the marijuana business at some point made a conscious decision to either form or become part of a group that was involved and actively participated in the various aspects of 'the business' in general. The two most prominent reasons for even being involved were either for the adventure or for the money or both. In both of those categories the risks and the rewards were great as were the consequences when one was apprehended. What really separated the men from the boys, however, was when the chips were down that only a few of us were able to take their punishment like a man and not succumb to the external pressures by becoming a government informant. In my opinion those who did cooperate and 'roll over' and become 'rats' were the lowest of the low, with either no moral compass, no conscience, simply greedy or a combination of all three at the expense of their business associates and usually lifelong friends who were double-crossed by these scoundrels. Individuals like Lou Villar, David Vaughn, Alan Logie, Donald McMichaels, Ciro Mancuso, Bruce Bibbero, Ed Lehmer, Phillip Byron and others became government witnesses and informants in order to minimize their own culpability at the expense of their friends, business partners and associates and even their lawyers in order to assist the government and be rewarded in being able to keep or get back at least some of their seized assets and/or to try and minimize or totally eliminate any potential jail time.

Usually for those of us who 'held our mud' the consequences were not nearly as bad as what we were threatened with by brow-beating government agents at the time of our apprehension. In order to defy 'the man' one had to be incredibly strong, have an uncompromising integrity and have a determination to stand on moral principles above all else. Usually if one rode it out, sentences were modified; with the passage of time, however, and as memories faded, some of those who cooperated were in a sense glorified in books and other media in order to somehow justify and mitigate their ruthless behavior. Although I think that I understand those motivations, I don't agree with them… I'm pretty sure however that 'my new best friend' former DEA agent Jim Conklin would have a completely different take on it!

As I mentioned earlier, it seems like everyone sees the world through a fish-eye camera lens, with themselves in the center and everything else distorted on the periphery. I'm no different, and this is my story as told from my perspective. Although there are some out there who might have a different perspective or recollection of the events I have described in this story, please remember this is my story as I saw and remember it.

This is really a story of daring adventure, living on the edge, and of the individuals who lived it. It is a story of adventures and misadventures and of what it really took to make it all happen. Although many of the names of the characters have been changed, for one reason or another, the story itself is a true account of what happened… as seen through my eyes and to the best of my recollection. Unlike several of my closest friends, I'm still alive and reasonably healthy enough to tell this story. Through the ups and downs and craziness of it all, I've always tried to keep a positive attitude, no matter what… even in my darkest hours.

February 1981

I received a letter written completely in Chinese. It was from the Research Embroidery Institute in Suzhou, China. Lacking the ability to read it, I took it to a Chinese friend of mine in San Francisco who read and translated it for me. The essence of the letter, written on fine parchment paper, said: the embroidery painting I had commissioned of my beloved dog Papi was completed. Once the remaining balance of $1,400 is received, the painting will be sent to your address.

I thought, 'Boy, now I'm really going to be taken for a ride!' But, I complied and sent the money as requested. I had now invested a total of $2,800 for a sight-unseen piece of artwork I'd commissioned some ten months previous.

About two months later I received word that the painting had cleared customs and I could retrieve it from a customs broker located near the San Francisco Airport. I picked it up later in the day.

It was rolled up, scroll-like, in a cardboard tube which was placed inside a wooden box to protect it during its voyage from China. I opened it and was completely blown away!

There before me was an exquisite embroidery painting and one of the most beautiful pieces of art that I'd ever seen. It was a two-foot by three-foot exact image of the three by five-inch photograph I had given the Institute nearly a year before. It looked exactly like the photograph, except it was a silk embroidery painting re-created from the original photograph capturing even the most minute detail in pure silk thread. Papi's image almost jumped off the painting, it looked so real, appearing as three dimensional. His regal pose was captured forever.

It took one person working eight hours a day for ten solid months to complete. From a distance, anyone who first sees it thinks, at first glance, it's a photograph, but up close everyone is completely taken aback when they realize it is indeed an embroidery painting composed of hundreds of thousands of individual strands of multicolored silk threads meticulously woven into a beautiful and timeless art treasure. Today it hangs in reverence in a special place and every time I look at it, I am reminded of all the memories of this story and of the special years I was lucky enough to have had with such an incredible being touching my life.

Gazing at it for the first time, my emotions got the better of me.
Papi had indeed come back to life.

1994

In 1994 I came up with the idea to write my story, though my mother pleaded with me not to do it while my father was still alive, since she knew that our family dynamics would have to be discussed and she didn't want to expose my father to that since he was now not in good health. Although I took notes during that time period, I acquiesced to her request.

On April 1, 2003, my mother passed away, followed by my father's death on December 7th of that same year. They had been married for fifty-eight years. To date they have both been dead for fourteen years, so it seems like enough time has passed so this story can finally be told.

The problem is, now they will undoubtedly roll over in their graves!

Fall 2014

After completing the majority of this story, I felt that there was still something missing and that was a perspective from the other side. It seemed that to be fair and more objective, a parallel view needed to be considered: the cops' side of the story. I did a little research and found former DEA Special Agent James B. Conklin, the agent primarily responsible for bringing down not only the Coronado Company but many of the major Thai weed smugglers, including myself. He had retired in the early 1990s and now runs his own private investigation service. His surprise in hearing from me after more than thirty years is an understatement, but he was very friendly, accommodating, supportive and helpful. He agreed to an interview.

In early December, I met and interviewed him face-to-face for over eight hours. Since I had last seen him at my trial in 1983, Jim had gained a little weight and lost most of his hair, but otherwise he seemed in great shape, his memory was as sharp as ever and he still has a great sense of humor. We discussed most everything I could think of including his background and personal life as well as details of the investigation, arrests and of my trial.

Jim had testified both as a prosecution and defense witness at my trial and recalled the details of the trial with great clarity. One point I found most interesting during our discussion was when he brought up what he and the prosecutor found to be the most incredulous part of my story: that when my dog Papi died and I had to leave Thailand in the middle of scoring the Neah Bay load to return home to try and settle down my distraught wife. He thought that tale I told during my testimony was complete B.S. The fact of the matter is, I was in court on the witness stand for nearly three days, spinning yarn after yarn about how I had nothing to do with the marijuana business and, in reality, pretty much the only true part of my testimony was the story of the dog. That revelation blew Jim's mind.

I would have liked to have also interviewed U.S. Customs Agent Rick Pierce but I found out that he had unexpectedly passed away in April of 2013. I can only believe that he finally 'blew a gasket' due to the unpredictable psychotic behavior that I and others witnessed of him during his fanatic pursuit of drug smugglers. Apparently he had retired from the U.S. Treasury Department as a senior special agent, but I guess that even in retirement he was still crazy and obsessed, which I am reasonably sure most likely somehow led to his ultimate demise.

Character Roundup

Marty Bibbero

Marty spent five years in the worst of Mexican prisons where he was brutalized and beaten regularly. He was released along with many other American prisoners in the 1977 Prisoner Transfer Treaty between Mexico and the United States. He returned to the United States a completely different person and due to the constant beatings on the head suffered serious inner ear damage leading to a 15-hour surgery to remove a cancerous tumor which had developed. He suffered terrible headaches and found himself addicted to and at the mercy of various forms of painkiller medicine. Marty and his younger brother Bruce together attempted to blackmail my father, Dick, during my trial. They threatened Dick, saying they would come forward and become prosecution witnesses against not only Dick and me but our grandfather as well, and they would tell the government that Dick along with our grandparents had helped me hide my money, if Dick wouldn't pay $300,000 for their silence.

Dick refused, saying to Bruce, "The next time I see you will be in hell." Little ever came of the threats aside from Bruce's anonymous call to the U.S. Attorney which resulted in my having to spend four extra days incarcerated at MCC San Diego; however both of the brothers were disowned from our family and precluded from any inheritance (except one dollar each), they might have otherwise received. Marty subsequently died of an overdose of sleeping pills in 1989. Following Bruce's cooperation with both the Santa Barbara Sheriff's Department and the FBI implicating several of his co-conspirators in a cocaine distribution scheme, Bruce went on to become a fly-by-night sports promoter and was later sued for numerous fraudulent sports promotion scams. In Bruce's case, 'a leopard never changes its spots.'

Joe Schroder

Joe was indicted in a second wave of indictments brought on by Lou Villar's cooperation and testimony to federal agents. He received a six-month sentence and was released on 5 years' probation in 1986. However, he didn't learn from his first encounter and went back to work in 1987 with Ciro Mancuso's smuggling organization. He was re-indicted in 1989. Joe, along with Mike Stallings, refused to cooperate and give testimony against anyone else. Both served almost two years in prison on contempt for not cooperating. Along with Joe's refusal to cooperate and give testimony against Ciro, his guilty plea earned him a ten year sentence. In an effort to further pressure Joe to cooperate, the Reno Justice Department jailed his innocent wife as well. That play failed, as she proved to be as strong as Joe and told them nothing. Very few, if any, significant others had the moral character or courage to hold their mud in the face of such pressure and she deserves a special debt of gratitude for such bravery. He ended up being fined $100,000 and serving more than seven years in prison both for the sentence he received and for the contempt charge. Following his refusal to testify, and after being ordered to serve a contempt sentence, Joe, with his usual smile, boldly and defiantly (or stupidly) remarked to the U.S. Attorney, to his face, while handcuffed and being led out of the grand jury room: "Well, if that's the punishment you guys are handing out for contempt, I guess I'll take one. Have a nice day!"

Following his release from prison in 1998, Joe went back to work as a truck driver, a skill he had learned while growing up in the agricultural area of Central California, then was able to join the trucker's union where he went on to become an official of the union. He traded in his cocaine habit for an equally obsessive habit of physical fitness and even today in his mid-60s maintains a remarkable physique of less than 5% body fat.

He still to this day pays $100 each month to the government as an agreed upon monthly amount to satisfy his fine. At the payoff rate of $1200 per year, it will take Joe a total of 83 years and 4 months to satisfy his obligation to the U.S. Government. This will theoretically make him debt free of this payoff just at the time to blow out the 133 candles on his birthday cake in the year 2081.

Willie Sherman

Willie managed to avoid any trouble with the law due to his remaining in the background and only being known by those individuals who had been caught but who wouldn't cooperate with the authorities, specifically Joe and me. Neither of us ever received even so much as a 'thank you' from Willie. He went back to work in his family's retail business for the next 25 years. However, his foibles of gambling, womanizing, and continued non-stop use of alcohol, cocaine and marijuana led to numerous visits to rehab facilities, several bouts of sexually transmitted disease, and the loss of over one million dollars spent in 30 years on drugs and gambling losses. In his mid-60s, three divorces and two children later, his facial appearance had changed due to a collapsed nose, the result of the deterioration of his nasal septum from years of cocaine abuse. Like Joe, Willie also had a large hole in what remained of his nasal septum, which he liked to display at parties by sticking a golf tee through it imitating the African Ubangi tribal custom of displaying a bone-through-the-nose. Even with his young good looks behind him, he still had a way with the women and was able to somehow defy both father time and the grim reaper as he continued to live life as usual with the same abandon as he always had.

However, on December 7, 2013, ironically exactly 72 years after Franklin Roosevelt declared December 7th as "A day that will live in infamy," Willie Sherman, 'The Professor', passed away. He couldn't have chosen a more fitting day to remember himself by in the circle of friends who knew and loved him. Seems like he did defy father time, as was quoted in his obituary calling him 'Peter Pan' (the boy who never grew up). Willie always claimed that he was living on borrowed time and nothing was going to slow him up. He always used to tell me that he was like 'the cat who had nine lives'… and he was… however, I guess in his propensity to push it to the limit, he tried to stretch it to ten lives, which is where he was finally met face-to-face with the grim reaper.

Willie was a lifetime San Francisco 49ers football fan and had had season tickets on the 50-yard line since he was a kid. The day after his death, his name was flashed in lights 'in memory' on the Jumbotron at Candlestick Park during the December 8th, 49ers vs. Seattle Seahawks game. Unfortunately Willie missed the 49ers victory coming on a 4th quarter field goal that propelled them into the playoffs. For the first time in years, he missed those as well!

Although in later years our paths went in different directions, over all the years he was probably my best friend. It broke my heart to see him as a man in his 60s continue doing the same things he'd done with reckless abandon as a young man and I guess I knew that somehow it would all catch up with him. Unfortunately it was sooner rather than later. I used to refer to him as Mr. Wizard: he knew something about everything and nothing about anything. His early death proved to me that he was truly the Professor… He knew so much about so little, he knew everything about nothing!

Phil Erikson

Phil was another of the original smugglers who managed to avoid getting into any trouble with the law for the same reason as Willie. Phil also was wise enough to get out of at least being on the front lines of the marijuana business and for all intents and purposes stayed out while he was still ahead, so that when Ciro decided to cooperate and try to expose his old childhood friend, the statute of limitations had already run, plus those closest to him, Joe and me, held our mud. Phil then retired to oversee the daily operations of his family's central California ranch.

Phil's late mother, Blanche, while at her granddaughter's wedding many years later, was actually the only person to ever thank me for keeping my mouth shut, doing my time in prison and not implicating her son, which would have been the easy way out for me.

From my perspective: unless you're actually put between a rock and a hard place and had to make tough decisions regarding your own freedom, no one can predict how one would react when push came to shove. Luckily, for Phil, he never had the misfortune to make such a decision.

Dave Killian

Following the debacle with my sailing yacht, *Mamamouchi*, Killian had the rigging repaired and took the boat to the South Pacific where he remained for several years meandering from Fiji to Tahiti and to the Marquesas Islands. After my bust, I realized I could no longer support Killian because of the astronomical expense in defending myself and from the financial devastation of my legal problems and divorce. Killian subsequently ran out of money. He then began selling various essential items off of the boat such as the life raft, the dinghy, winches, cooking utensils, radios, navigational equipment, and even sails in order to afford a plane ticket home and to survive. He abandoned *Mamamouchi* but was able to transfer title of it to one of the former crew members, Ed Lehmer, who used it for another smuggling venture in 1986. The once beautiful racing yacht *Mamamouchi* was last seen in San Francisco at the U.S. Customs dock abandoned and a mess beyond recognition. Ed Lehmer had forfeited *Mama* to the government as part of a deal to then turn state's evidence, informing on many of his friends, associates and crew members whom he'd smuggled with. On October 28, 1996, pursuant to a judicial order, a notice was published in the *Reno Gazette Journal* classified section[1] noticing the condemnation and forfeiture of SV *Mamamouchi* belonging to Edwin Lehmer.

Killian, now broke and without a home, went to Santa Rosa to live and care for his ailing mother until her death in the late 1990s. In 2006 he succumbed to AIDS and died peacefully in his mother's apartment.

Pat Suraghoomkol

In 1983 Pat was forced to leave the United States rather than face charges brought about by Lou Villar's ratting him out. He and Rebecca got married and returned to Thailand where he became a successful real estate developer. However, following his departure he developed a huge chip on his shoulder because he could no longer maintain the American lifestyle he had grown so accustomed to. He practically returned to Thailand in shame as he was not liked by any of his former Thai associates who wanted nothing to do with him. He also refused to see any of his former American friends. In 1989 I received a phone call from Pat who angrily threatened to tell the DEA everything about me if I didn't agree to send him hush money. I basically told him to get lost and hung up on him. It was the last I ever heard from my old friend and business associate. Through the grapevine and from researching on the internet, I learned Pat and Becky had had two daughters both of whom were educated in Oregon. Pat's thirty year resentment of his former friends and associates continues to this day. Some old habits never die, but this seems like an awfully long time to stay mad at anyone!

Ciro Mancuso

In his turnabout attitude, Ciro went from a previous position of 'never tell 'em anything' to 'tell them everything' to the feds as his way out. Ultimately it failed, however as a result of his cooperation hundreds of lives were ruined. Not only those who actually participated in his smuggling ventures, but wives, girlfriends, children, lawyers, accountants, parents, grandparents and associates of associates were ensnared by him. His new mantra was, "Don't be the last one to cooperate, because then you'll have nothing left to give them."

Following his release from custody he returned to Lake Tahoe and became a sort of cult hero. His redemption, derived from the money he was able get back following

---

1 Referenced Newspaper Articles, Item 25, Page 529.

his cooperation with authorities, included revitalizing the town of Truckee and being praised for doing so in the local newspapers. His legendary fame was further enhanced and became the subject of many magazine and newspaper articles through his daughter's skiing exploits wherein she became an Olympic athlete, winning numerous medals.

With the aid of both Phil and Joe divulging our successful trade secrets, Ciro was able to continue the Thai trip for another eight years and amass a fortune amounting to nearly two hundred million dollars. He stole over a million dollars from Pat, Phil and me on the *Drifter* load, claiming he'd lost that much in Mexico when Pat and I started our Thai trip. Subsequently when he ripped off the entire trip from us in 1979 he never offered us one cent in return. It was typical of his attitude and of the arrogance and ruthlessness he once cautioned me of long ago when I visited him in the Guadalajara Federal Prison.

In a small bit of poetic justice, along with millions of dollars in foreign banks, his beautiful home at Squaw Valley was seized and forfeited. It was sold at a government auction and purchased by his next door neighbor whose view of the mountains and valley had been ruined by the construction of Ciro's mansion. The longtime resident and neighbor hated Ciro and became even more infuriated that he had 'rolled' on all of his associates rather than taking his medicine like a man. He purchased the home and with the aid of dynamite and a wrecking ball blew up the house and reduced it to a pile of rubble and hauled the debris away in over 100 dump trucks. He merged the two lots and planted a beautiful garden where Ciro's edifice to his own arrogance once stood. It was rumored that he was often heard saying to anyone who'd listen: "After years of misery, I can only thank God that I've finally got my wonderful view back and now I don't have to look at that overbuilt piece of shit monstrosity next door or think of that so-and-so loser anymore."

Lou Villar

Louis Villar, like Ciro Mancuso eight years later, blazed a similar path by turning state's evidence against all of his associates and everyone he knew in order to save himself. He became the government's star witness and testified at my trial and at the only other subsequent trial of his former associates. For his cooperation, after less than six months in prison he was released and saved nineteen and a half years off of the twenty year sentence he would have surely been given. He got to keep over five million dollars of his ill gotten gains. However, unlike Ciro and fearing for his own life and safety, he chose to enter the witness protection program and acquire a new identity. He married his longtime young girlfriend who subsequently dumped him. He was rumored to be living in Eastern Oregon under an assumed name. His actual whereabouts and current activities are unknown although it has been reported that he still commiserates with his former lieutenant from the good old days and snitch partner David Vaughn.

I remember hearing through the grapevine that during a conversation while still incarcerated or shortly after his release from custody Lou was quoted as saying: "Someone else is going to do my time." This statement is not surprising coming from him. He was always in the shadows and virtually never on the front lines, but reaping huge profits on the backs of others. So, when the chips were down, his true colors where shown brightly, revealing the self centered, greedy coward and back stabber he really is.

In 2014 an article appeared in *GQ Magazine*[2] about The Coronado Company. Subsequently, it came to light that a well-known Hollywood producer was collaborating with a famous Hollywood actor to produce a movie about the Coronado Company centering around Lou Villar's role as the Coronado High School Spanish teacher who became a drug kingpin. It was rumored that Villar met with the movie producers to tell his story. Obviously after all these years of cowardly hiding in the shadows, the lure of future cheese was too great a temptation for him to pass up. The question is: Will his re-emergence into the spotlight bring him face-to-face with the countless people's lives he's ruined and those whose time spent in prison were the result of his cooperation for his own personal selfishness and financial gain at their expense? Only time will tell.

Bob 'Lights' Lahodny

Following his release from prison after serving six years, Lahodny became a successful stock day trader. He continued to dabble in marijuana and cocaine smuggling and both he and Eddie Otero were re-arrested in April of 1989 in connection with another smuggling venture. He then started an internet company to counsel others on the art of day trading. Always a great athlete, he continued to enjoy playing tennis and golf, however his smoking of cigarettes finally caught up with him and, at age 60 in October 2010, Bob Lahodny died of lung cancer.

Eddie Otero

Following his arrest and pleading guilty to numerous charges of smuggling, Otero was sent to federal prison to serve a ten-year sentence with an additional condition of lifetime probation. While in prison at the Metropolitan Correctional Center in San Diego, Otero became aware of a gang plot to murder a correctional officer and in effect saved the officer's life. He was given a reduced sentence for his valor and was sent to prison camp where he served out another two years. Following his release he set up an air conditioning business and began producing ozone generators for commercial and residential use. He patented several parts of his machinery and he built the business and produced his generators in a small shop in Palm Springs. This led to his producing his products in China where he made several trips and turned the small water and air purification business into a growing global concern, selling worldwide mostly on the internet.

He was always boisterous and loud mouthed and could always be seen smoking or chewing on a cigar. He loved offshore fishing. It was his passion and he often would take extended trips fishing for yellowfin tuna and mahi mahi in the Pacific Ocean off the Mexican Coast. Following Christmas with his family in 2012, Eddie and a few friends went on a four day pre-New Year's fishing trip leaving San Diego and headed out a few hundred miles to the prime fishing grounds in the Pacific waters. Two days

2 Referenced Magazine Articles, Item 4, Page 533.

out Eddie felt a horrible pain in his leg and collapsed on the deck of the fishing boat. Efforts to revive him by his mates failed and he died later in the day of what was later diagnosed as a massive heart attack.

Since the boat was two days out to sea, his fishing companions were obliged to head back to San Diego. In order to preserve Eddie's body and so it wouldn't start to decay and smell in the hot Southern California sun, they put him in the frozen fishing locker where he soon became frozen solid. Upon the boat's arrival back in San Diego the police and coroner were summoned to the dock as well as Eddie's wife to claim the body. As with such events at sea, an autopsy was required, but it would be impossible to preform such a procedure on a frozen carcass, therefore Eddie was taken to the morgue to thaw so the autopsy could be done. It was several days before his wife was able to claim the body and return it to Palm Springs, where he was buried.

Walter Brugger

Sometime shortly before Ciro's bust, Walter left the country for Switzerland. He was actually a Swiss citizen and was able to flee before being arrested. Brugger was however able to keep most of his liquid assets which were out of the country anyway. He did forfeit both his house on the beach in Kauai as well as his house overlooking picturesque Lake Tahoe. I received a call from him in the months following Ciro's bust and his subsequent cooperation. Walter was seeking help from any of his former associates in the marijuana business to attempt to countermand Ciro's accusations, implicating him in his drug smuggling activities, and was requesting that I, among others write letters to the Swiss and U.S. authorities stating in effect, "I didn't do it, and he didn't do it with me." I refused his request, telling him I'd just spent the past decade trying to extricate myself out of trouble and why would I want to commit perjury now and subject myself to further culpability, when so many others in Ciro's organization had cooperated and were ready at the government's behest to refute any such notion.

Brugger ended up spending about a year in a Swiss prison and upon his release he returned to a small Alpine Swiss town where he opened a local's restaurant.

Patrick "Butch" Hallinan

Pat's reputation as one of the finest criminal lawyers in San Francisco was subsequently tarnished as a result of Ciro Mancuso's cooperation as a government witness.

Following Mancuso's accusations that Hallinan was deeply involved in his continuing smuggling activities, Hallinan was able to fight fire with fire and he hired one of the best lawyers in the country to defend him. With a track record which included prosecuting Oliver North in the Iran-Contra scandal, John Keker was the right man for the job. He made mincemeat of every government witness including Mancuso, who was made to look like an arrogant fool and the 'con man' he was in front of the jury. In a mere four hours of deliberation, Hallinan was acquitted of all charges by the jury.

However the turmoil created in Butch's life over the period of several years in his own defense left him a broken man. His law practice was in shambles and his health was deteriorating. He retired a few years later, suffered a stroke and was later diagnosed with a very slow moving cancer which was literally eating him alive. Now 80 years old and in a weakened state, his mind is still sharp but his career as one of the top criminal lawyers is over. He told me that now he has a new appreciation of what a criminal defendant has to endure and said that it gave him a new respect of 'the other side'. Had he lost at trial, he would certainly have become the most famous jailhouse lawyer in history.

Even though he was found 'not guilty' and acquitted, Patrick appears to have lost at the life he once knew and is now suffering as another victim at the expense of Ciro's self centered, ruthless decision to throw him under the bus and save himself regardless of the consequences or the damage he has caused others to suffer. In essence Ciro Mancuso destroyed Patrick Hallinan.

Prior to his trial in Reno, I was subpoenaed to testify before the Reno grand jury. I refused to cooperate with the prosecution and only by sheer luck did I avoid more jail time. Even though I knew Patrick was innocent of the charges against him, I would have served time for contempt rather than to have somehow been induced and/or coerced to testify against Pat Hallinan. He told me that I would always be a welcome guest at his table.

The Team of Two Jims (Conklin & Nielsen)

The team of Two Jims achieved legendary status among their peers in law enforcement. Their diligence led to the total dismantling of the Coronado Company, from top to bottom and horizontally as well. They left no man standing, from the leadership at the top of the organization to the lowliest driver and gofer as well as investors and ancillary people, all were rounded up in their dragnet. No one came out unscathed. Jail sentences ranged from six months to ten or more years and the seizures and forfeitures resulting from their work amounted to tens of millions… but they weren't done.

Jim Conklin

It became clear to Jim Conklin that if he really wanted to make a serious dent in stemming the flow of Thai weed into the United States, following his success in bringing down the Coronado Company, he would have to physically go to Thailand and follow the trail wherever it led. Jim spent six years living in Thailand. Through his extensive network of connections at DEA in Bangkok and in the United States Embassy Jim was able to find out who the big players were in Thailand. During his six-year Thai stint, Jim was able to bust numerous individuals who were responsible for importing several hundred tons of Thai weed. Among his trophies were Brian Daniels, Michael Forewell, the Shafer brothers and the Colflesh brothers. He was also able to get to several sources of Thai weed. It was mainly through the efforts of Jim Conklin that the actual Thai weed industry itself in Thailand came to a screeching halt. The main big-time smugglers were all arrested and put out of business, so in effect the Thai connections had no one to sell to and the whole Thai weed industry came crashing down. This led to the proliferation of the home-grown marijuana industry mainly in California which took off like a rocket and is now a multi-billion dollar industry.

Jim retired from the DEA in 2000 and started his own private investigation business in Nevada and still works there to this day. He is now a grandfather and happily re-married following the demise of his first wife Nancy.

Jim Nielsen

Jim Nielsen, the brainiac of the pair, retired from the IRS several years after the Coronado Company arrests and trials. His love of cars never diminished and his collection of muscle cars grew, however, much to his dismay, he was never able to acquire the Shelby 427 Cobra from Lou Villar's collection.

Jim started his own forensic accounting investigation business which he ran successfully for over a decade. He retired in 2010 to spend more time with his family and his growing number of grandkids. He still lives in Southern California doing mostly charity work for the underprivileged.

Both of the two Jims look forward each year to getting together or at least speaking on the phone with one another on November 5th to commemorate the day of the CorCo bust.

Stan Yamamoto

Like everyone else who got caught in the Coronado dragnet, Stan's wife dumped him following his bust. Not surprisingly, so did all of the Tibetan 'holy hangers-on' who probably left in search of another meal ticket. His two main 'trusted' assistants 'B-Boy' and 'Mole' both quickly rolled over on him and sealed his fate. He was sentenced to five years in federal prison, spending most of his time at FPC Lompoc. During his time of incarceration, Stan worked out every day and built his rather small frame into a virtual hulk of rippling biceps, washboard abdominals and monstrous thighs. However, after his release, all of it melted away and he once again returned to his small stature.

From the experience, though, he learned his lesson and unlike Otero and Lahodny, he never went back into the business. He found a wonderful lady to keep him on the straight and narrow. His quest for the serious money from his African connections never materialized and evaporated when the well dried up. But he still never gave up hope and to this day, Stan still believes, one day his dream will come true. I told him: "Don't hold your breath."

John 'JQ' Quinn

JQ really never got out of the drug business. He went on to inherit his parents' family farm in the Central Valley of California where he became a legal pot grower servicing California's burgeoning medical marijuana business. All of his customers now have cards to be able to purchase his marijuana legally. After his harvest last year, JQ was attacked at the farm by a group of hooligans trying to steal his crop. He managed to fight them off, but not before many shots were fired and JQ luckily escaped without injury and without killing anyone, although the kitchen windows and back door were riddled with bullet holes. The incident was all caught on his surveillance cameras and he vowed to take it to the local police. He also says, next year's crop will be even better… hopefully his attackers will have moved on.

Cindy Smythe

Following our divorce's final proceedings in late November 1985, Cindy took her newfound riches and moved to Colorado to a millionaire's playground to attempt to mingle with the rich and famous. In 1989 and after a few short years, having gone from rags to riches then virtually having spent her way back to rags again with her fortune dwindling, Cindy began to sell off most of her belongings and found a job. Even with the anticipated sale of her possessions she realized she wouldn't have the amount of cash that she needed to buy into the area's low-cost housing where she thought she could still afford to live, so she contacted me for a loan and offered me first choice to buy back some of the artwork.

Since I was broke, my new wife as a gesture of goodwill agreed to dip into her savings to loan Cindy the money as well as buy back some of the artwork. However, after the money was transferred in good faith Cindy reneged, claiming I owed it to her and that if I persisted in attempting to get her to live up to her part of the agreement she would go to the IRS and tell them everything I'd done as well as try and collect a reward for her information. This extortion attempt failed when a mutual friend pointed out, and she realized it as well, that she would be culpable and liable for her part as a participant in the conspiracy. Instead of returning the loaned money, she reluctantly did send us some of the artwork and one Chinese carpet. However, amid a constant and continuing barrage of accusations, innuendos, and threats I'd finally had enough and, come what may moved on with my life. In the end Cindy moved back to the coast and hopefully found happiness with her ever growing menagerie of dogs and cats.

William 'Yorktown Billy' Greenberg

Although originally from New York City and the urban lifestyle, Yorktown Billy found city life much too confining after his retirement from the marijuana business. He moved up to the Mendocino Coast and became a commercial fisherman for several years. While fishing for salmon off the Northern Oregon Coast in the mid-1990s, Billy, one day, found himself in pea soup fog in the ocean at the mouth of the Columbia River near Astoria aboard his 35-foot fishing boat. Tending to his fishing lines, he glanced up just in time to see the bow of a 400-foot freighter emerge from the fog bank about 20 feet from the starboard side of his boat. Billy had just enough time to grab his super suit and dive overboard just as the freighter cut his boat in two. The fishing boat sank in less than one minute and Billy was lucky not to have gotten sucked into the freighter's prop. He was rescued from the freezing waters by another fisherman, but the incident ended his fishing career. He finally discovered the name of the freighter which had somehow sailed out of the shipping lanes when it struck him broadside. After much back-and-forth negotiation Billy received a substantial settlement from the Panamanian shipping company that owned the freighter.

Now, in his early 70s, he has never been happier. He now spends the winters in his camper on the beach in Mexico with his wife and their Brittany spaniel. He says if he never goes back to New York again, it will be too soon.

Father John Sorce

Father retired from the BOP (Bureau of Prisons) to live on the Monterey Peninsula. After I moved back there in 1988, we renewed our friendship and remained close friends until his death in 2011. While living on the Peninsula, Father worked as a priest at the Carmelite Monastery giving weekly mass and taking confession from the nuns who lived there. He became a friend of my family and loved to entertain my parents when they'd visit me when I lived in Carmel in the '90s. He said I was his success story, because I listened to his sage advice and never went back into the smuggling or drug business, like so many of his other prison disciples did.

There were many profound instances where Father Sorce had a great influence on my life, but one of the most was his introducing me to the Kosher diet while I was at FCI Tucson. Being Jewish I was legally entitled to not only attending weekly Jewish religious services but also to having a specially prepared Kosher meal delivered from a local Jewish restaurant at every inmate feeding thus avoiding my having to eat the regular prison slop that all of the other non-Jewish prisoners had to eat. The Kosher food actually tasted great in contrast to what other inmates were forced to eat and was one of the primary reasons that I was able to stay so healthy during my incarceration. Father truly saved my life in many ways and for that I will always be forever grateful to having known such a wonderful person and to his influence in substantially changing my life for the better.

Rick Bibbero

I'm still with Lu and we seem to have weathered the storm of my legal problems stemming from my 13 years in the marijuana business and the ten years of legal hassles following all of it. We've been happily married for over 25 years now and our love continues to grow each day as we look forward to our future together as we transition from middle to old age. Lu had a daughter as a young woman barely out of high school. The father abandoned both of them while Marci was an infant, and in 2004 I adopted her as an adult adoption. She has been a constant source of joy in my life.

One day she said to me: "Daddy, I think I'll quit my job, get a bunch of tattoos and piercings, become a druggie, steal your car and maybe spend some time in the pokey… just so you can see what it's like to be a real father to a true delinquent."

Even though it was said in jest and she's too responsible to go there, I deserve that.

Acknowledgments

This book took roughly three years to write and would not have been possible without the help and encouragement of Melissa Vaio and Marcia Bibbero-Hiegler. To my editor Leslie White, proofreader Dixie Cheek, and our prepress specialist, thank you, thank you. Your corrections, advice and constructive criticism actually made the book readable.

Others who put up with me by slogging through early versions included Leila Atkin, Matt Miller, Bill Stevenson, Mikey Bee, Steve Kovacs, Rick Barnett, Gary Johnson, Bruce Falkenborg, Paul Putzel, Carl Staub, Lauren Taylor, Joe Lerer and Pat Hallinan. Special thanks go to Brian Rohan.

The award for Original Inspiration for the story goes to Tony Lombardo. Many of the 'players' who also contributed, but whose real identities shall remain anonymous, include Little Fat, Beep, Post Festor, Mr. Ghee, Grover, Batman, Ünt, DM, DR, TK, Medium, Smiley Bob, Bugs and Digger.

Also special thanks go to Jim Conklin and Jim Nielsen who both provided me with valuable insights in Chapter 41, entitled *The Other Side*. Others in the government who helped me immensely to get beyond my past and who deserve special recognition and thanks for all their help, moral support and encouragement are retired U.S. Probation officers Fred Cheverria and Jose Guerrero, and the late prison chaplain Father John Sorce. And finally to my wife LaMoyne whose patience in putting up with me never wavered, with helpful insights even through countless bleary-eyed late nights of corrections and re-readings.

References

Referenced Newspaper Articles

1. *San Francisco Chronicle* 5/1/78, The Long Voyage of a Drug Ship by Rob Haeseler
2. *Seattle Times* 8/28/80, Riptide Foils Plot, 290 Bales of Marijuana Found Near Neah Bay Worth Millions by Ross Anderson
3. *San Diego Union* 2/3/83, Informant's Credibility Key As Drug Case Closes by Bill Ott
4. *San Diego Union* 2/4/83, Man Guilty of Drug Smuggling by Bill Ott
5. *San Diego Tribune* 2/4/83, Santa Barbara man found guilty in marijuana-smuggling conspiracy by William Polk
6. *San Diego Union* 2/5/83, 2nd Man Guilty in Pot Case by William Polk
7. *San Diego Union* 3/83, Man Sentenced to Seven Year Term in Marijuana Case by Bill Ott
8. *Los Angeles Times* 5/9/83, Millionaire Drug Dealer Makes Deal by Charles P. Wallace
9. *Santa Barbara News-Press* 1985, How Beneficial Is Letting A Suspect Go to Catch Another Wrongdoer? by Richard Aguirre
10. *San Francisco Chronicle* 4/23/86, S.F. Rock Attorney Arrested on Tax Charge by Francisco Garcia
11. *Reno Gazette Journal* 10/26/89, Nevada Drug Ring Smashed by Phil Barber
12. *Reno Gazette Journal* 10/27/89, 2 Arrests expected today; 11 Sought in Drug Ring Probe by Mike Henderson
13. *S.F. Chronicle* 10/29/89, Marijuana Conspiracy Rocks Tahoe Region by Tom Knudson
14. *Tahoe Daily Tribune* 4/19/90, Two More Indictments in Mancuso Case by Jeff DeLong
15. *San Francisco Examiner* 8/93, Lawyer Patrick Hallinan Arrested by Seth Rosenfeld
16. *Monterey Herald* 8/5/93, Patrick Hallinan to Be Arraigned by Kevin Fagan
17. *The Recorder* 8/16/93, The Case Against Hallinan by Howard Mimtz
18. *The Wall Street Journal* 8/31/93, Defense Lawyers Decry Attempt to Seize Law Firms in Drug Case by Wade Lambert
19. *The New York Times* 9/3/93, Indicted Lawyer Turns Suspicion on U.S. by Michael Chichi
20. *S.F. Chronicle* 10/8/93, U.S. Reveals Case Against Hallinan by Rob Haeseler
21. *The San Francisco Daily Journal* 1993, Defense Counsel is Depicted as Double Dealer by Rex Bossert
22. *S.F. Chronicle* 1993, Pot Smugglers Testify Against Their Attorney by Rob Haeseler
23. *S.F. Chronicle* 7/16/94, S.F. Attorney Faces New Criminal Counts by William Carlsen
24. *S.F. Chronicle* 6/28/95, Drug Kingpin Mancuso Gets 9 Years / Cooperation With Government Eased Punishment by Rob Haeseler
25. *Reno Gazette Journal*, 10/28/96, pg. 14, Notice of Forfeiture of SV *Mamamouchi*.
26. *Healdsburg Tribune*, 11/1/89, Pot Ring Entangles Local Man by Dan Murphy {see Jeff Welch on Page 503, 3rd paragraph}

Referenced Songs & Music

1. *Jumpin' Jack Flash*
   Performed by The Rolling Stones
   Songwriters: Keith Richards, Mick Jagger
   © Abkco Music Inc.
2. *White Rabbit*
   Performed by The Jefferson Airplane
   Songwriter: Grace Wing Slick
   © Universal Music Publishing Group
3. *Ride My See Saw*
   Performed by The Moody Blues
   Songwriter: John Lodge
   © Warner/Chappell Music, Inc.
4. *Legend Of A Mind*
   Performed by The Moody Blues
   Songwriter: R. Thomas
   © T.R.O. Inc.
5. *Bad Moon Rising*
   Performed by Creedence Clearwater Revival
   Songwriter: John C. Fogerty
   © The Bicycle Music Company
6. *Stairway To Heaven*
   Performed by Led Zeppelin
   Songwriters: Jimmy Page, Robert Plant
   © Warner/Chappell Music, Inc.
7. *Unbroken Chain*
   Performed by The Grateful Dead
   Songwriters: Philip Lesh, Robert M. Peterson
   © Universal Music Publishing Group
8. *Song of the High Seas* included in the Musical Score from *Victory At Sea*
   Performed by Erich Kunzel & Cincinnati Pops Orchestra
   Songwriters: Robert Russell Bennett & Richard Rodgers
   © BMG
9. *Memo To Turner*
   Performed by The Rolling Stones
   Songwriters: Keith Richards, Mick Jagger
   © Abkco Music, Inc.
10. *Dear Mr. Fantasy*
    Performed by Traffic
    Songwriters: Steve Linwood, Chris Wood, Jim Capaldi
    © Warner/Chappell Music, Inc., Universal Music Publishing Group, Cobalt Music Publishing Ltd., Rock and Roll Stew Music Ltd.
11. *Bali Hai*
    Performed by Juanita Hall in the movie *South Pacific*
    Songwriters: Rodgers and Hammerstein
    © BMG

12. *Hotel California*
    Performed by The Eagles
    Songwriters: Don Felder, Don Henley, Glenn Frey
    © Cass Country Music / Wisteria Music / Privet Music, Warner/Chappell Music Inc., Universal
    Music Publishing Group, Red Cloud Music
13. *Living In Oz*
    Performed by Rick Springfield
    Songwriter: Rick Springfield
    © Universal Music Publishing
14. *Dirty Laundry*
    Performed by Don Henley
    Songwriters: Don Henley, Danny Kortchmar
    © Warner/Chappell Music Inc., Cass County Music / Wisteria Music / Privet Music
15. *Tommy's Holiday Camp*
    Performed by The Who
    Songwriter: Keith Moon
    © Gowmonk Inc.
16. Musical Score from *Psycho*
    Performed by Joel McNeely & The Royal Scottish National Orchestra
    Songwriter: Bernard Herrmann
    © Masters Film Music, Vartse Sarabande Music
17. Old English Nursery Rhyme entitled Humpty Dumpty
    Original origins unknown
    Most notable version: Through the Looking Glass by Lewis Carroll 1872
18. *Won't Get Fooled Again*
    Performed by: The Who
    Songwriter: Peter Townshend
    © Spirit Music Group

Referenced Legal Research

1. Grand Jury Report, U.S. District Court Southern District of California, May 1981
2. Report of Investigation, Operation CorCo dated 2/22/82 Louis Villar debriefing by DEA Special Agent Marvin Mittleman, Special Agent James Conklin (DEA), Special Agent James Nielsen (IRS)
3. Report of Investigation, Operation CorCo dated 7/12/82, Alan Logie debriefing by DEA Special Agent Marvin Mittleman
4. Indictment Case #82-0572, U.S. vs Richard V. Bibbero Jr + 26 Defendants 8/3/82 Southern District Court Southern District of California
5. Trial Transcripts, 11 Volumes of U.S. vs Bibbero U.S. District Court Southern District of California 1/18/83 through 2/4/83
6. Federal Register 749 F.2d 581 U.S. vs Richard Bibbero 1984
7. Appeal of U.S. vs. Bibbero, 9th Circuit Court of Appeals, 10 Volumes 1983–1984
8. Petition of U.S. Supreme Court (Writ of Certiorari) U.S. vs Bibbero 1985
9. Grand Jury Proceedings–5 volumes U.S. Southern District of California 1984–1985
10. Report of Investigation–dated 12/12/88 Debriefing of Phillip Byron by DEA Agent Rick Wiley and DEA Special Agent Jack Bax North Lake Tahoe
11. Indictment Case #N-89-24-ECR–U.S. vs Ciro Wayne Mancuso + 17 Defendants 8/24/89 U.S. District Court District of Nevada
12. Superseding Indictment Case #N-92-61-ECR U.S. vs Edwin Lehmer + 12 Defendants 11/4/92 U.S. District Court District of Nevada
13. Indictment Case #S-93-237-DFL–U.S. vs Edwin Lehmer + 9 Defendants 7/14/93 U.S. District Court Eastern District of California
14. Superseding Indictment Case #N-92-61 ECR–U.S. vs Patrick Hallinan + 11 Defendants 8/4/93 U.S. District Court District of Nevada
15. Indictment Case #S-93-237-DFL–U.S. vs Edwin Lehmer + 14 Defendants 9/10/93 U.S. District Court Eastern District of California

Referenced Books

1. *Reefer Men* by Tony Thompson, 2008
2. *Blowback* by Michael Forwell with Lee Bullman, 2010
3. *Night Landing A Short History of West Coast Smuggling* by David Heron, 1999
4. *Thai Stick: Surfers, Scammers, and the Untold Story of the Marijuana Trade* by Peter Maguire & Mike Ritter, 2015
5. *Smoke Screen* by Robert Sabbag, 2013
6. *Royce's Sailing Illustrated*, Volume I by Patrick M. Royce, 1965
7. *American Practical Navigator* Volume 1 by Nathaniel Bowditch, 1962
8. *Ocean Passages For The World* Third Edition 1973 prepared by Commander H.L. Jenkins, O.B.E., D.S.C., Royal Navy & Hydrographic Department, Ministry of Defence, Sommerset, England, 1973
9. *Escape from Lecumberri* by Dwight Worker and Barbara Wilde, 2012
10. *Mr. Nice* by Howard Marks, 1996
11. *The Bandit of Kabul: Counterculture Adventures Along the Hashish Trail and Beyond* by Jerry Beisler, 2013
12. *Papillon* by Henri Charriére, Hart-Davis, MacGibbon 1970
13. *Survival in The Killing Fields* (Haing Nor: A Cambodian Odyssey) by Haing Nor and Roger Warner, 1988
14. *Oliver Twist* by Charles Dickens, 1838
15. *The Strange Tale of Dr. Jekyll and Mr. Hyde* by Robert Louis Stevenson, 1886
16. *Deep Water* by Katherine Nichols, 2016

Referenced Magazines Articles

1. *Latitude 38*, "A Loose Confederation," Volume 195, September 1993
2. *California Lawyer*, "Paranoid or Persecuted" by Michael Checchio, January 1994
3. *The American Lawyer*, "Fort Reno's Obsession" by Howard Mintz, May 1995
4. *Gentlemen's Quarterly Magazine*, "Coronado High" by Joshuah Bearman, July 2013

Referenced Television & Movies

1. *Psycho*, 1960 movie directed by Alfred Hitchcock
2. *PT 109*, 1963 movie directed by Leslie H. Martinson
3. *Jaws*, 1975 movie directed by Steven Spielberg
4. *Up In Smoke*, 1978 movie directed by Lou Adler and Tommy Chong
5. *The Frisco Kid*, 1979 movie directed by Robert Aldrich
6. *Escape*, 1980 made-for-TV movie
7. *60 Minutes* weekly TV show, Mike Wallace, *The Coronado Mob,* produced by Lowell Bergman, 1985
8. *Frontline TV series*, January 12, 1999 entitled *Snitch*
9. *Mr. Nice,* 2011 movie directed by Bernard Rose
10. *Locked Up Abroad*, 2012 *National Geographic* TV series
11. *The Perfect Storm*, 2000 movie directed by Wolfgang Petersen
12. *The Killing Fields*, 1984 directed by Richard Joffe
13. *Two Years Before The Mast*, 1946 movie directed by John Farrow
14. *South Pacific*, 1958 movie directed by Joshua Logan
15. *The Magic Christian*, 1969 movie directed by Joseph McGrath
16. *The Maltese Falcon*, 1941 movie directed by John Huston
17. *Cool Hand Luke*, 1967 movie directed by Stuart Rosenberg
18. *The Godfather*, 1972 movie directed by Francis Ford Coppola
19. *Victory at Sea*, 1952 TV series documentary
20. *Apocalypse Now*, 1979 movie directed by Francis Ford Coppola
21. *Midnight Express*, 1978 movie directed by Alan Parker

51382640R00296

Made in the USA
Columbia, SC
17 February 2019